Drawing Acts

Studies in Graphic Expression and Representation

Drawing Acts is about drawing, as both art and act. Taking the study of drawings beyond the traditional agenda of connoisseurship, David Rosand explores the significance of the making of drawings, the meaning in the line of the draftsman, and the re-creative dimension of critical response. The book focuses on drawings by artists such as Leonardo da Vinci, Raphael, Michelangelo, Rembrandt, Piranesi, Tiepolo, and Picasso, as well as on the history and theory of the medium itself. It seeks to establish new foundations for the criticism and appreciation of drawing, which is generally considered the most revealing record of artistic creativity, offering the most direct expression of the artistic self.

David Rosand is Meyer Schapiro Professor of Art History at Columbia University, where he also serves as chairman of the Miriam and Ira D. Wallach Art Gallery. Elected to the American Academy of Arts and Sciences, he is also a foreign member of the Ateneo Veneto in Venice. Best known for his research on the art of Venice – through publications such as *Titian and the Venetian Woodcut; Titian; Painting in Sixteenth-Century Venice: Titian, Veronese, Tintoretto;* and *Myths of Venice: The Figuration of a State.* He has also published in the area of modern art, notably *Robert Motherwell on Paper: Drawings, Prints, Collages.*

Drawing Acts

Studies in Graphic Expression and Representation

David Rosand
Columbia University

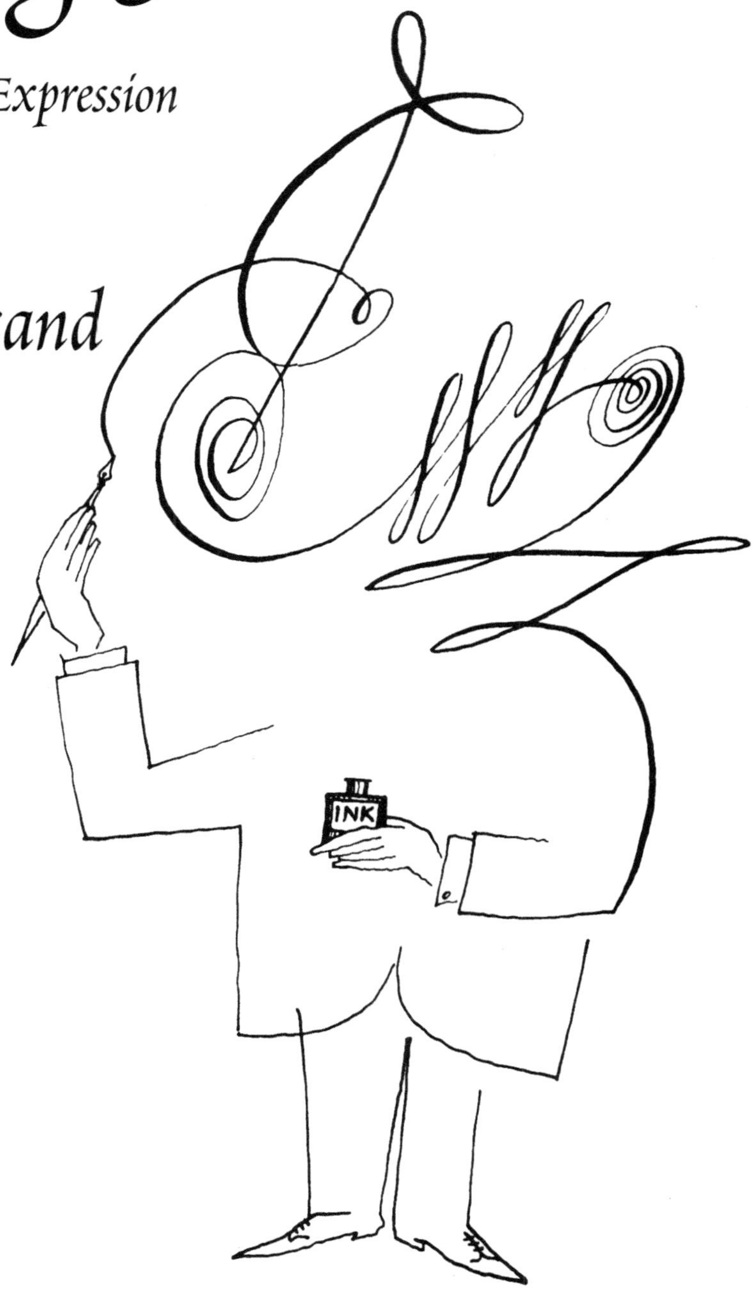

CAMBRIDGE UNIVERSITY PRESS

CAMBRIDGE
UNIVERSITY PRESS

Shaftesbury Road, Cambridge CB2 8EA, United Kingdom

One Liberty Plaza, 20th Floor, New York, NY 10006, USA

477 Williamstown Road, Port Melbourne, VIC 3207, Australia

314–321, 3rd Floor, Plot 3, Splendor Forum, Jasola District Centre, New Delhi – 110025, India

103 Penang Road, #05–06/07, Visioncrest Commercial, Singapore 238467

Cambridge University Press is part of Cambridge University Press & Assessment, a department of the University of Cambridge.

We share the University's mission to contribute to society through the pursuit of education, learning and research at the highest international levels of excellence.

www.cambridge.org
Information on this title: www.cambridge.org/9780521773300

Art page iii: Saul Steinberg, Signature (from The Passport, 1954).

First published 2002
Paperback edition first published 2016 (version 7, February 2024)

Printed in Great Britain by CPI Group (UK) Ltd, Croydon CR0 4YY, February 2024

Typefaces Aldus 10.5/14 pt. and Poetica *System* QuarkXPress® [GH]

A catalogue record for this publication is available from the British Library

Library of Congress Cataloging-in-Publication data
Rosand, David.
Drawing acts : studies in graphic expression and representation / David Rosand.
p. cm.
ISBN 0-521-77330-X
1. Drawing. 2. Drawing – Expertising. I. Title.
NC80.R595 2001
741 – dc21
2001025624

Publication of this book has been aided by a grant from the Millard Meiss Publication Fund of the College Art Association. MM

ISBN 978-0-521-77330-0 Hardback
ISBN 978-1-316-63752-4 Paperback

In memory of my father

Johan Herbert Rosand

1904–1997

Contents

Illustrations

Preface

drawing *n.* 1. The act or an instance of drawing. 2. The art of depicting forms or figures on a surface by lines. 3. A portrayal in lines on a surface of a form or figure.

Act, art, image: the several, related meanings of *drawing* offered by a standard dictionary of the English language (*American Heritage*) suggest the range of experience implicated in the word. That experiential range – from marking to viewing, creation to interpretation – is the object of these studies in the phenomenology of drawing. My concern is to expand the discourse on the art, to encourage a kind of sustained criticism that acknowledges the profound implications of tracing a line, of recording the motions of a hand, of making an image by direct extension of the body.

The study of drawings – "old master" drawings – has long enjoyed its own tradition, a tradition of conoisseurship, focusing, above all, on questions of attribution, dating, and function. That tradition, however, can seem terribly hermetic at times, closed to all but the officially certified in practice. Drawings, for good reasons of preservation, are kept locked in cabinets, guarded by their curators or keepers. This protective attitude has effectively kept them segregated, objects somehow precious beyond the paintings or sculptures they often prepare. Drawings, however, are generally assumed to reveal more about the creative process and the personality of the artist than those more finished products; they should therefore present a particularly profound challenge to critical interpretation. And yet, instead of being subject to continuing critical scrutiny they are briefly exhibited, attributed, catalogued – "published," as we say – and then reconsigned to the darkness of their solander boxes.

My hope is to open the discussion to a wider and deeper range of critical issues, to bring drawings back to the center of the discourse on representation, image-making, and self-expression. Such issues, of course, have always been fundamental to the appreciation of drawing, latent in the discourse of connoisseurship and its assumptions of the presence of the artist in his mark. By the first century Pliny the Elder, recording the studio lore of ancient Greek artistic tradition, rehearsed not only the etiology of painting in the drawn outline but the professional anecdotes that testify to a sophisticated awareness of the particular qualities of the line itself. Two lines emerge from Pliny's accounts that, together, epitomize the functional range of the drawn line as representation and expression: the line of Parrhasios, inflecting itself into space, and the line of Apelles, a sign of the presence of the artist himself. These alternatives establish the poles of graphic signification, of the line as illusion or reality, a reference to a fictional object of representation or the indexical trace of its own creator. Indeed, looking back over the history of drawing to Book XXXV of Pliny's *Natural History* only confirms that the formal semiotics and the phenomenology of our own century offer legitimate critical access to the art of the past.

The following chapters hardly pretend to offer a full introduction to the history and techniques of drawing. Rather, by concentrating on individual artists and problems, they aim to explore that range of issues implicit in graphic imaging. While seeking to move critical discussion beyond the inherited agenda of connoisseurship, I recognize that any expansion of the discourse must inevitably build upon the achievements of that tradition: its accumulated visual wisdom, its sensitivity to the complex workings of line, and its theoretical assumptions, namely, that the drawn mark stands as permanent record of the act of drawing and, ultimately, of the actor, the draftsman. The legacy of connoisseurship is not to be found in any single volume; the great connoisseurs were practical critics, not aesthetic theoreticians, and their true contributions are to be found in their attention to individual artists and individual drawings. Precisely such concentration on a particular drawing – attending to its constituent marks and graphic systems, responding to its particular interpretive challenges – leads to the kind of visual focus necessary to sustain any more ambitious critical enterprise.

That enterprise must engage the image dialectically. Criticism is in large measure a re-creative act, a rearticulation of the artist's activity, a retracing of gestures, of impulses and retractions. The connoisseurs of the past always assumed they were in dialogue with the artist, who revealed himself through his touch; the challenge was to discover the man behind the mark. That challenge, it seems to me, remains, even if we may no longer be comfortable with the traditional vocabulary; terms like "genius" or "taste" no longer seem adequate to the deeply personal complexities we sense in drawings by Leonardo da Vinci, Michelangelo, or Rembrandt. That a drawing is a revelation of the self may be an axiom we share with traditional connoisseurship, but the very notion of the self can hardly be taken for granted in our century. Nor can we remain satisfied with the Cartesian duality that maintained a continuing Platonizing transcendence in traditional commentary. As the direct record of motions of the body, a drawing inevitably takes us back to the drawing hand, to the body of the draftsman, in a kinesthetic circuit. Critical responsibility requires us to acknowledge the corporeal dimension of our response to a drawing, to the visible activity traced on the surface. Only then, by effectively retracing that activity in our imagination, can we participate in the experience of the drawing, that is, follow the imagining hand of the draftsman.

Having developed over the course of many years, these studies were initially tested in the lecture hall and seminar room; several generations of Columbia students, undergraduate and graduate, have collaborated in various ways in that development. My efforts at exploring a phenomenology of drawing first went public in 1977, when the late Agnes Mongan invited me to present a paper titled "Rembrandt's Reach and Other Observations on the Phenomenology of Drawing" at a session on drawings at the annual meeting of the College Art Association. That short paper grew, was presented on other occasions, a version published by the Drawing Society, and eventually emerged as Chapter Seven of this book. Chapter Three, on Leonardo, was first formulated as one of the Franklin Murphy Lectures delivered at the Spencer Museum of Art of the University of Kansas in 1986, and which were published as *The Meaning of the Mark* in 1988; it was further elaborated as a Special Lecture on Psychiatry and the Arts at the annual meeting of the American Psychiatric Association in 1993 and as a Julius S. Held Lecture at the Sterling and Francine Clark Art Institute. The drawing of Michelangelo, the subject of Chapter Six, was the theme of a paper presented at the 26th International Congress for the History of Art in 1986; it too was expanded through presentation on a number of subsequent occasions – as a University Lecture at Columbia University and another of the Julius S. Held Lectures in 1993. Aspects of "*Disegno:* The Invention of an Art," Chapter Two, were presented as a public lecture at Columbia in 1993 and in a paper to the international congress on Leon Battista Alberti in Paris in 1995. Parts of Chapter Eight, "The Antic Line," were tested in an inaugural lecture at Columbia in 1996.

Many of the ideas in these studies, then, have already received preliminary public airing, and I am grateful to my hosts for the invitations to present my evolving ideas and to the audiences who responded with helpful criticism: to the late Robert S. Liebert, M.D., and the Center for Psychoanalytic Training and Research at the College of Physicians and Surgeons of Columbia University; to the Drawing Center, the Drawing Society, the Frick Collection, the Department of Fine Arts of Harvard University; and to the New York Studio School and the University of Texas. I am especially grateful to Elizabeth Cropper, whose invitation to participate in a session at the 29th International Congress for the History of Art in 1996 encouraged a synthetic paper on "Remembered Lines," which led me to see beyond the horizon of the present project; her cochair was Paul van den Akker, whose own explorations into the history of drawing instruction assured me of a most responsive and sympathetic colleague.

The fullest public presentation of my ideas and the sharpest and most productive critical response took place in Paris in 1995 at the Centre d'Histoire et Théorie d'Art of the Ecole des Hautes Etudes en Sciences Sociales, where I offered a series of seminars under the title "Dessin/dessiner: Vers une phénoménologie du dessin." My hosts on that occasion were Daniel Arasse, Hubert Damisch, and Georges Didi-Huberman. To them, their colleagues, and their students I owe my deepest gratitude for providing a most challenging forum for testing ideas and exploring critical approaches to the study of art.

My art-historical study of old-master drawings began many years ago with the late Janòs Scholz, in a seminar held in the studio of that great collector and generous human being; it was there that, as a young graduate student, I first began to feel my way into those creations of past draftsmen, to touch old paper and to listen to it sing. That last phrase was echoed by another of my early mentors, until his death also my dearest colleague and friend, Michelangelo Muraro, who had a special feeling for the materiality of art. Among my Columbia teachers, two in particular guided me toward a clearer understanding of the many meanings of drawing: Julius S. Held, whose book on Rubens's drawings stands as a model of the most sensitive interpretive scholarship on the art and whose studies of Rembrandt demonstrate most profoundly its humanity, and Meyer Schapiro, who taught one the deepest meaning of the mark – both were true draftsmen in their own right. Charles de Tolnay, in a seminar many years ago, led a beginning graduate student into the world of Leonardo drawings and gave him the courage to confront them; I am sorry that I never thanked him properly.

Other friends and colleagues have guided me by the examples they have set and by their personal commitment: James Ackerman, whose encouragement and support over many years has meant more to me than he may have known; Stephen Addiss, who shared long and enlightening hours with me before his beloved calligraphy; Daniel Arasse, who has always challenged me by the critical intelligence of his own work and by his probing questioning of mine; John Elderfield, who has quietly enlarged our critical vision in the field of drawings; Michael Fried, who has long been exploring the phenomenological dimensions of image-making, and Leo Steinberg, who has articulated the manifold qualities of the drawn line with enviable sensitivity and precision. Each of them has shown me a way. Finally, I owe a very special debt to an artist who so generously shared ideas, experience, and friendship, as well as his art: Robert Motherwell talked art as eloquently and feelingly as he made it, confirming the meaning of the mark as personal expression.

Fellowships from the National Endowment for the Humanities in 1985–86 and 1991–92 enabled me to spend time in the drawing collections of Europe, just looking – and I am grateful to the curatorial staffs of those collections for facilitating my study of the drawings in their care, and especially to Jane Roberts, then curator of the print room at the Royal Library, Windsor Castle. In 1992, the legendary supportive hospitality of the Rockefeller Foundation's Study and Conference Center at Bellagiò afforded ideal time and place in which to write a draft of an introductory chapter.

For an embarrassingly long time I have owed this book to my children, who have been waiting for it with loving, if unrestrained, impatience, and to my wife, whose patience was of necessity greater and whose understanding, encouragement, and constant support helped bring the project to fruition. Above all, I have owed this book to my father, my first drawing master, to whose memory it is dedicated.

Drawing Acts

Studies in Graphic Expresssion and Representation

CHAPTER ONE

Criticism, Connoisseurship, and the Phenomenology of Drawing

> . . . I feel my hand move, turn, join, dive, and lift, and often, through the act of correction, delete or expand a line, taking the space right up to the margin, thus constructing from the apparently functional lines of the letters a space that is quite simply that of a work of art. I am an artist, not because I am representing an object, but, in a more basic sense, because in writing my body knows the joy of drawing on and rhythmically incising a virgin surface (its virginity representing the infinitely possible).
>
> – Roland Barthes[1]

Drawing is the fundamental pictorial act. To make a mark or trace a single line upon a surface immediately transforms that surface, energizes its neutrality; the graphic imposition turns the actual flatness of the ground into virtual space, translates its material reality into the fiction of imagination. Disrupting the emptiness, the mark activates the surface, disclosing dimensions latent in its suggestive blankness. Together, mark and surface participate in a dialectic exchange of positive and negative values, shifting object–ground relations. Dividing the space of its field, a line releases the allusive or generative charge of the surface – ancient Chinese calligraphers spoke of "generative paper."[2] Out of this pictorial physics is born the full range of painting's possibilities.

But drawing is not painting. By drawing we generally understand a pictorial structure more open than that of painting. Drawing tends to cover its supporting surface only incompletely; the ground retains its own participating presence in the image, just as the marks it hosts, and which so transform it, retain their autonomy. Ambivalence is an essential and functioning aspect of drawing. More insistently than the brush stroke in painting, the drawn mark resists surrender to the mimetic imperative, to pictorial illusion. Painting generally tends to incorporate its constructive units within a tighter texture of representational pretense, complicated by the always more elusive workings of color. In its simplest form, a drawing can be a single mark or line, on any surface – stone, ceramic, cloth, parchment, paper.[3]

Developed more complexly, drawing can indeed approach painting in its representational fullness, but it will always carry the traces of its surface construction; even when heavily worked, it will reveal the processes of its making and, ultimately, the nature of the surface on which it operates. Between its reality as material mark (pigmented substance applied to a particular ground, or an incision of the surface) and its mimetic responsibility in the creation of the visual fiction of an image (its individual role as bounding contour or its contribution to the collective effort of modeling) the drawn line exists, like the surface on which it is applied, *in potentia*. As a graphic sign it is both self-referential and representational, maintaining its own identity even as it alludes to something beyond itself, the object of representation. This semiotic ambivalence invites the interpretation that is requisite for its very functioning: the active participation of the viewer in constructing meaning.

The drawn mark is the record of a gesture, an action in time past now fixed permanently in the present; recalling its origins in the movement of the draftsman's hand, the mark invites us to participate in that recollection of its creation. That invitation to the viewer, to rehearse the creative gestures in his or her imagination, is a distinctive aspect of the appeal of drawing.

The meaning of the mark is the object of these studies. My theme is the phenomenology of drawing, the complex interrelation of marking and meaning, making and viewing. Just what does drawing signify? How does it mean? How is it experienced? These are central questions to be considered in the exploration of the possibilities of meaning in the art and act of drawing.

In the abstraction of geometry, a line is the locus of a point, a length without breadth. Reading that definition in a more active mode, we say that a line traces the progress of a point through space. But such an abstraction must be reified, realized visually before it acquires meaning in art, and that, of course, is our concern. The line that interests us is a drawn line, an extended mark made by an implement guided by a hand. To that kind of line, abstract idea embodied, we can respond personally and directly – although our response, in turn, may indeed lead us back to the abstraction. For in viewing a drawn line we follow the record of a path of motion, and our viewing involves, on several levels, a trajectory of vision, the movement of our eyes, and thus of our body. But we also, and even primarily, respond to the particular qualities of the line: to the way in which it was drawn, the nature of the marker's tracing, its material, the weight and velocity of the hand behind it, the physiognomy and affective resonance of the line. To these qualities we respond through the imaginative projection of our own body; indeed, it is that projection that assigns such values to the line. All of this, the full range from making to response, is implicated in the phenomenology of drawing.

Within the disciplines of art history, the connoisseurship of drawings has developed an impressive and most venerable tradition. Combining the subjective sensibility of the evaluating eye with objective research into the historical conditions of artistic production, it has seemed to offer a fully articulated methodological model for study of the art of the past. Monuments to its achievement are the great catalogues raisonnés, compendia of classification, in which the corpora of master draftsmen are described, ordered, and discussed according to the categories and values that have shaped and guided the agenda of connoisseurship: in particular, authorship, dating, and function. But once the drawings of an artist like Michelangelo or Rembrandt have been catalogued, the creations of the master distinguished from those of his disciples and imitators (however such distinctions might shift from one generation of connoisseurs to the next), once chronology has been established and function within the context of production clarified – what then? Is there a discourse beyond the catalogue raisonné? If so, how is it to be continued? One of the basic assumptions of traditional connoisseurship and appreciation is that drawings offer us the most intimate documents of artistic creativity and personality, but what exactly do we expect them to reveal?

Although our aim is to extend the study of drawings beyond the limits of its conventional agenda, we must, nevertheless, at the outset acknowledge our debt to traditional connoisseurship. Indeed, the same phenomena that have guided the observations of the connoisseur provide the foundation for a deeper critical enterprise. The draftsman's choice of medium, the flow of his line and the characteristics of his touch, the distribution of forms and accents over the page: these are some of the factors that determine graphic style, the primary object of connoisseurship. In its open structure, the relative autonomy of its marks and their resistance to representational obedience, drawing offers the connoisseur the possibility of studying the fundamental units of pictorial construction, of discerning and articulating the processes of representation. Such apparent clarity of structure would seem to permit a comparable clarity of analysis: we should be able to distinguish, describe, and categorize individual marks and marking systems, to determine with a certain precision the constituent elements of a style, eventually assigning to that style a name, that of its maker. More readily than painting, drawing promises to reward close analytical investigation of its surface structure. And yet, however it may hold out the prospect of objectifiable conclusion, its inevitable appeal is to subjectivity of response. Bernard Berenson, for example, after arguing the attribution of a problematic drawing to Michelangelo, developing his case on the basis of careful observation, finally abandons such objective pretense and concludes instead with an appeal to ultimate authority: the drawing is by Michelangelo because in his "heart of hearts" BB simply knows it to be so.[4]

1. *Ancient Lines*

. . . the boundary is a thing invisible.
– Leonardo da Vinci[5]

Although the connoisseurs of the eighteenth century brought a particular articulateness to the act of viewing, their effort was in fact the culmination of a very long history of awareness of the revelatory character of the marks of the hand. Certain truths about line had been established as axiomatic early in the Western pictorial tradition. The etiological myth of painting locates its origins in drawing, specifically in contour. All early accounts, as summarized by Pliny the Elder, "agree that painting began with the outlining of a man's shadow" (Fig. 1).[6] From that first primitive stage, of pure contour, art made steady progress toward tone and color. A significant step was taken when the daughter of Boutades of Sikyon, a potter, traced the outline of the shadow of her departing lover's profile (Fig. 2); her father filled in the outline with clay – the beginning of modeling.[7] Discovered in the tracing of a contour, painting developed out of drawing. And that etiology, no matter how

1. Joachim von Sandrart, *The Invention of Drawing*, from *Teutsche Academie der edlen Bau- Bild- und Mahlerey-Künste* (Nuremberg, 1675). New York Public Library.

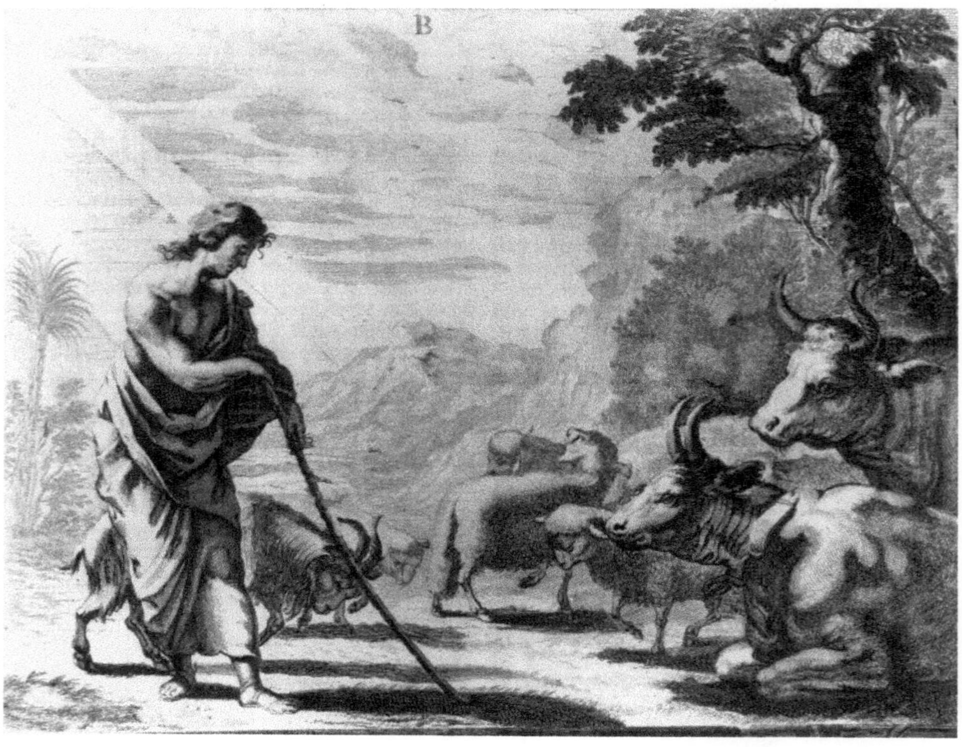

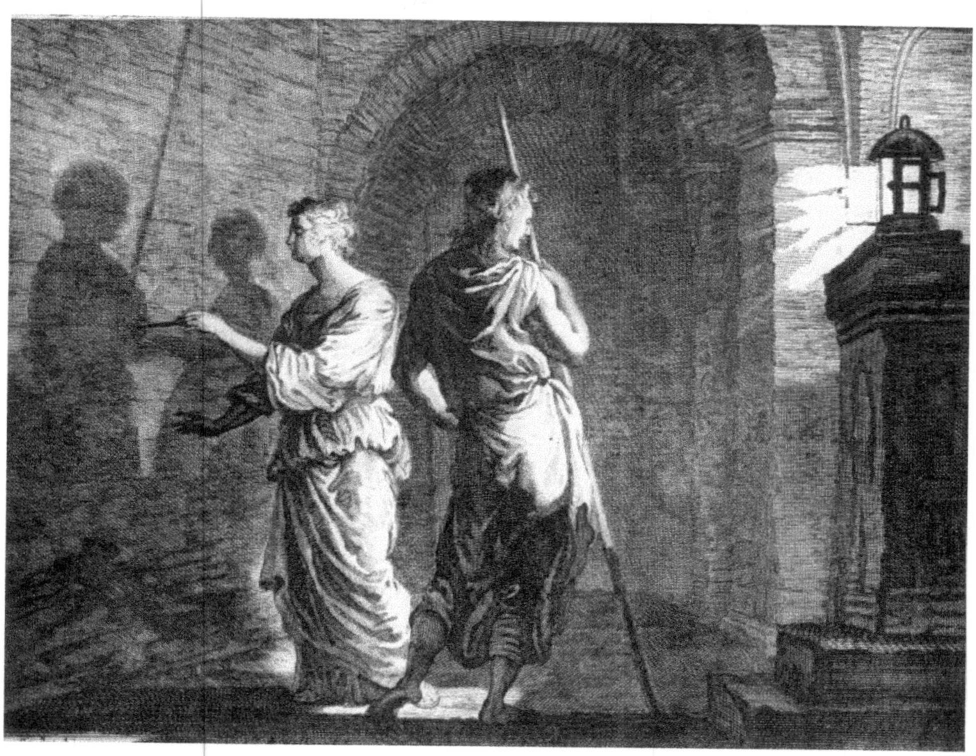

2. Joachim von Sandrart, *The Invention of Drawing,* from *Teutsche Academie der edlen Bau- Bild- und Mahlerey-Künste* (Nuremberg, 1675). New York Public Library.

melodramatically elaborated – as in the tale of the Sikyonian maid – proved technically more relevant and compelling than any competing myth.[8]

The distinction between outline and modeling – between schematic simplicity and tonal or chromatic complexity, surface reality and representational illusion – was to become fundamental in Western thought, with ethical implications that could charge aesthetic commentary with particular urgency. In line was to be found the essential truth of representation, the basic structure of idea, to which color could only add a superficial gloss of material nature, the appearance of a more contingent, less stable reality. Indeed, already in antiquity, in response to the full chromatic development of painting, there seems to have developed a sense of nostalgia for the primitive purity of linear expression. Associated with the sure measure of mathematics, with the proportions of creation, line appeals to the mind; color, on a baser level, appeals to the senses. This tradition, which runs from antiquity through the Middle Ages, serves especially in the Renaissance as the basis for a modern aesthetics based on drawing *(disegno):* "drawing," in the words of Matisse, "belongs to the realm of the Spirit and color to that of Sensuality."[9] The fuller implications of such an assumption find further eloquent twentieth-century expression in the words of the literary scholar Ernst Robert Curtius:

> Line is less material and more permanent than colour. It remains when colour fades. Colour is earthbound. Line reigns even in solar systems.

> Line can say more than colour. It fixes the contingent truths of contour and the eternal truths of mathematics. It can link everything with everything, can rely on the unconfined freedom of the abstract and the unsparing devotion to what is at hand. . . . the metaphysics of line are an aspect of poetic beauty.[10]

In his history of ancient painting the elder Pliny celebrated two lines in particular, each standing for basic qualities that were to prove essential to subsequent pictorial appreciation and analysis. The more famous of the two, and the more problematic, is the line of Apelles: a complex affair that was the result of professional competition of the highest order, the splitting of lines with an admired rival. The locus classicus for all such professional anecdotes, the story enacts the fundamental assumption of connoisseurship, the identity of the artist with and in his mark. It is worth narrating in full:

> A neat story is told of him [sc. Apelles] in connexion with Protogenes, who was living in Rhodes. Thither Apelles sailed, eager to see the works of a man only known to him by reputation, and on his arrival immediately repaired to the studio. Protogenes was not at home, but a solitary old woman was keeping watch over a large panel placed on the easel. In answer to the questions of Apelles, she said that Protogenes was out, and asked the name of the visitor: "Here it is," said Apelles, and snatching up a brush he drew a line of extreme delicacy [*linea summae tenuitatis*] across the board. On the return of Protogenes the old woman told him what had happened. When he had considered the delicate precision of the line he at once declared that his visitor had been Apelles, for no one else could have drawn anything so perfect. Then in another colour he drew a second still finer line upon the first, and went away, bidding her show it to Apelles if he came again, and add that this was the man he was seeking. It fell out as he expected; Apelles did return, and, ashamed to be beaten, drew a third line of another colour cutting the first two down their length and leaving no room for any further refinement. Protogenes owned himself beaten and hurried down to the harbour to find his visitor; they agreed to hand down the painting just as it was to posterity, a marvel to all, but especially to artists. It perished, I am told, in the first fire of the house of the Caesars on the Palatine. Formerly we might look upon it; its wide surface disclosed nothing save lines which eluded sight, and among the numerous works by excellent painters it was like a blank, and it was precisely this that lent it surpassing attraction and renown.[11]

Pliny then confirms Apelles' stature as master of the line, observing that the painter "made it an unvarying rule never to spend a day, however busy, without drawing a line by way of practice; hence the proverb": *nulla dies sine linea* – which, centuries later, was to grace the title page of many a printed drawing book.[12]

Few passages in Pliny's chapters on painting have so exercised interpreters. From the Renaissance on, Pliny's tantalizing description has continued to frustrate critics debating the exact nature of those famous lines. In the early Renaissance, Leon Battista Alberti, who disclaims telling stories like his ancient predecessor, alludes briefly to the legendary competition. Lorenzo Ghiberti, finding it difficult to believe that so learned a painter as Apelles would have demonstrated his art by anything as simple as a straight line, decides that what must have been at stake was a problem in perspective, a worthy pictorial challenge according to the values of the mid-Quattrocento. Indeed, most commentators since Ghiberti have sought to interpret those three competitive lines in a definitely pictorial light, as in some way representational – whether subtle contour or chiaroscuro.[13] Such interpretations, however, as Ernst Kris and Otto Kurz observed, "deprive the anecdote of its exemplary content – which is nothing other than sheer virtuosity."[14]

With a single stroke of the brush, Apelles left a mark of his presence. In that line Protogenes recognized the identity of his visitor. The line is the mark of the artist: at once a demonstration of his skill and testimony to his authorship, it is both work and signature, and thus a declaration of his professional self; as an index, a pure trace, it is without representational responsibility.

The second line celebrated by Pliny, however, is charged precisely with such responsibility. This is the line of Parrhasios, a painter "unrivalled in the rendering of outline," and this, Pliny adds, was "the verdict of artists." The appeal to professional judgment, so often made by Pliny in his search for authority, confirms the particular challenge and fundamental importance of outline:

> This is the highest subtlety attainable in painting. Merely to paint a figure in relief is no doubt a great achievement, yet many have succeeded thus far. But where an artist is rarely successful is in finding an outline which shall express the contours of the figure. For the contour should appear to fold back, and so enclose the object as to give assurance of the parts behind, thus clearly suggesting even what it conceals.[15]

The line of Parrhasios, this mimetic contour, will indeed prove to be the great challenge to artists: the single line that seems to disrupt the flatness of the surface, subtly inflecting itself into space, disappearing behind its own horizon. This quality of the line – what Leonardo da Vinci will call its *serpeggiare* – stands for the complex potential of line itself, a mark at once created and creating. In such a mark resides the fundamental truth of pictorial representation, its most primitive aspect. Whatever progress may have been made since the first outline was traced around a shadow, the very priority of that original inscribing gesture claimed a special status. The sophisticated advances of painting, advances in illusionistic representation, could be seen only as a loss of original virtue, leading to nostalgia for that early golden age of pure delineation:

> In ancient paintings the scheme of colouring was simple and presented no variety in the tones; but the line was rendered with exquisite perfection, thus lending to these early works a singular grace. This purity of draughtsmanship was gradually lost; its place was taken by a learned

> technique, by the differentiation of light and shade, by the full resources of the rich colouring to which the works of the later artists owe their strength.[16]

Like the conservative taste voiced by Dionysios of Halikarnassos, Pliny's celebration of the lines of Apelles and of Parrhasios testifies to an ancient aesthetic appreciation of the fine line, of the line as a test of artistic prowess.[17] Each of these lines, however, stands for a distinctive quality of marking. The line of Apelles is self-indicative; its reference is to itself, and, through itself, ultimately to its maker. The line of Parrhasios is pictorial, representational; although a display of art – and in that, of course, it too is self-demonstrative – its intended reference is ultimately to a notional reality beyond art. These two lines embody basic polarities of picturemaking: the mark on the surface and the illusion behind, graphic reality and representational fiction.

Whatever "exquisite perfection" and "singular grace" we may imagine informing the line of Parrhasios, the ultimate beauty of that line lay in its functional performance as a bounding line, its ability to inflect itself in space, to transcend and transform the flatness of the surface on which it was drawn – to become, in effect, one with the object depicted. The heritage of Parrhasios is renewed in those demonstrations of linear purity that mark the history of European draftsmanship, from the interlacing patterns of early medieval manuscript illumination to the elegant linearity of Gothic contour and the continuous traditions of drawing since the Renaissance – from Pollaiuolo, Leonardo, and Raphael through Ingres and Degas to Picasso and Matisse.[18]

Outline itself is an abstraction in nature, but not in art. Painters recognize that the contours imagined surrounding solid bodies have no reality in nature: "The outlines which show the shapes of surfaces of dense bodies are called contours and . . . do not have substance," as Leonardo declared, distinguishing the mathematical line from the drawn line.[19] But they also recognize them as necessary graphic fictions, essential to representation. The substance of the contour is itself the drawn line, the very materiality of the art. Its mimetic responsibility is realized in the act of being drawn, for the movement of the draftsman's hand is simultaneously a tracing on the surface and a probing of a world beyond.[20]

In the very character of the bounding line of the drawing we recognize the object, not seen but projected, imagined. Whether the line is sharp and even or irregular and varied, whether it rhythmically expands and contracts, whether its edges are neat or fade into the surrounding surface, whether its texture is smooth or rough, its trace continuous or broken, firm or tentative, thick or thin: such variables will inevitably inform representation, determining the quality or character of the object rendered as well as its relation to the ambient ground. Changes in contour – a thinning of the ink, a lessening of the density of chalk or crayon – may record the velocity of the drawing gesture, which, in turn, is measured over time as well as space, adding yet a further dimension to our experience of the line (Fig. 3). That velocity, moreover, may transfer to the depicted object, investing it with associated qualities, countering its own gravity and inertia. Or the kinesthetics may be reversed (Fig. 4). The draftsman's hand may move with slow deliberateness, or it may return to

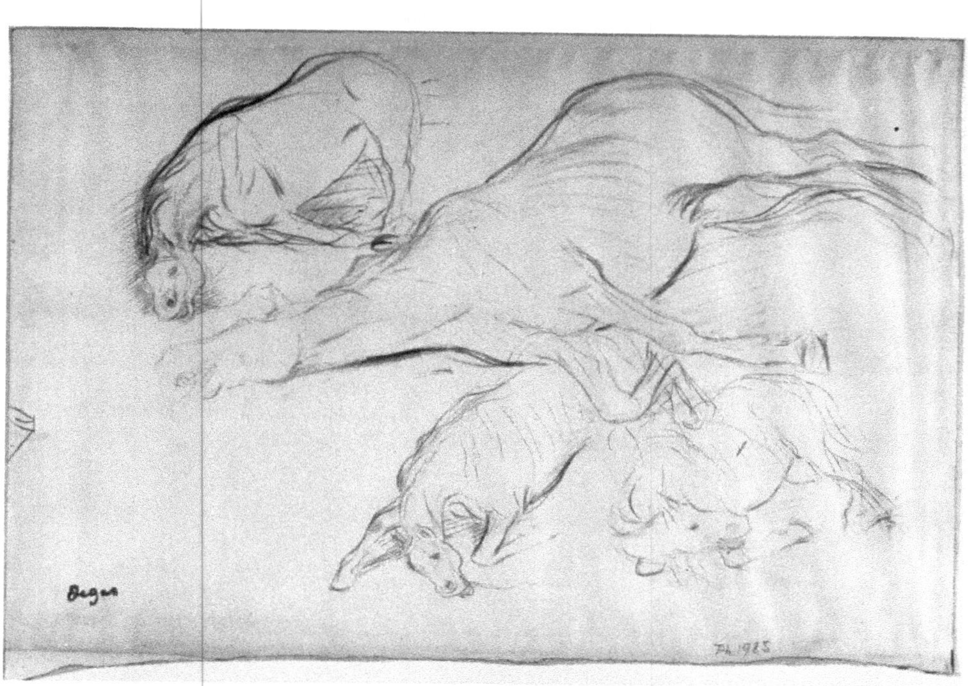

3. Edgar Degas, *Studies of Horses* (ca. 1866). Black chalk, 23.2 × 35.6 cm. Sterling and Francine Clark Art Institute, Williamstown, Mass. (1955.1391).

repeat its motion, thickening the substance of a line, adding to its material as well as visual weight; the resulting line might then brake its directional momentum, becoming by its very thickness less a directed trace than a spreading mark, an object in its own right. Such an expansion of its own inner field modulates the directional impulse of the line, effectively diffusing linear energy laterally, over a broader spread of surface. When a contour becomes so heavy, when it thickens across its directional axis, blunting its own momentum, we may speak of a "pictorialization" of the line – an extension into painting of the line of Parrhasios.

2. *The Desire of the Line*

> Draw a straight line and follow it.
> October 1960

– LaMonte Young
Composition 1960 No. 10[21]

Paul Klee opens his *Pedagogical Sketchbook* by introducing the concept of line as an independent force, a momentum: "An active line on a walk, moving freely without goal. A walk for a walk's sake" (Fig. 5). However apparently casual, this energy is directed: "The mobility agent is a point, shifting its position forward." In his sec-

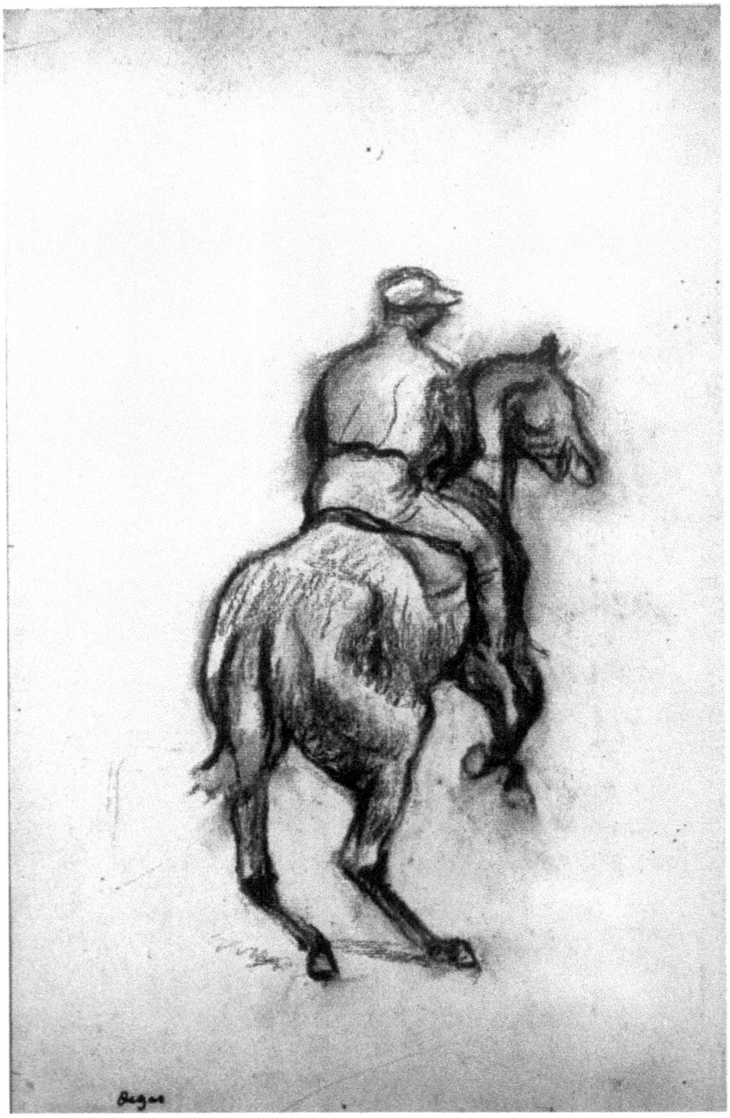

4. Edgar Degas, *The Jockey* (ca. 1898). Charcoal, 48.5 × 30 cm. Cleveland Museum of Art.

ond lesson (Fig. 6) Klee immediately constrains that Euclidean freedom, deliberately limiting the active line in its movement by establishing fixed points, bringing linear impulse under control and transforming "point progression" into "planar effect." Its initiating vectorial impulse interrupted, Klee's line willfully plots its irregular, unpredictable course. "Accompanied by complementary forms," it enters into varied relations with its surrounding field; "circumscribing itself" or engaging "secondary lines," it further complicates its relation to the ground, implicitly spatializing its path.[22]

Klee's demonstration, based on the axiomatic point-line-plane progression, participates in a long tradition of graphic speculation by artists fascinated by the trans-

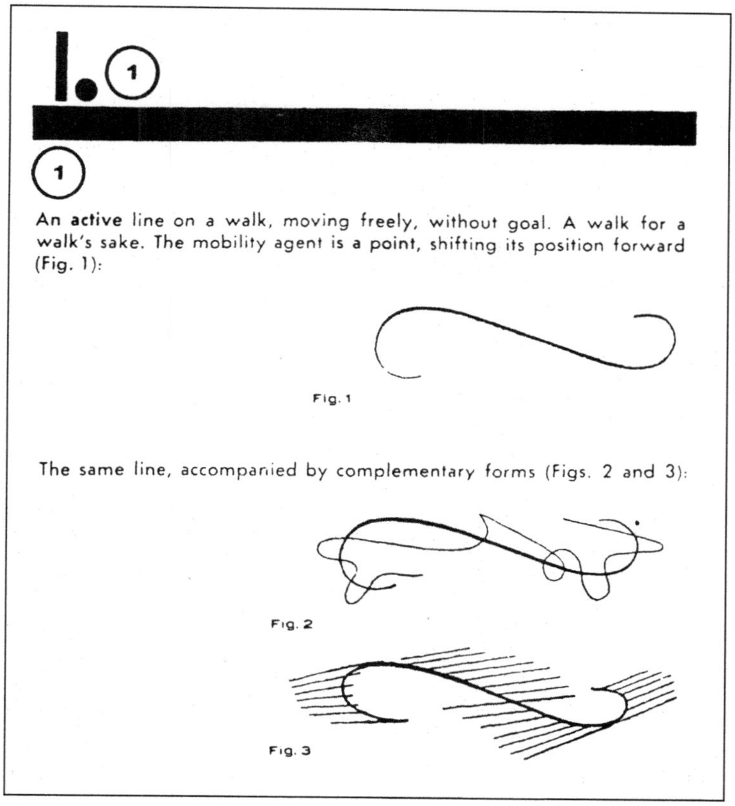

I.1

1

An **active** line on a walk, moving freely, without goal. A walk for a walk's sake. The mobility agent is a point, shifting its position forward (Fig. 1):

Fig. 1

The same line, accompanied by complementary forms (Figs. 2 and 3):

Fig. 2

Fig. 3

5. Paul Klee, from *Pedagogical Sketchbook* (1925; trans. Sibyl Moholy-Nagy, 1953), I.1.

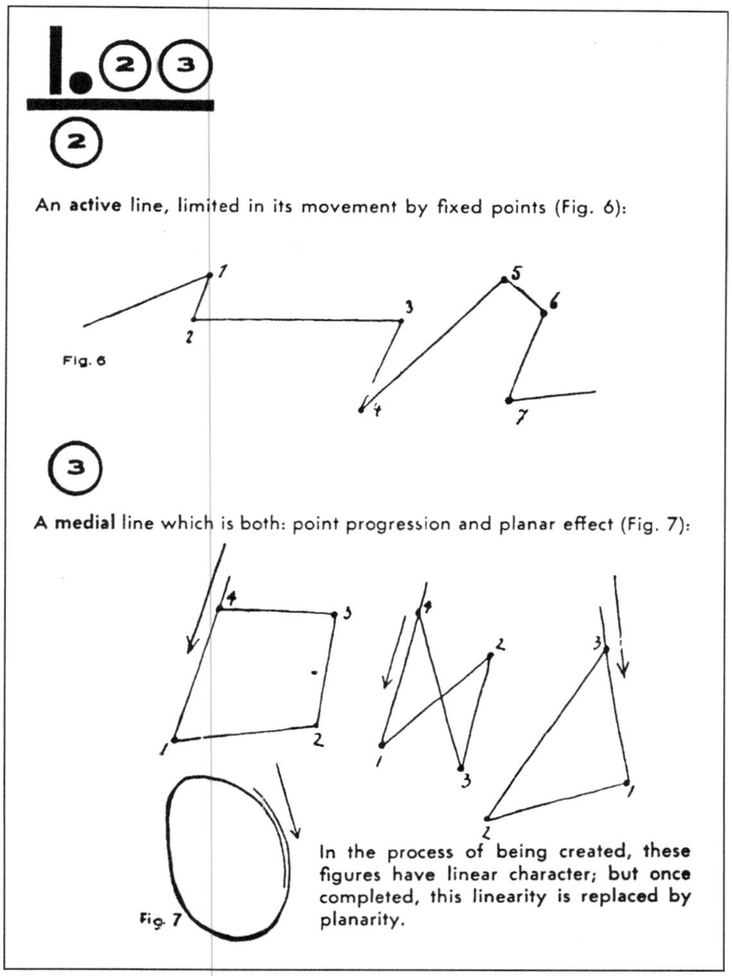

I.2 3

2

An **active** line, limited in its movement by fixed points (Fig. 6):

Fig. 6

3

A **medial** line which is both: point progression and planar effect (Fig. 7):

In the process of being created, these figures have linear character; but once completed, this linearity is replaced by planarity.

Fig. 7

6. Paul Klee, from *Pedagogical Sketchbook* (1925; trans. Sibyl Moholy-Nagy, 1953), I.2,3.

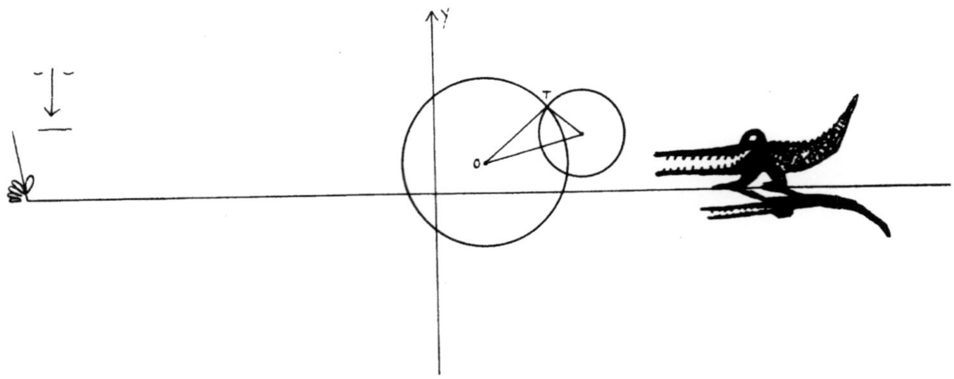

7. Saul Steinberg, *The Line* (detail) (from *The Labyrinth*, 1960).

formative power of line – from Alberti, Piero della Francesca, and Leonardo to Kandinsky, Picasso . . . and, of course, Saul Steinberg (Fig. 7). Artists do not speculate in the abstract, however. The line of their concern is a drawn line, traced by their own hand, and in the course of its making they can only become keenly aware of that pedestrian energy described in Klee's lesson. They know that linear momentum obeys no ready rule, that the trajectory of the line is open and that in such openness resides expressive potential.

The draftsman may begin a line with some goal in mind – whether to depict a particular object, jot down a compositional idea, or merely to break the surface tension of the paper. Once begun, however, the line itself begins to assert a certain will of its own, to challenge the guiding control of the hand, urging its own agenda. Out of that tension there can arise the most creative conflict, as the drawing hand, which may have become complacent in its purpose, is forced to decision. The initial energy of the hand, affected by its own physical extension and movement, inevitably flags: "The fatigue of one's hand as one draws is a perception of time," as Picasso summed up this particular truth of drawing.[23] The options available to the hand may lie anywhere between enforcing representational responsibility upon its own course and yielding to the momentum of the line itself. "One must always search for the desire of the line," Matisse taught, "where it wishes to enter or where to die away."[24]

Once begun, the line becomes more than a means toward an end. Insinuating itself into the drawing process, it insists upon its own role as protagonist, on establishing its own reciprocal relationship with its maker. Whatever initial intention may have inspired the making of a drawing, whatever external stimulus, the draftsman inevitably finds his attention being commanded by his own line. Whatever its intended function in the structure of representation, the line becomes an active participant in the act of drawing, in the processes of its own making, even asserting its own creative independence. And we, as viewers, acknowledge that independence when we respond to the reality of the drawn line, to its substance, its body and personality, its idiosyncratic and vagrant qualities. In searching for descriptive language adequate to our response, we invoke a full range of kinesthetic experience. Mixing metaphoric allusion and psychological perception, tactile sensation and somatic awareness, we assign values and qualities, affect and character, to lines and marks.[25]

The self-reflexivity of the drawn mark, alluding to its own making, quite naturally implicates the maker, returning us to an axiom of connoisseurship enacted in the line of Apelles: the presence in the drawing of the draftsman. In the assertion of its autonomy, its innate resistance to the purpose of representation, the line recalls the process of its becoming through the act of drawing, the gesture of the draftsman.

3. The Phenomenology of Drawing

> There is a tremendous difference between seeing a thing without a pencil in your hand and seeing it while *drawing* it.
> – Paul Valéry[26]

Drawing something is a complex action; it involves subject and object, perception and representation, eye and mind, and, most obviously – yet too often the neglected components in critical discussion – hand and body.[27] Nor is it merely a dialectical relationship between paired terms. Between perceiving eye and object there intercedes drawing itself, as both gestural sequence (act) and evolving configuration (art). Once the first mark disrupts the blank paper, the draftsman enters into a double dialectic: with the object before him (or the idea imagined) and with the emerging graphic construction itself. As the drawing develops, its demands upon the draftsman begin to take precedence over those of the object (or idea) before (or within) him; the drawing asserts itself as the main object of concern, the primary other in the subject-object relation.

The same object will be drawn differently by different draftsmen. We may be tempted to say that each "sees" a fruit differently. Such a locution, however, risks metaphorizing the verb, for we can hardly know what an other *sees*, only what he has represented. Through the drawing we can only know the draftsman, through whose vision we may believe we see the world. Moreover, as Leonardo will show us, the draftsman himself knows the world only by drawing it; the artist "sees" with hands as well as eyes, both sensory extensors of the body in the world.

Different modes of drawing represent different modes of knowing and understanding. The draftsman who bounds an object with a firmer contour, which, like a horizon line, implies the far side of the globe, continues the legacy of Parrhasios, his line "clearly suggesting even what it conceals" (Fig. 8). Such a drawing depends upon and reveals a certain confidence: not only in the firmly drawn line and in its ability to perform that complex representational function, but a confidence as well in the object represented, a faith, as it were, in the continuity of surface, in the existence of the far, unseen side. The very continuity of the line declares that belief.

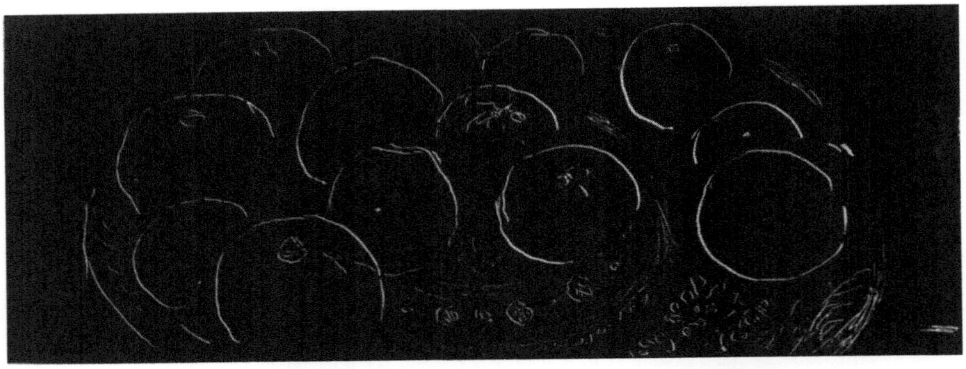

8. Henri Matisse, *Fruits on a Morrocan Plate* (1914–15). Monotype, printed in black 9.2 × 14.3 cm. Museum of Modern Art, New York. Abby Aldrich Rockefeller Fund. Photograph © 2000 The Museum of Modern Art, New York.

Conversely, the graphic shaping of an object through the accumulation of short, broken strokes that together suggest a boundary, not a contour but rather a liminal zone, reveals a different temperament (Fig. 9). The tentative probing recorded in that collectivity of touches betrays a kind of groping, a skepticism in search of assurance; in the exploratory sequence of strokes we read the haptic ambition of the drawing hand, the repeated attempt to reach the object, to secure it for the grasp. Even as we are ready to interpret the phenomenon in purely visual terms – as a graphic rendering of the idea of passage toward and beyond the bounding line, as a rendering of successive vantage points of that disappearing edge – we come

9. Paul Cézanne, *Apples and Pears* (1883–1887). Pencil and watercolor, 22.9 × 29.8 cm. Private collection.

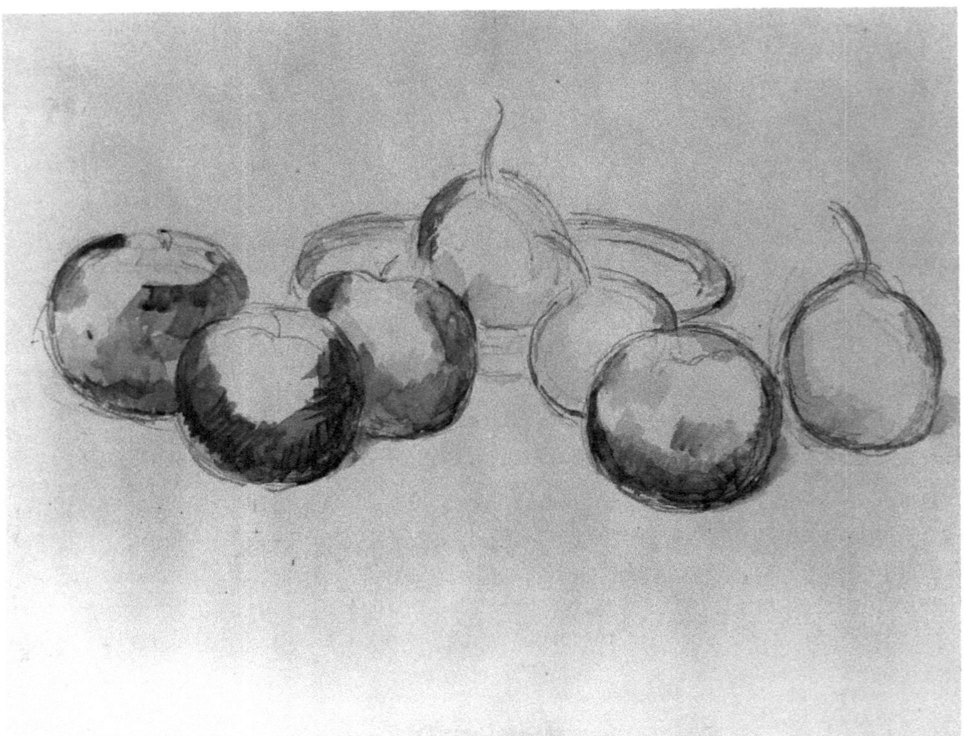

back to the gesture itself, as much the movement of the hand as of the eye. Interpretation involves us in the reconstitution of the act of drawing and, moreover, finds in that act the legitimate object of its own operation.[28]

"The painter 'takes his body with him,'" writes Maurice Merleau-Ponty, invoking Valéry. "Indeed," he continues,

> we cannot imagine how a mind could paint. It is by lending his body to the world that the artist changes the world into paintings. To understand these transubstantiations we must go back to the working, actual body – not the body as a chunk of space or a bundle of functions but that body which is an intertwining of vision and movement.[29]

That observation is even truer of drawing, where the movements of the body, actual and imagined, are more directly recorded by the tracing hand. What we here call the imagined movements of the body, however, refer to and ultimately depend upon the body-image of the viewer, that is, upon our tacit sense of our own body in the world, extending into the space around it and relating to other objects in that space.[30]

The act of drawing, in particular, at once is and records precisely that extension. The apple rendered accommodates itself to the hand that brought it into being; seen at a distance, it is made proximate through drawing, accessible to touch, prehended. More obviously, and on a larger scale, the drawing of a figure relates to the bodily situation of the draftsman. When the object of drawing is another human being the entire body is involved. The model's pose is internalized by the draftsman, measured against his own "body image" or "postural schema."[31] The peculiar tensions of the pose, the balance of the body, its relative stability or instability, especially as gauged against the norm of upright posture: these phenomena are instinctively felt, intuitively comprehended, rather than objectively analyzed.[32]

The analysis that occurs in the act of drawing, in the translation of perception to graphic mark, inflected contour or accentuated moment, is itself a response of the draftsman's body. The thirty-second pose in life-drawing classes acknowledges just that phenomenon: with little time for sustained visual analysis, the student is forced to take in the model in an instant, to comprehend and internalize the pose kinesthetically, to understand it in and through the very act of drawing it. And that experience is true even for longer poses. However attentively the draftsman may scan the model, searching out contours and surfaces, the record of the drawing itself is, we might say, more an expression than a representation, more an internal than an external match. With regard to "drawing from the life," Valéry theorizes "that the shapes our sight reveals to us as contours are produced by our consciousness of the concerted movement of our eyes as they register precise vision. This *registering* movement constitutes *line*." His conclusion: "Seeing lines is copying them. . . ."[33]

Drawing is (re-)enactment. So too is our response to drawing. Whether we are initially concerned with the mimetic function of the drawn line or with its calligraphic qualities as ornament, one aspect of its existence remains central: the line is a direct record of the draftsman's gesture. On a fundamental level, it involves us, as viewers, in the kinesthetics of the act of drawing: its qualities of direction, velocity, weight, its rhythm, pace, and inflection stand as permanent trace of the movement of the artist's hand – and of the body of which that hand is an extension.

More than the hand may be directly involved. Depending on the size of the field, the artist may be working only with his fingers, or from the wrist, or elbow, or shoulder. The swing and range of the marking implement will vary: the larger the scale of operation, the more of the body involved.[34] Thus, for example, the preliminary drawings *(sinopie)* done directly on the wall in monumental medieval and Renaissance fresco painting (see Fig. 13 on page 31) required the full engagement of the artist's body: the very act of drawing on that scale involves a kind of imitation *avant le figure,* so to speak; drawing itself becomes a playing out of the figural action being rendered. And the viewer surely responds more immediately and fully to a life-size figure represented by a series of graphic impulses, gestures of the creating body of the artist, than, say, to a thumbnail sketch.

The gesture of drawing is, in essence, a projection of the body, and, especially when viewing a drawing of the human figure, we are inevitably reminded of that. The conviction of such a representational image depends upon a kind of transference of energies felt. We might prefer to speak more conventionally of "imagination" or even of "mind," but the figures of an artist like Rembrandt are so intensely and fully realized in their summary graphic notation that our own response attests to what we may term the "mime" of drawing, the projection of self.

The drama is in the line. Meaning is generated in and by the act of drawing itself, for the act of drawing is already one of feeling.[35] In no other art – save, perhaps, dance[36] – are means and end, the how and what of significance, so perfectly identified. Responding to drawings, we make our way back, through line, to the originary impulse of the draftsman. Interpretation involves a connecting act of *re*-creation, the self-projection of the viewer *re*imagining the process of drawing.

This active role of the viewer – articulated by Leonardo as a private dialectic between the artist, as first beholder, and his emerging work – provides a further, complementary axiom of connoisseurship. The open structure of drawing, especially of the rapid sketch, invites the participation of the viewer; indeed, it requires such active response for the completion or realization of its significance. We may call upon a leading voice of early modern connoisseurship to speak for the tradition. Roger de Piles praises drawings that are "quickly executed and unfinished" as having "more spirit" and "good character"; such drawings lead the viewer to an appropriate response, for their unfinished state invites the imagination to "supply the missing parts," to fill in the spaces between lines. Each viewer thereby participates in the completion of the idea according to his own particular taste ("selon son Goût").[37]

Such engagement with suggestive graphic structure implicates the viewer in the creation of the drawing, as he or she is co-opted into supplying the missing parts by act of the imagination. But the drawing itself, as de Piles observes, takes the initiative in this exchange; it sets the viewer on the right path ("dans un bon chemin"), establishes the direction and momentum of interpretation. Only then can the viewer become an active agent in the completion of the design.

Interacting with the linear configuration of the drawing, the imagination of the viewer expresses itself in a corresponding mode. Drawing, as we have been emphasizing, is the record of a physical act. Its invitation is, on a primary level, to the body of the viewer, whose own response will necessarily involve a somatic dimension. "Looking long enough," as Ernst Kris has written, "one tends to become aware of a kinesthetic reaction, however slight; it may be that one tries, at first imperceptibly and later consciously, to react with one's body, or it may be that the reaction remains unconscious."[38] Following the linear patterns of a drawing, supplying continuity to the open gaps between points and lines, we engage the very energies and impulses that went into its making.

> From looking at a whirl of lines, from following them, we change imperceptibly from identification with the model into the stage in which we "imitate" the strokes and lines with which it was produced. To some extent we have changed roles. We started out as part of the world which the artist created; we end as co-creators: We identify ourselves with the artist.[39]

Within this epistemological circle of connoisseurship, draftsman, drawing, and viewer complete a circuit of identity. The viewer enacts the drawing, mimicking it with his body. Through the drawing the viewer meets the draftsman. Criticism, which is response articulated, imitates creation in reverse.[40]

4. *The Physiognomy of the Line*

> . . . gesture, like voice, reflects different emotions. . . . The gesture of the artist is in his line.
> – John Graham[41]

Suggesting more than it actually shows, the line of Parrhasios epitomizes the pictorial potential of the drawn line; reaching beyond its material limits, its reference is to something other than itself, to a bounded figure or to an imagined space beyond – inviting the imaginative projection of the viewer. The line of Apelles is retrospective; it refers back to the hand of its maker, and that self-reflexion makes it an emblem of connoisseurship: the line as trace, an index of authorial presence – inviting the imaginative recognition of the viewer.

It is the professional aspect of Pliny's account of Apelles' line that renders it a topos of such great resonance. The very formulation of the legend, involving professional admiration and courtesy, as well as competition, is calculated to pay tribute both to the artists and to the connoisseurs, those capable of perceiving and understanding true achievement in art. Such understanding puts the connoisseur in the studio; *addetto al lavoro,* he is an equal to the artist in the discourse on art, if not in its creation.[42] Thus, variations on the tale epitomize artistic talent in the most fundamental and apparently simple exercises: for example, the celebrated "O" of Giotto, the perfect circle drawn in a single stroke by the unaided hand.[43] To the uncomprehending such a display of virtuosity may be nonsense; to "those who understand" it will reveal the genius of the artist. In a sixteenth-century dialogue dominated by Michelangelo, Francisco de Hollanda summarizes the lesson as follows:

> . . . a good painter [*um valente home*], making a beginning with a simple outline [*um facil perfil*], will at once be recognized as an Apelles, if an Apelles he is; and for an ignorant painter, if he is an ignorant painter. In the eyes of those who understand, there will be need of no more, nor more time, or proof, or examination; they know that in a mere straight line Apelles was known by Protogenes, both immortal Greek painters.[44]

By his line shall an artist be known. This axiom of connoisseurship, proved in the professional studios of ancient Greece as part of the celebration of individual artistic achievement, has continued to inform the culture of critical appreciation from the Renaissance on. The competition between Apelles and Protogenes not only attested the special nature of artistic virtuosity and responsive sensibility, it confirmed the intimate identification of the artist with his mark. His basic handwriting, his *ductus*, became signature in the most immediate way, a graphic declaration of the presence of a particular persona. For the connoisseurs of the eighteenth century, the drawings of a master revealed his character most directly; through his touch we confront the unique quality of his genius. The etymological roots of the notion of style in *stilus*, in writing and the hand, are reconfirmed.[45] Style is signature – as Saul Steinberg so often reminded us (Fig. 10).

The notion that every artist represents himself in his work was fully articulated by the Renaissance, summed up in the adage "ogni dipintore dipinge se." Or, as Joachim Camerarius put it in his preface to Dürer's *Four Books of Human Proportion*, "The nature of a man is never more certainly and definitely shown than in the works he produces as the fruit of his art. . . . What single painter has there ever been who did not reveal his character in his works?"[46] We recognize the Renaissance roots of modern connoisseurship. Individual style means individual hand; the work of the artist is the work of the hand.[47]

5. The Legacy of Connoisseurship

. . . le style est l'homme même.
– Buffon[48]

Connoisseurship has always recognized the fundamental subjectivity of its operations, respecting intuition and celebrating the "good eye." In acknowledging drawing as a most personal statement, a direct expression of the character of the artist, it has, in effect, insisted on such critical subjectivity. Through a drawing, the connoisseur feels himself in privileged rapport with the artist, a meeting of two correspondingly fine and mutually confirming sensibilities.

On the eve of the eighteenth century, Roger de Piles summarized the basic assumptions of the appreciation of drawings, articulating those fundamental values that have informed connoisseurship to the present day. Drawings mark "the character" of the artist, revealing the nature of his genius, whether it is "quick or heavy," whether "his thoughts are noble or common," whether he has skill and "good taste." The painter who brings a picture to high finish may seek to hide behind the polished surface, disappearing behind its illusion, "but in making a drawing, he gives himself over to his genius, and reveals himself for what he is."[49]

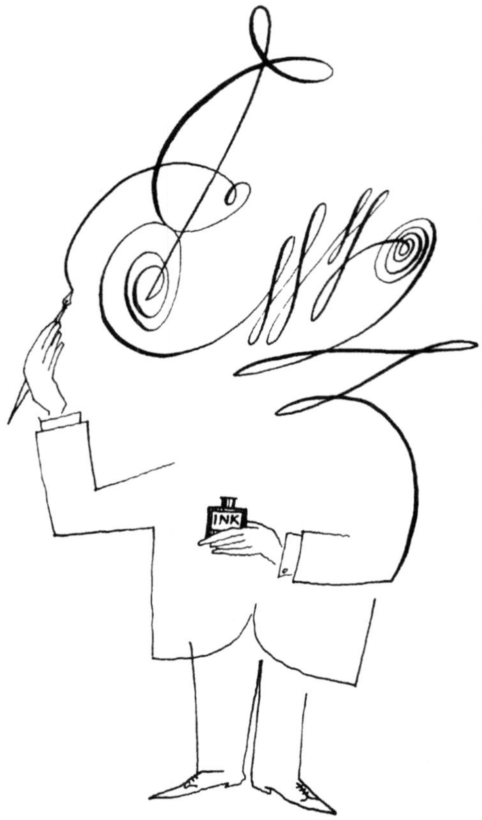

10. Saul Steinberg, *Signature* (from *The Passport*, 1954).

In drawings we most directly encounter the artist. The very openness of the medium denies the draftsman any place to hide and exposes him to us, unawares. Through its configuration of separate marks we gain a glimpse of his "character," his "genius," his "taste." And because those marks – of stylus, pen, chalk, or brush – are so physiognomically distinctive, comparable to individual handwriting, the study of drawings came to be considered the field par excellence for training in connoisseurship, the primary task of which was to distinguish "le caractère de la main."[50]

In the late nineteenth century, even as he sought to establish a new "scientific" basis for connoisseurship, Giovanni Morelli could not help but renew and reconfirm its traditional assumptions when he declared that in the drawings of the great masters "the whole man stands before us without disguise or affectation, and his genius with its beauties and its failings speaks directly to the mind."[51]

Since the sixteenth century it has been assumed that drawn marks, dependent as they are on the immediate recording impulse, take us close to the spontaneous act of creation, the moment of inspiration – "il furor dello artefice," as Giorgio Vasari phrased it early in the tradition.[52] The general assumption, already fully articulated in the Renaissance, is that the obedient hand of the artist gives visible form to an idea conceived in the mind: *idea, concetto, pensée* – such abstract terms have been constants in the vocabulary of commentary on drawing. But drawings are made by the hand, and our observations and interpretations must, of necessity, begin with the visible marks on the paper. Whatever we may think we know of the mind of an artist like Rembrandt, of his "inner vision," we can know only by attending to the stroke of his pen, that is, to the recorded movements of his hand.[53]

Still, beyond the mark on the paper, the material reality of the drawing, we do sense a realm of further possibilities. The drawn line offers an invitation to engage something beyond itself: on one level, of course, it points to the pictorial representation in the construction of which it participates; on another, in a less spatial and more temporal dimension, it leads not in the direction of illusion but, acknowledging the primary reality of the mark, toward the past of the drawing itself, the moments of its making.[54]

Well into the last century the dialectic between these antitheses has determined critical appreciation of drawing: "The vacillation between spirit and matter, artistic illusion and material object," in the words of Charles de Tolnay.[55] Indeed, this modern scholar maintains the assumptions and attitudes that shaped the traditions of connoisseurship in the eighteenth century, confirming their continuing relevance and affirming their validity:

> In a drawing the lines or brush strokes are not only elements of characterization for the forms but they have, at the same time, poetic value as expressions of the temperament, sentiment, or *état d'âme* of the creator. . . . a balance between spiritual and material aspects. . . . At one moment the beholder admires the beauty of the line as a purely material element made by human hand, while again he may be concerned with its expressive significance and see in it the illusionistic function which the artist intended. Because the handicraft and raw material are always apparent, a drawing seems to be a more intimate document. It is not yet completely liberated from the creator, nor from matter: it reveals an embryonic world.[56]

However romanticizing (or Platonizing) we may find his vocabulary, Tolnay's formulation nonetheless declares the openness of the situation: "Half matter, half spirit, the drawing is for us a symbol of a world in formation."[57] It implies the hermeneutic space in which interpretation operates, a space generated by the rich ambivalence – and, therefore, potential multivalence – of the mark as sign, trace, and index. It also suggests the responsive dynamics mandated by that openness, the necessity of interpretation, as the viewer negotiates the referential options of the line.

By the eighteenth century a distinctive language of connoisseurship had evolved. Refining the traditional vocabulary of critical appreciation, bringing Renaissance concepts to new focus and adapting them to new purpose, this language served the discourse of a culture of amateurs, a culture of taste and self-consciously aesthetic engagement. In the light of this culture, imitation yielded its primacy as a criterion of judgment to genius; a work of art became less transparent, less a window onto another world than a means of encountering the maker of the work.[58] The artist himself became the object of aesthetic experience, the work the sign of his presence. And it was especially in his drawings that such presence was felt: there, on paper, as Roger de Piles declares, "il s'abandonne à son Génie, & se fait voir tel qu'il est." That is why great collectors go beyond paintings to seek out drawings by the masters as well.[59]

Axiomatic to this attitude was a recognition of the work of art as self-expression. From the exalted notion of "genius," difficult to individualize with precision, de Piles invokes a psychologically more apprehensible one of "character." "This character," he explains, "consists of the manner in which the painter thinks things; it is the stamp that distinguishes him from others, and that he impresses on his works like the living image of his spirit. It is this character that stirs our imagination. . . ."[60] The way in which a painter thinks, that is, imagines the things of the world, induces us to imagine with him, to see the world through him. Through that mediated vision, then, we know the maker of the image. The artist imposes his "character" on the viewer as well as on the world represented.

Subsequent generations of connoisseurs elaborated the thesis of the artist-in-the-work. Seeking a more precise analytical vocabulary, they focused increasingly on the operations of the artist. Antoine-Joseph Dézallier d'Argenville, for example, while still invoking the Platonic fire of inspiration, searches for a creative dimension more accessible to analysis and practical criticism. Although rehearsing Renaissance commonplaces, he more deliberately lays out the interpretive space of connoisseurship to include both the ineffable qualities of genius and the mechanical operations of the hand; both are manifested most clearly in drawing:

> Drawings . . . are the first ideas of a painter, the first fire of his imagination, his style, his spirit, his manner of thinking. . . . An artist, in painting a picture, corrects himself and represses the ardor of his genius; in making a drawing, he throws out the first fire of his thought; he abandons himself to his self; he reveals himself as just what he is.[61]

Echoing and extending the discourse of de Piles, Dézallier d'Argenville continues to seek a balance between interior and exterior, spirit and body: "The character of the hand is the practice that each master forms in order to work; this hand must obey the thought, of which it is only the servant; the head makes the drawing, leading the hand, which then merely executes."[62] This celebration of manual obedience notwithstanding, the role of the hand in giving form to thought is indeed acknowledged. The operation of the hand is, after all, responsible for forming taste and for making the spirit intelligible.[63] And it is especially in the open form of the sketch that the character of the hand, the trait of the artist, is manifest to the true connoisseur:

> The great masters hardly finish their drawings; they are content to make sketches, or mere scribbles, which do not please the demi-connoisseurs, those who want something finished, something pleasing to the eyes. A true connoisseur thinks differently; he sees in a sketch a great master's very manner of thinking, of characterizing each object with a few strokes. His imagination, animated by the fine fire that determines the drawing, sees through what is missing; often it perceives what is not there and what should be there.[64]

Thus does the truly responsive viewer participate in the genius of creativity. How is one to discern the particular traits of a master? D'Argenville adduces the analogy, by then quite conventional, to penmanship. As the natural expression of handwriting clearly distinguishes one man from another, so an artist's style of drawing distinguishes his character from that of other draftsmen.[65] Seeking to discern the character of the artist in the operations of the hand, the connoisseur becomes ever more attentive to the constructive activity of the draftsman, the actual processes of marking, and to the individual mark. And it is in the immediacy and indeterminacy of the sketch rather than in the studied closure of the finished drawing that character is most legible; in the spontaneity of the instinctively drawn line, uncorrected and unpolished, is revealed the personal gesture of the inventing hand. Testifying to the creative presence of the artist, the individual marks of pen or chalk appeal to the imagination of the viewer; in and through his imaginative engagement, completing suggested form in his mind, the viewer becomes a participant in the creative process itself – "selon son Goût." Aesthetic experience thus pays compliment to both viewer and artist.

6. Beyond Connoisseurship

Recognition of the responsible hand, attribution, has always been the primary and most immediate concern of connoisseurship. Beyond that, the art-historical study of drawings, especially so-called old-master drawings, has focused on function, the purpose of drawing: its role in the production of other works of art or in the education of the artist or in his perfection. Indeed, within the broad Renaissance tradition, from the fifteenth through the eighteenth century, drawings were generally made for a specific purpose. With respect to production, they serve to develop or to present pictorial ideas, to clarify compositions, to study details, to enlarge or to transfer designs; with respect to professional education, artists drew to study other works of art, to learn the anatomy of the human figure or to understand other forms of nature, or they simply drew to keep their hand in practice – like Apelles: *nulla dies sine linea.* Before each drawing studied by the art historian, then, the question is appropriately asked: why was it done, toward what end?

Once asked, however, the question itself implies that the answer, which is usually obtainable as the result of proper art-historical research, is the end of the study. Once we have answered it – once we have determined, for example, that Leonardo made a drawing to investigate the movement of water, or that a sheet of sketches by Raphael served in the preparation of a particular painting, or that Michelangelo intended a drawing as a gift for a special friend, or that Rembrandt must have drawn this landscape from that specific vantage point – we tend then to assume that we have understood the drawing itself. Even when we consider the medium and technique of a drawing, we are satisfied once we have analyzed it as metal point or quill pen and bistre or iron gall ink or black or red chalk or a combination of them, or have determined that the paper is prepared or faded blue, that it was made in northern or central Italy. The answers to such questions give us the categories for cataloguing a drawing, and they may indicate a particular historical *raison d'être* for it, but do they offer fully satisfactory explanation? Do we not want a deeper account, a more genuinely critical understanding, one more commensurate with the richness of our experience of the drawing?

To declare that the meaning of a drawing lies essentially in its historical function not only ignores the complexity of that experience, thereby narrowing the possibilities of meaning, it effectively dislocates meaning itself. If we accept that the act of drawing is indeed what we respond to, then it is that that must become the object of critical attention. We owe it to our own experience to take the creating process itself as seriously as the created work, indeed, as an integral dimension of the work; as important, we owe it to the draftsman. The communication between us, between artist and viewer, occurs essentially through the graphic structures of a drawing: our present response to lines made by an artist sometime in the past. Our experience of the drawing involves the *re*-enactment of the drawing gesture, our mimic *re*-creation of the creative acts. Critical responsibility, then, must be to those originary acts, to the experience of the making, in which, we assume, lies the most profound, because most human, meaning of the work.

CHAPTER TWO

Disegno

The Invention of an Art

. . . we are building anew an art of painting.
– Leon Battista Alberti[1]

Drawing as an art is a discovery of the Renaissance. This is hardly to claim that the practice of drawing was unknown before the fifteenth century; modes of delineation had been the essential component of the pictorial arts since remote antiquity. Only in the Quattrocento, however, that is, in the early Renaissance in Italy, does drawing come to be consciously and programmatically recognized as a distinctive activity, fundamental to painting and the related visual arts and yet separate from them. Only in the early Renaissance does the practice of drawing become theorized, and this occurs as a consequence, intellectual and technical, of new attitudes toward painting and, ultimately, toward the painter. It relates both to the accommodation of the pictorial arts to the evolving cultural values of humanism and to the studio practices of a new generation of artists.

1. *Alberti's Finding*

The locus classicus for this phenomenon is the resonant little volume on painting written by Leon Battista Alberti in 1435. This first humanist treatise devoted to a traditionally mechanical art responds to and participates in the exciting new developments in painting in early fifteenth-century Florence. Just returned from family exile, Alberti recognizes and celebrates the artistic achievements and ambitions of the Florentines: "di nuovo fabrichiamo un'arte di pittura."[2] Rationalizing practice and articulating theoretical foundations for the art of Donatello, Ghiberti, Luca della Robbia, Masaccio, and, especially, Brunelleschi, to whom he addressed *Della pittura*, the Italian version of his text, Alberti structured his book on the model of ancient rhetorical treatises.[3] In his dedicatory letter he describes the division to Brunelleschi:

> You will see three books: The first, all mathematics, concerns the roots in nature from which arises this delightful and most noble art. The second book puts the art in the hand of the artist, distinguishing its parts and demonstrating all. The third instructs the artist how he can and should acquire perfect skill and knowledge in the art of painting.

In the first book, "tutto matematico," Alberti establishes the Euclidean basis for the art, demonstrating the simple geometry behind the recently invented system of artificial perspective that so radically distinguished the new painting of the Quattrocento from all that preceded it. Indeed, it was just this rationalization of pictorial rendering, the systematization of spatial representation, that inspired and permitted Alberti's search for the theoretical foundations of painting in optics and geometry. Taking his professional readers slowly through the fundamentals of plane geometry – from point, to line, to plane – he lays out the essentially linear base for representation, the determination of the foreshortened coordinated groundplane that will provide the standard of commensurability for the painter's composition. Mixing geometric theorems of similar triangles and optical theories of visual reception and perception, he describes painting as an intersection of the visual pyramid, a record of visual rays cut at a certain moment on their way to the eye. Perspective involves a seeing through and painting may therefore be analogized to a transparent window. Nonetheless, the goal of the system is less illusion than measure. Commensurability is the operative value, the predictability of proportion that permits rational control of perspectival diminution on the picture plane and adapts its grids and patterns to the subjective agent of the viewing eye (Fig. 11).[4]

In book 2, which "puts the art in the hand of the artist," Alberti's strategy shifts from the mathematical to the rhetorical, his inspiration from Euclid to Cicero and Quintilian. Again, the aim is a rational understanding of the art, the articulation of its fundamental principles. As in the overall structure of his treatise, Alberti follows the models of ancient rhetoric, dividing his art into three parts: "painting is composed of circumscription, composition, and the reception of light" (¶ 31). With this he postulates a tripartite definition of painting that will resonate through the Renaissance tradition of art theorizing. Translated as "disegno, comensuratio et colorare" by Piero della Francesca,[5] this aesthetic trinity will find its vernacular epitome in the sixteenth century as *disegno, invenzione,* and *colorire.* Alberti's *circonscrizione* articulates the very basis for *disegno,* for drawing in its functional sense as delineation, linear representation, and his paragraph on the term lays the foundation for subsequent critical appreciation of the art:

> Circumscription describes the turning of the outline [*l'attorniare dell'orlo*] in the painting. They say that Parrhasios . . . was most expert in this and had studied these lines most attentively. I say that one should take care that this circumscription is done with the most subtle lines, such that they can hardly be seen, like those the painter Apelles used to practice and compete with Protogenes. Circumscription is none other than the drawing of the outline [*disegnamento dell'orlo*], which when done with too apparent a line in a painting will look not like the margin of a surface but like a crack. I should like only the movement of the outline [*l'andare dell'orlo*] to be followed in circumscription; to this, I affirm, one must devote the utmost practice. No composition and no reception of light can be praised where there is not also good circumscription. Nor is it unusual to see a good circumscription alone, that is, a good drawing by itself be most pleasing [*cioè uno buono disegno per sé essere gratissimo*]. (¶ 31)

Alberti's brief disquisition on drawing is remarkable in several ways. Pillaging the anecdotal stores of antiquity, Pliny in particular, he moves from the historical celebration of the well-drawn line and the aesthetics of linear subtlety to injunctions concerning actual practice. Drawing is established as the foundation for painting. Without it neither composition nor coloring can succeed; but drawing itself has the potential to stand alone, independent of the other two terms. A subtle contour, Alberti recognizes – slipping from Apelles to Parrhasios – is a marvel to behold: a line across a surface that inflects itself spatially to transcend the flat reality of that surface, a line that has no equivalent in nature and therefore must seem not to exist even as it describes natural form – a paradox that will greatly worry and fascinate Leonardo da Vinci. Like ancient Pliny, Alberti too seems ready to celebrate the single line. In this passage he acknowledges the independence of drawing as an art. As the art of drawing emerges in its own right, with its own aesthetic values, Alberti explicitly confirms that autonomy: "cioè uno buono disegno per sé essere gratissimo."

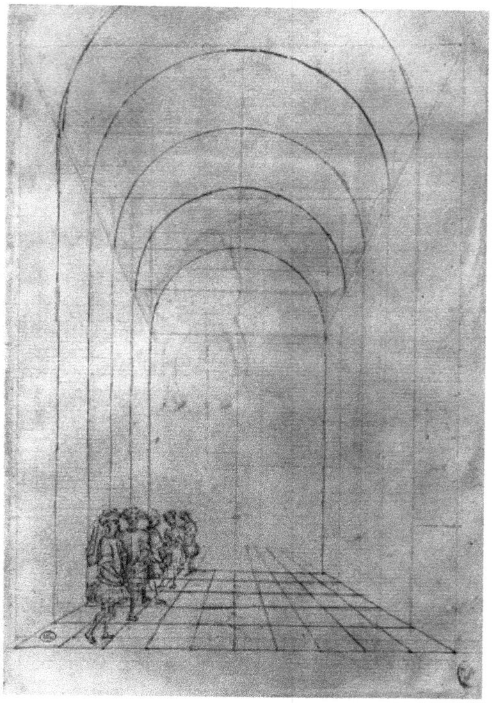

11. Pisanello, *Perspective Study.* Pen and brown ink over preliminary traces in metalpoint and stylus, with straightedge and compass, on paper washed in red, 25.2 × 17.4 cm. Musée du Louvre, Paris. Département des Arts Graphiques (inv. 2520).

Alberti's humanist predecessors and contemporaries had not exactly ignored drawing, but they recognized it strictly as a mechanical art. Only the anecdotal knowledge that the Greeks had held the practice in esteem sanctioned attention to it. Thus, for example, Pier Paolo Vergerio: "We are told that the Greeks devised for their sons a course of training in four subjects: letters, gymnastic, music and drawing. Now, of these," he feels compelled to observe, "drawing has no place amongst our liberal studies; except in so far as it is identical with writing (which is in reality one side of the art of drawing), it belongs to the painter's profession: the Greeks, as an art-loving people, attached to it an exceptional value."[6] In addition to the sanctioning example of antiquity, the virtues of fine penmanship – praised, and often practiced, by the humanists – could be appropriated on behalf of the art of drawing.[7] That art, however, remained part of the painter's manual practice.

In writing his treatise, its Latin version in particular, Alberti aimed to remove the mechanical stigma from the painter's art, to bring it into the circle of liberal studies. The new artificial perspective, presumably invented by Brunelleschi and certainly practiced on a monumental scale in painting by Masaccio, offered the means of defining the intellectual status of painting, for its mathematics required a certain mental as well as manual agility. Geometry, already securely established as a liberal art, provided the primary intellectual credentials for painting. Beyond that basic structure, however, beyond the definition of painting as intersection of a visual pyramid and hence as window, Alberti located the intellect of the art in the *istoria,* "the greatest work of the painter" (¶ 33). However problematic the notion may be – literally, "history" or "story," yet implying more than just a narrative subject – it is clear that Alberti associated *istoria* with composition, that is, with the challenge of figural design, as well as with theme or subject.[8] It is also clear that he assumed drawing as the basis of both, for his introduction of these topics opens with *circonscrizione,* "which pertains in no small way to composition." Composition itself is defined as "that rule in painting by which the parts are put together in a picture." This then leads directly to the celebration of "l'istoria" and to its analytic parsing: "parts of the *istoria* are the bodies; parts of bodies are the members; parts of the members are the surfaces." Reduced to its essential components in a taxonomy that leads from the human figure back to its constitutive planes, the *istoria* in turn leads logically back to drawing: "circumscription is none other than a certain rule for drawing the outline of the surfaces [*certa ragione di segnare l'orlo delle superficie*]. . . ."

Alberti has taken his discourse back to basics, to the actual drawing of contours. Although he never deals directly with strictly workshop matters such as how to cut a quill or draw with a lead stylus or how to tint paper – subjects prominent among the recipes in Cennino Cennini's *Libro dell'arte* of the previous generation – Alberti maintains a keen awareness of manual practice. This is particularly evident in his comments on the drawing of outlines, where a phrase like "l'attorniare del orlo" leads directly to the accomplishment of specific artists of antiquity and the injunction to make lines so subtle that "they can hardly be seen." The Euclidean line of geometry, the locus of a point, remains purely theoretical; the drawn line belongs to the more sensate wisdom of painting ("la più grassa Minerva" [¶ 1]), its material reality.[9]

In the space between theory and practice, between the mind and the hand, Alberti offers his final demonstration of circumscription, "cioè il modo del disegnare": the drawing of a foreshortened circle (¶ 34). One starts with a gridded square, that fundamental matrix of commensurability, in which the circle is inscribed (Fig. 12). Projecting that grid into perspective, one establishes a regular scale of diminution, a proportionate system that permits the transference of corresponding points from the undistorted schema. But marking and transferring a potentially infinite number of points of intersection would be tedious; therefore, having indicated only eight or so such points, "I continue the circle in the painting with my mind [*segno con ingegno il mio circulo*], guiding the lines from point to point." The work of ruler and compass must eventually be translated freehand, the mind guiding the hand across the gaps between points in the spatial projection of the circle. *Segnare con ingegno:* the phrase epitomizes the intimate rapport between hand and mind; it assumes the value of drawing in its highest ambition as a marking of the intentions of the intellect.

In book 3 of *On Painting*, on the artist himself, Alberti deals more directly, if briefly, with studio practice and especially as it involves drawing. In something of a humanist paraphrase of traditional guild injunctions, he calls upon the painter to be morally upright and learned in all the liberal arts, but above all in geometry (¶ 53). Moreover, the painter should be *letterato* and should associate with poets and orators, who share "many ornaments" with him and who have "a broad knowledge of many things," which "could be very useful in beautifully composing the *istoria*, whose greatest praise consists in the invention." Like "uno buono disegno per sé," so too "even without painting, a beautiful invention by itself is pleasing [*sola senza pittura per sé la bella invenzione sta grata*]." Following this affirmation of the independent value of invention, Alberti then offers his *ekphraseis* of the "Calumny of Apelles" and the "Three Graces" – a proleptic program for a Renaissance imagery yet to come.[10]

From these *invenzioni* he turns to the early training of the artist and the role of drawing in that program (¶ 55). Just as youths are taught to write by first learning the separate forms of the letters ("which the ancients call elements"), then syllables, and finally words, so too beginning painters should learn according to rule:

> First of all they should learn to draw well the outlines of surfaces, and here they would be practicing the first elements of painting. Then they should learn how to join together the surfaces, and then learn the individual form of each member, and commit to memory whatever differentiates each member.

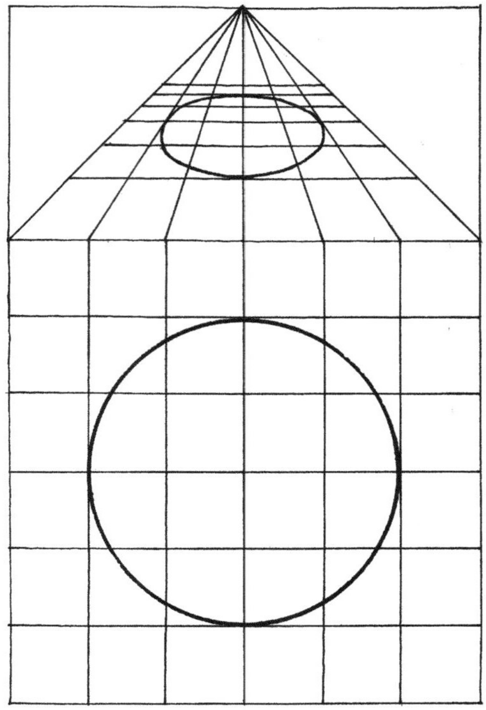

12. Construction of a circle in perspective according to Alberti.

Do not learn to draw on small tablets, Alberti admonishes, as though in direct critical reponse to chapter 5 of Cennino Cennini's *Libro dell'arte.*[11] He would rather have the youngster practice by drawing large, nearly equal in size to what is being represented. "In small drawings every large weakness is easily hidden; in the large the smallest weakness is easily seen" (¶ 57). "Anyone who knows how to paint a large figure well can easily form other small things with a single stroke [*in uno solo colpo*]." Behind this advice we sense the critical – if not necessarily practical – experience of mural painting, the grand tradition of fresco painting whose most recent triumphs, by Masaccio, were to be seen in the Brancacci Chapel and in Santa Maria Novella. Indeed, Alberti's counsel on preparing an *istoria* seems directed at such large public works and seems to take into account the very preparatory steps we can only infer in the absence of extant drawings:

> And when we have an *istoria* to paint, first we will carefully consider the means and the order to make it most beautiful; we will begin by making our drawings and models of the whole *istoria* and of each of its parts, and we will call upon our friends for advice about it. Thus we will do our best to have every part well thought out beforehand, so that there will be nothing in the work that we do not understand how to make or its location. And in order to have the greatest certainty, we will divide our models with parallels, so that in the public work we will take from our drawings [*congetti*], just as we draw upon our private commentaries for maxims and citations. (¶ 61)

From this rather compressed account we may infer a full range of preparatory activity, including the use of notebooks as repositories of motifs.[12] Above all, we are made aware of the function of drawings in the preparation of a "publico lavoro" – that is, mural or altarpiece – from compositional sketches on paper ("concetti e modelli"; Latin: "modulosque in chartis conicientes") and separate studies of individual parts through the final design squared for enlargement or transfer. Every decision will be thoroughly thought through, every detail brought under full control before the actual execution on wall or panel.

The one essential term missing from Alberti's account, but nonetheless very

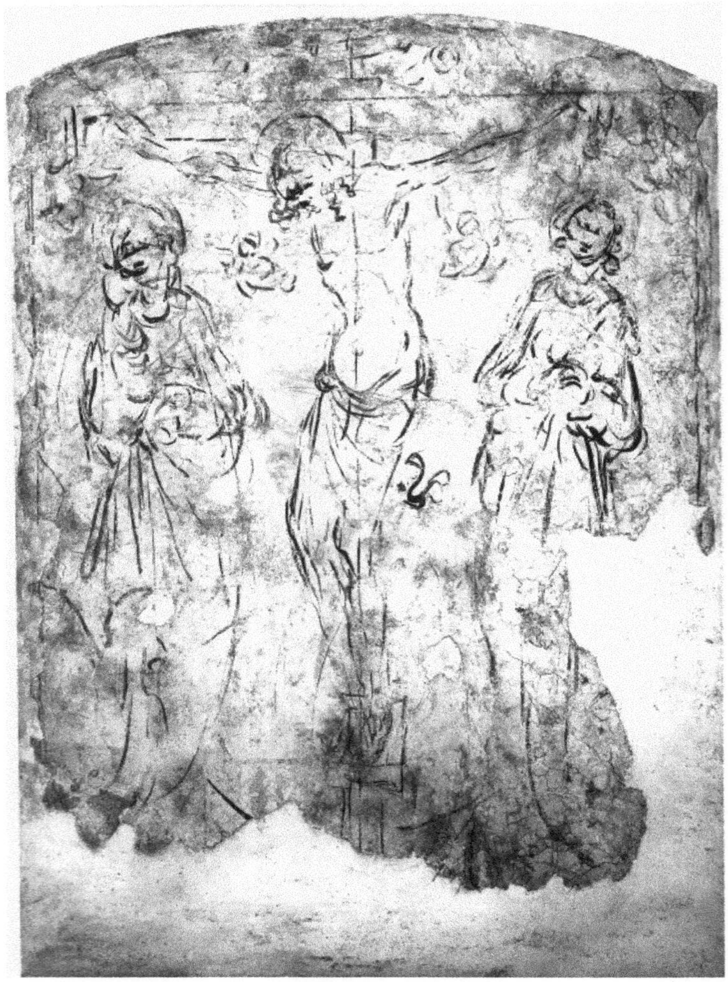

13. Parri Spinelli, *Crucifixion,* sinopia. Palazzo Comunale, Arezzo. Photograph Collection, Department of Art History and Archaeology, Columbia University. Gift of Millard Meiss.

much implicit in it, is the cartoon. For what Alberti here attests to is that crucial shift in practice from the freely sketched *sinopia,* a monumental drawing executed directly on the wall (Fig. 13), to the carefully prepared and exactly outlined cartoon, individual figures or even the full-size design worked out first on paper and then transferred mechanically to the wall or panel (Fig. 14).[13] The practice of squaring for enlargement and transfer is documented in frescoes by Masaccio (the *Trinity* in Santa Maria Novella) and Uccello (*Sir John Hawkwood* in the duomo of Florence).[14] Testifying to that practice, Alberti may also stand as witness to the use of the full cartoon, the monumental application of which we cannot actually document before Castagno's frescoes in Sant' Apollonia.[15] The cartoon stands as the culmination of a process of graphic preparation, of the development of pictorial ideas on paper; it is the point of arrival in a dialectical process of testing and correcting. What previous generations had done in large measure on the wall itself, drawing to scale with charcoal and then fixing with the brush, was now achieved first on paper, with stylus or pen, and then enlarged,

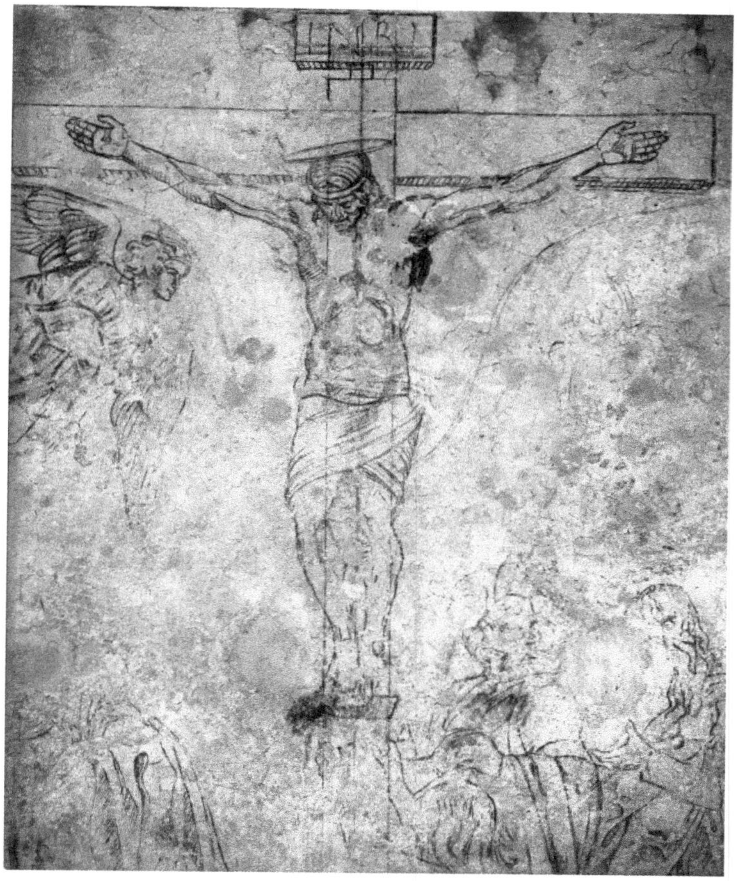

14. Andrea del Castagno, *Resurrection*, sinopia (detail). Sant'Apollonia, refectory, Florence. Photograph Collection, Department of Art History and Archaeology, Columbia University, New York. Gift of Millard Meiss.

on paper, before being transferred mechanically to the painting surface by either pouncing or incision.

At the very least, Alberti articulates the values that will render the cartoon central to the practice of fresco painting: the large-scale design, a composition whose contours are fully resolved, offered possibilities of control and precision that were central to his project. The development of the cartoon and the invention of mathematical perspective are both dependent upon clear linear structure; they are two aspects of drawing according to Alberti, and each represents a crucial step toward the rationalization of pictorial construction.

That Alberti had fresco painting in mind is further suggested by his following observation on speed of execution: "In making the *istoria* we should have that speed of execution [*prestezza di fare*] joined with diligence, so that we avoid the bother and tedium of working and that eagerness to finish things that makes us botch the work." With this call for the apparently oxymoronic combination Alberti, with certain awareness of ancient precedent, initiates a theme that will become central to later Renaissance criticism.[16] "Una diligenza congiunta con prestezza" is something he sought as well in drawing (¶ 59). "Never take up the stylus or brush without first having clearly worked out in your mind what it is you have to do and how you plan to do it; it will certainly be better to correct any errors with the mind than to remove them from the painting." Developing pictorial ideas beforehand in drawing enables speed of execution in painting. Drawing offers the possibility of testing the ideas formulated in the mind of the artist – in consultation, as Alberti would have it, with learned colleagues – and of correcting them in a dialectical process; for the mind in turn is stimulated by the practice of the hand: "The mind [*l'ingegno*] moved and warmed by exercise turns easily and more readily to work; and that hand follows most rapidly that is well guided by the sure rule of the mind."[17]

To acknowledge the degree to which he anticipates Leonardo and the later Renaissance hardly does justice to the originality of Alberti's thought or to its significance. In seeking the rational foundations of the art of painting, he goes beyond the geometry underlying perspective and representation and explores the processes of pictorial imagination. Recognizing drawing not only as foundational to learning and to practice but as an arena in which the artist first encounters his own creations, Alberti adumbrated a theory of drawing simultaneous with its new practical development in the early fifteenth century.

2. *Invenzioni* and Invention

A generation earlier, Cennino Cennini had already defined *disegno* and *colorire* as the foundation of the art of painting (cap. 4), but with drawing as the very basis of the course of study: "you begin with drawing" [*dal disegno t'incominci*] (cap. 5). Moreover, reaching out to the credentials of more privileged arts, he too had sought a theoretical sanction for his own:

> And it [sc. painting] justly deserves to be enthroned next to theory [*scienza*], and to be crowned with poetry. The reason is this: that the poet, with the theory that he has, is made worthy and is free to compose and combine together, or not, as he pleases, according to his inclination. In the same way, the painter is given freedom to compose a figure standing, seated, half-man, half-horse, as he pleases, according to his imagination [*secondo sua fantasia*]. (cap. 1)

Although lacking Alberti's humanist preparation and ambition, Cennini, before descending to his workshop recipes, managed to make high claims on behalf of the art of painting, "which calls for imagination and skill of hand, in order to discover things not seen (hiding themselves under the shadow of natural objects), and to fix them with the hand, making manifest that which does not actually exist" [*che conviene avere fantasia con operazione di mano, di trovare cose non vedute (cacciandosi sotto ombra di naturali), e fermarle con la mano, dando a dimostrare quello che non è, sia*]" (cap. 1). Cennini's declaration of inventive freedom for the artist celebrates precisely those disparate creatures imagined by painters that had been so mockingly condemned by Horace.[18] And, however obviously practical his advice, Cennini seems to be recalling Apelles' motto, *nulla dies sine linea,* when he counsels the advancing beginner to draw something every day, no matter how little, for such practice will lead to proficiency.[19] While rehearsing the various techniques and materials of drawing, Cennini too had recognized just how practice with the hand challenges the inventive mind of the artist: "Do you realize what will happen to you if you practice drawing with the pen? That it will make you expert, skillful, and capable of drawing out of your own head [*capace di molto disegno entro la testa tua*]" (cap. 13).

"Di trovare cose non vedute": even without the benefit of a classical vocabulary of *inventio* (*invenire:* to come upon or to find), Cennini had defined in the vernacular, *avant la lettre,* a central goal of Alberti's program. Toward this end Alberti advised the painter to frequent men of letters, in search of new *invenzioni,* discoveries of potential pictorial ideas. And so, too, did Cennini anticipate the role of drawing in that search, in the realization of a painter's *fantasia,* of the "molto disegno entro la testa."[20]

The new art celebrated and articulated by Alberti was founded on the principles of rational pictorial construction, but perspective and proportion were means toward a more ambitious end: the *istoria,* the great virtue of which "consists primarily in its invention" (¶ 53). In offering as models of *invenzioni* the *ekphraseis* of "The Calumny of Apelles" and the "The Three Graces," Alberti extended the program for a new art to include classical content as well as classical form. But that program, which we recognize as central to any notion of a Renaissance art, was not immediately realizable; it had to wait another generation or more. Not until later in the fifteenth century, in the work of artists like Mantegna and Botticelli, did such *invenzioni* find major pictorial expression, in painting on a large scale as well as in the newly developed graphic medium of engraving. In 1435 Alberti's pictorial vision was far ahead of standard humanist culture; the full resonance of his program could be appreciated only when that gap, which inevitably involved a lag in patronage, was closed.[21]

But Alberti was addressing two distinct audiences, as attested by the two versions of his treatise. *De pictura,* his Latin text, was dedicated to the courtly patron.[22] *Della pittura,* his Italian version, spoke directly to the artists themselves. Indeed, Alberti insists that he is writing as an artist for fellow artists, and there is every reason to believe that such a professional audience proved more immediately responsive than either prince or humanist. Alberti's invitation was to the painters, to join in creating a new art of painting: "di nuovo fabrichiamo un'arte di pittura" (¶ 26).[23] And the painters, without waiting for more intellectually enlightened patronage, evidently participated in the great enterprise on their own. They did so initially and primarily through drawing.

On one level, as we have recognized, Alberti was essentially codifying practice, articulating the theoretical principles and rational procedures underlying operations such as perspective construction and compositional development, from first sketches to cartoons for enlargement and transfer. His observation about drawing from "our private commentaries" (¶ 61) in developing public projects testifies to the use of graphic notebooks. Such albums, repositories of visual knowledge, were staples of any painter's workshop, collections of exempla, simile drawings, patterns

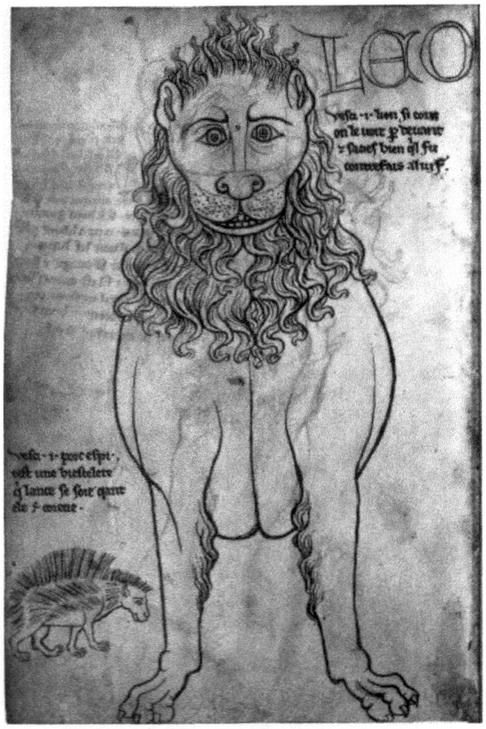

15. Villard de Honnecourt, *Lion and Porcupine.* Pen and brown ink over leadpoint and stylus on parchment, 24 × 16 cm. Bibliothèque Nationale, Paris (MS. Fr. 19093, fol. 48).

16. Giovannino de' Grassi, *Birds of Prey and Other Animals.* Pen and brown ink and wash over metalpoint, watercolor, on parchment, ca. 25.5 × 17.5 cm. Biblioteca Civica Angelo Mai, Bergamo (Cassaf. 1.21, fol. 4v).

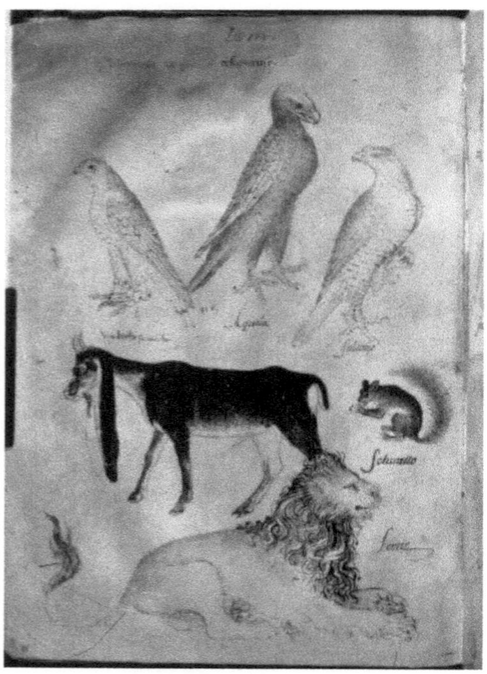

and observations copied from nature and from art, decorative details and compositional ideas. The tradition of these compendia – best known through examples such as the thirteenth-century album of Villard de Honnecourt (Fig. 15) and the late Trecento *taccuino* of Giovannino de' Grassi (Fig. 16) – is most richly documented in Alberti's own time by the collection of drawings assembled by Pisanello (Figs. 17, 18).[24] Cennini (cap. 29) advised the young painter to make a portfolio that would serve both to hold paper and as a kind of portable drawing board; in this way he could draw in "churches or chapels," copying works from which he will learn and at the same time assemble a store of models that will eventually enrich his own working capital. From a more purely Renaissance perspective, we may prefer to think of artists studying ancient sarcophagi for figural motifs (Fig. 19) or, like Brunelleschi and Donatello, drawing antiquities in the Roman Forum.[25] Still, if the objects studied represent a new set of cultural values, the practice and the goal remain essentially the same: the constitution of a body of visual knowledge recorded. From such basic working stock the painter or sculptor might supply the "variety and abundance" that were requisite for a successful *istoria.*

One set of Quattrocento drawing books in particular distinguishes itself from the older tradition: the two volumes left by Jacopo Bellini, today in the British Museum and the Louvre.[26] Larger and more ambitious than most such collections, their contents are also more original and challenging, assembling acquired material and original creations, traditional motifs and pictorial innovations. There are studies after nature, including one closely observed watercolor of an iris; studies of lions that seem to have been drawn from the living model (Fig. 20), others inspired by known sculptural monuments (Fig. 21), and still others that belong to exempla of an earlier modelbook (Fig. 22);[27] decorative motifs collected from the same late medieval source mix with modern studies of classical antiquities. For the most part, however, Bellini's own pages are devoted to full compositional ideas, figural action often located in elaborate architectural settings or in expansive landscapes. Many of these compositions represent standard themes of Christian narrative – scenes from the life of the Virgin and Christ: the Nativity, the Adoration of the Magi, the Crucifixion, the Lamentation; images of popular saints: John the Baptist

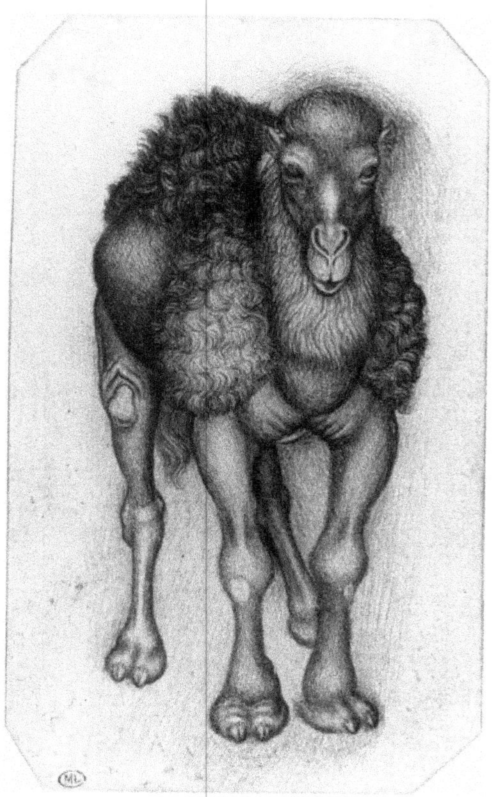

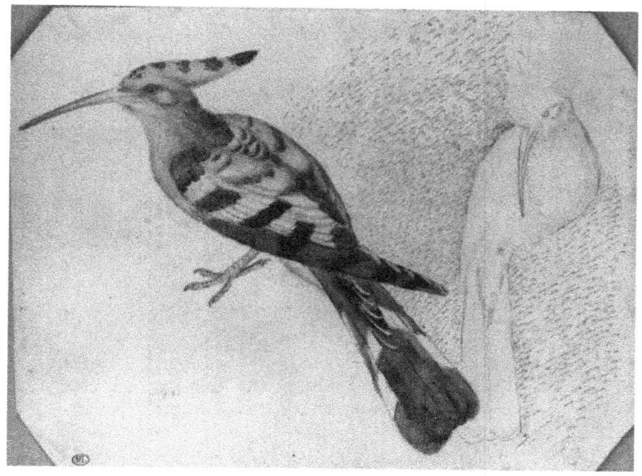

17. *(left)* Pisanello, *Camel.* Pen and brown ink over metalpoint on cream-colored prepared paper, 16.8 × 10.2 cm. Musée du Louvre, Paris. Département des Arts Graphiques (inv. 2399).

18. *(above right)* Pisanello. *Two Studies of a Hoopoe.* Pen and brown ink over preparatory design in leadpoint, brush and brown wash and watercolor, heightened with white, 16.1 × 21.7 cm. Musée du Louvre, Paris. Département des Arts Graphiques (inv. 2467).

19. *(below)* Pisanello (studio). *Studies after Ancient Sarcophagi.* Pen and brown ink over metalpoint on parchment, 19.3 × 27.2 cm. Musée du Louvre, Paris. Département des Arts Graphiques (inv. 2397v).

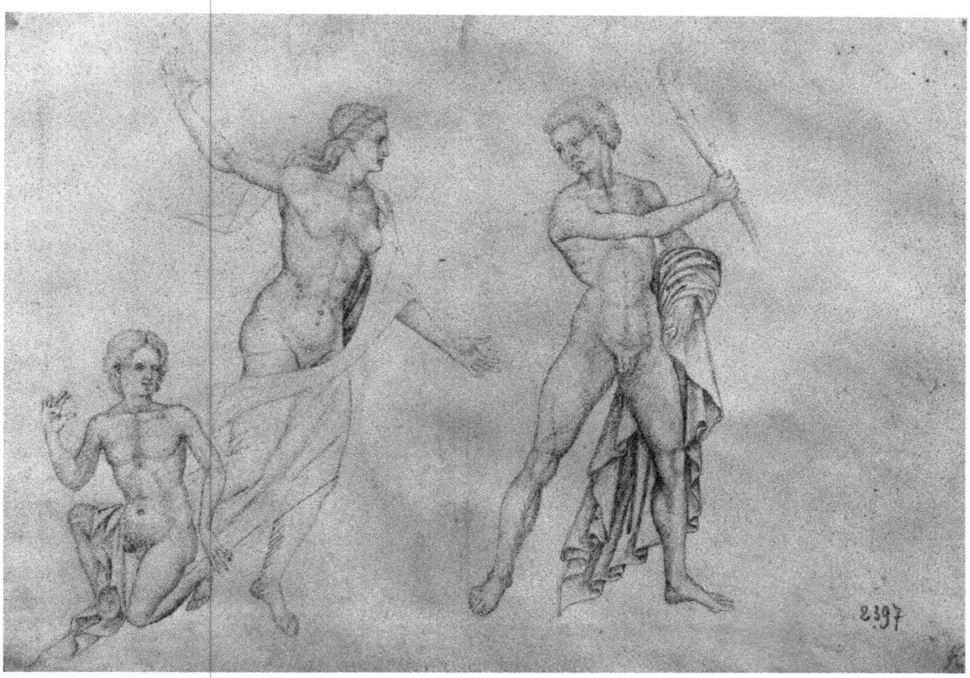

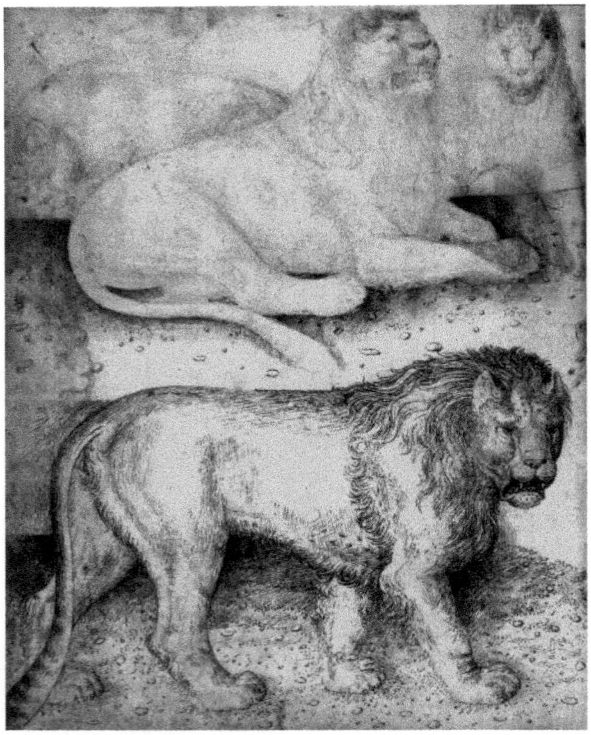

20. *(left)* Jacopo Bellini, *Studies of a Lion.* Leadpoint on white paper, later partially gone over in pen and greenish wash, 41.3 × 33.5 cm. British Museum, London (1855-8-11-1 verso [fol. 2v]).

21. *(below)* Jacopo Bellini, *Lion Attacking a Horse.* Leadpoint on white paper, 41.3 × 33.5 cm. British Museum, London (1855-8-11-6 verso [fol. 7v]).

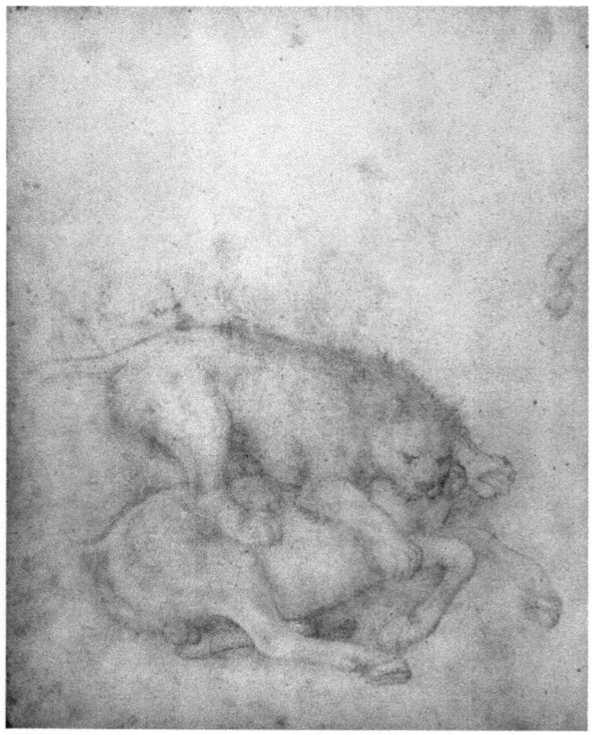

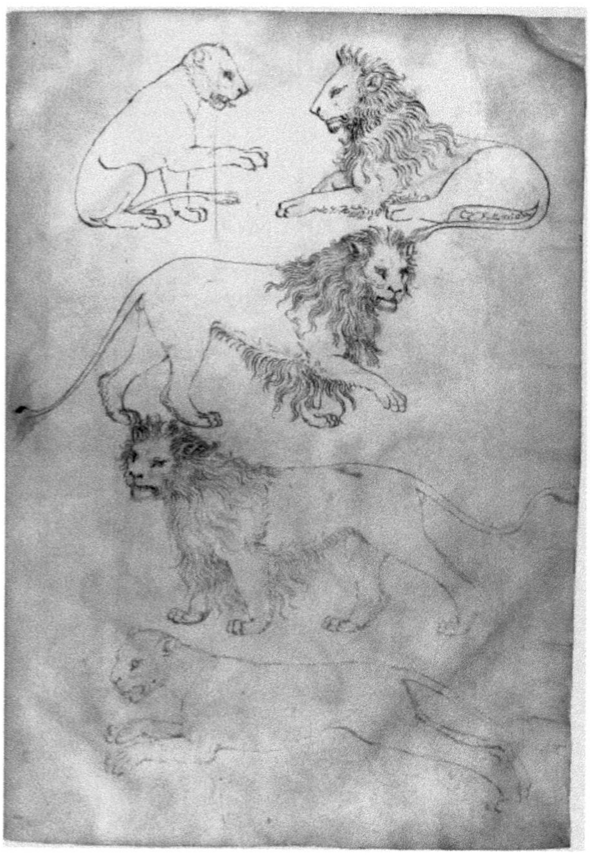

22. *(left)* Anonymous Fourteenth-Century Venetian, *Five Lions.* Pen and brown inks over leadpoint on parchment, ca. 42.5 × 28.7 cm. Musée du Louvre, Paris. Département des Arts Graphiques, (R.F. 1539 verso [fol. 77v]).

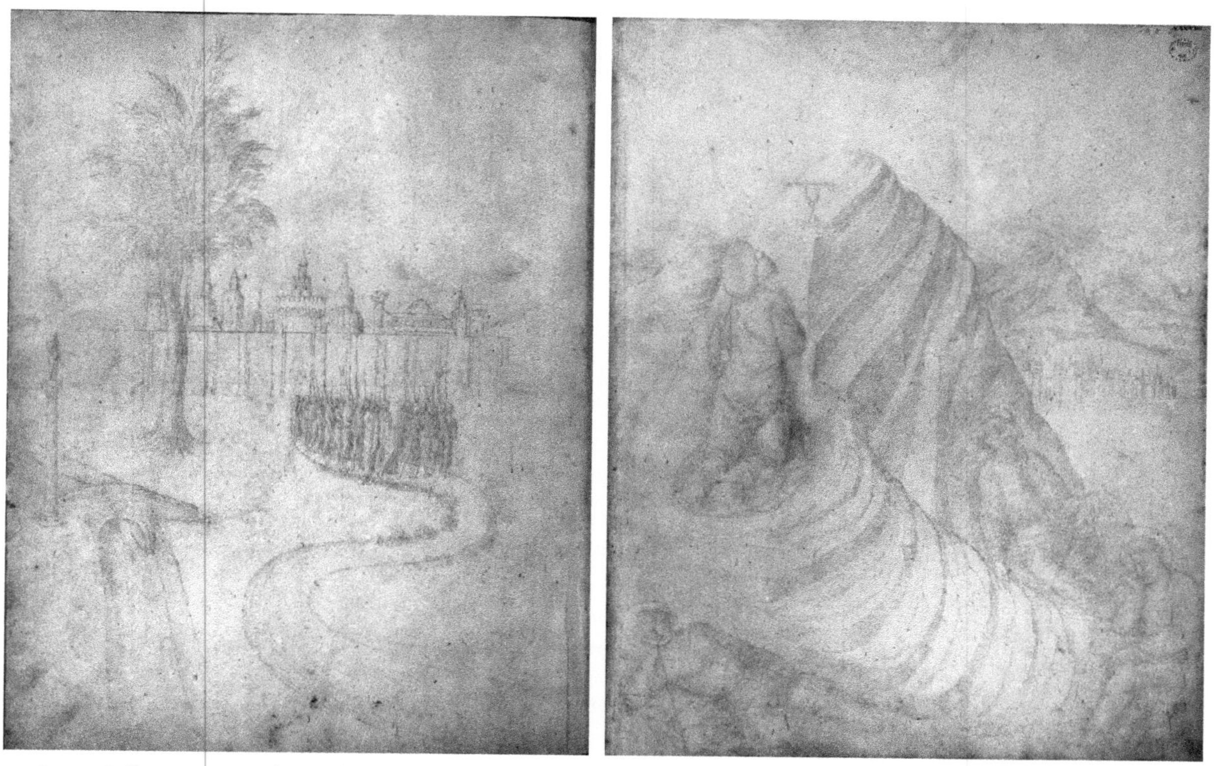

23. Jacopo Bellini, *Agony in the Garden.* Leadpoint on white paper, 41.3 × 33.5 cm, each. British Museum, London (1855-8-11-42 verso-43 [fols. 43v–44]).

preaching, Jerome in the wilderness, George slaying the dragon. Others are, in every sense, more fanciful: problems in architectural perspective, simple and complex; warriors in combat, knights on horseback, courtly tournaments; studies of tomb monuments; pagan subjects from classical antiquity, generally bacchic and satyric. With very few exceptions – the Agony in the Garden (Fig. 23) being the most celebrated, having been adapted in painting by Jacopo's son-in-law, Mantegna, and his son Giovanni – these compositions seem not to have served as models for paintings. Indeed, for the most part they seem ill suited to painting for reasons either formal or thematic. The religious subjects share a conventional iconography, but the dominance of setting over figures, which sometimes seem an afterthought, renders many of the compositions awkward models for painting. When the figures do aspire to a certain monumentality, this is often in classical subjects for which painting had yet to offer the opportunity of realization.

Like the recommended subjects of Alberti's proleptic program of antique *istorie,* Bellini's profane and pagan essays *all'antica* anticipate the pictorial culture of the next generation; they hardly coincide with the expectations of standard patronage of painting toward the mid-Quattrocento. Rather, they present themselves as pure inventions of the artist's imagination, new subjects inspired by a new cultural ambition or deliberately novel solutions to traditional themes. Appended at the end of the Paris book of drawings is an index of its contents written in a fifteenth-century hand.

Although it will not submit to too precise philological scrutiny, the vocabulary describing the subjects represented is suggestive.[28] Drawings of the Adoration of the Magi, for example, are labeled *storie* in a fairly prosaic sense: number 32 depicts "la storia de I magi ch[e] vien per tre vie" (Fig. 24), number 34 "la storia di magi con molte figure" (Fig. 25). A scene of the triumphant Bacchus (no. 40), however, is described as "una Istoria de Bacho con uno caro di trionfo chel tira" (Fig. 26). The "story" of the Three Magi is exactly that, a well-known, received tale.[29] The subject of Bacchus, on the other hand, is *una istoria,* a pictorial invention in an apparently Albertian sense. So, too, number 41, "una Istoria de pasion senza Iladri," seems deliberately to present (or rather, to have presented, since the drawing itself is no longer preserved) a variation on a conventional subject: the Crucifixion without the flanking thieves – presumably in a landscape setting, for the Crucifix alone would require no such comment (Figs. 27, 28). Through such variation a composition could lay claim to a certain inventiveness; at the very least, the nomination calls specific atten-

24. Jacopo Bellini, *Adoration of the Magi.* Pen and brown ink over metalpoint on vellum, ca. 28.7 × 42.5 cm, each. Musée du Louvre, Paris. Département des Arts Graphiques (R.F. 1497 verso-1498 [fols. 31v–32]).

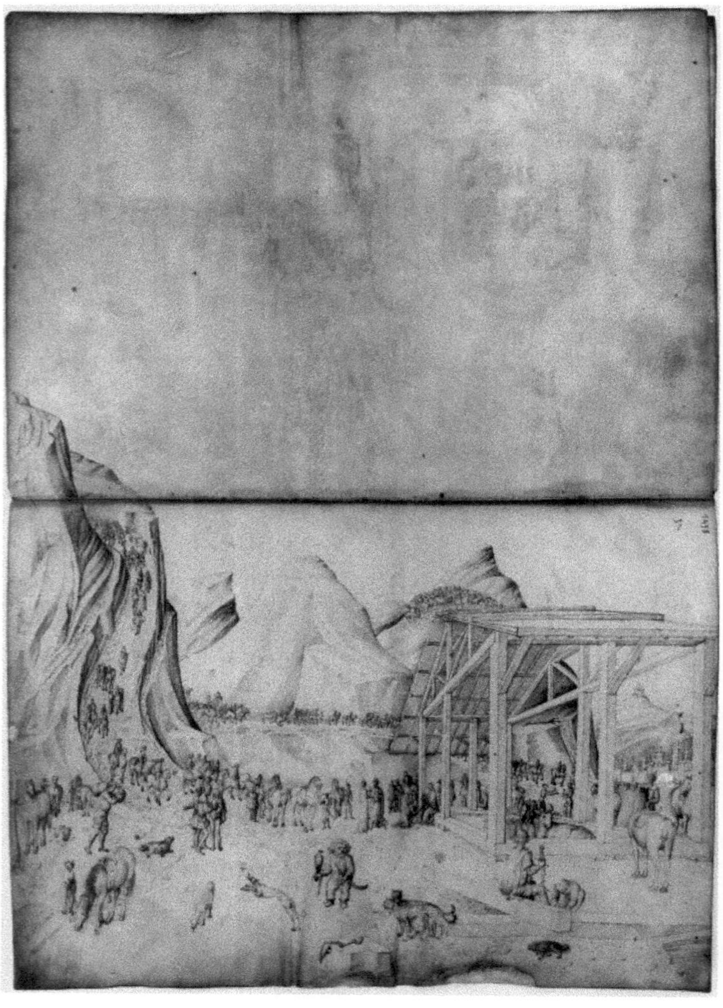

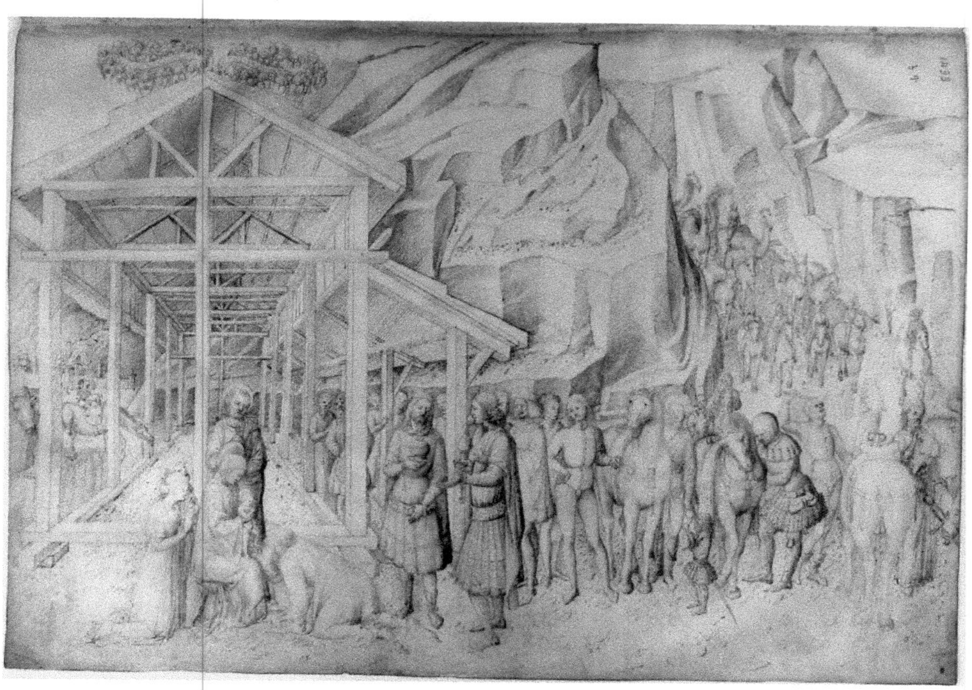

25. Jacopo Bellini, *Adoration of the Magi.* Pen and brown ink over metalpoint on vellum, ca. 28.7 × 42.5 cm. Musée du Louvre, Paris. Département des Arts Graphiques (R.F. 1499 [fol. 34]).

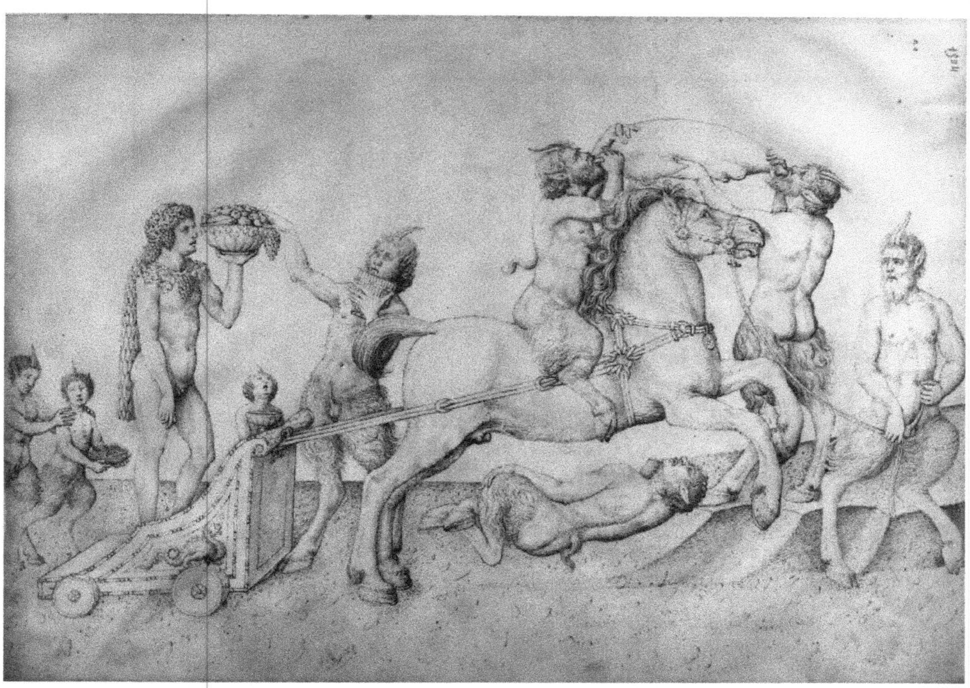

26. Jacopo Bellini, *Bacchus and Satyrs.* Pen and brown ink over metalpoint on vellum, ca. 28.7 × 42.5 cm. Musée du Louvre, Paris. Département des Arts Graphiques (R.F. 1504 [fol. 40]).

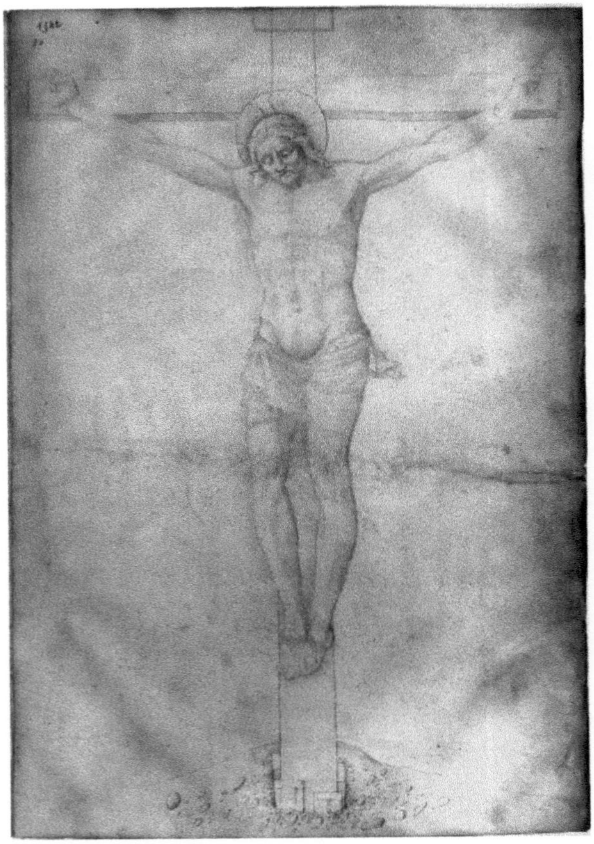

27. Jacopo Bellini, *Christ on the Cross*. Metalpoint, partially gone over with pen and brown ink on parchment, ca. 42.5 × 28.7 cm. Musée du Louvre, Paris. Département des Arts Graphiques (R.F. 1542 [fol. 80]).

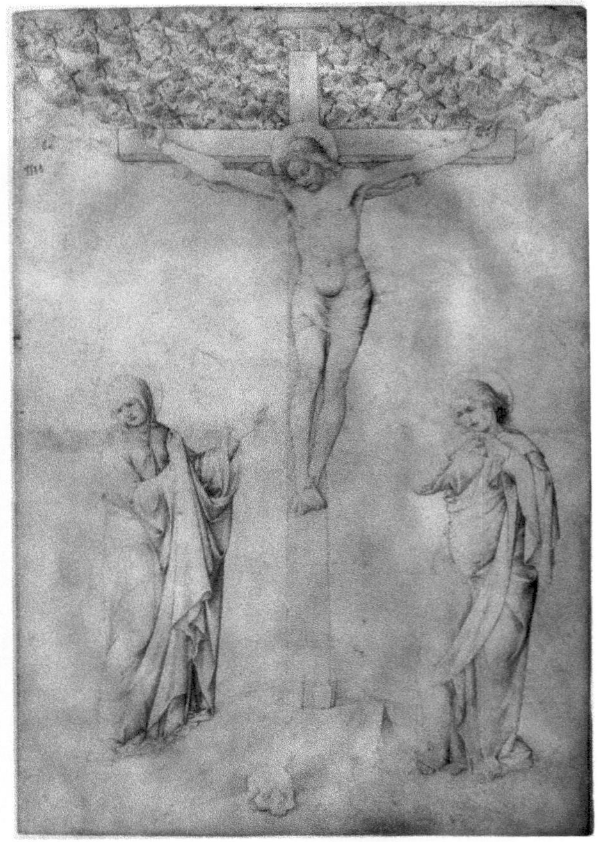

28. Jacopo Bellini, *Christ on the Cross with the Virgin Mary and St. John*. Pen and brown ink over metalpoint on vellum, ca. 42.5 × 28.7 cm. Musée du Louvre, Paris. Département des Arts Graphiques (R.F. 1523 [fol. 60]).

tion to an aspect of the design thought worthy of special note. There is a difference between a well-known subject *(la storia)* and a newly invented one (*una storia*).[30]

Through Bellini's two drawing books there runs a series of representations of the Crucifixion that collectively present inventive variations on a basic theme: the Crucifix with or without the thieves (Figs. 29, 30), with or without a crowd or mourners (Fig. 31),[31] with or without attendant angels (Figs. 27, 28, 32), seen proximately or distantly, frontally or obliquely, symmetrically or asymmetrically (Figs. 33, 34, 35).[32] Each drawing offers a different treatment, and the range of solutions far outstrips the opportunities that might have been offered by potential commissions for paintings, whether for altarpieces or predella panels. Rather, we are aware of an artist exploring the possibilities inherent in a particular subject, testing dramatic and formal options and probing creatively beyond the boundaries of traditional imagery, searching out new details in the narrative sources – such as the opening of the tombs at the death on the cross (Matthew 27:52) (Figs. 29, 30).[33] Drawing provides the arena for such exploration; it is the medium of Bellini's invention.

By the end of the fifteenth century, drawing will be joined by another medium in this function. Printmaking may legitimately claim to be an essentially original art of

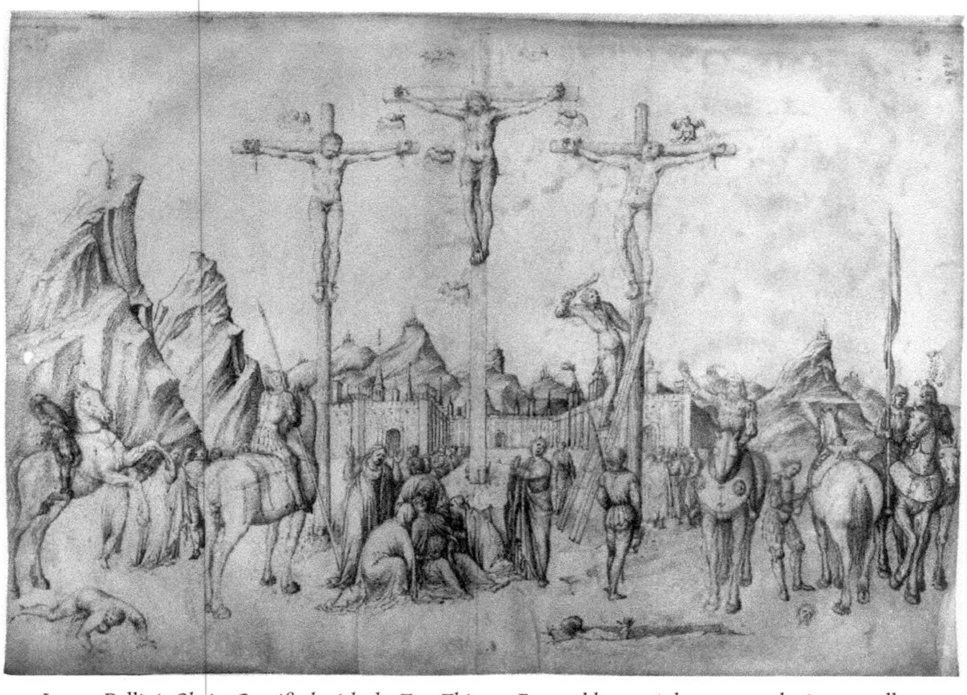

29. Jacopo Bellini, *Christ Crucified with the Two Thieves*. Pen and brown ink over metalpoint on vellum, ca. 28.7 × 42.5 cm. Musée du Louvre, Paris. Département des Arts Graphiques (R.F. 1486 [fol. 19]).

30. Jacopo Bellini, *Crucifixion*. Pen and light brown ink, brown wash, over metalpoint, yellow wash, on vellum, ca. 28.7 × 42.5 cm. Musée du Louvre, Paris. Département des Arts Graphiques (R.F. 1505 [fol. 41]).

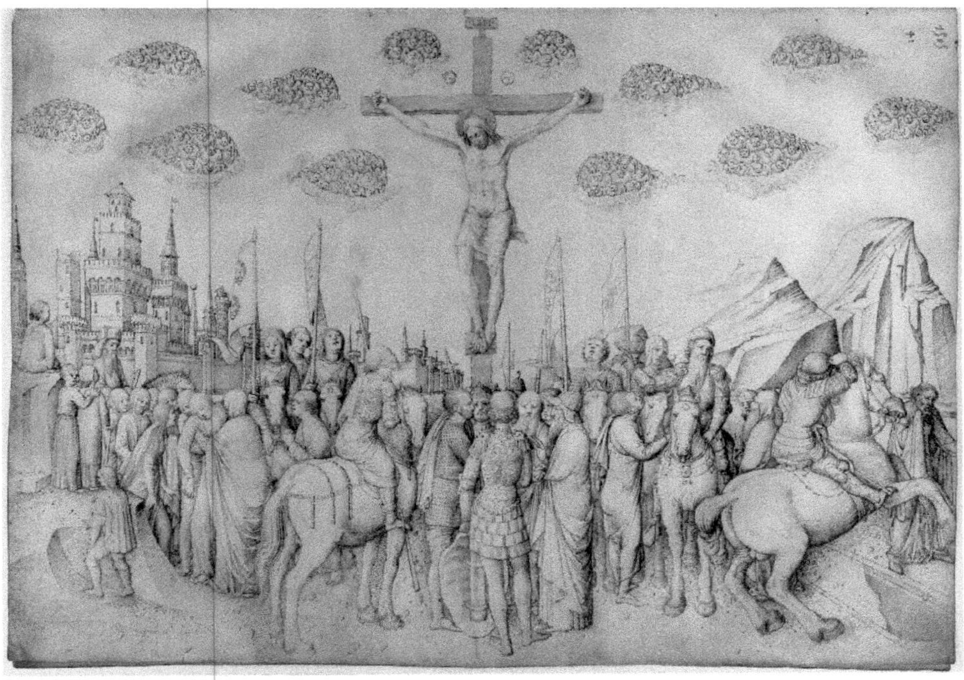

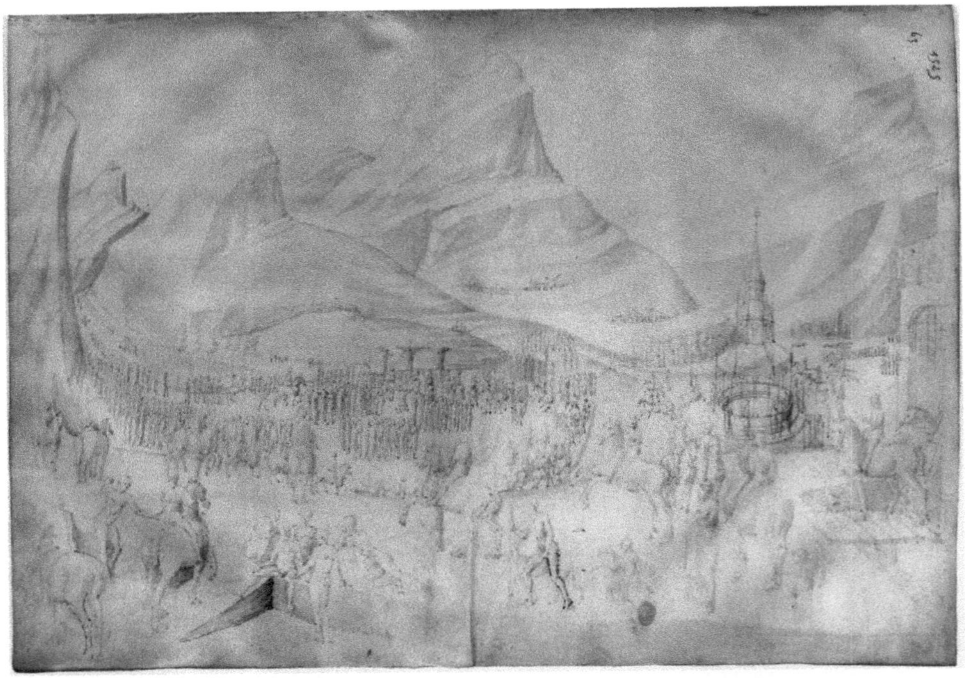

31. Jacopo Bellini, *Golgotha*. Brush and gray-brown ink on vellum, partially reworked in pen and brown ink, ca. 28.7 × 42.5 cm. Musée du Louvre, Paris. Département des Arts Graphiques (R.F. 1525 [fol. 63]).

32. Jacopo Bellini, *Crucifixion with Mary Magdalen at the Foot of the Cross*. Leadpoint on white paper, 41.3 × 33.5 cm, each. British Museum, London (1855-8-11-0 verso-1 [fols. 1v–2]).

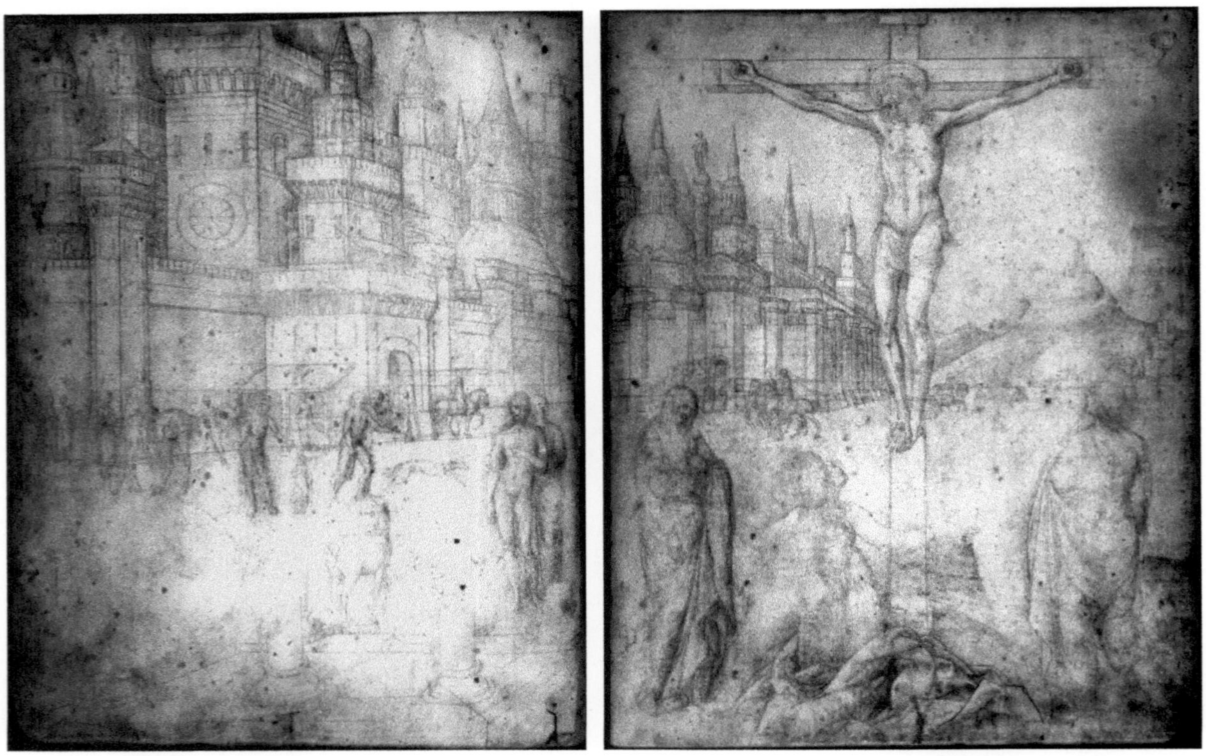

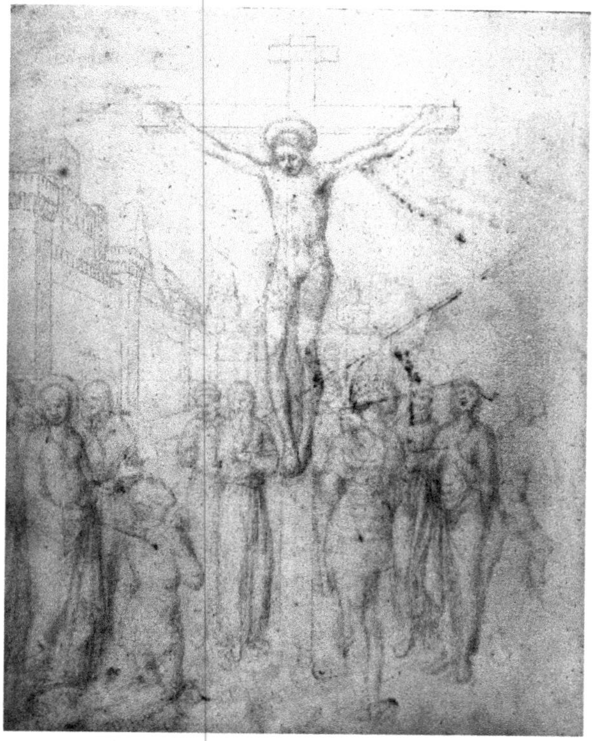

33. Jacopo Bellini, *Crucifixion.* Leadpoint on white paper, 41.3 × 33.5 cm. British Museum, London (1855-8-11-85 verso [fol. 86v]).

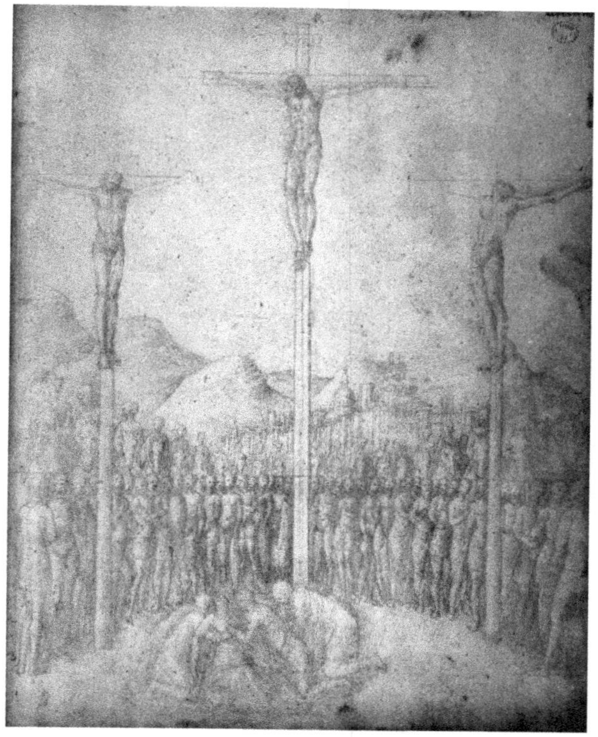

34. Jacopo Bellini, *Christ Crucified with the Two Thieves.* Leadpoint on white paper, 41.3 × 33.5 cm. British Museum, London (1855-8-11-77 [fol. 78]).

35. Jacopo Bellini, *Christ Crucified with the Two Thieves.* Leadpoint on white paper, 41.3 × 33.5 cm, each. British Museum, London (1855-8-11-74 verso-75 [fols. 76v–77]).

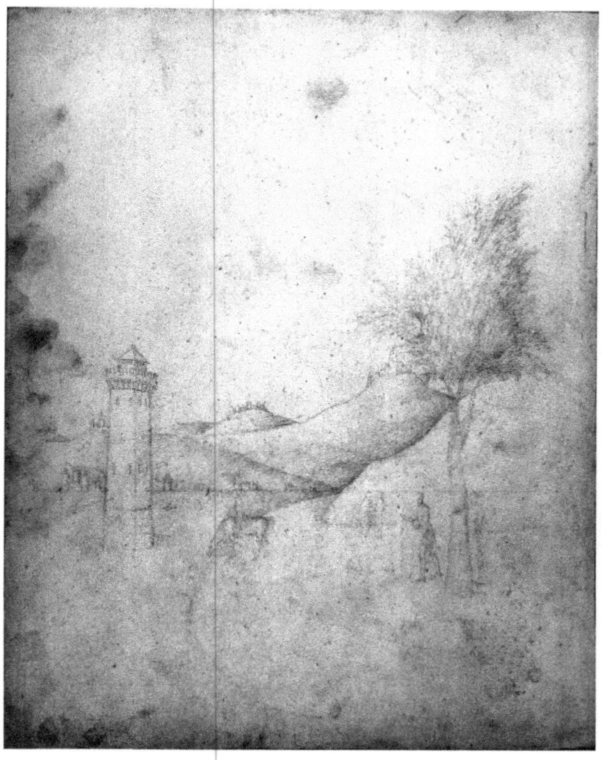

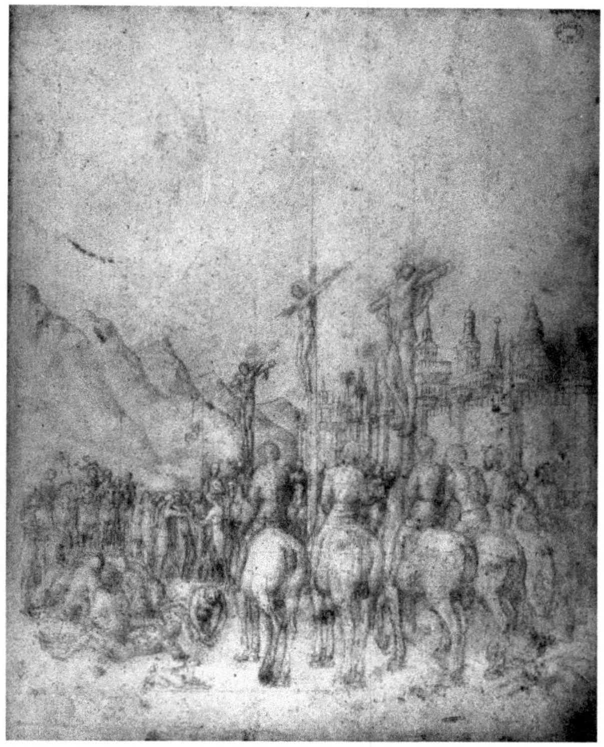

the Renaissance. Whatever its prehistory, its full development depended upon the invention of the printing press, both for the new technology itself and for its cultural consequences. We recognize the crucial role of printing in the emergence of what historians generally call the early modern era, a term that may better represent the full dynamic of the fifteenth century than "Renaissance," with its necessarily retrospective implications. Among the technological phenomena that transformed the civilization of Europe in this period were two of direct concern to our topic: the commercially viable production of paper and the invention of movable type. Dependent upon paper, printing in turn created an increasingly exigent market for its manufacture. Together, they enabled the creation of a new kind of reading public.[34]

The printed image participated in that cultural transformation, playing a critical role in the shaping of a new kind of visual literacy. As the printed book both created and was sustained by a new reading public, so the printed image entered into a complex exchange with its audience. Or perhaps we should say, audiences: for the sheer variety of types of printed image – sacred and secular, didactic and diverting, narrative and decorative – attests to a multiplicity of function and appeal. The print was a means for the broad dissemination of knowledge, cultural and, in specific regard to our theme, visual knowledge.[35] Indeed, among the most important buyers of prints were the artists themselves: we may recall the young Michelangelo copying Schongauer's *Temptations of St. Anthony* or Dürer himself drawing after engravings by Mantegna and Pollaiuolo (Figs. 36–41).[36] From the very beginning of its modern development, the printed image declared itself a model of invention. Engraving, in particular, became the special field for demonstrating and disseminating the painter's *invenzioni.*

The same generation of artists that eventually realized Alberti's ekphrastic program of *istorie* discovered and exploited the potential of the print as a vehicle for the display of inventive talent. The leading figure in this campaign, a pioneering explorer of the new medium, was Andrea Mantegna, celebrated as "el più belo desegnatore e inventore."[37] Behind such designations, and informing this vocabulary, lies the essential theoretical construct first adumbrated by Alberti, the tripartite constitution of the art of painting as *disegno, invenzione,* and *colorire.* Whatever ambivalence may have enriched the first of these terms, enabling it (as we shall see) eventually to assume absolute priority, *disegno* always stood in intimate relation to *invenzione;* it was the basic means of visualizing the latter, of giving visible form to idea. These two could function perfectly well without color: as Alberti had admitted, "uno buono disegno," a pure line drawing, alone, could be a fully self-sufficient expression. That is, in effect, just what engraving offered, and Mantegna's fame as *disegnatore* and *inventore* was secured by the engravings of his designs that circulated throughout Italy – and, presumably, beyond the Alps.

Trained in the classicizing culture of the university town of Padua, Mantegna became the humanist artist par excellence.[38] He seems deliberately to have taken up the inventive challenge manifest in the drawings of Jacopo Bellini, his father-in-law. But Mantegna explored the thematic possibilities of pagan subject matter with an expressive purpose and cultural precision well beyond the vision of the older mas-

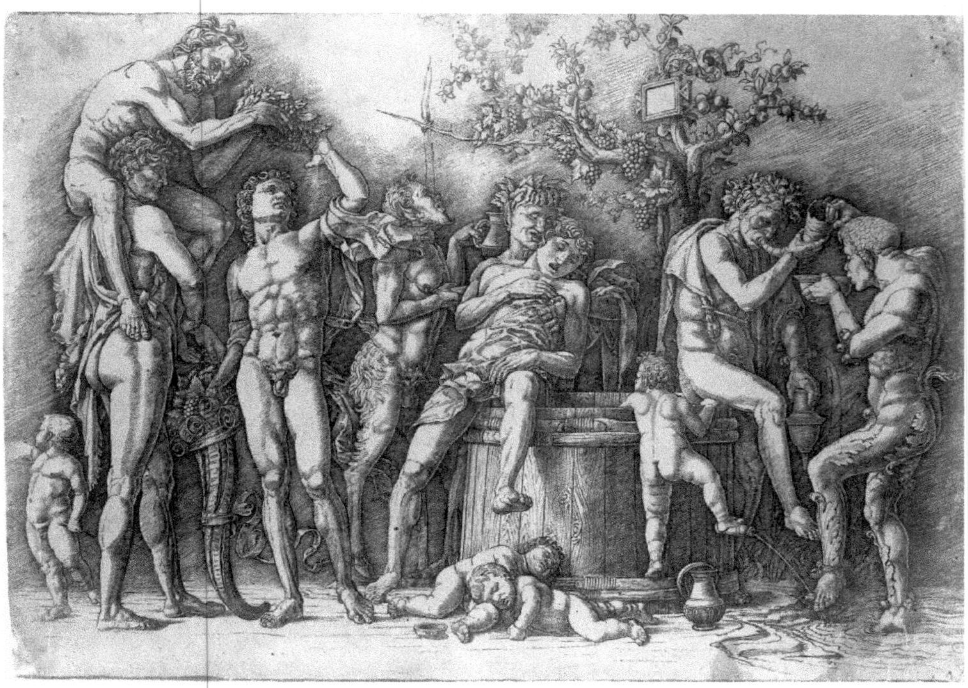

36. Andrea Mantegna, *Bacchanal with a Wine Vat*. Engraving, 29.9 × 43.7 cm (plate: 33.5 × 45.4 cm). Metropolitan Museum of Art, New York. Rogers Fund and the Elisha Whittelsey Collection, Elisha Whittelsey Fund, 1986 (1986.1159).

37. Andrea Mantegna, *Bacchanal with Silenus*. Engraving, 29.9 × 43.7 cm (plate: 33.5 × 45.4 cm). Devonshire Collection, Chatsworth. Reproduced by permission of the Duke of Devonshire and the Chatsworth Settlement Trustees.

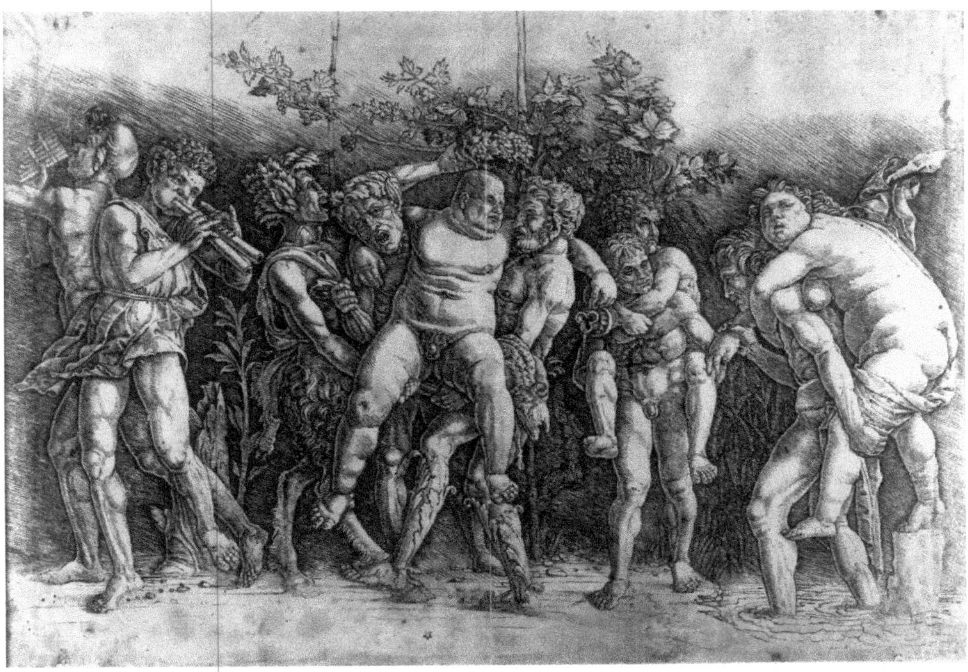

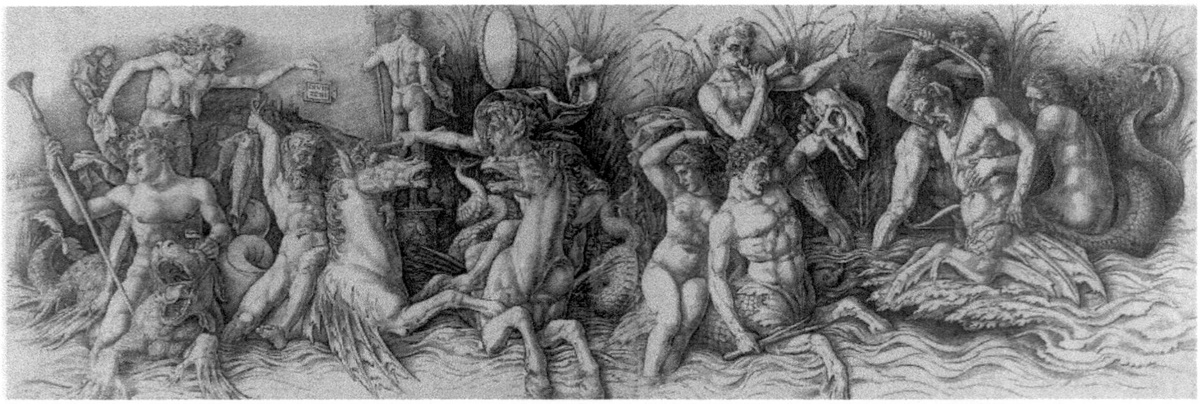

38. Andrea Mantegna, *Battle of Sea Gods.* Engraving, 28.3 × 82.6 cm (two plates: left, 34 × 44.5 cm; right, 34 × 45.5 cm). Devonshire Collection, Chatsworth. Reproduced by permission of the Duke of Devonshire and the Chatsworth Settlement Trustees.

ter. If his engravings representing Bacchus, Silenus, and bacchanalia (Figs. 36, 37) seem to present no particular iconographic problems, the subjects of designs like the *Battle of Sea Gods* (Fig. 38) continue to elude definitive identification. Evidently no ready illustration of received classical text, such imagery seems, rather, dedicated to demonstrating the artist's own fertile imagination, his ability to invent *all'antica.*[39] Engravings like these must have invited attentive reading, challenging the viewer to interpretation, to match wits with the artist; they required a connoisseurship of the mind as well as of the eye. In such images Alberti's hopes for the painter to establish himself as a man of high culture are fully realized.

39. Antonio Pollaiuolo, *Battle of Nude Men.* Engraving, 42 × 60.4 cm (platemark). Cleveland Museum of Art, Purchase from the J. H. Wade Fund, 1967.127.

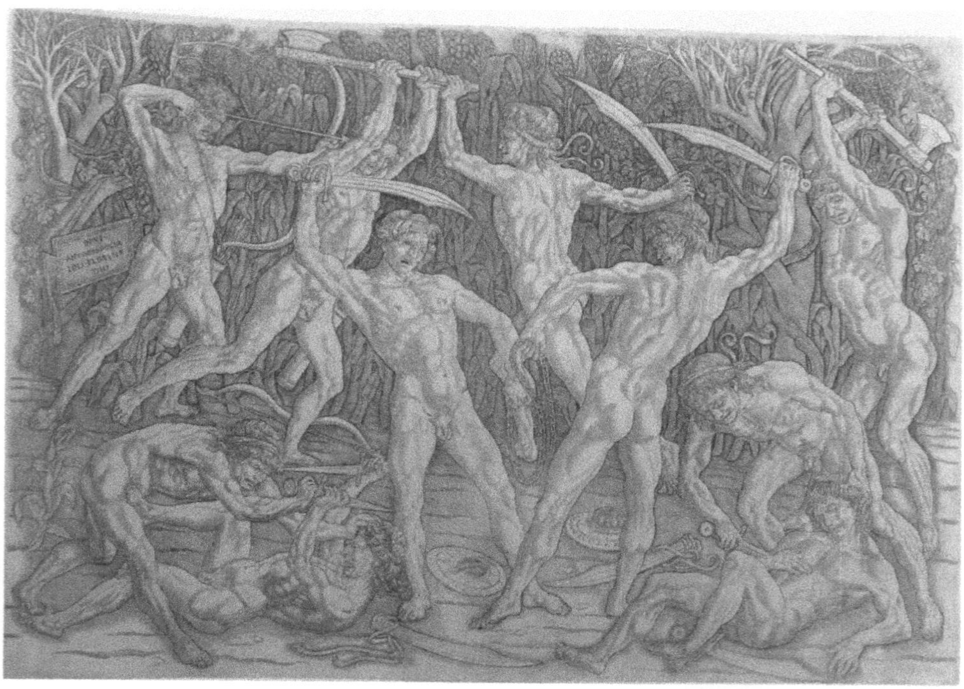

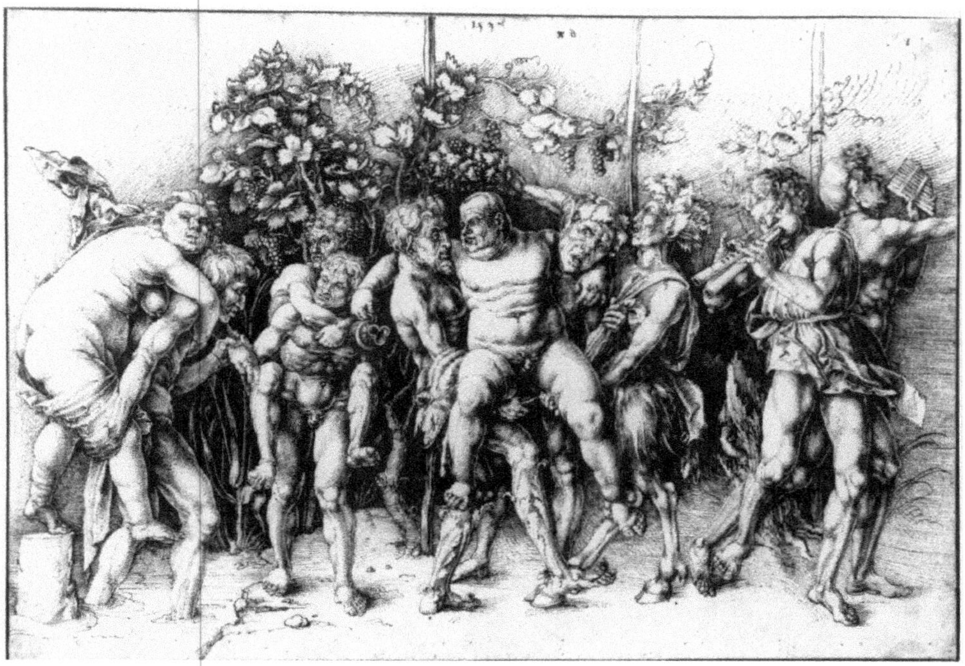

40. Albrecht Dürer, *Bacchanal with Silenus,* after Mantegna. Pen and brown ink, 29.8 × 43.5 cm. Graphische Sammlung Albertina, Vienna (inv. 3060 D 33).

41. Albrecht Dürer, *Battle of the Sea Gods,* after Mantegna. Pen and brown ink, 29.2 × 38.2 cm. Graphische Sammlung Albertina (inv. 3061 D 34).

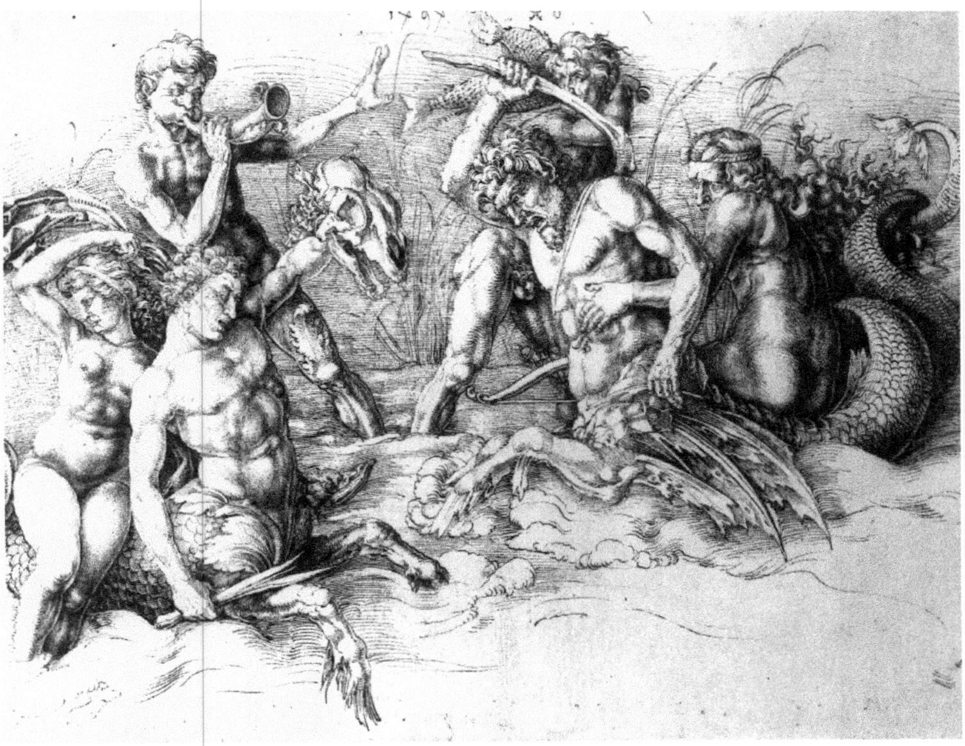

Similar observations may be made of what is perhaps the most ambitious engraving of this generation, Antonio Pollaiuolo's monumental plate representing a *Battle of Nude Men* (Fig. 39). It too has proved resistant to exact interpretation, and yet it is clear in the intention of its aggressive anatomies, suggesting itself as a model of *invenzione* and *disegno*. Whatever the exact subject – if there is one in a conventional literary sense – Pollaiuolo's engraving presents itself as a model of drawing, that is, a demonstration of the artist's knowledge of the anatomy of the male body and of his controlled ability to render that knowledge – frontal and dorsal as well as foreshortened. His *ingegno* is displayed in the very design, in the furious yet harmonious action of the figures and in the affect of their expression. Even as it functions as anatomical exemplum, however, a model to be studied by other artists, the battle scene here assumes its still larger academic role, as a challenge and test in pictorial composition.[40]

Pollaiuolo's engraving of figures in combat, like Mantegna's *Battle of Sea Gods*, elaborates a thematic motif that had become a standard topos in the late Quattrocento. Such imagery afforded the opportunity to choreograph affective action, to compose a group of bodies expressing the passions of the soul, and through such exercise to demonstrate one's talent (*ingegno*) as both *inventore* and *disegnatore*. Hardly confined to graphic art, this role of the battle is reinforced by antecedent and parallel traditions of similar scenes in relief sculpture, ancient and modern, and these find monumental pictorial culmination in the great Florentine battle murals of Leonardo and Michelangelo (Figs. 42, 43, and Fig. 87 on page 92).

42. Leonardo da Vinci. *Sketches for the Battle of Anghiari*. Pen and brown ink, 14.5 × 15.2 cm. Gallerie dell'Accademia, Venice (inv. 215A).

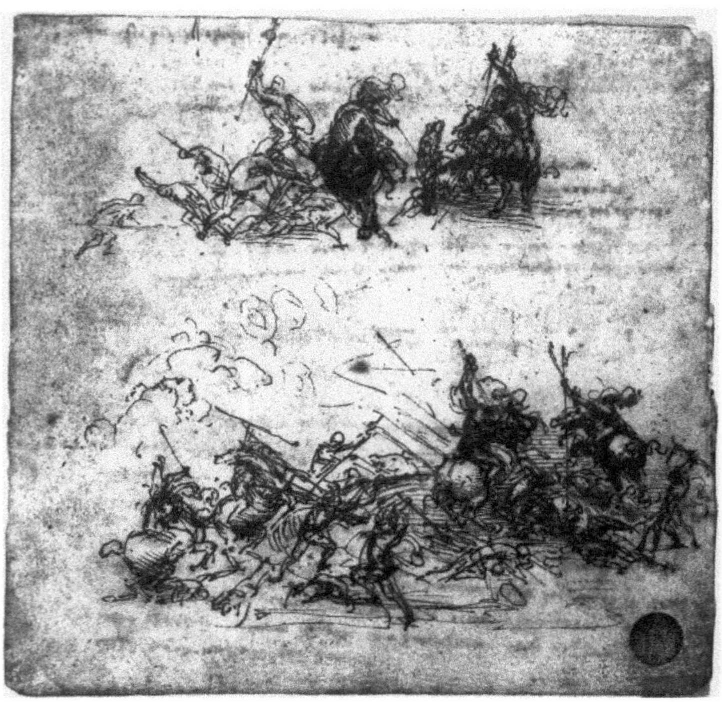

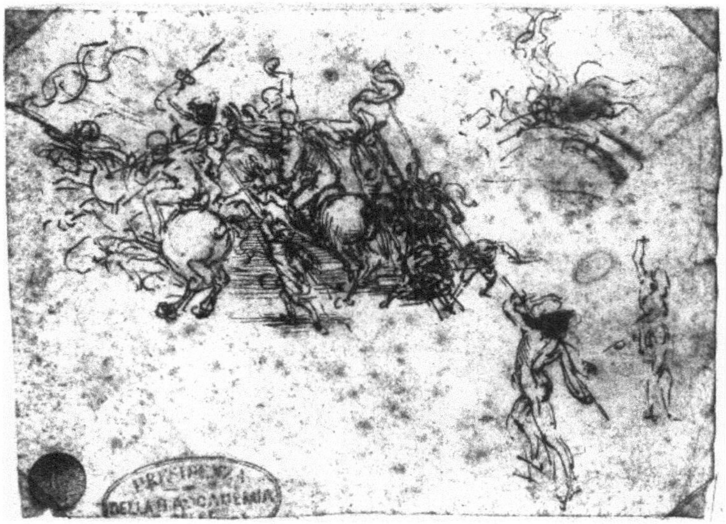

43. Leonardo da Vinci, *Sketches for the Battle of Anghiari.* Pen and brown ink. 10.1 × 14.2 cm. Gallerie dell'Accademia, Venice (inv. 216).

Its special relation to graphic art, however, is confirmed by one particularly eloquent engraving of the early Cinquecento, the *Massacre of the Innocents* designed by Raphael and engraved by Marcantonio Raimondi (see Figs. 121, 122 on pages 126–27). We shall return to consider the graphic language of this print, its linear system, in Chapter Four; what commands our immediate attention is the collaboration itself, which is so explicitly recorded in the signatures. The inscription on the wall to the left declares that Raphael of Urbino invented the design: "RAPHA/VRBI/INVEN." Below, Marcantonio's monogram, "MAF" (*Marc'Antonio Fecit*), affirms his responsibility as engraver of the plate. The *Massacre of the Innocents* is one of the earliest printed examples of the formula *invenit,* or *inventor,* a term that represents full acknowledgment of the legitimacy of separating *invenzione* from *disegno,* distinguishing idea, which is fully represented by the print, from its immediate execution, which was originally conceived in and as drawing by the "inventor" himself.[41] Marcantonio's engraving of the *Massacre of the Innocents* offers direct access to the invention of Raphael.

This very practical distinction between invention and execution, between ideation and realization, finds sanction in the theoretical structure originally articulated by Alberti and then standardized in Renaissance discourse on painting. Even as the tripartite definition of painting was becoming fixed in the literature on art, prints were functioning in a special way to validate and substantiate what had begun as a notion adapted from rhetoric. The designs that an artist engraved, or had engraved, were the products of his imagination; their publication made possible the broader distribution of those ideas, the fruits of invention. In this sense authorship becomes a particular issue in the visual arts, and it is worth noting that the copyright privilege, conceived to encourage printers and publishers by protecting their work against competitors, copyists, and pirates, applied to printed images as well as to books. For the printmaker this meant legal recognition of his invention – and, at least according to Vasari, allowed even a *forestiero* like Dürer in Venice some (small) recourse against the blatant plagiarism of Marcantonio.[42]

3. Leonardo's Discovery

By the end of the fifteenth century, then, the processes of artistic creation and production had been subjected to fairly rigorous and rational analysis. The established use of mathematical perspective toward the beginning of the century had effectively initiated that systematization, providing a geometric basis for pictorial composition. By the middle of the century, the use of the carefully worked out cartoon had further contributed to the methodical rationalization of artistic production, an ordering that was to achieve its most celebrated and influential operation in the Roman studio of Raphael.

As a corollary to these developments, at once prerequisite and consequence, drawing assumed an increasingly important and precise role in the preparatory process. Drawing became the acknowledged arena of invention. We have already discerned in Alberti's "concetti e modelli di tutta la storia" an early testimony to the special role of preliminary compositional designs, first ideas to be tested and, in the dialectical light of critical judgment, modified and improved. Moreover, in urging a certain rapidity of execution – "quella prestezza di fare," the rendering of things "in uno solo colpo" – Alberti seems to have recognized the special appeal of the more open work, its suggestive invitation to viewer projection. Rendering the expressive features of the face rapidly, avoiding finicky closure, leads the observer to imagine more than he actually sees ("sempre seguire cose molto pronte e quali lassino da pensare a chi le guarda molto più che egli non vede" [¶ 42]).[43] Commenting on what we may assume was studio practice, and turning practice into precept, Alberti was articulating the mechanics of graphic creation.

The potential for discovery that Alberti sensed in the dynamics of drawing was to become the very center of concern for Leonardo da Vinci, who, in profoundly personal ways, comes to embody these evolving modern notions about drawing. Observing the world around him with resolutely analytic vision, Leonardo quite naturally included himself among the phenomena to be studied. More knowingly and thoroughly than Alberti, he subjected the creative experience, his own experience, to intense scrutiny. Making his own practice the object of study, describing and commenting on his own creative habits, Leonardo significantly extended the range of aesthetic discourse. Among the most celebrated passages in his draft treatise on painting are those counseling rapidity and roughness in sketching compositional ideas: "The sketching of narrative scenes [*il bozzar delle storie*] should be rapid, and the limbs not too detailed; be content with only the [general] position of the limbs, which you can finish at your leisure, when it pleases you."[44] That Leonardo is describing his own practice is eloquently attested by his own sketches

(Figs. 42, 43, and Figs. 55, 56, 59, 60 on pages 70–72). These represent a new order of apparent disorder, forms and relationships only barely discernible within the skelter of self-effacing lines. Such drawings – which Alberti can hardly have anticipated when he recommended working up the *istoria* with "quella prestezza di fare" – are a long way from the *diligenza* that will be necessary for their eventual realization as finished paintings. In composing *istorie,* Leonardo instructs,

> do not separate the parts of your narrative with sharp lines, or that will happen to you which happens to many painters, who want every little stroke of charcoal to stand [*sia valido*]. These may well acquire riches but not praise for their art, because many are the times when the body of the living creature so represented does not move in a way representative of its thoughts and emotions. But having painted a finished, beautiful, and agreeable arrangement of the limbs, it seems to the artist a damaging thing to alter those limbs, putting them higher or lower or farther back or forward. Men such as these do not deserve any praise at all for their knowledge.[45]

Then, in a move that is only slightly disingenuous, he invokes the poet's compositional fury, not his inspiration but his penmanship:

> Now, have you never considered how poets compose their verses? It does not annoy them, just because they have written beautiful letters, to erase some of their verses, then writing them out again better. Therefore, painter, compose the parts of your figures arbitrarily, then attend first to the movements representative of the mental attitudes of the creatures composing your narrative painting, rather than to the beauty and goodness of the parts of their bodies. Because you must understand that if such an unfinished composition [*componimento inculto*] turns out to be consistent with your invention, it will satisfy all the more when afterward it is adorned with the perfection appropriate to all its parts. I have seen clouds and stains on walls which have given rise to beautiful inventions of different things; although these stains were completely lacking the perfection of any part, yet they did not lack perfection in their movements or other actions.[46]

As he surely recognized in his own experience, drawing a figure rapidly was more likely to realize the affect imagined by the draftsman. It was assumed, of course, that the artist had full control over the anatomical details necessary for bringing the figure to completion in painting, with the requisite *diligenza.* But that finish should be arrived at on the basis of the first rough idea, the initial visualization of imagined intention.[47] In his own drawings Leonardo recognized (as do we) that the very action of the draftsman's hand most effectively projected the "movimenti apropriati alli accidenti mentali" of his imagined figures. The intimate rapport between *ingegno* and *mano* that had already been intuited by Alberti (¶ 59), becomes ever more dynamic in Leonardo's evolving aesthetic. His "new discovery, an aid to reflection, . . . very useful in stimulating the mind to various discoveries [*nuova inventione di speculatione . . . à destare lo ingegnio à varie inventioni*]," appeals directly to the projective faculty of imagination: Look into the rough surfaces and variegated patterns of

> the stains of walls, or the ashes of a fire, or clouds, or mud, or like things, in which, if you consider them well, you will find really marvelous ideas. . . . the composition of battles of animals and men, various compositions of landscapes and monstrous things, such as devils and similar creations, because the mind is stimulated to new inventions by obscure things [*perche nelle cose confuse l'ingegnio si desta a' nove inventioni*]. . . . (McM ¶ 76, c. 35v)

In the intense dialectic of the artist's creative practice the rough sketch, the *componimento inculto,* functions like those surfaces. Product of the imagination, the sketch in turn serves to stimulate that same faculty, inspiring variations on itself, *nuove invenzioni.* Drawing, for Leonardo, involves both invention and recognition – and, as we shall see, cognition. Mediating between the imagination of the artist and the visible world, between interior and exterior worlds, drawing becomes ever more central to artistic creation – which, toward 1500, and not only for Leonardo, appears increasingly as an open process.[48]

Sketching per se was not Leonardo's personal discovery, of course. The tracing hand in search of form – tentatively setting down contours, exploring variations on its own structures, questioning and modifying initial decisions – is to be found in earlier drawing, especially in the revealed *sinopie* of Italian mural painting (Fig. 13). Indeed, toward 1400 the continuing pattern book tradition underwent important transformations, in the North as well as in Italy, as a freer, more tentative touch in drawing increasingly replaced the closed, absolute contours of the older exempla (cf. Figs. 15, 16).[49] Such, we may imagine, was the practice that inspired Alberti's observations on open form. Leonardo's particular contribution was to perceive the principle behind such practice and to recognize its larger implications. Like Alberti, he theorized practice, and in so doing he in turn opened new creative vistas for himself, which he shared with that generation of artists whose achievements we tend to group under the rubric High Renaissance.

Product of the rapid motion of a hand seeking to set down the mind's quicker imaginings, the sketch can present a relative chaos of lines. *Schizzare* implies a sudden spurt or splash of liquid, and Leonardo evidently used the Italian word only once, on a book of collected horse studies, undoubtedly in pen and ink, for the cartoon of the *Battle of Anghiari,* a book marked "libro dj chauallj sc[h]izati pel cartone."[50] Generally, however, Leonardo used other terms to indicate a design roughly blocked out [*abbozzato*] or set down with just a few quick strokes *(brevi segni).* These immediate extensions of the artist, he recognized, guaranteed a surer affect: if the movements of the body do indeed reflect the movements of the soul, then the latter will find most effective expression through the moving body of the draftsman.

The sketching hand extends imagined feeling, projects and records the "accidenti mentali," as the the artist himself participates in the imagined drama of his *istoria*. Just how involved Leonardo himself was in the movements, physical and psychical, of his imagined battle of Anghiari is apparent in those *cavalli schizzati* (Figs. 42, 43).

It is precisely the speed of the sketch, executed by the practiced hand, that relates it so intimately to the designing mind. Validated by its immediacy, its *prestezza* and deliberate lack of *diligenza*, the sketch testifies to the fertility of the artist's imagination, to the rich storehouse of imaginings in his mind. Without the hand, idea remains invisible, unrealized and unrealizable; to take shape, *fantasia* requires *operazione di mano*. "Molto disegno entro la testa tua": Cennini's happy phrase, we recall, results directly from the practice of drawing with the pen. More than a century later, the notion will be filled out and summarized by Albrecht Dürer:

> For the imagination of a good painter is full of figures [*inwendig voller vigur*], and were it possible for him to live forever he would always have from his inward "ideas," whereof Plato speaks, something new to set forth by the work of his hand.[51]

Leonardo, however, was unique in his articulate appreciation of the dialectical complexity that existed between the sketch, as "componimento inculto," and the sketcher, at once active and reactive. No other commentator, not even a practicing contemporary like Dürer, probed his own experience with such demanding intensity; no other was so free of cultural convention in his most personal analysis of artistic creativity. And yet Leonardo was indeed speaking for his contemporaries as well, for that generation of artists – and connoisseurs – who were coming to value the documents of the creative process as much as its final crafted product. By the middle of the sixteenth century the position of the sketch had become codified within an elaborated aesthetic system. The first step in the graphic development of a pictorial concept, it also came to represent the critical link with pure idea.

That priority of the sketch finds full declaration by 1550 in Giorgio Vasari's technical prologue to his *Vite*. *Schizzi*, Vasari begins, are a kind of first drawing ("una prima sorte di disegni") in which figural postures and the overall form of the composition are established as a rough draft made in the form of a blot ("in forma di una macchia"). The products of the inspired mind of the artist ("dal furor dello artefice"), they are set down ("espressi") quickly to test the spirit of his ideas.[52] Confirming a basic shift in values that occurred between the Quattrocento and the Cinquecento, Vasari elevates this graphic production to the level of Platonic inspiration. The notion of creative fury, transferred to the pictorial arts, endows them with the highest privilege, permitting a new concept of artistic genius to enter the critical vocabulary – with the celebration of a Michelangelo as "divine" ("Michel, più che mortale, Angel divino," as Ariosto sang [*Orlando furioso*, XXX.2]). No longer the learned mathematician of the early Renaissance, Alberti's ideal, the new, post–High Renaissance artist represents a more subjective and irrational set of values; his art depends less upon commensurability and control than upon the irrationality of inspiration, the intervention of a power beyond the reach of human reason.

Nowhere is this distinction more eloquently figured than in Raphael's *School of Athens*, in the contrast between the painter's self-portrait and the image of Michelangelo as Heraclitus: Raphael associates himself with the Euclidean measurers, with the architect Bramante as Euclid, open and gregarious; the brooding, melancholic Michelangelo, opposite, is represented as totally alone, self-involved, pen in hand, awaiting the inspiration of a higher source. In this fresco Raphael traces that fundamental shift in the conception of the artist as creator, from Albertian humanist to Platonic genius.[53]

Drawing, as the agency by which idea first finds form, was central to this conception of inspiration. The impulsive pen lines of the sketch recorded the creative fury of the inspired artist, testified to a creative energy barely under control; the very immediacy of the sketch, its casual disregard of pictorial decorum, confirmed its credentials. Bold and burning ("tutto fiero ed acceso"), it was the graphic document of that heated moment of inspiration, the draftsman's *afflatus*.[54] This assumption of direct access to the creative mind through drawing becomes axiomatic in the subsequent history of critical appreciation of the art, essential, ultimately, to the theory and practice of connoisseurship.

4. The Father of the Arts

Like the workshop-oriented Cennini, who defined the two fundamentals of painting as "il disegno e'l cholorire," Leonardo too divided painting into only two principal parts: line and color, or shading (McM ¶¶ 101, 102). And if he debated with himself as to their relative importance, deciding now for drawing (McM ¶¶ 102, 106), now for color (McM ¶¶ 107, 435), he hardly doubted the significance of *disegno* ("cioe lineamenti che circondano le figure de corpi finiti") as the art fundamental not only to to pictorial mimesis but to the painter's very imagination:

> But this *disegno* is of such excellence that it not only investigates the works of nature, but infinitely more than those that nature produces. . . . And for this reason we conclude that *disegno* is not only a science but a deity whose name should be duly commemorated, a deity which repeats all the visible works of God the highest.[55]

More than a generation earlier Lorenzo Ghiberti had declared *disegno* to be "il fondamento e teorica" of the arts of painting and sculpture. In a still more ambitious mood, he included "teorica disegno" among the liberal arts to be mastered by both sculptor and painter.[56] Alberti's lead is here taken up to assert directly the new status of the visual arts.

Alberti's tripartite definition of painting, based on ancient rhetorical models, and his presentation of the art in *Della pittura* had assigned a definite priority to drawing: "circonscrizione" precedes "composizione" and "ricevere di lumi." That priority, which will be retained in subsequent definitions from Piero della Francesca to Vasari and beyond, derived from both theory and practice. In the geometric model of Alberti's aesthetic scheme line follows point; as the first Euclidean element to attain visibility, line is the basic grapheme, the primary unit of pictorial language. This was the theory that glossed practice.

In Piero's treatise on pictorial perspective the definition of painting follows Alberti, with a slightly altered vocabulary: the three parts of painting are "disegno, commensuratio et colorare." The first consists of the contours bounding form; the second, corresponding to Alberti's "composizione," regards the proper, proportional location of those bounded forms. Announcing his intention to focus on "commensuratione," which he calls perspective, Piero admits that it will be necessary to include something of "disegno," without whose lines there can be no perspective.[57]

Line makes form possible. It is the beginning of representation, of the "works of nature" as well as of "infinitely more" (Leonardo's words) residing in the mind of the artist, his *fantasia*. Just as Piero had to fold *disegno* into his consideration of composition, so Leonardo, in his binary definition of painting, implicitly incorporates composition, as well as invention, in *disegno:* It is through drawing that the artist discovers the ideas in his mind, through drawing that he can begin to see and confront those Platonic figures that fill his head, in Dürer's suggestive image. Essential in theory and in practice, drawing acquires still grander status as the *fons et origo* of the visual arts: "detta teorica è orgine et fondamento di ciascuna arte," as Ghiberti declared.[58] *Disegno* comes to be recognized not only as the means of realizing idea but as the very source of idea itself.

What remained implicit in the art theory of the Quattrocento, even in Leonardo's enthusiastic observations, became fully revealed in the culturally more ambitious pronouncements of the Cinquecento. In the course of the sixteenth century artists and men of letters elevated the concept of *disegno* to the highest levels of aesthetic worship. For example, in a little book entitled *Il Disegno* (1549), the Florentine Antonfrancesco Doni could openly declare its divinity. *Disegno* is "divine speculation," which produces a most excellent art, and the "first *disegno* is the invention of the entire universe, imagined perfectly in the mind of the first mover," the primal act of modeling and coloring.[59] The rhetorical logic of traditional aesthetic discourse, already pushed to daring extreme by Leonardo, leads to an inevitable conclusion: if God is indeed the first maker (*deus artifex*), then the same creative principles must have applied from the beginning.[60] Creation itself, as Leonardo already knew, stood as the great witness and monument to the primal energies of *disegno*.

The 1540s saw a flurry of publications on the arts, including the first printed editions of Alberti's treatise on painting.[61] In Florence during this decade the aesthetics of the visual arts attained a new level of public discussion, spurred in part by the questioning of Benedetto Varchi regarding the relative merits of painting and sculpture, but perhaps above all by the sheer phenomenon of Michelangelo. Varchi's academic prodding encouraged artists to voice opinions and values that otherwise might have remained tacit, working assumptions lying just below the threshold of articulation.[62] In their responses to Varchi, the artists publicly acknowledged *disegno* as the foundation of their arts and their common bond.[63]

The most resonant and influential text to come out of this ambience of aesthetic reflection and self-reflection is Vasari's *Vite,* the pioneering monument of art historiography. It is Vasari – significantly, a working artist – who most effectively addresses *disegno* in both theoretical and practical terms. Summing up more than a century of speculation on the topic in one vivid genealogical image, he declares it the father of the three visual arts.

> In that *disegno,* father of our three arts, Architecture, Sculpture, and Painting, proceeding from the intellect, derives from many individual things a universal judgment, it is similar to a form or rather idea of all the things of nature, which is most singular in its measure; for not only in the bodies of humans and of animals but also in plants, in buildings, in sculpture and in painting, does it know the proportion of the whole to the parts and of the parts to one another and to the whole. And seeing that from this knowledge is born a certain conception and judgment, so that there is formed in the mind that something which then expressed with the hands is called *disegno,* one can conclude that this *disegno* is none other than a visible expression and declaration of the inner conception that one has and of that which others have imagined in the mind and given form to idea.[64]

Vasari and his contemporaries were heirs not only to the previous generations of artist-writers, going back to Alberti and Cennini, who had explored *disegno* as theory. They were also direct witnesses to the practical triumph of the art of drawing in the High Renaissance of Leonardo, Raphael, and Michelangelo. The great achievement of these masters stood as eloquent testimony to the divinity of the art – even as their own drawings offered the demonstrations that were to serve as ideal academic models.

The mutual dependency of *operazione di mano* and *fantasia* remained a constant dialectic in the aesthetic discourse of the Renaissance. Discussions of *disegno* invariably begin with contour but then, following the expansive momentum of the term itself, reach out to include composition and invention. Following the conventional definition of painting as "disegno," "invenzione," and "colorire," Paolo Pino (1548) further divides *disegno* into four parts: "giudicio," "circumscrizzione," "pratica," and "retta composizione," the last of these synthetically encompassing the other three as full pictorial expression. Like Alberti (whose work he had disparaged as more about mathematics than painting), although with much less consistency and rigor, Pino follows the constructing sequence from surfaces to members to bodies to full design.[65] "Giudicio" is innate, a talent that the painter, like the poet, must be born with, although exercise might still allow him to master "circonscrizzione," that is, the outlining and shading of figures ("il profillare, contornare le figure e darle chiari e scuri"); through "la pratica" the artist acquires "buona maniera nel disegnare." Similarly, for Lodovico Dolce (1557) *disegno* comprehends more than its initial definition as "the form that the painter gives to things that he is imitating, a varied turning movement of lines which form the figures." Without that primary forming, invention itself is impossible: "Nor is it enough for a painter to be a good inventor if he is not equally good as a draftsman [*disegnatore*], for invention is represented by form, and form is none other than *disegno*."[66]

The acknowledged master of this art, without peer, was Michelangelo. His association with *disegno* played an essential role in the absolute elevation of the concept in the Cinquecento, for he himself was "il Maestro delle tre arti del disegno," indeed, "il Padre" of them all.[67] The divinity ascribed to the concept was shared by the artist.

The notion that the several visual arts depend on and from *disegno* – already a cultural commonplace for the courtiers of Castiglione[68] – found institutional confirmation in Florence in the creation in 1563 of the first academy of fine arts, the Accademia delle Arti del Disegno, with Grand Duke Cosimo de' Medici and Michelangelo himself as *capi*. The common paternity of the three arts – painting, sculpture, and architecture – legitimized their grouping as *arti del disegno*. The very concept of the "fine arts" depends upon the discourse we have been following, the recognition of the foundational status of drawing in theory and in practice and of *disegno* as a guiding principle, an idea.[69]

The academy was especially the inspiration of Vasari, and it is from Vasari as well that we have clearest testimony of another kind of institutional acknowledgment of the centrality of *disegno:* the collection of drawings. Vasari himself was hardly the first collector of drawings; we have already observed the visually literate audience that emerged by the end of the Quattrocento, an audience interested in graphic inventions, drawings and prints; artists themselves tended to be among the most avid collectors.[70] But Vasari's collection was systematic in a new way, keyed to his biographical and historical project. For each of the artists whose life he recorded he sought products of his hand. Entered in Vasari's *libro de' disegni*, those drawings were dutifully attributed and mounted on large folios, singly or in groups, set in elaborately drafted frames of his own design (Fig. 44). Taken from their original studio context – although it was to that creative context that they continued to bear witness – these sheets were set apart as fully independent works of art. Whatever their original purpose, they now served a new function, aesthetic and art-historical, documenting individual style. Accompanying the further elaboration of *disegno* as theory in the sixteenth century, collecting attests to a more practical evaluation of drawing as an art. The well-turned line, the studied pose, and the sensitively modeled surface were appreciated as qualities of *buon disegno;* the rapidly scrawled *macchia* of the sketch was valued as a permanent record of an

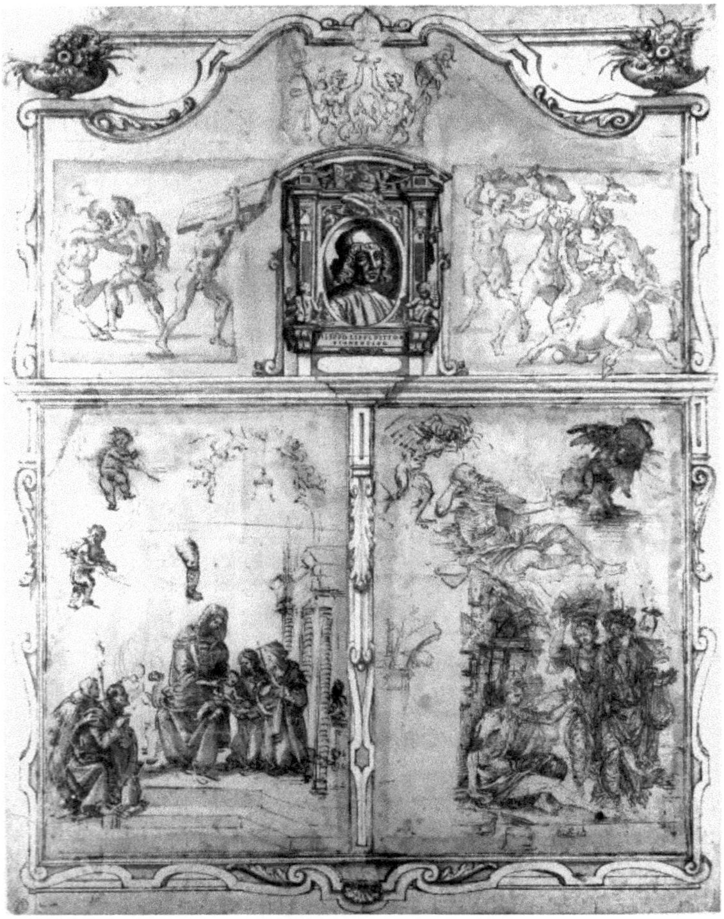

44. Filippino Lippi, *Five Sheets of Sketches,* from Vasari's *Libro de' disegni,* 56.5 × 45 cm (including Vasari's frame). Christ Church, Oxford (OBS 36 recto).

inspired moment of creative fury. Viewing a drawing afforded privileged access to the creative process. The old polarity of *diligenza* and *prestezza di fare* invited new appreciation.

By the end of the sixteenth century *disegno,* as the central concept in the visual arts, had become subject to increasingly intense theorizing, supported and encouraged by the very ambivalence of the term. Signifying both the specific physical act of the draftsman (drawing) and the larger notion of design (composition), *disegno* operated in an aesthetic space between matter and idea, between the sensual and the spiritual. And that polarity, as we have seen, offered rich ground for aesthetic speculation. What was only vaguely intuited in Cennini's "molto disegno entro la testa," what was haltingly Platonized in Dürer's good painter "inwendig volle vigure," becomes more deliberately articulated. On one of his designs for an emblem of the Accademia del Disegno (Fig. 45), Benvenuto Cellini inscribed a simple epitome of the tradition: "*Disegno* is of two kinds: the first is that which is made in the *Imaginativa,* and the second, deriving from it, is that which is demonstrated with lines."[71] This first kind of drawing emerges as the fully developed and independent concept of *disegno interno,* the idea in the mind of the artist. And, like pure idea, it requires material realization in order to be apprehended by the senses, that is, *disegno esterno.* Only through the physical act of drawing, with base material like ink or chalk, can idea be made visible – Alberti's "più grassa Minerva."

The deification of the art and the concept achieves its rhetorical culmination in Federico Zuccaro's capricious etymological conceit, where *Disegno* is, literally, the sign [*segno*] of God [*Dio*] in man: *DI,SEGNO,O,* the seal of His holy name.[72] It is Zuccaro who, with scholastic elaboration, most fully articulates the distinction between the two modes of *disegno.* He further distinguishes three categories of *disegno esterno,* "one natural and two artificial": The first is nature itself, to be imitated by art; the second, "disegno artificiale esemplare," is human artifice, with which we form inventions and *concetti* historical and poetic. The third is also artificial but "fantastico," and it includes all the "bizarrie, capricci, invenzioni, fantasie e

45. Benvenuto Cellini, *Design for the Seal of the Accademia del Disegno.* Pen and brown ink, brush and brown wash, heightened with white, 30 × 21.7 cm. Staatliche Graphische Sammlung, Munich (inv. 2247).

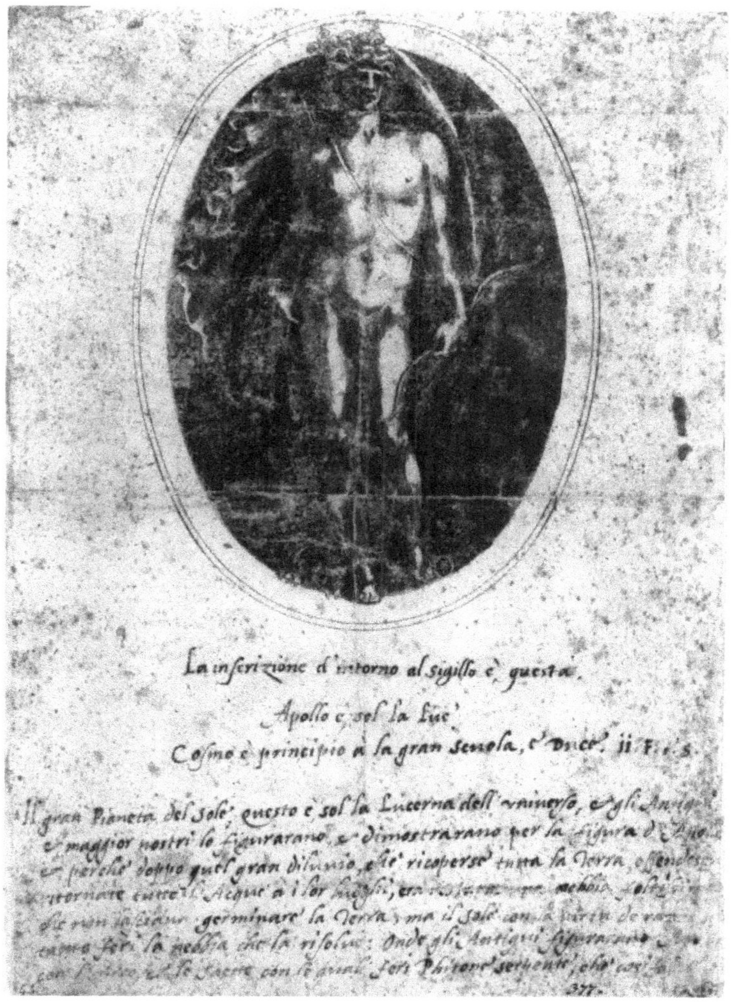

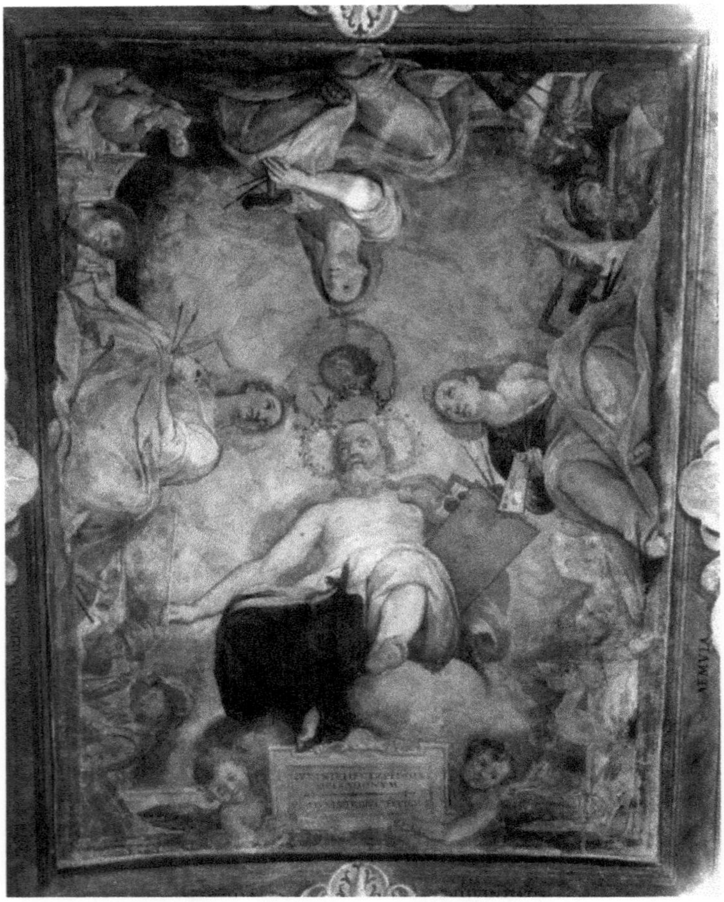

46. Federico Zuccaro, *Allegory of Disegno*. Sala del Disegno, Palazzo Zuccaro, Rome. Photograph: Bibliotheca Hertziana, Rome.

ghiribizzi dell'huomo."[73] And with this final distinction Zuccaro, while summarizing earlier aesthetic assumptions, effectively opens the way to a fuller acknowledgment of the *capriccio* as a creative mode – a theme to which we shall return.[74]

For all the philosophical rhetoric brought to the discussion by intellectually ambitious academics like Zuccaro – who in his own palace figured the father with his three daughters (Fig. 46)[75] – a basic truth remains: *Disegno* is fraught with contradiction and ambivalence, located as it is at the very boundary between mind and hand, idea and form.[76] This truth, a discovery of the Renaissance, has shaped the subsequent history of drawing, its practice and its critical appreciation.

CHAPTER THREE

The Handwriting of the Self
Leonardo da Vinci

It is said that every painter paints himself.
– Girolamo Savonarola[1]

In both theory and practice, the pivotal figure in the history of drawing in the West is Leonardo da Vinci. From his own experience as a draftsman Leonardo elaborated a series of observations that, collectively, constitute a fully articulated theory of drawing. It was in and through his own practice that he discovered and named the sketch. Watching his own drawing hand – alert to its operations, aware of the demands made upon it, of the expectations that impelled it, and of its own willful instincts – he made it the subject of continuing inquiry. Drawing, he came to recognize, was his means of seeing and knowing, of relating to and controlling the world. The analysis of his own drawing afforded him a way of confronting himself. Any study of his drawings, then, inevitably leads to that confrontation with the artist.

1. *Inscribing the World*

As the son of a notary, Leonardo probably learned his letters and formed his hand well at an early age. His earliest dated work is a drawn prospect of the Arno valley, a key monument in the development of landscape representation (Fig. 47).[2] An inscription dates the drawing precisely to the feast day of Santa Maria della Neve, the fifth of August 1473 ("dì di s.ta Maria della Neve / addj 5 daghossto 1473"). Scripted with a notarial flourish that declares its documentary function with quasi-official ostentation, the text sits proudly in the upper left of the paper, its graphic weight balancing the mounting crowns of foliage to the right. Such calligraphic indulgence suggests a special satisfaction taken in forming his letters, a skill, we presume, Leonardo developed under the early tutelage of his father, ser Piero da Vinci. But the text is entirely backwards, in mirror-writing, scripted from right to left. Leonardo, perhaps the most notorious lefty in history, stubbornly refused in his writing to accommodate society's convention. The inscription exists in a state of double tension: with the perspective art of the drawing that it documents and with the writing art of the father and his culture.

A view from on high of a plain stretching past surrounding hills to the distant horizon, Leonardo's drawing offers a clear statement of the ambitious spatial reach of early Renaissance pictorial representation. The pen moves in complexly suggestive ways. Rapid, contained patterns of impressionistic yet disciplined scribble establish the foliate crowns of trees as atmospheric volumes; other, bolder and more cursive strokes define more rugged arboreal growth. Leonardo's pen has reinforced the nearer contours of the rocky terrain that drops precipitously and sinuously from the high plateau of the draftsman's vantage. The assertive visual strength of those lines affirms their materiality and, therefore, proximity: their appeal is tactile; available to the touch, they are (we imagine) within reach. Beyond the graphic density of this foreground level stretches the cultivated plain; in the distance, reaching to the horizon, plowed fields structure and measure progress through space. Composed of patterns of receding orthogonals, these units evoke the system from which they have been adapted: perspective representation. The spatial construct of Leonardo's drawing, then, combines a number of strategies, a number of penmanships – and inks. The perspective declaration of the distant fields confirms the spatial implications of the foreground penwork.

If the full design of Leonardo's drawing may be seen as a monumental elaboration of the representational principle inherent in the spatializing line of Parrhasios, the inscription hanging on the surface in the upper left recalls the indexical character of the line of Apelles: the line as signature. Without mimetic function, the inscription, in witnessing the work, records the presence of the maker, traces the

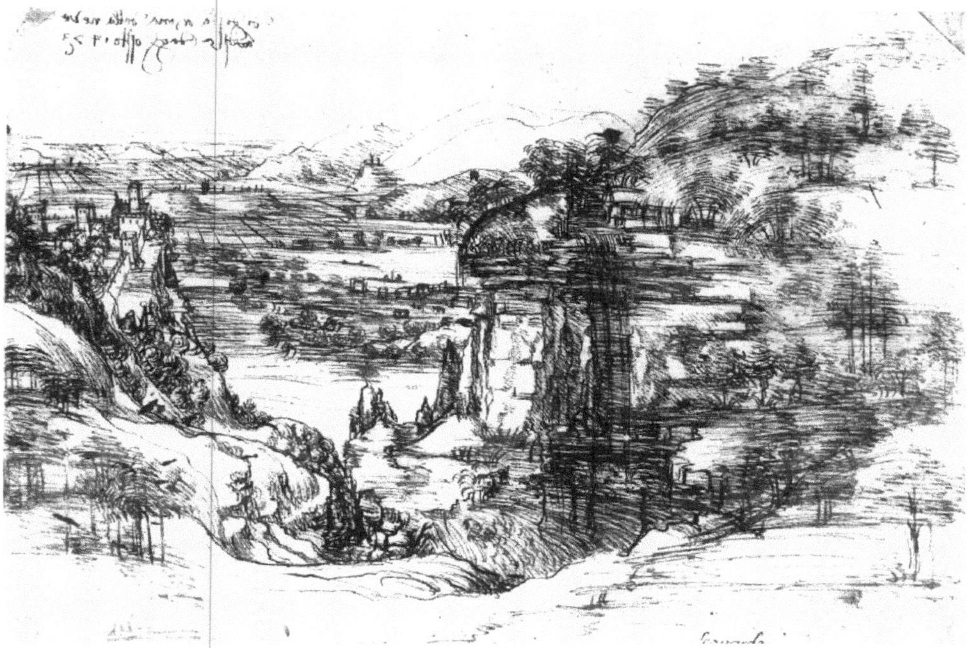

47. Leonardo da Vinci, *View of the Arno Valley*. Pen and brown inks, 19.6 × 28.7 cm. Gabinetto Disegni e Stampe degli Uffizi, Florence (no. 8P).

movement of his hand – at a precise moment in time, but then holding that moment in perpetuity. The linear self-indulgence of its quasi-Gothic calligraphy confirms the inscription's self-reflexivity.[3] That it is in mirror-writing may not be surprising in view of Leonardo's left-handedness, but it should not be taken for granted. It may seem natural for a *mancino* to write backwards, thereby obviating the awkward twist of hand otherwise required to avoid smearing wet ink. But the culture frowned upon such supposedly unnatural acts; children cursed with left-handed preference were forcibly corrected – including, evidently, artists like Michelangelo and Sebastiano del Piombo.[4]

Leonardo was the firstborn, though illegitimate son of a prominent notary in Florence, a professonal master of documentary script. It seems hardly fortuitous that the son picked up certain writing habits from the father, not only graphic, like a taste for the declarative flourish, but verbal as well: *In dei nomine* ("In the name of God") will become one of Leonardo's favorite, casual, and usually abbreviated notations, indulged in for its own cursive pattern. Being illegitimate, the son was barred from succeeding to his father's respected profession, and his willful development of left-handed mirror-writing can hardly be considered without awareness of that situation. Perhaps the clearest indication of its relevance is offered by Leonardo's own recording, twice, of his father's death: "A dì di luglio 1504, mercoledì a ore 7 morì Ser Piero da Vinci, notaio al Palazzo del Podestà, mio padre, a ore 7, era d'età d'anni 80, lasciò 10 figlioli maschi e 2 femmine"; and again: "Mercoledì a ore 7 morì Ser Piero da Vinci a dì 9 di luglio 1504." Each of these notations is written in the conventional manner, from left to right.[5]

The first of these entries drew the attention of Freud in his psychoanalytic study of Leonardo. He was struck by the "pedantic exactness" of the passage and the "prominence given to numbers." He read as a sign of Leonardo's "affective inhibition" the repetition of "at 7 o'clock." This "perseveration," as Freud termed it, concealed and suppressed the emotional weight of the report, displacing it "on to the most indifferent detail."[6] In light of the subsequent debates over Freud's interpretation of Leonardo, it is especially unfortunate that the psychoanalyst was evidently unaware of the script itself, of Leonardo's deliberate reversal of his *mancinismo,* his temporary obedience to the dominant conventions of legibility in recording the death of his father – so prominently identified professionally as "notaio al Palazzo del Podestà." When Leonardo abandoned his natural mirror-writing, it was to make himself legible to an other. To whom was he addressing himself here? Even more than perseveration, then, the handwriting itself may be charged with the "affective colour" of these words.

Interestingly, Freud's earliest fascination with Leonardo seems to have been linked to just this aspect of the artist, in which he found a clue to other dimensions of his personality. In 1898 he wrote to Fliess that "perhaps the most famous left-handed individual was Leonardo, who," he adds, "is not known to have had any love-affairs."[7] Whatever the value of the implications here for an etiology of homosexuality, Freud's initial observation at least recognizes a definite significance to Leonardo's hand.

The inscription on the landscape drawing of 1473 is the earliest extant example of Leonardo's penmanship. The graphic pride of its elaborated calligraphy, its self-declarative character, attests to the special weight assigned it by the twenty-one-year-old artist. In its intimate relationship to the drawing it documents, the inscription initiates the dialectic of word and image, of writing and drawing, that will animate and impell Leonardo's activity as a draftsman.[8]

Leonardo's next preserved dated drawing (Fig. 49), from five years later, is a torn sheet featuring two male heads confronting one another and inscribed, fragmentarily, near the bottom, late in the year 1478, December or possibly November.[9] A longer inscription filling the upper portion of the originally folded paper (Fig. 50) records the artist's affection for a certain Fieravanti di Domenico in Florence, "my most beloved companion as though he were my . . ." ("Fieravanti di Domenicho in Firenze e chompar / amantissimo quanto mio . . ."); the ellipsis may be indicative of the emotion, or even anxiety(?), with which it was penned. The two facing heads, so poignantly juxtaposed, seem either commentary on or illustration of the written confession – although they very likely preceded the writing. Just below that inscription we encounter for the first time the formula that will become such a frequent graphic notation in Leonardo's marginalia: *In dei nom[ine]* – and again we are reminded of his notarial paternity.[10] Then, below that, Leonardo repeats his comparative declaration of affection, abbreviating "amant[issimo] quanto." The final flourish of this brief inscription, a continuous loop stabilized by two vertical strokes, floats somewhat ambiguously on the surface. Following the word

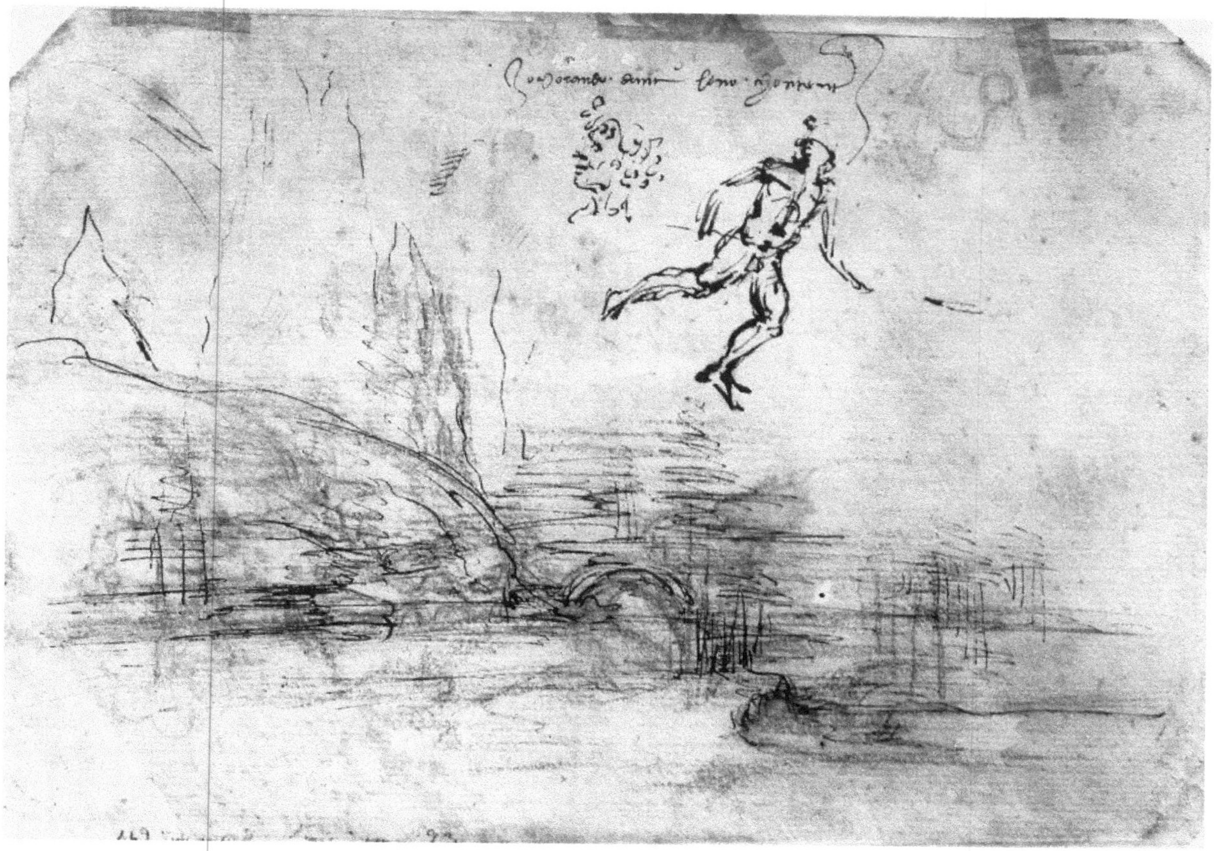

48. Leonardo da Vinci and another hand, *Landscape and Other Sketches*. Black chalk, pen and brown ink. Verso of Fig. 47.

"quanto," but evidently carrying no alphabetic reference, it remains illegible, enjoying a certain graphic independence; mingling with the pen strokes defining the hair of the virile profiled head, it nonetheless does not actually participate in the drawn image. Pictorial or scriptorial? Its visual ambiguity testifies to the intimacy of writing and drawing as marking gestures.

Below the two heads is the fragmented inscription that dates the drawing and also relates it to a number of other projects: "[Decem(?)]ber 1478. I began the 2 Virgin Marys" (". . . bre 1478 Inchominciai le 2 Vergine Marie") (Fig. 51). These words – like those below ("e chompa . . . in Pisstoya") – are also written in a kind of exaggerated notarial hand. Such calligraphic indulgence, which can turn a document into a work of art, extends the momentum of the letter beyond the written line into the surrounding field of the page; it encourages a certain controlled fancy in the pen – or, more accurately, the hand guiding the pen. In the case of Leonardo's writing on this sheet that momentum claims new – or, renewed – energy: the flourish detaches itself from the initiating letter (Fig. 52), liberating itself from the legible responsibilities of writing; a gesture has assumed a life of its own. Writing has become drawing.

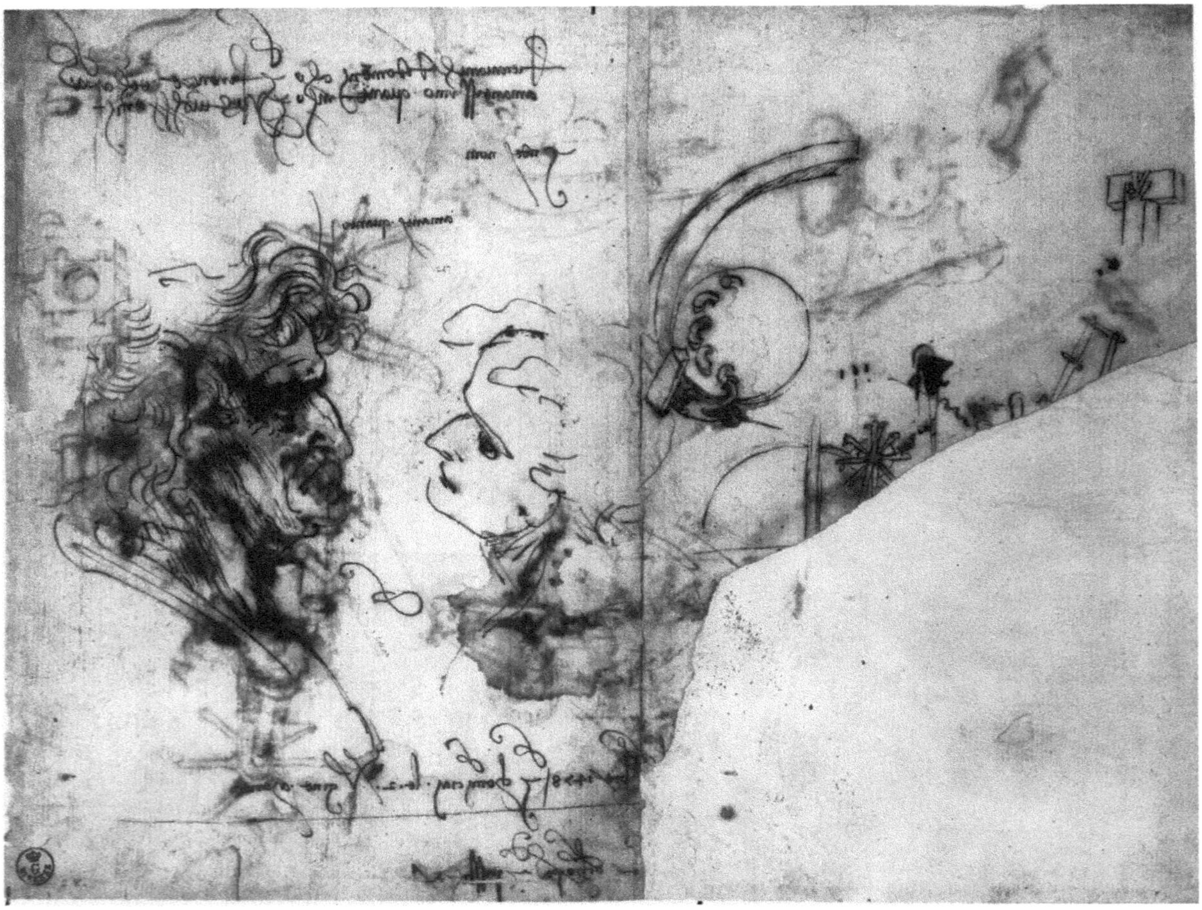

49. Leonardo da Vinci, *Studies of Heads and Machines*. Pen and brown ink, 20.1 × 26.7 cm (irregularly torn). Gabinetto Disegni e Stampe degli Uffizi, Florence (no. 446E).

Literally taking off, repeating itself as an independent graphic exercise, the flourish leaves the word behind, and in so doing discovers and explores its new potential as grapheme. Above all, freed from scripted constraint, it more insistently asserts the spatial implications of drawing; it becomes a line in space. The pen declares its own will: an initial small curve continues on its elegant course, defining the surface over which it runs. Then it turns back upon itself, a movement natural to the alphabetic course of writing. But as soon as it crosses its own previous path – and without the governing verbal context of the letter/word – the line declares the challenge of pictorial art, its ambiguity. Does the line pass over or under? No matter: it has transcended the absolute flatness of the paper. As soon as the line has crossed itself, forming a loop, it participates in what may be called the "spatialization" of linear movement.[11] However it may seem a mere doodle for Leonardo, this calligraphic impulse nonetheless functions as an epitome of the act of drawing – what we have heard Paul Klee describe as "an active line on a walk, moving freely, without goal," but whose path is clearly controlled by the habits of the trained hand.

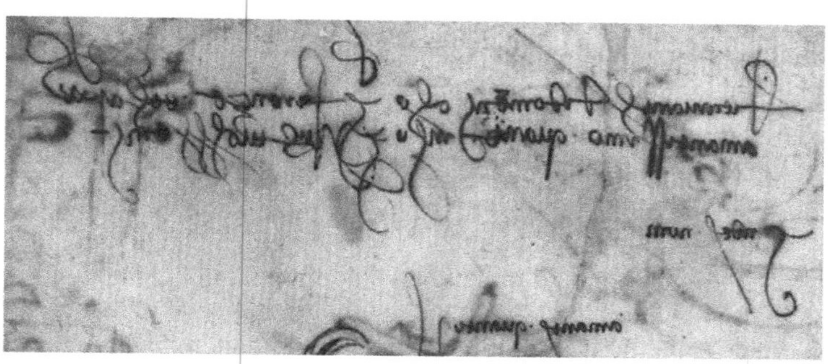

50. Leonardo da Vinci, *Studies of Heads and Machines,* detail of Fig. 49.

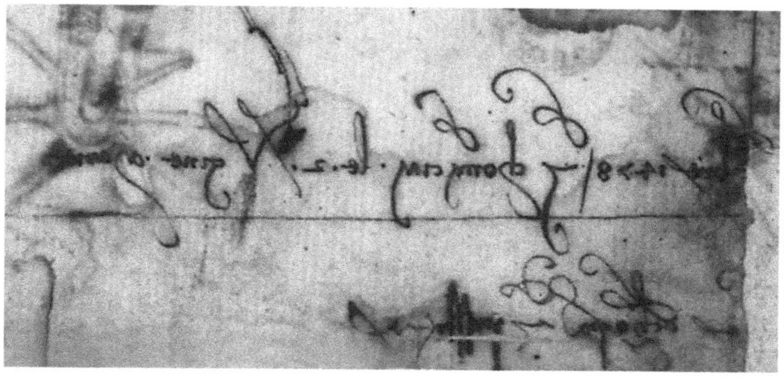

51. Leonardo da Vinci, *Studies of Heads and Machines,* detail of Fig. 49.

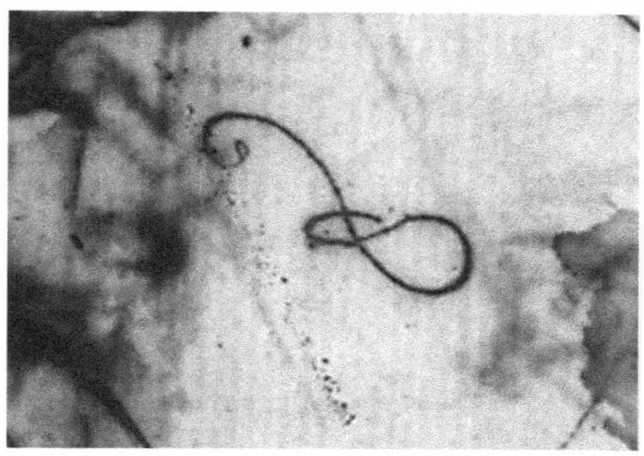

52. Leonardo da Vinci, *Studies of Heads and Machines,* detail of Fig. 49.

2. *A Generation Drawing*

Doodle: "An aimless, more or less automatic scribble, outline, design or improvised sketch traced while one is mentally occupied with something else" (*Webster's New Collegiate Dictionary*). It is the word often used to describe Leonardo's marginal graphic activity, the notations, pictorial and scribal, that fill the peripheral areas of his drawings, but most densely and compellingly on the grand sheet as in the Royal Library at Windsor (12276), which probably also dates from about 1478 (Figs. 53, 54).[12]

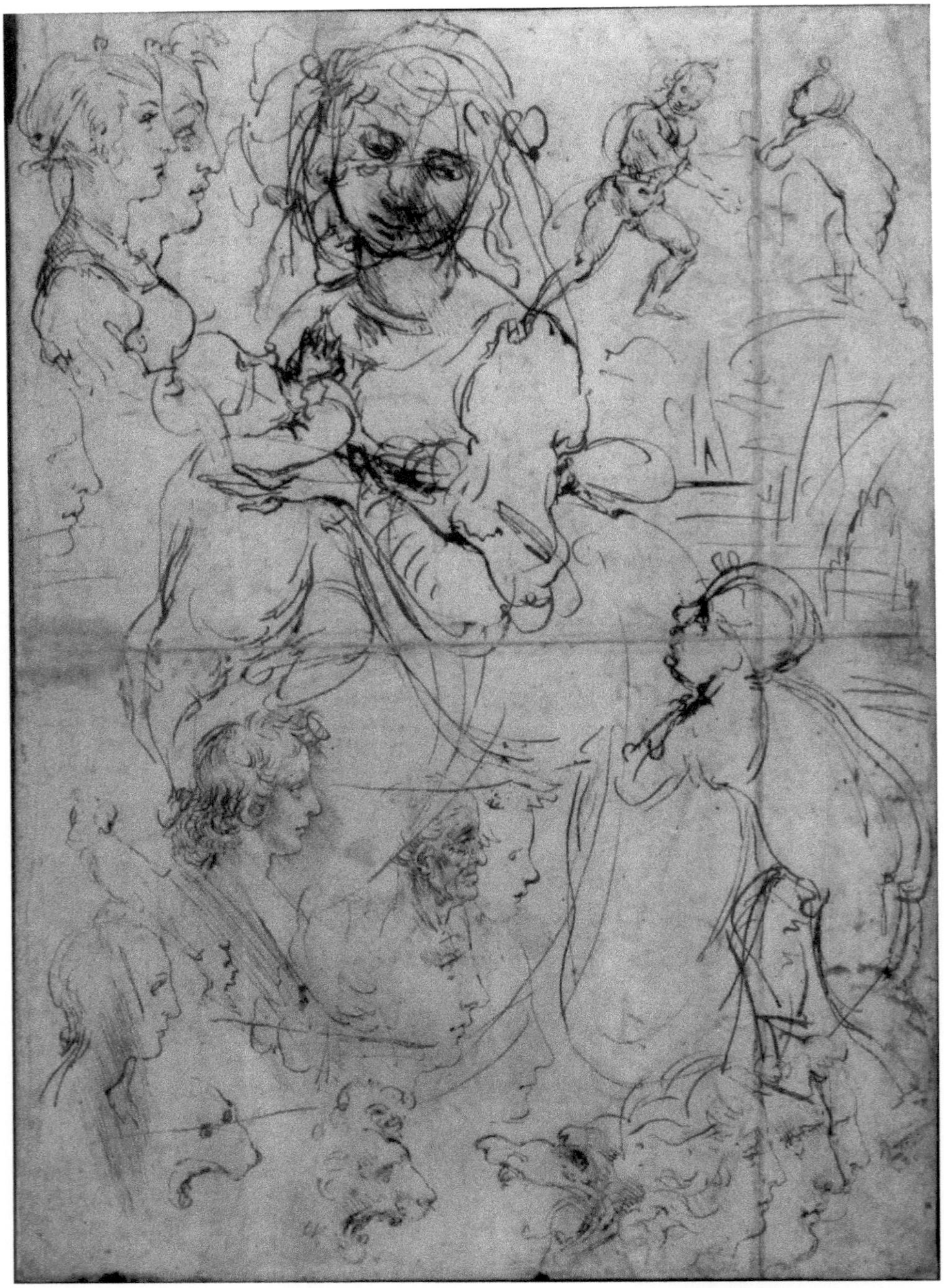

53. Leonardo da Vinci, *Madonna and Child with the Infant St. John the Baptist and Other Studies.* Pen and brown ink, 40.4 × 29.1 cm. Royal Library, Windsor Castle (no. 12276r). The Royal Collection ©2000, Her Majesty Queen Elizabeth II.

The central motif on the recto, Virgin and Child with the infant Saint John the Baptist, may well prepare one of those two compositions of the Virgin Mary that Leonardo recorded on the Uffizi drawing (Fig. 51). Such images seem hardly to call for comment; they were the bread-and-butter subjects of any Renaissance workshop. Probably a few years earlier, about 1475, Leonardo had painted the *Virgin and*

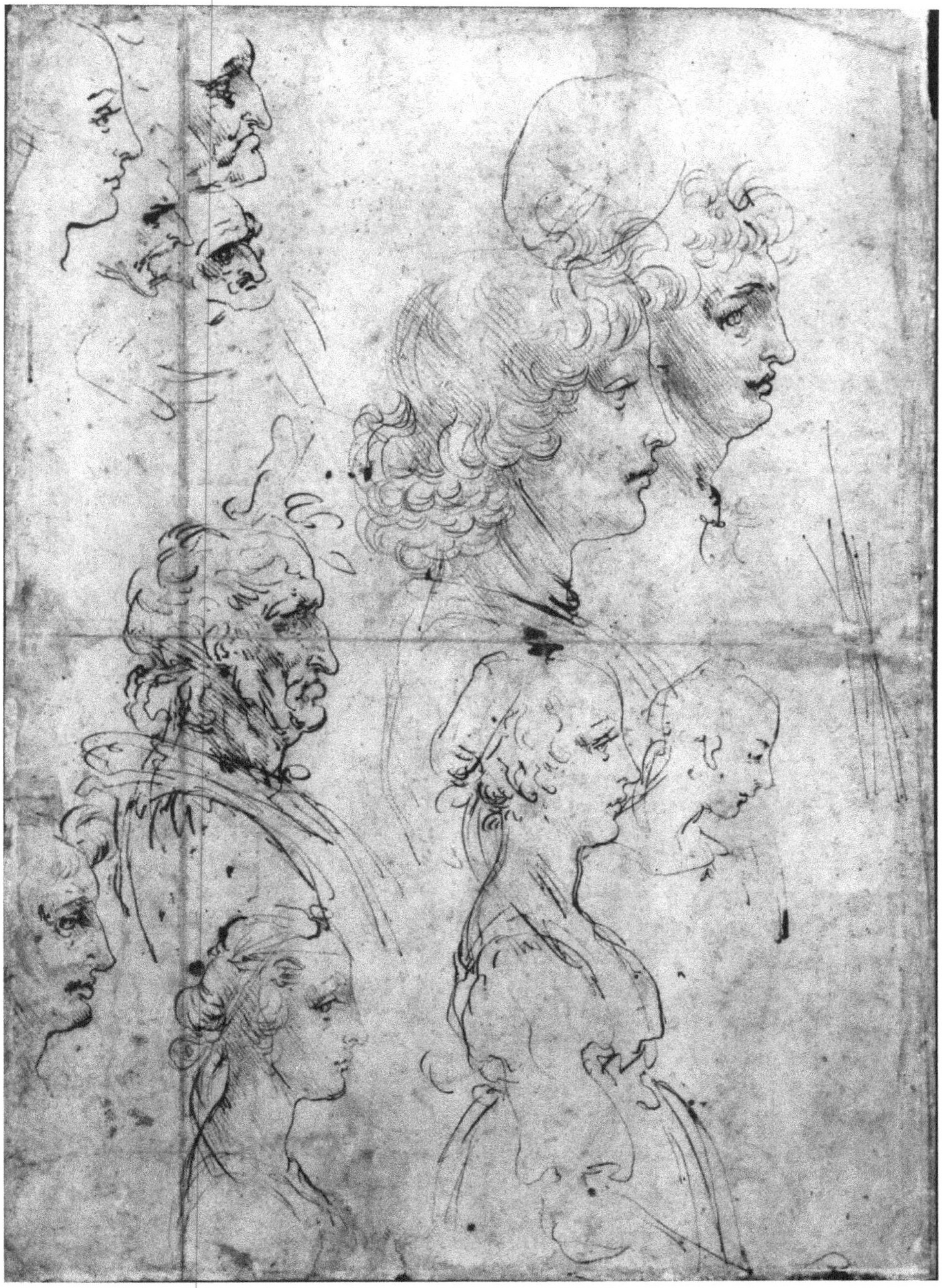

54. Leonardo da Vinci, *Studies of Heads in Profile.* Pen and brown ink. Verso of Fig. 53.

Child with a Carnation (Munich, Alte Pinakothek); although it is still an exercise in the mode of his master Verrocchio, Leonardo's hand and imagination reveal themselves in the subtlety of its formal rendering and, especially, in the distant landscape. More relevant to a date of about 1478 is the *Benois Madonna* (St. Petersburg, Hermitage): less rigid in conception, it introduces the vitality of serpentine movement, formal and dramatic, that is so crucial to Leonardo's achievement.

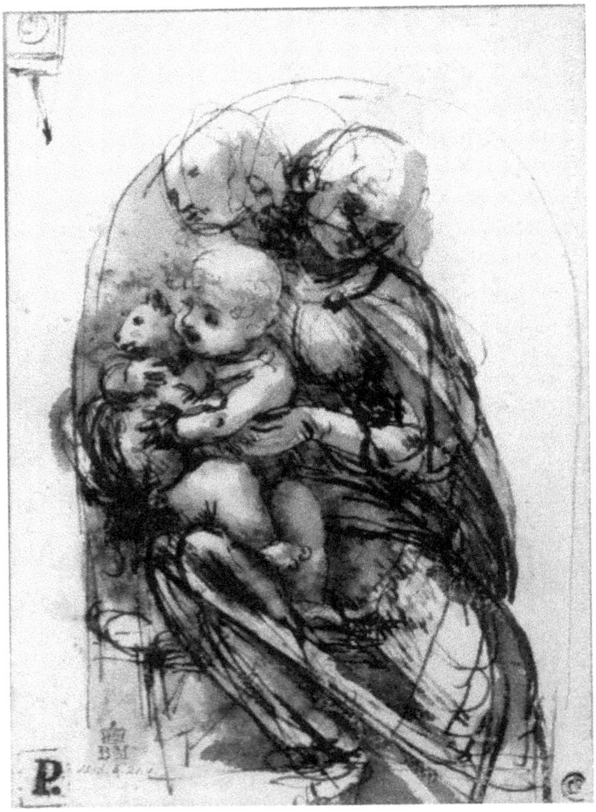

55. *(left)* Leonardo da Vinci, *Madonna and Child with a Cat.* Pen and brown ink, brush and wash over preliminary stylus sketch, 13.2 × 9.5 cm. British Museum, London (1856-6-21-1).

56. *(below left)* Leonardo da Vinci, *Madonna and Child with a Cat.* Pen and brown ink. Verso of Fig. 55.

57. *(below right)* Leonardo da Vinci, *Studies for a Madonna and Child with a Cat.* Pen and brown ink over black chalk or charcoal (upper study), 27.4 × 19 cm. British Museum, London (1860-6-16-98).

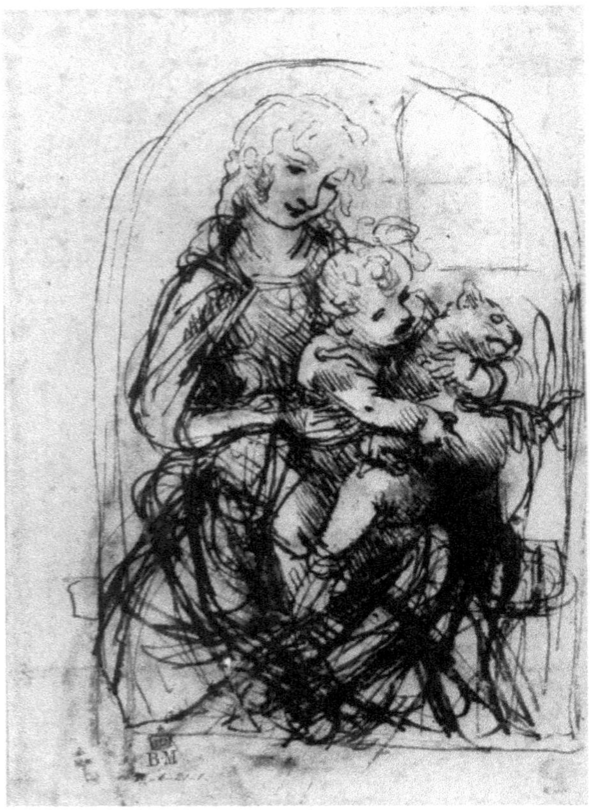

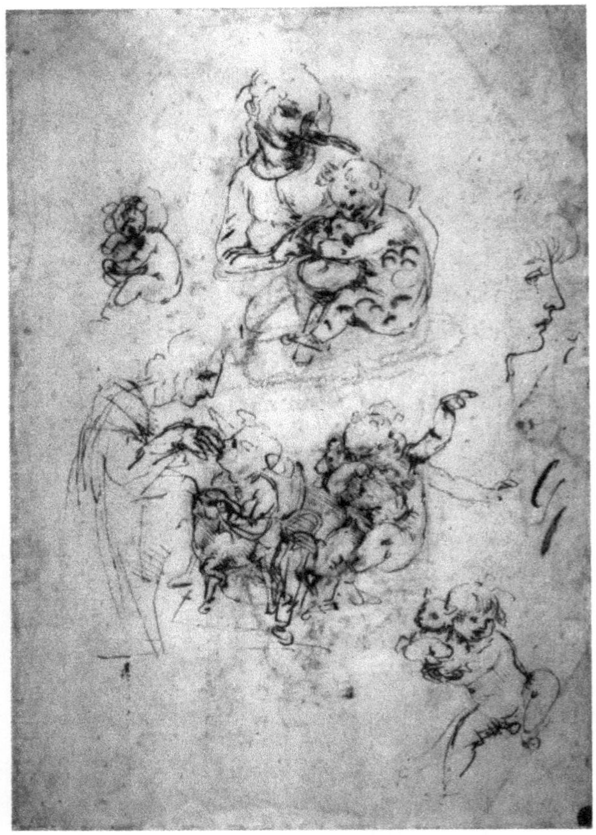

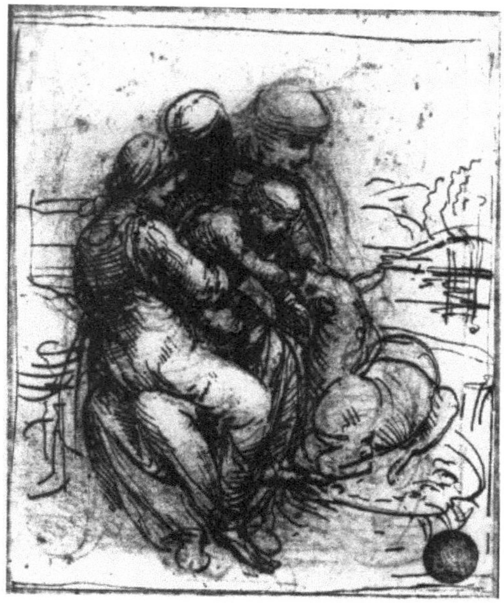

58. Leonardo da Vinci, *Madonna and Child with St. Anne and a Lamb.* Pen and brown ink over black chalk, 12.2 × 10 cm. Gallerie dell'Accademia, Venice

That movement, with its active psychological exchange, serves as the basic motif in Leonardo's graphic investigations of this most central theme in Renaissance painting. His playful introduction of a cat into the composition served as the occasion for such movement through a series of drawings (Figs. 55–57), and the role of the animal was to acquire greater import in the substitution by the symbolically more apposite lamb; the addition of the figure of Saint Anne, Mary's mother, completed the generational sequence (Fig. 58)[13] – these graphic meditations culminating eventually in the painting of the *Madonna and Child with St. Anne* (Fig. 59). With the introduction of additional figures, complicating the standard iconographic situation, Leonardo created new possibilities of figural interaction, new kinds of formal challenge and, therefore, of psychological consequence. Perhaps his most affectively resonant solution involved the introduction of the young Saint John the Baptist (Figs. 60, 61), an innovation that returns us to the folio at Windsor (Fig. 53).[14]

Leonardo initiated the drawing with the study of a kneeling Virgin holding the Child that fills the recto of the sheet. It is a remarkable image in many ways. Here, Leonardo actually seems to be inventing the motif of San Giovannino, the infant Baptist, so intimately approaching his holy cousin and his aunt. Earlier Florentine artists, like Fra Filippo Lippi, had already introduced the young Baptist, a patron saint of Florence, into scenes of the adoration of the Christ Child.[15] It was Leonardo, however, who brought Giovannino into such intimate rapport with the holy pair, who brought him into the family. This innovation will become an important part of Leonardo's legacy, especially to Raphael, who was to appropriate the motif and make it very much his own in a series of paintings from his Florentine years, when he directly encountered Leonardo. As a significant part of that legacy, Raphael evidently learned from Leonardo the great challenge of thematic variation, modulating an original invention with subtle art, and, of course, thereby inflecting the basic theological core with new human meaning.[16]

59. Leonardo da Vinci, *Madonna and Child with St. Anne and a Lamb.* Oil on panel, 168 × 130 cm. Musée du Louvre, Paris.

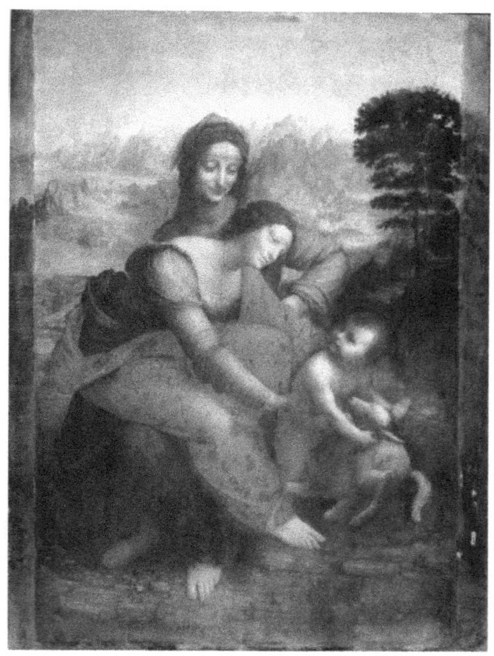

In its sequence of thought, its probing of possible formal variations, Leonardo's graphic invention of the motif betrays a fascinating awareness of the psychological consequences of such variation. In the initial idea, of the Virgin

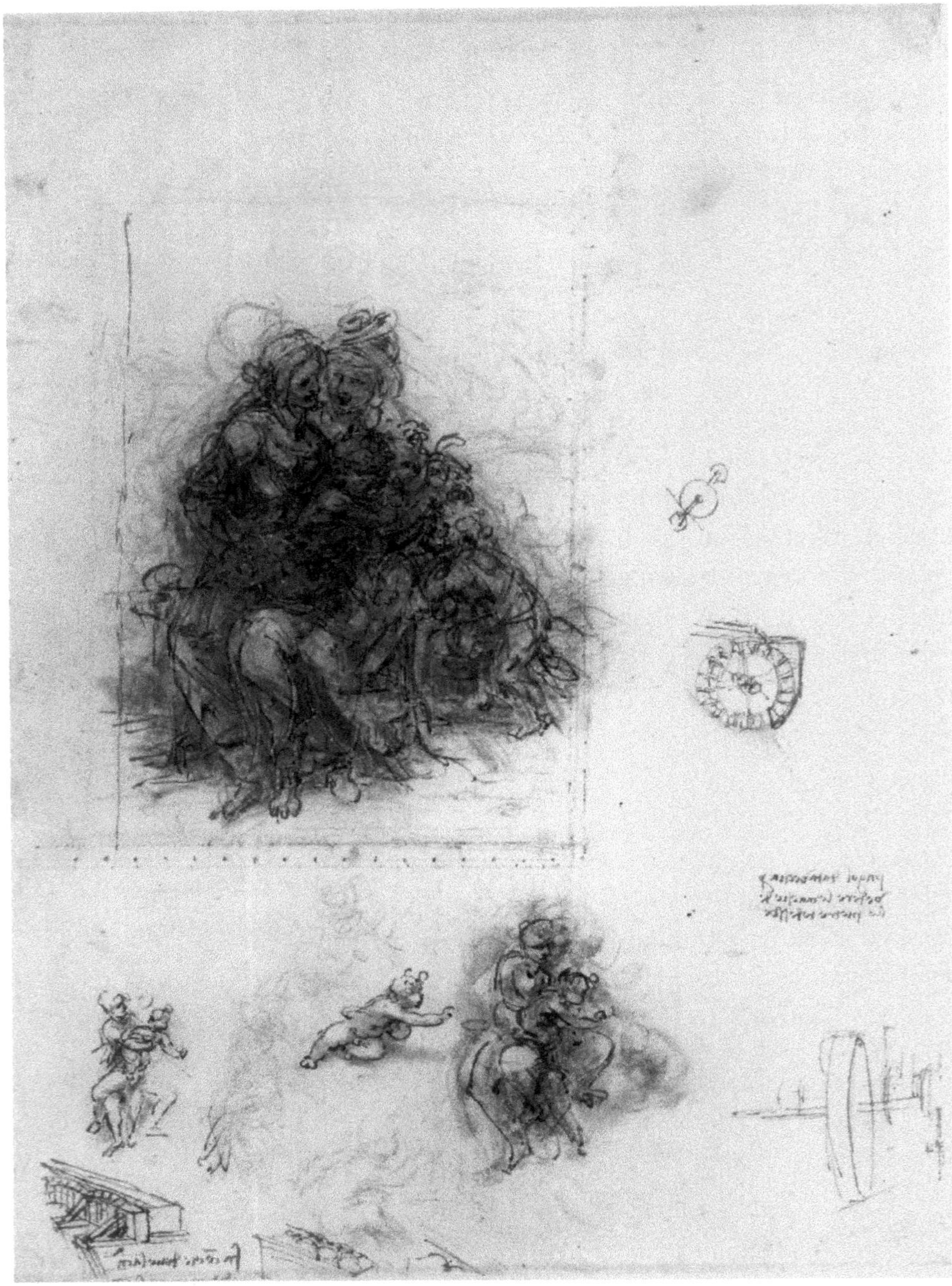

60. Leonardo da Vinci, *Studies for a Madonna and Child with St. Anne and the Infant St. John the Baptist.* Pen and brown ink, brush and wash over black chalk, 26.7 × 20.1 cm. British Museum, London (1875-6-12-17).

nursing the Child, the two were alone; the mother's head, inclining to the left, was directed toward the Child, whose profile returned her attentive gaze (Fig. 62). Then, in his most inventive stroke, Leonardo added the figure of young cousin John, an outsider entering the scene from the right. The introduction of the infant Baptist called for response, formal and dramatic, from the Virgin. Turning her head away from the nursing Child, she now acknowledges the presence of the importunate

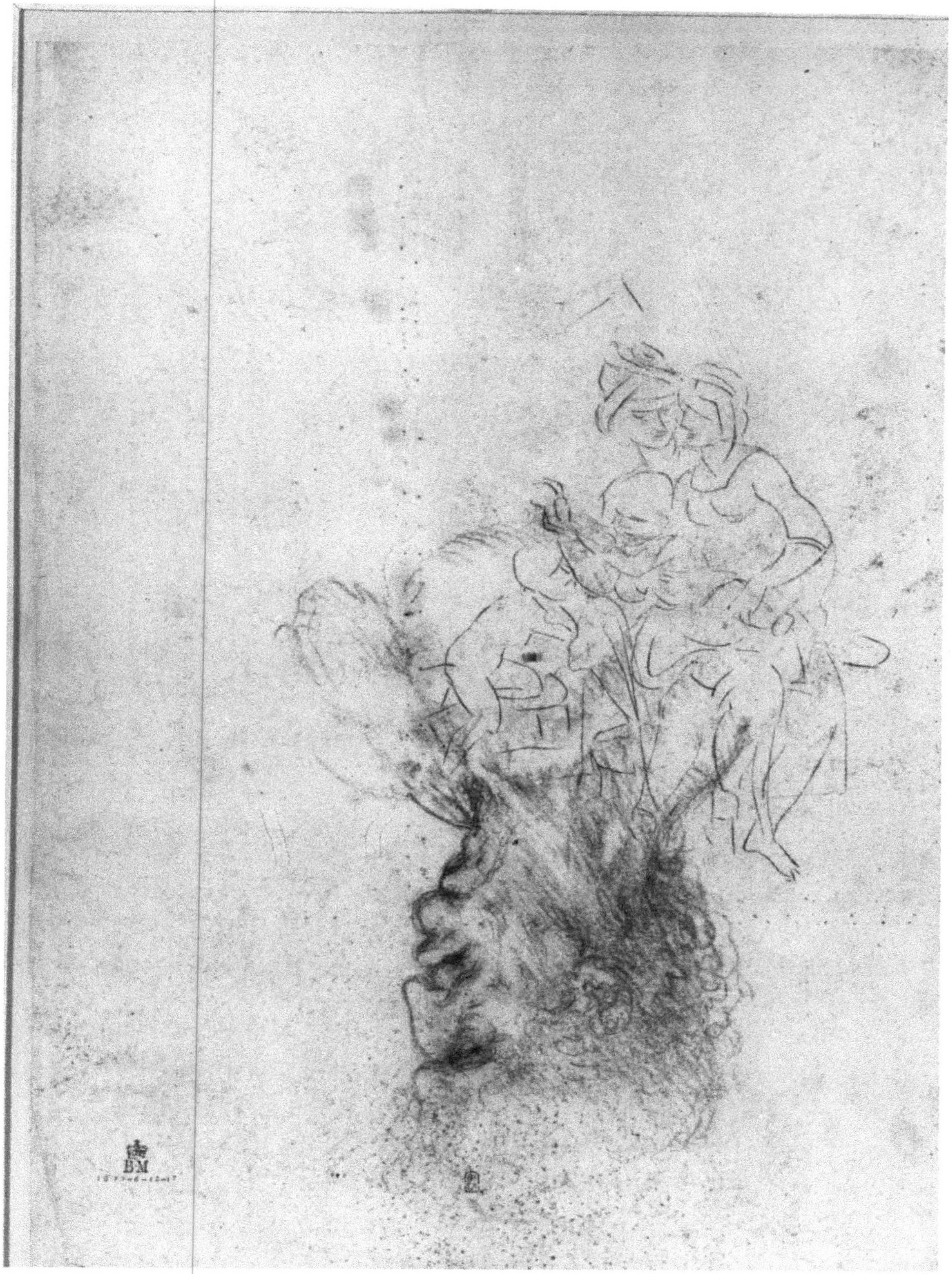

61. Leonardo da Vinci, *Male Head in Profile and Tracing of a Madonna and Child with St. Anne and the Infant St. John the Baptist.* Black chalk and stylus tracing. Verso of Fig. 60.

interloper. Actually, we can trace an intermediate position within the linear complexity of her head: lightly penned in schematic fashion is a more frontal view. Upon this palimpsest of alternative heads, then, Leonardo imposed a final resolution through the insistent hatching and strengthening contours of the third. This kind of shifting activity was to be explored more deliberately from the living model, as in a sheet of metalpoint studies of the head of a woman in which both model and view-

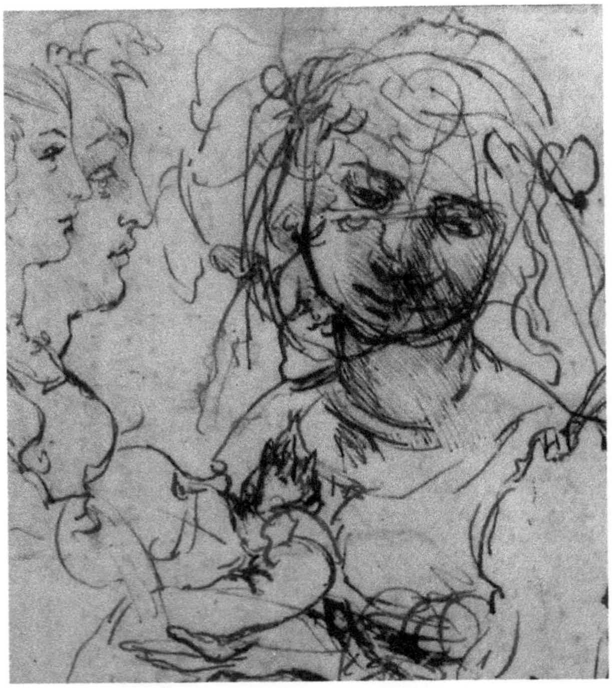

62. Leonardo da Vinci, *Madonna and Child with the Infant St. John the Baptist,* detail of Fig. 53.

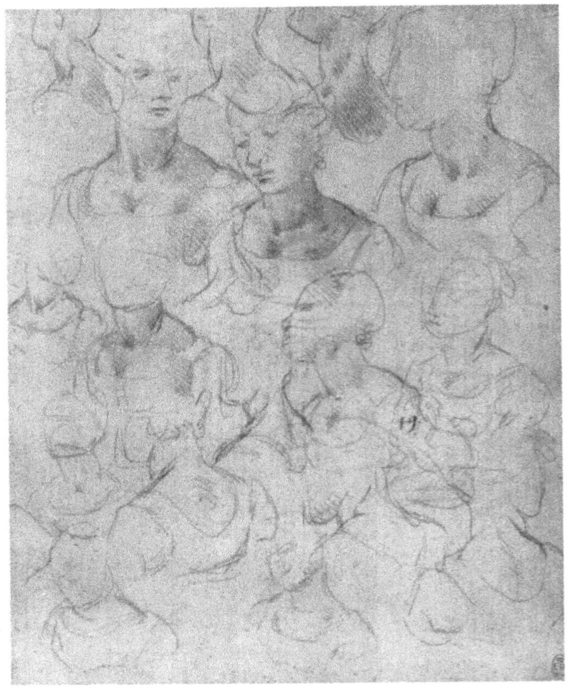

63. Leonardo da Vinci, *Studies of a Woman's Head and Bust.* Metalpoint on pink prepared paper, 23.2 × 19 cm. Royal Library, Windsor Castle (no. 12513). The Royal Collection ©2000, Her Majesty Queen Elizabeth II.

ing eye seem to be in motion (Fig. 63), but it was conceived – or, better, first discovered – in the fluid plasticity of the sketch, in the projected imaginings of the pen.

To articulate the landscape space of this holy encounter, in the area above Saint John Leonardo indicated with a few strokes the kind of jagged formations that were also to be developed in more meticulous drawings (Fig. 64) and were, eventually, to find painted realization some five years later in the *Virgin of the Rocks* (Fig. 65) – where, not incidentally, Saint John may be said to have displaced Jesus in intimate proximity to the mother figure.[17] Higher still in the Windsor drawing, above those rocky peaks, in the upper right corner, Leonardo repeated the figure of Saint John and then, apparently, added a more aggressively striding older (adolescent?) male nude who seems calculated to counter the momentum of the adoring (and presumptuous?) Baptist (Fig. 66).

Even without Freud's analysis of Leonardo's complex family situation and its supposed consequences, and the subsequent psychoanalytic literature on the problem, we can hardly fail to recognize the charged implications of the artist's iconographic inventiveness: in the divided attention of the mother, itself confirming, even while inviting, the rivalry of the children, one privileged at the breast, the other seeking access – his temerity overtly rebuked in the encounter of the upper right. If drawing does indeed reveal the artist most directly, as we generally assume, what then does Leonardo reveal of himself in this family drama of sibling competition? The reconciliation of the two children may indeed be iconographically, theologically inevitable, and Leonardo effects it with, literally, touching conviction in the London cartoon

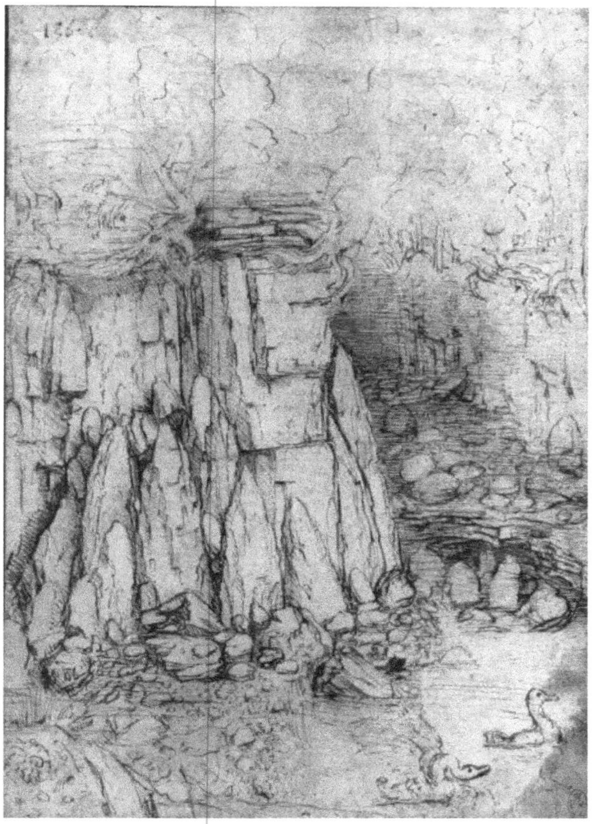

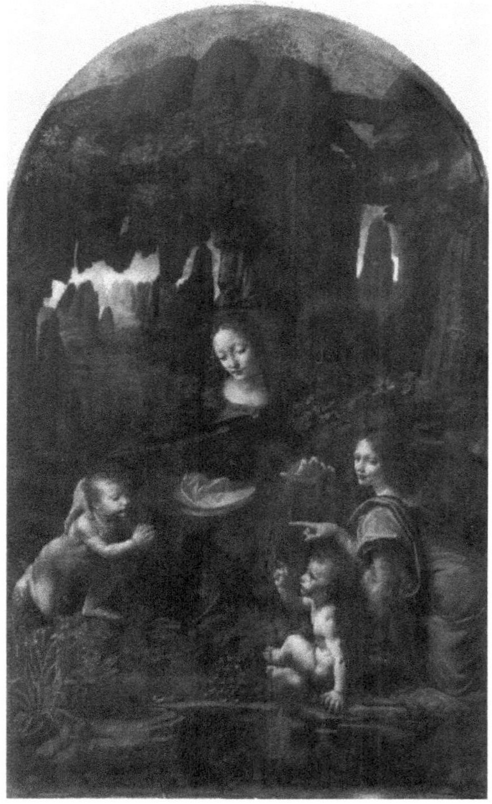

64. *(above left)* Leonardo da Vinci, *Rocky Landscape with a Stream*. Pen and brown ink, 22 × 15.8 cm. Royal Library, Windsor Castle (no. 12395). The Royal Collection ©2000, Her Majesty Queen Elizabeth II.

65. *(above right)* Leonardo da Vinci, *The Virgin of the Rocks*. Oil on panel, 199 × 122 cm. Musée du Louvre, Paris.

66. *(below)* Leonardo da Vinci, *Madonna and Child with the Infant St. John the Baptist*, detail of Fig. 53.

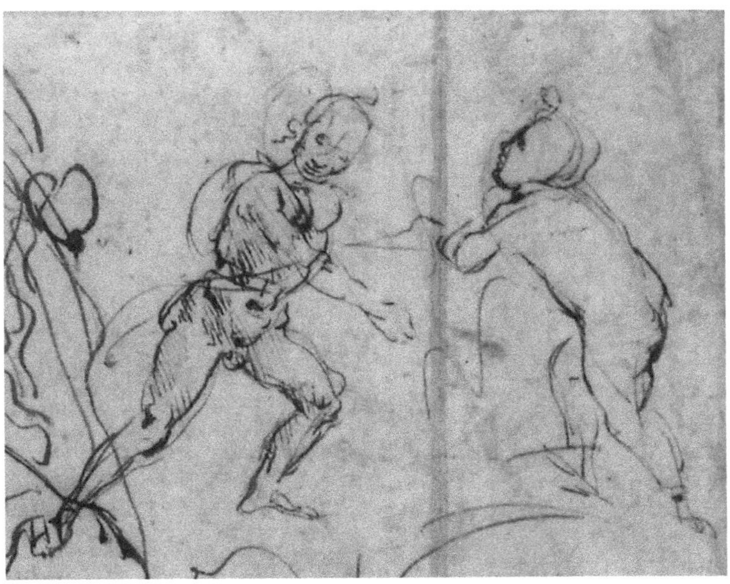

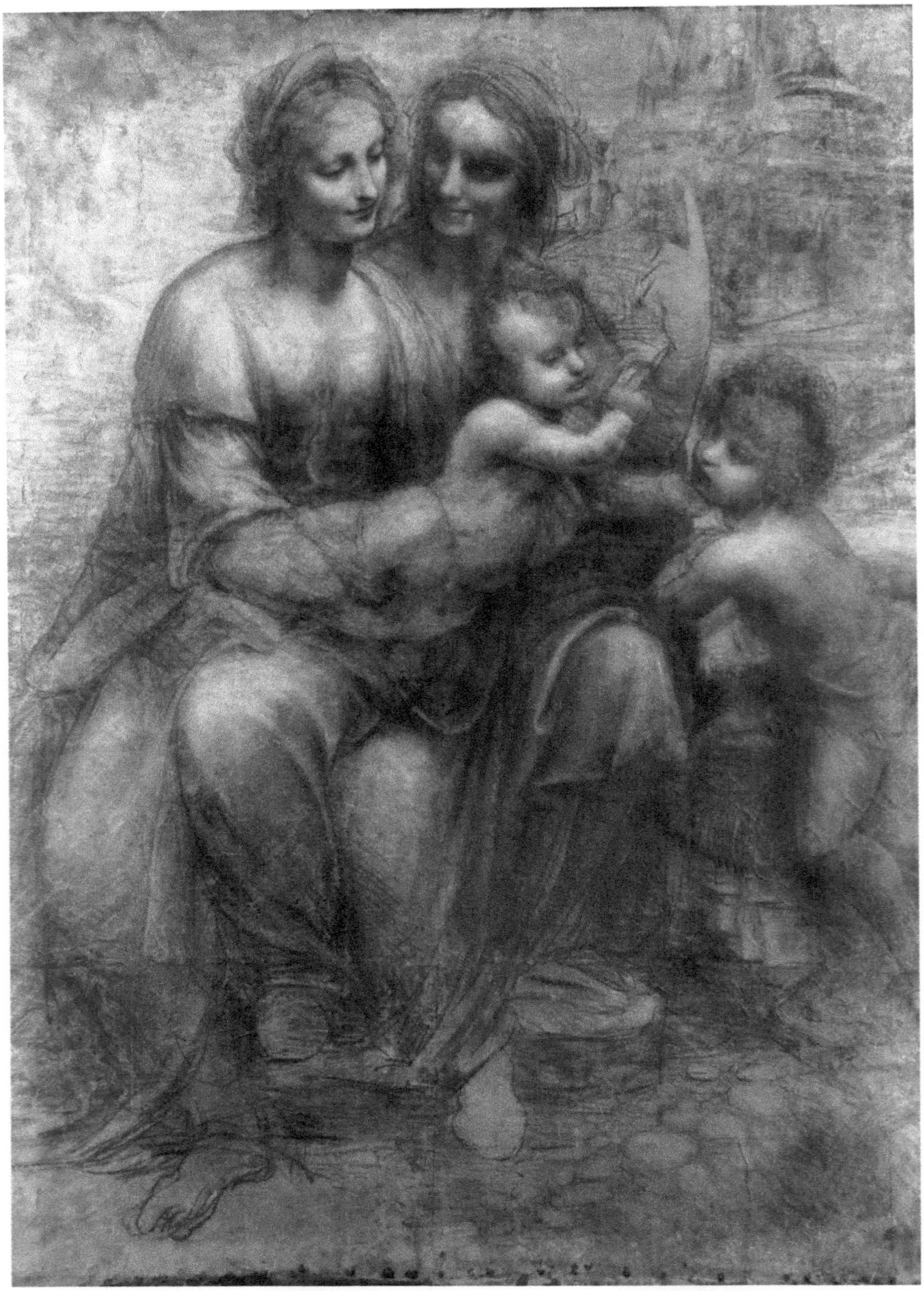

67. Leonardo da Vinci, *Madonna and Child with St. Anne and the Infant St. John the Baptist*. Charcoal on brown paper, heightened with white, 139 × 101 cm. National Gallery, London.

nearly thirty years later (Fig. 67). Still, the artist seems always to display a particular sensitivity to cousin John's marginal family status. We can hardly avoid acknowledging the psychic dimension of the artist's imagining – and, as I am suggesting, the psychological resonance of the drawing itself.

There is yet another remarkable aspect to this rendering of the nursing Madonna, who kneels and thereby offers an extended thigh as support for the Child: Leonardo has drawn her lower limbs nude. Now, we know from a series of impressive drawings, really paintings, on linen that Leonardo cast draperies over small armatures to study the patterns of the folds (Fig. 68). And we might recall that a generation earlier Leon Battista Alberti had recommended that in dressing a figure one should first draw it nude and then enfold it in garments, but Alberti refers quite explicitly to a male figure.[18] Yet not even Leonardo's drapery preparations, generally for a seated female figure, sanction the indecorous rendering of the spread legs of the Virgin. Leonardo himself seems to have been unable to ignore his own indiscretion, for in the space of that opening he drew the profile of an infant's head, issuing in graphic rapport with the contour of the mother's curving thigh (Fig. 69). The parallel head of an old man, although apparently drawn before the child, seems, in the highly unusual softness of its profile, actually to have been inspired by an infant's lines.

I know of no other drawing of the Virgin Mary by Leonardo that is so anatomically explicit – although his later scientific studies will lead him to investigate with pioneering and obsessive thoroughness the female anatomy in its procreative functions.[19] The formal concept of a kneeling female nude may be related – although at some remove – to the crouching Venus of ancient art, but Leonardo then would have transferred her generational powers to Mary. It was just that generational aspect of the motif that charged it and kept it alive in Leonardo's art. Some twenty-five years later it reemerges, retaining the essence of its original context, in studies for *Leda and the Swan* (Figs. 70, 71).[20]

Unlike other Renaissance artists – Michelangelo, for example (see Fig. 177 on page 190) – Leonardo was uninterested in the actual copulation of immortal bird and mortal woman. Rather, his fascination was with the issue of Jupiter's avian passion: Leda, with her swan, displaying the double twin progeny. Although he eventually painted her standing

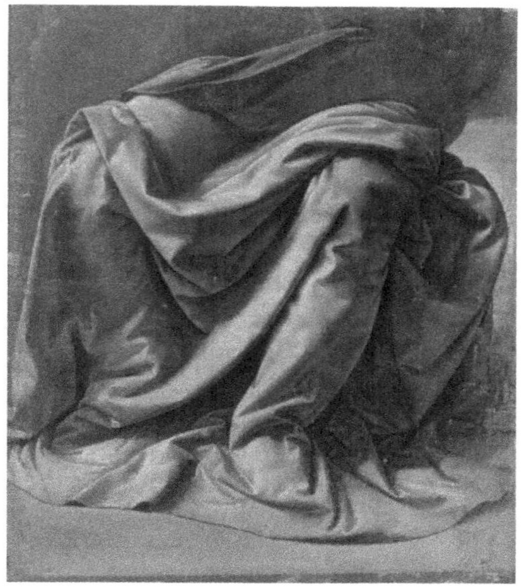

68. Leonardo da Vinci, *Study of Drapery for the Legs of a Seated Figure.* Brush and brown paint on linen, heightened with white, 26.6 × 23.4 cm. Musée du Louvre, Paris. Département des Arts Graphiques (inv. 2255).

69. Leonardo da Vinci, *Madonna and Child with the Infant St. John the Baptist,* detail of Fig. 53.

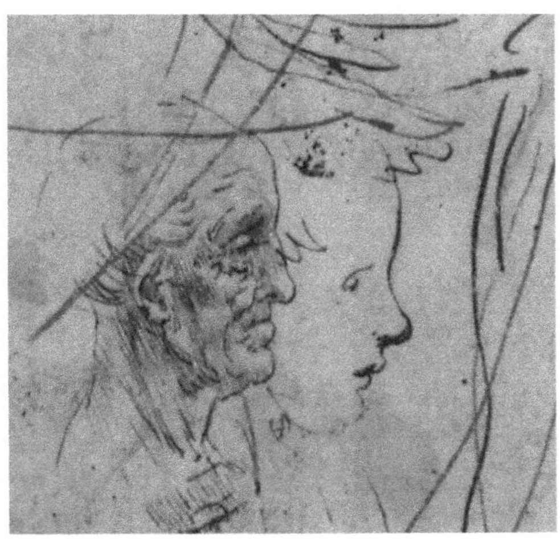

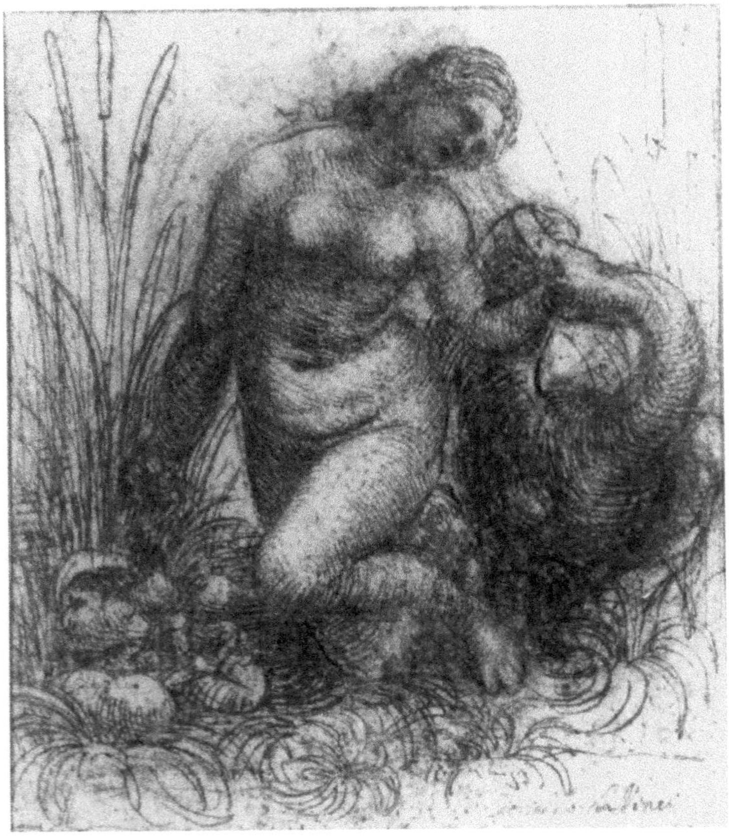

70. Leonardo da Vinci, *Leda and the Swan.* Pen and brown ink over black chalk, 12.5 × 11 cm. Museum Boijmans Van Beuningen, Rotterdam (inv. no. I-466).

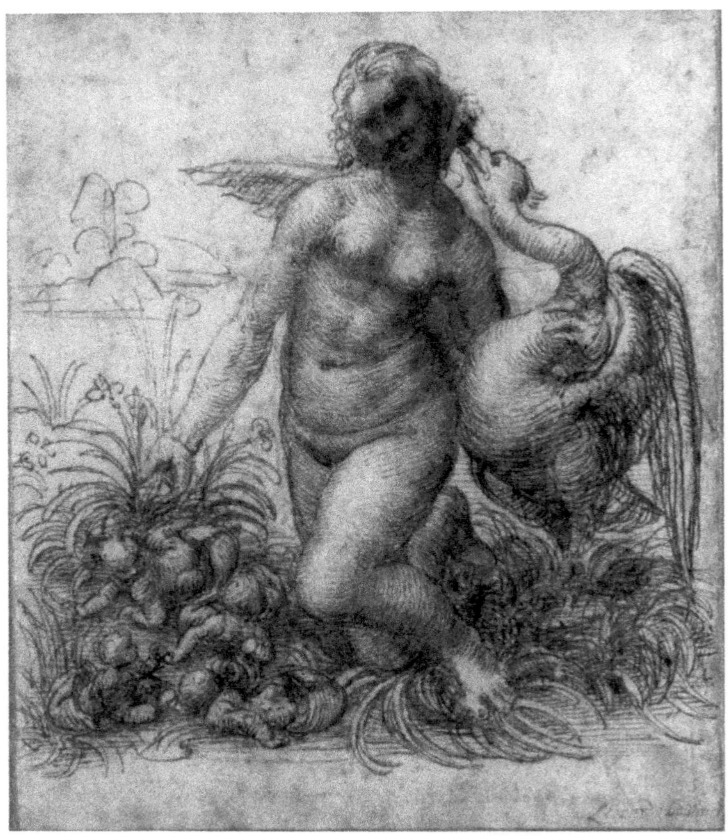

71. Leonardo da Vinci, *Leda and the Swan.* Pen and brown ink, brush and wash over black chalk, 16 × 13.9 cm. Devonshire Collection, Chatsworth (no. 717). Reproduced by permission of the Duke of Devonshire and the Chatsworth Settlement Trustees.

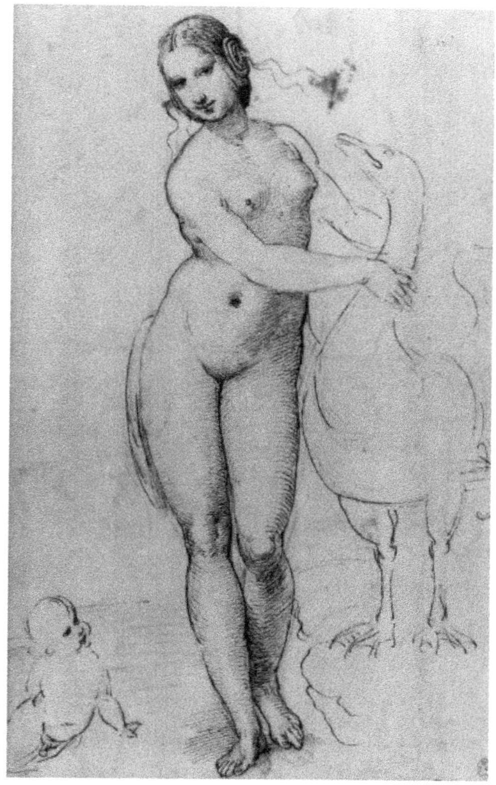

72. Raphael, *Leda and the Swan,* after Leonardo. Pen and brown ink over preliminary sketch with the stylus, 30.8 × 19.2 cm. Royal Library, Windsor Castle (no. 12759). The Royal Collection ©2000, Her Majesty Queen Elizabeth II.

– in a composition known to us only through variant copies (Fig. 72) – Leonardo's initial representations of the theme involved a kneeling Leda, simultaneously embracing the swan and displaying the hatching offspring, as in the drawings in Chatsworth and Rotterdam. But his first thoughts, in fact, did not include the great swan (Fig. 73). In these small sketches the kneeling serpentine Leda is more exclusively maternal, accompanied only by her children (Fig. 74–76). It is as though the Virgin of Windsor 12276 had turned, displacing the child on her thigh – precisely as she does in Leonardo's later development of the theme, in the London cartoon (Fig. 67) and the related sketch in the British Museum (Figs. 60, 61). Birthing Leda was prefigured in the nursing Virgin Mary.

3. *Marginalia*

Even beyond its central study, however, Windsor 12276 reveals itself as a proleptic repository of themes and motifs in Leonardo's art. That the artist's pen reached deep into his self to give graphic form to psychic preoccupations and fantasies is further confirmed by the sketches surrounding the main figural group on the folio (Fig. 53) and those on the verso (Fig. 54).

Leonardo's favorite and most typical doodle – although that must now seem hardly an adequate word for such an accomplished performance – took the form of

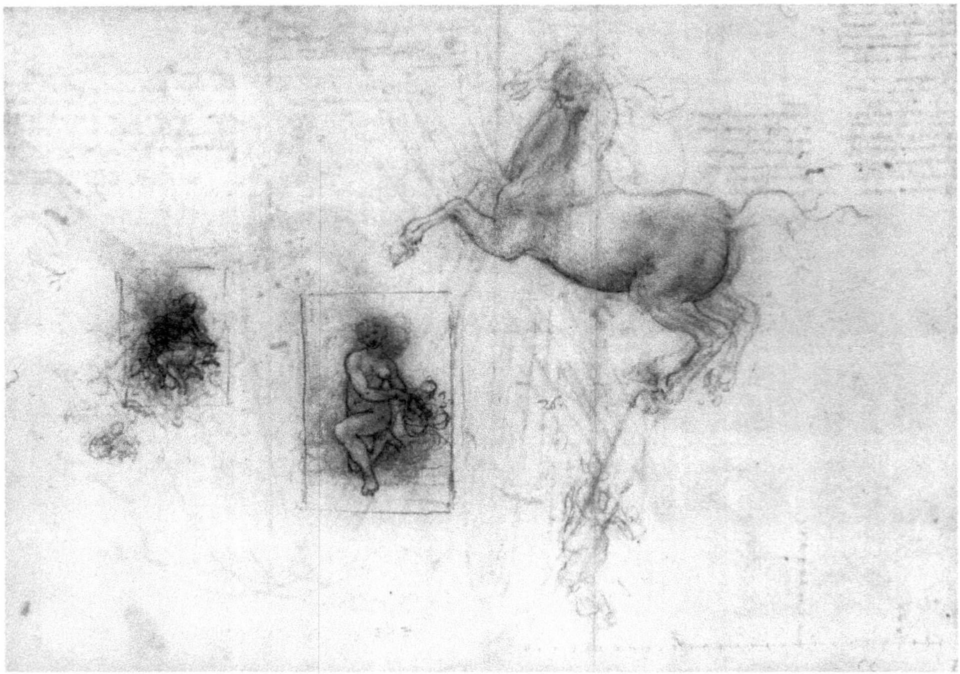

73. Leonardo da Vinci, *A Rearing Horse and Studies for the Kneeling Leda*. Black chalk partly drawn over with pen and brown ink, 29.3 × 41.3 cm. Royal Library, Windsor Castle (no. 12337). The Royal Collection ©2000, Her Majesty Queen Elizabeth II.

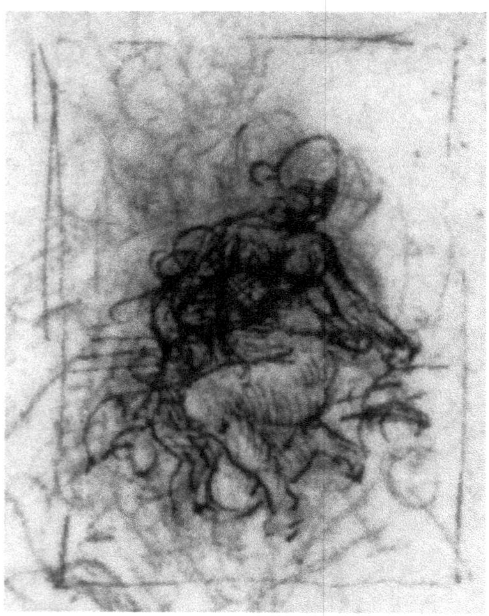

74. Leonardo da Vinci, *Study for the Kneeling Leda*, detail of Fig. 73.

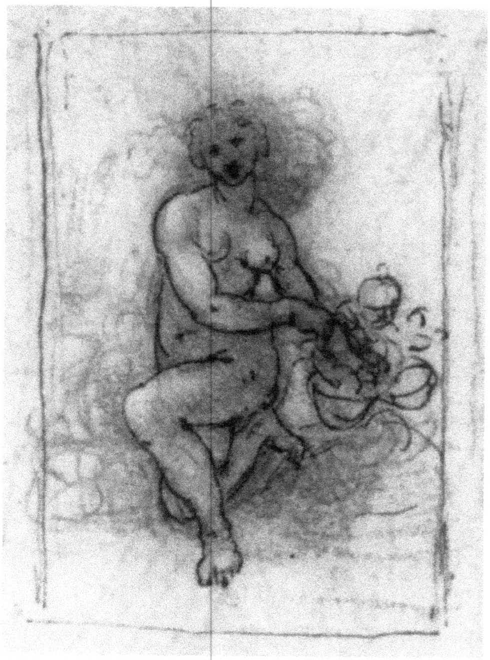

75. Leonardo da Vinci, *Study for the Kneeling Leda,* detail of Fig. 73.

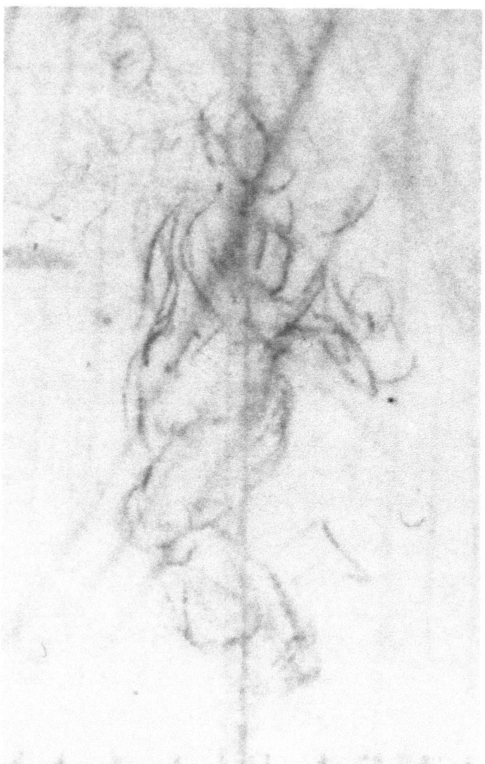

76. Leonardo da Vinci, *Study for the Kneeling Leda,* detail of Fig. 73.

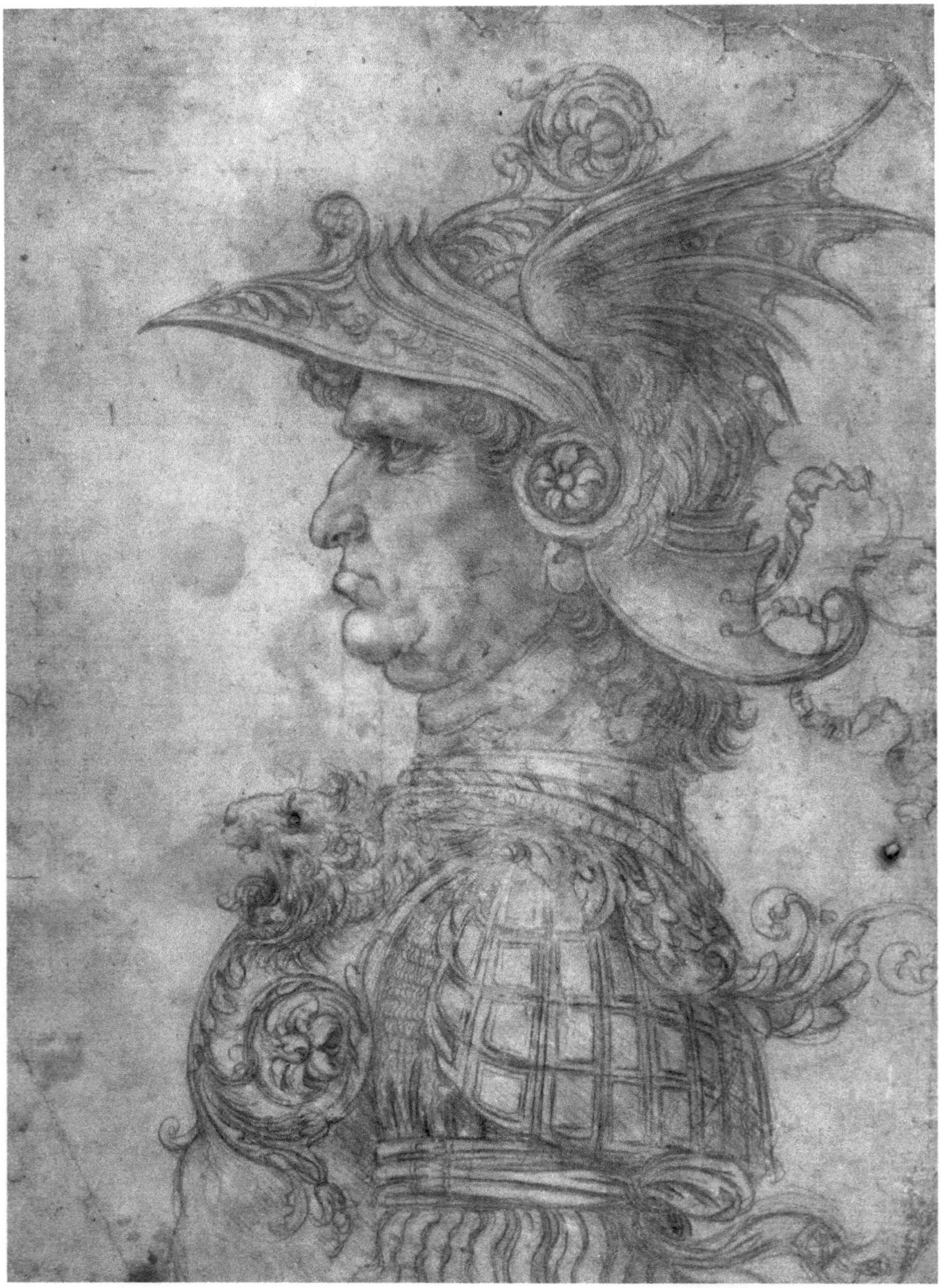

77. Leonardo da Vinci. *Head of a Warrior in Profile*. Metalpoint on cream-colored prepared paper, 28.5 × 20.7 cm. British Museum, London (1895-9-15-474).

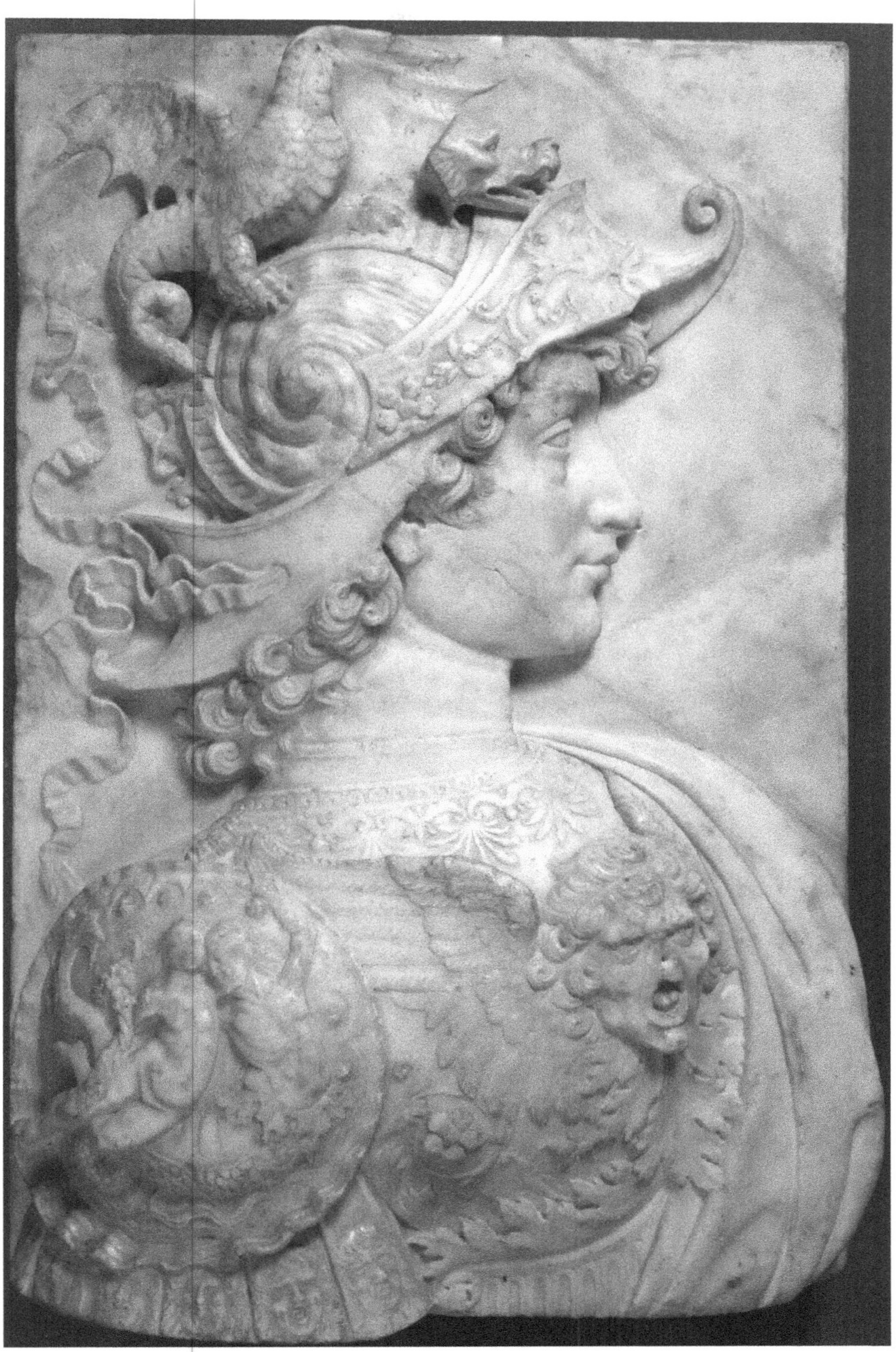

78. Andrea del Verrocchio(?). *Profile Head of Alexander the Great.* Marble relief, 55.9 × 36.7 cm. Washington, D.C., National Gallery of Art.

a face in profile. Two basic complementary types appear: an epicene youth and an older, frowning warrior (Fig. 77). Whatever their relationship to Quattrocento Florentine art in general and to Verrocchio in particular (Fig. 78),[21] both have been taken to represent projections of different aspects of Leonardo's own self, "the two hieroglyphs of Leonardo's unconscious mind," as Kenneth Clark phrased it, "the two images his hand created when his attention was wandering."[22] For all its classicizing purity, the youthful head – characterized by languidly lidded eyes, slightly distended nostrils, sensuously fleshed lips – has been assumed to reflect in some way the features of the young artist himself, who was so celebrated for his own physical beauty and grace, as well as strength.[23] The recurring presence of that young profile in the margins of Leonardo's drawings and the apparent ease with which its contour flowed from his pen require explanation and interpretation. To account for this phenomenon with reference to workshop training and practice, ascribing the motif to lessons learned in the studio of Verrocchio, seems inadequate.[24] Leonardo's fascination with faces will develop into an ambitious study of human physiognomy, but to ascribe such programmatic intention to these early profiles is to ignore the affect of their insistent repetition, the apparent automatism of their return. They seem such a natural product of Leonardo's drawing hand, the graphic expression of something more personal. It is Leonardo himself who encourages us to consider seriously the resemblance between the draftsman and his creatures.

Every painter paints himself: that commonplace of Renaissance culture was fully experienced by Leonardo himself, and he specifically counseled correctives to such automimesis. He thought it the most dangerous vice of the painter, frustrating his proper ambition to imitate nature in all its variety, not merely to replicate one particular example of creation. Speculating on the phenomenon, Leonardo found an explanation in terms of traditional faculty psychology:

> Having often considered the cause of this defect, it seems to me one must conclude that the soul which rules and directs each body is really that which forms our judgment before it is our own judgment. Thus it has developed the whole shape of a man, as it has deemed to be best with long, or short, or flat nose, and definitely assigned his height and shape. This judgment is so powerful that it moves the painter's arm and makes him copy himself, since it seems to that soul that this is the true way to construct a man. . . .[25]

The frequency with which he returned to the issue in his notes, repeating and refining the formulation, persuades us that his concern was based – like most of this knowledge – on his own direct experience, self-knowledge derived from the practice of his own art. It is "our judgment which guides the hand in the creation of the outlines of figures" (McM ¶ 437).[26] Our own bodies deceive us, distorting our judgment and leading it to believe that all nature reflects our particular physiognomy and proportions.[27] Despite his own counsel and impulse toward variety, however, Leonardo's profiled marginalia, with their remarkably limited range of variation, testify to the

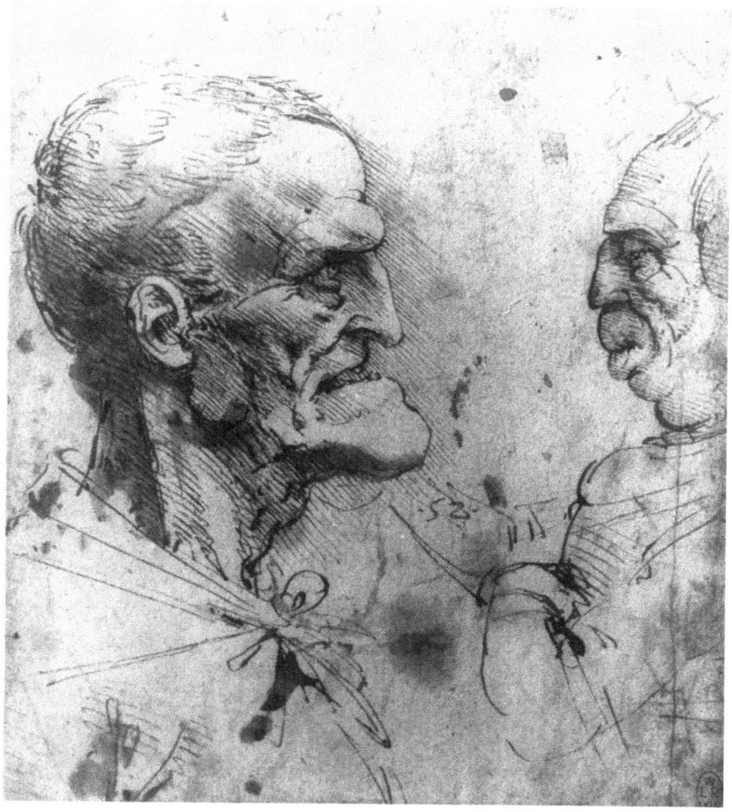

79. Leonardo da Vinci. *Two Grotesque Heads.* Pen and brown ink and some wash, 16.3 × 14.3 cm. Royal Library, Windsor Castle (no. 12490). The Royal Collection ©2000, Her Majesty Queen Elizabeth II.

powerful hold of such automatic self-representation. The repetition itself strongly suggests that what he penned in the margins of his drawings were, in some fundamental sense, reflections of his own particular beauty – the supposedly aimless pen returning quite naturally to the forms and image of its master.

What concerns us most immediately, however, is not the fact of such marginal repetition – nor its relation to a Florentine stylistic ambience or to the antique – but rather its mechanism, the guiding of the hand. The verso of Windsor 12276 is dedicated exclusively to profile heads, old and young, male and (unusually) female (Fig. 54). What had been marginal on the recto, and on the Uffizi fragment of 1478, here dominates the field as the central purpose of the page. Between the polar types of the fair adolescent and the leathery elder with his "nutcracker" profile (Kenneth Clark's happy characterization) Leonardo explored a full range of the ages of man; his rare female profiles in this context are generally restricted to ideally beautiful young women – not until the grotesques will he distort that beauty. On the two sides of the Windsor sheet that range does ineed extend from infancy to old age. Often, as in the Uffizi drawing (Fig. 49) and in his later grotesques (Fig. 79), he would set his profiles into a kind of confrontation or dialogue, juxtaposing young and old, beautiful and ugly, male and female.[28] In this he was anticipating the advice he was to offer in his treatise on painting: "in narrative paintings," he counseled, "one ought to mingle direct contraries so that they may afford a great contrast to one another, and all the more when they are in close proximity; that is, the ugly next to the beautiful, the big to the small, the old to the young, the strong to the weak, all should be varied as much as possible and close together" (McM ¶ 271). The dialectic was Leonardo's preferred mode.[29]

On the Windsor sheet he was already indulging his taste for contrasts, but the programmatic exploration of the profile head in this case seems less dramatically motivated; it seems rather a more deliberately graphic operation. There are, of course dramatic contrasts and oppositions – for example, in the confrontation of lion and dragon (Fig. 80) or in the immediate juxtaposition of infant and old man below the open legs of the Virgin (Fig. 69). But the two profiles dominating the upper right quarter of the verso establish a different procedure (Fig. 81), the basic one that returns us to the act of drawing itself. Here, and in the sequence of three profiles in the lower right corner of the recto (Fig. 82), Leonardo makes his theme the profile per se, that is, the contour. Even the abbreviated "In dei nomine" just below the neck of the second profile on the verso confirms the primacy of linear thinking, epitomizing by its very self-indulgence the mechanics as well as aesthetics of the operation.

All the heads face to the right, as we might expect of a left-handed draftsman: the natural way to draw a profile is from within, the hand moving inside the head, internally generating the curving contour outward, from the wrist. Starting with the classically idealized profile of a youth, Leonardo then moved to vary it (Fig. 81). He exaggerated slightly the curves of the nose and mouth, added weight to the chin, and thereby gave additional force and age to the head. The alignment of parallel profiles, variations on an initial theme, becomes in Leonardo's marginalia more than a doodle precisely because it is never quite an aimless exercise. However casually he might have set down the first statement, no matter how automatic the gesture may seem – or may actually have been – Leonardo's drawing of profiles assumes a systemic logic and purpose in the course of its development. Indeed, precisely the graphic logic of the operation, its studied variation on a linear motif, will make it a standard exercise in later drawing curricula (cf. Figs. 131–33 on pages 135–37).

We can follow this logic in the sequence of heads in the lower left corner of the recto (Fig. 83). At the margin he drew a typical profile head, not quite as refined of feature as some of its more elegant siblings, perhaps, but still a handsome youth. The particular falling curve of its front contour, from the high forehead through the slight inflections of brow and bridge to the tip of the nose, establishes a specific linear motif. That motif is then picked up, not in any of the other neighboring human profiles, but rather in the two successive heads of a snarling lion. The sequence of curves that determined the initial profile has been modified in rhythm but nonetheless maintained in essential structure; the angle of their progress has

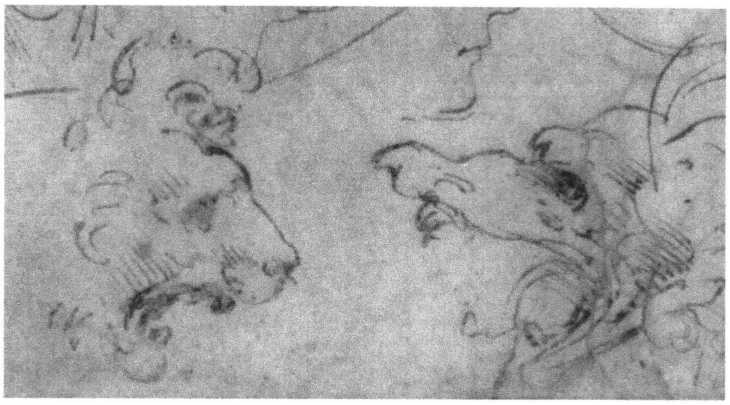

80. Leonardo da Vinci, *Madonna and Child with the Infant St. John the Baptist,* detail of Fig. 53.

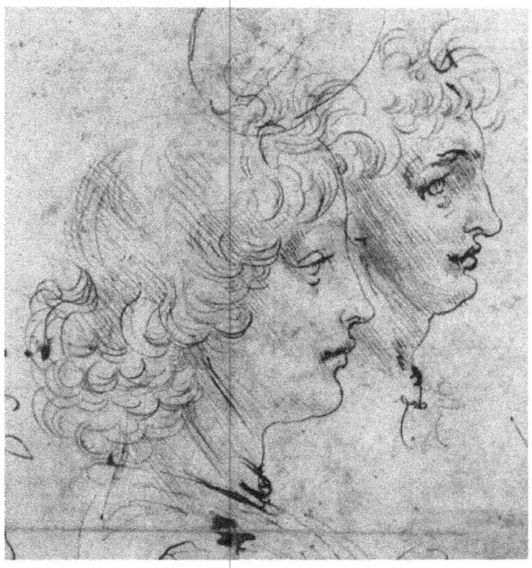

81. Leonardo da Vinci, *Studies of Heads in Profile,* detail of Fig. 54.

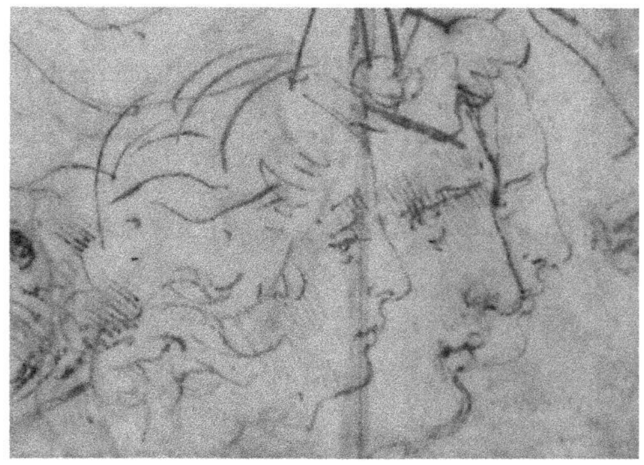

82. Leonardo da Vinci, *Madonna and Child with the Infant St. John the Baptist,* detail of Fig. 53.

83. Leonardo da Vinci, *Madonna and Child with the Infant St. John the Baptist,* detail of Fig. 53.

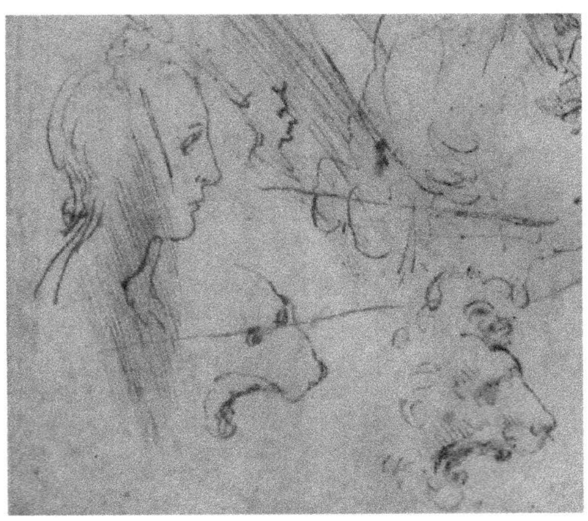

been flattened to accommodate the new feline representation. This is just the kind of analogy that will eventually guide Leonardo's researches in comparative anatomy and physiology.[30] Here, however, the comparison is inaugurated not yet out of scientific curiosity but by a certain graphic momentum. It is the act of drawing that provides the essential continuity from one form to another in this instance, from human to leonine.[31] On a somewhat different level, the answering dragon, countering the leonine challenge, attests to Leonardo's active commitment to the dialectic of contrast we have already observed. But the assertively dynamic calligraphy of this beast's profile, indulging in its own vitality, suggests that, again, the creative momentum resides in the drawing impulse; the information being varied is carried by the line itself.

Eventually, Leonardo codified the results of his researches in his treatise on painting (Fig. 84). In his notes he distances himself from his own operations, enough to permit objective commentary on subjective experience, and to formulate some ruling order of principle behind it; he seeks to understand his own experience through a kind of self-analysis. Offering advice on the drawing of profiles, he focuses on the four different physiognomic features: nose, mouth, chin, and forehead. Matching the variety of forms known to his pen, he formulates an elaborate taxonomy of nasal types and subtypes. Three basic categories are distinguished: straight, concave, and convex, and these in turn are further divided into three or four variations. Leonardo's aim was less to categorize nature in all its variety than it was to aid in *drawing* those features, and in particular in drawing them from memory. His categories are intended to serve as graphic *aides mémoires* to the draftsman: each type represented not only a particular nasal structure but also a particular movement of the drawing hand.

4. *Remembered Lines*

The titles of these paragraphs typically read: "Method for remembering the shape of a face" (McM ¶ 415) or "Of making a man's portrait in profile after having seen him only once" (McM ¶ 416). Throughout these passages Leonardo is concerned with remembering the features of faces, with drawing them from memory. Indeed, it becomes quite clear that for him drawing was, in effect, memory. "The painter ought to study methodically and not leave anything without fixing it in memory . . ." (McM ¶ 66).

The mnemonic property of the profile had been recognized in the practices of portraiture since antiquity, enacted in the tracing of the shadow of the departing lover. Between record and recollection lies a temporal dimension that comes to epitomize a special power of images. Alberti celebrated that "divine force" of painting, "which not only makes absent men present, as is said of friendship, but moreover makes the dead seem almost alive. . . . Certainly, the face of one long dead lives a long life through

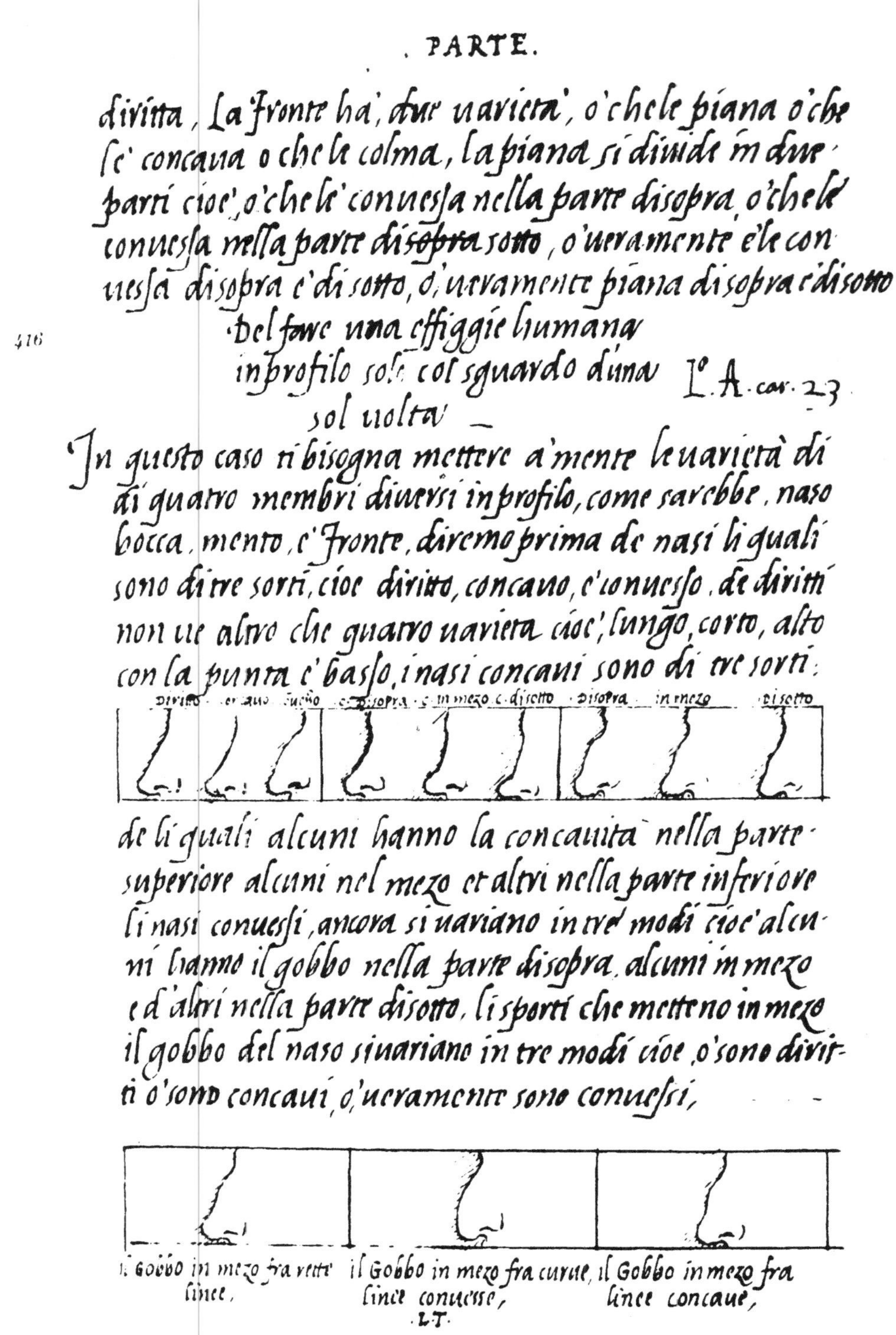
. PARTE.

diritta, La fronte ha due varietà, o che le piana o che
le concava o che le colma, la piana si divide in due
parti cioè, o che le convessa nella parte disopra, o che le
convessa nella parte disopra sotto, o veramente è le con
vessa disopra e di sotto, o veramente piana disopra e disotto

416 Del fare una effigie humana
in profilo sol col sguardo d'una L.A. car. 23
sol volta

In questo caso ti bisogna mettere a mente le varietà di
di quattro membri diversi in profilo, come sarebbe, naso
bocca, mento, e fronte, diremo prima de nasi li quali
sono di tre sorti, cioè diritto, concavo, e convesso. de diritti
non v'è altro che quattro varietà cioè, lungo, corto, alto
con la punta e basso, i nasi concavi sono di tre sorti;

de li quali alcuni hanno la concavità nella parte
superiore alcuni nel mezo et altri nella parte inferiore
li nasi convessi, ancora si variano in tre modi cioè alcu
ni hanno il gobbo nella parte disopra, alcuni in mezo
e d'altri nella parte disotto. li sporti che metteno in mezo
il gobbo del naso si variano in tre modi cioè, o sono dirit
ti o sono concavi, o veramente sono convessi,

il Gobbo in mezo fra rette linee, il Gobbo in mezo fra curve linee convesse, il Gobbo in mezo fra linee concave,

L.T.

84. *Libro di Pittura di M. Lionardo da Vinci, pittore et scultore fiorentino.* Biblioteca Vaticana (Codex Urbinas Latinus 1270, carta 108v).

painting."[32] And the effigy that most characteristically preserved the essential features of the absent, the form that most insistently impressed itself upon the memory, was the profile. Defined absolutely by its outline, by which it first fixed fugitive shadow, securing physiognomic clarity, the profile readily fixes itself in memory.

The acquisition of a physiognomic repertoire was, of course, essential to the painter of *istorie;* developed essentially through the practice of drawing, it provided raw natural material to be refined by the imagination. As Vasari was to phrase it, through drawing one fills the mind with beautiful ideas and learns to imagine ("fare a mente") all the things of nature, without having to have them physically before one's eyes.[33] Central in every way to the pictorial imagination, drawing functioned as the synthesizing agent in the dialectic complexities between hand and mind, hand and eye, eye and mind. Long before Vasari, we recall, Cennino Cennini had recognized the dynamics of the imagining activity of the painter, who must combine imagination and skill of hand in order to discover things never before seen and, most important, to be able to fix them with the hand ("fermarle con la mano"). The fluidity of pen and ink especially facilitates the artist's imagination, enriching the storehouse of the mind ("capace di molto disegno entro la testa tua").[34]

For the Renaissance artist, drawing became an act at once mimetic and mnemonic, a means of knowing the world and of preserving that knowledge. The practice of drawing entailed committing the forms of nature, external forms, to memory, internalizing them in the mind. From such an inventory of remembered forms, the artist could then create newly imagined worlds – epitomized, for example, by Leonardo's eclectic dragon, itself a model of the Horatian grotesque (Fig. 85).[35] "No man shall ever be able to make a beautiful figure out of his own thoughts unless he hath well stored his mind by study," as Dürer was to affirm. A "well-practised artist," he continues, "hath no need to copy each particular figure from the life. For it sufficeth him to pour forth that which he hath for a long time gathered into him from without."[36] The beauties of the world, God's own creation, must be internalized to establish that source of potential images; such inventions are re-creations of figures stored in the mind, remembered beauty. Leonardo himself, constantly contemplating his own practice, his own experience, makes memory a leitmotif of his treatise. And the essential mnemonic means is drawing, contour in particular. At night or during dark winter evenings the painter is to commit to memory those natural forms he has studied during the day or during the summer: "when you are in bed in the dark, to exercise the imagination," he recommends "recalling the outlines of forms you have already studied . . . fixing these things in the memory" (McM ¶ 65). Leonardo was struck by the evident clarity of forms imagined in the dark: "Why," he wondered, "does the eye see a thing more clearly in dreams than with the imagination being awake?"[37]

Beyond his scientific interest in physiognomic expression – and, I would add, prior to it – Leonardo's own practice as a draftsman exploited the profile as linear exercise.[38] His earliest drawings establish the sequence of profiles as a mode of lin-

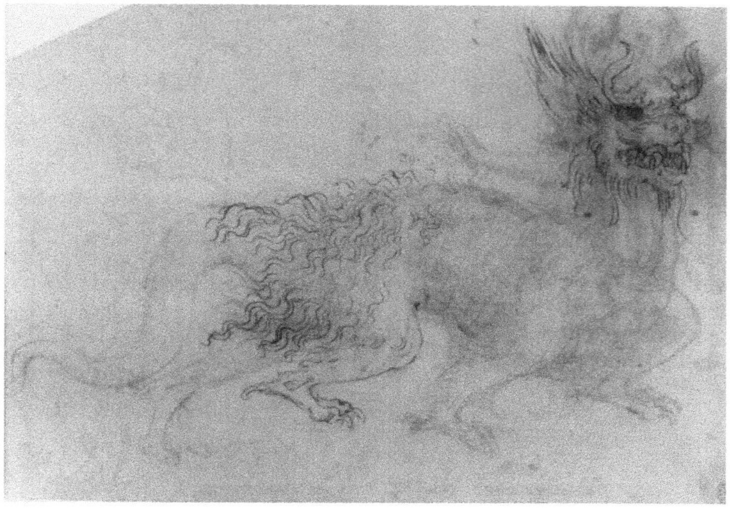

85. Leonardo da Vinci, *A Dragon.* Black chalk and pen and brown ink, 18.8 × 27.0 cm. Royal Library, Windsor Castle (no. 12369). The Royal Collection ©2000, Her Majesty Queen Elizabeth II.

ear variation; for Leonardo, the motif itself informs the line with physiognomic affect. Drawing the profile becomes a test of graphic memory.

It is true, of course, that Leonardo systematized his growing knowledge of natural forms, that his studies were spurred by his own dialectical habits of inquiry. These led to bold analogic formulations, most grandly of the macro-/microcosmic reflection, and to searching for parallels among the species of the animal world – especially human, equine, and leonine (Fig. 86).[39] Leonardo's interest in comparative anatomy achieved a dramatic and culminating focus in his studies for the *Battle of Anghiari,* in which his ambivalent fascination with the savagery of war (this "pazzia bestialissima," as he called it [McM ¶ 266]) found such effective expression through bestial analogy (Fig. 87) (it seems perfectly appropriate to illustrate the central motif of Leonardo's lost composition with the famous copy by Rubens, who, more than any other student of Leonardo, understood the expressive dynamics and motives of the Florentine master). Man and horse, the protagonists of Leonardo's great battle picture, both partake of that leonine fury that serves to set the physiognomic model for such rage.[40] Needless to say, these visual parallels were explored and confirmed experimentally in Leonardo's extensive notebooks.[41] But we have already encountered this analogy in his drawings some twenty-five years earlier, in the Windsor sheet that has been the center of our attention: even the shrieking warriors of the *Battle of Anghiari* find their earliest formulation there, as Leonardo, following leonine instinct, realizes the bellicose potential latent in his grimmer profiles (Fig. 88).

And our experience of the earlier man–lion transmutation (Fig. 83) alerts us to the fundamentally graphic nature of Leonardo's thought. His investigation of the physiognomic mechanics that functionally united the aggressive rage of man and beast grew out of knowledge first discovered in and through the exploring pen. That earlier

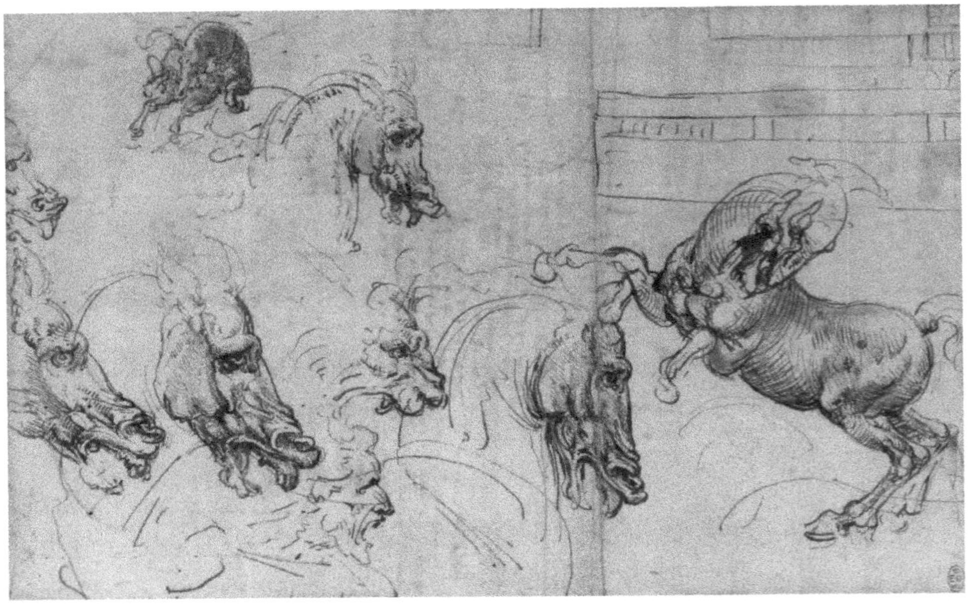

86. Leonardo da Vinci, *Horses and Other Studies for the Battle of Anghiari.* Pen and brown ink and wash, with traces of black and red chalk, 19.6 × 30.8 cm. Royal Library, Windsor Castle (no. 12326). The Royal Collection ©2000, Her Majesty Queen Elizabeth II.

87. Peter Paul Rubens, *Battle of Anghiari,* after Leonardo. Pen and brown ink and wash over black chalk, heightened with gray and white body-color, 45.2 × 63.7 cm. Musée du Louvre, Paris. Département des Arts Graphiques (inv. 20271).

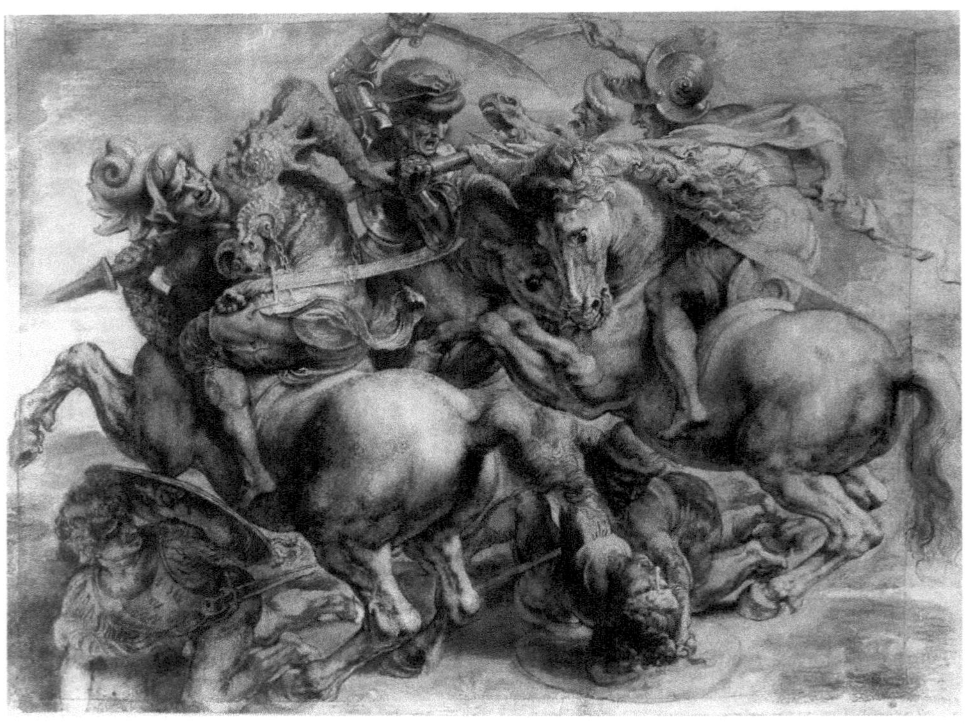

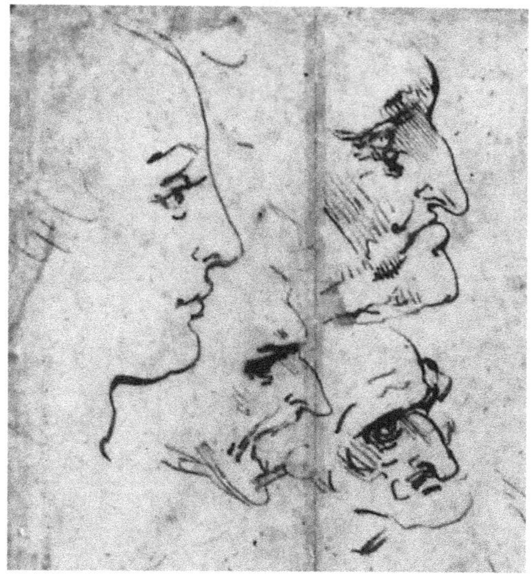

88. Leonardo da Vinci, *Studies of Heads in Profile*, detail of Fig. 54.

discovery – a resultant variation on a contour line, part of the apparently purposeless but nonetheless pointedly imaginative wandering of hand and mind together – was invoked to new purpose decades later. Commenting on just this kind of operation, Leonardo wrote in his treatise of "those reflections and considerations that, continually appearing before the eyes, give material to the memory to be stored" (McM ¶ 74). That storehouse of images, he recognized, was the creation of an imagination fed on the constant observation of nature. And the key to its function, he argued, was in drawing. "How to memorize well" is another typical rubric in his treatise: "When you wish to remember something you have studied," he advised, "do this: when you have drawn the same object so many times that you have it in your memory, try to execute it without the model" (McM ¶ 66). Through drawing the artist discovered forms, and through drawing he committed them to memory. The act of drawing served to create and record, and it was also operationally essential for the retrieval of those images stored. And in particular, it is in and through the contour line that he commits them to memory.

Those profiles that populate Leonardo's drawings throughout his career may be seen as doodles, unmeditated products of the aimless pen. Or, we might prefer to see them as the archetypical images drawn from Leonardo's graphic memory. For a painter who so prized his art's ability to emulate and even to surpass nature in the variety of its creations, Leonardo's own creations – as we have been observing – display remarkable continuities and repetition of forms. The rearing horse turning back upon itself, for example, seems an invention central to the very conception of the *Battle of Anghiari*, uniquely proper to it, until we recall its appearance much earlier in Leonardo's oeuvre, in the background of the panel of the *Adoration of the Magi* that remained unfinished when he left Florence for Milan in 1481 (Figs. 89, 90). Clearly, it was a form that came naturally to Leonardo's mind – and hand (Fig. 91).[42] Long before the Florentine mural project, Leonardo was extending the serpentine dynamics of this rearing horse into battle, in the background of the abandoned painting and, before that, in a series of studies of combat with a

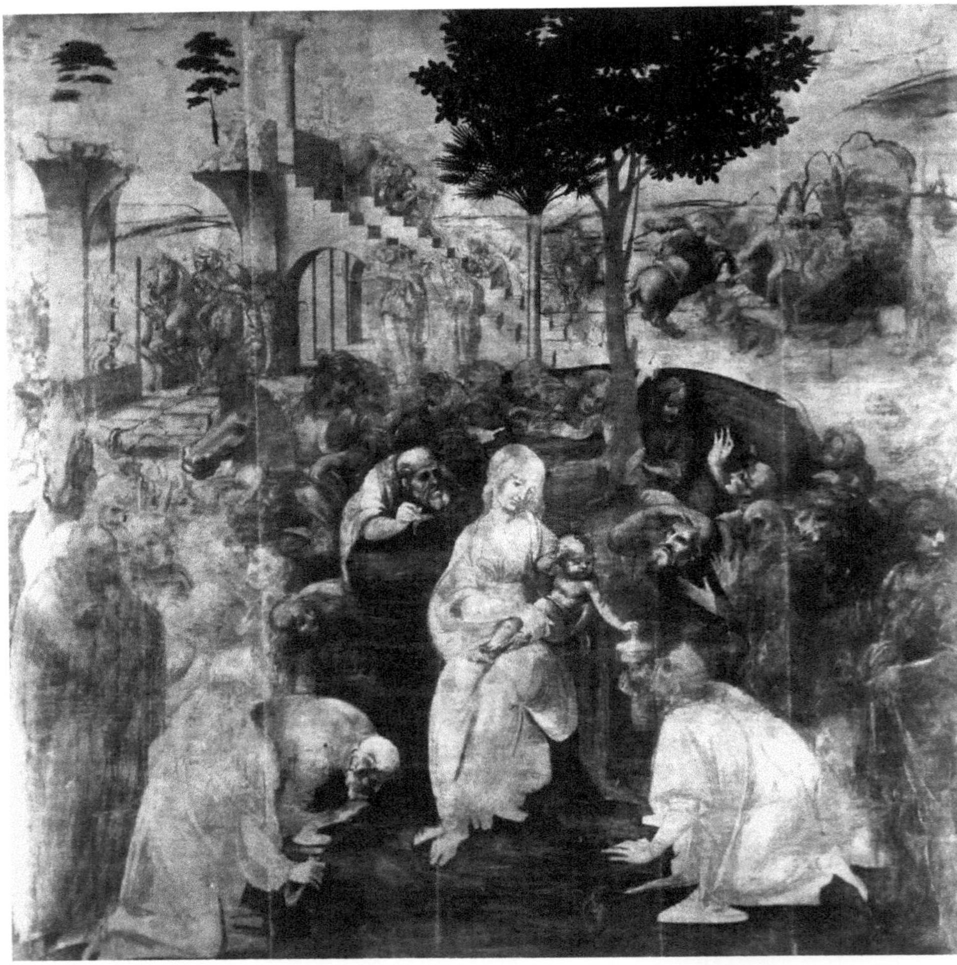

89. Leonardo da Vinci, *Adoration of the Magi.* Oil on wood panel, 246 × 243 cm. Galleria degli Uffizi, Florence.

90. Leonardo da Vinci, *Adoration of the Magi,* detail of Fig. 43.

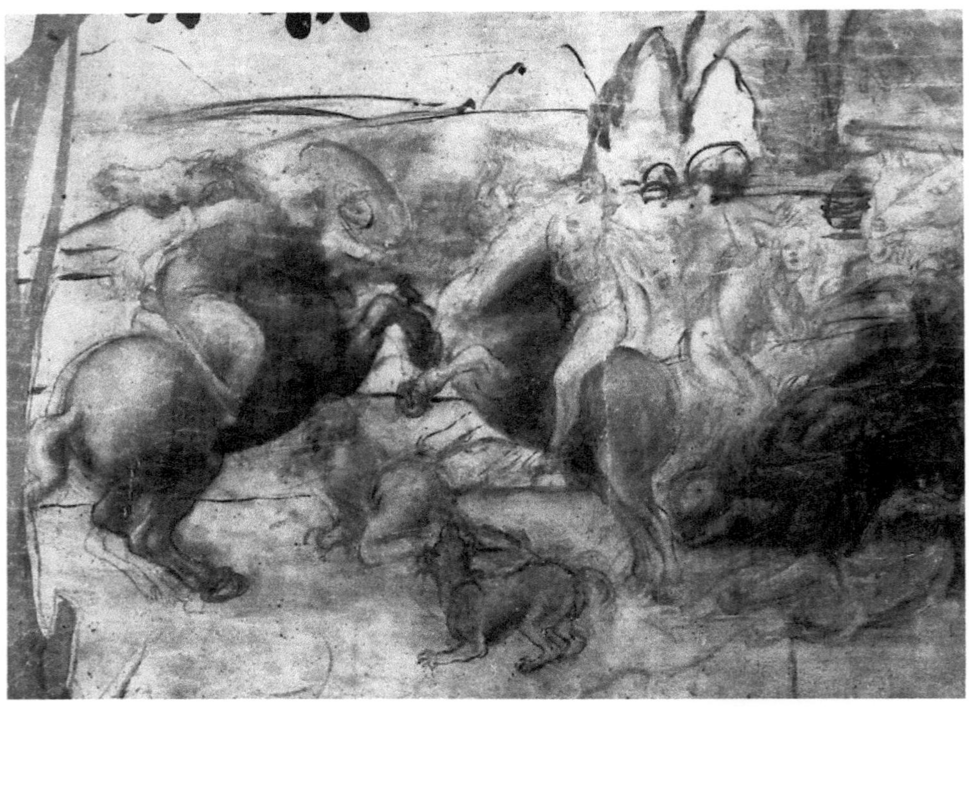

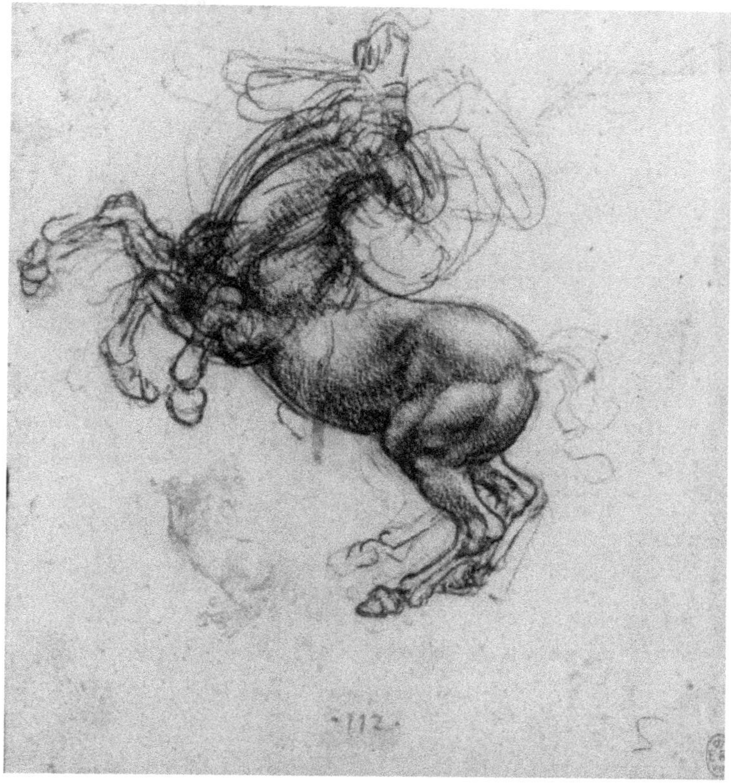

91. Leonardo da Vinci, *Study of a Rearing Horse.* Red chalk with some traces of pen and brown ink, 15.3 × 14.2 cm. Royal Library, Windsor Castle (no. 12336r). The Royal Collection ©2000, Her Majesty Queen Elizabeth II.

92. Leonardo da Vinci, *Dragon Fight.* Pen and brown ink, brush and wash over preliminary linework with stylus, 13.9 × 19 cm. British Museum, London (1952-10-11-12).

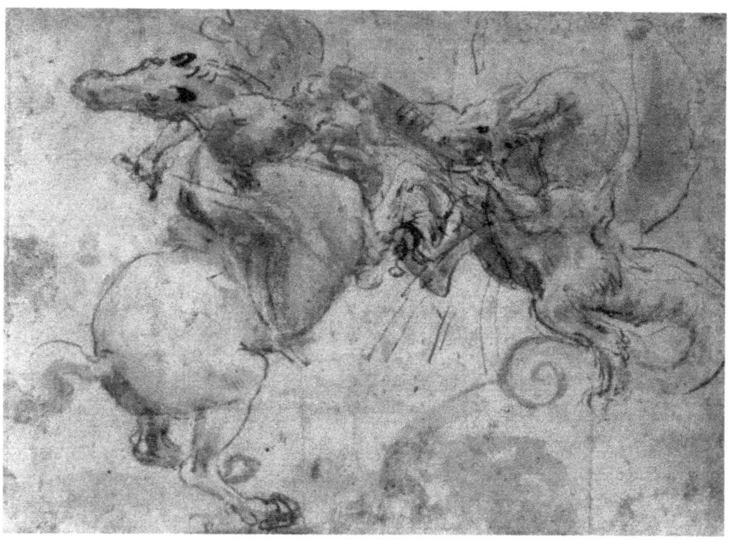

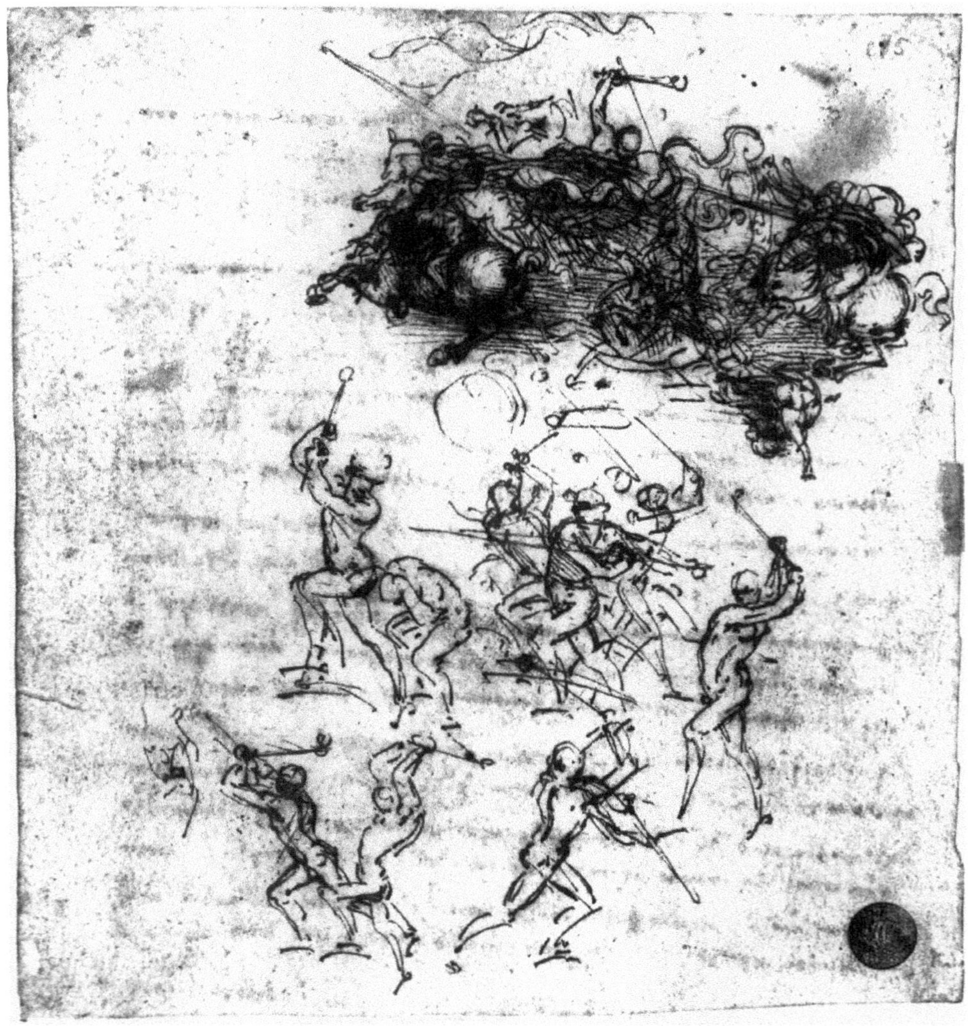

93. Leonardo da Vinci, *Sketches for the Battle of Anghiari*. Pen and brown and black ink, 16 × 15.2 cm. Gallerie dell'Accademia, Venice (inv. 215).

dragon, variations on a Saint George motif (Fig. 92).[43] And it is hardly incidental that the dragon motif too finds an early statement at the bottom of Windsor 12276 (Fig. 80).

The gyrations of this equine form, its complexity of conflicting centrifugal and centripetal forces, are themselves part of the essential Leonardo. On a larger pictorial scale they inform the entire composition of the battle for the standard.[44] And yet, as the many preparatory studies for that composition attest, these energies are, we would say, graphically generated (Fig. 93).[45] Originating in the process of drawing, they assume a guiding function in Leonardo's imagination, determining his sense of composition (Fig. 94) but also conditioning his study of the various forms of nature.[46] Indeed, it might be argued that the cohesive unity of design that Vasari, long before Wölfflin, had isolated as a characteristic of High Renaissance composition was itself the product of such intensely concentrated exercises in drawing: the

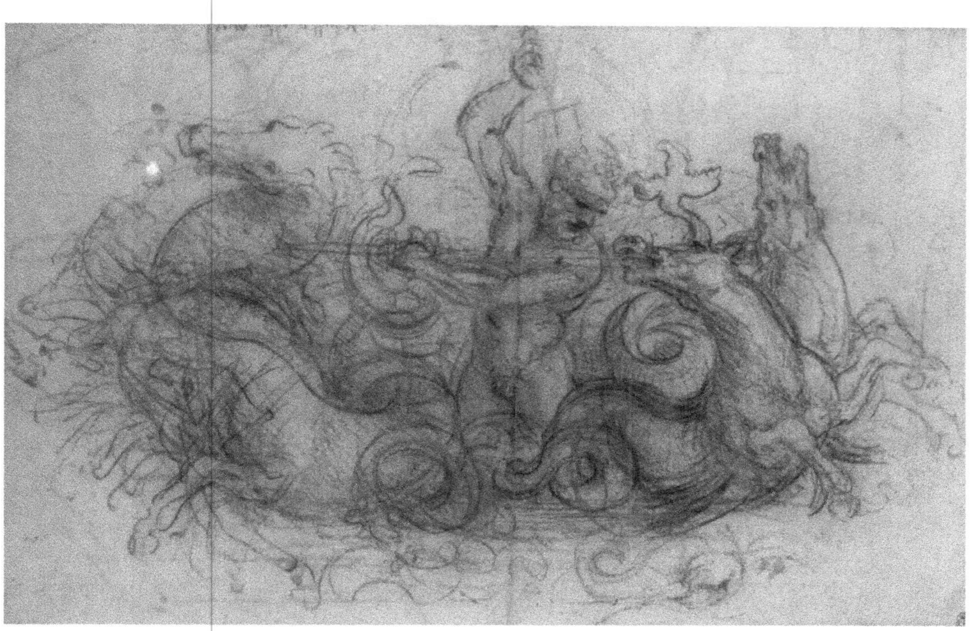

94. Leonardo da Vinci, *Neptune*. Black chalk, 25.2 × 39.2 cm. Royal Library, Windsor Castle (no. 12570). The Royal Collection ©2000, Her Majesty Queen Elizabeth II.

compact formal coherence of the small-scale sketch transposed to the monumental scale of painting.

5. *Drawing and Knowing*

It was toward 1500, and especially following his return to Florence and in the context of such Florentine projects as the battle mural, that Leonardo fully acknowledged the determining quality of certain complex forms, the spiraling ovoid in particular (Figs. 70, 71, 93, 94). Even as it presents a certain calligraphic elegance, the sinuous line that is the basic constituent of this form more deliberately asserts its three-dimensional (Parrhasian) implications: its curve functions stereometrically in the modeling of solids and spatially in the creation of volume.

In effect, Leonardo had come to discover a correspondence between the form of motion in nature and the motion of his own hand in drawing. A basic linear structure became his way of both seeing and recording, and it is hardly unique in the history of art that hand and eye so acknowledge their mutual dependence. With pen or chalk in hand Leonardo saw better. Through graphic gesture he could make visible those forces of nature that seemed to lie beyond the threshold of normal perception. Most impressively, he could see and record the complex movements of water because he could impose upon the natural phenomena his own graphic formulae. Analysis is in the act of drawing; nature accommodates art.

Of all Leonardo's water studies the great spiral blossoming of whirlpools at Windsor (12660v) stands as a culminating achievement of drawing (Fig. 95).[47] The accompanying text seeks to provide verbal explanation of the hydrodynamic forces here represented, the impact of a cascade:

> The movements of the falling water after it has entered the pool are three in kind and to these must be added a fourth, which is the movement of the air that is drawn into the water by the water. And this is the first, and let it be the first to be defined; and let the second be that of the air drawn into the water, and the third the movement of the reflected waters after they have yielded up the compressed air to the other air; when the water has risen in the shape of large bubbles it acquires weight in the air and hence falls back onto the surface of that water, penetrating it as far down as the bottom. The fourth is the swirling movement on the surface of the pool of the water that returns to the place of its impact since it lies at a lower level between the falling and the reflected water. There is to be added a fifth motion called the welling motion, which is the movement of the reflected water when it carries up the air to the surface that was submerged with it.[48]

Leonardo's effort to describe verbally the forms of movement in water is marked by a certain awkward urgency as he seeks to subject that apparent chaos to the order he knows must be there. In his penetrating essay on these studies of movement in water and air, E. H. Gombrich quotes the full text in order to stress "that a drawing like this must be read as a diagram visualizing Leonardo's theoretical propositions rather than a kind of snapshot achieved by a miraculous pair of eyes."[49] Such alternatives seem to me to miss the point. Leonardo's "theoretical propositions" were hardly formulated verbally on the basis of direct observation. This drawing is no mere "diagram," no post facto illustration of a text. The graphic clarity of this complex structure is the product of Leonardo's seeing pen: only by drawing did he truly come to understand; only through drawing was his vision clarified. Whatever his theoretical propositions, they were formulated in and through graphic representation. His text can only provide an explanatory gloss on the drawing. We are reminded of the challenge Leonardo himself sounded on one of his anatomical drawings: "With what words, O writer, will you describe with similar perfection the entire configuration which the drawing here does?"[50] Words, finally, really were not this artist's medium.

In this grand drawing of complex liquid energies Leonardo offers the most satisfying image of the forces of the heaviest of the "spherical" elements. The spiraling motions and countermotions that he saw in the movements of water could not but participate in the dynamics of the larger sublunar universe.

He worked with water, and he came to know it in all its most destructive manifestations.[51] Water, he wrote, "wears away the lofty summits of the mountains. It lays bare and carries away great rocks. It drives away the sea from its ancient shores. . . ." In the margin Leonardo glossed this inventory of water's power: "col tempo ogni cosa va variando" ("with time everything changes").[52] And he translated this dramatic awareness into his own grand vision of cataclysm, the later series of deluge drawings (Fig. 96).[53] Leonardo realized this vision by escalating the graphic structures of his

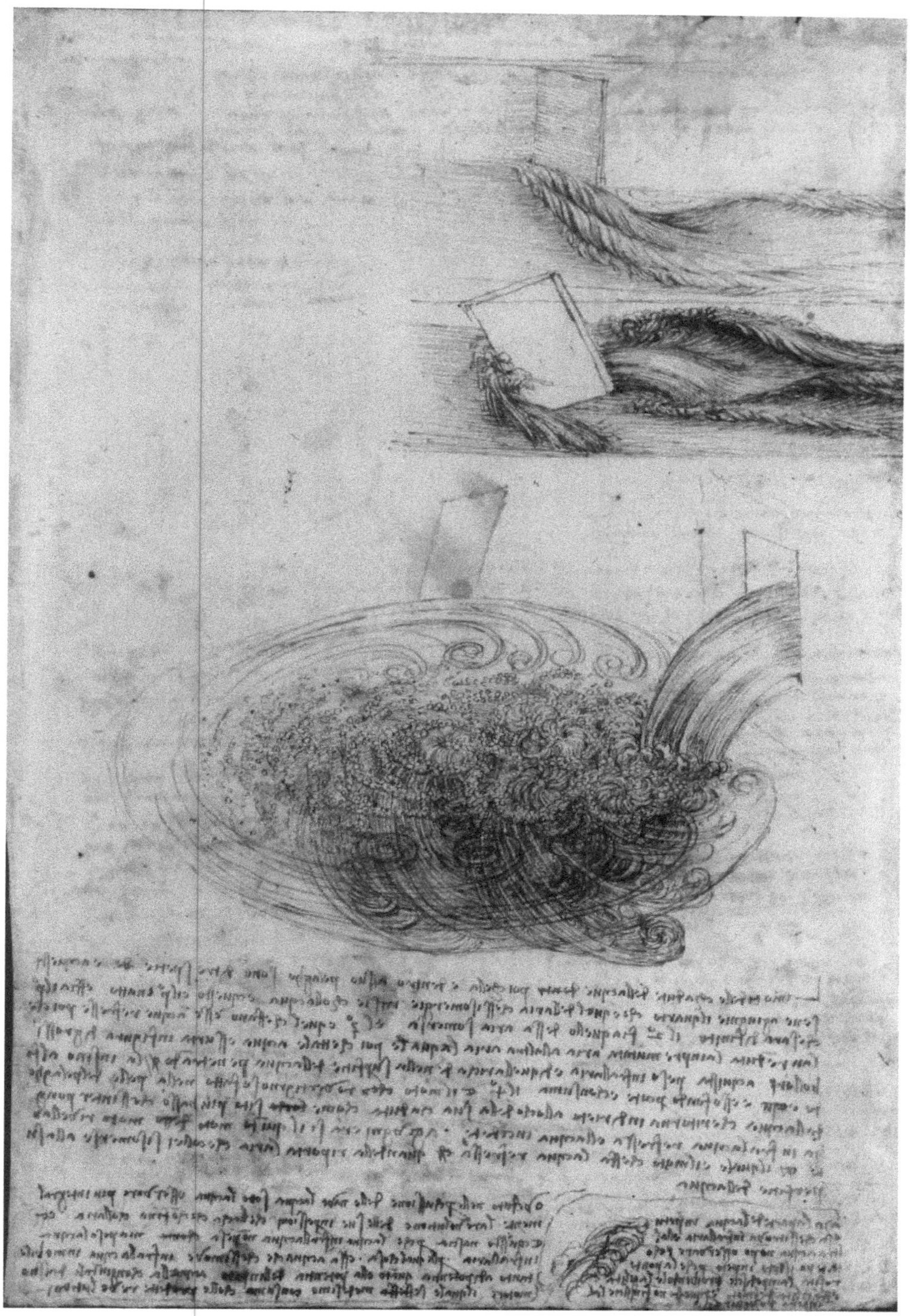

95. Leonardo da Vinci, *Studies of Water.* Pen and brown ink over traces of red chalk, 29.8 × 20.7 cm. Royal Library, Windsor Castle (no. 12660v). The Royal Collection ©2000, Her Majesty Queen Elizabeth II.

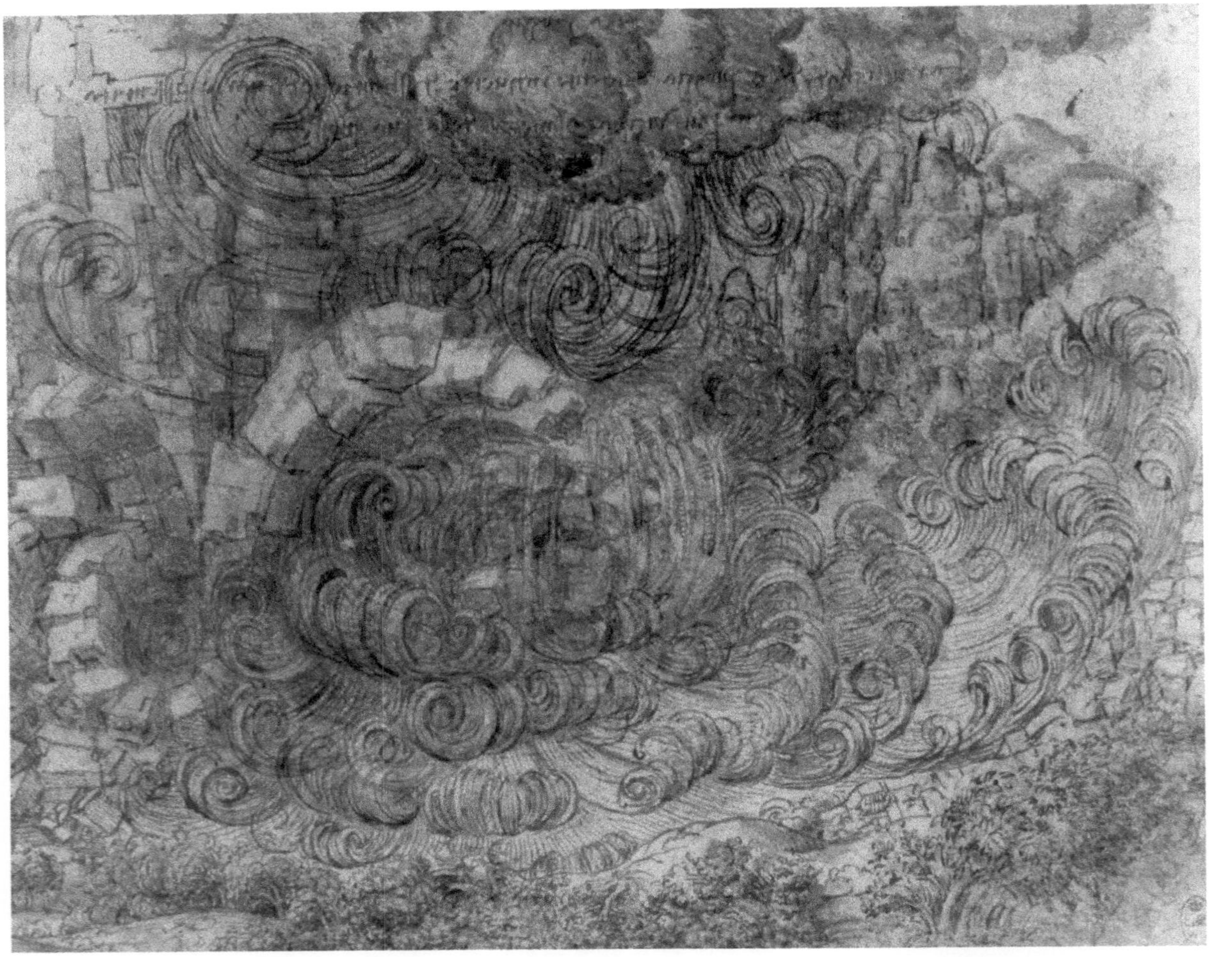

96. Leonardo da Vinci, *Deluge*. Pen and black and yellow ink, brush and wash over black chalk, 16.2 × 20.3 cm. Royal Library, Windsor Castle (no. 12380). The Royal Collection ©2000, Her Majesty Queen Elizabeth II.

water studies to a monumental scale, transposing them from a microcosmic to a macrocosmic key. The same great whirlpools now shape the air, and their impact forces the earth to yield and in its destruction to join in the revolutions of spiral upheaval.[54]

And with these same structures Leonardo imposed order on still another phenomenal scale, on the unruly curls of man (Figs. 97, 98).[55] Clearly, spiral or, more accurately, helical motion – extended in space and turning back upon itself (what he had analyzed as a movement "revertiginoso dechonpossto") – was basic to his vision of the dynamic forces of nature. His graphic analyses led him to search out the essential linear unit of such motion, the single curve in space (Figs. 99, 100). Helical motion, simultaneously driving to close its own cycle and to progress through space, transformed the double vectors of the screw – and Leonardo was long fascinated by Archimedes' invention[56] – into a form of fuller volume: an ellipsoid tense with the contradictions of its own internal forces. That form itself is beautifully epitomized in Leonardo's drawing of a star of Bethlehem (Fig. 101), the floral equivalent to the blossoming whirlpool.[57]

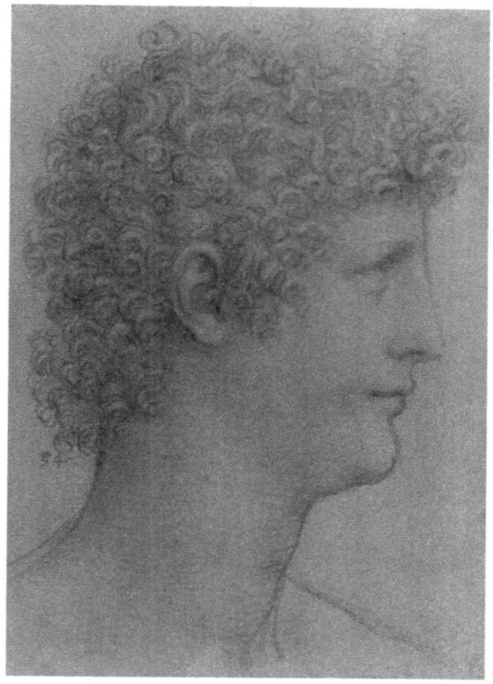

97. Leonardo da Vinci, *Profile of a Youth.* Red chalk with some touches in black chalk on red prepared paper, 21.7 × 15.3 cm. Royal Library, Windsor Castle (no. 12554). The Royal Collection ©2000, Her Majesty Queen Elizabeth II.

98. Leonardo da Vinci. *Old Man in Meditation and Studies of Water.* Pen and brown ink, 15.2 × 21.3 cm. Royal Library, Windsor Castle (no. 12579). The Royal Collection ©2000, Her Majesty Queen Elizabeth II.

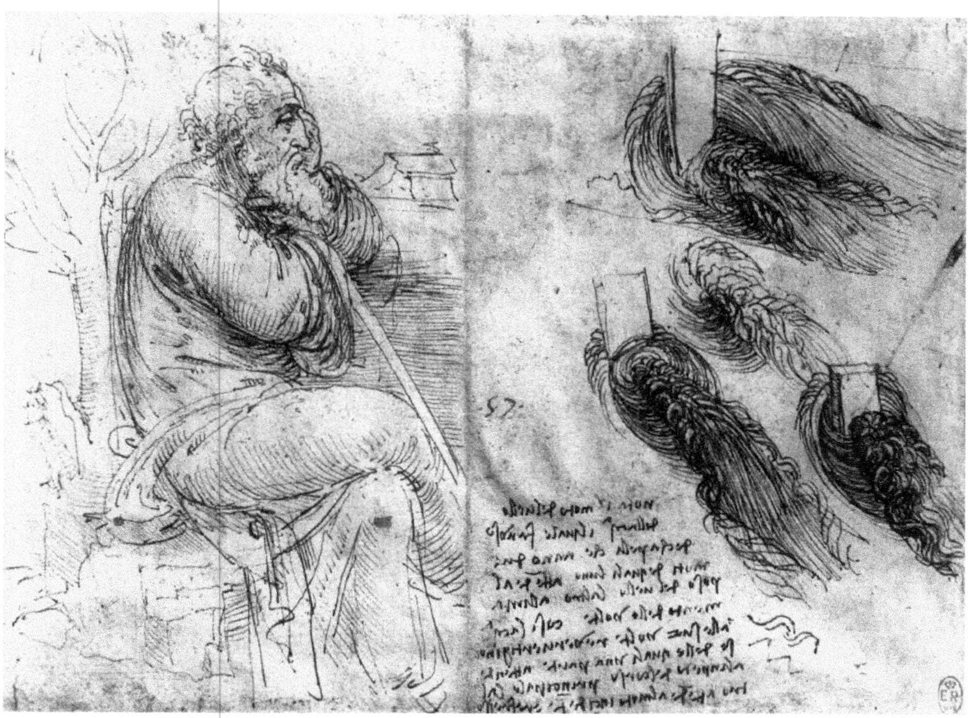

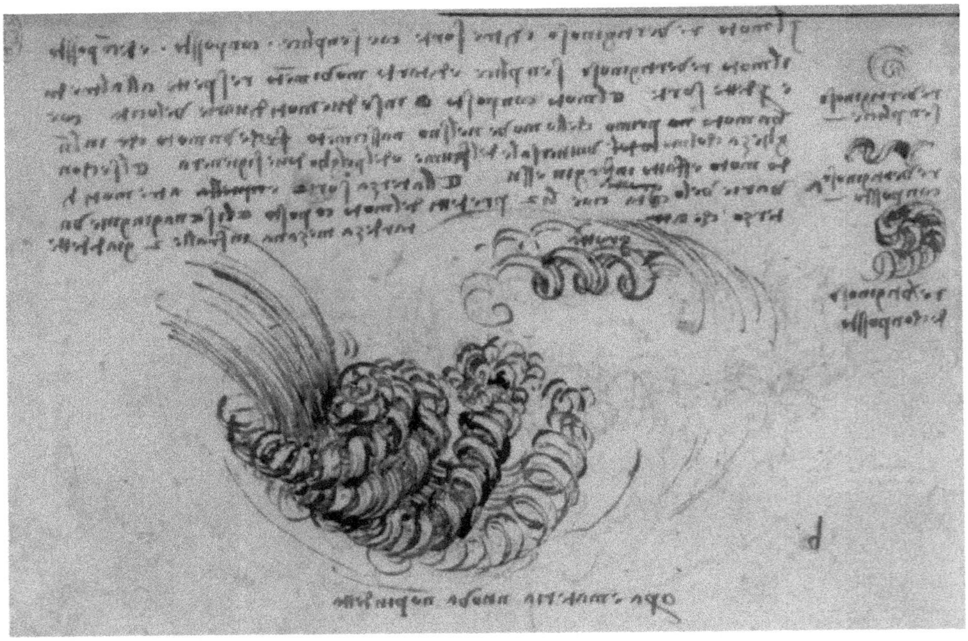

99. Leonardo da Vinci, *Studies of Water*. Pen and brown ink over red chalk, 21.5 × 16.1 cm (detail). Royal Library, Windsor Castle (no. 12663). The Royal Collection ©2000, Her Majesty Queen Elizabeth II.

100. Leonardo da Vinci, *Studies of Water*. Pen and brown ink, 8.8 × 10 cm. Royal Library, Windsor Castle (no. 12666). The Royal Collection ©2000, Her Majesty Queen Elilzabeth II.

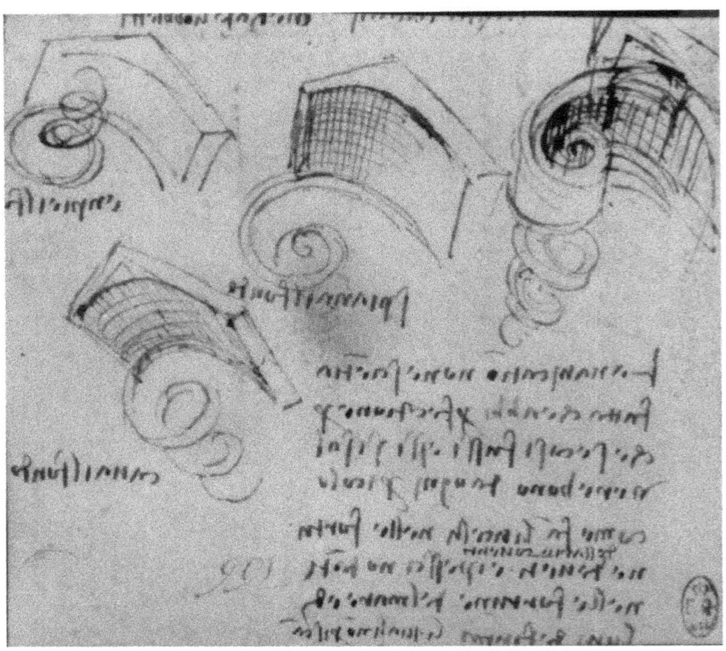

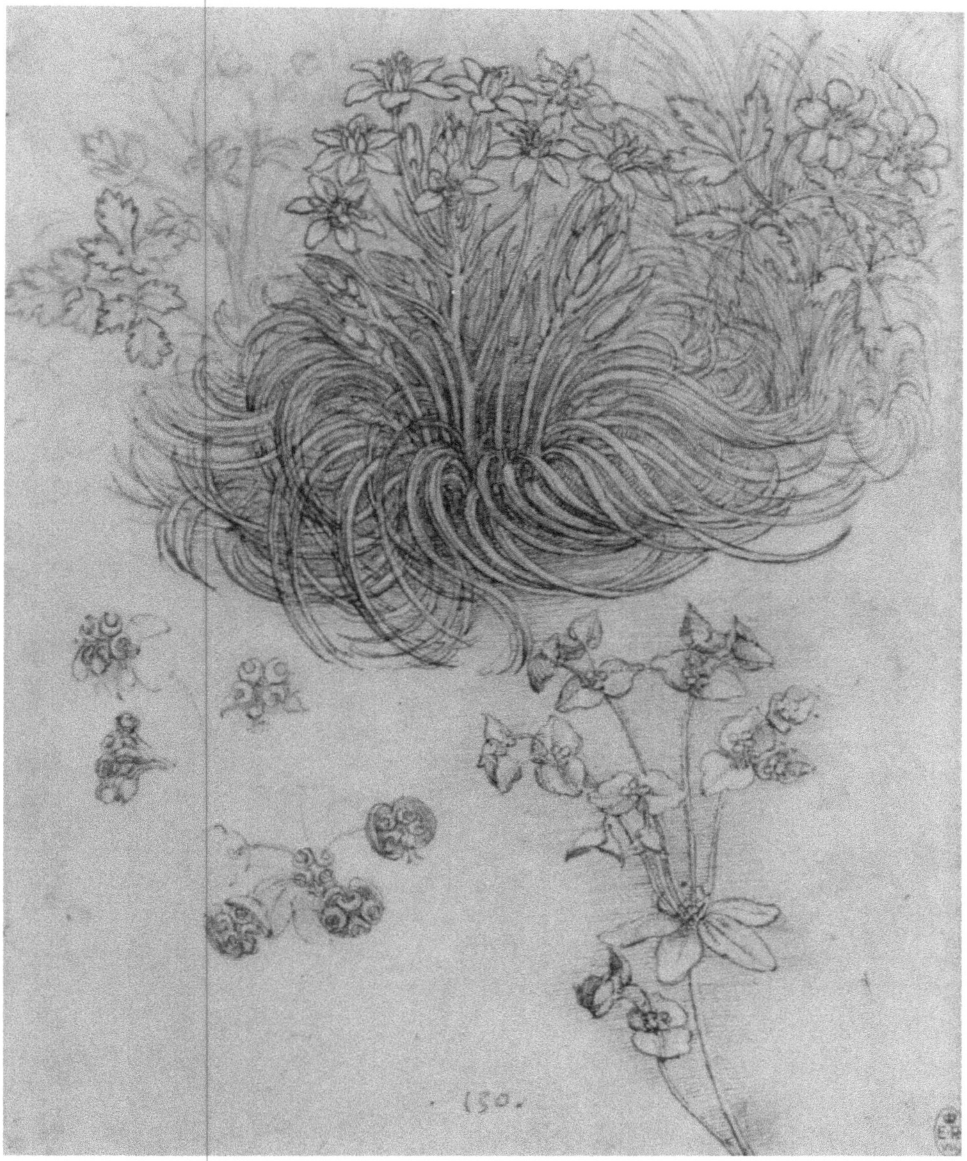

101. Leonardo da Vinci, *Star of Bethlehem and Other Plants.* Pen and brown ink over red chalk, 19.8 × 16 cm. Royal Library, Windsor Castle (no. 12424). The Royal Collection ©2000, Her Majesty Queen Elizabeth II.

Through the controlled formal vocabulary he had devloped in drawing, Leonardo imposed a graphic order on the apparently chaotic forces of nature.[58] Leonardo knew what he could draw.

Although much of his natural investigation took the form of a kind of vector analysis, it may be something of an exaggeration to say that Leonardo saw the world in line. Certainly as a painter he knew very well that outlines did not occur in nature, that they could only be considered a useful convention, a convenient graphic fiction.[59] Yet, for all his deep pictorial concern with aerial perspective, *sfumatura,* and chiaroscuro, he still could conceive of the world as a dynamic lin-

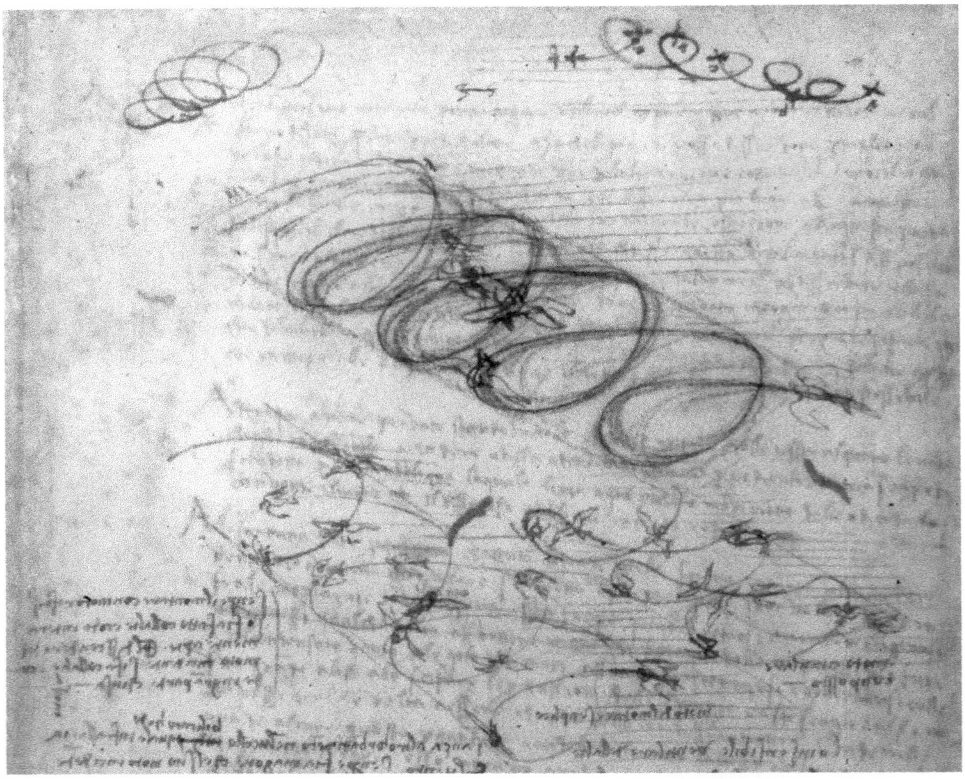

102. Leonardo da Vinci, *Studies of the Flight of Birds,* Codex Atlanticus, new fol. 845r (detail). Biblioteca Ambrosiana, Milan.

ear system. "The air is full of infinite lines," he wrote (about 1492), "straight and radiating, intersected and interwoven, without their displacing one another; and they represent for every object the true form of their cause."[60] And in his studies of the movement of air and the flight of birds he seems determined to record patterns of that linear dynamic (Fig. 102). One example of his linear analysis seeks to discover and record the complexity of such movement, to synthesize in a single linear form the three aspects of line that he discerned and categorized: essentially, straight, curved, and spatial (Fig. 103). This drawing carries the proud inscription, "Body born of the perspective of Leonardo da Vinci, disciple of experience." And it goes on to declare its purpose: "Let this body be made without relation to any body, but out of simple lines only" – the linear generation of form, we might say.[61]

Leonardo's observations on line are, understandably, as varied as the functions of line itself. Within the more immediate pictorial contexts of drawing, he notes the responsibilities of line to suggest even as it delineates: "The contours of any object should be considered with the most careful attention, observing how they twist like a serpent. These serpentine curves are to be studied to see whether they turn as parts of a round curvature or are of an angular concavity" (McM ¶ 115). Or, elsewhere in the treatise on painting, again with respect to outlines, he urges the painter to "note in what direction they turn . . . what portion twists toward one side or the other, and where it is more or less clear and therefore broad or fine [*larga o' sottile*]" (McM ¶ 63). In these observations he shifts easily from the contour envi-

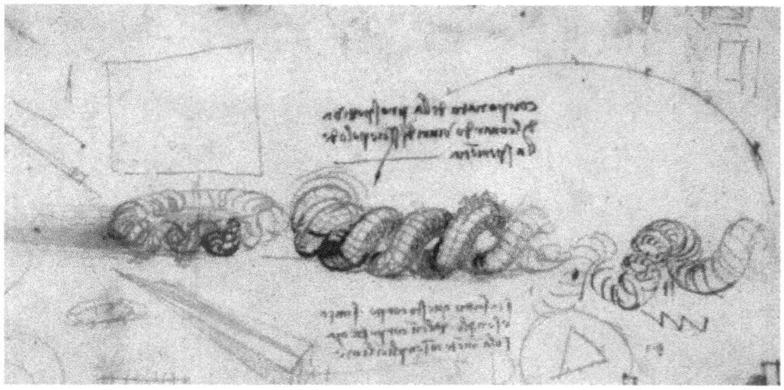

103. Leonardo da Vinci, *Spiral Forms,* Codex Atlanticus, new fol. 520r (detail). Biblioteca Ambrosiana, Milan.

sioned in nature to the drawn outline. Indeed, the two merge, as they must, in his mind: even in writing, Leonardo thinks quite naturally in graphic terms.

Seeing and making are simultaneous acts for Leonardo. His observations on contour at once comment on its function in the representation of natural form and recognize the actuality of tracing that line, the physical act of drawing it. To talk of the ability of an outline to suggest spatial structure is already to implicate the way in which it is rendered – to extend the art of Parrhasios. To talk of it being "più o men'euidente" or "così larga o' sottile" is to acknowledge the manner of its making, that is, the gesture of drawing. In one passage in the treatise Leonardo directly addresses the issue; it is a passage that more essentially than many others translates that act into words. Under the rubric "On drawing an object" he offers the following: "When you are drawing and beginning a line, be sure to look over the whole body that you are representing for whatever may lie in the direction of the line you have begun" (McM ¶ 114).[62] It seems an innocent enough counsel, but it testifies to its author's profound awareness of the act of drawing as an extension into the world, a process of seeing, knowing, and possessing, of that mutuality of hand and eye – and body.

From the perspective of studio practice this must seem obvious. Anyone who has ever drawn an object has experienced the fullness of engagement demanded by the act, the degree to which the eye anticipates the hand, precedes it, a sensory scout exploring the terrain, whose probing extends the potential reach of the hand. The object being rendered, the form coming into being on the paper, comes to exist as a body confronting that of the draftsman, existing in a space that is implicitly a continuum with his or her own. The act of drawing, then, is necessarily an act of projection, of self-projection.

Two drawings of horses may serve to clarify these issues. One, in metalpoint on blue prepared paper, a study related to the equestrian monument to Francesco Sforza, dates toward 1490 (Fig. 104).[63] The other, part of a sheet of studies in pen and ink for the battle mural that we have already met, takes us to about 1503 or 1504 (Fig. 105). Differences in style between these two drawings are naturally, in part, a function of differences in medium. Metalpoint is handled differently from pen. Over a surface specially prepared to abrade the passing metal, the implement is dragged; the mark, a result of that interaction, is strengthened by repeated passing of the point rather

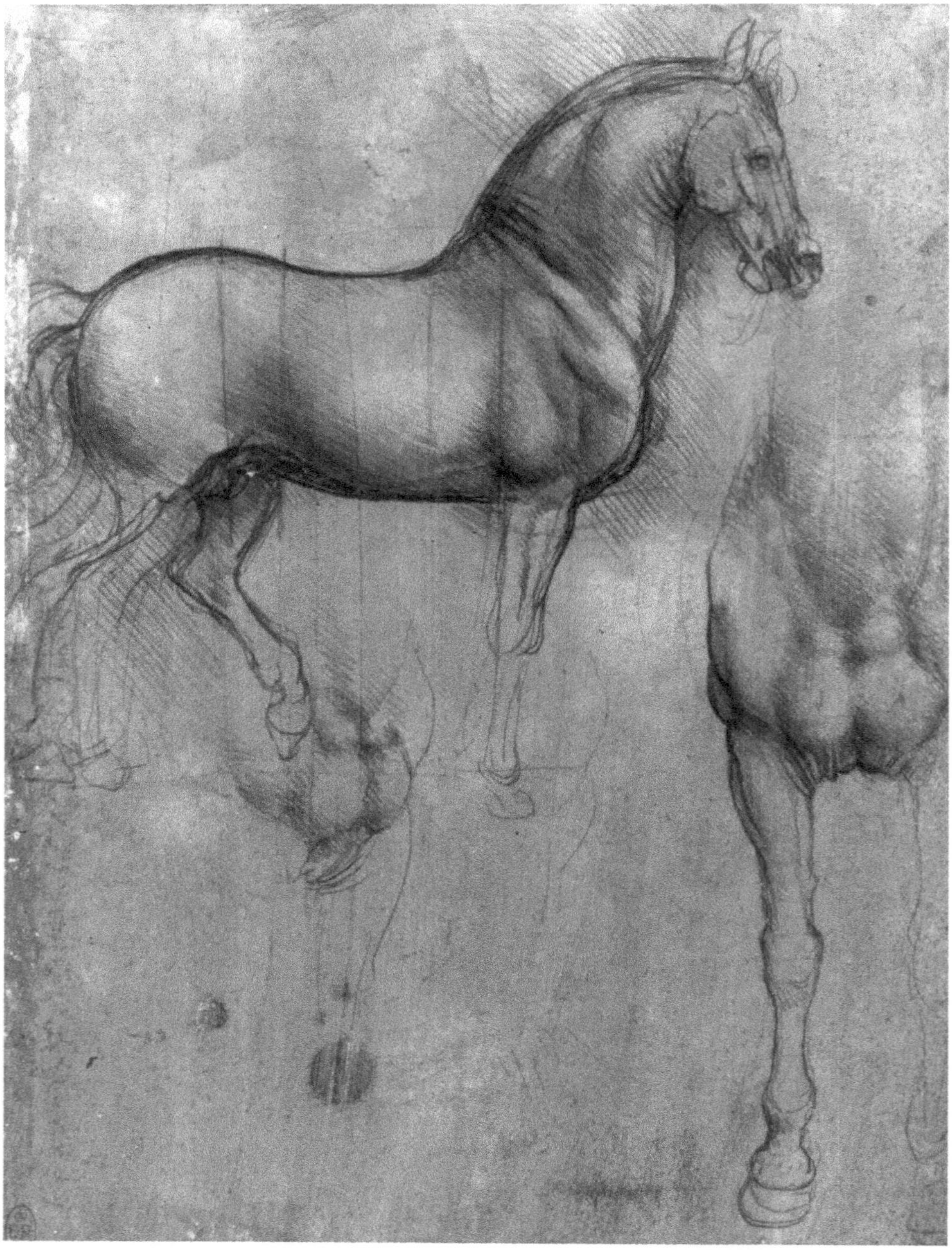

104. Leonardo da Vinci, *Studies of a Horse.* Metalpoint on blue prepared paper, 21.2 × 16 cm. Royal Library, Windsor Castle (no. 12321). The Royal Collection ©2000, Her Majesty Queen Elizabeth II.

than by added pressure or impulsive accentuation – which would only threaten the prepared surface of the paper.[64] The resulting style – which in its general aspect is typical of the late Quattrocento and not unique to Leonardo – is that delicate tissue of parallel lines running diagonally across the blue field. Those lines function to model solid form and to shadow surrounding space; running across both, they establish the overall unity that is a hallmark of both style and technique. The very delicacy of touch works to discover and display with a certain steadiness of purpose the variations of surface relief in the objects rendered and, by extending beyond those objects,

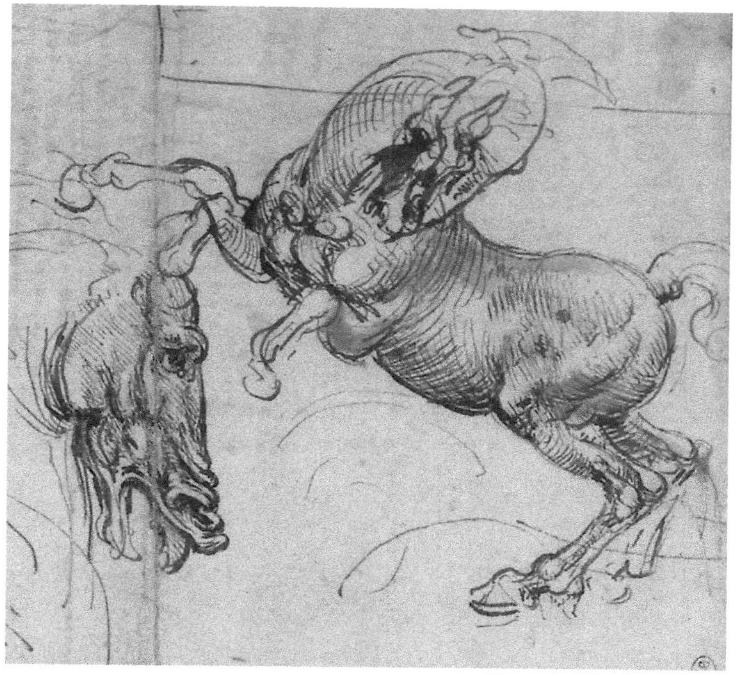

105. Leonardo da Vinci, *Horses and other Studies for the Battle of Anghiari*, detail of Fig. 86.

to establish the atmospheric continuum that further convinces us of their existence in space. As the execution is relatively slow and deliberate, so too is our own exploration of the forms given to our vision. Technique mediates knowledge.

Drawing in pen permits a very different set of possibilities, essentially of more varied movement and more dynamic gesture. But it is not just that the study of the rearing horse for the *Battle of Anghiari* is rendered more energetically and in pen that determines its essentially different character. The variety allowed the drawing hand is really directed by the task set: the rendering of an organic solid turning in space. Leonardo's pen follows the twisting stereometry of the animal's bulk. From the beginning, line shares in the fiction, identifies with the object rendered as it adheres to the surface of the horse's body. Indeed the pen's chief responsibility seems to be precisely that, to hold tight and not let go as it follows the curving planes of horseflesh.[65]

Differences in style, without question: but the question is bigger than style. Leonardo's mode of drawing is, as I have been proposing, a mode of knowing. Demanding to know more of the world out there, the artist has developed a way of rendering that not only satisfies that demand but makes it possible. This kind of penmanship probes deeper, with deliberate intensity and with an energy that is more than just graphic. Fundamentally tactile, it explores by touch, seeking a hold on what it renders. The earlier style, whether executed in metalpoint or in pen, offered a system of visually suggestive linear pattern (Fig. 106);[66] its procedure involved a tentative probing of reality, a cumulative stroking of it into existence. The later penmanship is concerned less with such deliberate teasing of form from ground, less with atmospheric, pictorial space than with physical realization (Fig. 107).[67] Now the stress is on touch, or grasp, rather than vision, on proximity rather than distance – in the terms of Alois

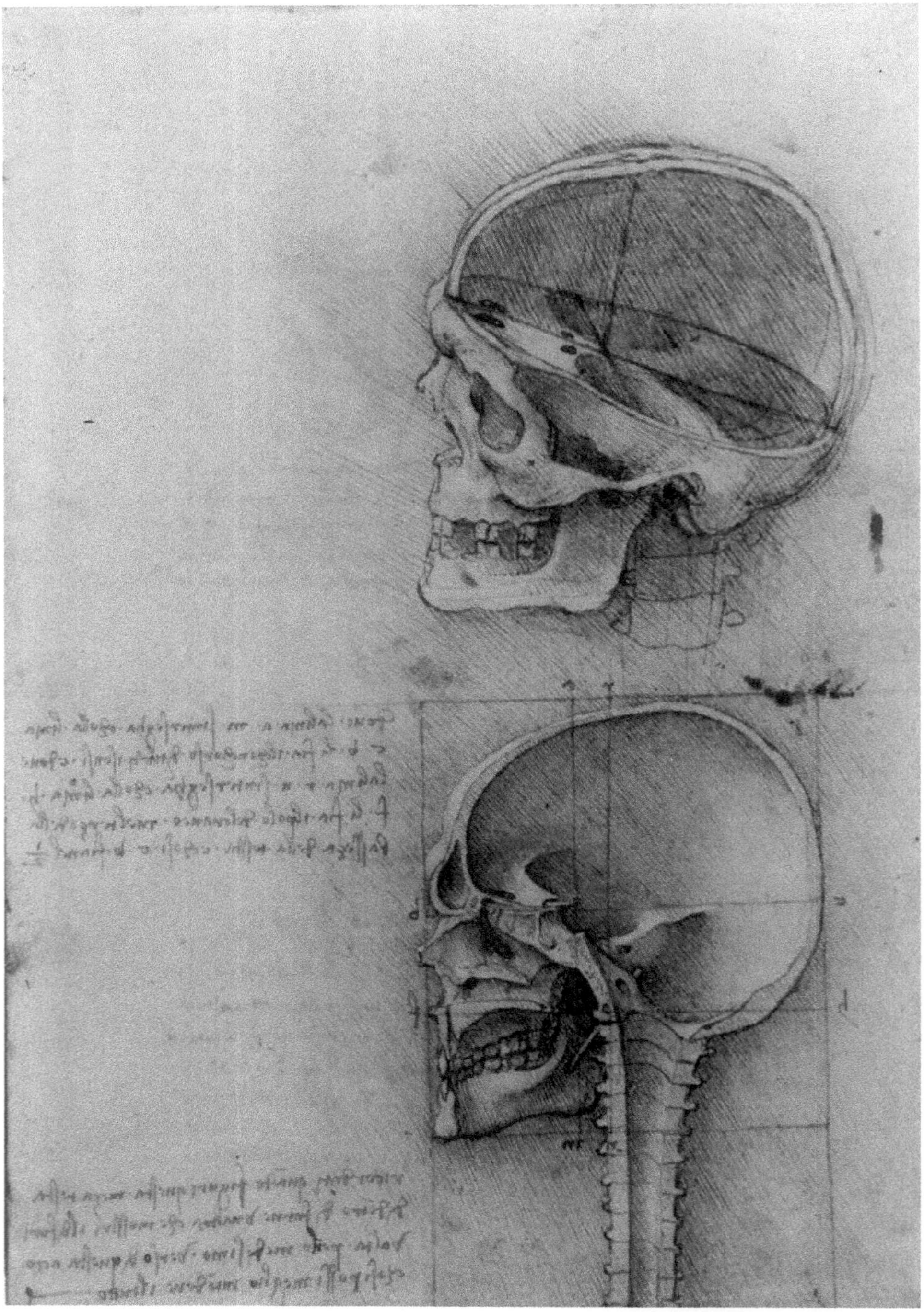

106. Leonardo da Vinci, *Studies of a Skull in Section.* Pen and brown ink over black chalk, 18.8 × 13.4 cm. Royal Library, Windsor Castle (no. 19057). The Royal Collection ©2000, Her Majesty Queen Elizabeth II.

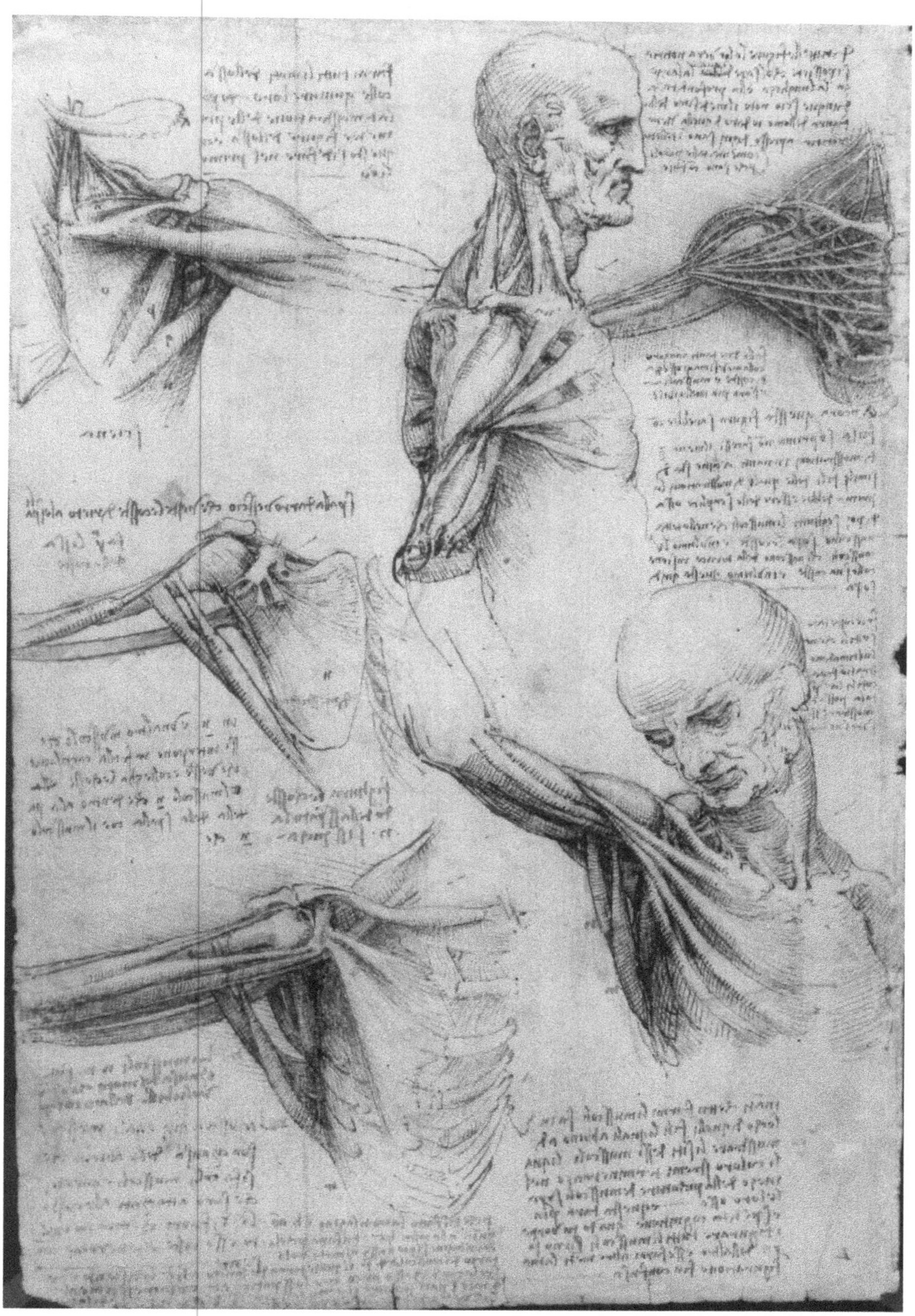

107. Leonardo da Vinci, *Studies of the Shoulder Muscles.* Pen and brown inks with some wash over black chalk, 29.2 × 19.9 cm. Royal Library, Windsor Castle (no. 19003v). The Royal Collection ©2000, Her Majesty Queen Elizabeth II.

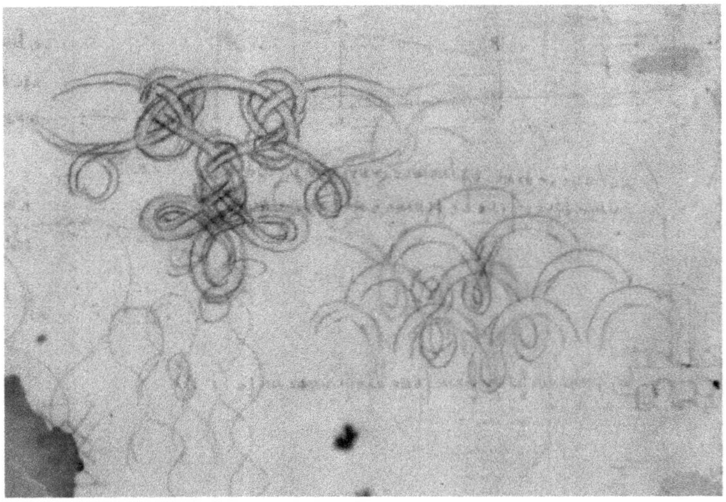

108. Leonardo da Vinci, *Interlace Patterns*. Red chalk, 27.4 × 19.4 cm (detail). Royal Library, Windsor Castle (no. 12351v). The Royal Collection ©2000, Her Majesty Queen Elizabeth II.

Riegl, on haptic rather than optic qualities.[68] In each case, however, the line is a means of reaching out.[69]

Drawing is a way of seeing and knowing, and the quality of what is seen and known changes with the mode of drawing. Drawing records what has been seen and is known, but not after the fact: it is simultaneous with and, for the draftsman, identical to perception.

The course of a line's making is a process of exploration; its progress is a progress into the world. Long before Klee described the point as "the mobility agent . . . shifting its position forward," Leonardo had demonstrated his awareness of just this function of the line as a probe, but for him it was of necessity directed. Although he certainly appreciated its appeal as pure tracing or calligraphy (Fig. 108),[70] it was precisely the exploratory responsibility of a line that gave it purpose;

109. Leonardo da Vinci, *Mortars Firing Stones*. Pen and brown ink, brush and wash, 32.9 × 48 cm. Royal Library, Windsor Castle (no. 12275). The Royal Collection ©2000, Her Majesty Queen Elizabeth II.

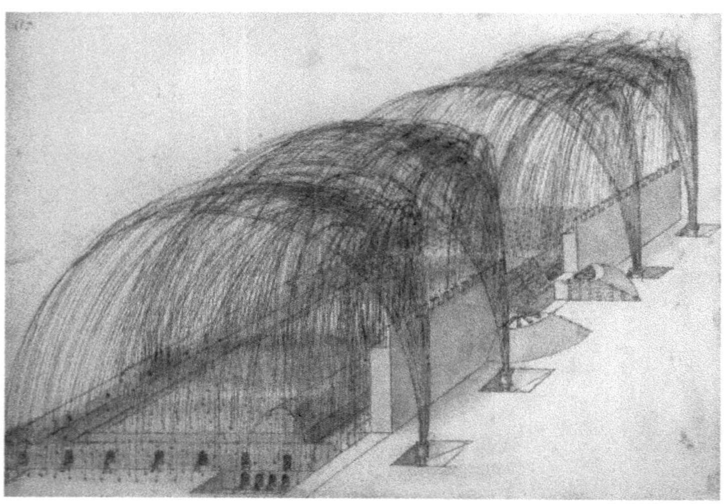

its extension into the world made visible vectors of force and energies otherwise unperceivable by the eye (Fig. 109).[71] Line made the world imaginable.

In elaborating his arguments on behalf of painting in the *paragone* with poetry, Leonardo celebrated the eye as the privileged organ of perception. "The eye is the window of the human body through which the soul views and enjoys the beauties of the world. Because of it the soul in its human prison is content, and without it this human prison is its torment . . ." (McM ¶ 34). To the standard Platonizing physiology he added his own exploratory enthusiasm. The eye was a means of extension: "It carries men from the east to the west, it has discovered navigation. . . ." And the lead of the eye, he continues, is followed by the hand.[72] Following it, the drawing hand will travel toward those distant horizons. In practice, however, the eye is urged on by the hand.

"A line is made by the movement of a point." Leonardo begins one of his typical observations with this geometric axiom. But he then transposes the abstraction to the realm of lived reality: "the point may be compared to an instant in time, and the line may be likened to the length of a certain quantity of time, and just as a line begins and terminates in a point, so such a space of time."[73] Time with a length – what Valéry was to call the *chronolysis* of space.[74] Whether or not such a concept was adapted from Roger Bacon, it must have assumed a more powerful meaning for an artist with a pen in his hand, seeking to know the world through and as drawing. The moments of a line, the time of drawing – as Picasso put it, quite concretely: "The fatigue of one's hand as one draws is a perception of time."[75]

In a lecture "On the Nature of Vision," delivered in 1912, Oskar Kokoschka confessed: "Without intent I draw from the outside world the resemblance of things; but in this way I myself become part of the world's imaginings."[76] Through the act of drawing the draftsman reaches out, puts himself in active touch with the world, projects himself. To draw a line is to extend oneself into the world, to know it, and to recognize one's self.

CHAPTER FOUR

Raphael and the Calligraphy of Classicism

. . . una linea sola non stentata
– Baldesar Castiglione[1]

A single sheet of pen studies for a group of Madonna and Child marks a particular moment in the development of Raphael as draftsman (Fig. 110).[2] Although each of the sketches set down here was eventually to be further elaborated and realized in painting – the *Bridgewater Madonna* (Fig. 111), the *Colonna Madonna* (Berlin, Staatliche Museen), the *Large Cowper Madonna* (Washington, National Gallery of Art) – they cannot be considered "preparatory" in any directly intentional sense. Rather than steps toward the solution of a particular, commissioned project, they seem to offer rephrasings of the basic compositional problem itself.

Indeed, for Raphael, as for Leonardo, the theme of Madonna and Child, bread-and-butter subject for any Renaissance workshop, afforded an ideal field for graphic exploration. If not quite *componimenti inculti,* these drawings nonetheless constitute a generational complex; they represent the kind of creative graphic activity that Leonardo practiced and theorized. And the British Museum sheet, executed probably around 1507–8 in Florence, does indeed conform to the older master's example in its confluence of ideation and realization. By the mid-sixteenth century Raphael himself was to stand as the exemplar with regard to preliminary sketching of compositional ideas. Inspired by his subject and trying out his *fantasie* in preliminary sketches, the painter, advises Lodovico Dolce, should follow the example of Raphael and not be satisfied with a single design but should develop several alternatives from which eventually to select. This was the way of Raphael, "so rich in inventiveness, who always worked out a narrative (*una historia*) in four or six different ways, each one different from the other, and all were full of grace and well constructed."[3]

Raphael came to Florence in 1504 expressly to learn, "per imparare," as his letter of introduction stated.[4] But to suggest that he was consciously applying a lesson learned would be misleading, for the drawing itself, by its organic integrity and natural dynamic, testifies rather to the realization of a potential already inherent in Raphael's own draftsmanship. The impact of Leonardo upon the young Urbinate was undoubtedly important, as Vasari recognized in his account of Raphael's development. Raphael does seem to have realized himself as an artist through a process of stylistic emulation and appropriation: moving from Perugino to Leonardo to Michelangelo, growing with each step until he achieved his own mature High Renaissance classicism. But such encounters with the art of other masters were essentially catalytic experiences for an artist of such innate talent – and ambition. Lessons in composition, chiaroscuro, foreshortening, and anatomy of course were to be had from Leonardo and Michelangelo in Florence, and, deliberately seeking out such instruction, Raphael clearly profited from his studies. Drawing, however, is the most elementary activity of pictorial art. No matter how teachable, it is the primary expression of ability, and the most personal. It was (according to Vasari's account) the very young Raphael's "maniera del disegnare" that recommended him to Perugino.[5] And that is precisely what we encounter in the British Museum studies. It is the effortless movement of his pen that convinces us that this mode of drawing can be no application of another's procedure, no appropriation of an external model, but is very much an extension of Raphael himself. These sketches record a process of personal discovery. In the pen line itself we recognize both the style and the artist.

1. The Circling Hand

A basic motion informs the overall design of this sheet as well as its smaller constituent elements, a generally circular motion. From the circling movement of Raphael's pen form is generated, revealing itself in and through the repetition of

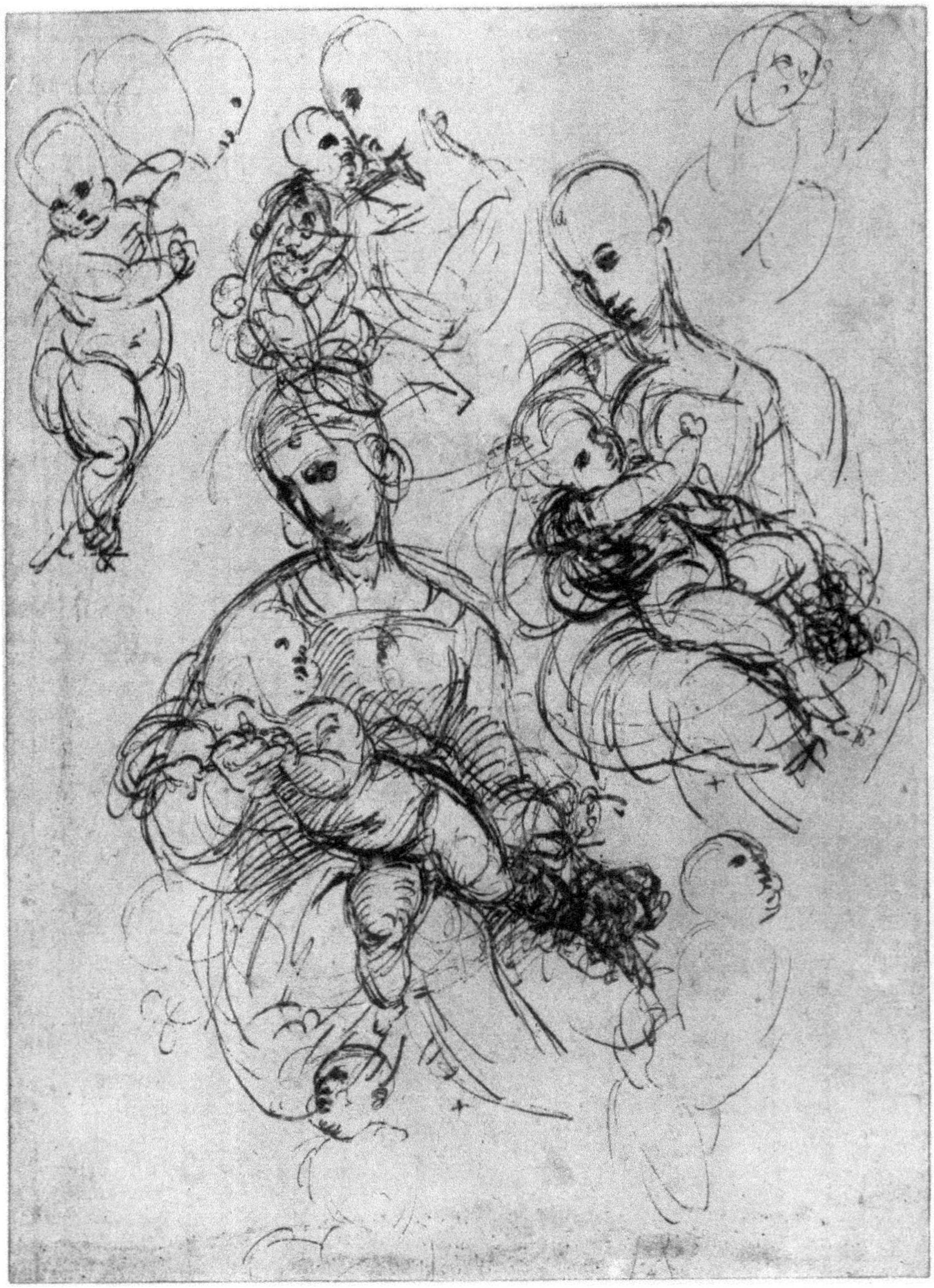

110. Raphael, *Studies of the Virgin and Child.* Pen and brown ink, over some traces of red chalk, 25.4 × 18.4 cm. British Museum, London (Ff. 1–36).

that same movement. Two arcs create an oval – a head, an arm, a thigh, an infant's belly. Repeated contours, motivated by a search for linear closure, transcend outline to build up a sense of form in space; the bundled lines themselves resonate that space even as they hug the solids they define. Leaving patterns of nearly parallel arcs, the same curving movement creates tone and models form, to which the regularity of this concentric hatching assigns a simple stereometry.

We readily follow the draftsman's progress on this sheet, beginning with the central dominant group. Here, in a pose that recalls inventions of both Leonardo and Michelangelo, the child strides across the mother's lap, as if squirming to escape that protective nest, and yet turning back to acknowledge her maternal concern. From the bare markings in the margins, we imagine Raphael's opening movements, the simple arcs that define the basic oval of the Virgin's head. And we follow Raphael's repeated tracing of the contours, his pen moving to either side of the initial tentative line. By that process of expansion and contraction figure and ground fuse into a shared continuum as paper is imaginatively transformed into solid and void. The circling action of the pen finds in its own motions the potential for form, and out of those motions it creates form, establishing a basic design unity in which we recognize style: "the constant form . . . the constant elements, qualities, and expression . . . in the art of an individual."[6]

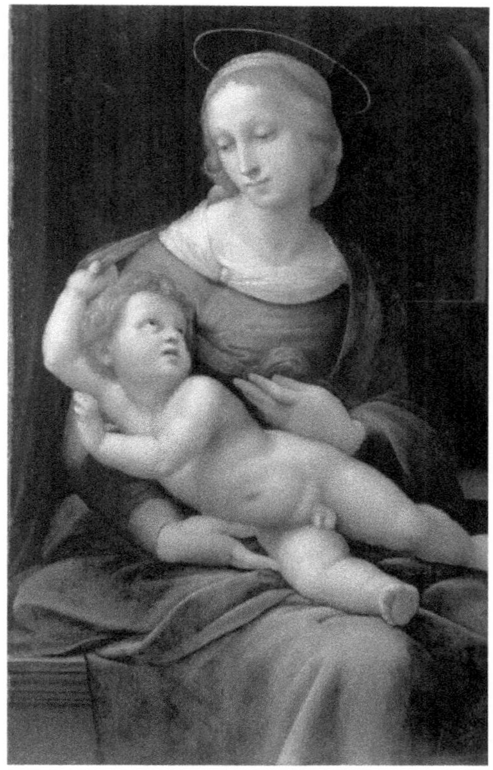

111. Raphael, *The Bridgewater Madonna.* Oil on panel, transferred to canvas, 81 × 56 cm. National Gallery of Scotland, Edinburgh.

The same gestures that establish the maternal container generate the child within; his own movements conform with the larger contours of his mother. He is realized from and through the same circulating graphic energies. Even the contrapposto of his body, striding to the left as his head, obeying the indications of his mother's contour, turns back and inward; within this linear dynamic, their two faces are fixed momentarily by the axis of exchanged glances. Out of the traces of the moving pen come both the larger sense of stability and containment and the internal agitation; out of its *pentimenti* comes action, most obviously in the changing relationship of mother's hand to infant's foot. Dramatic narrative, figural motion on however small a scale, is produced by the drawing hand.

From this central group, then, the circling pen extends its forming impulse to other open areas of the paper. Concentrating on the space to the right, it produces a variant on its initial discovery: Here the child is turned, its body meeting the mother's; the pair is more internally focused as only his head now looks away from her, out to the beholder. In this group, too, the essential values result from the motions of the pen. Density of application, an overlapping of lines, again focuses moments of sustained and sustaining contact, where maternal hands support the infant; the looping calligraphy encircles the foundational thigh of the Virgin, the rapid tracing of the pen mimicking the draped surface of its volume.

Along the top of the paper the space between these two major groups invited further graphic thinking, and the draftsman responded with a still more intimate coupling of mother and child, reinventing the venerable Byzantine type of the

Madonna of Compassion (*Eleousa*) or of Sweet Embrace (*Glykophilousa*). And next, in the upper left corner, yet another thematic variant comes into being in response to the particular shape of the vestigial field: a fully vertical child along the margin of the page.

The dialectic nature of this process, one positive form or open space provoking a response, is perhaps most striking in the still skeletal sketches in the upper corners of the field: one angled head answered contrapuntally by another, one arc by another. The energy carrying this process is essentially graphic. Once set in motion, the restless but purposeful pen fills the paper, trying the formal possibilities latent in its own circulation. And in that generally circular motion we recognize not only the source of unity of this particular sheet of sketches but also an essential quality of Raphael's classicism, the formal dialectic holding in precarious balance the particularized reality of nature and the formal ideality of a larger ordering geometry.

The organic quality of that style we call High Renaissance, what for Vasari was the modern style – initiated by Leonardo and perfected by Raphael, spurred by Michelangelo – finds an essential expression in drawing. In describing the principles of this "new pictorial form," Heinrich Wölfflin noted "the capacity to see parts collectively and simultaneously, the power of grasping the variety of things in the field of vision as a single unit, which links up with a type of composition in which every part of the whole is felt to have its necessary and inevitable place within that whole."[7] What will be realized on a more monumental scale in painting, the harmonious subordination of the parts to the whole and the isomorphic correspondence of the two, we find naturally produced in drawings like those on the British Museum sheet – as in Leonardo's pyramidal groupings for the *Madonna and Child with St. Anne* (Fig. 59) or his ovoid sketches for the *Battle of Anghiari* (Figs. 42, 43, 93). The linear impulses of drawing cohere into form and thereby establish, however roughly, the fundamental compositional structures that will be further refined in painting. Thus, the curving profile of the central group in the British Museum sheet of studies, the strong collective contour that so firmly contains the Child within the mother, will be refined and more deliberately elaborated in the *Bridgewater Madonna* by the upraised arm of the Child grasping the Virgin's mantle (Fig. 111). By his pose, he now actively participates in the closure that was first conceived in and through the drawn stroke. Whatever the dramatic refinement and the accommodation to a different pictorial scale and medium, the essential compositional idea was born in and through drawing. We may readily imagine how these same motions of the drawing hand naturally generated ideas for tondo compositions,

112. Raphael, *Madonna della Sedia*. Oil on panel, diameter: 71 cm. Galleria Palatina, Palazzo Pitti, Florence. Photograph: Alinari/Art Resource, New York.

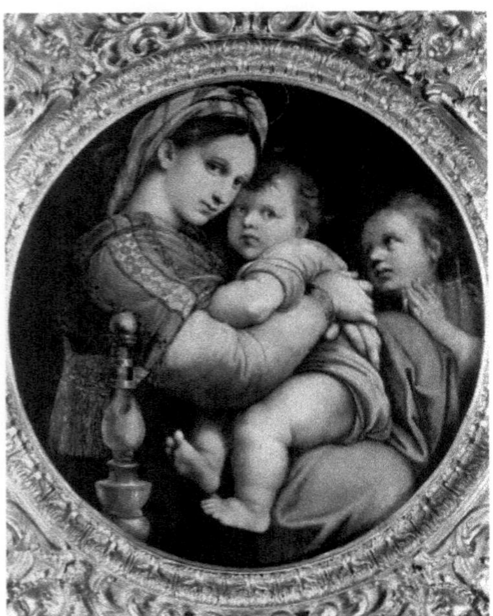

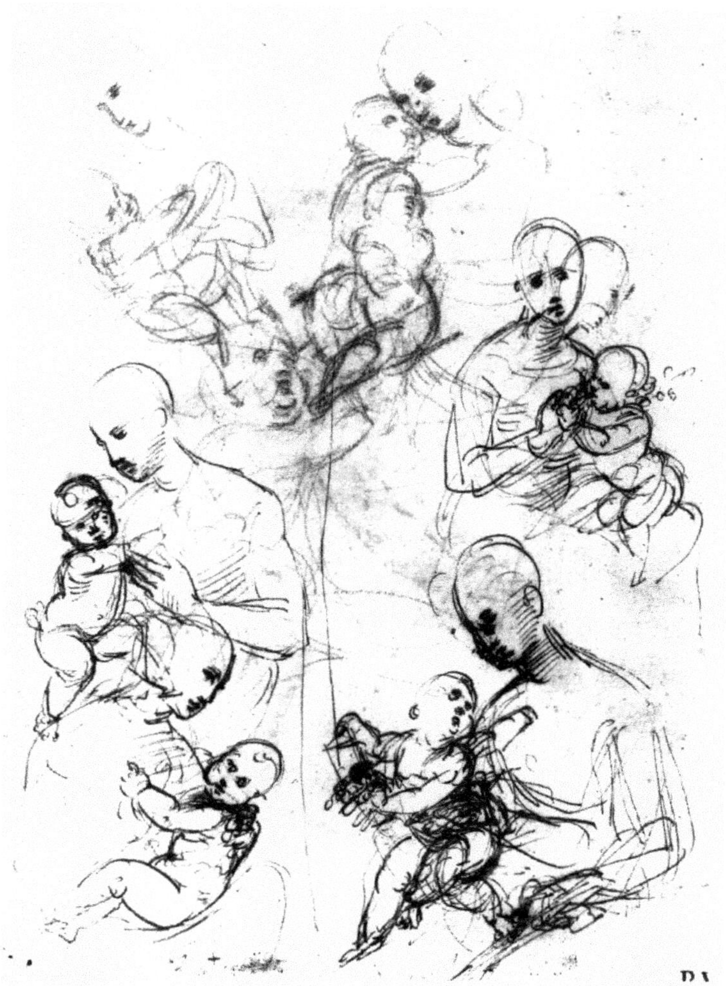

113. Raphael, *Studies of the Virgin and Child.* Pen and brown ink, red chalk, 26 × 19.2 cm. Graphische Sammlung Albertina, Vienna (IV, 209).

especially Raphael's fullest realization of the structure, the *Madonna della Sedia* (Fig. 112).[8]

The special nature of the British Museum sheet emerges more clearly in comparison with a page of studies that presumably followed it (Fig. 113).[9] Raphael continued to develop the ideas generated in those initial sketches. Evidently working first in red chalk, he took up the top marginal group of Madonna and Child in sweet embrace; a larger version of this motif fills the center of the paper, which is then varied slightly, but on a smaller scale, just above. Then, to the left and still in red chalk, he began working with the second large motif on the British Museum sheet, the child lying in the mother's arms but looking outward – eventually realized in the *Colonna Madonna.* These red-chalk sketches are of a different order from their originating models; effectively replicating the original inventions, their lines record not the search for form but rather a schematic reduction of form

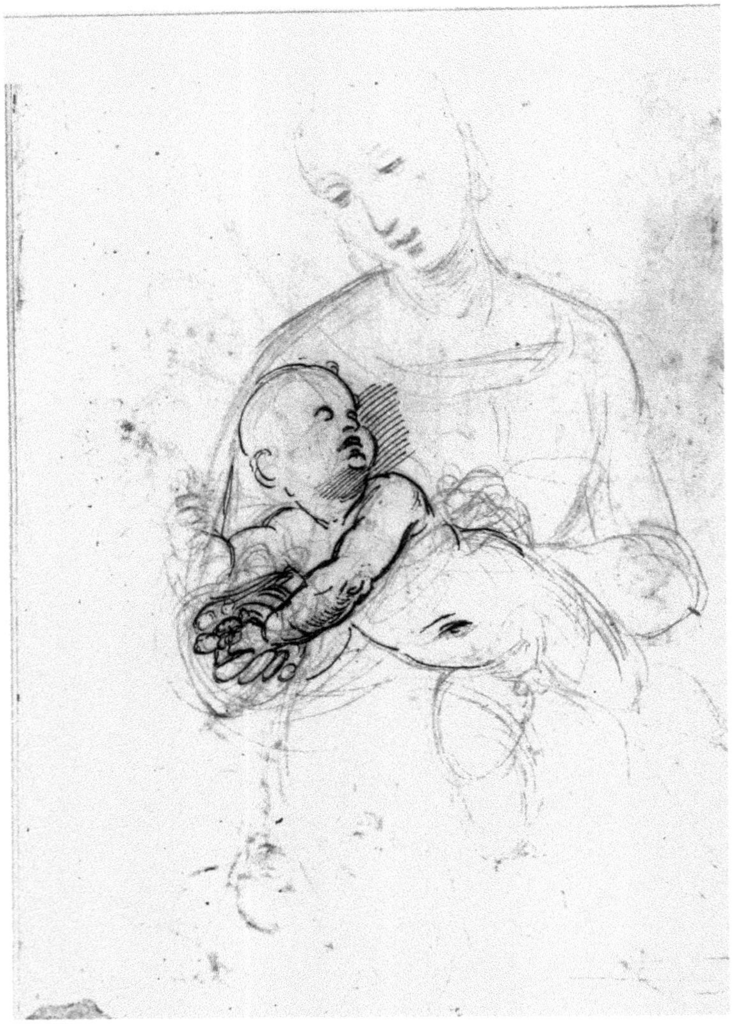

114. Raphael, *Study of the Virgin and Child.* Pen and brown ink over metalpoint on pink prepared paper. Verso of Fig. 113.

already discovered, and now recalled. A similar quality distinguishes the pen drawings on the lower portion of the Albertina sheet. These are not informed by that circular searching motion of the British Museum sketches; instead, the figures here are set down with contours relatively secure, with a more predetermined, fixed sense of form. Dependent as they are on preceding inventions, these separate groups do not manifest the same organic, or dialectic, relationship to one another.

This distinction, a function of the different stage in the development of pictorial idea, becomes especially evident on the reverse side of the Albertina sheet: a more deliberate elaboration of the central motif of the British Museum drawing (Fig. 114).[10] Constructed first in metalpoint and then partially reinforced in pen, it is now more recognizably a preparatory drawing for the painting it will become. Different graphic energies, less open and probing, are at work here, in drawings that are in

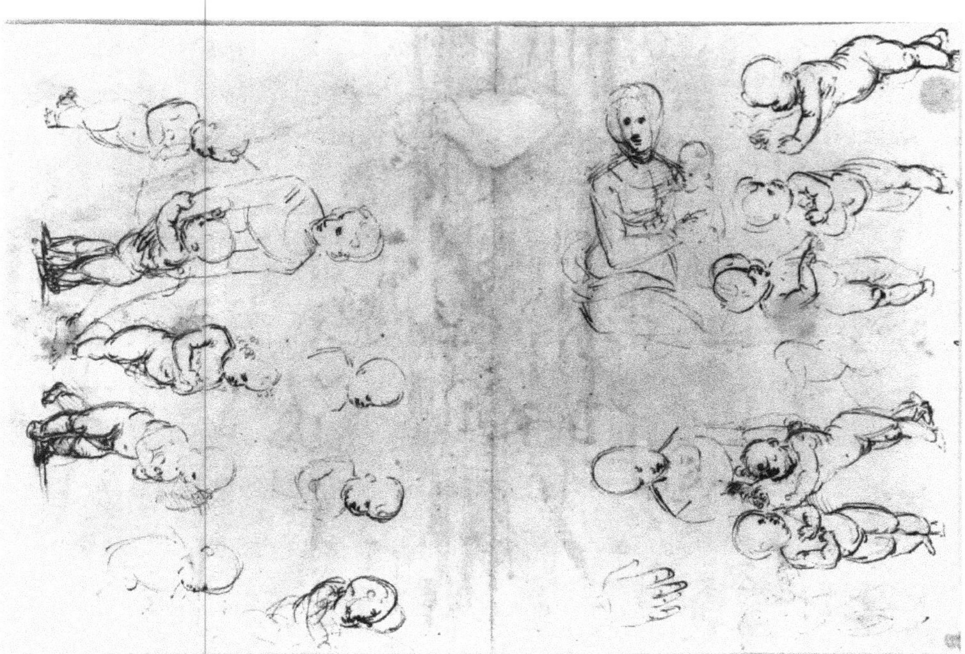

115. Raphael, *Studies for the Madonna of the Meadow*. Pen and brown ink over stylus, 36.2 × 24.5 cm. Graphische Sammlung Albertina, Vienna (IV, 207).

effect one step, or more, removed from the original moment of graphic inspiration – *dal furor dello artefice.*

Its organic quality is what distinguishes the British Museum sheet from Raphael's other Florentine studies of the same motif. His studies for the *Madonna of the Meadow* (Figs. 115–18), for example, do indeed explore variations on a basic theme, but the relationship among these several drawings is, we might say, essentially thematic rather than organically graphic.[11] That is, the variations grow out of an already developed notion of the dramatic narrative inherent in the encounter of the infants Jesus and John around the dominant figure of the Virgin. These deliberately studied variations of pose are premeditated rather than discovered in the act of drawing; each remains a quite discrete unit on the page – not unlike the motifs of an earlier generation's drawn pattern books. Indeed, as in many of Raphael's more elaborated drawings, the initial sketching here was done with a blind stylus, whose incised patterns were then edited by the pen selecting those lines to be preserved for still further development.

Even in these drawings of different function, however, we are aware of the dominance of the oval as the shape and shaper of Raphael's pictorial vision. Art-historically, we may recognize this as part of his own Umbrian heritage, part of the tradition into which he was born and which was reinforced by his close encounter with Perugino and then by his Florentine study of Fra Bartolommeo as well as Leonardo. Raphael's developed penmanship is, understandably, the product of forces both personal and cultural, natural instinct nurtured and refined within a larger matrix of values – aesthetic, intellectual, social.

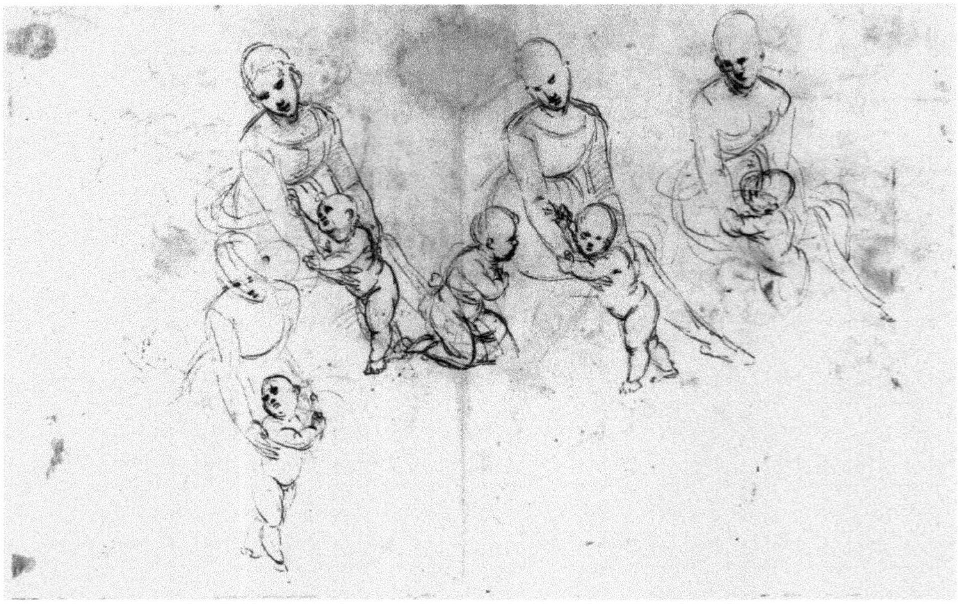

116. Raphael, *Studies for the Madonna of the Meadow.* Pen and brown ink over stylus. Verso of Fig. 115.

117. Raphael, *Studies for the Madonna of the Meadow.* Pen and brown ink, 25 × 19.4 cm. Devonshire Collection, Chatsworth (no. 783). Reproduced by permission of the Duke of Devonshire and the Chatsworth Settlement Trustees.

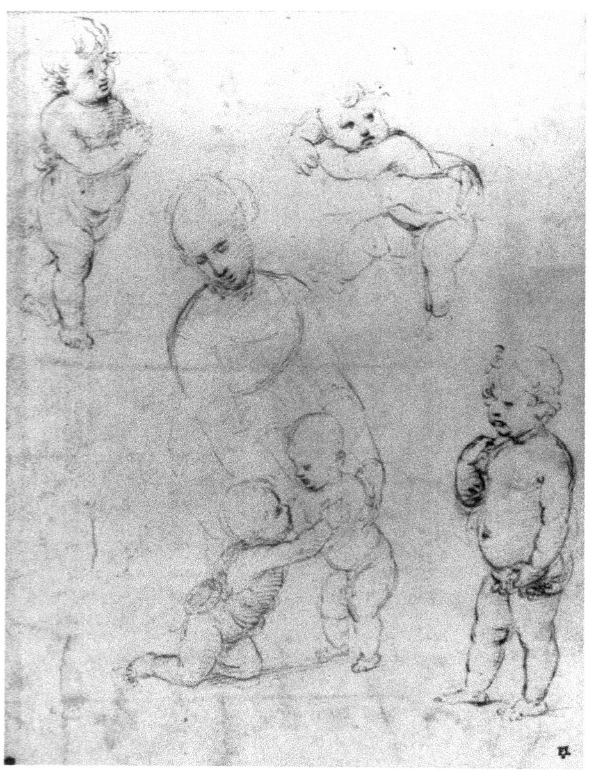

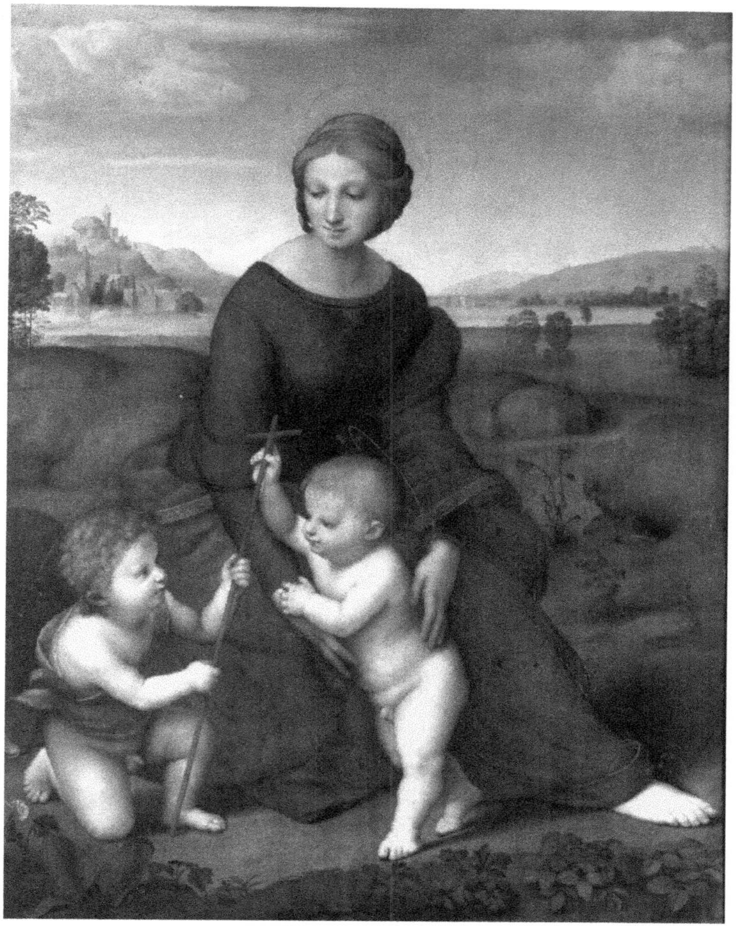

118. Raphael, *Madonna of the Meadow.* Oil on panel, 113 × 88 cm. Kunsthistorisches Museum, Vienna.

2. *Inflected Circles*

The ideality of the circle, with its single center and circumference with neither beginning nor end, had assumed a privileged position in the symbolic geometry of the religious imagination as the perfect representation of the divine. In theology's paradoxical transcendence of geometry, God was a sphere of which the center is everywhere and the circumference nowhere (Empedocles).[12] Adding Christian sanction to ancient pagan models, this reading of the form redirected Renaissance architectural thought to the circle as the ideal base for church planning.[13] In painting, too, it assumed a governing force in compositional thinking from the early Quattrocento, manifested with great early clarity in the work of Masaccio.[14]

For artists, the fundamental supporting text was, of course, Vitruvius, who brought the correspondence between the microcosm of man and the macrocosm of the universe to fine focus in the image of the ideally proportioned human body: adapting itself to both circle and square, the two basic geometric forms. Renaissance fascination with the Vitruvian formula found no more imaginative or beautiful expression than in Leonardo's famous drawing (Fig. 119), in which the artist's own fascination with the impossible challenge of squaring the circle is in effect resolved through the human body.[15] Indeed, it is precisely the body's relation to these fundamental forms that attests to the special nature of man: the quadripartite values of the square, traditionally corresponding to the structures of this sublunar universe (four elements, four temperaments, four seasons), manifest his humanity; the perfection of the circle declares his divinity. Actively reconciling these two systems, Leonardo's Vitruvian figure affirms the Christian duality of man: the impossible squaring of the circle, accomplished here through the human figure, becomes in effect a manifestation of the Incarnation.[16]

The values implicit in Leonardo's drawing find monumental pictorial expression in Raphael's *Disputa,* perhaps the most articulate and secure exposition of the doctrine of Transubstantiation in any medium, literary or pictorial (Fig. 120). Through the Incarnation God became Man, assuming bodily form and substance; in the consecrated host of the Eucharist that body remains perpetually present on earth. Raphael realizes this essential tenet of the faith through geometry: in the descent of golden circles – from the sphere of heaven, through the persons of the Trinity, down to the monstrance on the altar and the wafer within it – and in the shift from heavenly circle to earthly rectangle. In the heavenly sphere itself, governed by circular form, a further distinction is made: between the perfect circle viewed *in maestà,* undistorted discs of gold, and the form seen in perspective, foreshortened, subject to the laws of natural vision and rendered here in natural colors – the cloudbank of the host of biblical figures, early saints, and first martyrs of the Church. Nowhere in Renaissance painting does the circle more fully realize its symbolic meaning and expressive potential.[17]

Just this inflection of the circle, between the flat geometric perfection of its heavenly (Platonic) form and the distorted ellipse of its earthly appearance, returns us to Raphael's drawing and "la bellezza della figura circolare."[18] The form generated through the circling motion of the pen is rarely of circular perfection; as that motion responds to the conception of a figure, elongating its path along a dominant axis, it yields shapes that are rather oval or elliptical. In those shapes we recognize the ellipse of the foreshortened circle, the spatial extension of the ideal form into the real world, its tilting from the picture plane. We recall that for Alberti the rendering of the circle represented a test of freehand drawing. The circling momentum – or, better, intention – of the draftsman's hand passes beyond the plane; it is, from the start, a projection into space. Even as the pen outlines shape, it reaches beyond and behind its own delimiting line – in Parrhasian mode – over the horizon of contour. Circle and sphere, perfect geometric forms, belong to an ideal realm; the ellipse is the form of the natural world, in its approximating imperfection, and of pictorial mimesis. To the degree that it recalls its geometric origins as undistorted ideality, it serves to idealize the nature that it represents. This is essential, a graphic key, to Raphael's classicism, that measured balance in his art between the natural and the ideal. Larger cultural values confirmed and encouraged the innate course of his drawing.

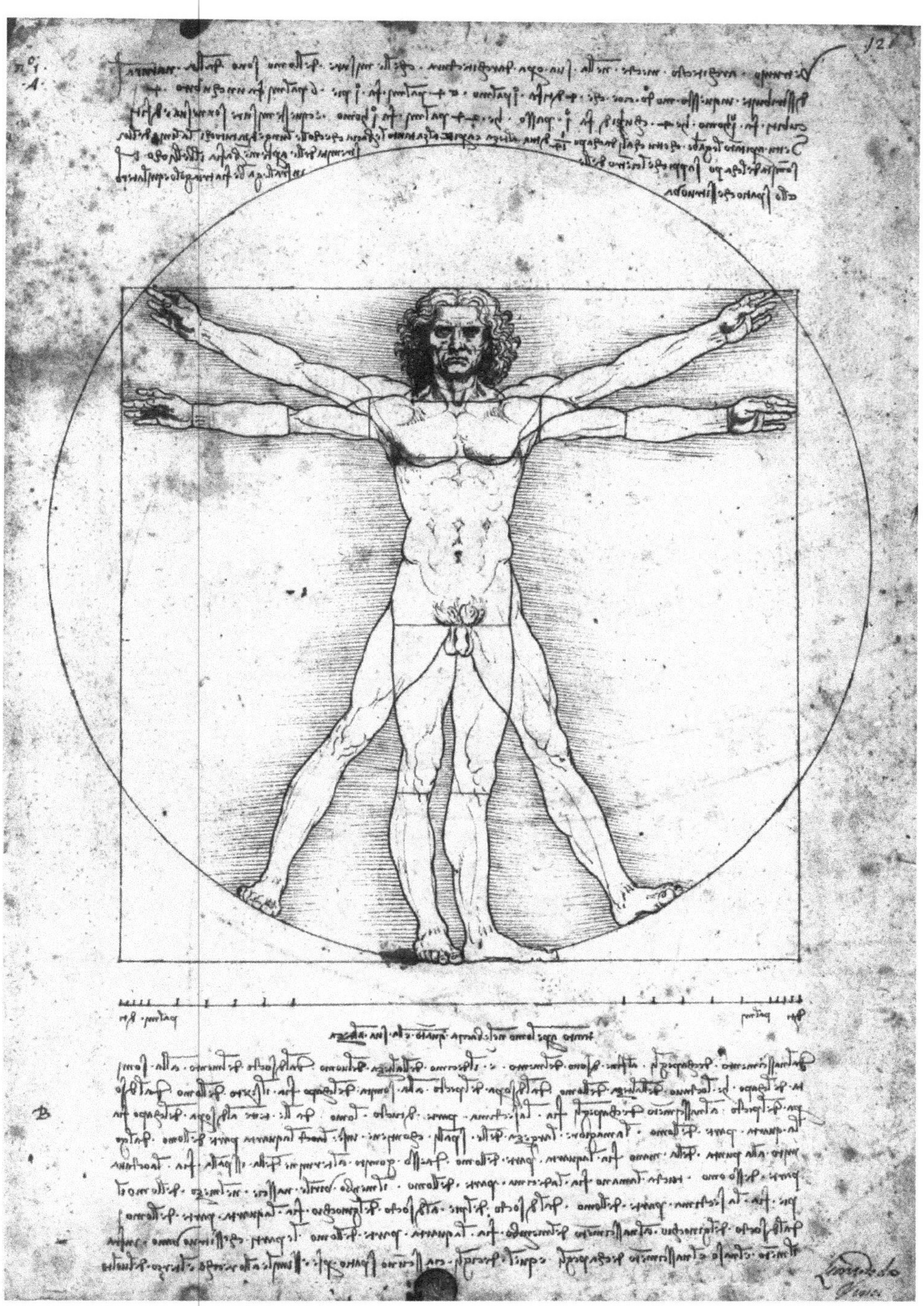

119. Leonardo da Vinci, *The Proportions of the Human Body according to Vitruvius.* Pen and brown ink, traces of brush and brown wash, over *spolvero* transfer, stylus and compass construction, 34.3 × 24.5 cm. Gallerie dell'Accademia, Venice (inv. 228).

3. *Linear Grammar/Linear Grace*

Between the flat surface of the paper and the curving line drawn on it lies the realm of mimetic possibility. In the dialectic tension between the two, where the single line implicitly breaks through the flatness and spatializes the surface, we find the fundamental dynamics of pictorial representation. Precisely in that dialectic Raphael seems deliberately to have proved his classicism. Subjecting linear structure to rigorous analysis, he developed a relatively systematic grammar for his graphic language – "a chastened flow of line," as Wölfflin so nicely phrased it on behalf of High Renaissance style.[19] Most draftsmen, of course, work out such systems naturally, as graphic instinct becomes routine habit in and through practice. Raphael's self-analysis, however, was encouraged under particular circumstances, near the beginning of his career in Rome.

It was then, around 1510, that he had to accommodate his own drawing style to the needs of engraving. Having decided to use Marcantonio Raimondi's burin as a means of broadcasting his own *invenzioni,* Raphael took special care in preparing the design of the *Massacre of the Innocents* (Fig. 121). Of the several related drawings that survive, one in particular is especially revealing of the artist's strategy (Fig. 122).[20] Fully modeled through systematically developed patterns of hatching, this pen drawing seems almost an approximation of the engraver's art. It is not, however, that Raphael has sought to preempt the engraver's task by exactly anticipating the burin's work. Rather, by assigning such full pictorial responsibility to linear pattern, he established a basic example for the engraver; the drawing offers instruction in graphic procedure. Those patterns themselves participate in two different systems of modeling: one, more optical, is composed of parallel diagonal lines that fall broadly and flatly over form; the other, more haptic, consists of parallel curves that hug the forms they model. The first recalls the systems of Quattrocento graphics – the engravings of Pollaiuolo or Mantegna, for example. The second, modeling stereometrically, develops from Raphael's own circling penmanship – which is in turn related to Leonardo's of his second Florentine period.[21]

From such drawings Marcantonio learned the lessons of graphic classicism, the regularity of linework that imposed a distinctive order on represented form, an order that derived less from the differences of natural objects depicted than from an a priori aesthetic. In Dürer's engravings, by contrast, linear system is so refined and particularized that it seems to coincide with the idiosyncracies of represented form and surface – without, however, compromising its own systemic integrity.[22] Unlike that influential model, the graphic language that Raphael taught to Marcantonio asserts its generality; its regularity claims a certain independence. Just as Raphael's figures in their reductive ideality of form – as well as in the generalizing truth of their nudity, physiognomic expression, and costume – aspire to a classicism above natural accident, his linear structures claim aesthetic value beyond any merely imitative function. Confirming the classicism of his style, the very regularity of Raphael's penmanship provided a basic grammar of linear expression for Marcantonio's burin.

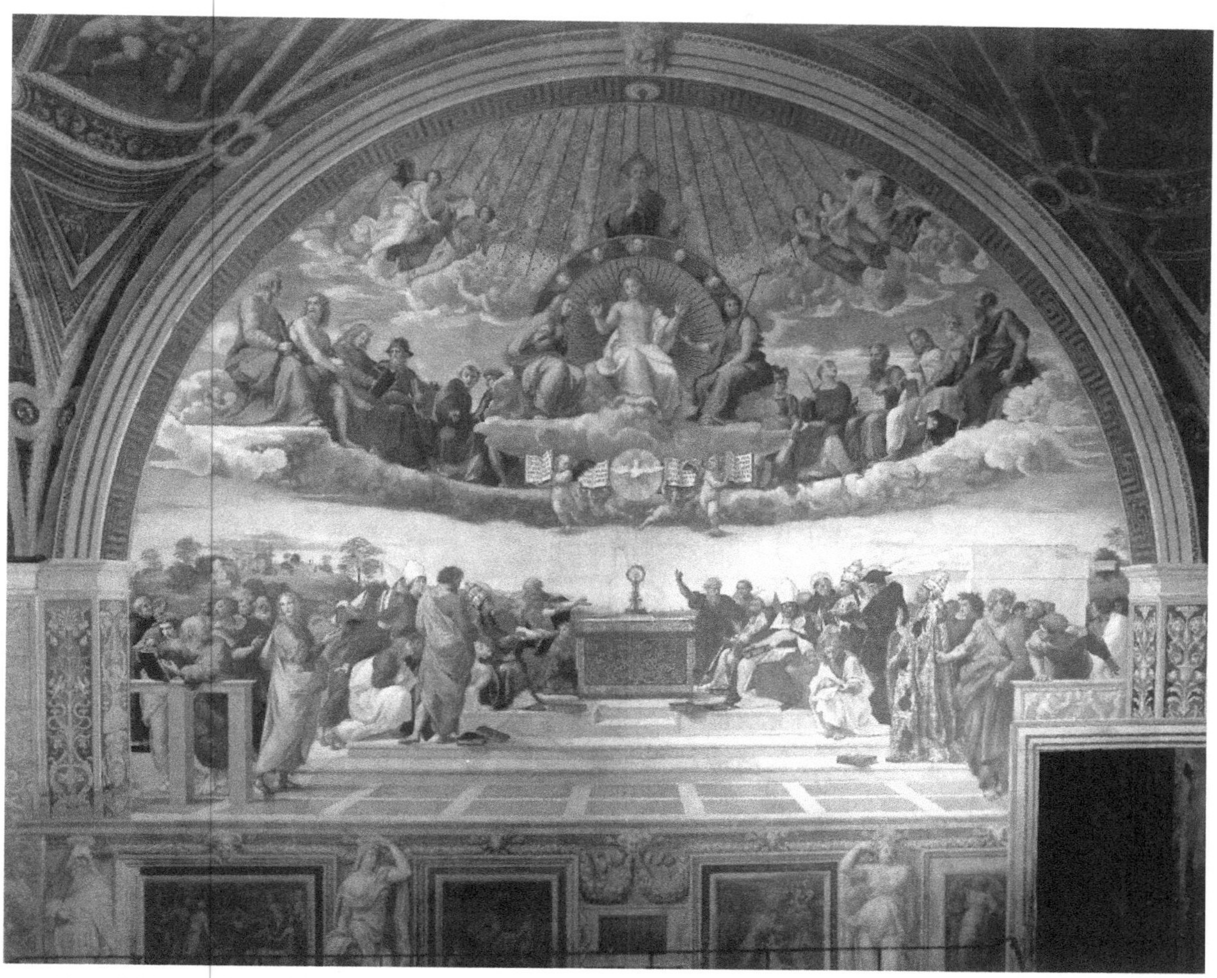

120. Raphael, *Disputa*. Stanza della Segnatura, Vatican Palace, Rome. Photograph: Musei Vaticani, Archivio Fotografico.

Before his association with Raphael, Marcantonio's engravings reveal a pictorialism based on the eclecticism of his studies – the simple linear patterns of niello prints attributed to his first master, Francesco Francia; the studied varieties of Dürer; the fine patterning of Lucas van Leyden. As a technique, engraving mandates a certain regularity, a repetition of motions of the burin building tone out of extremely fine line. On that technical foundation, however, Raphael taught Marcantonio's burin a particular respect for formal and pictorial surface. He effected the engraver's passage from the last vestiges of a Quattrocentesque *maniera secca*, with its sharp modeling, to a truly modern style; a longer and more flexible line created smoother and more subtle modulations of tone, yielding that "rilievo, dolcezza e grazia" that were the hallmarks of the new style. Upon the various patterns of the engraver's representational grammar, Raphael imposed a new and higher order. Such linear structures, while modeling individual forms, remained responsible as well to their own integrity; aware of their own visible role in establishing style, they obeyed the rules of their own system. Raphael harnessed the natural curving grace of the burin's *taille* to his own sense of classical form. In this regard,

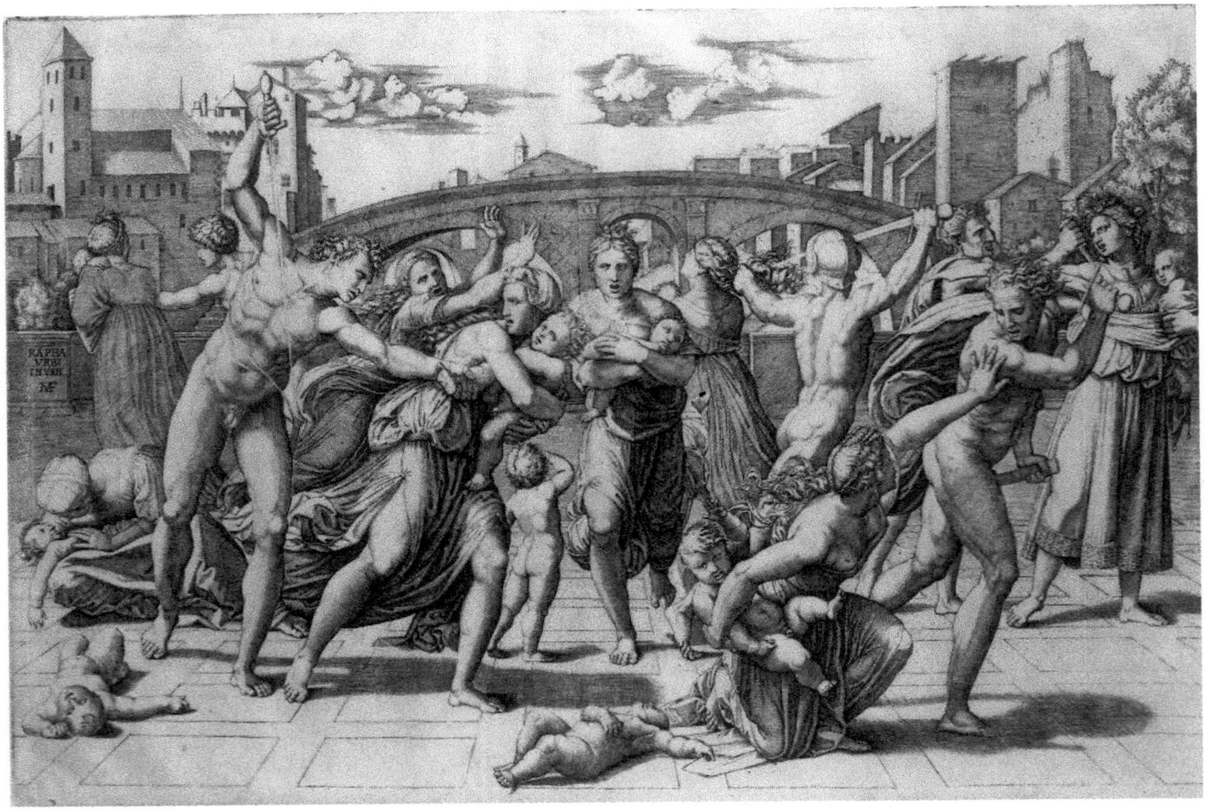

121. Marcantonio Raimondi, *Massacre of the Innocents*, after Raphael. Engraving (B.XIV,21–24,20), 28 × 42.5 cm. Metropolitan Museum, New York. Rogers Fund, 1922 (22.67.21).

another observation of Wölfflin's regarding "the new pictorial form" seems apt: "It now seems that a new sympathy has been aroused for the line in itself, as if it were now conceded that it has a right to live its own life."[23]

Until new technologies assumed responsibility for reproducing pictorial ideas, Marcantonio's engraving stood as exemplar, "the *ne plus ultra* of the profession," as George Cumberland could still claim in 1827, in *An Essay on the Utility of Collecting the Best Works of the Ancient Engravers of the Italian School.* Cumberland's appreciation of Marcantonio's "careful labours" recognized precisely their fidelity to both the formal idea and the technical realization of Raphael:

> for no one since his time has so well adapted the stroke of the graver, or line of the Print to forms; no one has better understood depth, character, or correctness of outline (that absolutely necessary qualification), in which so many have been deficient; insomuch that it is difficult not to believe that Raffael himself sometimes directed the graver, and that to his refined taste and judgment we owe a great many of the superior excellencies with which these Prints abound.[24]

Three centuries after Raphael's enterprise observers still knew how to read in Marcantonio's engravings the *disegno* as well as the *invenzione* of the master himself.

Creating models for Marcantonio, we may assume, made Raphael all the more

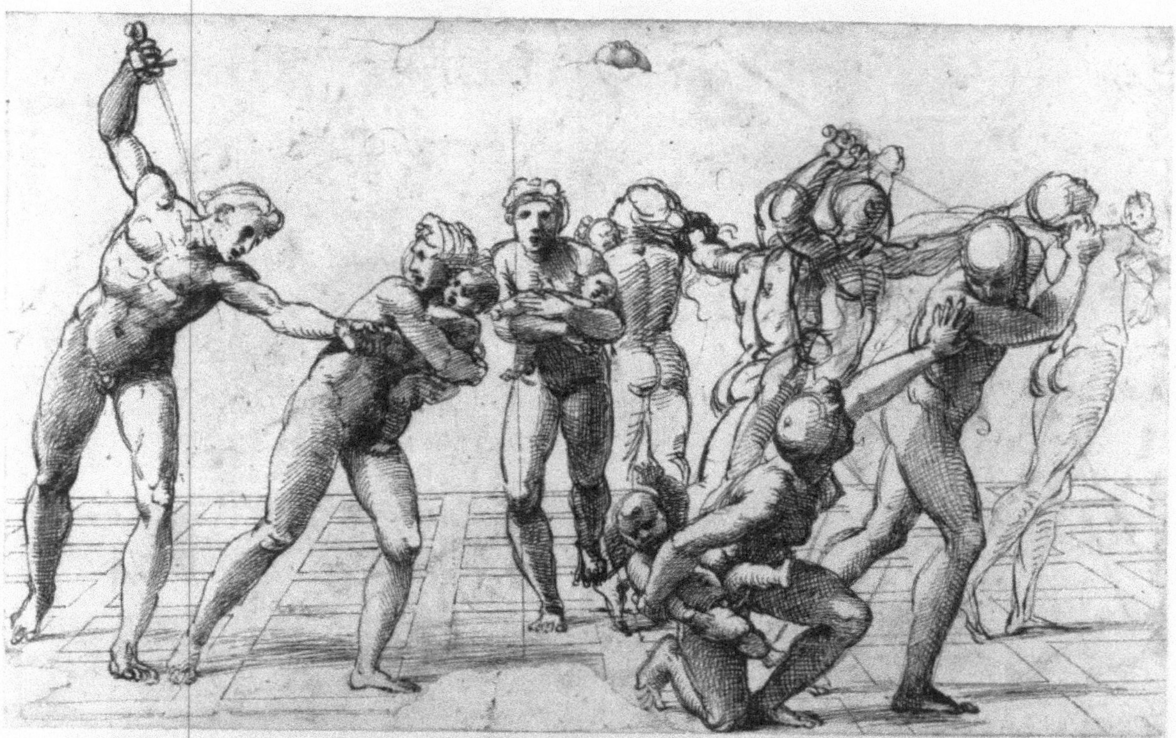

122. Raphael, *Study for the Massacre of the Innocents*. Pen and brown ink, red chalk, pricked for transfer, 23.2 × 37.7 cm. British Museum, London (1860-4-14-446).

conscious of the responsibilities and possibilities of line. The contrapposto of his *Lucretia* embodies the values prized in his art (Fig. 123). Her slow serpentine turn around her own firm axis balances movement and stasis; filling the field, the simultaneous frontal address of her body to the picture plane (and the viewer) passes with almost unnoticed ease into the near profile of her turned head; an equilibrium is maintained between natural imitation and high artifice.[25] Epitomizing the classicism of Raphael's art, these are qualities that inform the basic constituent of that art, his line. For Raphael's line, even at its most decorative, is fully plastic. Informing the very conception of his figures (Fig. 124),[26] it generates a space around itself, transcending the flat surface of the paper without, however, violating the integrity of that surface.

Disegno, to quote Lodovico Dolce once again, "is the form given by the painter to the things he is imitating; and it is really a turning movement of lines in various ways, which give form to the figures."[27] That identity of drawing and form, of line and figure, commonplace though it be, reflects a profound reality of drawing as representation. Implicit in Dolce's observation are values that had already been recorded, we recall, by Pliny in praise of Parrhasios: an outline that expresses the contours of the figure is the true test of an artist, a contour that seems to pass behind and so enclose the object, "thus clearly suggesting what it conceals." In drawing an object an artist will quite naturally tend to inflect his outlines toward

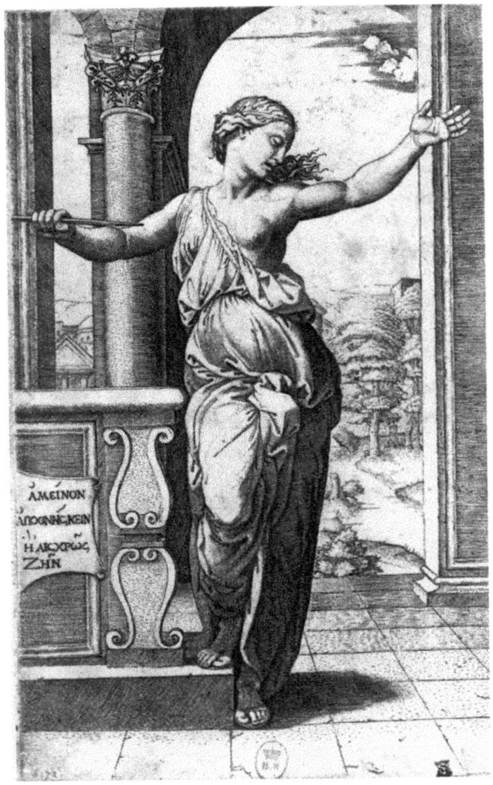

123. Marcantonio Raimondi, *Lucretia,* after Raphael. Engraving (B.XIV,155, 192), 21.7 × 13.3 cm. Bibliothèque Nationale de France, Paris.

such spatial suggestiveness, as the very act of drawing as representation involves the imaginative exploration of mind and hand together. Leonardo, as we have seen, was particularly aware of the complex spatial dimensions of a line, as must any practicing artist be as he projects an object onto and beyond the flat surface on which he draws. Even if the ultimate practical goal is the single fixed contour of the cartoon (Vasari's "buon disegno di linee girate [che] circondano la figura"), the tracing and retracing of an outline represents more than a search for that purely graphic boundary. Rather, the repeated motions of the draftsman involve a tactile exploration, a feeling beyond the horizon line of form to the other, unseen side. Each stroke of the pen or chalk represents a new contact, each variation a slightly different point of view – or angle of approach and (imagined) touch.

In a drawing by Raphael, the flow of lines and the flow of form identify with particular ease (Fig. 125).[28] Fluency of figural action depends as much on the mellifluous movement of the draftsman's hand as on the actual poses struck by the imagined bodies, on a concinnity between the two. Bundled contours of red chalk here maintain an openness of boundary that enables them to transcend the flatness of the paper and spatially encircle the forms they contain. Patterns of internal modeling, following the notional surfaces they define, transfer their own linear energies to those surfaces. Or, where the patterns are more regimented systems of long parallel hatching, they may announce themselves as tonal impositions on form, shadows cast across a surface, affirming a reality of atmospheric spatial extension. The slow sinuosity of Raphael's line, its unforced course, matches that same qual-

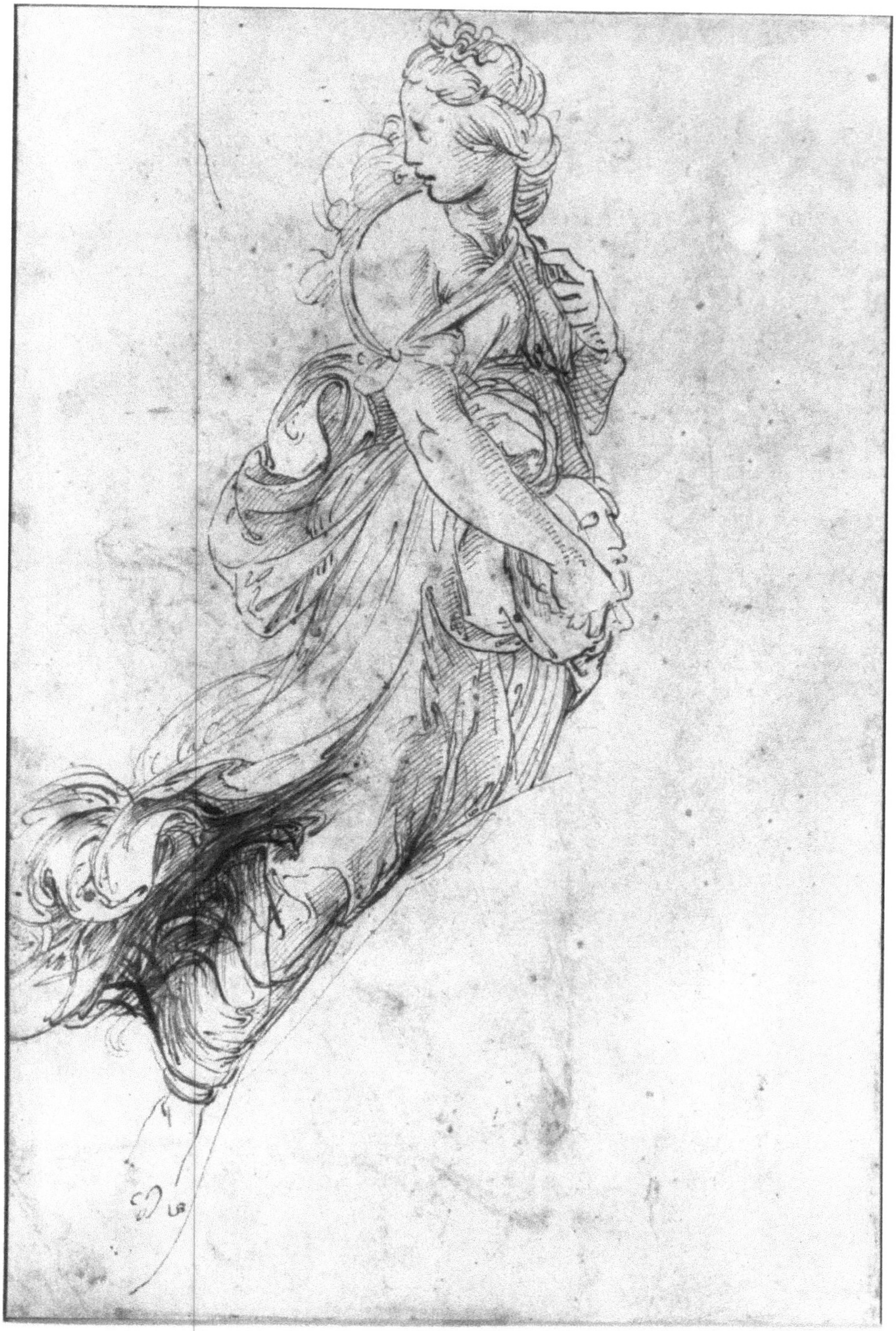

124. Raphael, *Study for the Figure of Melpomene.* Pen and brown ink over traces of black chalk, 33 × 21.9 cm. Ashmolean Museum, Oxford (P.II, 541).

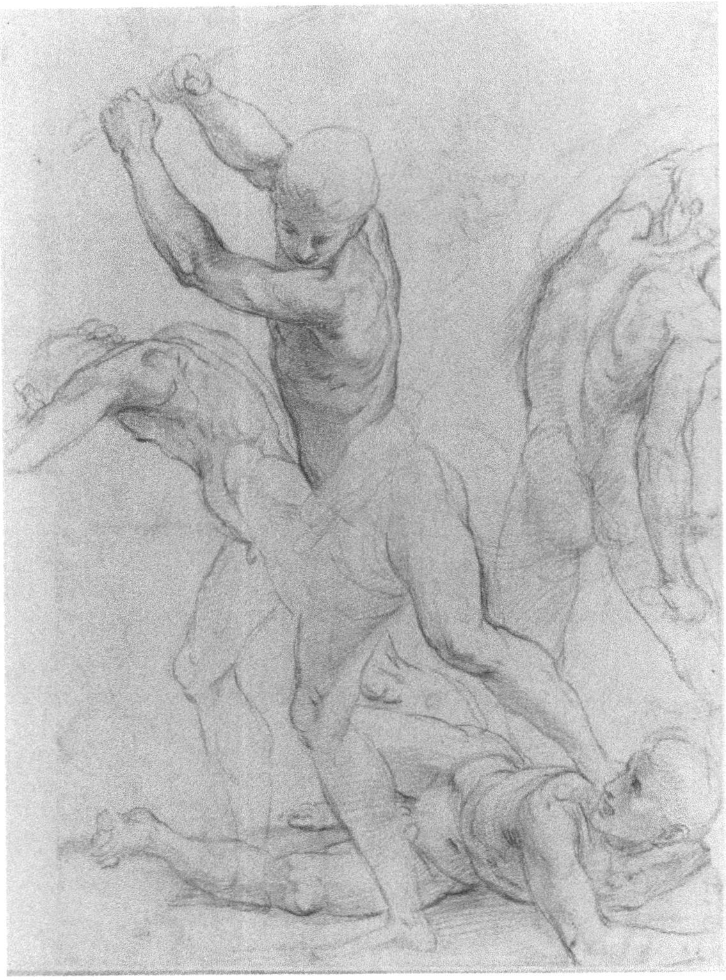

125. Raphael, *Combat of Nude Men*. Red chalk over stylus, 37.9 × 28.1 cm. Ashmolean Museum, Oxford (P.II, 552).

ity in his figural conception, the easy strain of athletic grace: calligraphy and choreography in mutally expressive operation. This quiet but persuasive fulfillment of mimetic function by line epitomizes that *grazia* recognized as the special virtue of Raphael's art and person, a grace of comportment, manifesting itself in the movements of the artist and his creations. Like Apelles, Raphael possessed that "grace, called *charis* in Greek," and his figures, like those of the ancient master, manifested that same rare quality of charm *(venustà)*, which is so hard to define.[29] The easy transference of the term between artist and art, identifying one with the other, assumed the relationship that was to form a basic principle of connoisseurship.

Perhaps no drawing of Raphael's more profoundly embodies the grace of figural line that underlies his very sense of form than the study for the personification of Poetry on the vault of the Stanza della Segnatura (Fig. 126).[30] With exquisite subtlety she turns about her own vertical axis in quiet serpentine flow, an organic contrapposto delicately balancing shifts of weight, axis, and body address. Raphael first drew this figure with a blind stylus, incising her form into the paper in freely swung curves that testify to his sense of her fullness. As in his pen sketches of Madonna and Child (Fig. 110), only now on a larger scale, the circling motion that guides the draftsman's initial search lays the essential formal foundation – the oval here assuming a particularly sensual function in defining the distended abdominal core of the torso. Over that sensuously schematic armature of the stylus drawing, Raphael then developed the figure in black chalk, adding material substance to flesh out pictorially the initial skeletal design.

The final squaring for enlargement registers the ultimate purpose of the drawing, as a step in the preparation of a larger decorative project. Transferred to the roundel of the vaulted ceiling of the Stanza della Segnatura, the figure adapts itself to its monumental architectural setting (Fig. 127); the sensuous flow of her contrapposto is straightened, her posture made more tectonic and formal, her address to the plane more direct. In addition, however, that squaring affirms a basic reality of the drawing: it is the projection of a figure on a flat plane. Pretending to no representational illusion – indeed, explicitly denying it – such coordinates declare the surface of the paper itself. And it is precisely against that measured reality that we ultimately gauge the figure's slow serpentine movement, her controlled turning from the frontal plane and displacement of notional space.

Leonardo had quite determinedly investigated the nature of the serpentine line, recognizing its generating energies, and he had already realized its principles in figural pose, postulating an aesthetic that was to provide a foundation for figural style through the sixteenth century. Breaking from the stable coordinates of the frontal plane, the *figura serpentinata* manifests, on a larger scale, those very qualities of spatialization that were to be sought in the effective contour – the line of Parrhasios. Revealing several aspects of itself in the helical course of its contrapposto, such a figure, depicted on a flat surface, cannot but evoke the *paragone* between painting and sculpture. In this respect, the *figura serpentinata* becomes aesthetically charged, a polemical demonstration of pictorial art.[31]

Within a dramatic context, such a figure is poised to assume a narrative complexity as well, as in the chorus of mothers in the *Expulsion of Heliodorus*. Raphael's drawings for two members of this chorus, while exploring the narrative dimensions of the serpentine pose, offer still clearer demonstration of that spatial quality of contour that enables such dramatic conception (Figs. 128, 129).[32] In the more exerted of these poses (Fig. 128), the extreme torsion of the figure recalls its origins in a circling motion of the imagining hand. Her companion on the verso of the same sheet (Fig. 129), less radically tensed, offers as the essential graphic epitome of her conception the graceful contour of her turning neck. Studied again to the right as an isolated problem, that line summarizes the entire formal issue. As her neck is the pivot of dramatic action here, the critical moment of turn back into space, so its outline carries the full responsibility of spatialization – folding back, enclosing the object, and "clearly suggesting what it conceals." The isolation of such a motif is very much a draftsman's choice.

In the graceful movement of the drawn line, its slightest inflection suggesting a turn into space, is to be found the germ of Raphael's larger figural notion. Again,

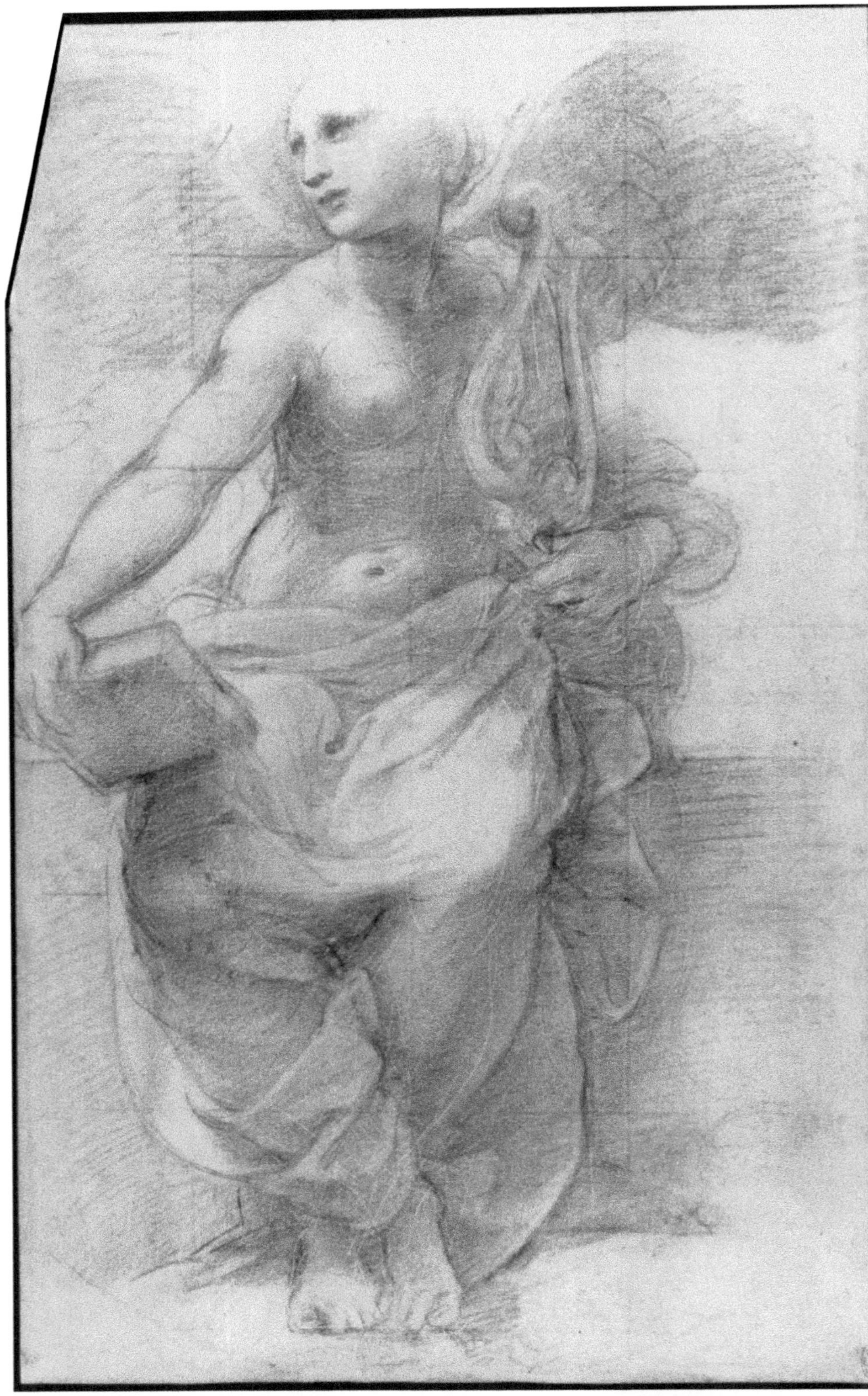

126. Raphael, *Personification of Poetry.* Black chalk over stylus, squared in black chalk, 35.8 × 22.7 cm. Royal Library, Windsor Castle (no. 12734). The Royal Collection ©2000, Her Majesty Queen Elizabeth II.

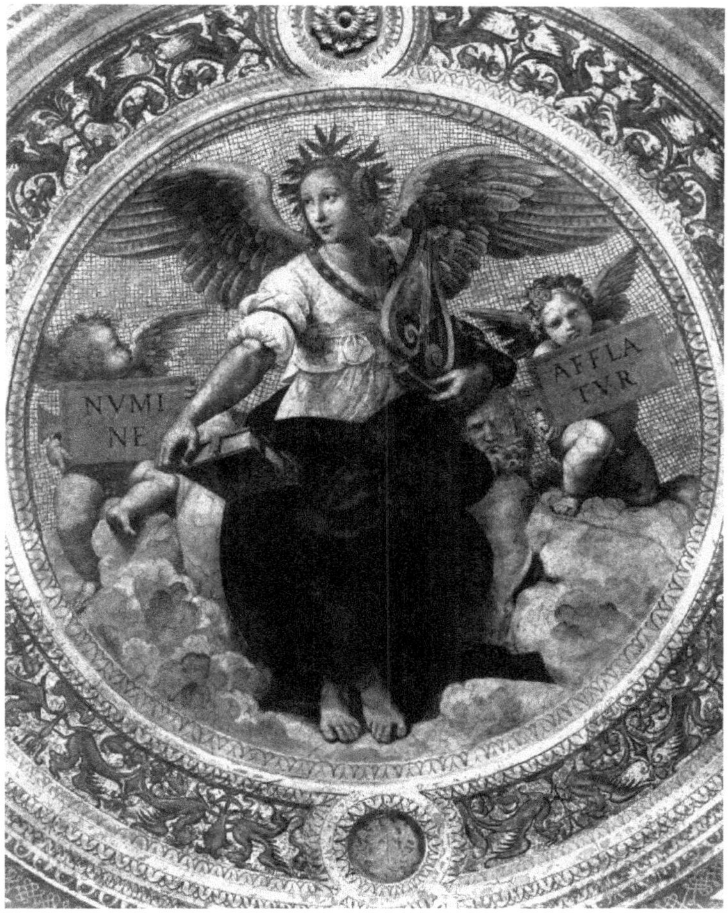

127. Raphael, *Personfication of Poetry.* Stanza della Segnatura, Vatican Palace, Rome. Photograph: Alinari.

the movement of the draftsman's hand informs that of his projected figure. From such concinnity of execution and expression, of the body imitating and the body imitated, arises the naturalness of Raphael's figures, their ease of motion, their celebrated grace. When such a union of movements was later discerned in Parmigianino, he was declared a Raphael *redivivus.* The spirit of the one was said to have passed into the body of the other, for that youth combined rare artistic talent with personal courtesy and grace, as had Raphael.[33] In the drawings of Parmigianino, as in those of Raphael, grace of line is reciprocally shared by the drawn mark and the figure drawn, each endowing the other with its own traits (Figs. 124, 130).[34] In "la leggiadria penna," as Guido Reni referred to Parmigianino, sensuousness of line, its swelling rhythm and caressing imitation, most explicitly declares the sensuality of delineated form.[35] Even more deliberately than his namesake, the new Raphael explored the expressive character of contour as well as the spatial implications of its serpentine potential. The profile of the face offered the ideal exercise for testing the variability of contour (Fig. 131). In this, as in his exploitation of the sketch as an arena of invention, Parmigianino was extending the example of Leonardo.[36] Indeed, the sequence of parallel profiles seems an entirely natural practice for the

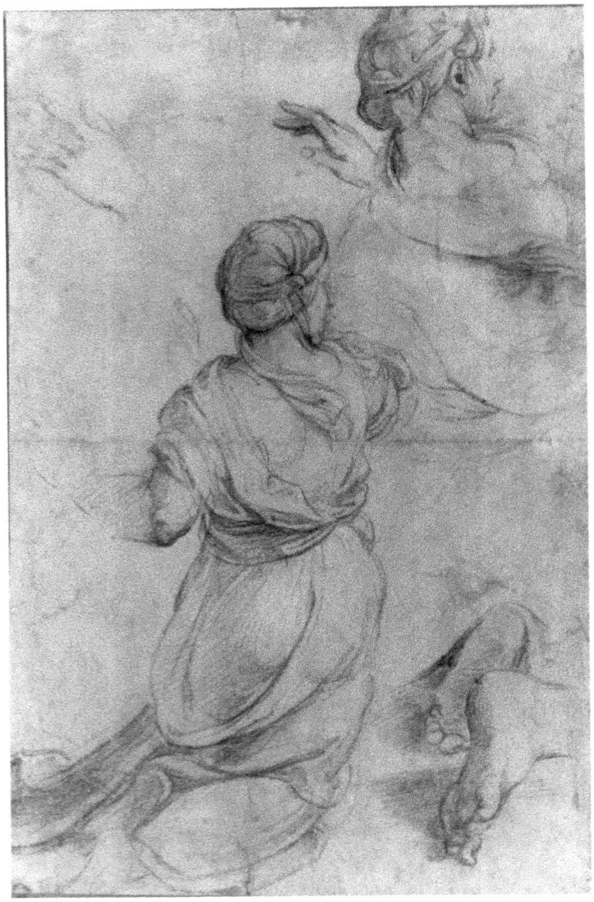

128. Raphael, *Studies for the Expulsion of Heliodorus from the Temple*. Black chalk, 39.5 × 25.8 cm. Ashmolean Museum, Oxford (P.II, 557).

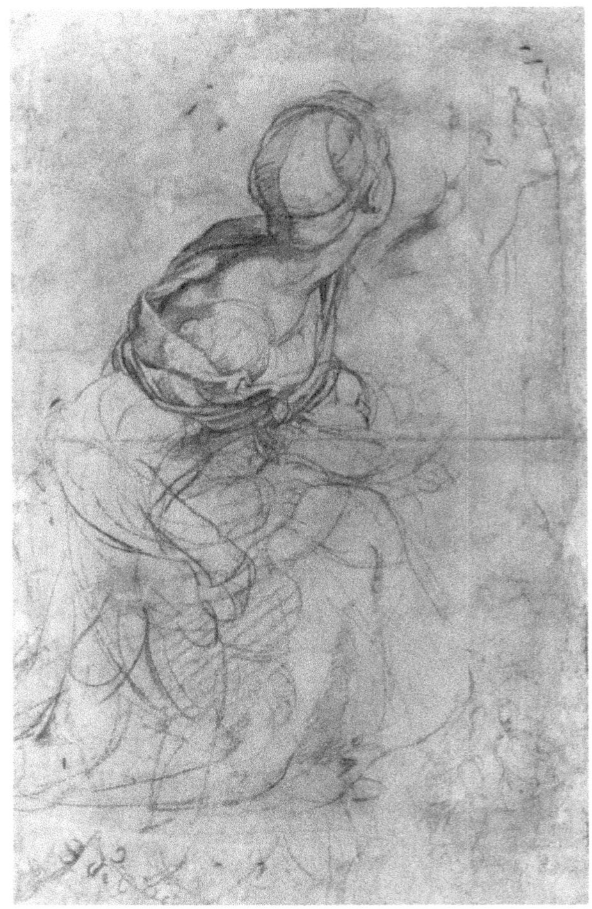

129. Raphael, *Studies for the Expulsion of Heliodorus from the Temple*. Black chalk. Verso of Fig. 128.

130. Parmigianino, *Study for the Madonna dal Collo Lungo.* Pen and brown ink on pink-tinted paper, 8.5 × 6.6 cm. British Museum, London (1905-11-10-62).

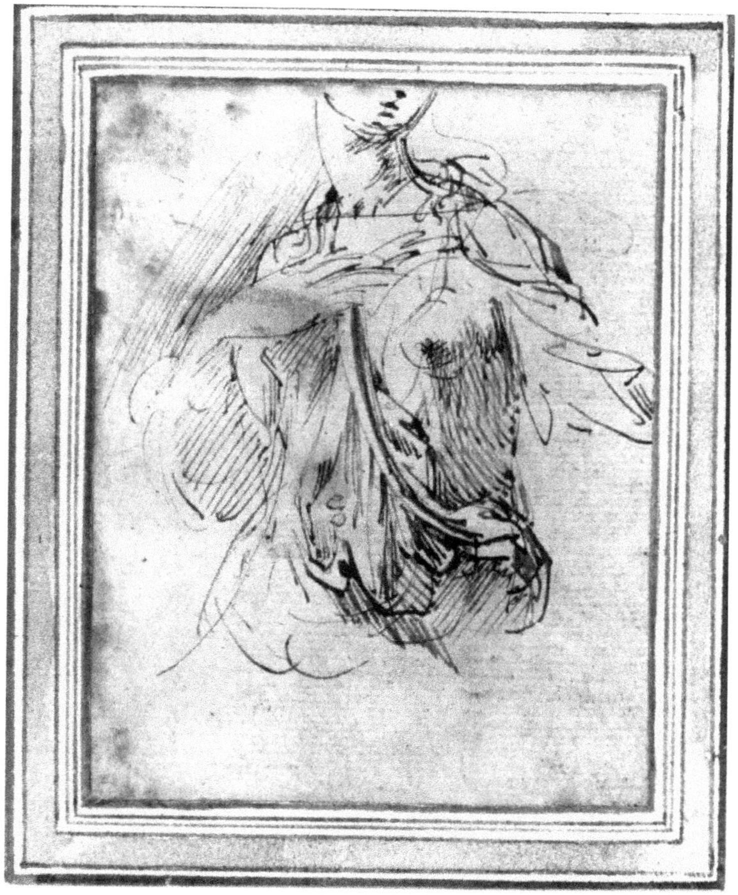

131. Parmigianino, *Four Female Heads in Profile.* Pen and black ink, 8.8 × 10.5 cm. Royal Library, Windsor Castle (no. 0526). The Royal Collection ©2000, Her Majesty Queen Elizabeth II.

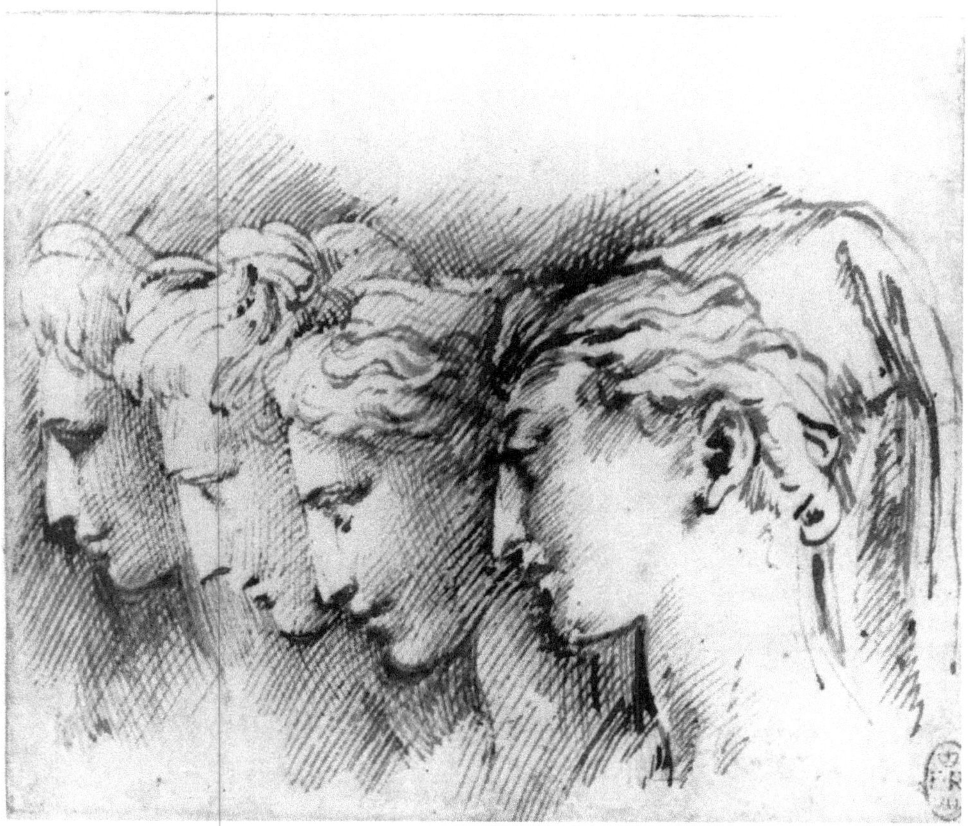

draftsman, offering the occasion for bringing to focus the meandering hand (Fig. 132), and the fundamental pedagogic function of this structure became codified in later printed drawing manuals (Figs. 133).[37]

4. *Connoisseurship of the Line*

Raphael's ability to turn a line – to find the balance between contour and form, surface pattern and spatial volume – was recognized as central to his achievement. Paolo Giovio singled out just that quality in his praise of the artist, who succeeded so well "in drawing contours and the boundaries between areas of color, and in softening and toning down the excessive harshness of colors."[38] Modulation of form and color, the smooth transition that avoids abruptness – the "rilievo, dolcezza e grazia ne' colori" that Vasari cited as criteria of the modern style[39] – these qualities begin with *disegno,* with line. Raphael's "maniera leggiadra e gentile" (Dolce) resulted from the apparent effortlessness of his drawing, the harmonious dialectic of defining line and form defined; the easy turn of his serpentine figures was a natural consequence of his turning line. The line of Parrhasios continued in the Renaissance to be the sign of singular talent.

Defending Raphael's *facilità* against the *difficultà* and *terribilità* of Michelangelo, critics like Dolce celebrated the pure artifice of his art; they argued the difficulty of such facility. Raphael's was the art that hides art. "E' arte a nasconder l'arte": Dolce's aesthetic declaration was directly inspired by the social aesthetics of Baldesar Castiglione's *Cortegiano* (1528), the locus classicus of High Renaissance notions of style and comportment – itself inspired by the model of the visual arts – and the authoritative text for the following generations. And it was Dolce who most purposefully applied Castiglione's resonant neologism, *sprezzatura,* to the art of painting, calling for the avoidance of too much diligence in execution and for a certain appropriate casualness ("una certa convenevole sprezzatura").[40] The discourse is fully Castiglione's, developed from his argument on behalf of grace and against affectation:

> But, having thought many times already about how this grace is acquired (leaving aside those who have it from the stars), I have found quite a universal rule which in this matter seems to me valid above all others, and in all human affairs whether in word or deed: and that is to avoid affectation in every way possible as though it were some very rough and dangerous reef; and (to pronounce a new word perhaps) to practice in all things a certain *sprezzatura* [nonchalance], so as to conceal all art and make whatever is done or said appear to be without effort and almost without any thought about it. And I believe much grace comes of this: because everyone knows the difficulty of things that are rare and well done; wherefore facility in such things causes the greatest wonder; whereas, on the other hand, to labor and, as we say, drag forth by the hair

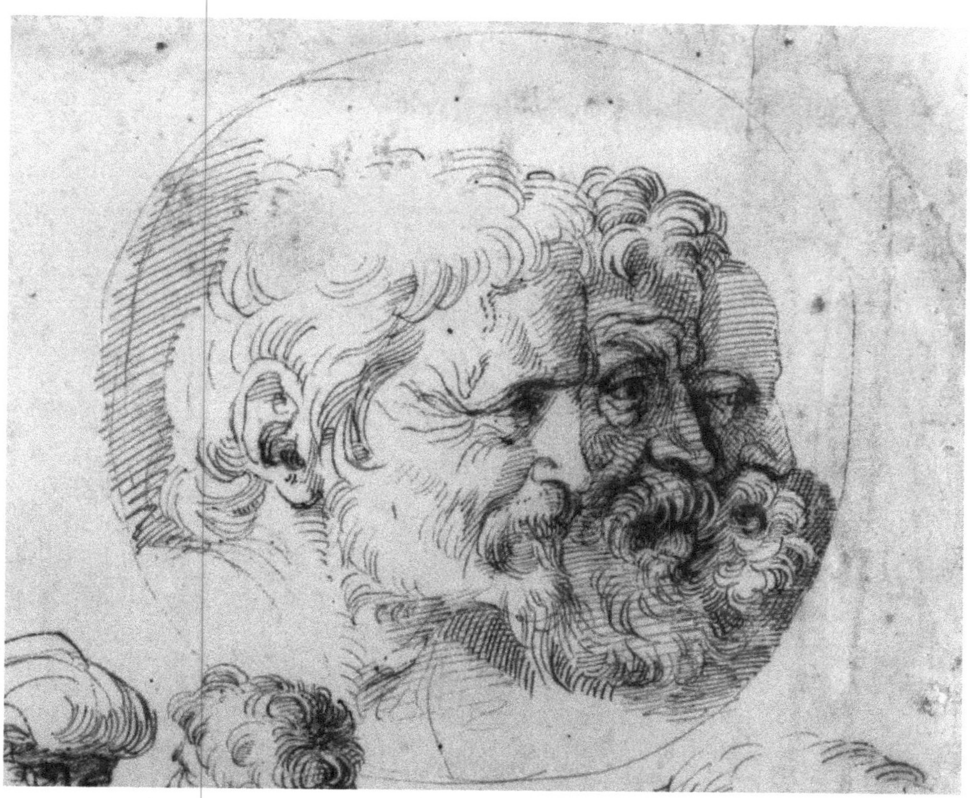

132. Agostino Carracci, *Group of Figures, Studies of Animals and Heads in Profile*. Pen and brown ink, 40.5 × 30.6 cm (detail). J. Paul Getty Museum, Los Angeles (86.GA.726).

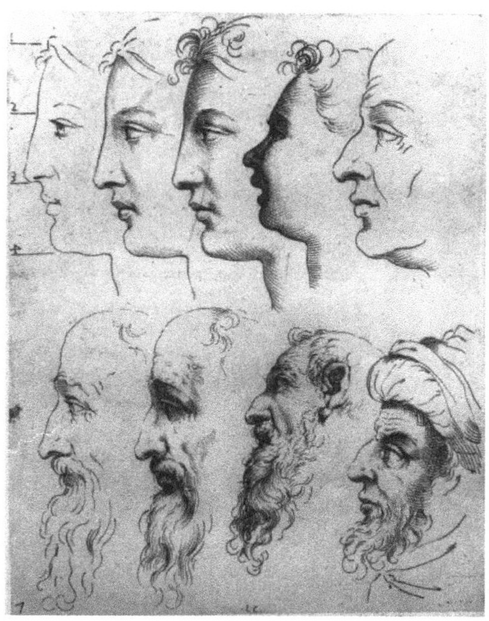

133. Luca Ciamberlano, after Agostino Carracci, *Heads in Profile* from *Scuola perfetta per imparare a disegnare. . . .* Engraving (B.XX,18,160,11), 17.4 × 12 cm. British Museum, London. Photograph Collection, Department of Art History and Archaeology, Columbia University.

> of the head, shows an extreme want of grace, and causes everything, no matter how great it may be, to be held in little account.[41]

Apparent effortlessness, ease and facility, the masking of application: this is true art, which is at once the source and manifestation of grace. In the movements of the body it manifests itself as "quella sprezzata desinvoltura," that easy nonchalance of the naturally graceful body.[42] With its theological as well as social resonance, grace (*grazia*) was the term above all others applied to Raphael, to his person as well as to his art. *Sprezzatura,* the true source from which grace springs ("il vero fonte donde deriva la grazia"), is what distinguished ancient Apelles from Protogenes, who was guilty of overdiligence, not knowing when to take his hand from the panel.[43] Castiglione's invocation of the ancient Greek painters brings the argument directly into the studio:

> Often too in painting, a single line which is not labored [*una linea sola non stentata*], a single brush stroke made with ease [*un sol colpo di pennello tirato facilmente*] and in such a manner that the hand seems of itself to complete the line desired by the painter, without being directed by care or skill of any kind, clearly reveals that excellence of craftsmanship, which people will then proceed to judge, each by his own lights.[44]

Appreciating the natural movement of the line, Castiglione here assumes that basic tenet of connoisseurship: by his line shall the artist be known. And that notion invariably found early sanction in the legendary competition between Apelles and Protogenes, the contest of lines.

The Renaissance variant on that Plinian topos was the story of the "O" of Giotto, which returns us to the circle. Giotto's celebrated demonstration of his mastery, apocryphal though it may be, epitomizes the aesthetic and social values of the culture that perpetuated the story. When asked to submit a sample of his work for papal consideration, Giotto took up a brush and drew a circle, telling the puzzled emissary to take that to his holiness. The artist chose a circle to represent himself. His freehand rendering was indeed a display of virtuosity, and Vasari is careful to describe the mechanics of this performance – how Giotto transformed himself into a compass by steadying his arm against his body and, with his wrist as pivot, moving only his hand, turned a perfect circle: "Eccovi il disegno."[45] Generating that most perfect geometric form from his imperfect body, the artist shows himself to operate in a Platonic realm; mimesis is here the imitation not of nature but rather of the higher universal idea. All the values of the circle are implicated in Giotto's demonstration. His ability to create such pure form represents the ultimate claim to the most audacious of Renaissance epithets for the artist, vaunted by both Alberti and Leonardo: *alter deus.*[46]

The scenes of incomprehension, protest, and final appreciation that make up the narrative of the Giotto story – proving the obtuseness of the pope's man (who thought the artist was joking) and, by contrast, the aesthetic infallibility of papal judgment (recognizing the rarity of the talent demonstrated) – are socially revealing. The master painter tests the connoisseur. In Giotto's divinely controlled line could be seen all the virtue of his art – by those who could see.[47] As Francisco de Hollanda, returning to the classical source and ostensibly quoting Michelangelo himself, neatly summarized the situation: "in a mere straight line Apelles was known by Protogenes."[48] The line is recognized as the natural expression of the artist, an extension of his very person, and the means by which the viewer gets to know him. In this most elementary expressive sign the artist reveals himself by demonstrating his art. Pliny's tale of the Apelles–Protogenes competition, we recall, was cast in the most professional terms, of both technical virtuosity and sensitive connoisseurship. The story is recounted, yet again, by Paolo Pino to exemplify the necessity of the painter being possessed of a swift but steady hand, which can only be a natural gift ("La prontezza e sicurtà di mano è grazia concessa dalla natura").[49] From such grace flows a naturally graceful line, the virtue of which, its facility, will be apparent to "the eyes of those who understand."

Those who understand had been practicing their judgment on painting and painters throughout the Renaissance, seeking the words with which to characterize and appreciate individual style. A vocabulary generally reapplied from ancient rhetorical tradition enabled humanists to become art critics, as in Cristoforo Landino's distinguishing celebration of the Quattrocento painters of Florence, set out in the preface to his commentary on the *Divine Comedy* (1481).[50] That apparent precision of language served as the basis for a broader cultural participation, as discriminating knowledge of art and artists became de rigueur for the gentleman, and lady, of the Renaissance. In a culture that increasingly expressed itself in the serious intellectual banter of the dialogue, critical judgment necessarily required recognition of the relativity of perfection. "Consider," invites Count Ludovico da Canossa in Castiglione's *Cortegiano*, "that in painting Leonardo da Vinci, Mantegna, Raphael, Michelangelo, and Giorgio da Castelfranco are most excellent; and yet they are all unlike one another in their work: so that in his own manner no one of them appears to lack anything, since we recognize each to be perfect in his own style."[51]

That sense of the relativity of style guided Vasari in the creation of his *Libro de' disegni*, the most reasoned and ambitious collection of drawings assembled in the Renaissance. As he explains in the course of his *Lives*, it was his intention to have representative works by as many of his subjects as possible: the history of art through the history of drawing.[52]

5. *Penmanship*

In the brief epilogue to the second edition of his *Lives*, Vasari addresses his fellow artists ("L'autore agli artefici del disegno"). Paying quick tribute to those predecessors whose writings had served him – Ghiberti, Ghirlandaio, Raphael – he explains that he has always measured such written sources against the works of art themselves. Only through long practice, he continues, can one come to know the various styles ("le varie maniere") of different artists. To support what will become a truism of connoisseurship he draws an analogy to handwriting: One comes to recognize individual pictorial style just as a practiced secretary gets to know the different penmanship of his professional colleagues and as everyone recognizes the letters of their closest friends and relatives.[53] Vasari's explicit recognition of handwriting as an individual trait similar to the individual character of an artist's style participates in a long comparative tradition – from Pliny to de Piles and beyond.[54]

More particularly, writing was comparable to drawing, an association prompted, in part, by technical consideration: both were practiced with the same instrument, the pen. But the comparison was extended further, and quite logically, in acknowledgment of the similarity between the two manual acts. Even as they denied *disegno* a position among the liberal arts, fifteenth-century humanists were forced to deal with its claims, which boasted antique pedigree.[55] And the virtues of fine penmanship, praised – and often practiced – by the humanists, were inevitably appropriated on behalf of the art of drawing.

Alberti had already invoked writing as a model for teaching the principles of drawing: from letters to syllables to words.[56] Leonardo, too, invoked the analogy in his pedagogic admonition to proceed step by step.[57] Later in the sixteenth century it was argued by Giovanni Battista Armenini that not only should the young aspiring artist be trained in letters, that is, be literate, but that early training in writing would serve well as a foundation for drawing:

> . . . for those who are accustomed to write with a fine hand are considered to have made a certain good beginning in drawing. The better they write, the greater promise they show in drawing. . . . The skill which children, through continual practice, acquire in handling the pen well and in forming good letters will make the imitation of drawings easier since one learns to write in part through the imitation of another's letters.[58]

Parmigianino, according to Vasari, demonstrated his natural inclination toward drawing when he was first being taught to write: having pen in hand he immediately began to make marvelous drawings.[59]

Erasmus himself, in a dialogue on handwriting, understandably reversed the analogy, recommending that drawing should be taught as a way of loosening the hand and making it appreciative of linear shaping:

> Boys should be so taught this subject that they feel they are playing, not studying. For some masters teach writing with such severity that the pupils learn to hate letters before they can make them. It will, therefore, be useful to give them occasional training in drawing. Many are attracted spontaneously to this art because they delight to express what

> they recognise and to recognise what others have expressed. Just as trained musicians have a superior enunciation even when they are not singing, so a man whose fingers are trained to draw lines of every shape will construct letters with greater ease and facility.[60]

However casual, the humanist's acknowledgment of the play element in the handling of the pen and of the foundational role of linear exercise reflects a post-Leonardo appreciation of the art of drawing.

The elementary procedures for learning to write through the imitation of good models are essentially mechanical and belong to a venerable workshop context. Indeed, even as artists began preparing for publication those pedagogic pattern books intended to teach aspiring draftsmen to construct the human figure from its parts, Renaissance writing masters were publishing such primers for their own art.[61] Perhaps the most celebrated of these penmen was the apostolic secretary Ludovico degli Arrighi, called Vicentino. His relation to Raphael, though apparently tangential, is interesting. In a well-known letter of 15 August 1514 the artist wrote to thank Marco Fabio Calvo for sending the manuscript of his Italian translation of Vitruvius. Raphael was looking forward to designing a frontispiece for it and filling in the figures for which space was provided. The manuscript had been delivered to him by the calligrapher himself, Ludovico Vicentino, for whose work Raphael expresses his admiration: "schritto de bellissima lectera."[62]

The *bellissima lettera* for which Arrighi was justly famous was his cursive, or chancery, hand. More rapid and flowing, less formal and ceremonial than Gothic, more graceful and elegant than *lettere mercantesche,* this script had developed in an epistolary context, for letters written *brevi manu.* Arrighi set out to teach "il modo & regola de scrivere littera corsiva over cancellarescha" to a larger audience through a little book published in Rome in 1522: *La Operina di Ludovico Vicentino da imparare di scrivere littera cancellaresca* (Fig. 134, 135). The following year he published *Il modo de temperare le penne,* which taught the beginner how to cut the quill, to "tune the instrument" of his art (Fig. 136, 137).[63] Arrighi's pen, like that of the High Renaissance draftsman, follows the impulse of its own linear momentum, within intuitive rules of balance that respect the field of available space.

His lessons in forming cursive letters begin with the basic strokes of the pen, one flat and thick ("piano et grosso"), the other slanting and thin ("acuto et sottile"). From such elements, he proceeds to the formation of letters. He describes which of them begin with the thick stroke, which with the thin; which are written in a single stroke, which require two, and how to vary the stroke in forming complex curves. He discusses the proper height of letters, their just spacing and ideal slant. Within the established rules, however, Arrighi's lessons are as relatively free and flowing as the cursive script itself. Thus, if *p* and *t* are allowed to rise above their equals it is simply because it looks better that way to him: "a l'occhio mio assai piu

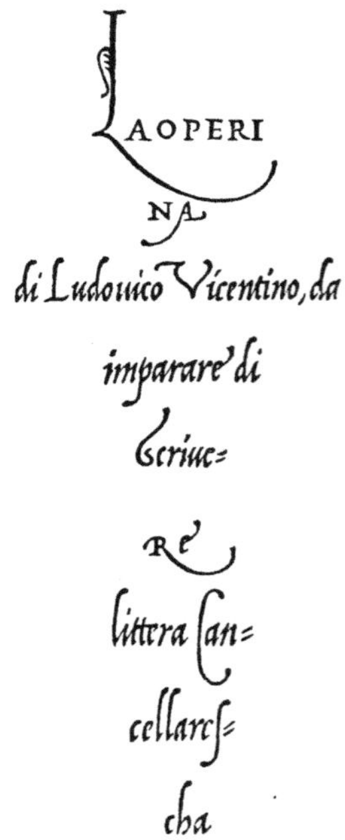

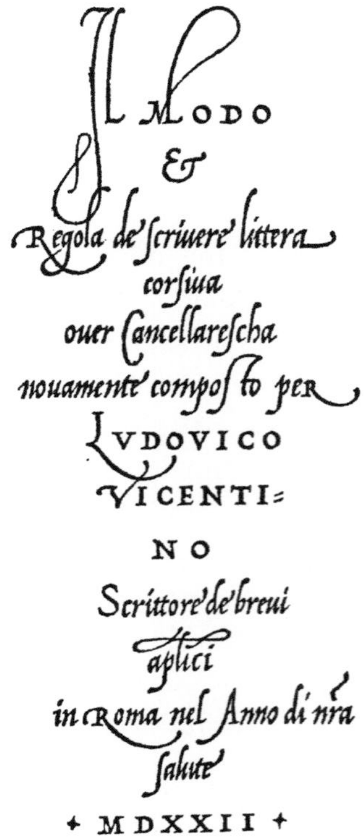

A

134. *(above)* Ludovico degli Arrighi, *La Operina di Ludovico Vicentino da imparare di scrivere littera cancellaresca* (Rome, 1522).

135. *(above right)* Ludovico degli Arrighi, *Il modo & regola de scrivere littera corsiva over cancellarescha nuovamente composto per Ludovico Vicentino.*

136. *(right)* Ludovico degli Arrighi, *Il modo de temperare le penne* (Rome, 1523): *Il coltellino per temperare le penne. . . .*

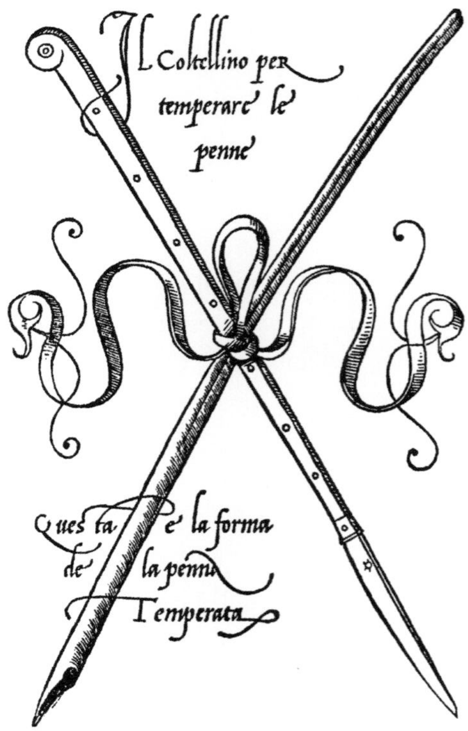

satisface."[64] In the matter of spacing, the superiority of judgment to rule is even more explicitly affirmed:

> Make sure that from line to line the distance of anything you write in chancery letters is neither too wide nor too narrow, but in between, and the distance from word to word equal to the width of an *n:* From letter to letter within the ligature, there should be as much white as within the legs of the *n.* But because it is almost impossible to follow this rule, try to check with your eye, and to satisfy it, which will serve you as an excellent compass.[65]

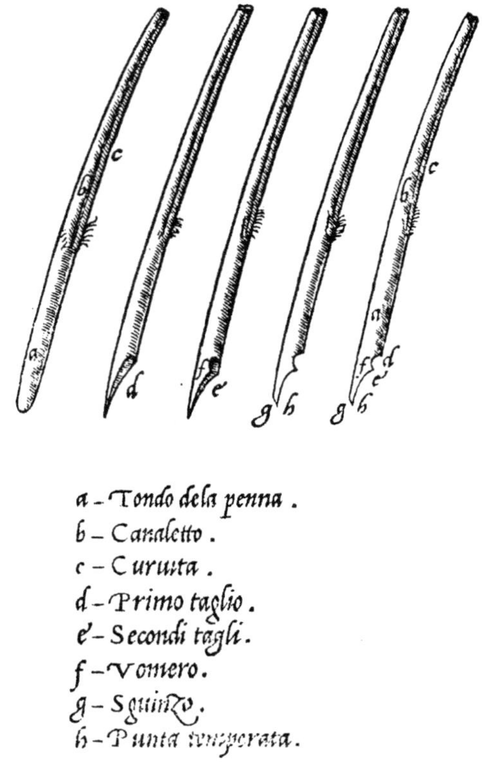

137. Pens, from Ludovico degli Arrighi, *Il modo de temperare le penne.*

The judgment of the eye: we recognize a central theme in the aesthetics of the later Renaissance, most famously expressed in Michelangelo's declaration, reported by Vasari, that the artist should have the compass in his eyes, not in his hand. The point is made initially in regard to Michelangelo's figural proportions, his creation of figures of nine, ten, twelve, or even thirteen heads, guided by a sense of grace not to be found in nature. Transposing the discourse, quite legitimately, from human figure to architectural column, Michelangelo is said to have relied more on grace than on measure.[66] This is the license that, in the *proemio* to the third part of his *Lives,* Vasari postulated as essential to the modern style: that certain freedom from rule that is nonetheless obedient to rule, that judgment of the eye that, not subject to precise measurement, informs figures with a grace beyond measure ("una grazia che eccedesse la misura").[67]

The oval form, so naturally produced by the circling motion of the draftsman's hand, extends and rebalances the perfect measure of geometry toward a more organic grace. Such transformative adjustment of the ideal absolute to the reality of human movement is essential to fine calligraphy. Indeed, Arrighi offers *in nuce* the clearest critical analysis of High Renaissance grace in graphic production, addressing directly the geometry of letters and its necessary manual transcendence. The fine cursive hand shapes its letters in an oblong parallelogram and not in a perfect square ("quadretto oblungo et non quadro perfetto"), "because to my eye the cursive or chancery lettter ought to partake of the long and not of the round" (Fig. 138).[68] Within the pedagogic intent of his project, Arrighi thus brings to focus precisely the operations we observe in the pictorial calligraphy of Raphael (Fig. 110), operations subsequently even more marked in the penmanship of Parmigianino (Fig. 130). In the draftsman's oblong canted forms, geometry is extended beyond the stasis of its Platonic perfection. And the motion of that extension, the motion of the pen, sets form into motion, vivifies form. Effectively spatializing basic Euclidean form, the pen takes it toward that grace beyond measure.

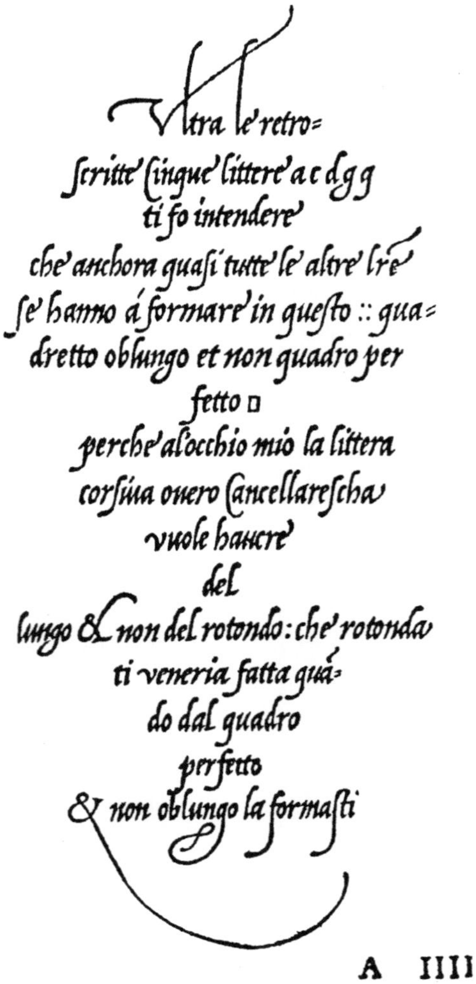
Vltra le retro=
scritte cinque littere a c d g q
ti fo intendere
che anchora quasi tutte le altre l're
se hanno á formare in questo :: qua=
dretto oblungo et non quadro per
fetto ▭
perche al occhio mio la littera
corsiua ouero cancellarescha
vuole hauere
del
lungo & non del rotondo: che rotonda
ti veneria fatta quá=
do dal quadro
perfetto
& non oblungo la formasti

A IIII

138. Ludovico degli Arrighi, *La Operina di Ludovico Vicentino,* fol. A IIII.

Castiglione's enunciation of a Renaissance aesthetic continues to resonate, with special application, in the literature on the visual arts. It seems perfectly appropriate that one of its earliest expressions should relate to *l'arte della penna,* for in the single unforced line was to be found the highest value of that aesthetic, the natural grace embodied first and foremost in Raphael.

CHAPTER FIVE

Disegni a stampa
The Printed Line

. . . in which technique those most gifted in *disegno* have a more ample field in which to display their talent.

– Giorgio Vasari[1]

Printing is the technology that defines the civilization of early modern Europe; it is a Renaissance invention. Movable type and the resulting possibilities of the diffusion of knowledge transformed the intellectual and cultural world, and, almost immediately, the new technology implicated the creation and distribution of visual knowledge as well. First through the older medium of the woodcut and then through engraving, the printed image redefined standards of visual literacy throughout Europe.[2] Constructed entirely of clearly defined linear patterns, prints in effect trained the eye in the discernment of

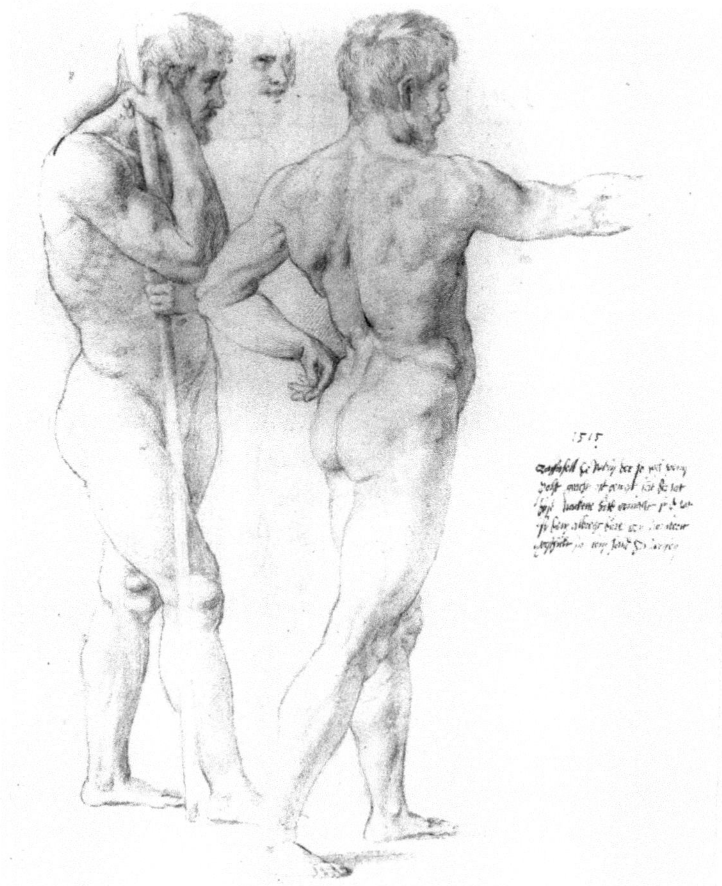

139. Raphael, *Figure Studies for the Battle of Ostia.* Red chalk over stylus, 40.3 × 28.1 cm. Graphische Sammlung Albertina, Vienna (V, 17575).

If the philology here requires modification – "disegno a mano" is, after all, a rather precise Italian equivalent to "Handzeichnung" – Panofsky's reading of the situation does emphasize the broader implications of such terms. Dürer, he reminds us, placed just such a synecdochic value on the hand as representative of the artist and his art. On the drawing that Raphael had sent him as a gift in 1515 (Fig. 139) he added his famous inscription after the artist's death: "Raphael of Urbino, who was so highly esteemed by the Pope, has made these nudes and has sent them to Nuremberg, to Albrecht Dürer, in order to show him his hand."

On the assumption that the drawing Raphael sent was a studio production, attributable to Giulio Romano, Panofsky may have tended to exaggerate the distinction between German and Italian values:

> For Raphael it was a matter of course to present his German colleague with the best available specimen of a *style* for which he felt responsible, no matter whether the manual execution was his or a pupil's. Dürer, on the contrary, took it for granted that an Italian master, whom he respected and loved, could only have wanted to "show him his *hand*" – the hand of an individual chosen by God.

Although the drawing in question has generally been restored to Raphael, Panofsky's point retains a certain validity, if we read *style* as *invention*, which, as in Marcantonio's engravings after Raphael, is not necessarily bound to medium or to manual execution.[8]

We have already seen how Raphael's invention of the *Massacre of the Innocents*, developed through a series of *disegni a mano* (Fig. 122), was translated into Marcantonio Raimondi's *disegno a stampa* (Fig. 121). Although the distinction between design and execution is explicitly acknowledged in the signatures on this engraving, the issue remains inherently problematic in the printmaking of the earlier, pioneering generation of Italian artists of the late Quattrocento. Even Pollaiuolo's proud declaration of responsibility for his *Battle of Nude Men* ("OPVS ANTONII POLLAIOLI FLORENTINI") may offer no absolute guarantee that the engraving itself is indeed *di propria mano* (Fig. 39). We are only sure of having before us the master's invention. And the total absence of signature on the engravings associated with Mantegna has caused scholars to wonder whether or not that master ever actually handled the burin himself – although those engravings most compellingly attributable to him reveal an exceptionally original and inventive use of the burin, at times handled with the flexibility of a pen: the mark of an amateur engraver, perhaps, but one of genius (Figs. 36–38).[9]

The difference from German contemporaries could not be stronger in this regard, even if in many cases we know only the initials of the master. Dürer, whose own monogram became itself a significant contribution to European visual culture, never failed to document his graphic production, drawings as well as prints, with signature and date (Figs. 40, 41). His engravings, on which he invested so much time and energy, represent the surest conjunction of inventive and executive skill, of *ingegno* and *arte*.[10]

It is not at all unlikely that Pollaiuolo, like so many Florentines trained in the goldsmith's craft, did indeed engrave his own plate of the *Battle of Nude Men*. Vasari declares as much, although his commentary is concerned primarily with the larger scope and function of the print: a demonstration of Pollaiuolo's mastery of anatomy, a model of both *invenzione* and *disegno* intended especially to serve fellow *artefici*.[11] Although we still lack a full picture of the early public for prints, we do know that artists themselves, on all levels, were among the earliest and most assiduous collectors of these *disegni a stampa*. Widely distributed, prints assumed the role of the older modelbook or collection of *simili* and *exempla*. Marcantonio published several series of small and sometimes technically unambitious engravings of apostles and saints specifically, according to Vasari, for the use of those poor painters who were weak in *disegno* and who could use such models as cribs.[12] But Vasari also makes it quite clear that the appeal of prints went beyond a purely professional audience to include amateurs who took particular delight in such graphic imagery.[13]

The relationship between the two media of graphic representation, drawing and printmaking, was an intimate one. Initially duplicating drawings, prints in turn became models for drawing; the technically necessary clarity of their linear structures offered an ideal primer for the beginning draftsman. In 1494, Dürer, still young but hardly a novice, acquired lessons in Italian classicism by copying engravings by Mantegna (Figs. 40, 41). Although impressive for its original and subtly inflected burin work, especially in contours, Mantegna's engraving style participates in that general late Quattrocento graphic manner built upon a systematic screen of diagonal hatching. In his art, however, that manner is carried to new levels of commitment and consistency, achieving remarkable richness of pictorial effect. As similar units of parallel lines model form, cast shadow, or create ambient space, the surface continuities they establish transcend mimetic function. The planar insistence and material consistency resulting from such regularity evoke a sculptural relief aesthetic, an important allusion in Mantegna's classicism, in drawing as well as engraving. As later in the quite different engraving aesthetic of the Raphaelesque Marcantonio, regularity of linear structure assumes a key role in the definition of style.

Although he followed the basic contours of Mantegna's engraving, Dürer brought to the rest of his study – that is, the modeling and shading – his own personal graphic dialect: an unclassical *Handzeichnung,* we might say. In its particularizing quality, in the small-scale concentration of its modeling stroke, its loops and hooks, its refusal to subject the natural but irregular curve of the drawing gesture to the discipline of the straight line – in all this, his mode of drawing was indeed unclassical. Although more than a difference in media is involved, in this contrast between German and Italian sensibilities, the comparison does remind us of the technical and material dimensions of style. Dürer's searching pen stroke, in its flexible response to the intricacies of form, seems to go well beyond the metal-bound capabilities of the engraver's burin. It is Dürer himself, of course, who will eventually teach the burin new lessons in responsive organic description.

Aside from their demonstration of classical *inventio,* Mantegna's engravings reaffirmed for the young German a critical lesson in contour – ultimately, a lesson extending the line of Parrhasios. Internal hatching is not brought all the way to the contour, leaving a border of light within the bounded form (Fig. 140); this softening of the edge allows the modeled planes to break the surface tension of the flat paper and begin their turn into space. Developing this technique of opening and thereby spatializing contour, Dürer made it very much his own in all graphic media, in pen drawing (Fig. 141) as well as engraving and woodcut (Fig. 142). Through his own prints, in turn, the lesson was then reintroduced to Italy, as artists in the sixteenth century looked to the German master for lessons in graphic representation (Figs. 143–45).[14]

In elevating the ambitions and capabilities of the burin, Dürer developed a complex and subtle vocabulary of graphic terms suitable to the representation of the

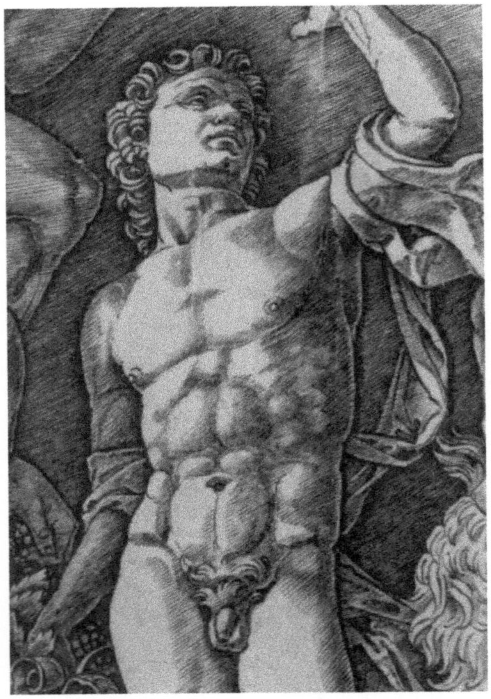

140. Andrea Mantegna, *Bacchanal with a Wine Vat.* Engraving, detail of Fig. 36.

glories of a visionary realm as well as the fullness of the visible world: systems of curves and parallels, of cross-hatching at varied angles, of different lengths of line, of dashes, flecks, and stippled dots – and, as important, the most creative use of untouched white paper. Articulating techniques and demonstrating strategies of linear representation, his prints became basic texts in the graphic education of artists throughout Europe.[15] In Benvenuto Cellini's *Discorso sopra l'arte del disegno,* typically, discussion of pen drawing culminates with the invocation of Dürer. Drawing with the pen – creating shadow through dense cross-hatching and light by tracing fewer lines, leaving the white paper itself for highlights – is the most difficult kind of drawing, and few are the draftsmen who have mastered the technique.

> And this kind of drawing inspired engraving with the burin on copperplate, so that today one sees so many prints in circulaton; among these the best executed ever seen, that is the best engraved, are those of Albrecht Dürer of Germany.[16]

Pen drawing, with its reliance on linear patterns and hatching, was invariably compared to engraving, but the slow deliberateness of the engraver's art, its necessary patience and diligence, could hardly satisfy a drawing aesthetic that so appreciated *prontezza di mano.* The first mode of drawing for Giovanni Battista Armenini is drawing with the "pen on white paper, hatching only where the shadows are seen, similar to those designs made on copper plates."[17] But, even though he recommends

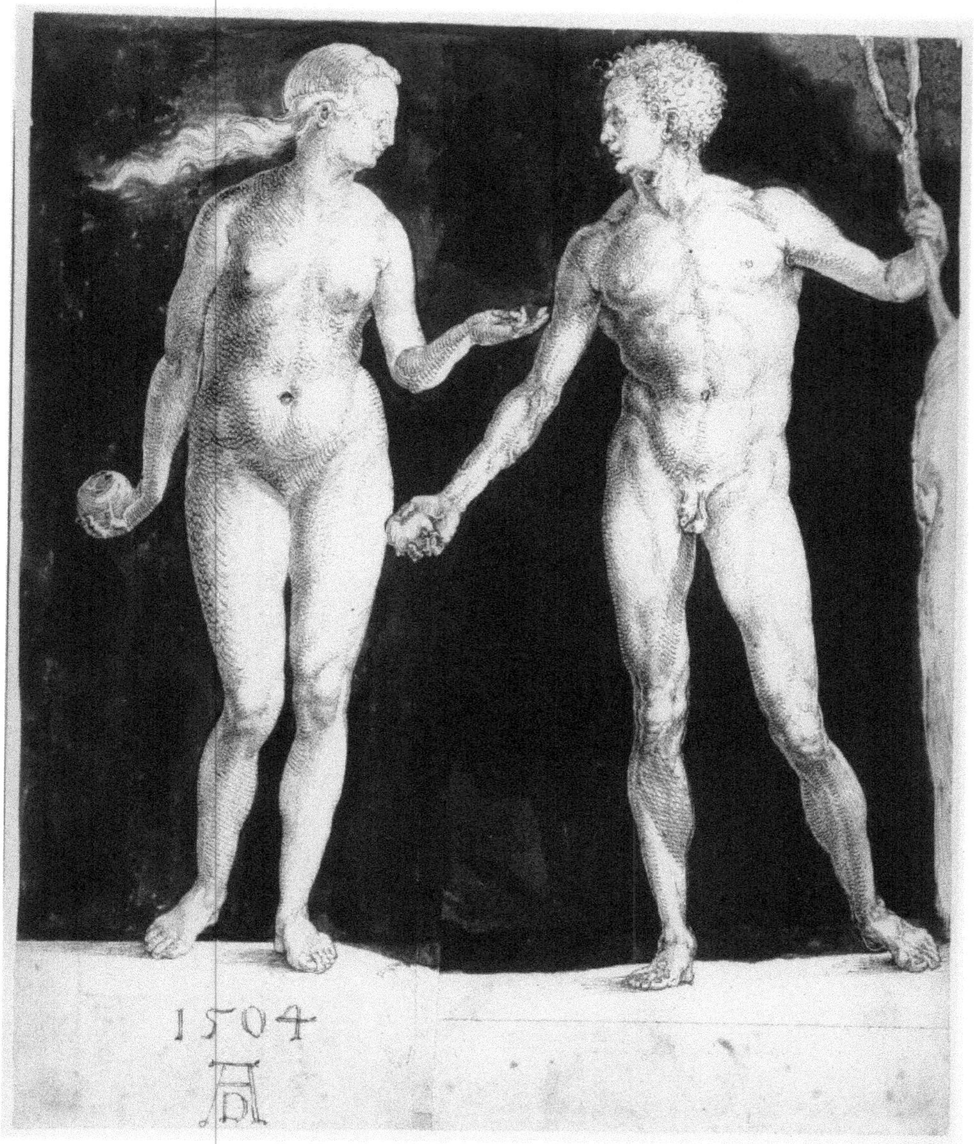

141. Albrecht Dürer, *Adam and Eve*. Pen and brown ink, brush and brown wash, corrections in white, separate pieces of paper joined, 24.3 × 20 cm. Pierpont Morgan Library, New York (no. I,257d).

copying engravings as models, Armenini explains that such deliberately worked linear structures are not appropriate for the draftsman:

> . . . I do not mean, nor do I counsel anyone to become enamored of those very minute strokes which may be seen in some prints, such as those of Albrecht Dürer. For one wastes time by not knowing how to avoid that kind of minuteness of line, which, although quite beautiful, is useful only to engravers, but not to those who draw, who must be shown ways that are quick and without effort.[18]

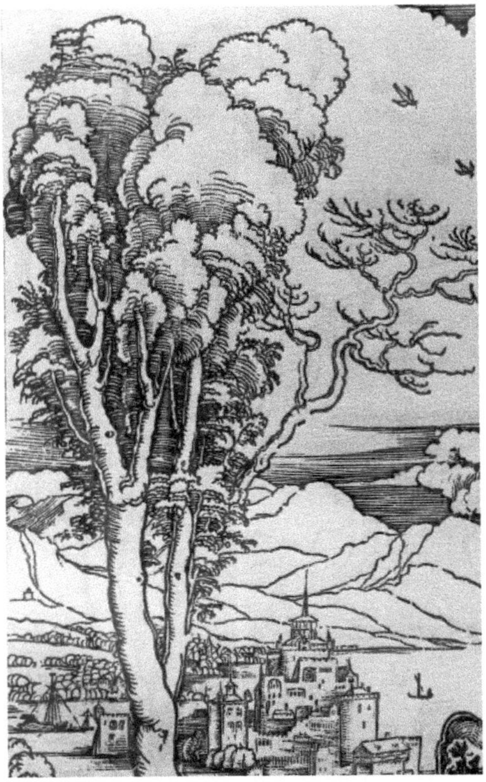

142. Albrecht Dürer, *Samson Rending the Lion.* Woodcut, 38.2 × 27.8 cm. (detail). Metropolitan Museum of Art, New York. Gift of Julius S. Morgan, 1919 (19.73.255a).

143. Ugo da Carpi, *The Sacrifice of Abraham,* after Titian. Woodcut in four blocks, 80 × 106 cm. Kuperfstichkabinett, Staatliche Museen Preussischer Kulturbesitz, Berlin.

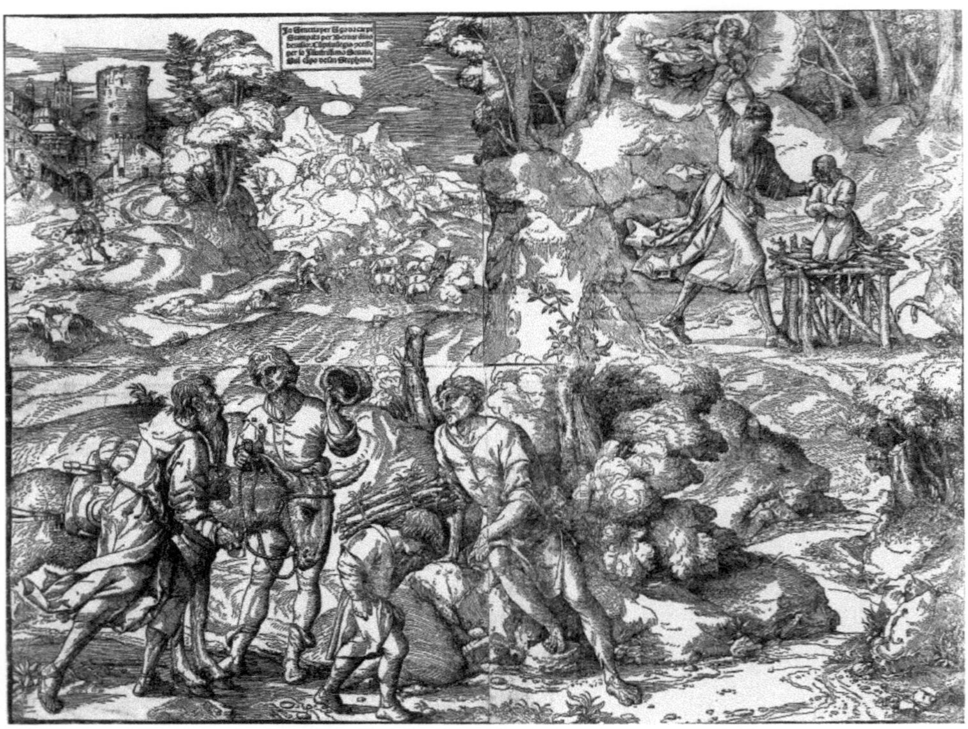

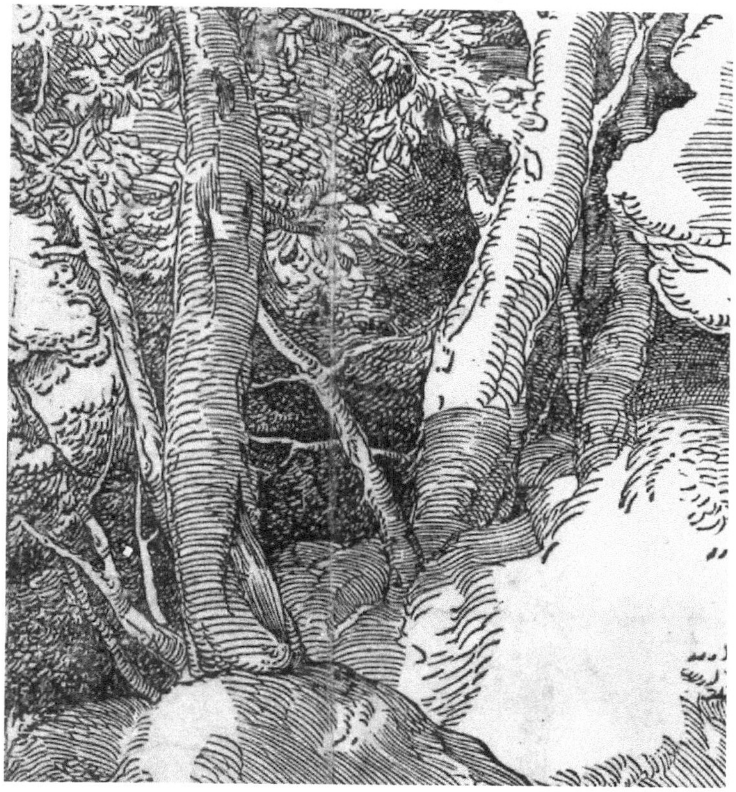

144. Ugo da Carpi, *The Sacrifice of Abraham*, after Titian. Woodcut, detail of Fig. 143.

145. Titian, *Group of Trees*. Pen and brown ink, with traces of black ink, 21.8 × 31.9 cm. Metropolitan Museum of Art, New York. Rogers Fund, 1908 (08.227.38).

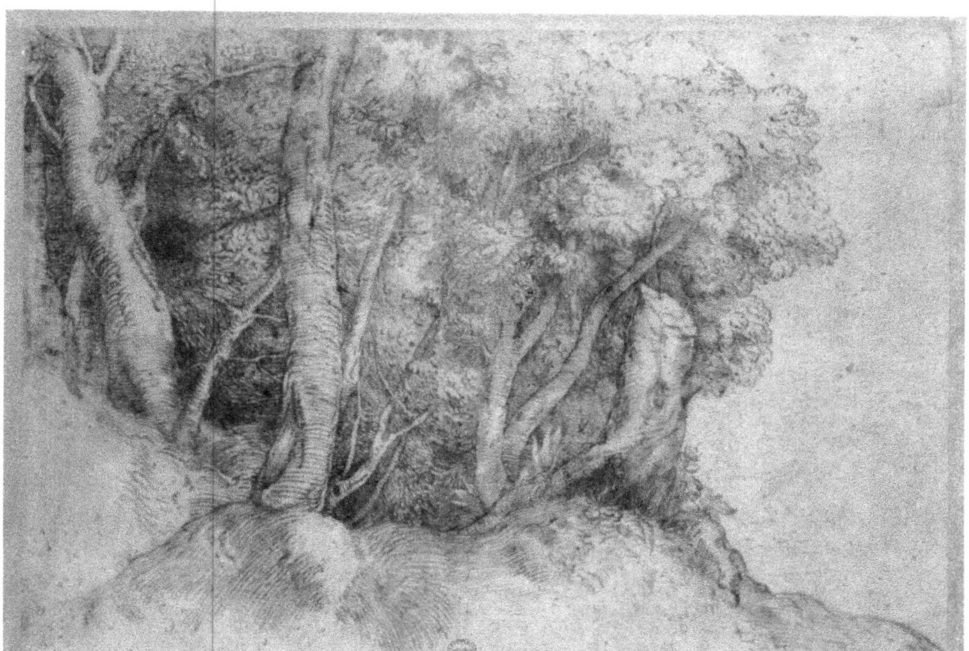

Despite the Italian criticism of his minute lines, it is precisely in Dürer's invention of linear system that we may recognize the particular classicism, as it were, of the German engraver's art (Fig. 146). Within the scope of his own committed naturalism, Dürer achieved a wondrous balance between mimesis and artifice, that is, between the responsibility of line in representing natural form and its participation in larger graphic patterns and sequences that create and guarantee aesthetic coherence. That balance is, in its way, the northern equivalent to – and, in the very regularity of its varieties, an inspiration for – the graphic classicism achieved by Marcantonio's burin under Raphael's guidance. The tension between these two linear functions, or allegiances, so precariously held in Dürer's engravings, represents a particular moment of classical balance in the history of engraving. It was not to be maintained.

Inspired by Dürer and challenged by his example, engravers of the later sixteenth century discovered and explored the expressive potential of their own instrument. And as they did so the line of the burin asserted itself increasingly, exploiting and indulging in its own natural grace (Fig. 147). The elastic *taille* – swelling and tapering, elegant in its subtle inflection – was a direct product of the engraving process: the entry of the burin into the copper, its deepening and widening path, gradual resurfacing, and final withdrawal. Recording the burin's progress, the resultant line was informed by a long, attenuated rhythm, of expansion and contraction, a gracefully curving taper. Naturally serpentine, this line simultaneously enjoyed its calligraphic quality as ornamental surface decoration and asserted its spatial prerogative as representation. The triumphant, and fully self-conscious, master of this linear aesthetic was Hendrick Goltzius, who, within his own art, defined the rules of the *paragone* between pen and burin and visually argued both sides of the debate (Fig. 148).[19]

Ever since Cennino Cennini had promised that its practice would lead to "molto disegno entro la testa tua," pen and ink had been acknowledged the most demanding and, therefore, most rewarding of drawing media, the most difficult to control and the most difficult to correct. Drawing with the pen alone, leaving the untouched paper to serve as highlight, Vasari declares, is difficult and thus a true demonstration of the draftsman's mastery ("con la penna sola, lasciando i lumi della carta, che è difficile, ma molto maestrevole").[20] Purely linear, it is the most graphic mode of drawing. Its marks retain their individual presence even as they participate in larger systems; in this binary responsibility of the line lies the aesthetic potential of the medium. To create a design in which both the single line and the complex pattern demonstrate their self-expressive capabilities even as they work toward a common mimetic end: that was the great challenge.

From the example of the engraver's burin, in the course of the sixteenth century, the draftsman's pen learned to exploit its own rhythmic possibilities, to record the varying pressure, slant, and pace of the drawing hand, to coordinate those linear rhythms, weaving them into modulated surface patterns. Adjusting the angle of its curved cross-hatching yielded longer, more flexible lozenge interstices, which might then be further complicated by the addition of a dot or dash (Fig. 149). By

such graphic structures; beyond simply making pictures more available, prints taught lessons in the fundamentals of *disegno,* the basic systems of drawing, even as they articulated the distinction between its manual operations, the realization of the image, and its conception, the invention of the artist.

1. The Hand and the Press

Addressing the reader about to learn his *littera corsiva over cancellarescha,* Ludovico degli Arrighi explains that since he was hardly able to produce enough manuscript copies of his work ("questa nuova inventione de lettere") to satisfy the demand, he has taken advantage of the new technology of the printing press and had it printed. If, despite his best efforts, the woodcut rendition (by Ugo da Carpi) is not entirely faithful to his original penmanship, he begs the reader's indulgence, for printing ("la stampa") cannot fully represent the living hand ("la viva mano").[3] The master penman here acknowledges the particular tension that informs the relationship between drawing and printing, between the line drawn by hand and its mechanical replication. This distinction between "la stampa" and "la viva mano" becomes fairly standard in the course of the sixteenth century, as the rich ambivalence of *disegno* permits the term to be used for both drawings and prints.

The very ambitious collector-dealer Jacopo Strada, for example, describes his purchase from the widow of Perino del Vaga of "due casse di dissegni . . . tutti fatti a mano" – including many by Perino's master, Raphael of Urbino.[4] Strada had been shown the entire legacy of *disegni* left by Perino, and his acquisitive isolation of those "made by hand" confirms what one would have expected of any later Renaissance artist's estate: namely, that it contained at least as many prints as drawings. The same was true of amateurs. In Venice, the inventories of the great collection assembled by Gabriele Vendramin included, among much else, Giorgione's *Tempesta,* paintings by Titian, drawings by Raphael, and entire print series by Dürer; in addition to drawings, there are listed hundreds of "dissegni a stampa de rame et legno" (i.e., engravings and woodcuts). Conserved together in the same portfolios, books, or rolls, these various *disegni* were described as either "disegni a mano" or "disegni a stampa."[5] "Disegni stampati" is the term Vasari uses, for example, in reference to the etchings of Battista Franco.[6]

Such terminology casts interesting historical light on Erwin Panofsky's observation, the conclusion to his grand monograph on Dürer,

> that no European language has an equivalent for the German words "Handriss" and "Handzeichnung" ("hand-drawing") which stress the fact that the hand of an individual person has rested on this very piece of paper, imparting to it a sentimental value not unlike that of a personal souvenir or even a relic – a hand-written letter, a hand-signed document, a hand-embroidered handkerchief.[7]

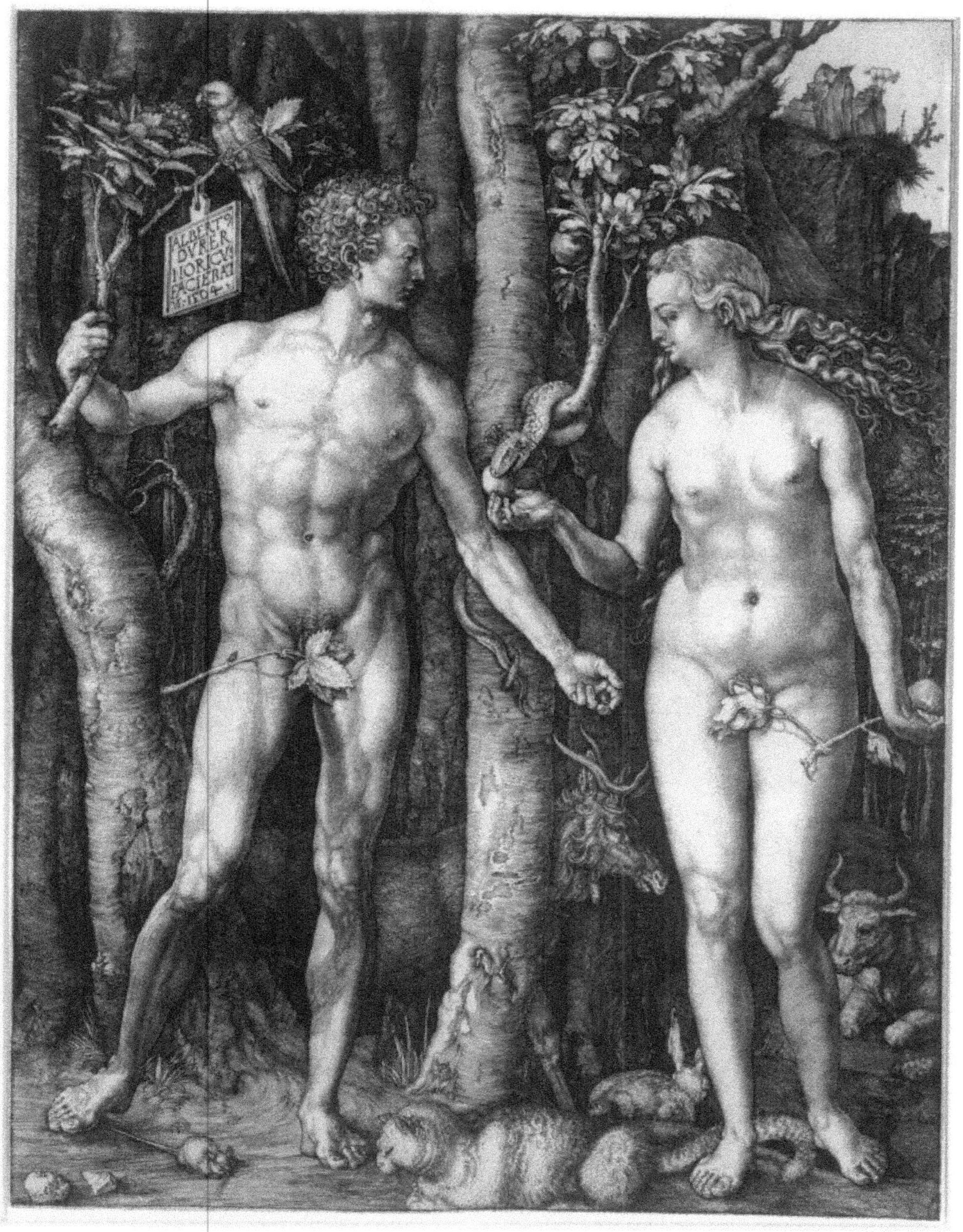

146. Albrecht Dürer, *Adam and Eve.* Engraving, 25.1 × 19.4 cm. Museum of Fine Arts, Boston. Centennial Gift of Landon T. Clay, 1968. Courtesy, Museum of Fine Arts, Boston.

this technique shadow could be enriched by infusing it with light – another of Dürer's lessons. Achieving finer tonal modulation through stippling or extending the life of a line through a dissipating dotted sequence further accommodated modeling patterns to surrounding contour, so that outline itself seemed inflected into space. Through such technical feats did pen drawing meet the challenge of engraving. In particular, the pen learned to mimic the long and graceful curve of the burin's line, as the burin, in its turn, tested itself against the most elaborate calligraphic exercises of the scribal pen. Triumphant in this graphic aesthetic is line

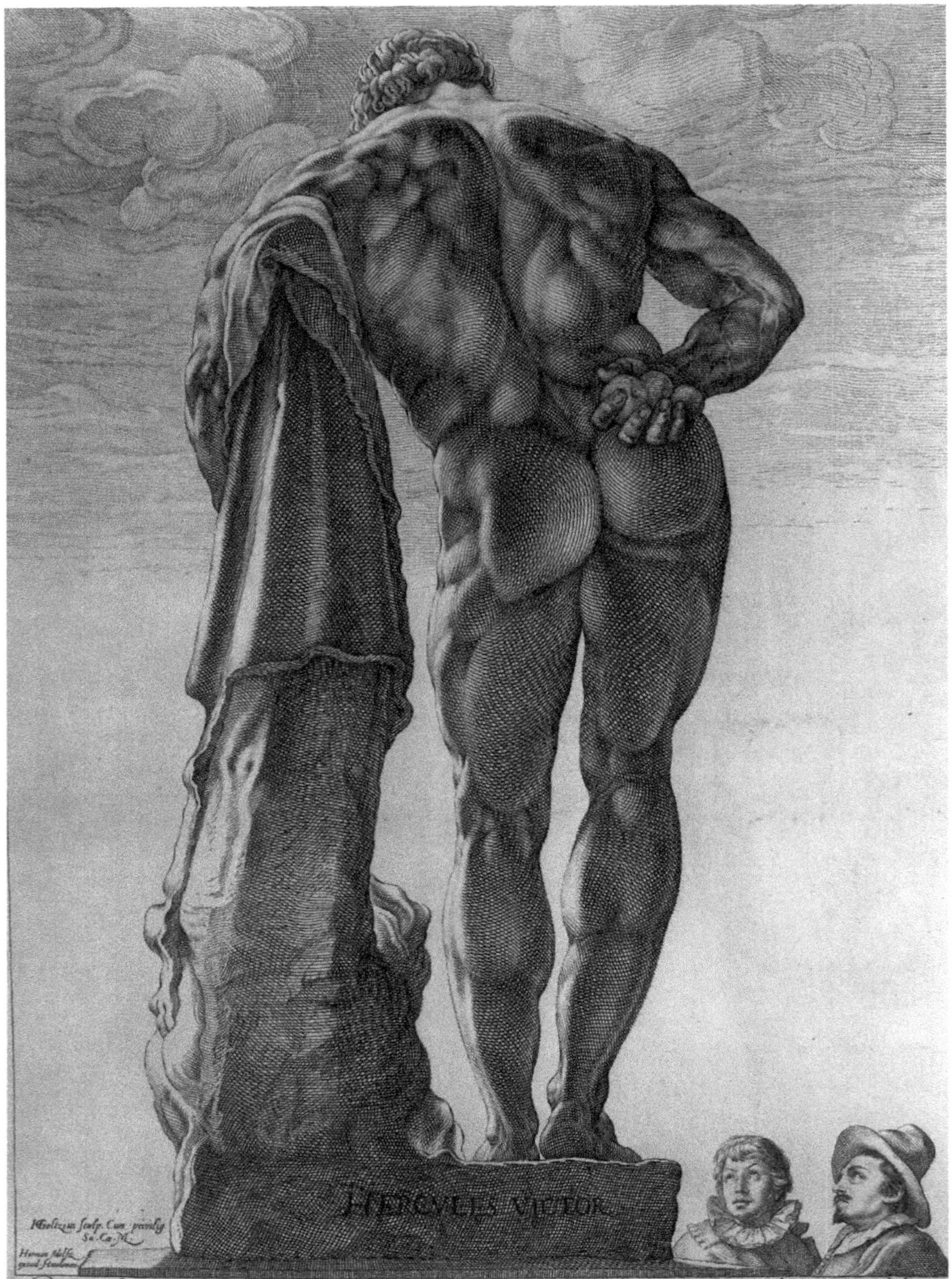

147. Hendrick Goltzius, *Farnese Hercules*. Engraving, 41.5 × 29.5 cm. Metropolitan Museum of Art, New York. Gift of Henry Walters, 1917 (17.37.59).

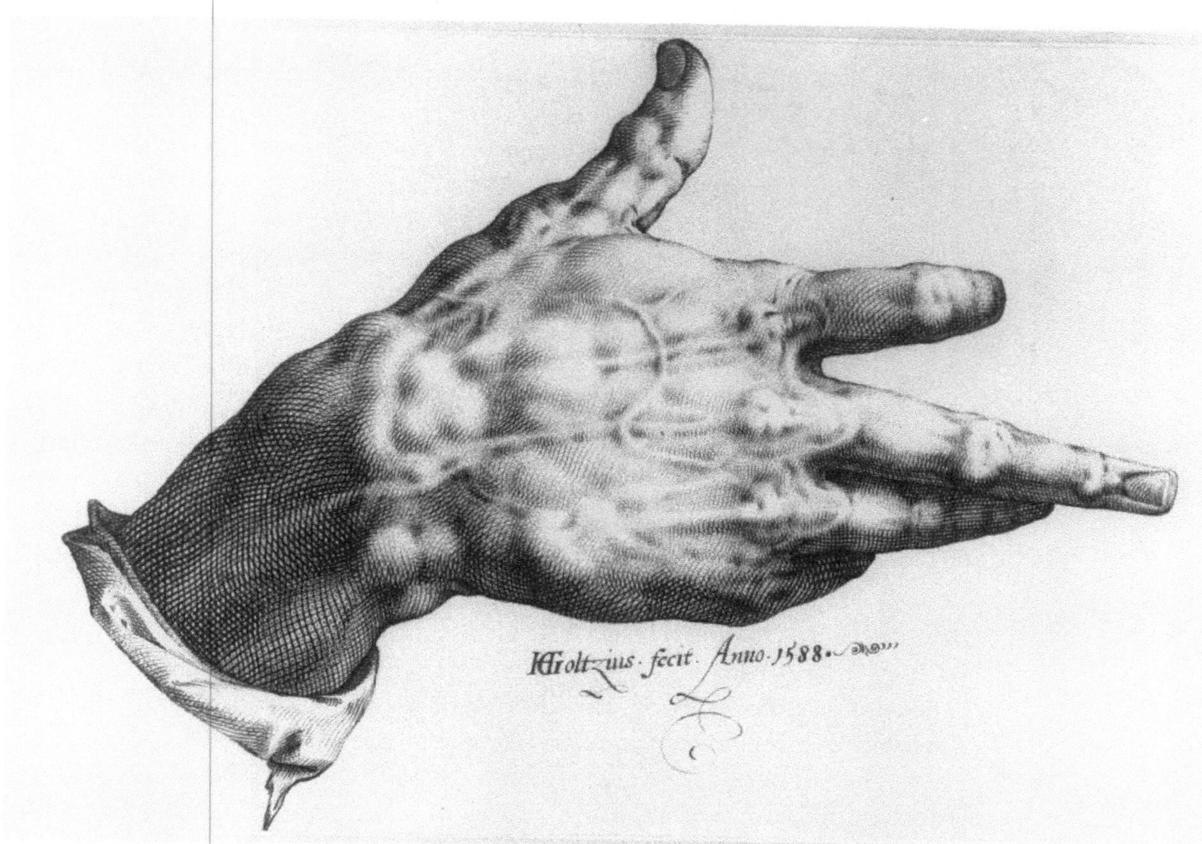

148. Hendrick Goltzius, *"Goltzius's Hand."* Pen and brown ink, 22.9 × 32.8 cm. Teylers Museum, Haarlem (no. N 58).

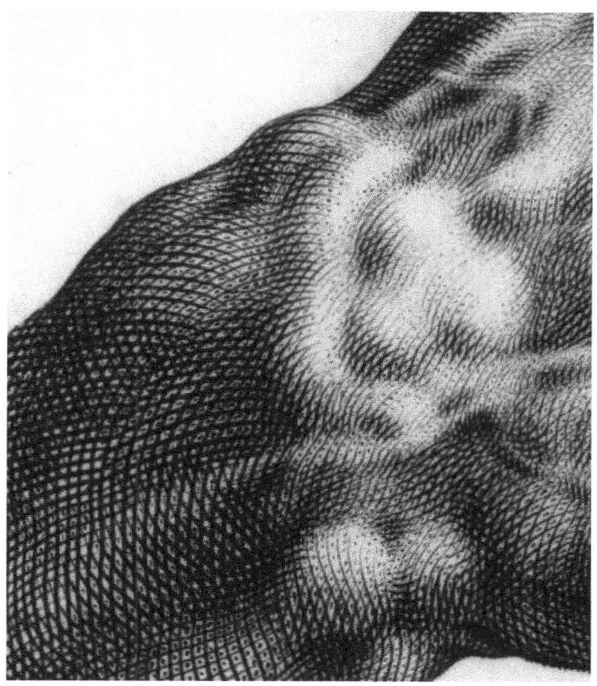

149. *"Goltzius's Hand,"* detail of Fig. 148.

itself, which imposes its own sinuous values on the very forms represented, stylizing nature into art – the kind of art called *di maniera* or "Mannerist."

Moving between engraving and drawing, Goltzius elevated the art of the pen to a monumental level. His pen eventually challenged painting itself, extending the ground of its operations beyond paper to the more precious surface of parchment – itself a declaration of the permanence as well as the preciousness of the art – and then to the larger field of prepared canvas.[21] On whatever support, however, Goltzius's "pen works" represent the triumph of the draftsman's line. However the pen may have been educated by the burin – and Goltzius was absolute master of both – these demonstrations of the art of line proclaim a shared graphic aesthetic, especially appealing in the artifice of its language and sophisticated syntax to a particular class of connoisseurs. Virtuoso displays of linear art, celebrations of manual dexterity, these *Penwercken* testify most explicitly to *l'ingegno della mano.*

2. *The Line Transformed*

Ludovico degli Arrighi's cursive script was not replicated by the burin; his penmanship was imitated not in engraving but in woodcut, a procedure that puts a very different light on the relationship between *la viva mano* and its printed diffusion. In the *intaglio* process of engraving, the burin incises its own lines into the copper plate, and those grooves take the ink that will print the design. In engraving there is a direct correlation between the incised line and the printed image, which records the actual movements of the burin across and through the plate. The engraver's task is analogous to the draftsman's in that he too is building complex patterns directly out of line – as Goltzius so eloquently demonstrated. By contrast, the woodcut involves a process of indirection; it creates line in a very different way.

Oldest of the arts of graphic reproduction, the woodcut is a relief print. On the prepared surface of a block of wood, generally sawn along the grain, a design is either drawn directly or, more normally, transferred from a drawing on paper.[22] The "negative" areas surrounding the lines of the drawing are then cut away, leaving only those parts of the design actually to be printed; the ink is applied to those uncut surfaces, which stand out in relief from the rest of the block. A carving process, the woodcut involves the "liberation" of the drawn line from the wood, a consequence of which may be a certain transformation of the line itself. Cutting requires several moves of the blade, which operates from outside the line. The original drawn line was internally generated, conceived as and by the single stroke of the pen; now freed on all sides and defined, as it were, externally, it thus becomes a more fully independent and more deliberately bounded mark. Moreover, the minimum thickness of the line is effectively limited by several practical factors: the nature of the wood itself and the physical pressure it must withstand during the printing process. The early woodcut mark, then, is typically rather broad, and its imagery tends toward a directness of statement quite distinct from the finer patterns produced by the burin in engraving.

Historically, the skill of the cutter has been measured by his fidelity to the designing draftsman's line. Thus, in the German *Ständebuch,* or "Book of Trades," published in 1568, Jost Amman's illustration of *Der Formschneider,* a woodblock cutter, is accompanied by the following verses of Hans Sachs:

> I am a wood-engraver good,
> And all designs on blocks of wood
> I with my graver cut so neat,
> That when they're printed on a sheet
> Of paper white, you plainly view
> The very forms the artist drew:
> His drawing, whether coarse or fine,
> Is truly copied line for line.[23]

That such a goal could be imagined and articulated was entirely due to Dürer and his radical transformation of a relatively modest graphic art into one of major pictorial ambition. By the final years of the fifteenth century, Dürer had realized the potential of the woodcut as the reproducible equivalent of drawing; he discovered in the medium not only a graphic language of new variety and eloquence but also a remarkably effective means of self-expression on a broad scale, a means of giving the widest circulation to the creations of his pen (Fig. 150). Furthermore, he recognized the degree to which the graphic arts permitted a greater freedom of invention than did the normally more traditional art of painting, more public in scope and specially commissioned. Printmaking invited the exploration of the visionary and the fantastic. Mantegna and Pollaiuolo had already exploited engraving's invitation to invention, as, a generation before, Jacopo Bellini had exploited drawing.

Dürer's "reform" of the woodcut has been sensitively described by Erwin Panofsky in terms of organically relating contour and internal modeling, of overcoming the functional disparity that had characterized the work of his immediate predecessors in Germany:

> The hatchings were no longer permitted to appear as schematic series of stiff, indifferent strokes or to fuse into indistinct masses, nor were the contours confined to the function of mere boundaries. Both were subjected to the discipline of what may be called "dynamic calligraphy," and were thereby reduced to a common aesthetic denominator. . . . He taught woodcut lines to behave like the prolonged, elastic *tailles* produced by Schongauer's burin. They were made variable in length and width, they learned to move in curves significant both from an ornamental and representational point of view, and, above all, they acquired the capacity for swelling and tapering so as to express organic tension and relaxation. Thus hatchings as well as contours were transformed into flexible and expressive "modelling lines," with equal emphasis on the concepts of "line" and "modelling."[24]

Dürer taught the woodcut, in effect, to follow the dynamic impulse of his own pen, so that he could exercise fully his natural inventiveness in designing for the medium. In the comment following his listing of the German's engravings, Vasari, for all the

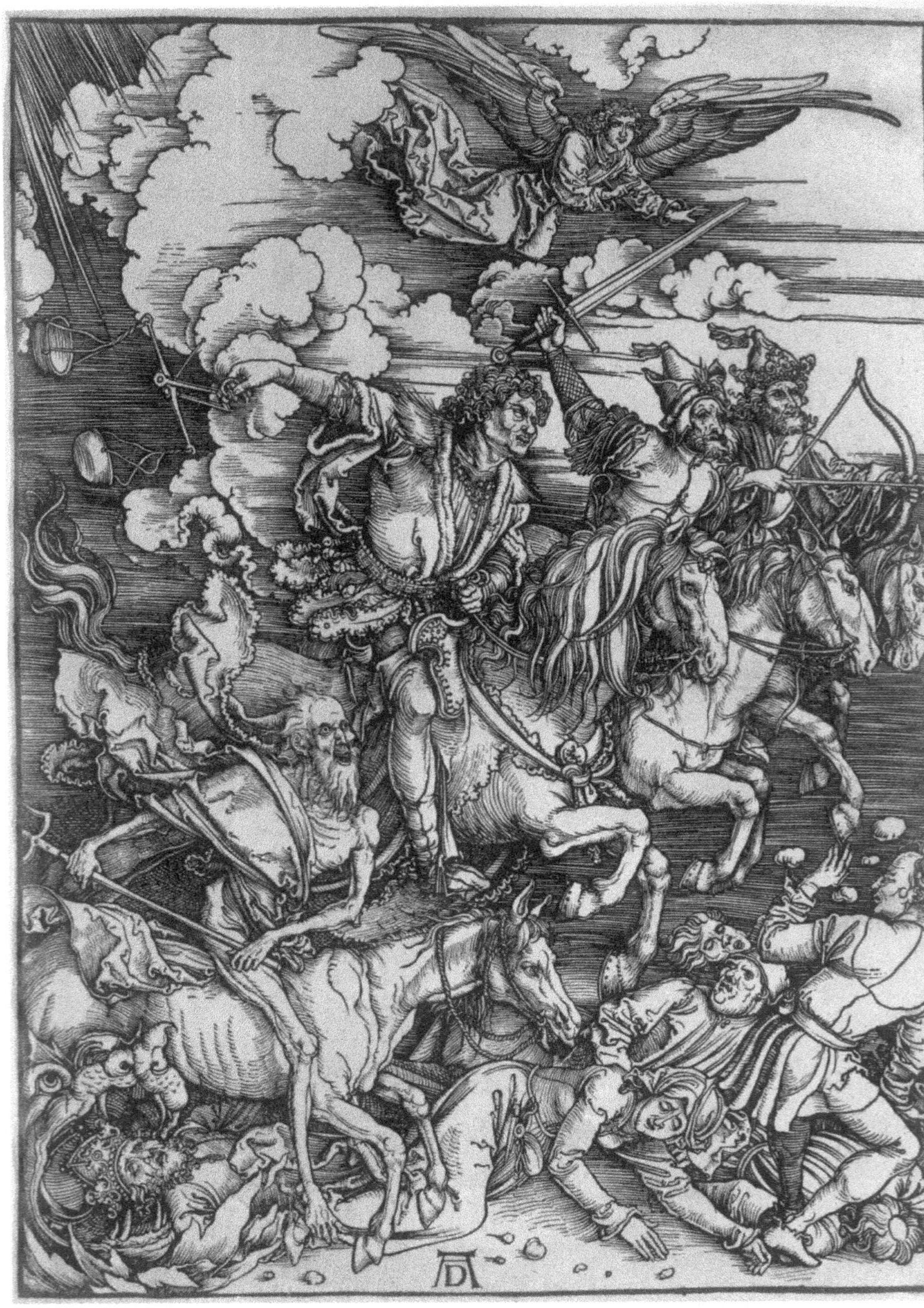

150. Albrecht Dürer, *The Four Horsemen of the Apocalypse*. Woodcut, 39.2 × 27.9 cm. Museum of Fine Arts, Boston. Bequest of Francis Bullard, 1913.

historical inaccuracy of his account, rightly recognized this intimate relationship between drawing and printmaking. Impatient with the time consumed in engraving and having so many ideas to express, writes the Italian critic from his own particular vantage, Dürer turned to the woodcut, a medium in which "those who have a real talent for drawing have a more ample field in which to demonstrate their skill."[25]

More than his engravings – whose many fine lines were criticized by Armenini as a waste for the draftsman – Dürer's woodcuts provided absolutely clear models of linear structure. As Vasari recognized, they were indeed replicas of pen drawings. But only by being his own cutter could Dürer assure the faithful translation of his design by the knife, that the original pen drawing was "truly copied line for line." (Later in his career, when he did use assistants for the cutting, even though he had trained a workshop to meet his high standard he deliberately accommodated his drawing to such translation, by reducing the demanding complexity of his linework.) In so far as he made the woodcut obedient to the pen, Dürer, we might say, rendered the medium transparent – although his special delight in the complex exchanges of black and white, especially within deep shadow, cannot but pay tribute to the virtuoso exercise of the blade. As Hans Sachs testified, fidelity to the drawn model was to remain the highest ambition of the woodcut.

There was, however, an alternative xylographic aesthetic. It developed in Italy, in Venice in particular and around the drawing style of Titian.[26] Here the initiative was taken not by an ambitious artist who was also his own publisher but by professional publishers and printers. A master like the young Titian may have supplied the design, but the work was produced by the publisher, who held the copyright to it. The ambition of the Italian projects lay more in size and scale of production than in technical refinement of execution. Titian's earliest design for a woodcut was probably for a *Triumph of Christ,* a processional frieze printed in ten blocks and measuring nearly nine feet in length (Figs. 151–53). His grandest design, the *Submersion of Pharaoh's Army in the Red Sea,* printed in twelve blocks, measures over four by seven feet (Fig. 154).[27]

151. After Titian, *The Triumph of Christ.* Woodcut in ten blocks, 38.5 × 266.3 cm (detail). Bibliothèque Nationale de France, Paris.

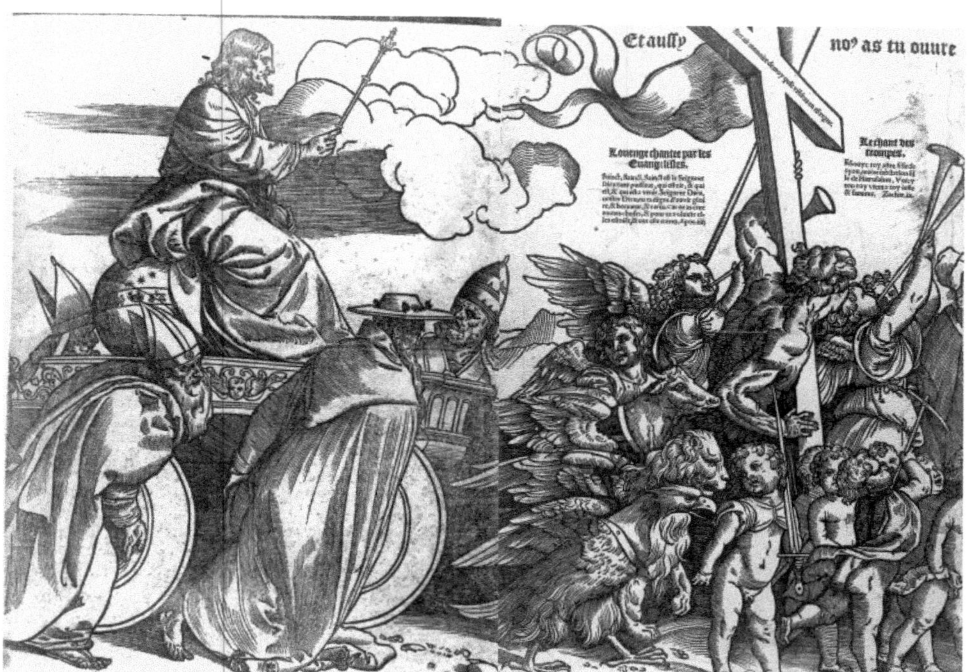

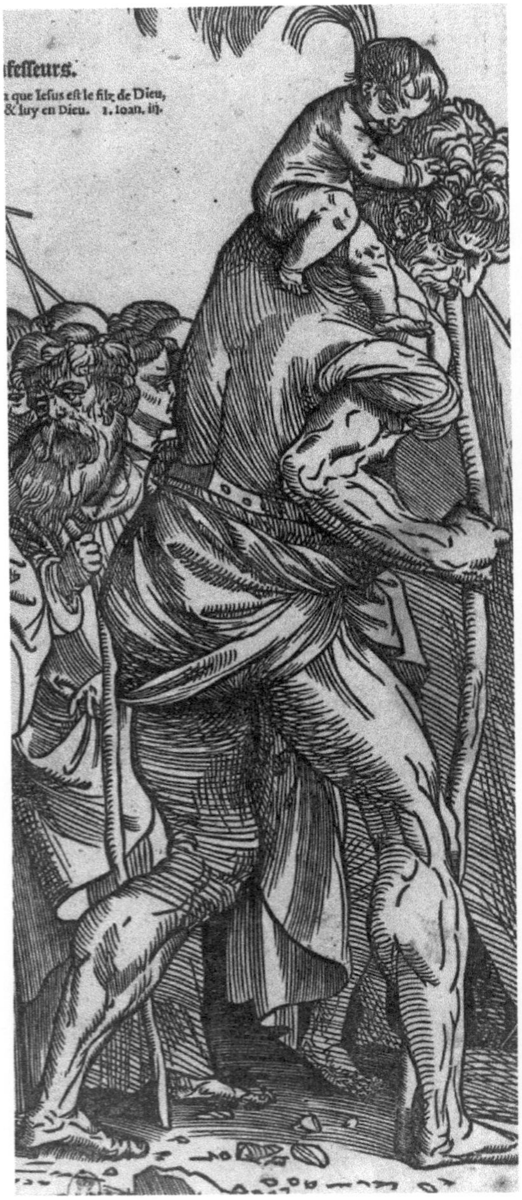

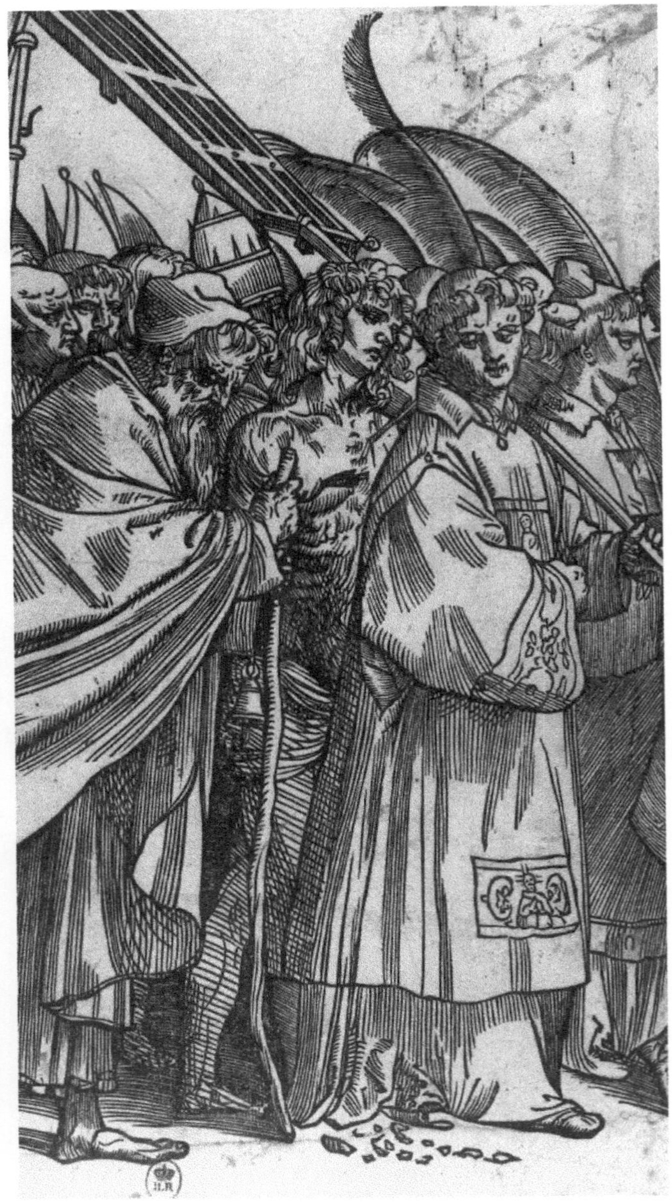

152. After Titian, *The Triumph of Christ*. Woodcut (detail).

153. After Titian, *The Triumph of Christ*. Woodcut (detail).

For graphic images on such a monumental scale Titian undoubtedly supplied the woodcutters with designs less meticulously prepared than Dürer's. Some of his surviving pen drawings suggest the kind of linear structures the craftsmen may have faced: energetic, irregular, governed by rules less deliberate than the German's (Fig. 155). From such tangled webs of lines the cutter would have had to find and pick out the linear patterns to be set into relief. The best of them apparently learned to deal with Titian's manner of drawing; others, unable or unwilling to cope with such graphic energies, fell back on the relatively simple systems of parallel hatching that had become traditional to their trade and thereby betrayed their model. The most impressive parts of the *Triumph of Christ*, figures like that of St. Christopher (Fig. 152) or St. Sebastian (Fig. 153), give us some record of what Titian's original pen drawing may have been like: rendered in vigorous strokes, informed by a graphic energy correlative to the organic force of nature. In certain, relatively more studied areas, however – the beasts of the evangelists, for example (Fig. 151) – the designer seems to have followed the lesson of Dürer's unification of "descriptive" and "optical" lines, to use Panofsky's functional distinction. But it is especially in his freer calligraphy – for example, in the internal modeling of the body of St. Sebastian – that Titian offers an equivalent, a bold Venetian alternative, to Dürer's "transformation of black lines and white intervals into negative and positive symbols of the same entity, namely, light."[28]

Although always keenly aware of Dürer's example, Titian forged for himself a new kind of graphic vocabulary. In designing the *Red Sea* (Fig. 154), he was operating on a scale well beyond any models but his own *Triumph of Christ* – and, before that, Jacopo de' Barbari's monumental *View of Venice*.[29] The design of the *Sacrifice of Abraham*, another large woodcut, in four blocks, had evidently been prepared with separate drawings for individual details and sections (Figs. 143–45).[30] For the *Red Sea*, in contrast, Titian seems to have drawn across the entire surface, either in a full-size cartoon or, more likely, on the blocks themselves. This is most clearly suggested by the great strokes of which the divine cloud is constructed (Figs. 156, 157). Even in the smaller articulation of details in the foreground landscape, where his pen defines tide-eaten rocks, pebbles, bark, and foliage (Fig. 158),

154. After Titian, *The Submersion of Pharaoh's Army in the Red Sea*. Woodcut in twelve blocks, 122.5 × 221.5 cm. Metropolitan Museum of Art, New York. Harris Brisbane Dick Fund, 1927 (27.54.87–98).

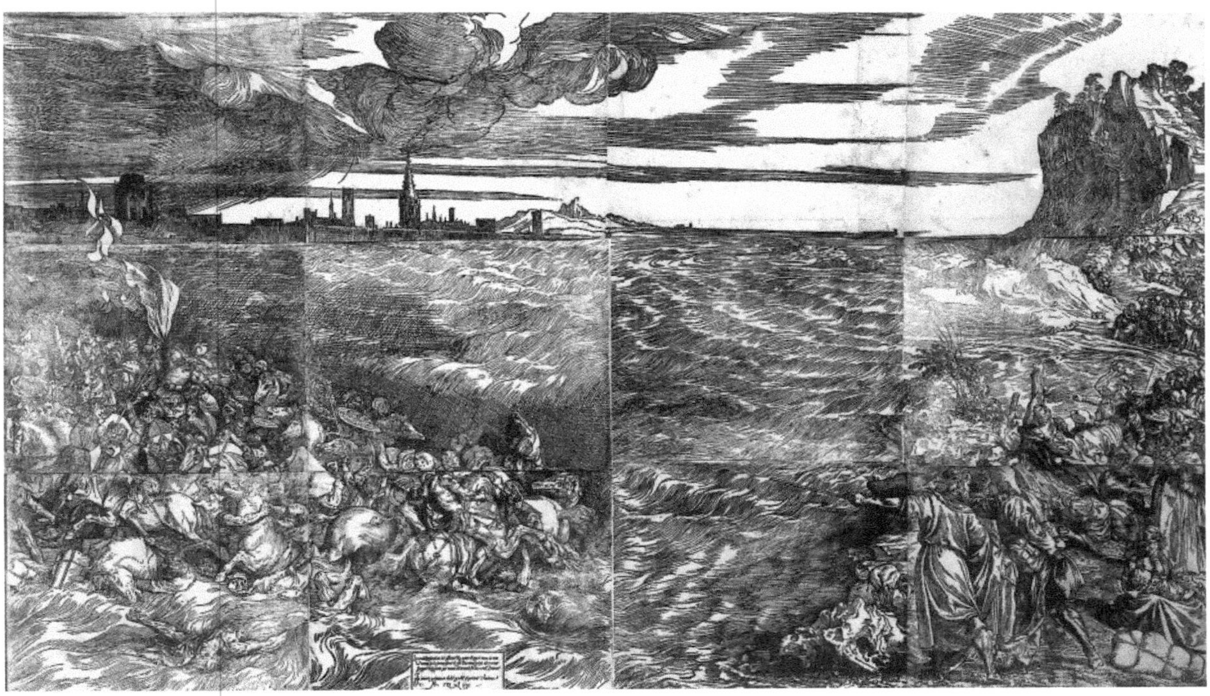

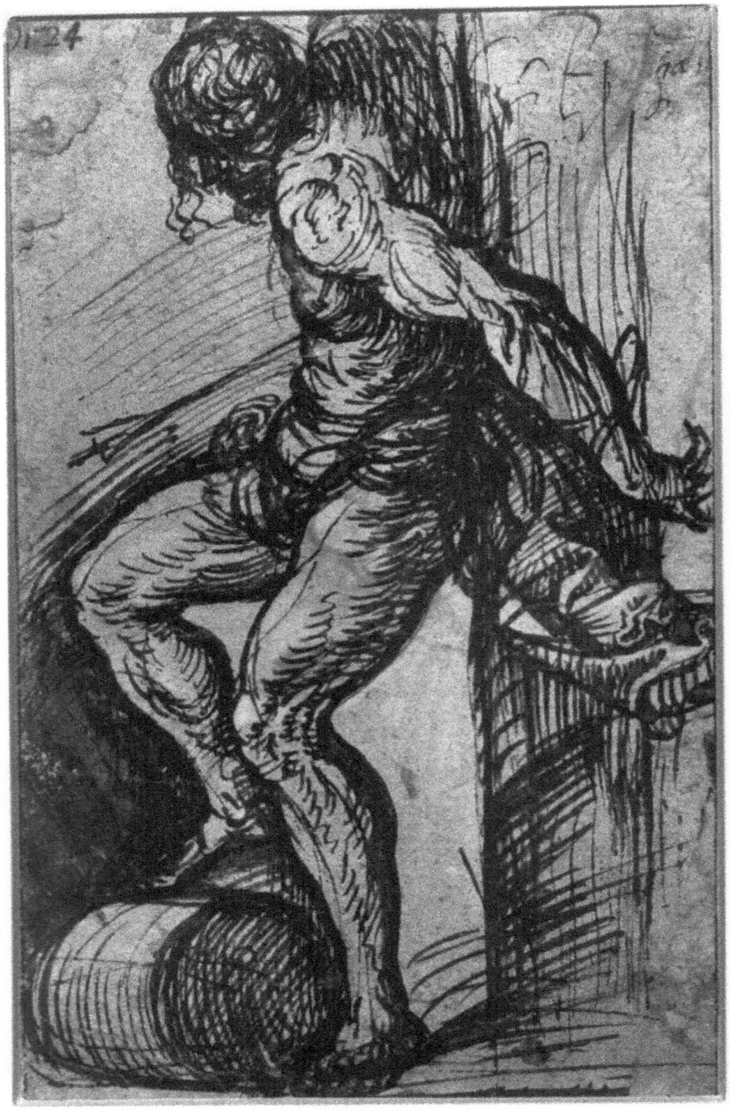

155. Titian, *Study for St. Sebastian.* Pen and brown ink, brush and wash, on blue paper, 18 × 11.5 cm. Frankfurt am Main, Städelsches Kunstinstitut, inv. no. 5518.

Titian drew with broad, free strokes. His use of cross-hatching, literally fluid in its effects in the rendering of rippling waves, achieves an extraordinarily abstract richness in the synthetic structures of the great rock (Fig. 159).

Titian's original design, a graphic mural that must have been one of the most ambitious pen drawings of the High Renaissance, owes its organizational unity and power as much to the sheer sweep of the pen itself as to its overall compositional construction. The draftsman set himself a variety of representational problems – land and seascape, cloud and rock, figures and animals – so that in many ways the *Red Sea* seems a studied response to the sophisticated printmaking of Dürer. And its solutions involved a correspondingly varied and sensitive use of the pen. Light and

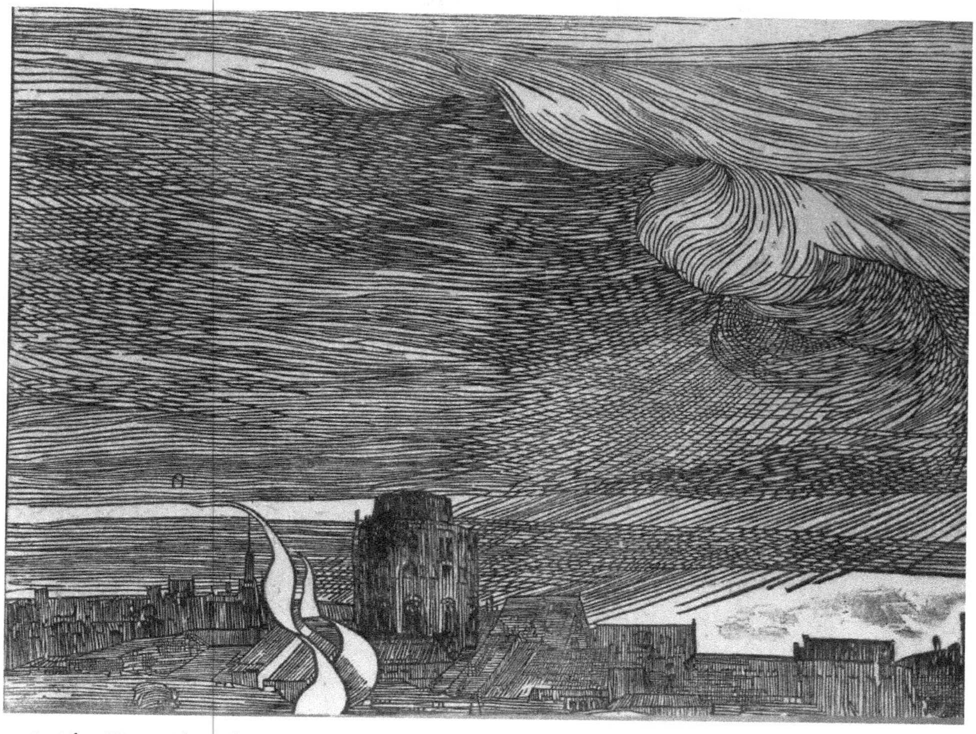

156. After Titian, *The Submersion of Pharaoh's Army in the Red Sea.* Woodcut (detail). Cleveland Museum of Art. John L. Severance Fund (52.296).

157. After Titian, *The Submersion of Pharaoh's Army in the Red Sea.* Woodcut (detail). Cleveland Museum of Art. John L. Severance Fund (52.297).

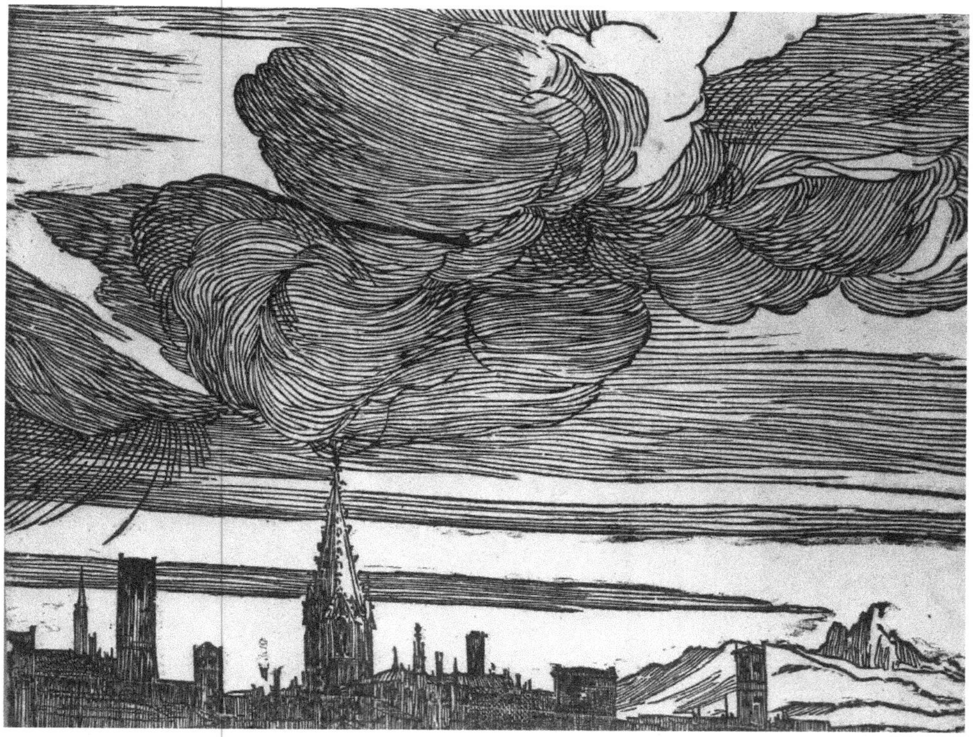

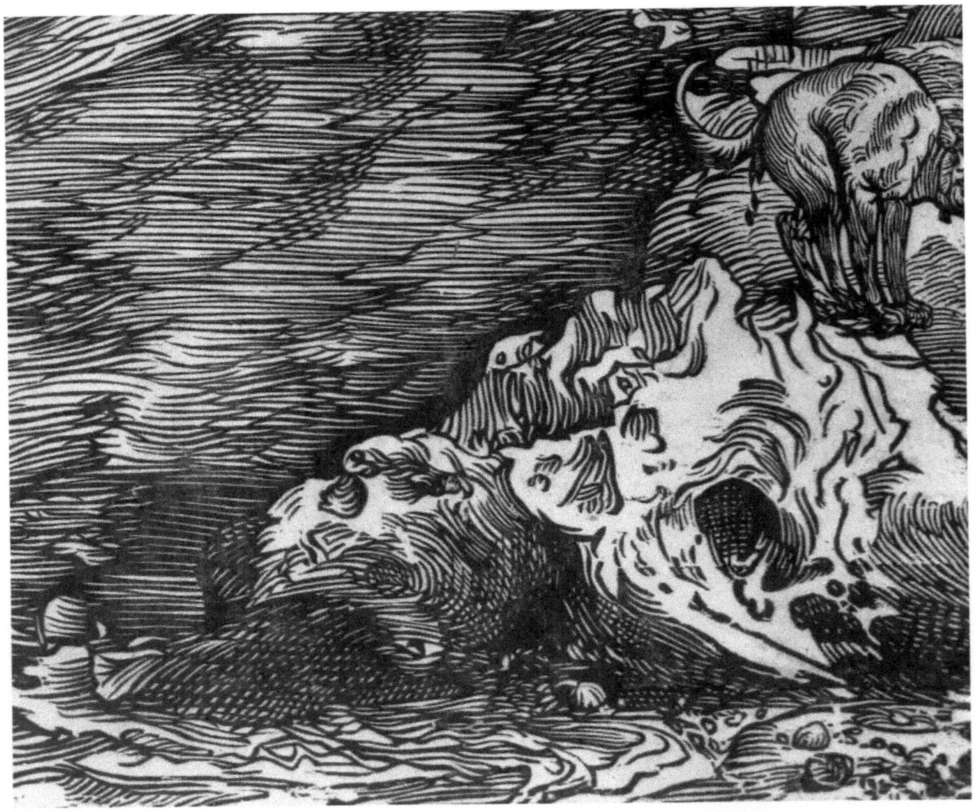

158. After Titian, *The Submersion of Pharaoh's Army in the Red Sea.* Woodcut (detail). Cleveland Museum of Art. John L. Severance Fund (52.306).

dark, central protagonists to the narrative, are handled with a precise control all the more remarkable for the very scale of the drawing. For each area – from the thunderous closing of the sea to the gentler waves rippling at the shore, from the grandly divine cloud sweeping up out of Egypt to the massive cliff silhouetted against the serene brightness of the clearing sky – Titian found the suitable graphic pattern, the appropriate system of stroke and hatching, varying from a subtlety approximating the effects of the engraver's burin to a ruggedness of form expressive of the glyptic nature of the xylographic medium itself. Nowhere does the pen flag in the energy of its creative function; every mark records the force of the original gesture.

For a clearer sense of what kind of drawing may have confronted the cutter(s) of the *Red Sea* blocks we might turn to Titian's pen study for the figure of St. Sebastian in the Brescia altarpiece (Fig. 155). Although the design for the woodcut may have been somewhat more finished, one can sense in this figure the special challenge to xylographic translation. Some of the most powerful, expressionistic effects in the heads among Pharaoh's drowning host seem to be the result of working from such models (Fig. 160); moving within the intricate calligraphy, the cutter's blade crystallizes the irregular, organic patterns of swirling, searching lines, seeking the lozenges of white that are the resultant corollary of their interlacing activity. Out of the dynamics of this process, the dialectical conflict between pen and knife, the final graphic resolution preserves the vitality of the original model, if not its exact linework.

In the dark waters engulfing the Egyptian army, the block cutter may have played an even more active interpretive role, for these cross-hatched patterns in particular document the creative intervention of the knife. The drawing – obviously executed "gagliardamente e con molta prestezza"[31] – had originally consisted of a series of linear continuities; these were disrupted in the cutting process. Picking out the white between the crossed lines, the cutter naturally worked on separate fragmented units, "negative" spaces, and instead of maintaining the continuity of the pen line he produced a mosaic structure of distinct and individual tesserae, each one of a slightly different shape. This irregularity, resulting from the dynamic interplay between two different instruments, yields a surface of sparkling effect, a darkness shimmering with flecks of light. Irregularity might even be termed a basic constructive principle in this graphic aesthetic – manifesting itself most impressively in the structure of the great rock protecting the Israelites (Fig. 159).

This principle lies at the core of Titian's contribution to the woodcut's graphic language, an alternative to Dürer's calculated control and more ornamental calligraphy. In certain ways the *Red Sea* reaches back beyond Dürer to a more primitive stage in the development of the art (Fig. 161), for it was by the precision and reg-

159. After Titian, *The Submersion of Pharaoh's Army in the Red Sea.* Woodcut (detail). Cleveland Museum of Art. John L. Severance Fund (52.299).

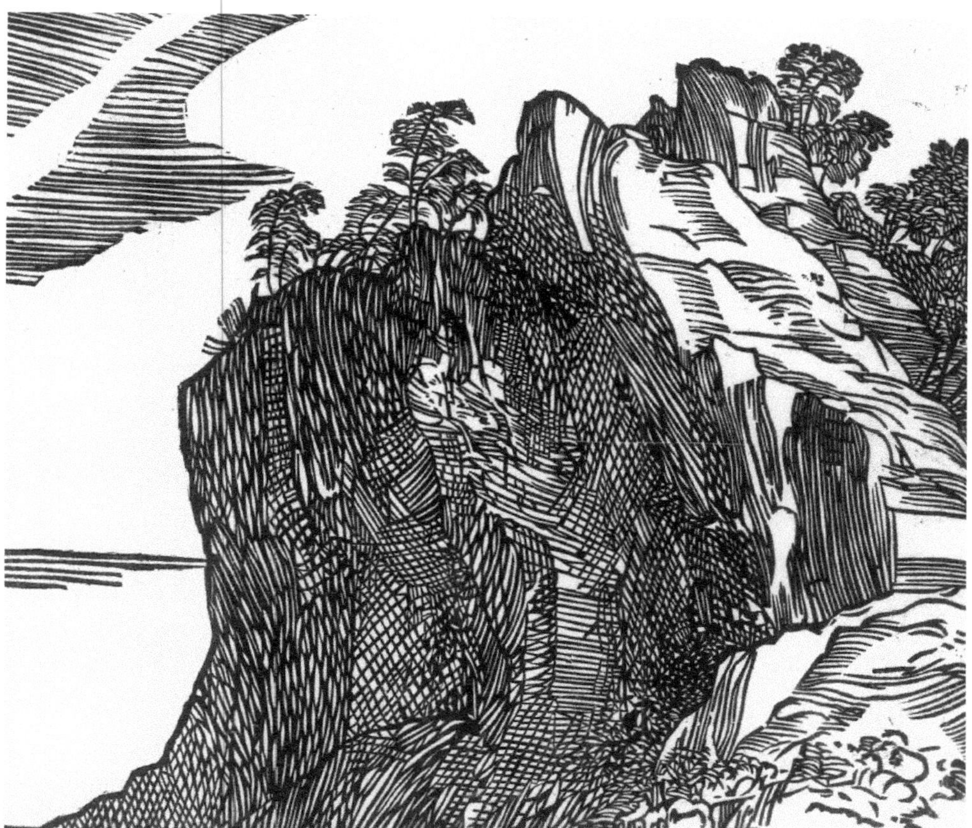

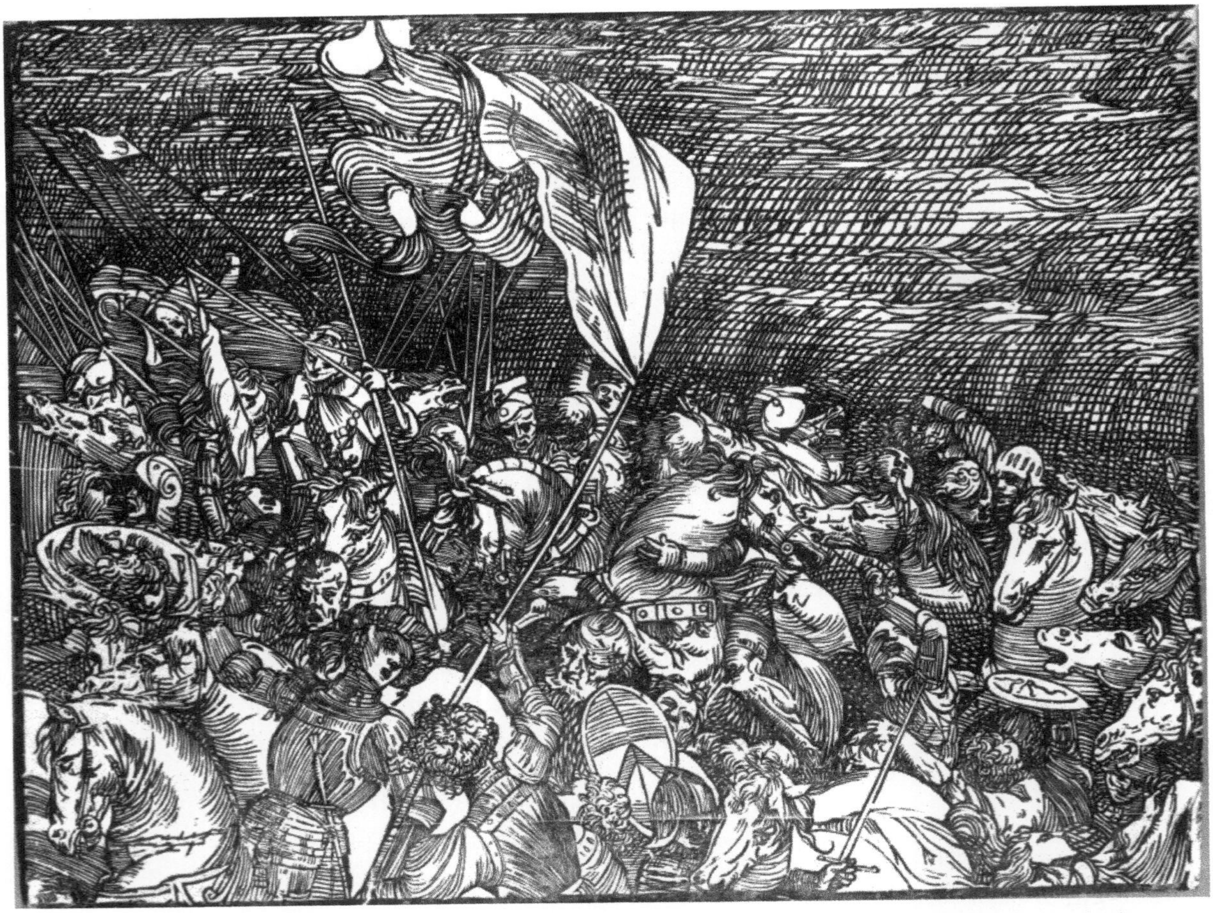

160. After Titian, *The Submersion of Pharaoh's Army in the Red Sea.* Woodcut (detail). Cleveland Museum of Art. John L. Severance Fund (52.300).

ularity, the subtle inflections of his directed linear systems that the German reformer had led the woodcut to a more sophisticated cultural level. Titian seems almost deliberately to be seeking the cruder power, the raw expressiveness that characterized the more popular traditions of the medium. Defining and epitomizing the aesthetic values of the Venetian woodcut in the first decades of the sixteenth century, Titian's great print offers the fullest expression of an essentially Venetian graphic dialect. At once preserving the energies of the basic drawing and recording the very carving process by which it is realized, its complex of black and white marks, broadly impressionistic in effect yet retaining the individual force of each stroke, is the graphic equivalent to the Venetian *pittura di macchia,* the mode of free and open painting that Titian was to contribute to the history of art.[32] Even before he had fully exploited these possibilities in painting, Titian was testing them in his graphic art, in the assertive freedom of his drawing style and in the woodcuts that reproduced his designs.

Titian liberated energies latent in the xylographic medium itself. Dürer's standard in his reform of the woodcut was set by the refinement of engraving and according to the perceptual scale of the book, the requirement of proximate legi-

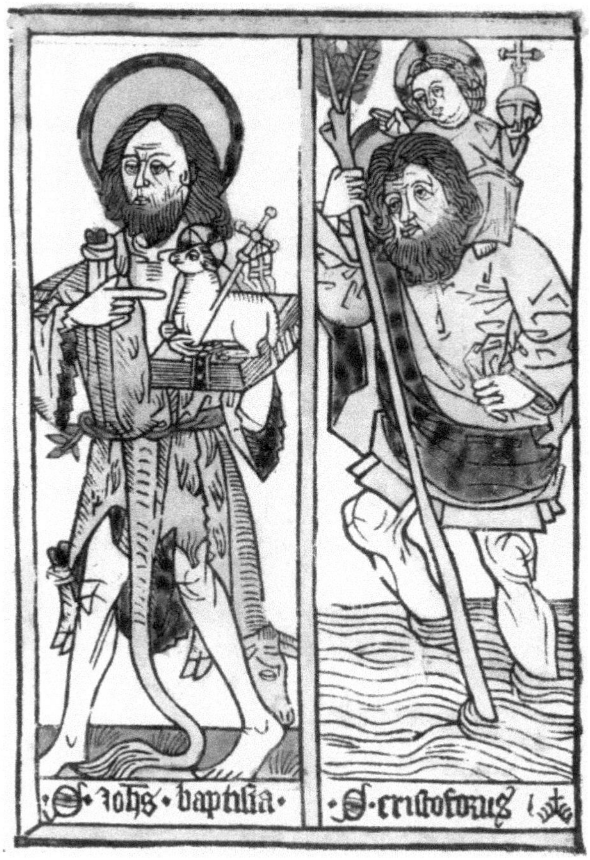

161. German, Fifteenth Century, *St. John the Baptist and St. Christopher.* Woodcut, hand-colored in red lake, yellow, green, pink, gray, brown, and tan, 28.5 × 19 cm. National Gallery of Art, Washington (1943.3.617 [B-3171]). Photograph ©2000 Board of Trustees, National Gallery of Art.

bility and the decorum of the study. Titian's graphic boldness, on the other hand, responded to more monumental circumstances; a woodcut like the *Red Sea* operated on a mural scale, to be seen from a certain distance. In Dürer's cutting the virtuosity of the knife disappears in its very success in rendering the drawn line. Titian's looser design invites the knife to leave its own signature, to impose its own language on the line in translation, transforming linear continuity into broken edges, curves into facets. Defined from outside, the line loses some of its organic integrity as pen trace and becomes instead a more blatant, irregular mark. And yet by this very dialectic we are made all the more aware of linear structure itself.

3. *The Sketched Plate*

In both engraving and woodcut, then, the drawn line is transformed technically, mechanically. The engraver's burin essentially substitutes its own line for that of the drawn model; it creates its own logic and order of representational system. If the woodcut professes a certain fidelity to the drawing it reproduces, the drawn line nonetheless suffers inevitably the indignity of the blade, which cannot but, by its slicing and chiseling, betray the organic flow of the pen, of *la viva mano*. Both media, engraving and woodcut, involve physical operations that are natural to their materials – incising into metal, cutting away wood – and that are fundamentally different from the natural action of the drawing (or writing) hand guiding a pen. Hence the history of printmaking is documented by signatures that distinguish the hand that designed (*delineavit*) from the one that incised or carved (*incidebat* or *sculpsit*), a distinction (if not a vocabulary) we encounter most explicitly in Marcantonio's execution of Raphael's design.[33]

One printmaking technique, however, records the direct intervention of the draftsman himself: etching required – at least at the first stage of design – no special craft skill beyond the ability to draw. The artist drew directly on the prepared plate, using a sharpened metal instrument instead of a pen. The point of the needle scratched through the covering ground revealing the metal beneath; the plate was then exposed to acid, which corroded only the exposed metal of the design, leaving grooves to be inked as in engraving. True, the procedures of the acid biting required a certain technical control, as did the preparation of the protective ground, especially to avoid foul biting, and one had to be careful about the spacing of lines to avoid undercutting by the acid. Nonetheless, etching was much less laborious and time consuming than either engraving or woodcut. It was essen-

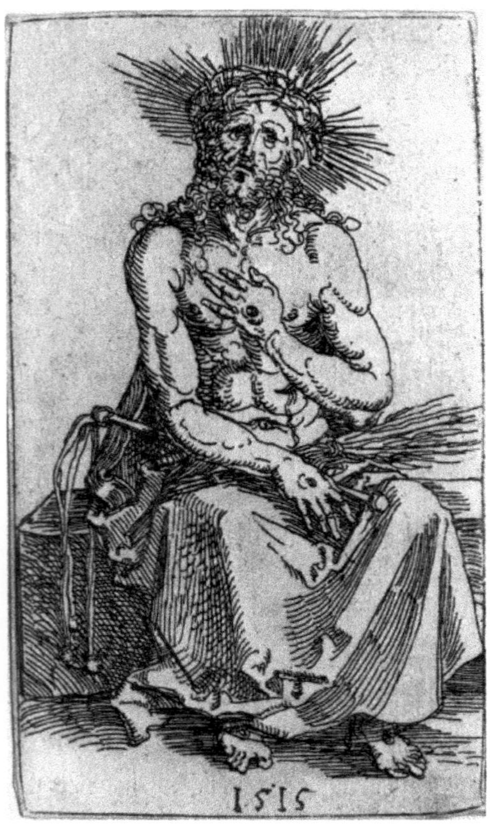

162. Albrecht Dürer, *Christ as Man of Sorrows*. Etching, 11 × 6.5 cm. British Museum, London.

tially like drawing, and therein lay its special appeal to painters.[34]

The fact that the artist *draws* directly on the grounded plate, was a crucial point for Vasari. In his laconic paragraph on etching he emphasized how much easier it was than engraving, but he noted as well the different character of the acid-bitten line, much less clean than the burin's incision.[35] A highly valued virtue of engraving, as we have seen, was the clarity of its line and of its linear structures, a direct product of the burin's neat incision. The corrosive action of acid on a metal plate, on the other hand, produced a line roughly bitten at its edges, less precisely inflectable, less elegant than the engraved *taille* (Fig. 162). As if in response to that criticism, etching masters in the seventeenth century developed techniques – such as a hard ground and instruments like the *échoppe* – that allowed the production in etching of a line neat and flexible enough to rival the burin and imitate the graphic decorum of engraving (Figs. 163, 164). But originally, in the earlier sixteenth century, the primary virtue of etching lay in its facility, in the directness of its design, its function not as the reproduction or imitation of drawing but rather as drawing itself.

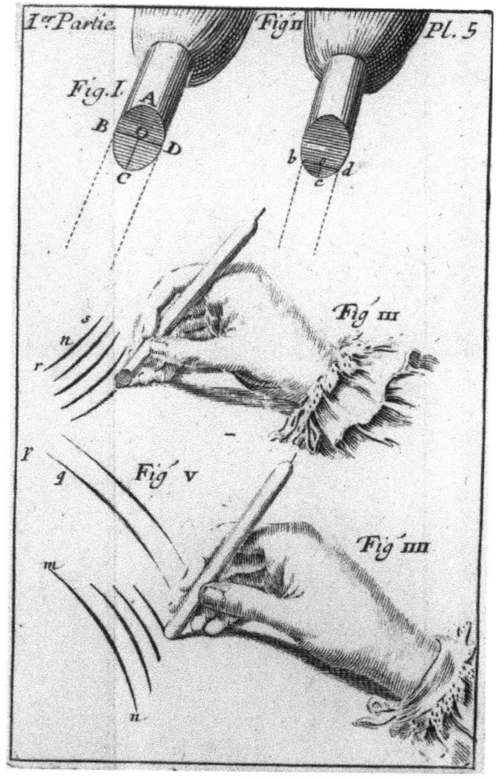

163. Abraham Bosse, L'échoppe. Plate 5 from *Traicté des manières de graveur en taille douce* (1645; ed. 1758). Engraving, 20.3 × 12.7 cm. Metropolitan Museum of Art, New York. Gift of Lincoln Kirstein, 1963 (63.568.61).

Continuing his comments on etching, Vasari singles out as his first examples of the medium several works by Parmigianino "che sono molto graziose." Parmigianino was indeed the first Italian *peintre-graveur* to produce a significant body of prints in etching, the first painter to recognize the expressive potential of the medium. Despite experiments by Dürer and other German artists, as well as efforts by Marcantonio to mix etching and engraving,[36] it was Parmigianino who in exploring the medium recognized its inherent quality as *disegno.* Interestingly, what may be his first essay in the medium, a *Sleeping Cupid* (Fig. 165), derives from the figure of the central dead infant in the Raphael–Marcantonio *Massacre of the Innocents* (Fig. 121).[37] From that engraving – and possibly from Marcantonio himself – Parmigianino learned the graphic language of printmaking, the control of line and fleck and dot that creates tone out of black and white. Very quickly, however, he adapted the etching needle to his own fluid mode of drawing. Etching, he found, preserved the impulses of his drawing hand and, therefore, permitted immediate registration of the imaginings of the creative mind – that "cervello capriccioso" which, according to Vasari, is what led the young Parmesan artist to take up printmaking in the first place.[38]

Etching, like drawing, afforded a means to "sfogare i capricci" – as Vasari said of

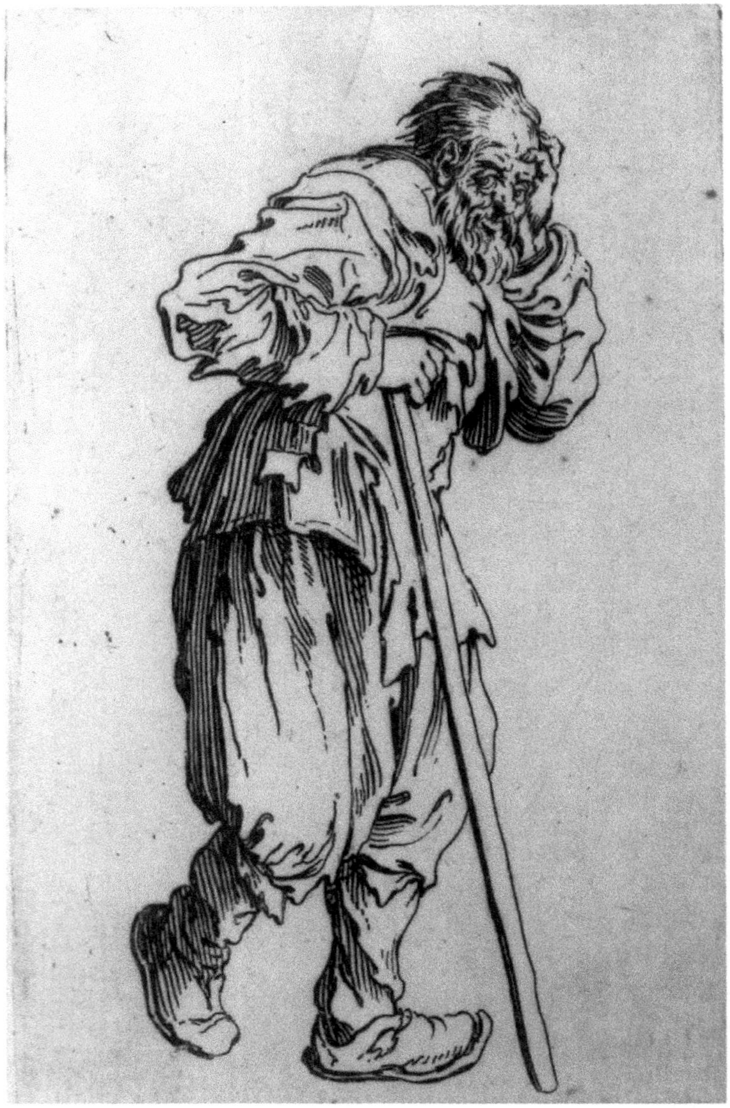

164. Jacques Callot, *Beggar with a Stick*. Etching, 13.8 × 8.7 cm. National Gallery of Art, Washington. Rosenwald Collection (1949.5.299 [B-15,605]). Photograph ©2000 Board of Trustees, National Gallery of Art.

Dürer's printmaking. These were not images made on commission or to serve any other function than to demonstrate the artist's talent as both *disegnatore* and *inventore* (Fig. 166). Like drawings, Parmigianino's etchings represented the "concetto che si ha nell'animo"; more particularly, like sketches, they retained the "furor dello artefice," that first fire of invention. In the developing appreciation of the free sketch Parmigianino's etchings must have played a critical role in educating an audience in the values of an open graphic aesthetic. Their loose linework and general openness of facture, testimony to the rapidity of execution, were fixed and replicated in and through the print medium. It was the etchings he had in mind

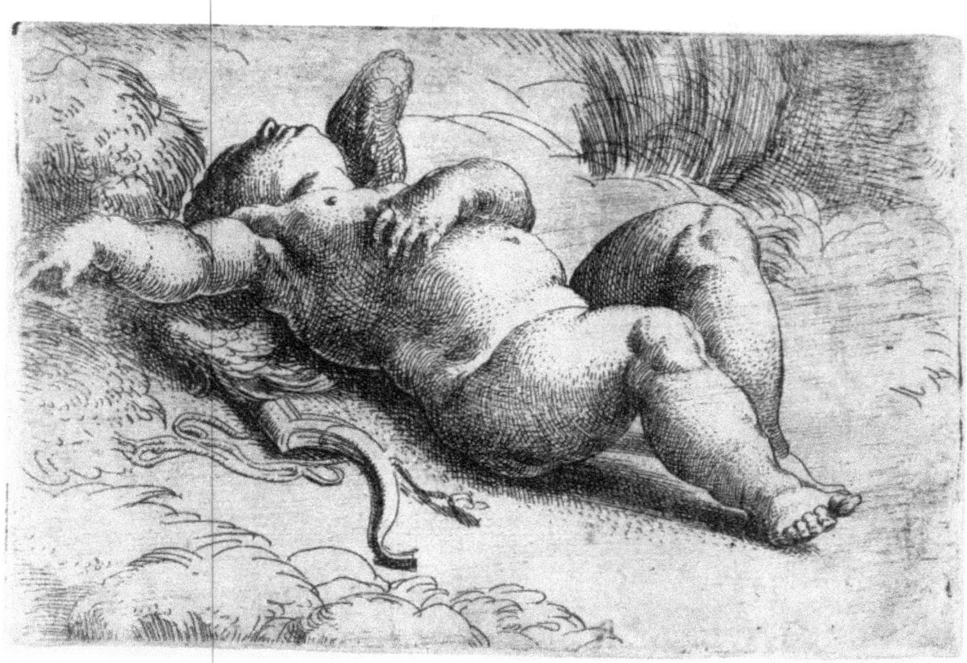

165. Parmigianino, *Sleeping Cupid.* Etching, 7.3 × 11.4 cm. British Museum, London (1855-2-14-78).

when El Greco noted that Parmigianino was "born to show through his sketches or scratchings what is called beauty and grace in figures."[39]

Sketching and scratching: the relationship goes beyond the assonance of the two terms in English. Both imply a certain haste, a lightness of touch, a tentative, even casual marking gesture. Indeed, more than a generation before etching was fully claimed by painters, drypoint had afforded the draftsman a means of drawing directly on the plate. Using a sharpened metal instrument, the artist scratched his design into the metal. Although an *intaglio* technique like engraving, drypoint offered a profoundly different experience and effect. The engraver's burin, held firmly against the palm of the hand, pushes into and through the plate, neatly lifting a curling strip of metal from the incised groove. The drypoint needle is held like a pen; pulled across and scratching the surface, it displaces metal to either side of its course. In printing, that resulting burr spreads the ink beyond the scratched line proper, bleeding the tone and thereby softening the sharpness of the line. This tonal transformation of line, however, was good for only a few impressions, for the burr would inevitably wear off in the process of printing.

Such direct intervention on the plate relates drypoint technique to engraving, and engravers used it to add finishing touches or tone to their work. Mantegna may have exploited drypoint in this way, to modify his engraved plates by softening their linear structures.[40] But one artist contemporary with Mantegna, an anonymous northerner whom we call the Housebook Master, made much more ambitious use of the technique and has left a corpus of some ninety images executed in drypoint (Fig. 167).[41] Ranging in subject from the religious and the moralizing to the comic, parodic, and fantastic, these designs were evidently made to "sfogare i suoi capricci." The liveliness of touch of the Housebook Master's drawing needle informs his interpretation of even the gravest religious themes. The graphic informality of its quick flecks and scratches, fundamentally different from the more decorous regularity of engraving (Fig. 168), is a constant reminder of the drawing hand. Drawings attributed to the master reveal a similar kind of light touch, quick and nervous, somewhat hesitant, without, however, being timid. The vitality of each mark contributes to that of the larger image; the rapidity and apparent casualness of its application record a pace and rhythm of execution that create a sense of moment.

The Housebook Master's graphic touch participates in that aesthetic of openness, of form and facture, developing throughout much of Europe toward 1500 and which will include a comparable loosening of technique in the work of Bosch in the Netherlands and Giorgione in Italy, and which finds its most articulate voice in Leonardo. Epitomizing that aesthetic is the sketch, the image closest to the generating moment of inspiration. Still inchoate but "tutto fiero ed acceso," this

166. Parmigianino, *A Youth and Two Old Men.* Etching, 12.1 × 9.4 cm. British Museum, London (1855-2-14-81).

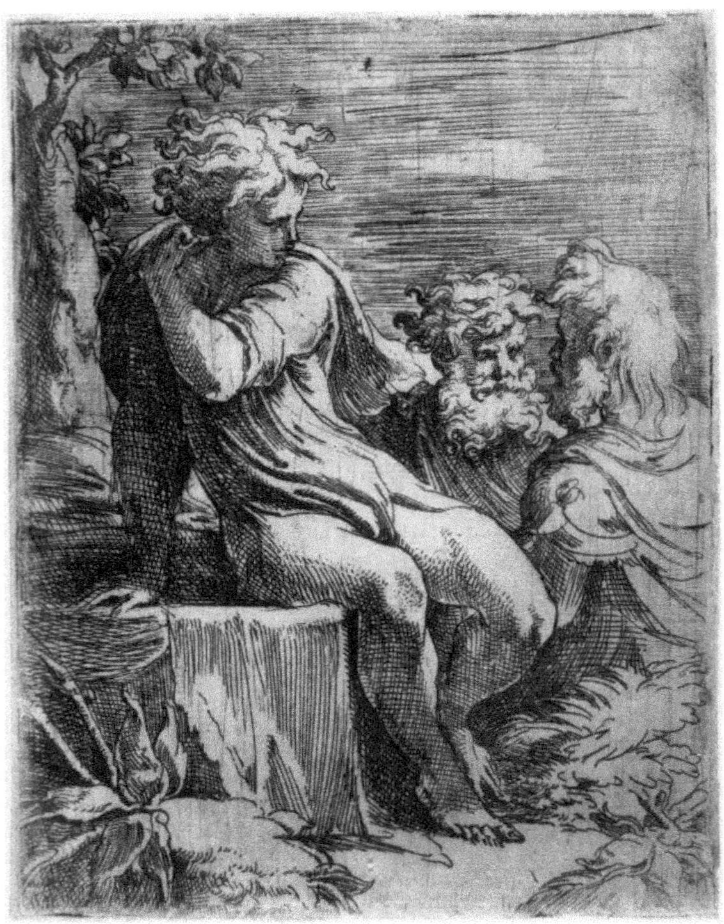

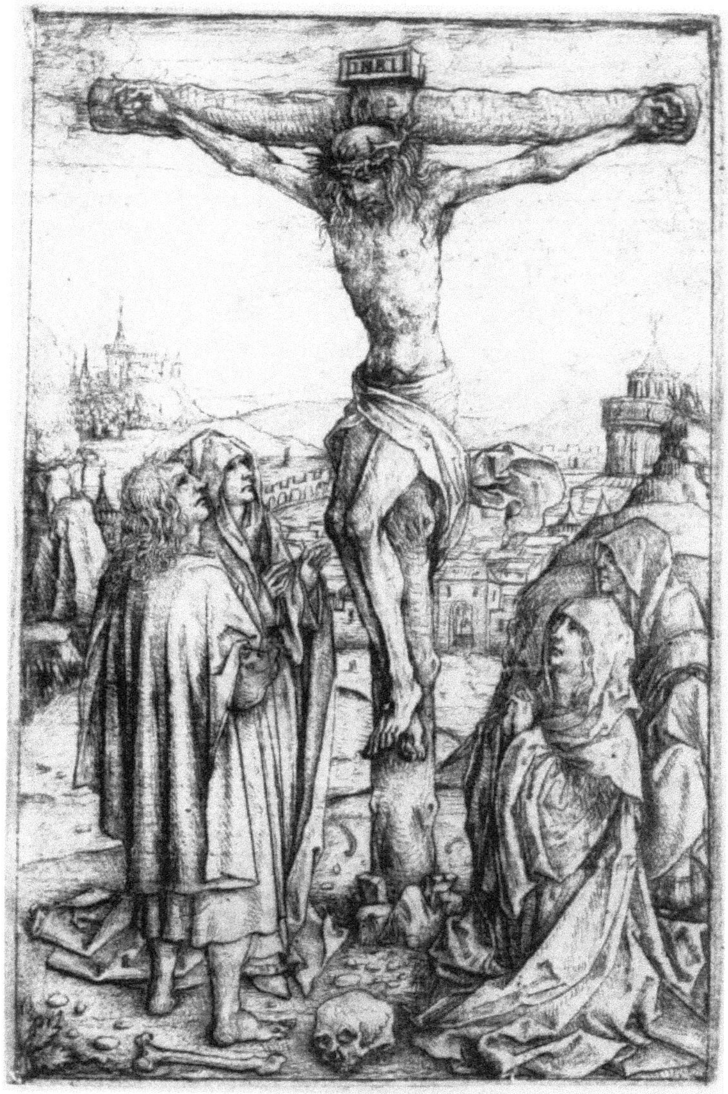

167. Housebook Master, *The Crucifixion with St. John and the Holy Women.* Drypoint, 15.5 × 9.9 cm. Rijksmuseum, Amsterdam.

exploratory mode extends its values to drawing in a more general way, validating the open structures of graphic representation. The etchings of Parmigianino disseminated not only his own figure style but this aesthetic as well, which was confirmed by their very popularity.

Following his lead, Andrea Schiavone pushed the print medium still further, experimenting with combinations of techniques (Fig. 169). Schiavone seems to have used drypoint extensively, reinforcing its light lines through etching. He often manipulated plate tone through deliberately controlled wiping or applied a wash of color to his prints with the brush, thereby returning to a *disegno a stampa* some quality of *la viva mano.* As a draftsman, Schiavone hardly rivaled Parmigianino, and this relative weakness seems to have encouraged a heavy investment in linear pattern that can seem excessive at times. His plates can appear overworked, as though the designer had little confidence in the expressive capacity of line itself; rarely do we encounter a single line asserting its own aesthetic presence, "una linea sola non stentata." The effect is, rather, pictorial: a very busy drawing hand producing form out of broad and sometimes quite irregular areas of massed lines. And it is that graphic activity, the sheer concentration of the needle, that establishes the vibrant surface of Schiavone's prints and that keeps the motions of their making so evident – including the many accidental scratches that testify to a certain casual attitude toward the plate. If his haste of execution failed to appeal to Vasari, who could only condemn such disorder, it could nonetheless be appreciated

168. Martin Schongauer, *The Crucifixion.* Engraving, 28.6 × 43 cm. Amsterdam, Rijksmuseum.

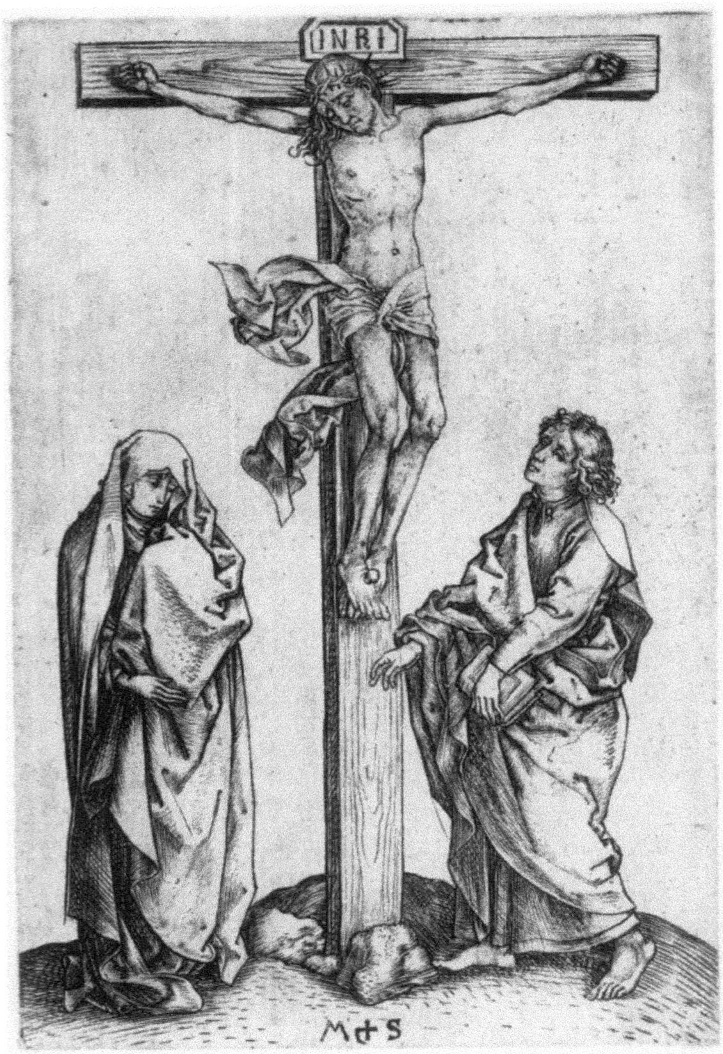

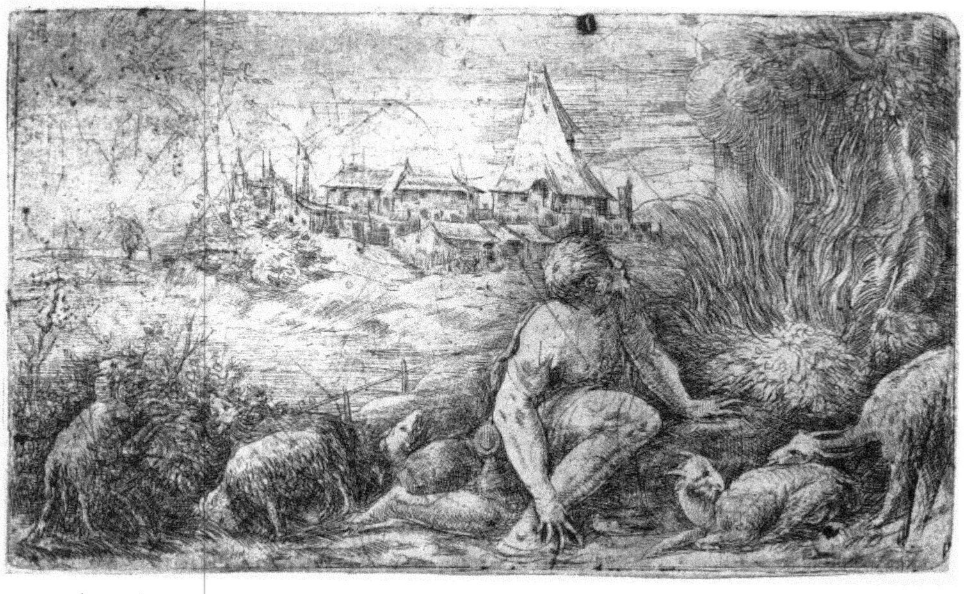

169. Andrea Schiavone, *Moses and the Burning Bush*, second state. Etching, 12.5 × 21.6 cm. Metropolitan Museum of Art, New York. Harris Brisbane Dick Fund, 1927 (27.78.2[26]).

in light of the very aesthetic Vasari himself had helped to articulate, as a sign of "il furor dello artefice."[42]

The *peintre-graveur* who most fully realized the expressive potential of working directly on the plate, in etching and drypoint, was, of course, Rembrandt. In etching, he invented an incredible range of linear systems, each responsive to a particular mimetic function but also asserting enough graphic independence to testify to the invention itself. Rembrandt found the copper plate as congenial as paper. His casually produced plates are like sheets from a sketchpad (Fig. 170): assorted images, more or less fully rendered, sometimes barely scratched, in different orientations. He turned the copper plate as frequently as necessary to gain a proper approach to the available space. And what may have been casual practice at the beginning nonetheless became fundamental style in his more mature work.[43] As in drawing so in etching: lines built up toward a dense central image but dissipate into the surrounding blankness of untouched surface toward the margins. Following the increasing density of linework toward the core, one follows the very processes of graphic representation, of drawing itself.

Rembrandt's scribbling, so apparently casual and even haphazard, acquires system through its participation in the larger order of the image (Fig. 171). Each area of hatching, by its own impulse seems to have been generated by its own graphic energy; each seems to run its own course, as the hand swings through its rhythmic coverage. Coming together, overlapping, these separate units reinforce one another; by their distinction they affirm the independence of their neighbors, even as they surrender that independence to the common cause of representation. Out of apparent graphic chaos comes a larger order in the field.

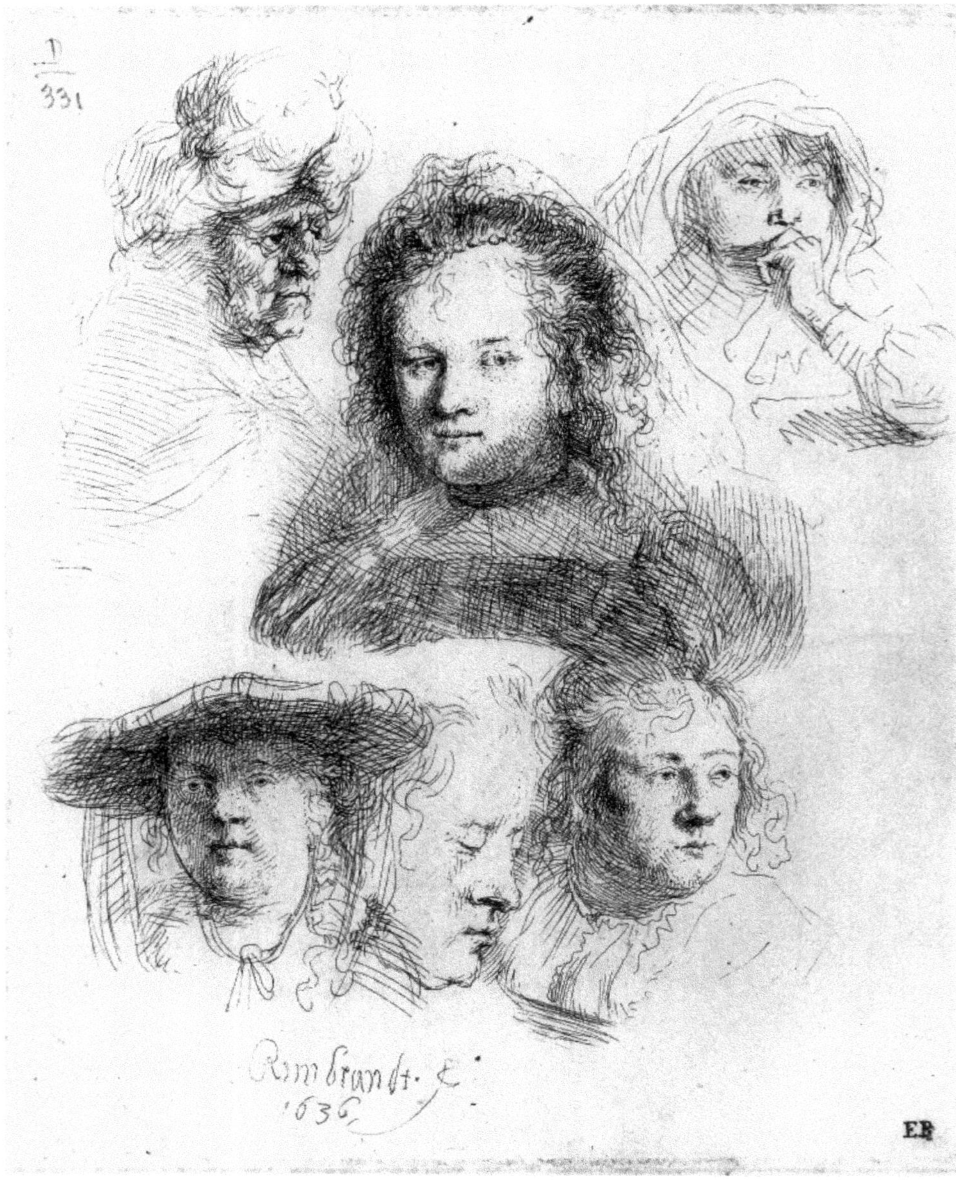

170. Rembrandt, *Studies of the Head of Saskia and of an Old Woman.* Etching, 15.1 × 12.6 cm. Museum Het Rembrandthuis, Amsterdam.

Rembrandt's direct intervention in the printing process involved creative inking and wiping of the plate as well as the selection of particular and unique papers. Like Schiavone and, more relevantly, his own compatriot Hercules Seghers, Rembrandt reclaimed for printmaking the vitality of the lively hand. No printmaker, before or after, subjected a plate to such constant transformation – developing a design, modifying it, reworking it on small and large scale, burnishing out entire areas, until the copper surface could presumably suffer no further attention (Figs. 172, 173).[44]

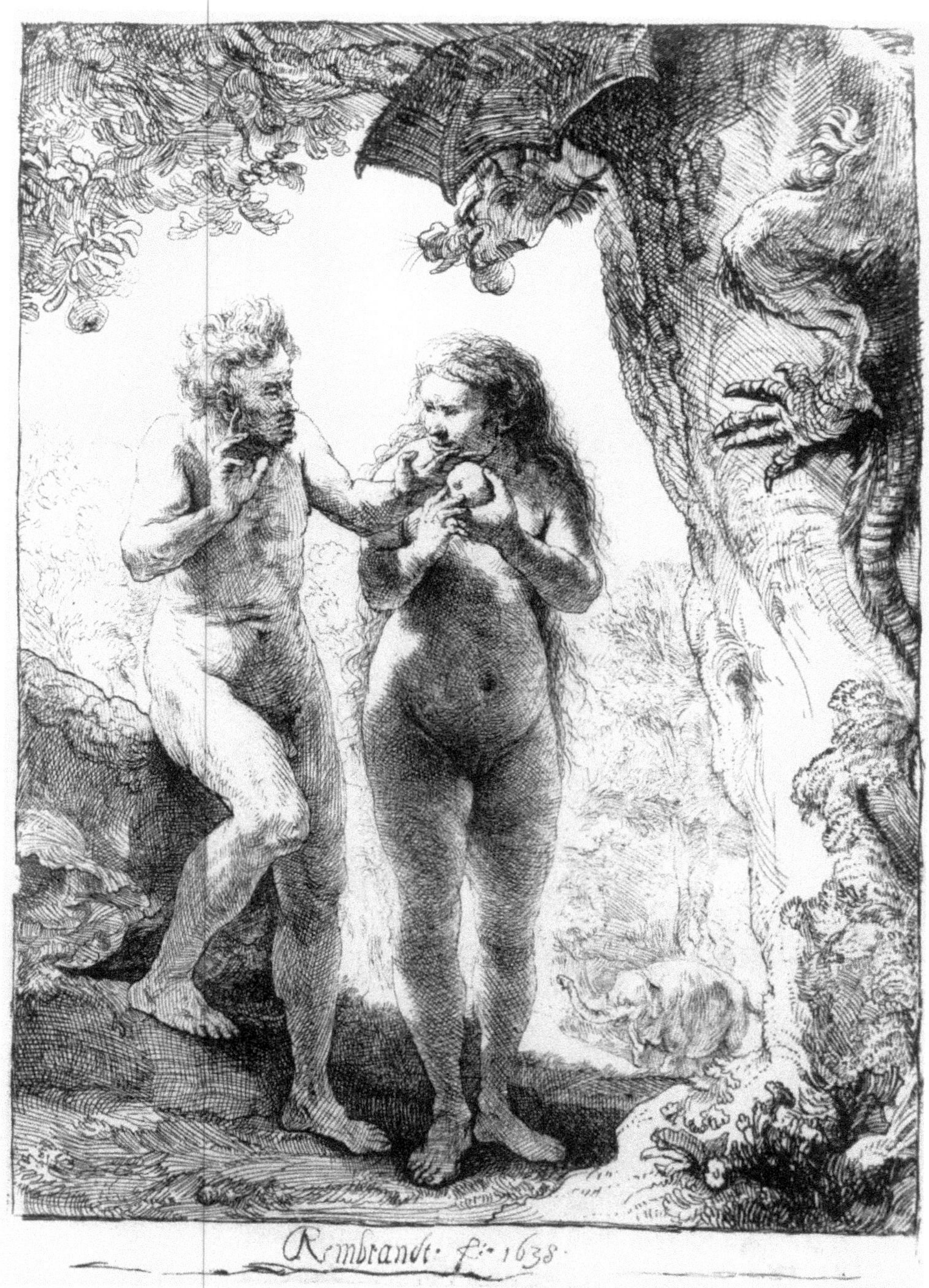

171. Rembrandt, *Adam and Eve,* second state. Etching, 16.2 × 11.6 cm. Museum Het Rembrandthuis, Amsterdam.

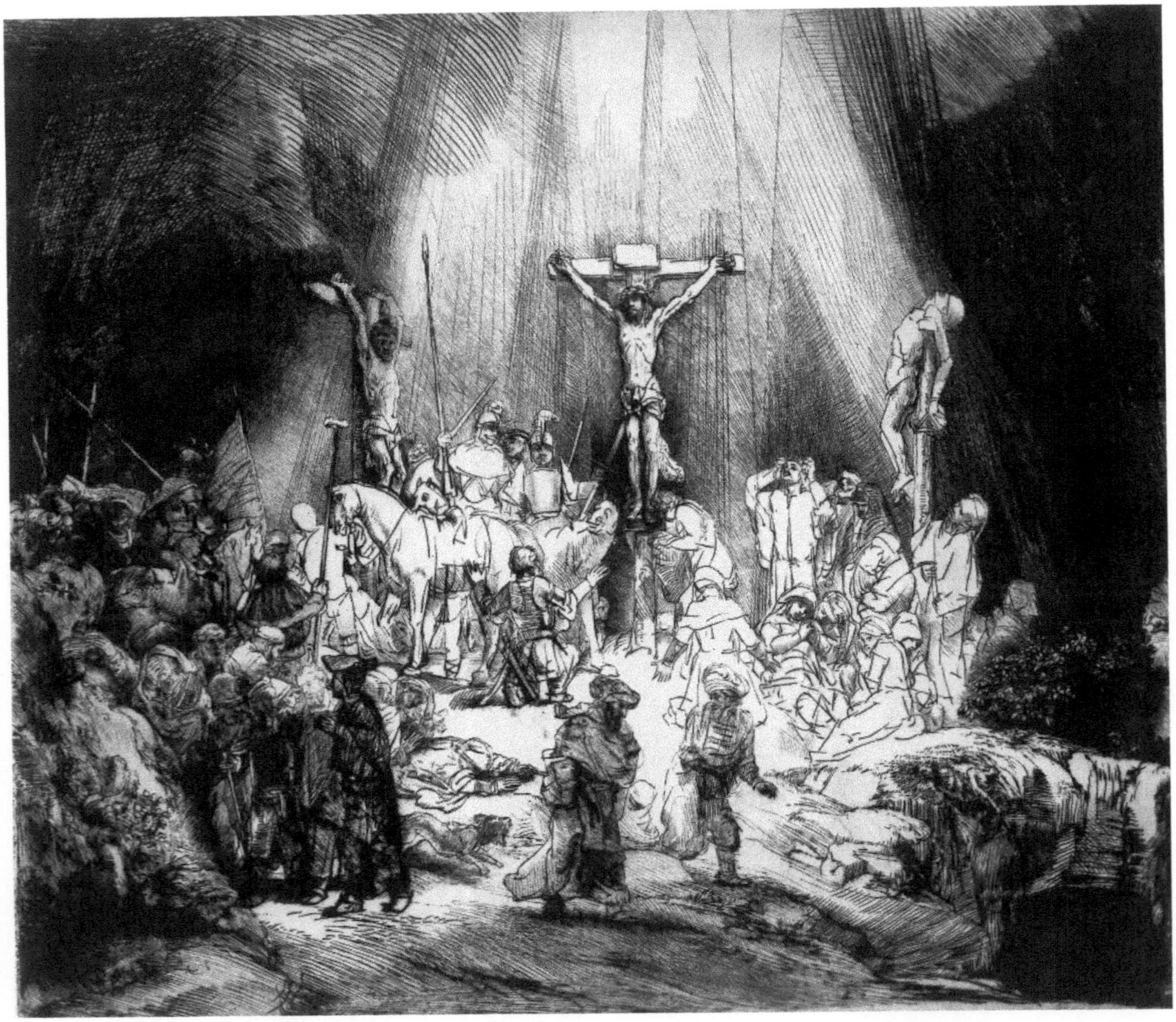

172. Rembrandt, *The Three Crosses*, first state. Drypoint and burin, 38.5 × 45 cm. The Pierpont Morgan Library, New York (B.78,I). Photo: David A. Loggie.

Toward the end of his career as printmaker, Rembrandt abandoned etching altogether to devote himself exclusively to direct engagement with the copper through drypoint. Out of the dialectic between needle and copperplate he created a graphic style of complex simplicity. Drawing on and in the metal, he appropriated the obdurate resistance of the latter to his own purpose. The resulting stiff lines that became the simple contours of his figures lent those same figures a formal nobility, an archaic quality that compressed expression into the most rigorous efficiency. Although it informs Rembrandt's late painting and drawing as well, especially his drawing with the reed pen, this "breadth and squareness of execution"[45] offers eloquent testimony to the physical endeavor, and ultimate triumph, of *la viva mano.*

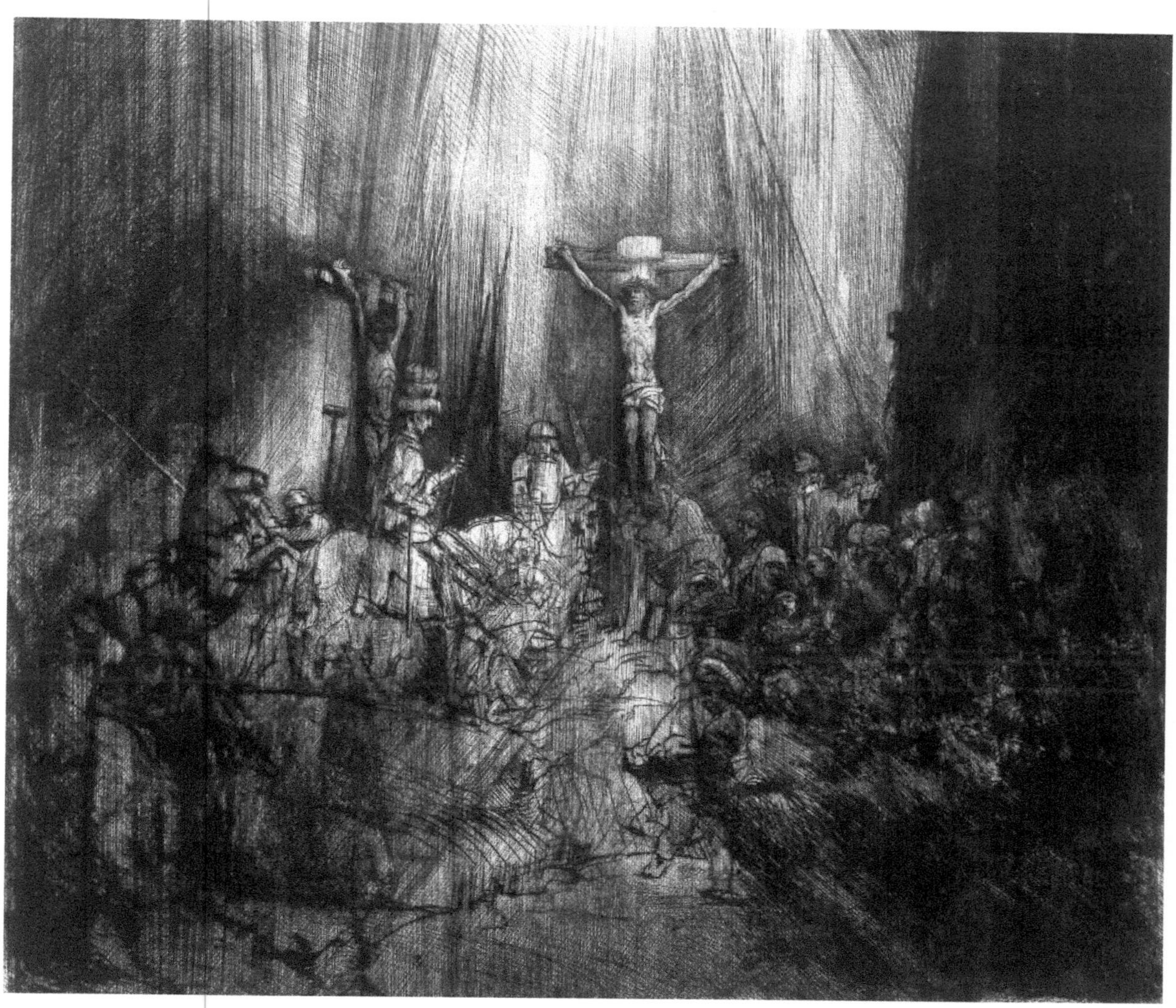

173. Rembrandt, *The Three Crosses,* fourth state. Drypoint and burin, 38.5 × 45 cm. The Pierpont Morgan Library, New York (B.78,IV). Photo: David A. Loggie.

CHAPTER SIX

Michelangelo
The Urgent Gesture

la penna al buon voler non po gir presso.
– Petrarch, *Rime sparse* XXIII

In a monograph on Michelangelo, published over a century ago but still among the most resonant in the vast bibiliography on the artist, John Addington Symonds recapitulated a basic assumption of connoisseurship: "If we seek to penetrate the genius of an artist," he wrote,

> . . . probing his personality to the core, as near as this is possible for us to do, we ought to give our undivided study to his drawings. It is there, and there alone, that we come face to face with the real man, in his unguarded moments, in his hours of inspiration, in the laborious effort

> to solve a problem of composition, or in the happy flow of genial improvisation. . . . The simplicity of a sketch, the comparative rapidity with which it is produced, the concentration of meaning demanded by its rigid economy of means, render it more symbolical, more like the hieroglyph of its maker's mind, than any finished work can be.[1]

Whatever our fascination with "a painted picture or a carved statue," Symonds continues, "we shall never find exactly the same thing, never the involuntary revelation of the artist's soul, the irrefutable witness to his mental and moral qualities, to the mysteries of his genius and to its limitations."

However uncomfortable we might feel with such language following the *fin d'un autre siècle* – after all, what postmodernist would not blush at mouthing words like "genius" or "soul," let alone "real man"? – Symonds's late romantic belief in the artist in the work professes an aesthetic creed central to the Western tradition at least since the Renaissance and rooted in classical antiquity. We have been following it from the *linea summae tenuitatis* of Apelles through the "O" of Giotto to the appreciative enthusiasm of a critic like Roger de Piles.

That drawn marks, dependent as they are on the immediate recording impulse, take us close to the spontaneous act of creation has been assumed since the sixteenth century. And we continue to recognize in the rapid sketch a document of the moment of inspiration or, still in the Platonizing vocabulary of the Renaissance, of creative fury. It is just this appreciation of spontaneity that comes to privilege the sketch over the finished drawing, as the more immediate and therefore more self-revealing creative document.

Although very much a master of the inspired sketch, Michelangelo challenges the exclusive claims to authenticity of that mode of drawing. Famously – or infamously – shortly before his death he is known to have burned many of his drawings. His motivation, according to Vasari, was to hide the labor that went into his art, so as not to appear less than perfect himself.[2] Within a culture that had developed a taste for the unfinished work, for the sketch that revealed and recorded the mechanics of the creative process, Michelangelo seems determined to deny such public access to himself. The visual and physical realization of the idea in the mind ("sì grandi e terribili concetti" [Vasari]) was indeed a struggle and, too often, a frustration. The graphic groping of the sketch, an awkward and tentative beginning, was not something to be shared. No artist of the Renaissance so jealously guarded the operations of his hand and yet was so attentive to those operations, so painfully aware of their ambitions and failures. "I have heard him say that he never draws a line without remembering whether he has ever drawn it before," writes Ascanio Condivi, the master's amanuensis, adding that if, perchance, the great draftsman ever did repeat a line he would erase it before it could be seen by anyone.[3] The biographer's account of Michelangelo's most tenacious memory ("tenacissima memoria") leads then to the artist's most powerful imagination ("potentissima virtù immaginativa") and to his frustrated dissatisfaction with his own work, with the failure of his hand to give adequate form to the inner ideas of the mind.[4]

Whatever his self-doubt and self-protectiveness, Michelangelo was nevertheless quite ready to send out into the world a certain kind of drawing: elaborately executed graphic gifts, self-conscious models of *buon disegno.* Indeed (pace Symonds), in such highly finished designs Michelangelo allows, deliberately demonstrates, precisely the revelation of the artist, but now a voluntary revelation of the soul. His fully rendered images in black or red chalk represent a very special category of drawing for him in which he invested his most intimate feelings and to which he did indeed confide his self. They affirm the position of the art of drawing both within a general cultural system and as a deeply personal phenomenon.

1. Father of the Arts

Within the evolving art theory of the Renaissance, drawing had become identified with the creative process itself: from the earliest sketches of an idea through the further elaboration of the composition in more sustained studies of individual motifs to the final finished design or cartoon.[5] By the sixteenth century, as we have seen, *disegno* was firmly fixed at the center of Renaissance art theory, acknowledged as the foundation of the visual arts. The "father" of the arts of painting, sculpture, and architecture, *disegno* is the essential creative or formative faculty that unites these arts. In the aesthetic rhetoric of the Renaissance, it is what the artist shares with God (*deus artifex*), the first maker. *Disegno* could be defined as "divine speculation," the operations of the inventing imagination. Standing as the great witness and monument to its primal energies was Creation itself. On earth, that creative faculty found its fullest incarnation in one artist, the absolute master of all three *arti del disegno,* the "divine" Michelangelo – "Michel, più che mortale, Angel divino" (Ariosto, *Orlando furioso,* XXXIII, 2). Vasari bore witness to the aesthetic worship of his age. Indeed, for no other artist of the Renaissance did drawing assume such a deeply personal function, as expression and communication. Hailed as both *padre* and *maestro* of the three arts of *disegno,* Michelangelo became the personification of *disegno* and, as such, its most authoritative spokesman.[6]

Vasari's biography of Michelangelo opens with a vision of divine aesthetic mercy in which *disegno* is the form assumed by grace and Michelangelo is its bearer:

> . . . the most benign Ruler of Heaven in his clemency turned His eyes to the earth, and, having seen the immense uselessness of all those labors, most ardent studies but fruitless, and the presumptuous self-satisfaction of men, which is farther from truth than darkness from light, in order to redeem us from such errors, determined to send down to earth a spirit with universal ability in every art and every profession, who, working by himself alone, would demonstrate just what is perfection in the art of *disegno. . . .*[7]

In an inspired transposition of the Christian salvation myth, Vasari rehearses the efforts of artists since Giotto to imitate the greatness of nature and attain perfect artistic understanding. Looking down upon earth and seeing the presumption and futility of their efforts, the benign Ruler of Heaven, taking pity upon these poor mortals, resolved to save them from their errors by sending into the world an artist who was master of every art and whose own work would be a revelation to mankind of "the perfection of the art of *disegno.*" Before then proceeding to cite the several manifestations of that art – painting, sculpture, and architecture – Vasari acknowledges its technical modality: Michelangelo first demonstrates the perfection of *disegno* precisely "in delineation of contour and shading" ("nel lineare, dintornare, ombrare e lumeggiare").[8]

By thus giving priority to the graphic base of its operations, Vasari, always the practicing artist, clearly founds his religious celebration of Michelangelo's *disegno* in the functional act of drawing.

2. *Drawing for an Other*

Modern connoisseurship has continued that worship, but in its concern with the relevant art-historical issues – of attribution, dating, and function – it has tended to slight the act itself. True, most Renaissance drawings were made with ulterior motive; they were developmental, preparatory steps toward final realization in another medium, and we can understand them best within the problem-solving context of their function. Other drawings, however, were made as independent works of art, complete in themselves. Such were the drawings Michelangelo made as gifts for presentation to those closest to him, those he loved. Deliberate examples of *buon disegno,* these highly worked models of draftsmanship in black or red chalk were created as objects of independent aesthetic value and social purpose or, late in his life, religious purpose. Profoundly self-expressive – more personal than professional, we might say – the deep meaning of these drawings, as I shall argue, resides in their making, in Michelangelo's graphic procedures, in the very act of drawing.[9]

The most famous group of such drawings, celebrated and copied soon after their completion, were those Michelangelo made for Tommaso de' Cavalieri, the handsome young Roman noble who became the object of the older artist's affection. Michelangelo expressed himself to Cavalieri in both poetry and drawing, as well as through an exchange of letters. Vasari reports that the artist made many incredibly beautiful sheets in black chalk and in red chalk for this aesthetically inclined youth; four were of mythological subjects: a *Rape of Ganymede,* a *Punishment of Tityus,* a *Fall of Phaethon,* and a *Bacchanal of Children,* in addition to "teste divine" and a large portrait of Cavalieri, "un cartone, grande di naturale."[10]

At least two of these drawings were sent as presents for Christmas 1532, initial offerings of friendship from the fifty-seven-year-old artist to the noble youth. This was Michelangelo's opening gesture to this unique "light of our century." Recognizing the presumption of being "the first to move," he speaks of the offerings he hopes and promises to make for his young lord.[11] On January 1, 1533, Cavalieri replied, honored that such a great master would take an interest in him and, significantly, in his own artistic endeavors; Michelangelo had evidently been shown some of Cavalieri's drawings. The young man explains that he is currently ill but hopes to be well enough within a few days to pay a visit to Michelangelo. Meanwhile, he writes, he will console himself by spending at least two hours a day contemplating the two drawings ("doi vostri desegni"): "the more I gaze upon them, the more they delight me," and, he adds, he takes comfort in the promise of seeing further works by his admirer.[12]

It is generally assumed that the two drawings in question correspond to the first two mythologies mentioned by Vasari, the *Rape of Ganymede* and the *Punishment of Tityus*, and that these two subjects were conceived by Michelangelo as a pair. The *Tityus* is almost certainly the drawing preserved in the Royal Library at Windsor Castle (Fig. 174).[13] The composition of the *Ganymede*, however, is known only through copies and, to complicate matters, in two different formats: the horizontal composition, depicting only the handsome shepherd and the ravishing eagle, is best known in a version, also at Windsor, attributable to Giulio Clovio (Fig. 175);[14] the vertical format, which includes a lower landscape with the shepherd's staff and bag and abandoned dog and sheep, is represented by a drawing in the Fogg Art

174. Michelangelo, *The Punishment of Tityus*. Black chalk, 19 × 33 cm. Royal Library, Windsor Castle (no. 12771). The Royal Collection ©2000, Her Majesty Queen Elizabeth II.

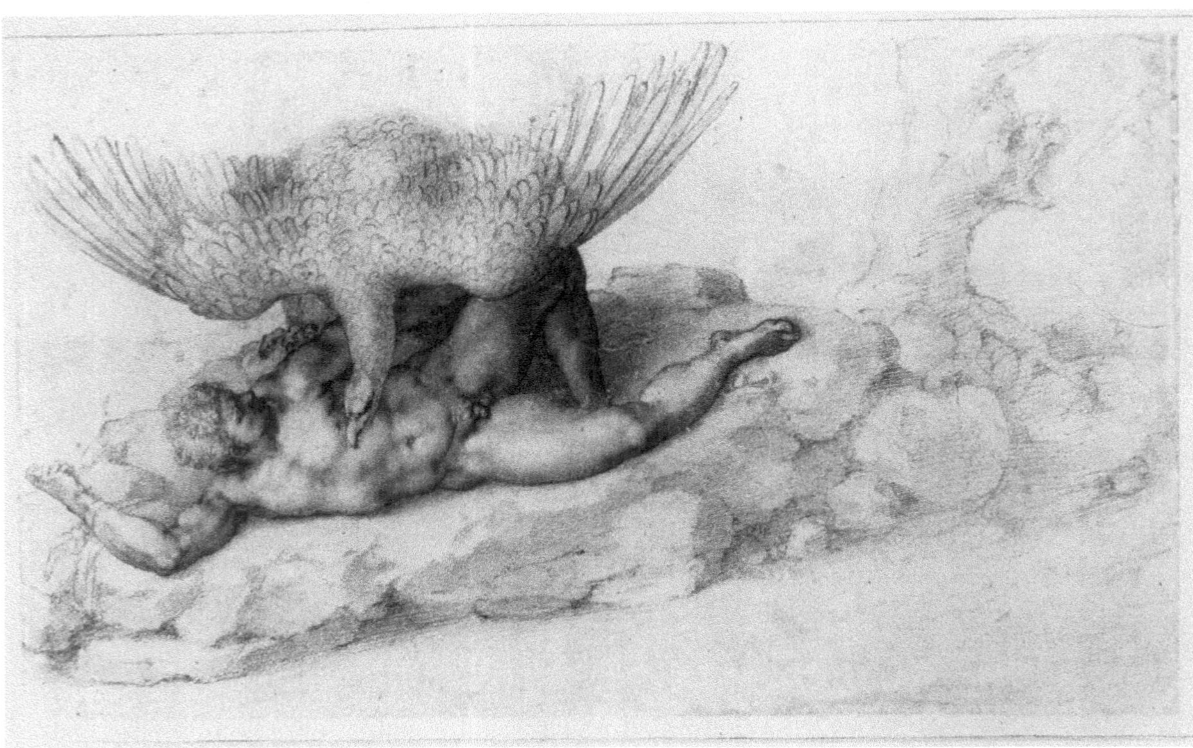

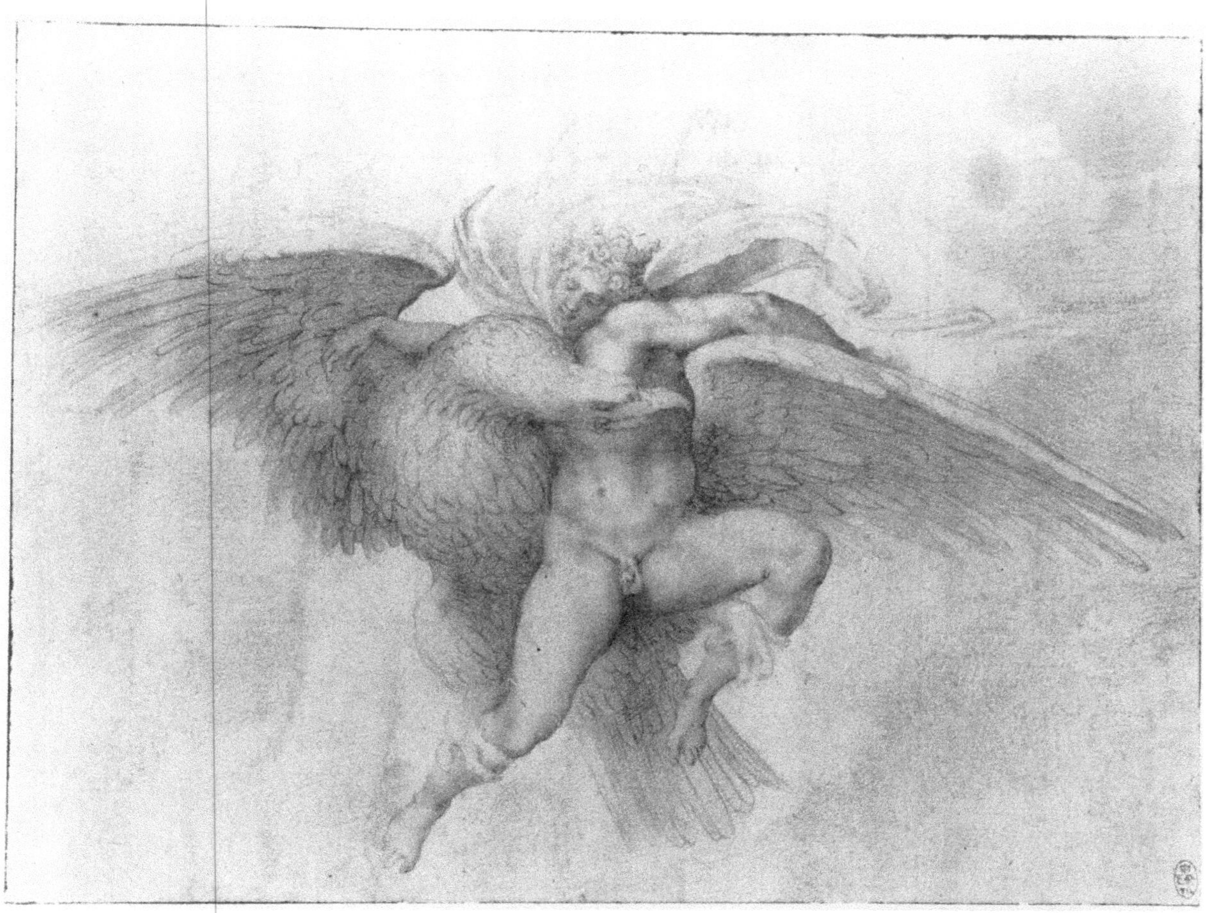

175. Giulio Clovio, *The Rape of Ganymede,* after Michelangelo. Black chalk, 19.2 × 26 cm. Royal Library, Windsor Castle (no. 13036). The Royal Collection ©2000, Her Majesty Queen Elizabeth II.

Museum (Fig. 176). Although the latter has been attributed to the master himself, it too seems rather a copy: the contours of Ganymede's torso and the arching neck of the eagle lack the torsion that one finds even in Clovio's drawing, and the internal anatomical modeling seems inarticulate, suggestively fudged rather than patiently constructed.[15] The simple outlines of the lower zone imply that Michelangelo may never have fully developed that part of his design. Both versions of the *Rape of Ganymede* were copied often in a variety of media, graphic and glyptic, and there seems little reason to doubt Michelangelo's inventive responsibility for both. But which was made for Cavalieri?

The fuller version, with the lower pastoral landscape and abandoned dog (cf. Virgil, *Aeneid,* V, 257), presents a binary structure of high and low that invites moralizing interpretation. The body borne heavenward on the wings of the god was early taken as a figure of the soul. Such spiritual transport is denied to the beast below, creature of mere matter only and condemned to purely terrestrial existence.[16] Lacking that lower earthly contrast, the horizontal version of the *Rape of*

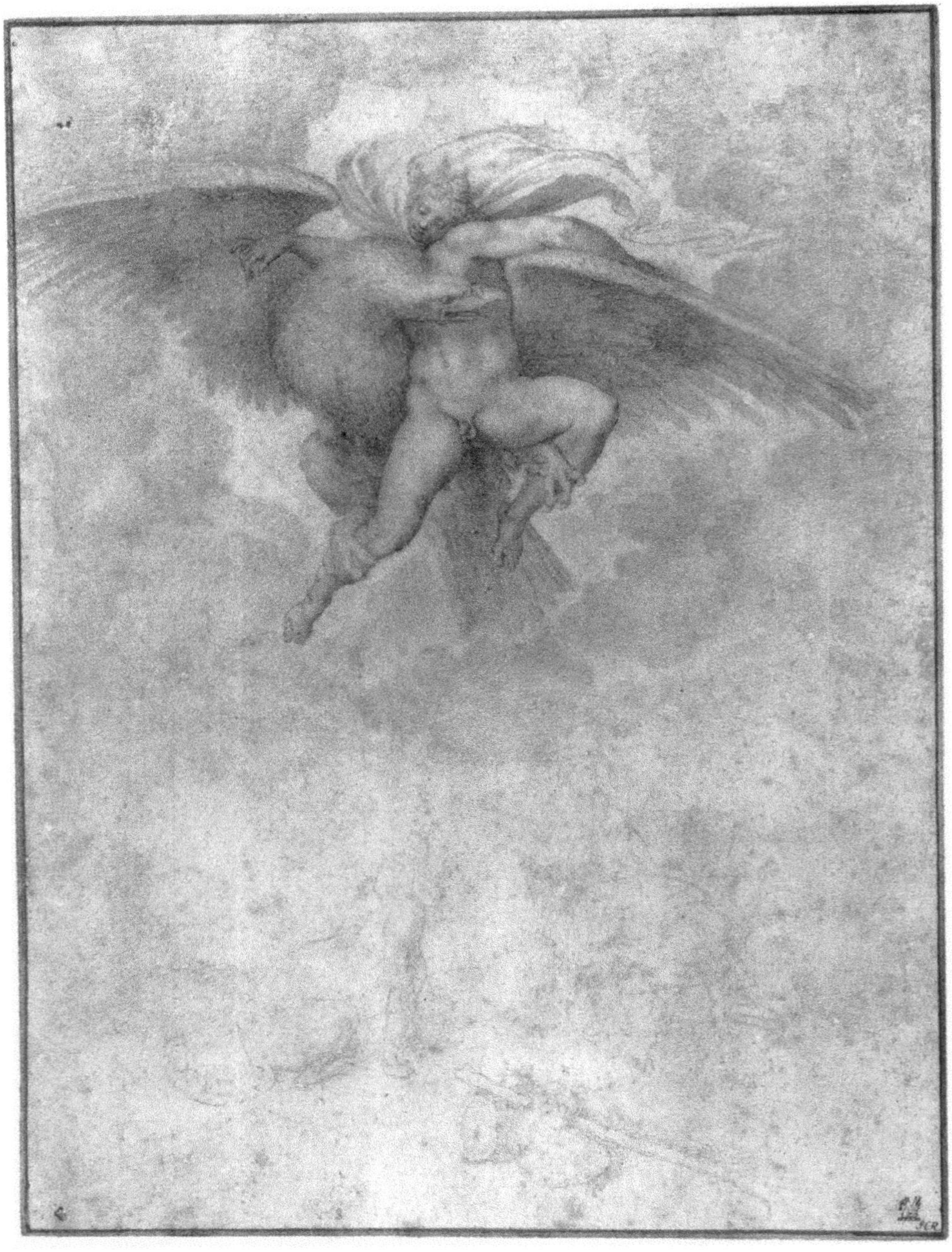

176. Michelangelo (?), *The Rape of Ganymede.* Black chalk, 36.1 × 27 cm. Fogg Art Museum, Harvard University Art Museums, Cambridge, Mass. (acc. no. 1955.750).

Ganymede seems to require some comparative complement to its heraldic declaration of divine love; it seems to require the *Punishment of Tityus.*[17]

In format and design these two compositions appear clearly complementary: one figure is horizontal, earthbound, the other, vertical and soaring heavenward; of the two large birds, one is threatening and destructive, the other caring and protective. These essential dichotomies encourage a dialectical reading of the pair. Within the context of their Renaissance culture, they offer themselves as a Michelangelesque version of the Neoplatonic theme of sacred and profane love, an interepretation insistently explored by Erwin Panofsky – and just as insistently denied by critics who would deny the interpretive challenge inherent in any mythological image of the Renaissance.[18]

Tityus, the son of Earth, was damned in Hades for his lustful assault upon Latona, mother of Apollo and chaste Diana. As punishment, his liver, the seat of carnal passion, was to be devoured by vultures for eternity. The mythic sinner, victim of his own sexual appetite, became in the Renaissance a symbol of love's torment, specifically of the agonies of sensual desire.

Ganymede, on the other hand, beloved of Jupiter, ascending to heaven on the wings of the god, symbolizes "the ecstasy of Platonic love, powerful to the point of annihilation, but freeing the soul from its physical bondages and carrying it to a sphere of Olympian bliss," to quote Panofsky's enthusiastic words. Michelangelo himself verbalized just that imagery in a sonnet addressed to Cavalieri, in which he envisions

> . . . one soul in two bodies made eternal,
> both rising to heaven with the same wings;
>
> (. . . un'anima in duo corpi1 è fatta etterna,
> ambo levando al cielo e con pari ale)[19]

Panofsky has well described the beautiful cup-bearer elect to the gods: ". . . in a state of trance without a will or a thought of his own, reduced to passive immobility by the iron grip of the gigantic eagle, the posture of his arms suggesting the attitude of an unconscious person or corpse, and his soul really *rimossa dal corpo. . . .*" But, we may wonder, in Michelangelo's art can the soul ever really be removed from the body? Is his conception of Ganymede unequivocally closer to Xenophon's moral reading, according to which the myth allegorically denotes the superiority of mind over body and the name itself is said to have its etymological roots in the Greek words for "to enjoy" and "intelligence"? Or may not Michelangelo's image actually accord better with Plato's explanation of the myth as an invention of the Cretans, a transparent justification of homosexual love, specifically between men and boys? In a revealing footnote dedicated to the possible classical prototypes for the design, Panofsky observed, with knowing innocence, that "no representation prior to Michelangelo shows Ganymede so firmly held in the grip of the eagle."[20] Without undue prurience, we recognize in this drawing a definite physical functionalism of pose, avian as well as human: Ganymede's loving eagle is in every sense the homosexual counterpart to Leda's swan (Fig. 177) – the two avian forms of divine love had been paired on ancient Roman sarcophagi.[21]

Even accepting that *Tityus* was presented to Cavalieri as a pendant with the *Ganymede*, there may be internal reason to question whether the design was originally conceived and executed with the noble youth in mind. On the reverse of the drawing the essential contours of the splayed Tityus have been traced and, the

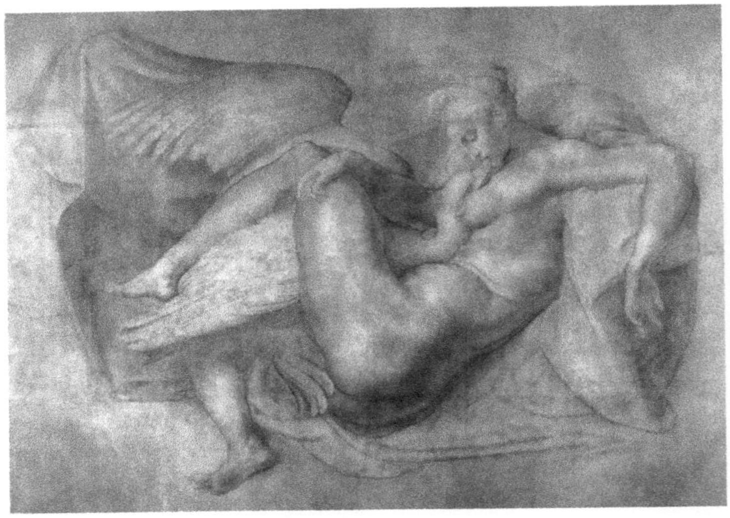

177. Rosso Fiorentino (attr.), *Leda and the Swan*, after Michelangelo. Black chalk, 170.1 × 248.8 cm. Royal Academy of Arts, London.

sheet rotated ninety degrees, thereby transforming the ancient giant into a resurrected Christ (Fig. 178). This translation of sinner into savior appears as a particularly charged example of the kind of figural operation common in Renaissance studio practice: the reversal of a figure to achieve an added dividend on the original invention. Assuming Michelangelo's own responsibility for this inflection, we may wonder at such an exercise on a drawing intended as a gift for another. This exploitation of invention suggests rather that the drawing remained in the studio, at least briefly, before being intended for Cavalieri.[22]

The tracing itself, however, is not entirely faithful to the contours of the recto: the upraised arm and the extended leg have both been straightened, adapting the figure to its new orientation, of vertical ascent. Knowingly schematic in its anatomical rendering, the new figure represents a pivotal moment in Michelangelo's graphic thinking. On the one hand, it recalls the type of resurrected figure that Michelangelo had designed for Sebastiano del Piombo's Lazarus and relates thematically to figures of the risen Christ that he had been developing at this same time, in the early 1530s (Fig. 179); on the other, formally it anticipates those figures that were soon to become a center of imaginative attention, the thundering Jupiter of the *Fall of Phaethon* (Figs. 180–82) and the judicial Christ of the *Last Judgment* (Figs. 183, 184). The verso transfiguration of Tityus, then, and the absorption of the new risen Christ into Michelangelo's figural vocabulary, must have been achieved before he decided to offer the drawing to Cavalieri.[23] That offering was made, presumably, along with the *Ganymede*. Whether or not they were the only offering made at the end of 1532, the pairing of the two drawings would have reinforced the interpretive dialectic that seems built into their structural relationship and confirmed by the poetic and epistolary correspondence between the artist and the object of his affection.

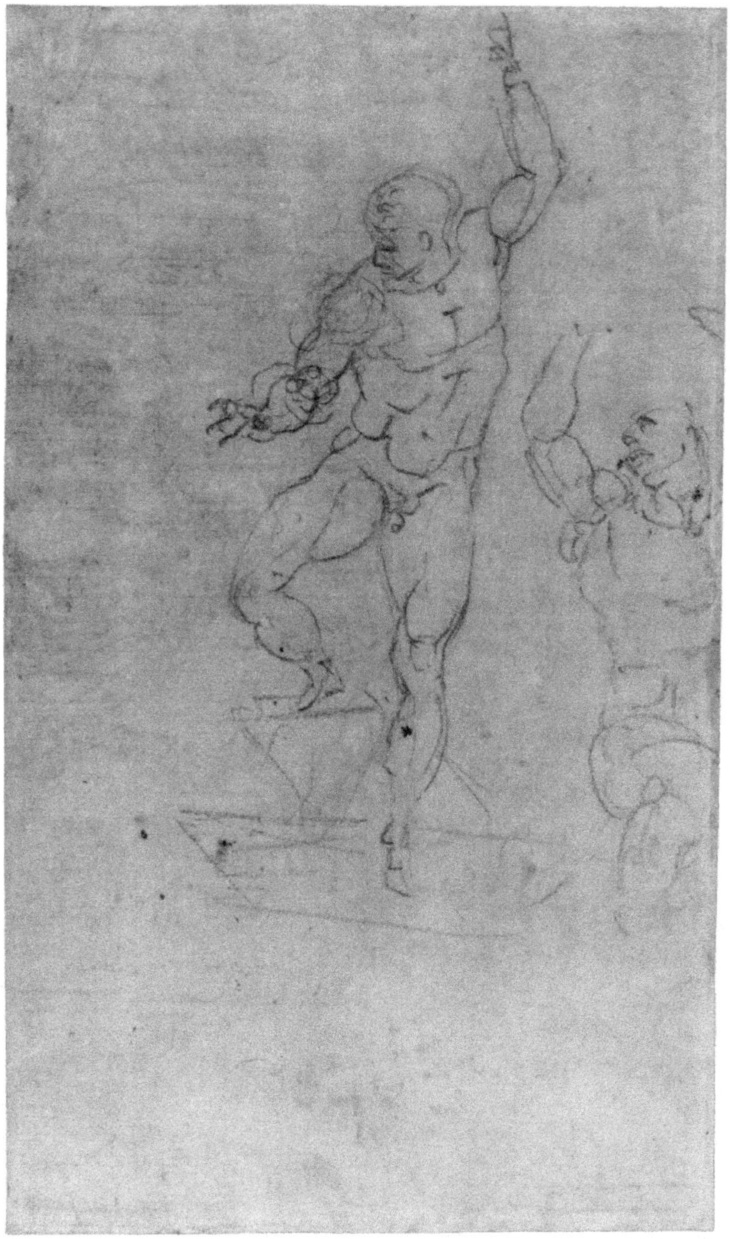

178. Michelangelo, *The Risen Christ*. Black chalk. Verso of Fig. 174.

Michelangelo's passion for human beauty was well known to his contemporaries. Its implications were evidently the subject of gossip, leading his faithful biographers to defend the purity of his intentions. Condivi is the first to confront the rumors:

> He has also loved the beauty of the human body as one who knows it extremely well, and loved it in such a way as to inspire certain carnal

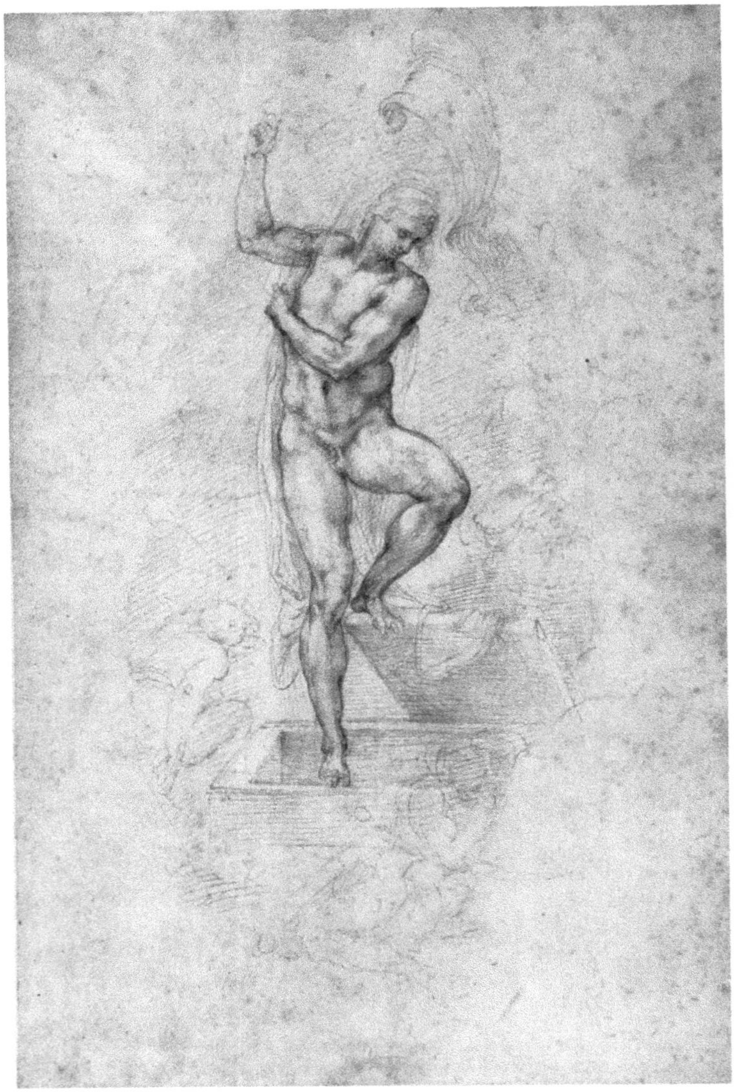

179. Michelangelo, *The Risen Christ.* Black chalk, 40.6 × 27.1 cm. British Museum, London (1887-5-2-119 [Wilde 53]).

men, who are incapable of understanding the love of beauty except as lascivious and indecent, to think and speak ill of him. It is as though Alcibiades, a very beautiful young man, had not been most chastely loved by Socrates, of whom he was wont to say that, when he lay down with him, he arose from his side as from the side of his father. I have often heard Michelangelo converse and discourse on the subject of love and have later heard from those who were present that what he said about love was no different than what we read in the writings of Plato. As for me, I do not know what Plato says on the subject, but I do know very well that, in all my long and intimate acquaintance with Michelangelo, I have never heard any but the most honorable words cross his lips,

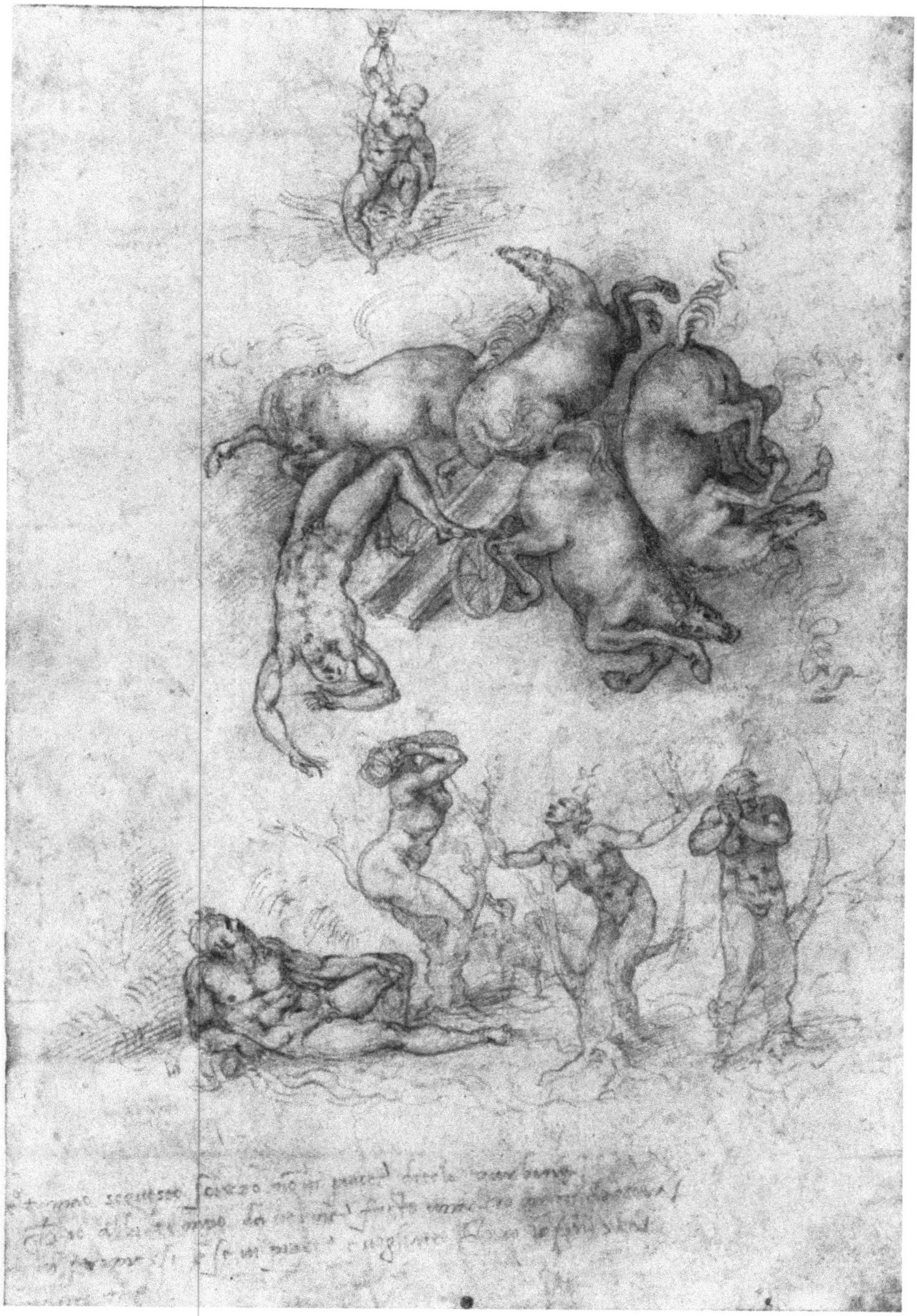

180. Michelangelo, *The Fall of Phaethon*. Black chalk, 31.3 × 21.7 cm. British Museum, London (1895-9-15-517 [Wilde 55]).

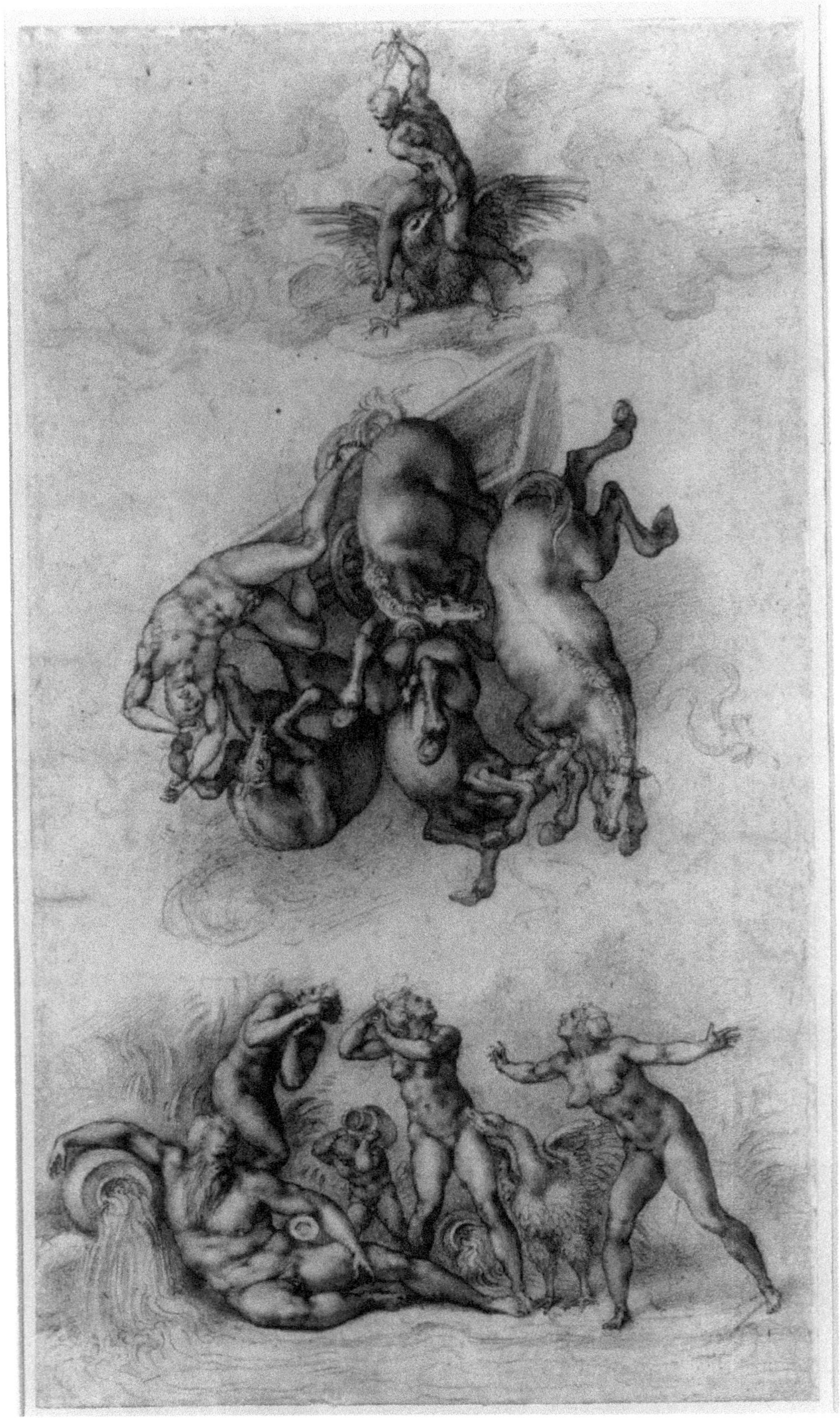

181. Michelangelo, *The Fall of Phaethon*. Black chalk, 41.3 × 23.4 cm. The Royal Library, Windsor Castle (no. 12766). The Royal Collection ©2000, Her Majesty Queen Elizabeth II.

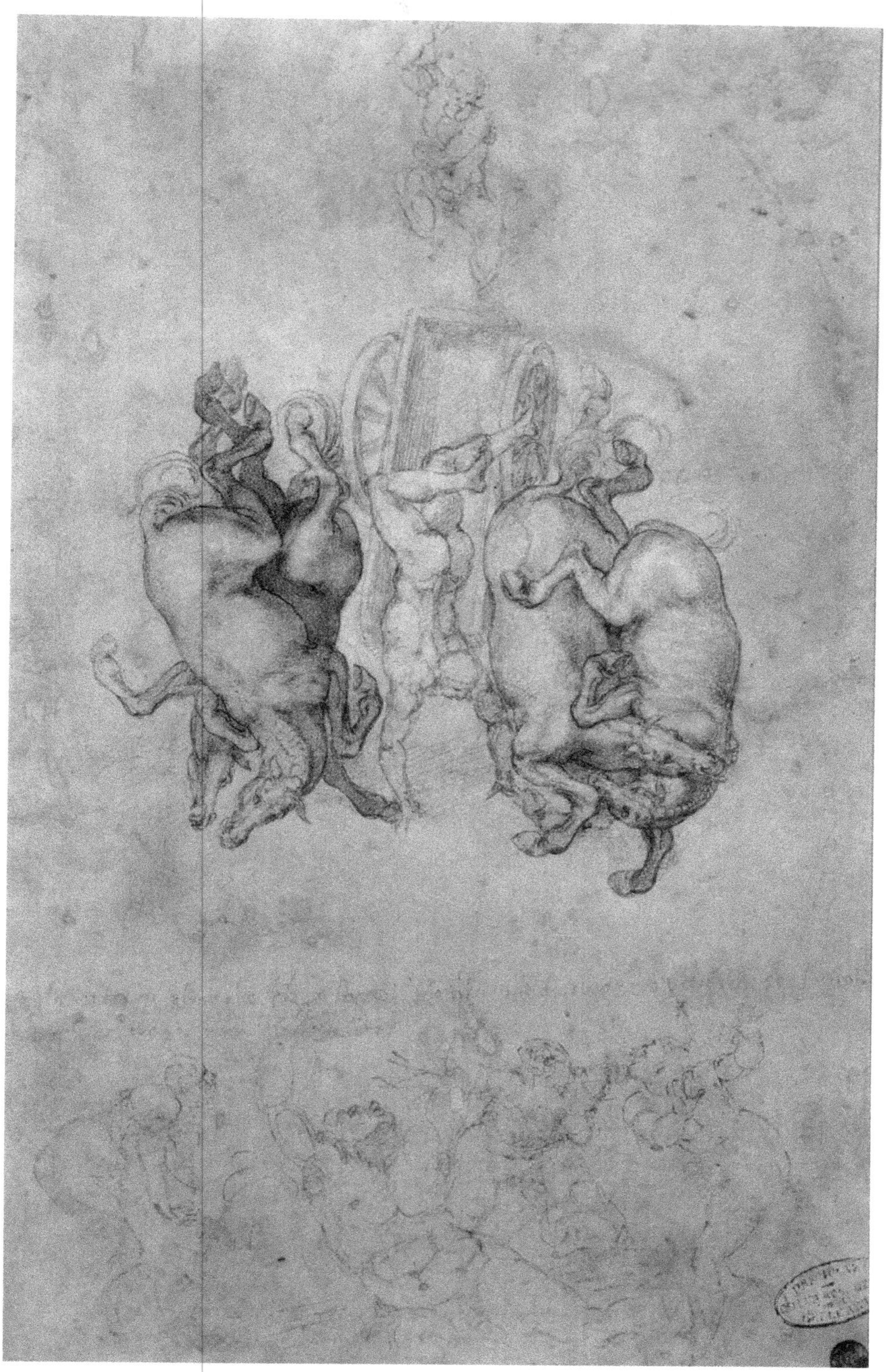

182. Michelangelo, *The Fall of Phaethon*. Black chalk on paper discolored brown, 39.3 × 25.5 cm. Gallerie dell'Accademia, Venice (no. 177).

> such as have the power to extinguish in the young any unseemly and unbridled desire which might spring up. And that no foul thoughts could have arisen in his mind is evident from the fact that he has loved not only human beauty but everything beautiful in general.[24]

Taking up the defense in the second edition of his life of the artist, Vasari emphasizes the purely professional aspect of Michelangelo's love of human beauty, "per la imitazione dell'arte," and he stresses the austerity of his lifestyle as proof of his innocence of "pensieri lascivi e disonesti."[25]

That Michelangelo's Platonizing language may indeed have been inspired by amorous desire hardly detracts from the loftiness of its sentiment. Rather, precisely in that paradox lies a source of the profundity of his art: the tension between the physical and the spiritual, the real and the ideal. That tension, resolved only in the art itself, accounts for its affective power. Michelangelo's gift drawings are not images commissioned by a patron or determined by an iconographic program devised by some humanist adviser. Grounded in his own personal culture, they are direct expressions of his own feeling, as spontaneous in their way as the most rapid of sketches, for all their finish. Indeed, such *buon disegno*, with its dedicated care of execution, is absolutely integral to their meaning. Inspired by love, these drawings were given with the timorousness of a lover. And when he in turn received some word from the beloved Cavalieri, Michelangelo poured his gratitude into a sonnet that acknowledges the bartering function of his sensual drawings and his own hopeful expectations of the deal:

> What great, indecent usury it would be,
> giving you such shameful pictures,
> to have in return persons beautiful and living
>
> (Che sconcia e grande usur saria a farla,
> donandoti turpissime pitture
> per rïaver persone belle e vive. [G 79])

The remarkable iconography of the drawings given to Cavalieri embodied a confession of deep feeling, an expression made possible only by the sanctioning controls of the conventions of Renaissance Neoplatonism – although the querulous embarrassment of the poem seems uncomfortably aware of the limits of such sanction. Anxiety and doubt constituted part of Michelangelo's relationship with Cavalieri.[26] In the draft of a letter from the very end of 1532 Michelangelo confesses his embarrassment at having taken the initiative, of having been "the first to move" ("primo a muovere"). "Read the heart and not the letter," he asks; the pen can hardly give adequate expression to his feelings, he adds, quoting Petrarch: "la penna al buon voler non può gir presso."[27] Michelangelo's drawings – even more than the sonnets, we may imagine – represented an urgent extension of himself to a beloved. Intended as affective exchange, they were meant to serve as means of

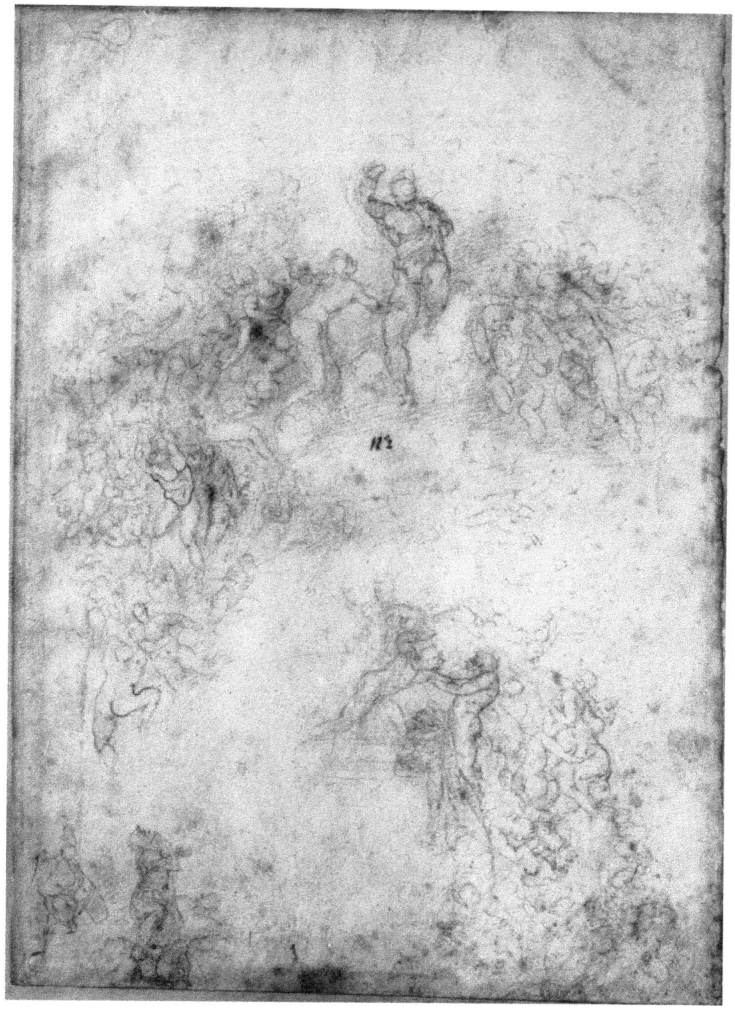

183. Michelangelo, *Compositional Study for the Last Judgment.* Black chalk, 41.4 × 30 cm. Casa Buonarroti, Florence (no. 65F-r).

self-expression, of communication within the most intimate social context. And we, in interpreting these drawings, can hardly ignore any aspects of that context, least of all their actual making.

Beyond the social conventions of poetry and philosophy, then, beyond the varied implications of mythological iconography, a further dimension grounds Michelangelo's gift drawings in lived experience. That dimension is, in a quite technical sense, artistic: technical, but no less profoundly personal. In naming Cavalieri as the most beloved of Michelangelo's special friends, Vasari wrote that the master's ostensible, public motive in making these "stupendous" drawings for the young man was to offer him lessons in drawing.[28]

The traffic pattern of the several versions of the *Fall of Phaethon* would seem to document that intent. Once again, the artist expressed himself through ancient myth, likening his own amorous daring to the tragic ambition of overreaching

Phaethon, whose hubris in attempting to drive the chariot of Helios, his father, led to his own destruction – as well as to the transformation of others and of part of the earth. The essential iconography, following Ovid's narrative (*Metamorphoses*, II, 1–400) is established in the first of the drawings, that in the British Museum, which the artist himself calls a "sketch" (Fig. 180).[29] To save the earth from further destruction, Jupiter brandishes in his right hand the thunderbolt that hurls the panicked charioteer from the solar cart. Below, the reclining rivergod Eridanus marks the site of his fall (the Po); Phaethon's lamenting sisters, the Heliades, are transformed into poplars and his brother, Cycnus, into the swan. An inscription on this sheet records the artist's opening offer: "Messer Tommaso, if this sketch doesn't please you tell Urbino [his servant] so that I may have time to have another done by tomorrow evening as I promised you; and if you do like it and want me to finish it, send it back to me." ("[Mess]e^{r} tomao se questo scizzo no[n] ui piace ditelo a urbino [acci]o / ch[e] io abbi tempo d auerne facto un altro doma[n] dassera / [co]me ui promessi e se ui piace e uogliate ch[e] io lo finisca / [rim]andate me lo.") Whatever Cavalieri's response, Michelangelo evidently "finished" his design by rendering it anew in the more compact and highly finished version in the Royal Library at Windsor Castle (Fig. 181), which Cavalieri enthusiastically acknowledged in a letter of September 6, 1533.[30]

A third, more problematic rendition is in the Accademia in Venice (Fig. 182); it too bears an inscription, much rubbed, that may be read as another offer to redraw: "I have drawn it as well as I could; however, I am returning yours to you . . ." (". . . lo ritracto el meglio ch[e] o saputo . . . vi rimando il vostro . . . un altra volta . . .").[31] It has been suggested that this sheet actually represents Cavalieri's own effort to imitate the master, a diligent pupil's exercise, but it is hard to imagine the amateur draftsman attaining the perfection of finish we find here in the rendering of the horses.[32] To account for that evident perfection, it has also been suggested that the sheet is the product of a joint effort: Cavalieri responsible for the schematic initial drawing, Michelangelo for the finished horses.[33] Despite the discrepancies in execution, the more roughly sketched Jupiter and the grieving Heliades are rendered with confidence; their energy and urgency seem the product of an inspired hand, one responsive to its subject, and the receiving figure of the river, rising from his bed, enacts the role of choral leader with dramatic conviction. Accepting Michelangelo's authorship of the entire sheet, then, we are left with the question of its position within the sequence. Is the Venice drawing an intermediary stage between the versions in London and Windsor, or does it follow them, a further thought on the topic? Jupiter himself seems closer to the Christ of the *Last Judgment* (Fig. 184), the cartoon of which was evidently completed before the death of Pope Clement VII in September 1534, and the small figures on the verso, revealed after the recent restoration, also seem to relate in their compressed gravity and downward reach to studies for the Sistine mural. Indeed, the entire composition of the Venice drawing, with its axial formality, suggests its closer association with the *Last Judgment*.[34]

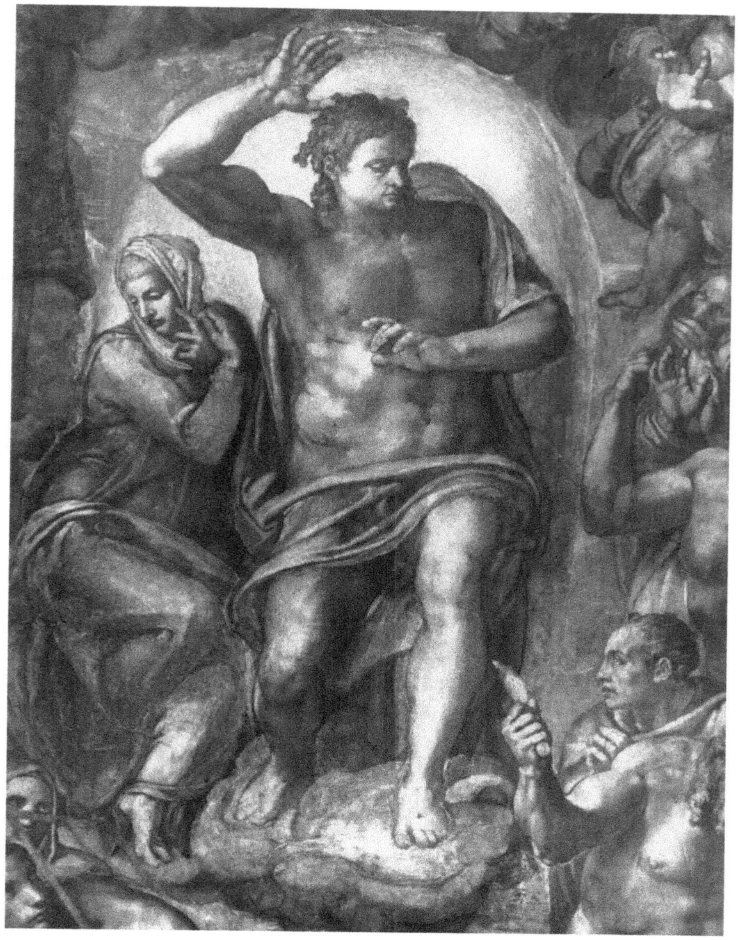

184. Michelangelo, *The Last Judgment* (detail). Sistine Chapel, Rome. Photograph: Alinari/Art Resource, New York.

Whatever its exact message, the inscription, like that on the British Museum sheet, further testifies to an active correspondence. Like the letters and the poems, these drawings were an effective, and even more highly charged, means of communication between the older artist and the young nobleman.

In that exchange, however, medium and message are one. Cavalieri's response, in his first letter to Michelangelo, of January 1, 1533, was that of a connoisseur, an amateur – a lover of art, as Vasari described him. We recall the pleasure he took in these graphic presents and his vow to spend several hours a day contemplating them.[35] Style and technique in these drawings, achieving the highest levels of craft, do indeed invite the most careful scrutiny. Testifying to a special dedication of execution, to a high level of finish, which, however, assumes a meaning beyond the skill involved, beyond the exercise of art. Not only were the images of an intensely suggestive iconography – the hubris of the charioteer representing that of the enamored draftsman – but the polished style of such *buon disegno* represented a certain concentration of creative energy. In these drawings technique itself becomes a sign of personal commitment: an act of love.

That Michelangelo's drawings were to be studied long and carefully is further confirmed by another of his favored friends, the pious Vittoria Colonna, widowed Marchesa of Pescara. Of his design of *Christ on the Cross* (Fig. 185) she wrote how this crucifix

> has crucified in my memory whatever other pictures I have ever seen. One cannot conceive of an image better made, more living or more finished, and certainly I could never explain how subtly and marvellously it is executed. . . . I have looked at it carefully in the light, with the lens and with the mirror, and I have never seen anything more finished.[36]

3. *Making as Meaning*

Nor have modern connoisseurs failed to respond to the technical finish of these drawings, despite the general preference for the more open sketch as "an art of improvisation." Admitting to just that prejudice in his commentary on the Cavalieri drawings, Bernard Berenson proclaimed that, in drawing,

> the highly elaborated, smoothly finished design is likely to be either a failure or an absurdity – a failure when the contours, through lack of spontaneity, have lost their instantaneousness and sparkle; an absurdity when fully modelled, for then the effort really ceases to be draughtsmanship and becomes a kind of painting, a kind of pastel painting.[37]

John Addington Symonds, more passionately engaged with the artist and more personally responsive to his loving gesture, expressed greater appreciation of the sensuality of Michelangelo's graphic surface: "It is impossible," he wrote,

> to describe the refinements of modulated shading and the precision of predetermined outlines by means of which these incomparable drawings have been produced. They seem to melt and to escape inspection, yet they remain fixed on the memory as firmly as forms in carven basalt.[38]

We recall, as undoubtedly did Symonds, the language of Vittoria Colonna.

But in admiring the technique of these drawings, modern students have often failed to look carefully enough. Rather, a serious misapprehension about Michelangelo's drawings was perpetuated, one that has effectively blocked deeper access to his art. I refer to the myth of "stippling," the notion that to achieve the remarkable degree of tonal modulation in his finished drawings Michelangelo resorted to a pointillist technique, slowly and patiently building up his surfaces by the application of thousands of tiny dots. Symonds himself introduced the term – indirectly, per-

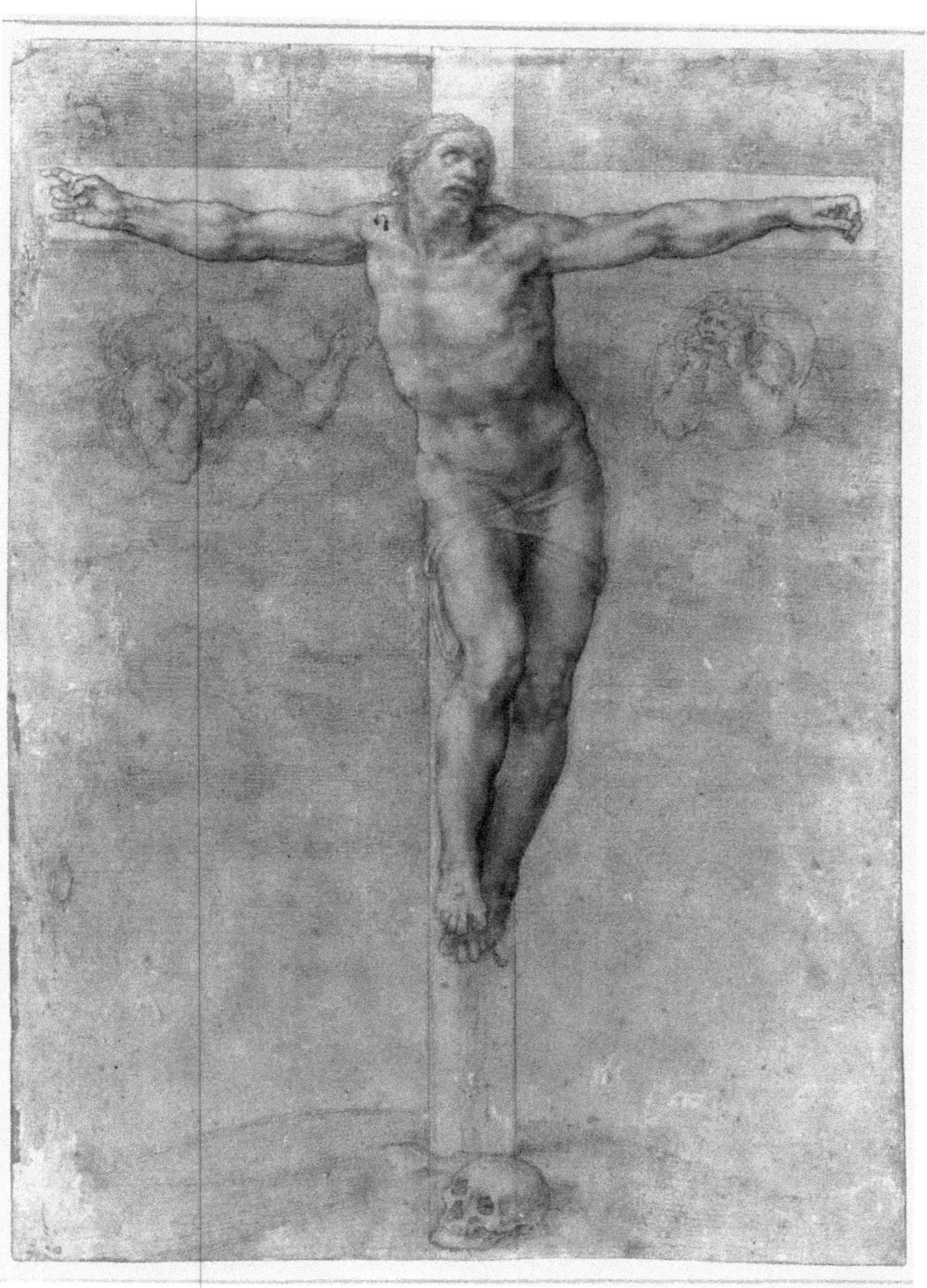

185. Michelangelo, *Christ on the Cross*. Black chalk, 37 × 27 cm. British Museum, London (1895-9-15-504 [Wilde 67]).

haps – in discussing the *Archers* (Fig. 186), a drawing not known to have been made for Cavalieri but carrying a comparable message of attraction and desire.[39] Symonds praised the "rounding and modelling [of] the nude with those soft stipplings and granulated shadings which bring the whole surface out like that of a bas-relief in

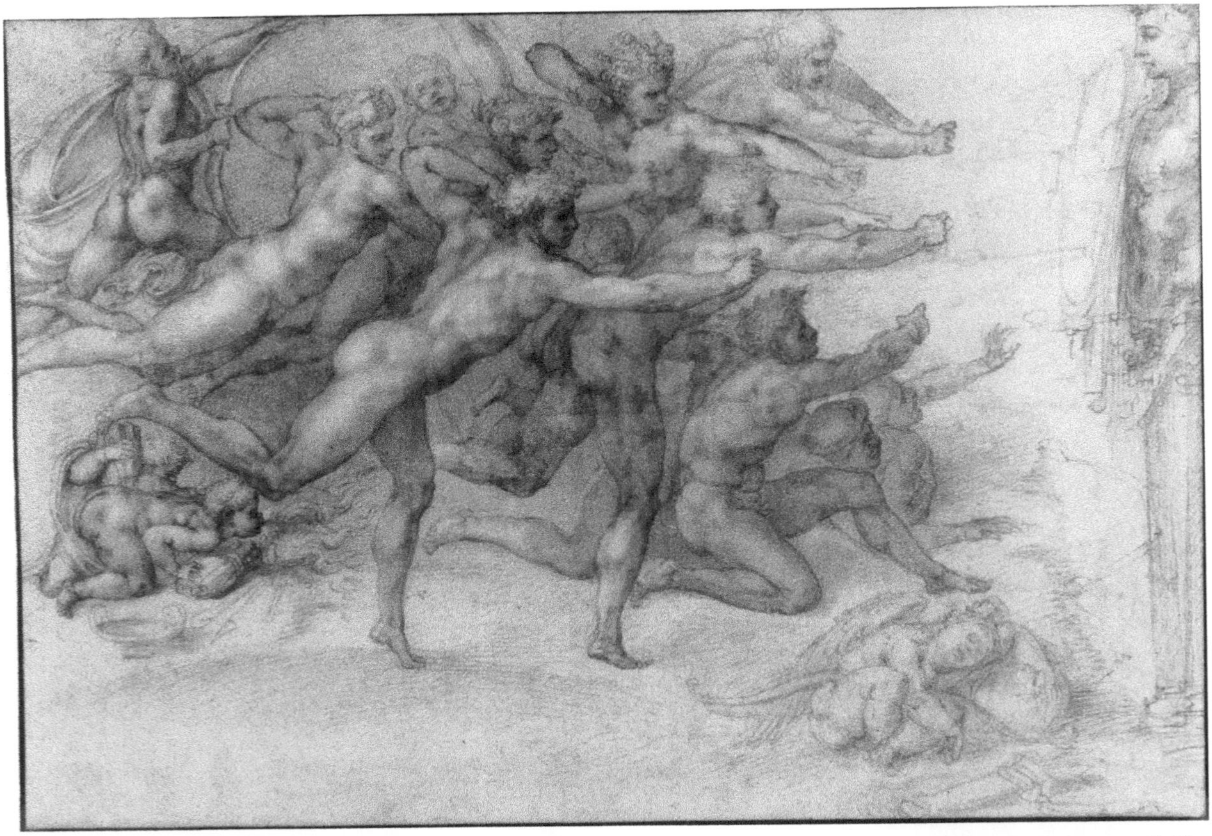

186. Michelangelo, *The Archers*. Red chalk, 25.7 × 37.2 cm. Royal Library, Windsor Castle (no. 12778). The Royal Collection ©2000, Her Majesty Queen Elizabeth II.

polished marble."[40] The observation recalls Vasari's sensitive response to the fine chiaroscuro of another red chalk drawing, the *Bacchanal of Children* (Fig. 187), which was made for Cavalieri.[41] Vasari compared the shading here to a kind of tonal mist, breathed on rather than applied by hand: "not even by breath," he wrote, "could one achieve a finer blending" ("col fiato non si farebbe più d'unione").[42]

It is significant that the conceit of breathing tone on paper developed in direct response to Michelangelo's Cavalieri drawings, particularly, the *Rape of Ganymede*. In Francisco de Hollanda's fourth dialogue on painting, the copy of Michelangelo's design (Fig. 175) by which Giulio Clovio "first won renown at Rome," initiates a discourse on the illuminator's art: "a method of working by means of certain dots, which I call atoms, like a woven veil; they seem a mist drawn over the face of the painting. . . ." The invention of this technique in Italy is allowed Clovio, but the Portuguese author claims that he had, as a youth, "by myself discovered this way of illuminating with atoms and mist which Don Giulio was using at Rome."[43] Significantly, Clovio's *Ganymede* is described as "illuminado de sua mño sobre o debuxo . . . muito suavemente lavrado. . . ." Cavalieri, we know, shared his Michelangelo drawings, allowing them to be copied in various media. By 1538, the putative date of the dialogues recounted by de Hollanda, one of those drawings

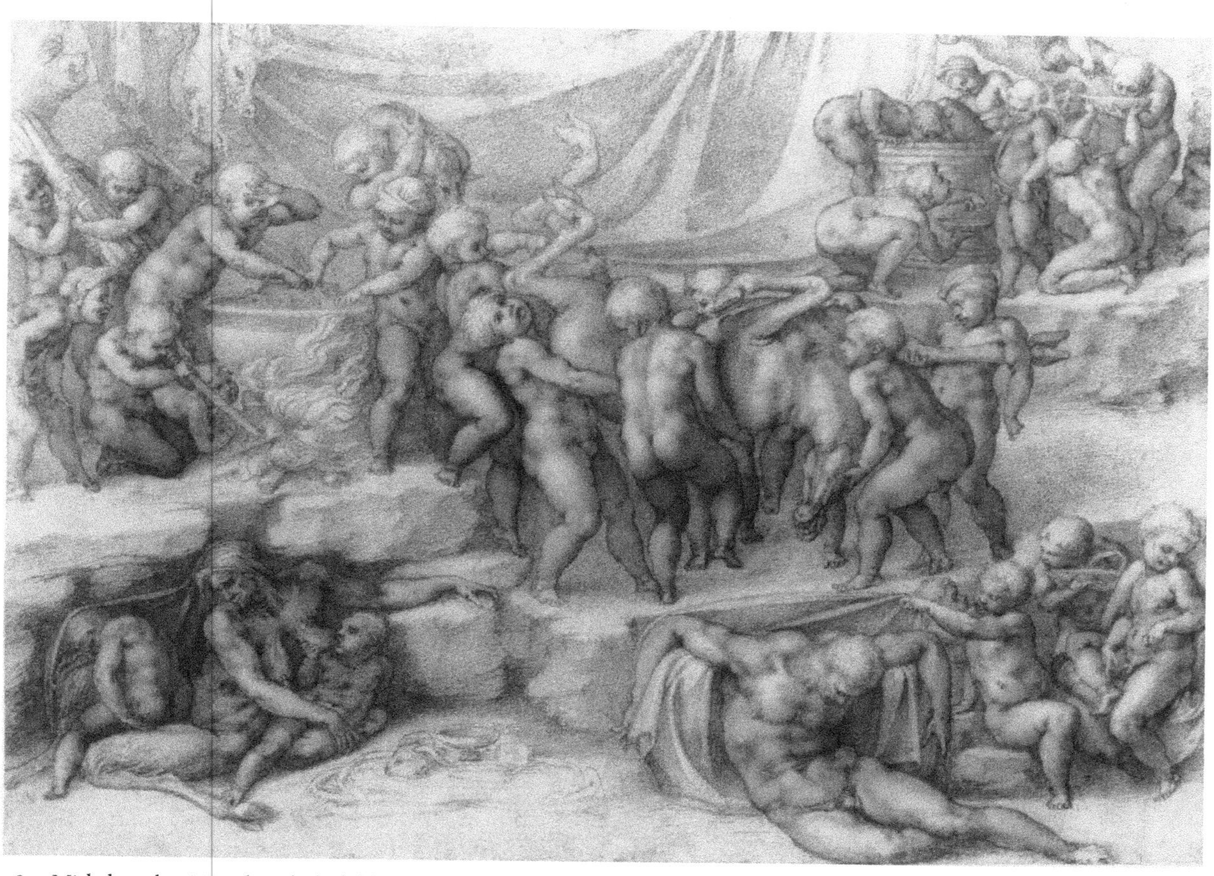

187. Michelangelo, *A Bacchanal of Children*. Red chalk, 27.4 × 38.8 cm. Royal Library, Windsor Castle (no. 12777). The Royal Collection ©2000, Her Majesty Queen Elizabeth II.

had inspired a new art of illumination in Rome, Giulio Clovio's "maniera di figure piccole," which was indeed an art of stippling.[44]

That association with the miniaturist's art has, unfortunately, conditioned modern critical vision of Michelangelo's own finished drawings. Johannes Wilde, a scholar who contributed so much to our knowledge of the artist's drawings, consistently isolated "the delicacy of technique introduced by Michelangelo, and reserved for this class of drawing: they are stippled in a laborious process."[45] With regard to the Windsor version of the *Fall of Phaethon* (Fig. 181), Wilde concluded that "work on such a sheet must have required several weeks."[46] And yet Michelangelo himself, in the note on the British Museum *Phaethon* (Fig. 180), offered to have another version done by the next day. Even if the artist meant another "sketch," the truth is, there is no stippling to be found in Michelangelo's drawings.[47]

Nor should critics have needed microscopic investigation to realize that. The question transcends the niceties of catalogue description and exhibition wall labeling, for at issue is the very basis of the critical interpretation of drawing. First of all, stippling is not a chalk technique. It is a process associated with shading in pen and ink and, especially, in intaglio printmaking (Fig. 188), where the spacing of individual marks or dots controls tonal effect. It would be redundant in chalk. The granular effect observed in Michelangelo's drawings is the natural result of the interaction between the substance of the medium and the texture of the support, between the granules of chalk and the tooth of the paper. Michelangelo modeled his anatomical forms not by any patient dotting process, but rather by passing and repassing his chalk over the surface in ever denser concentrations of hatching (Figs. 189, 190).[48]

In the context of the gift drawings, above all, technique is crucial for meaning and interpretation, for technique mediates importantly between the artist and his creation. Moving over the paper, for the duration of its contact the drawing hand remains responsive to the feeling of its own movements. Evoking form from paper, each stroke affirms, even as it defines, the reality of that form. The intent is plastic: to shape the flatness of paper. The drawing hand is a forming hand. As Pierre-Jean Mariette, the greatest of the eighteenth-century connoisseurs, recognized in Michelangelo's finished drawings, "He caresses what he makes" ("Il caresse ce qu'il fait").[49]

There is an important difference between creating graphic form through a system of dots and through a sequence of strokes. Stippling involves a certain distancing of the draftsman from the emerging image. Each dot is made as a tiny independent mark, equal in value to every other dot; its application hardly engages the draftsman kinesthetically, except in that the very repetitiveness of the technique may try both patience and eyesight. It is only the final collective result of the individual dots, contingent upon their concentration, that yields the illusion of form. Between the activity of making and the image made there is a gap – as de Hollanda

188. Giulio Campagnola, *Venus Reclining in a Landscape.* Engraving, 11.9 × 18.3 cm. Cleveland Museum of Art. Gift of the Print Club of Cleveland (1931.205).

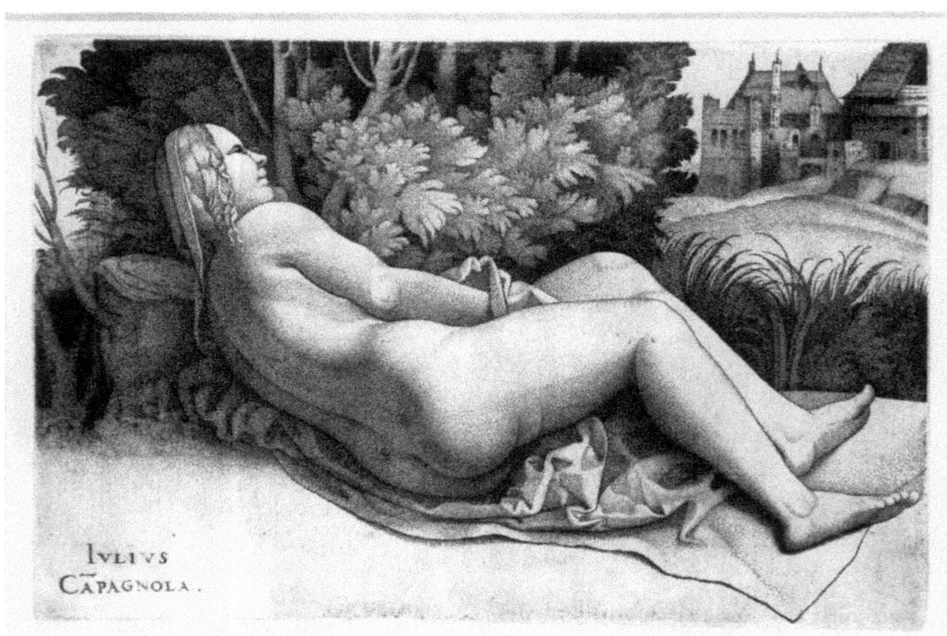

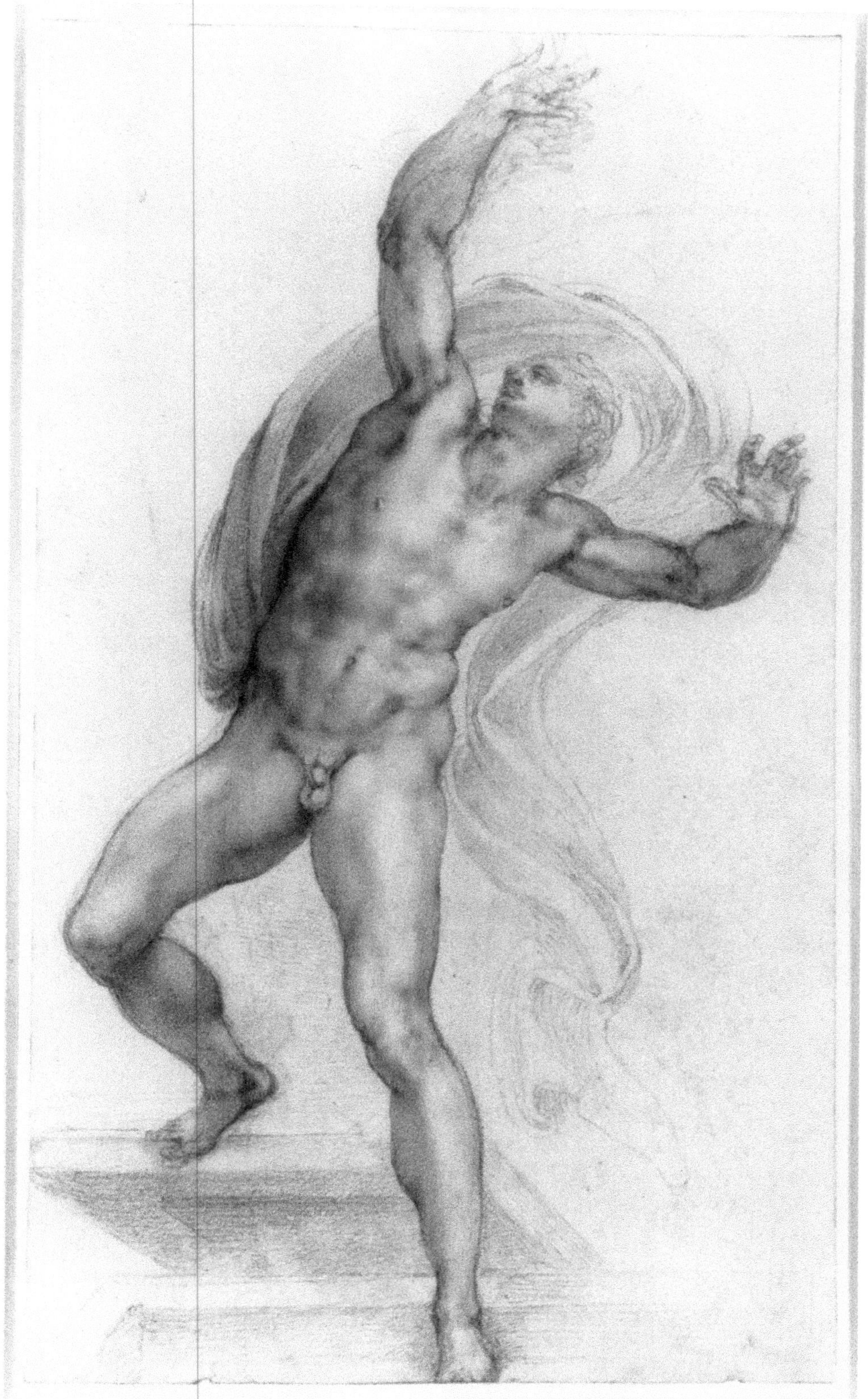

189. Michelangelo, *The Risen Christ*. Black chalk, 37.3 × 22.2 cm. Royal Library, Windsor Castle (no. 12768). The Royal Collection ©2000, Her Majesty Queen Elizabeth II.

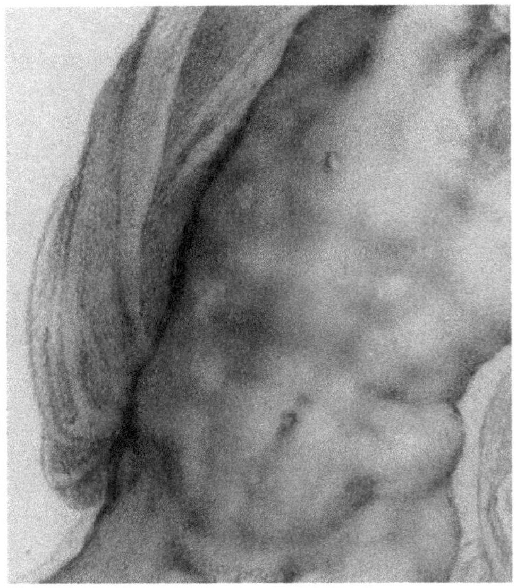

190. Michelangelo, *The Risen Christ*, detail of Fig. 189.

boasted, the image seems a miraculous appearance, not to have been made by hand (*acheiropoieton*).[50]

Modeling through hatching, that is, through patterns of more or less parallel lines, affords an essentially different experience. That difference is less the function of the final resulting impression than of the process itself. Each stroke of the chalk runs a course over the surface of the paper, over the represented form. Tracing that course, the draftsman's hand remains engaged in the form itself, in touch with the body coming into being – and we can hardly avoid thinking of the genesis of the figure in Michelangelo's own sculpture (Fig. 191). The drawing itself records, even as it enacts, the emergence of that body, its gradual definition from initial tentative outlines through the securing of contour to the internal articulation of form. The process of formal realization is continuous and more active, involving a more sustained and therefore committed gesture. There is a tactile and therefore somatic dimension to stroking the chalk that keeps the artist in constant, responsible and responsive touch with his emerging creation. Michelangelo was no miniaturist.

In the physical engagement of such a graphic process time counts. Each stroke is a progress toward a mimetic end; it also represents a duration or, to quote Leondardo, a "space of time," a sustained period of contact with the drawing, of commitment to it. The very speed of the stroke betrays that commitment, revealing the kind of attention devoted to the form depicted. In the *Punishment of Tityus* (Fig. 174), for example, the claw-rooted stump of hell at the right receives a different kind of graphic attention than that accorded the body of the giant: its hatching pattern is broader, lines longer, space more open. True, such rapid execution is suggestively atmospheric and locates its object in a secondary space. But it is precisely that sense of distance, placement beyond tactile reach, that distinguishes this motif from the central figure. The body of tortured Tityus is rendered more patiently, with finer and more deliberate strokes; the drawing hand has lingered long over

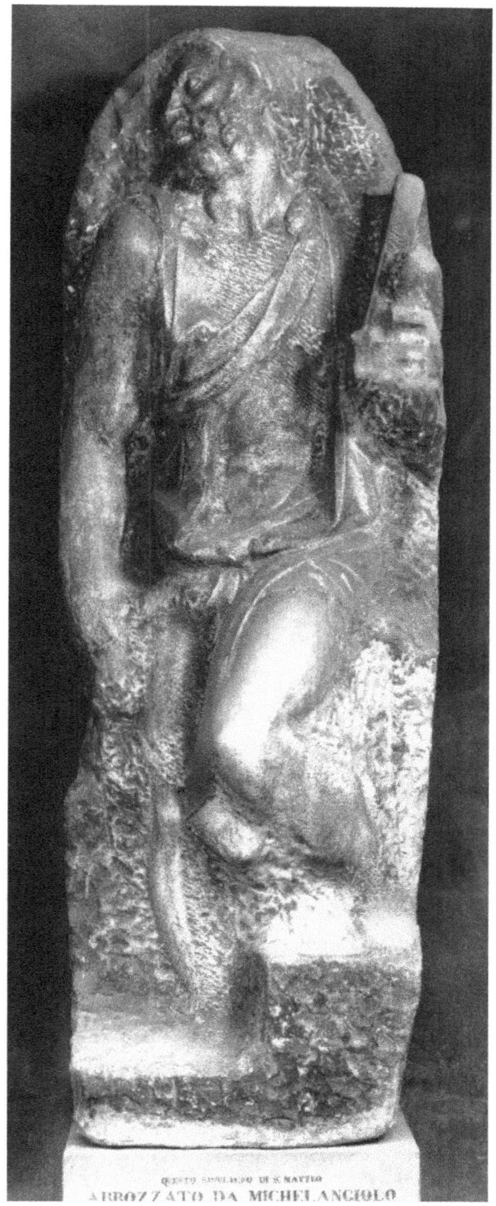

191. Michelangelo, *St. Matthew.* Marble. Accademia delle Belle Arti, Florence. Photo: Alinari/Art Resource, New York.

this body. Such quality of attention testifies to the nature of the draftsman's own personal investment in the drawing.

What Michelangelo put into his drawings for his beloved friends was more than just painstaking effort. The meaning of those drawings for him – a meaning, we may assume, that he intended to convey to their recipients – involved more than *invenzione,* more than iconography certainly, but also more than the formal finish of *disegno.* In every sense, these drawings were gestures of friendship, and the very gestures of their making can only have meant much to their maker. Drawing was for Michelangelo a means of personal expression, an extension of himself toward an other. Making already signified meaning.

4. *Drawing as Prayer*

The transformation of the carnal sinner Tityus into a resurrected Christ assumes a still greater resonance when considered in the light of Michelangelo's creative ambivalence about his own state of grace. For Michelangelo the human body, the nude male body, represented the basic and exclusive term of art, of all the arts – including architecture, whose proper study, he insisted, begins with anatomy. He saw, thought, and felt through and with the body – "persons beautiful and living," as he poetically confessed with embarrassment to the handsome Cavalieri. Vasari wrote that Michelangelo "greatly loved human beauty," carefully adding, we recall, "for its imitation in art; for only by copying the human form, and by selecting from what was beautiful the most beautiful, could perfection be achieved in art." For all their good intentions in moving to protect the master's reputation, Michelangelo's biographers can only seem naïve in their insistent denial of any lasciviousness or impropriety in his focus on the human form. For a profoundly religious man, as Michelangelo was, such a commitment to the body was inevitably fraught with conflict, with consequences of the deepest significance and, we may say, risk.

From his earliest *Pietà* (Fig. 192), in which the body of Christ assumed simultaneously a new ideality and an unprecedented sensuality, through the internalized

192. Michelangelo, *Pietà*. Marble. St. Peter's, Vatican City. Photo: Alinari/Art Resource, New York.

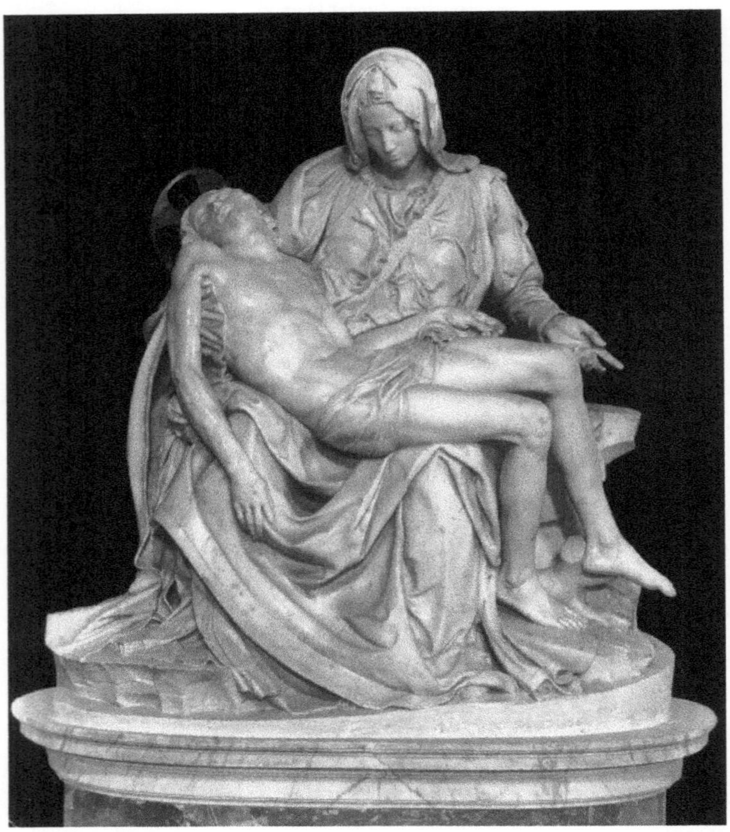

drama of body–soul agony figured in his creations for the tomb of Julius II (Fig. 193), Michelangelo gave sensible form to the beautiful microcosm that reflected the larger moral dynamics of the universe. And even though he later professed recantation of that youthful aesthetic, that classicizing dedication to the human form, his deepening religion could only force him to seek ever closer rapport with one body in particular, that of his Savior. In the sculptural group he intended for his own tomb (Fig. 194) the artist rendered himself in the role of Nicodemus, thereby guaranteeing his own perpetual contact with the body of Christ.

Michelangelo had already transferred his graphic affection, as it were, to that body in the drawings he made for Vittoria Colonna, such as that crucifix which crucified in her memory all other images she had ever seen (Fig. 185). In her close scrutiny of that body, that most "finished thing" – "in the light, with the lens and with the mirror" – the pious marchesa passed easily from aesthetic detachment to religious engagement, if such a distinction ever existed for her. Or for the artist himself. Whatever qualms he may have had about the propriety of the pagan bodies made with such loving care for Tommaso de' Cavalieri, those "shameful pictures" ("turpissime pitture"), Michelangelo harbored doubts of a different kind regarding his imaging of the *corpus Christi*. Here his rendering of the body involved passions of a different order – different, but hardly unrelated.

Late in his life, when he was about eighty, Michelangelo made a series of drawings of Christ on the Cross that manifest most resonantly the special meaning of the act of drawing in the hands of the avatar of *disegno* (Figs. 195–99). These drawings seem to transcend any practical function; the sheer complexity of their surfaces frustrates the legibility requisite for such purpose.[51] Rather, the essential qualities that bind them as a group, including technique and size, suggest that they are the products of a more or less sustained campaign, conscious variations on a theme – although the aestheticizing implications of such a notion might at first seem to violate the spirit of these images. Above all, these drawings impress by their highly worked surfaces – indeed, overworked, even to the point of Berensonian "absurdity," becoming, as he might have objected, "a kind of painting." Varied in their enactment of response to

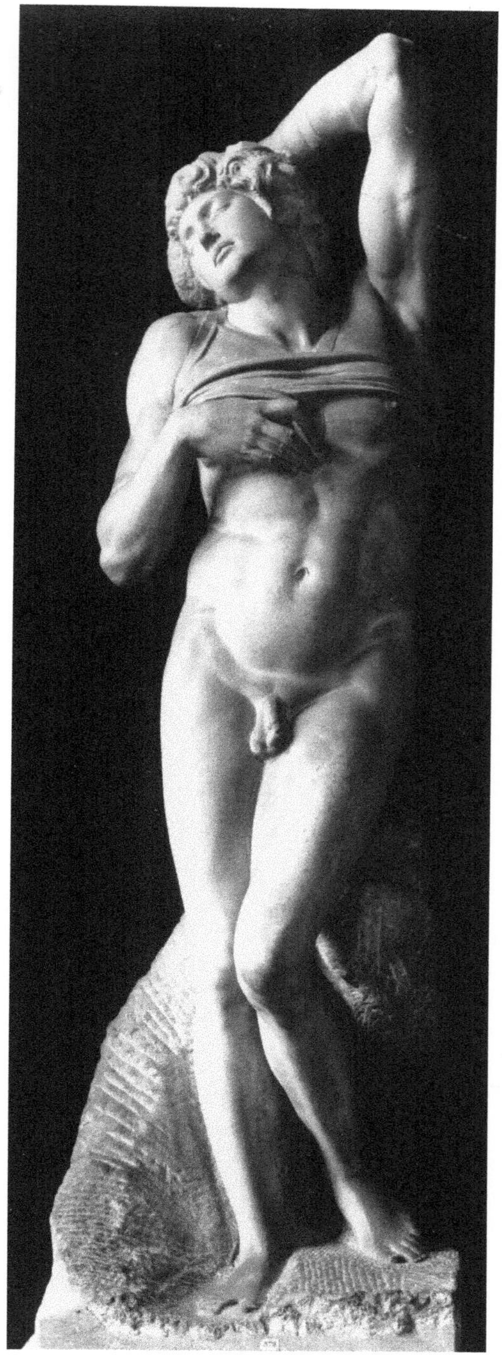

193. Michelangelo, *The Dying Slave.* Marble. Musée du Louvre, Paris. Photo: Alinari/Art Resource, New York.

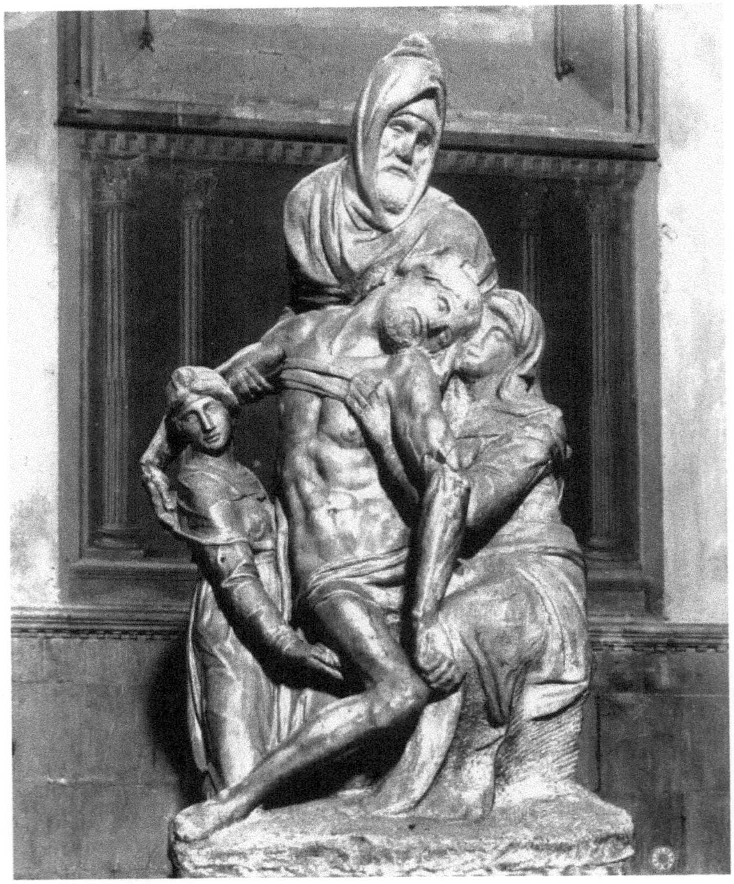

194. Michelangelo, *Pietà (The Deposition of Christ)*. Marble. Museo dell'Opera del Duomo, Florence. Photo: Alinari/Art Resource, New York.

the sacrifice on the cross, they all focus, understandably, on the body of Christ, a concentration that is material as well as visual.

Drawing with black chalk, and building upon a prepared surface – not an uncommon practice for him[52] – Michelangelo constructs his forms with that tremulous touch characteristic of the aging draftsman, almost as though he were at first hesitant to disturb the paper. Once in, however, he seems hardly able to stop. From those bundled contours he proceeds to ever denser patterns of hatching, carving relief surfaces out of the paper. The chalk is stroked, rubbed, covered over again and again by its own retracings and spread by the artist's finger. White, both chalk and paint, is used for further modeling and, more critically, for corrections, the two functions mingling in final effect. The process is a complex one, and its complexity is recorded in the confusing density of the rendered surface, as forms are redrawn and modified to near obliteration. The physicality of the surface is further stressed by the incised lines of the stylus, used especially to score the axes of the cross or to fix its contours. In the most moving of these graphic images (Fig. 199) intersecting arcs intriguingly locate the position of the cross arms: scoring with a pair of compasses enigmatically plots the top line of the arm of the cross and, implicitly, locates the protagonists

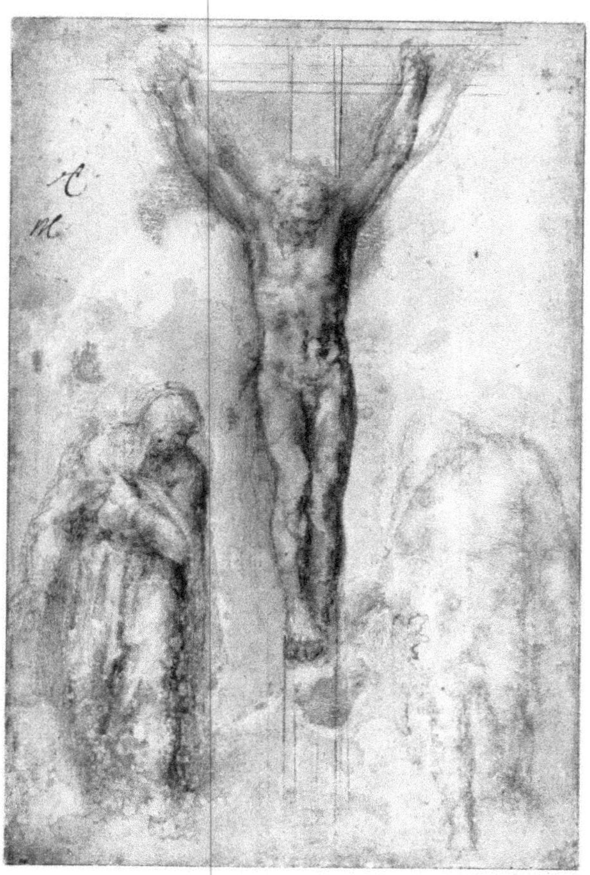

195. Michelangelo, *Christ on the Cross between the Virgin and St. John.* Black chalk, brown wash, white paint, 43.2 × 29 cm. Musée du Louvre, Paris. Département des Arts Graphiques (inv. 700).

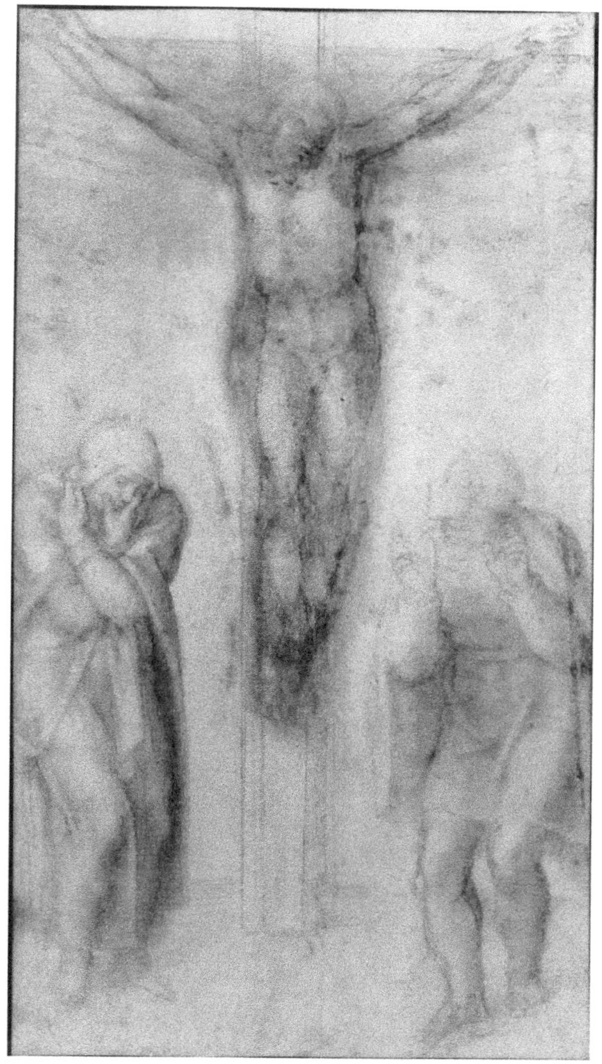

196. Michelangelo, *Christ on the Cross between the Virgin and St. John.* Black chalk, white paint, 38.2 × 21 cm. Royal Library, Windsor Castle (no. 12775). The Royal Collection ©2000, Her Majesty Queen Elizabeth II.

within the circumferences of two intersecting circles (Fig. 200). Whatever the rationale for such geometrical ordering, it is important to note that the turning of the compass and the application of the ruler follow the figural design.

In these drawings Michelangelo conceived the figure first and then accommodated the cross to it. Indeed, as much as the figures, the cross itself was varied and adjusted; the modifications of form and axial orientation, recorded in the multiple scoring of its outlines, destabilize the cross, even as its ruled contours add a sense of structure to the overall field. These repeated mechanical lines, some of them ghosted through partial erasure, seem to echo the shimmering repetitions of contour surrounding the figures themselves. The mourners at the foot of the cross, the Virgin and Saint John,

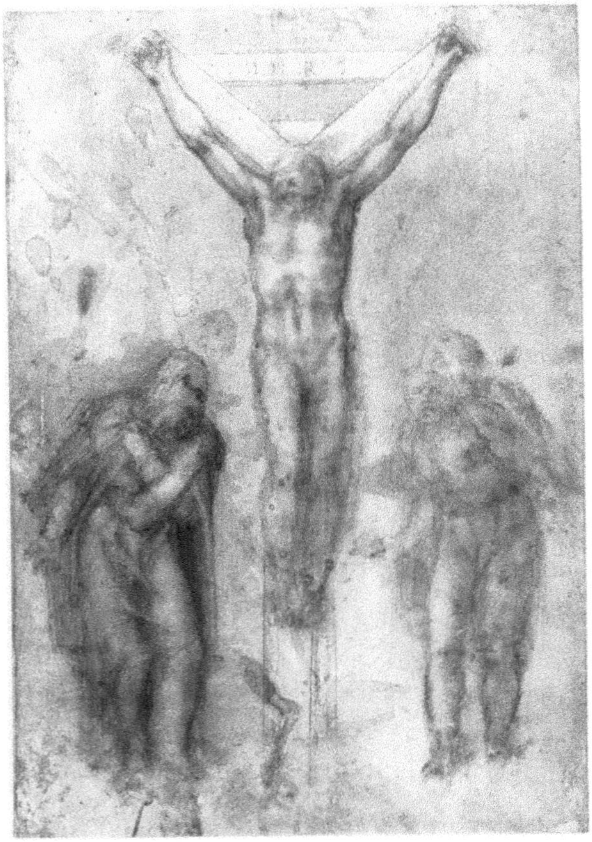

197. Michelangelo, *Christ on the Cross between the Virgin and St. John.* Black chalk, white paint, 41.3 × 28.6 cm. British Museum, London (1895-9-15-509 [Wilde 81]).

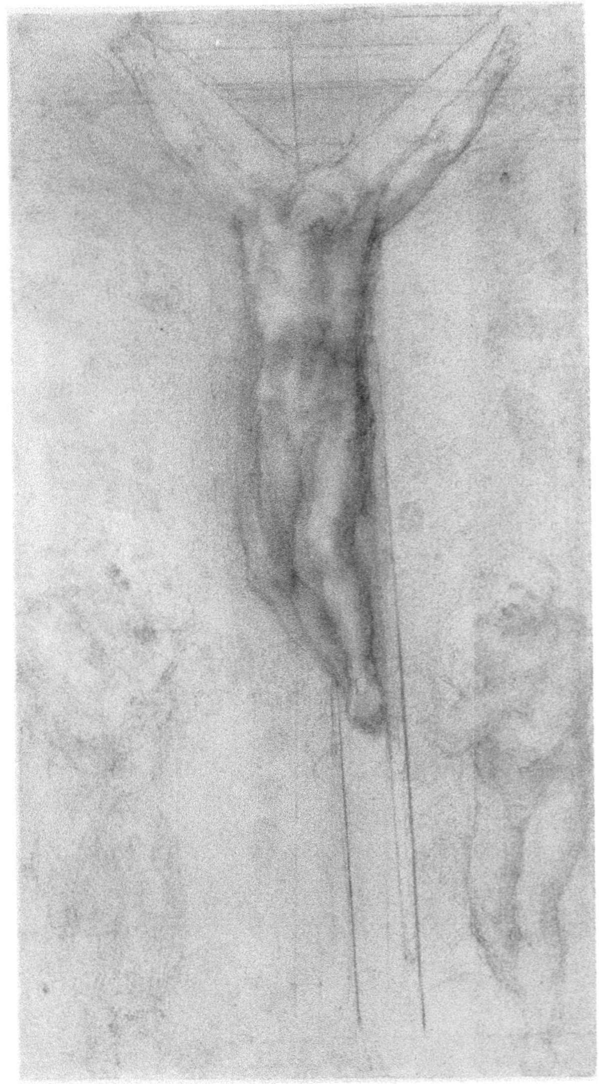

198. Michelangelo, *Christ on the Cross between the Virgin and St. John.* Black chalk, 40.5 × 21.8 cm. Royal Library, Windsor Castle (no. 12761). The Royal Collection ©2000, Her Majesty Queen Elizabeth II.

respond emotionally to the sacrifice and share their response directly with the viewer. As these figures are reworked, they tend to withdraw, to internalize their gestures and concentrate their physical and psychic energies. And that tendency toward compression suggests a certain sequence in the execution of these drawings, culminating in the British Museum sheet in which Mary, moving ever closer to her Son, finally fuses with him through their shared contour (Fig. 199).

In discussing these late religious drawings as "inner prayers," Charles de Tolnay has written that the "external and material image of Christ" has here been "supplanted by the internal spiritual image."[53] Such a response, however sympathetic it may be to us, seems, again, to focus on the final image to the exclusion of the process

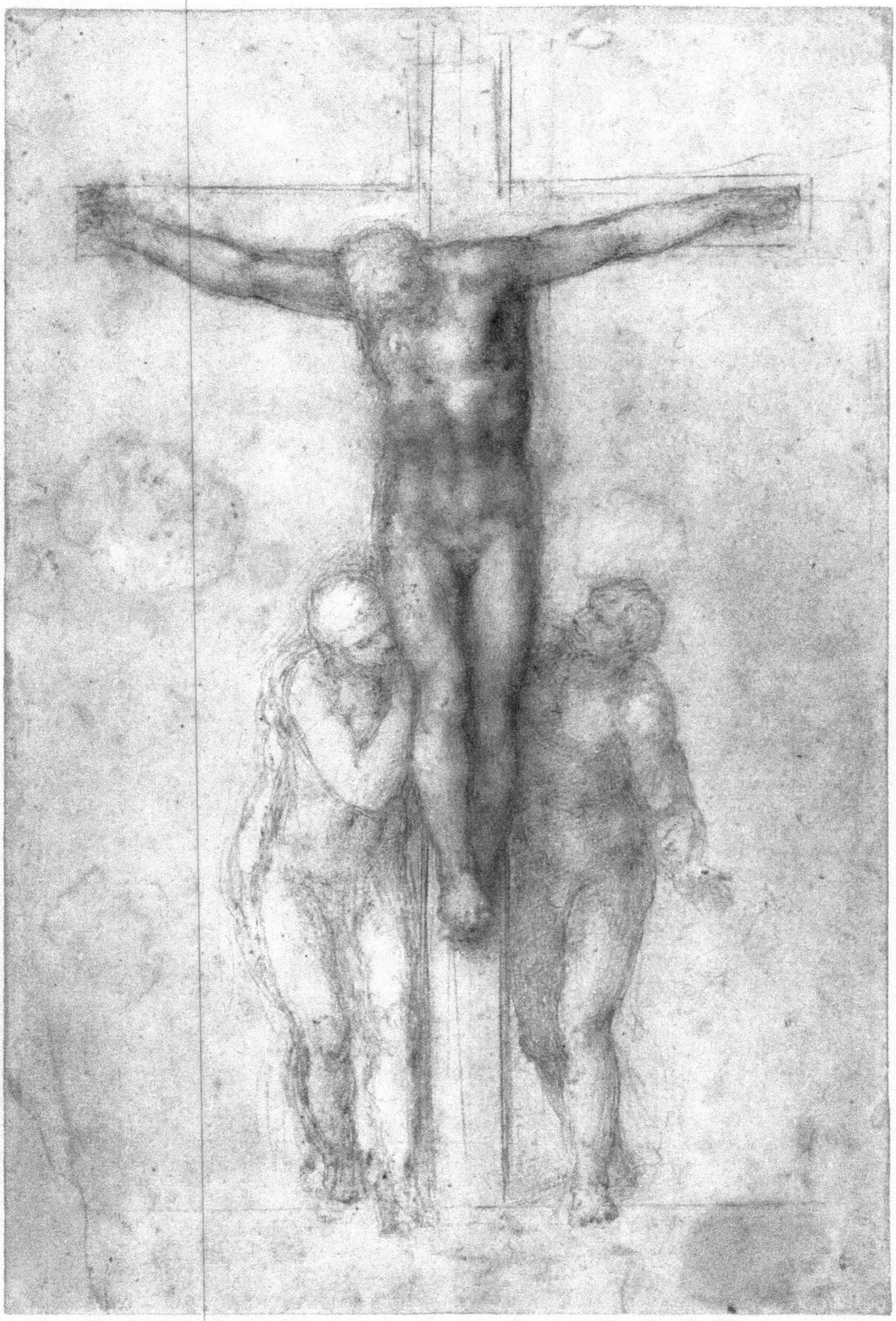

199. Michelangelo, *Christ on the Cross between the Virgin and St. John*. Black chalk, white paint, 41.2 × 27.9 cm. British Museum, London (1895-9-15-510 [Wilde 82]).

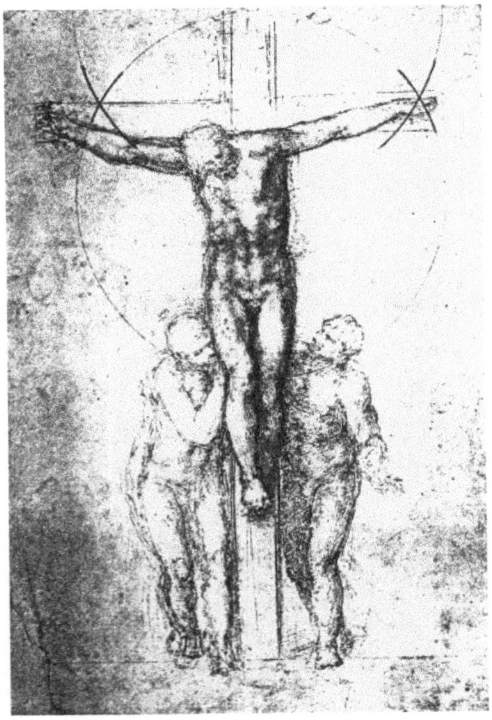

200. Michelangelo, *Christ on the Cross between the Virgin and St. John* (with compass marks indicated).

of its creation. If anywhere in Michelangelo's graphic corpus, it is here that medium and message are one. The Crucifixion drawings represent, in effect, the culmination of Michelangelo's *buon disegno,* but now transformed and transcended: overdrawn to excess, surfaces are rougher, more insistently worked, more desperately covered. Materiality of surface, a constant reminder of the operations of the drawing hand, cannot but become a record of the physical presence of the draftsman. Through the manipulation of his medium, Michelangelo shapes, and thereby knows, the body of his Redeemer. To quote Mariette again, "C'est la chair même." It is flesh itself, but flesh now assumes Eucharistic resonance.

The graphic complexity of the surface, its essential tactility, suggests a reluctance to let go, to lose touch with that body. The act of drawing has become an act of devotion. And the compulsive application of the one becomes the urgency of the other. The materiality of this experience is what we feel in the physicality of image in Michelangelo's late religious poetry, in which we hear the anguished yet always powerful voice of a penitent in longing search of his God. Both the poetry and the drawings are heard as private meditations, prayers of a deeply felt, desperate piety. Yet even as Michelangelo denies his art of the body, desiring to free his own soul from material bondage, the poetry itself returns us to the physical; even as he remains grounded in the flesh, the artist reaches toward heaven with the same aspiring energy that informs his own creatures:

> I pray, my Lord, offer me that chain
> with which is linked every heavenly gift:
> faith, I mean, to which I strive and urge myself,
> but whose full grace, through my own sin, I miss.
>
> (Deh, porgi, Signor mio, quella catena
> che seco annoda ogni celeste dono:
> la fede, dico, a che mi stringo e sprono;
> né, mie colpa, n'ho grazia intiera e piena. [G 289])

Already in the *Last Judgment,* which transformed the altar wall of the Sistine Chapel into a permanent monumental reminder of our end, Michelangelo had given pictorial form to that heavenly chain of faith, by which the elect do indeed rise to heaven (Fig. 201). And in the same fresco, created in the years immediately following his initial encounter with Cavalieri, the artist depicted his own features, famously, in the flayed skin of Saint Bartholomew (Fig. 202), a conceit he shared in a sonnet for Cavalieri:

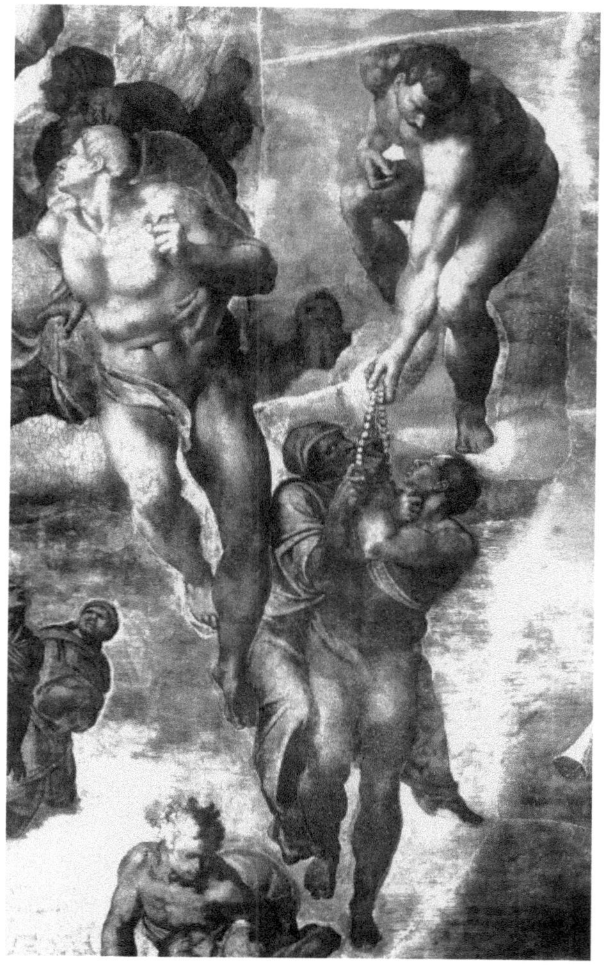

201. Michelangelo, *The Last Judgment* (detail). Sistine Chapel, Vatican City. Photo: Alinari/Art Resource, New York.

only through death might one be called truly reborn
. . .
. . . as a serpent sheds its skin on a rock,
so through death might I change my state.

(e sol per morte si può dire ben nato
. . .
. . . come serpe al sasso si discoglia,
pur per morte potria cangiar mie stato. [G 94])

Nearing the end of this life and fearing for the next, Michelangelo begins to address himself directly to his God; acknowledging the error of his pagan ways – when he worshiped art as "idol and monarch" – he turns to the one source of salvation and asks:

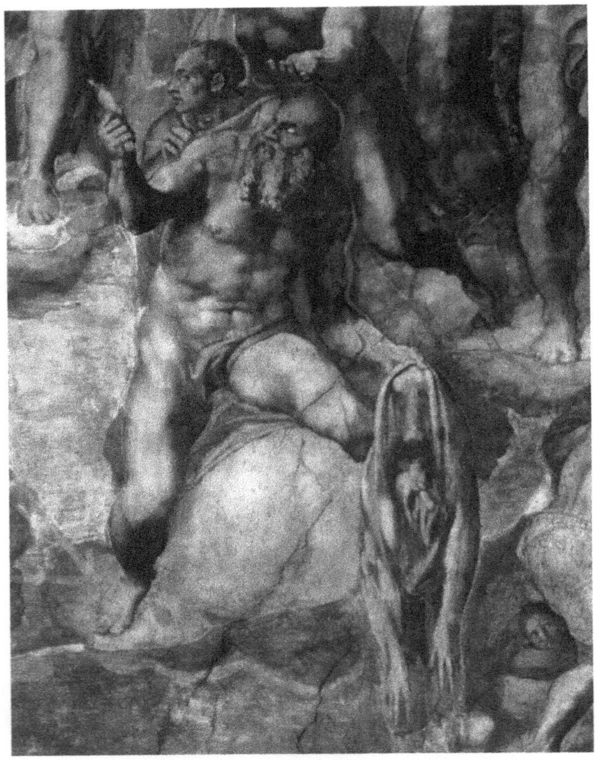

202. Michelangelo, *The Last Judgment* (detail). Sistine Chapel, Vatican City. Photo: Scala/Art Resource, New York.

Those amorous thoughts once so light and vain,
what are they now that I am nearing two deaths?
Of one I'm sure, the other threatens me.
Neither painting nor sculpture can any longer
calm my soul, now turned toward that divine love
who on the cross opened his arms to embrace us.

(Gli amorosi pensier, già vani e lieti,
che fien or, s'a duo morte m'avvicino?
D'una so 'l certo, e l'altra mi minaccia.
Né pinger né scolpir fie più che quieti
l'anima, volta a quell'amor divino
c'aperse, a prender noi, 'n croce le braccia. [G 285])

It is true that the late drawings "look almost transparent, as if they were illuminated by a diffused light," as Tolnay has written, that "they seem to emanate a soft aura which at once surrounds them and isolates them," that "the distinction of the forms dissolves at the periphery into the underdetermined." And yet these bodies can never become "purely spiritual realities" – much less Berenson's irreligious "ideated sensations . . . of . . . almost ambrosial repose."[54] The intense longing for the body of the Savior, which here, through shared contour, presses the Virgin into a special bond of union with her Son (Fig. 199), partakes of that physical urgency that so animates the imagery of the poems. Finally, however, the materiality of the surface itself, its insistent tactility, betrays the physical presence of the draftsman, the marks of a hand in search of form, a process of groping, caressing, of coaxing form from out of the depths of the paper. It is, we might say, the touch of the sculptor himself, here modeling and molding, patting and testing surface, always in direct contact with the forming image.[55]

That groping with the chalk becomes an essential stylistic aspect of the very last drawings by Michelangelo: for example, in the study of a standing Madonna and Child in the British Museum (Fig. 203). The repeated search for the bounding line here expands beyond the requirements of contour, as the echoing strokes of the chalk reverberate in both directions: concentrating toward the core, they compress to contain the body drawn; expanding from that core, they radiate a field of energy surrounding the figure. The spread of touch is remarkable and suggests the very tentative motion of the draftsman's probing hand, reaching out, unsure of just when chalk will meet paper. In this context, of the always problematic concept of an *Altersstil*, Michael Hirst has recalled the reports of the aging artist's presbyopia, his difficulty in working at close range.[56] The diagnosis would seem to be confirmed by the haptic quality of the very late drawings, their emphasis on securing touch. Whether or not this open manner is "based on a disturbance of motor movement caused by a tremor," as Alexander Perrig has argued, the impression is of an effort to bring the drawing gesture under control.[57] And yet, for all its essential plasticity, the drawing is completed with a most effective pictorial touch: the core of the figure established, Michelangelo applied a system of diagonal hatching to model form and to stretch a veil of shadow across the opening of the Virgin's legs. The drawing itself remains a record of the draftsman's trembling gesture, a surface marked by the nervous touch of chalk seeking to locate the form it is in the process of defining. Contained within the enveloping aureole of strokes, Mother and Child vibrate with the energies of that touch, fused in the luminous effect of their graphic medium.[58]

A comparable fusion of Christ and his Bride/Mother operates in a different medium in the sculptural group Michelangelo intended for his own tomb (Fig. 194), a *Pietà* that manifests as well his own deeply felt need to stay close to the body of Christ.[59] Having abandoned that work and given it away, the artist immediately acquired another block of stone and began working it, according to Vasari, "so that he could spend time each day with the chisel."[60] Indeed, having brought a second *Pietà* to completion, toward the very end of his life the artist began recarving the group and, as one witness reports, he was still working on it ("studiando sopra quel corpo della pietà") six days before his death (Fig. 204).[61] The spectral presence of this marble image, its holy figures reduced to a common core, seems to offer eloquent testimony to Vasari's report: *nulla dies sine malleo*, not a day without hammer, without chisel – the sculptural equivalent of Apelles' motto. The old

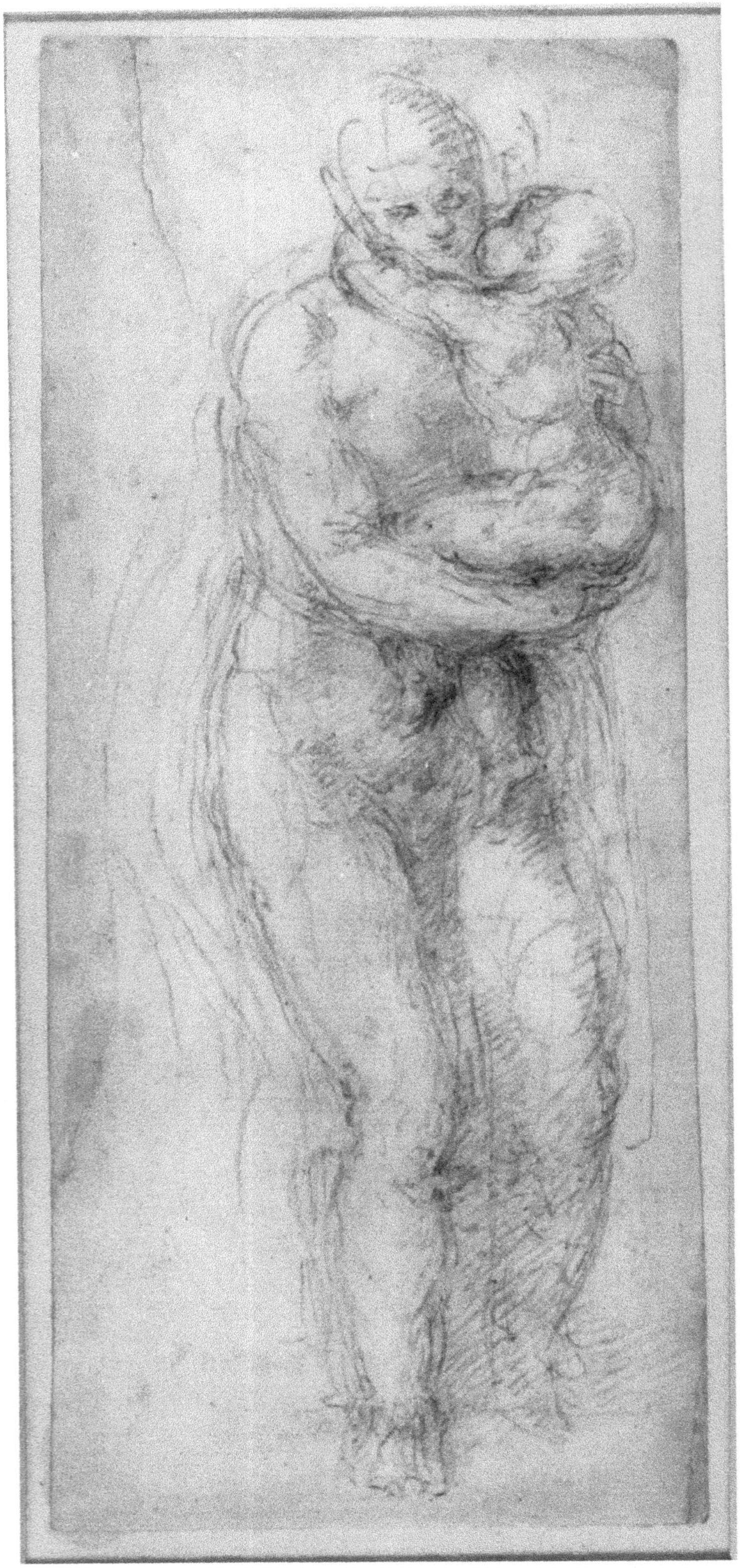

203. Michelangelo, *The Virgin and Child.* Black chalk, 26.6 × 11.7 cm. British Museum, London (1859-6-25-562 [Wilde 83]).

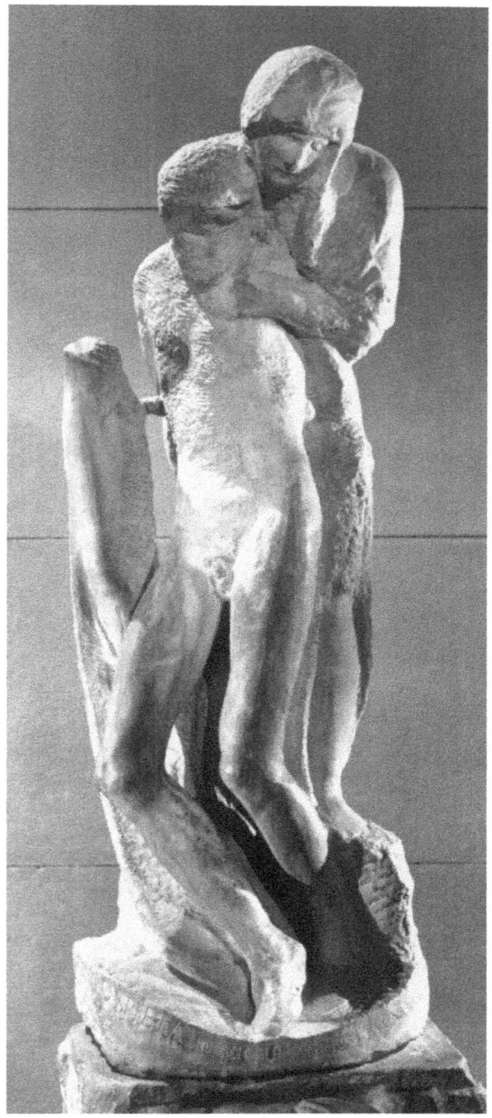

204. Michelangelo, *The Rondanini Pietà*. Marble. Castello Sforzesco, Milan. Photo: Scala/Art Resource, New York.

stonecarver evidently needed to keep his hand in it, but the nearly destructive results of that radical revision, like the overwrought state of the Crucifixion drawings, confirm that the need was more than purely professional.

Although made for himself, Michelangelo's Crucifixion drawings, like the finished drawings he made for Tommaso de' Cavalieri and for Vittoria Colonna, are nonetheless addressed to an other, but one now divine. As the addressee of his poetry changes from mortal beloved to divine Savior, the corporal object of the draftsman's desire has become that most significantly mortal of human bodies. Offering himself through his art, Michelangelo spoke to the other through drawing. For us to hear his voice clearly, we must attend to the workings of his hand.

CHAPTER SEVEN

Rembrandt's Reach

. . . everything represented so naturally that one can read the meaning from the very penstrokes themselves.

– Arnold Houbraken[1]

Execution after all is a kind of miming.

– Paul Valéry[2]

In his rendition of painting's etiological myth Calderón de la Barca ascribes the invention of the art to a group of bathing boys, one of whom began tracing with his finger the outline of the shadow of another cast on the sand. Thus, "painting's first workshop was light, its first sketch shadow, and its first surface sand, its first brush the boy's finger, and its first artist the youthful exuberance of chance."[3] The Spanish poet, whose legal defense of the art of painting was made in 1677, might almost have had in mind Rembrandt's etching known now as "La Petite Tombe" (Fig. 205). The preaching Christ looks down in a kind of wonderment at the only

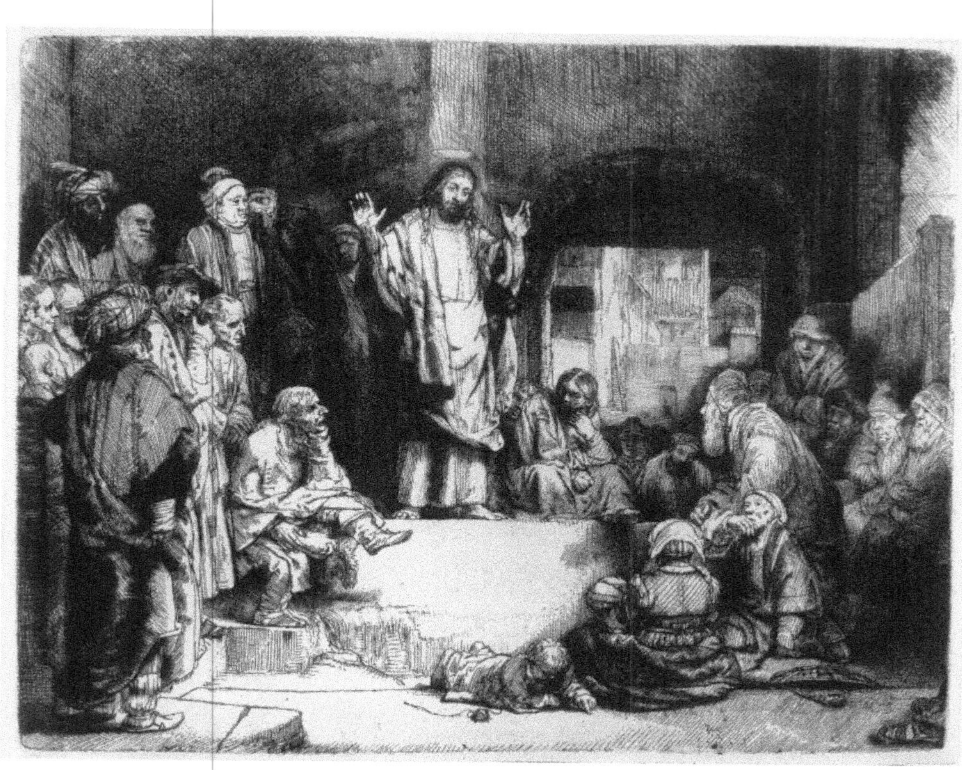

205. Rembrandt, *Christ Preaching* (*"La Petite Tombe"*) (ca. 1652). Etching with burin and drypoint, 15.5 × 20.7 cm. (B. 67). Metropolitan Museum of Art, New York. Bequest of Mrs. H. O. Havemeyer, 1929. H. O. Havemeyer Collection (29.107.18).

figure in the crowd who ignores him: a child lying on his stomach, his back to the Savior, idly running his finger through the sand (Fig. 206). While the assembled listeners are attentive to his words and presence, the preacher's own focus and his light, is on the child below, who remains oblivious to this privileged attention: "Suffer little children, and forbid them not, to come unto me" (Matthew 19:13–15).[4] The drawing finger of this little draftsman leaves no visible trace on the ground, although the curling string of his abandoned top itself represents a drawn line; his finger seems only to follow the edge of his own shadow. In this innocent reenactment of the myth of the origins of painting, Rembrandt – who had often represented his own son Titus in the act of writing or drawing – affirms a truth of drawing: that it is a direct extension of the draftsman's body, a projection of the self into the world.[5]

1. *The Mime of Drawing*

Ogni dipintore dipinge se. No artist more than Rembrandt validated that Renaissance commonplace, for no other artist (before Picasso) so consistently projected himself into his art – consciously and unconsciously. From the very beginning of his career Rembrandt made of his own face an academy, in which his studies

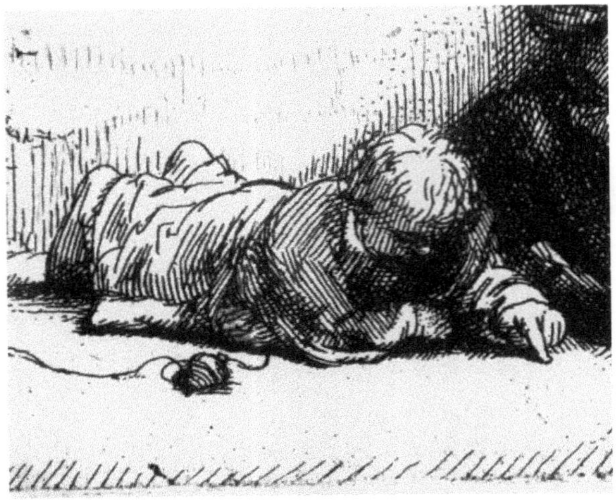

206. Rembrandt, *Christ Preaching* (*"La Petite Tombe"*), detail of Fig. 205.

extended beyond anatomical structure to physiognomic expression of the most varied kind (Figs. 207, 208). In paintings, drawings, and, especially, etchings, the young artist found his most ready and responsive model in the mirror. There, out of his own self, he created and confronted an other, a being in whom he discovered that self and through whom he fantasized the psychic life necessary to his art of history painting. From the mirror to the imagined stage of pictorial narratives Rembrandt translated his own visage, becoming himself an active participant, for example, in the stoning of Saint Stephen or in the elevation of Christ on the cross or in the descent. In the course of his career he cast himself in many roles, from chorus to protagonist, as witness, sinner, saint. And, even more overtly, in the lifelong series of self-portraits in which he costumed himself in imagined scenarios without such explicit scripts; in these images sartorial strangeness serves to establish an objective distance between self and other, allowing Rembrandt to serve as Rembrandt's model.[6]

Rembrandt's practice became theoretical precept in the treatise written by his onetime student Samuel van Hoogstraten. In the painting of the passions, Hoogstraten counsels, "one must reform oneself totally into an actor." Explicitly recommending the study of the artist's own expression in the mirror, "where you are simultaneously the performer and the beholder," he observes that here "a poetic spirit is necessary in order to imagine oneself in another's place."[7]

In neither theory nor practice was Rembrandt's procedure unusual, however. Renaissance art theory, building on ancient rhetorical tradition, taught that the painter who wishes to move the passions of the beholder – and that, it went without saying, was his highest goal – must first feel them himself. What was true for Horace's classical orator held for the modern painter: "If you want to move me to tears, you must first feel grief yourself; then . . . your misfortunes will grieve me too. . . . Pathetic language is appropriate to the face of sorrow."[8] And in the Baroque other artists as well sought appropriate physiognomic models in the mirror:

Bernini, for prime example, who to capture the grim determination of David, is said to have studied his own grimacing features in a mirror held by his exalted patron, Maffeo Barberini, and who, before depicting the martyrdom of Saint Lawrence, is said to have thrust his own limb over a fire that he might feel the pain himself and thus better understand and more effectively render the suffering of the saint. Domenichino, too, had turned himself into an actor, playing out the roles of the figures he was painting, making their *affetti* his own. And in this he was extending the lessons of the Carracci, for Agostino in particular taught that figures would appear stiff and artificial unless the artist understood them through his own physical imitation.[9] An age of pictorial high drama expected its artists to perform with conviction.

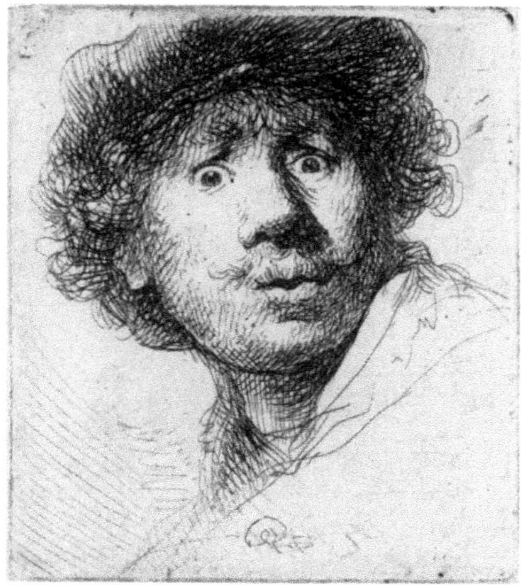

207. Rembrandt, *Self-Portrait in a Cap, Open-Mouthed and Staring* (1630). Etching, 5.1 × 4.6 cm. (B. 320). Museum Het Rembrandthuis, Amsterdam.

Rembrandt's theatrical ability, his talent at miming the passions, was legendary, ever since Constantijn Huygens celebrated the young painter's superiority in "judgment" and in "liveliness of emotion." Huygens's example is the early (1629) painting of *Judas Returning the Thirty Pieces of Silver*, in particular the gesture of the despairing Judas: "Judas maddened, howling, begging forgiveness, yet not hoping for it, or reflecting any hope in his countenance, his expression frightening, his hair tangled, his clothes torn, his limbs twisted, his hands clenched to the point of blood, prostrate on his knees on a random impulse, his body twisted by every pitiful hideousness. . . ."[10] Rhetorical as it is, Huygens's own response testifies both to the expressive aims of history painting and the expectations of its beholders, and to their own imaginative participation in its affect, to their own projections of feeling.

208. Rembrandt, *Self-Portrait, Open-Mouthed, as if Shouting* (1630). Etching, 8.3 × 7.2 cm. (B. 13). Rijksmuseum, Amsterdam (inv. RP-P-1962-8).

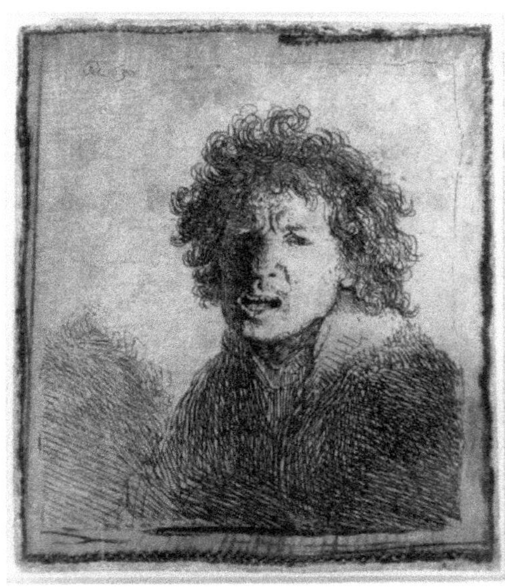

Rembrandt himself, in his only recorded comment on the ambition of his art, confirmed its affective intent: writing to Huygens of the religious pictures he was painting for the stadholder, he declared his preoccupation with expressing "the greatest and most natural emotion" ("die meeste ende die naetuereelste beweechgelichkheijt").[11] Whether *beweechgelickheijt* translates more appropriately as "motion" or "emotion," an object of debate among scholars, seems irrelevant, for the two terms were natural pictorial complements: "the motions of the countenance doe best expresse the state of the mind," as Franciscus Junius summarized another Renaissance commonplace.[12] If Rembrandt's own face served

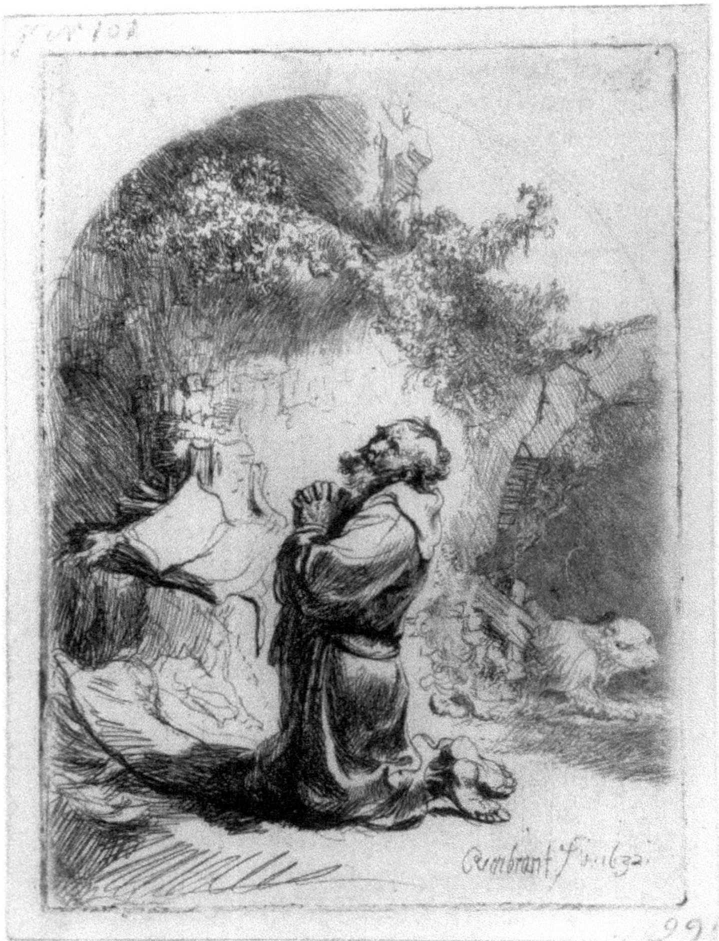

209. Rembrandt, *St. Jerome Praying: Arched Print* (1632). Etching, 10.8 × 8.0 cm. (B. 101). British Museum, London.

him as a model in which to discover proper physiognomic expression, expression was hardly limited to the face. As attested by Huygens's projective response to the despairing Judas, it was the motions of the full body that spoke with special force from the stage of painting. Indeed, however impressive the contorted features of his countenance, the tortured soul of this Judas reveals itself in the agony of his twisted limbs, especially his hands, "clenched to the point of blood." This motif will remain a powerful – and influential – element in Rembrandt's expressive vocabulary, and we may assume that he came to know it less from any model, living or art-historical, than from his own intense imitation.[13] The tension we, like Huygens, respond to in the agonized body of Judas is fully felt and was, presumably, so felt by its creator. Rembrandt the actor must have played Judas for Rembrandt the painter, at least on the internal stage of the body's own imagination.

That the intensity of the experience was somehow epitomized in those tightly clenched hands seems confirmed by the number of related representations Rembrandt produced in the years following the painting of Judas, especially etchings of

Saint Jerome in prayer (Fig. 209). In each of these images the hands, fingers painfully interlocked, focus the energies of the body, as an internal physical node and synecdoche for the emotional agony of the kneeling penitent. Rembrandt continually reinvented the motif, and with increasing conviction in the less overtly theatrical, more introverted conception of his later art (Fig. 210).[14]

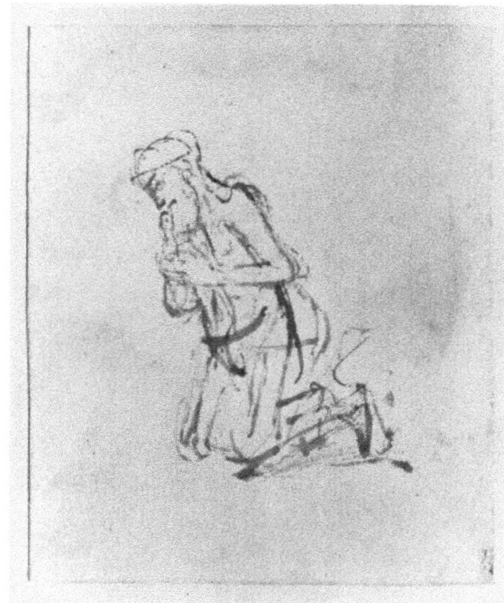

210. Rembrandt, *Old Man Kneeling in Prayer* (ca. 1650). Pen and brown ink, 10.3 × 8.5 cm. Ashmolean Museum, Oxford (P.I, 184 [Benesch 859]).

Among Rembrandt's early drawings, one (of ca. 1635) seems particularly close in imagination to the Judas: a compositional sketch of Jacob's extreme response to the sight of Joseph's blood-stained coat (Fig. 211). Relatively modest in size (17.2 × 15.5 cm), like most of his dramatic drawings, this sheet accommodates a remarkable concentration of energies. The grieving father throws himself back in his chair, his face twisted in lamentation, his hands tightly clasped "to the point of blood."[15] As in the despairing Judas, physiognomy and anatomy combine to create a figure in extremis, the expression of the face punctuating a statement writ large by the radical dislocation of the body. Indeed, the momentum of that dislocating thrust culminates in, even as it is carried by, the dense impacting of expressive forces produced by the close juxtaposition of face and hands. In the residual space to the upper right, Rembrandt tests alternative responses of Jacob: first, a variation on the energized agony, less internalized, with the face cast upward, appealing now to heaven; and then collapse, as Jacob sinks into himself, in emotional exhaustion. Evidently living through the story with his pen, Rembrandt narrates it in his own imagination; each variation signals a different moment in what we can read as a sequence of response, progressively resigned. Graphic continuity, the progress of drawing, becomes narrative sequence.[16]

Franciscus Junius – whose *De Pictura Veterum libri tres* was published in Amsterdam in 1637, in English the following year and in Dutch translation four years later – might almost have had Rembrandt in mind when he wrote about the need of the painter, like the poet, to have "a strong and well-exercised Imagination." Even more evocative of Rembrandt is his description of the way painters will consider seriously the subject at hand, "as if they were present at the doing, or saw it acted before their eyes; whereupon feeling themselves well filled with a quick and lively imagination of the whole worke, they make haste to ease their overcharged braines by a speedie pourtraying of the conceit."[17]

"Speedie pourtraying," rapid execution, is precisely what conveys the urgency of Jacob's drama in Rembrandt's drawing. The old man's back-breaking agony comes across as much through the force of Rembrandt's lines as through the pose itself; physical intensity is a function of drawing. More than merely representing the motions of the body, the pen activates them: its swiftness sends Jacob back; its concentration articulates physiognomic expression, and the dense pooling of ink, a coming together of lines that weights and shades form, concentrates the pressure at the uncomfortable juncture of head and shoulder. Surrounding the agonized Jacob, his sons are rendered even more swiftly but to more generalized purpose; their choral function is confirmed by the standing figure framing the scene at the left, apparently in direct dialogue with Jacob. Possibly the son charged with presenting the coat to the father – the lines of his drawing, arching and broken, establish the solicitation of his affect – this tall figure is transformed into pure repoussoir by the final application of wash. Lending pictorial body to the rapidly penned son, running across the ground and up to offer shadowed support to the centrifugal figure of the unbalanced father, the wash spatializes the entire scene, establishing a frontal, proscenium plane. A typical framing gesture in Rembrandt's graphic staging, such broadly brushed areas of shadow simultaneously declare the flat surface of the paper and define a virtual depth extending beyond that surface. In this duality the wash recapitulates on a large scale the ambivalence of every mark on the sheet, the tension between graphic reality and pictorial illusion.

As the narrative logic of the progression of alternative solutions confirms, Rembrandt thought with pen in hand. His exploration in the Jacob drawing is a draftsman's search; it took place on the paper as an integral part of the drawing process, imagination and hand moving in tandem. Hoogstraten, again presumably rehearsing lessons learned in Rembrandt's studio, recommended that in the evening the student devote himself to "drawing many histories from the imagination [*uyt de geest*]." "Sketch and sketch again," he urges, "and play out the history first in your thoughts. . . ."[18] Arnold Houbraken, a further generation removed from that studio, celebrates "hundreds of [Rembrandt's] sketches wherein the passions of the soul in all kinds of situations are so explicitly and artfully shown. . . . Anger, hatred, sorrow, joy, and so on, everything represented so naturally that one can read the meaning from the very pen strokes themselves."[19]

Precisely: meaning is generated by the stroke itself. Although he certainly studied living models, in and out of the studio, and posed them in the outlandish costumes that distanced them from contemporary Amsterdam, Rembrandt found the truest theater of dramatic subjects in his own imagination. Those subjects, we sense, were enacted not so much on miniature stages in the studio but on the drawing board.[20] The passion of lamenting Jacob finds expression through the medium of the pen; it is the passions of the draftsman's hand that so move us.

More is involved here than a simple contrast between drawing after life (*naer het leven*) and drawing from the imagination (*uyt de geest*) – or, a variant category, from memory (*van onthoudt*).[21] Even if Rembrandt did pose models in narrative situations, even if he did counsel his pupils to feel their way into the roles of fictional personages, to imagine the passions of others, the drawings he himself made operate on their own, essentially graphic terms. Whatever the scene before him, or in his mind, Rembrandt eventually lived the drama on the paper. His imagination worked dialogically. His creatures, given voice through pen stroke, are social beings; even those alone on the page seem to need to communicate, to speak or to listen.

A torn sheet in Berlin (Fig. 212) testifies eloquently to the graphic impulse of

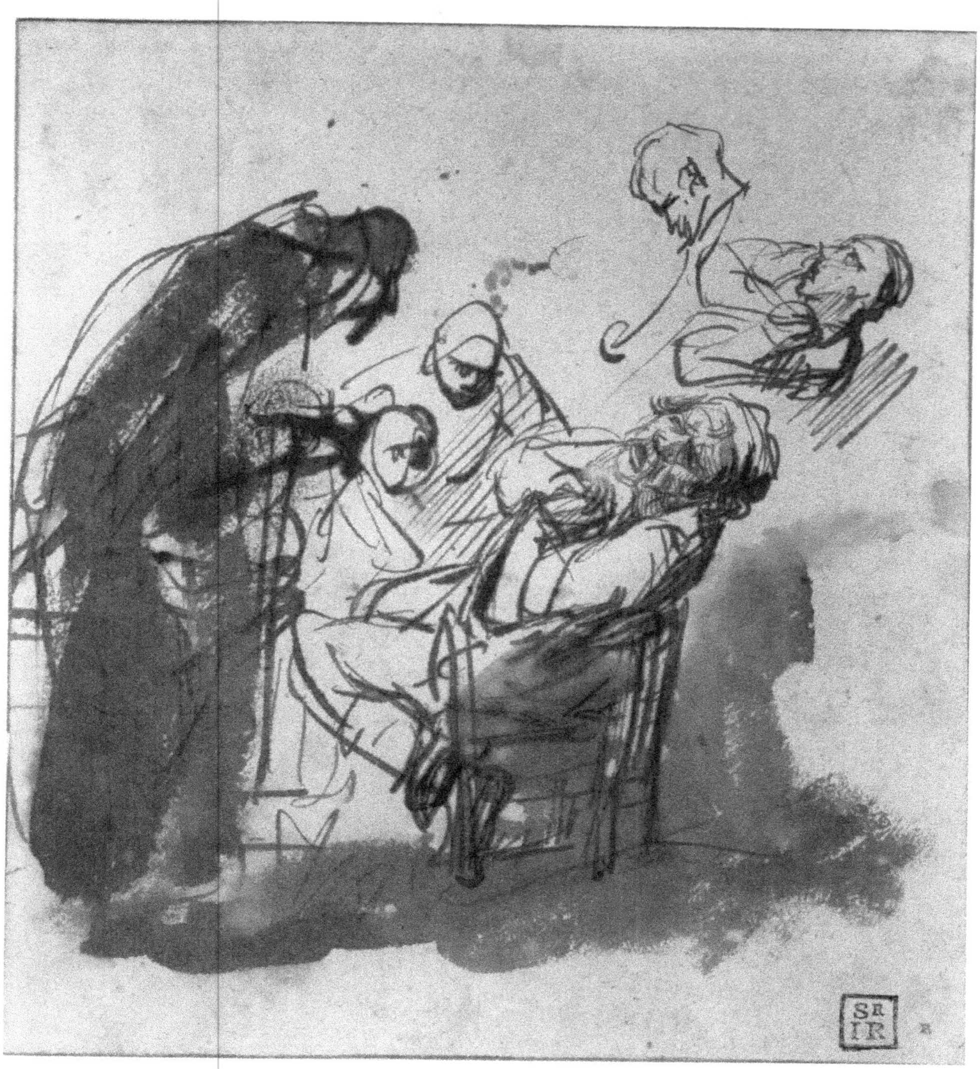

211. Rembrandt, *Jacob Lamenting at the Sight of of Joseph's Blood-Stained Coat* (ca. 1635). Pen and brown ink, wash, 17.2 × 15.5 cm. Kupferstichnkabinett, Staatliche Museen zu Berlin, Preussischer Kulturbesitz, Berlin (KdZ 5213 [Benesch 95]). Photo: Jörg P. Anders.

Rembrandt's imagination. The drawing comprises a group of costumed women and men. Six of the eight look to the right with varying degrees of attentiveness, from aggressively focused to deeply thoughtful to somewhat casual or even suspicious. Members of a typical Rembrandt audience before a compelling preacher, they were probably preparatory to the painted monochrome of the *Preaching of Saint John the Baptist* (Br. 555).[22] Each figure responds to the word in an individual way; even the two who turn to the left, their heads fit into interstices, assume roles in this context, contrariness suggesting skepticism or doubt. Our own reading of this drawing, then, readily assigns psychological values to the individuals and hence to the group. The narrative unity we ascribe to them is a function of the visual coherence we perceive in the overall design of the group, and that coherence is a direct product of Rembrandt's active pen.

As in the marginal variations on Jacob's lament, so too in this densely impacted

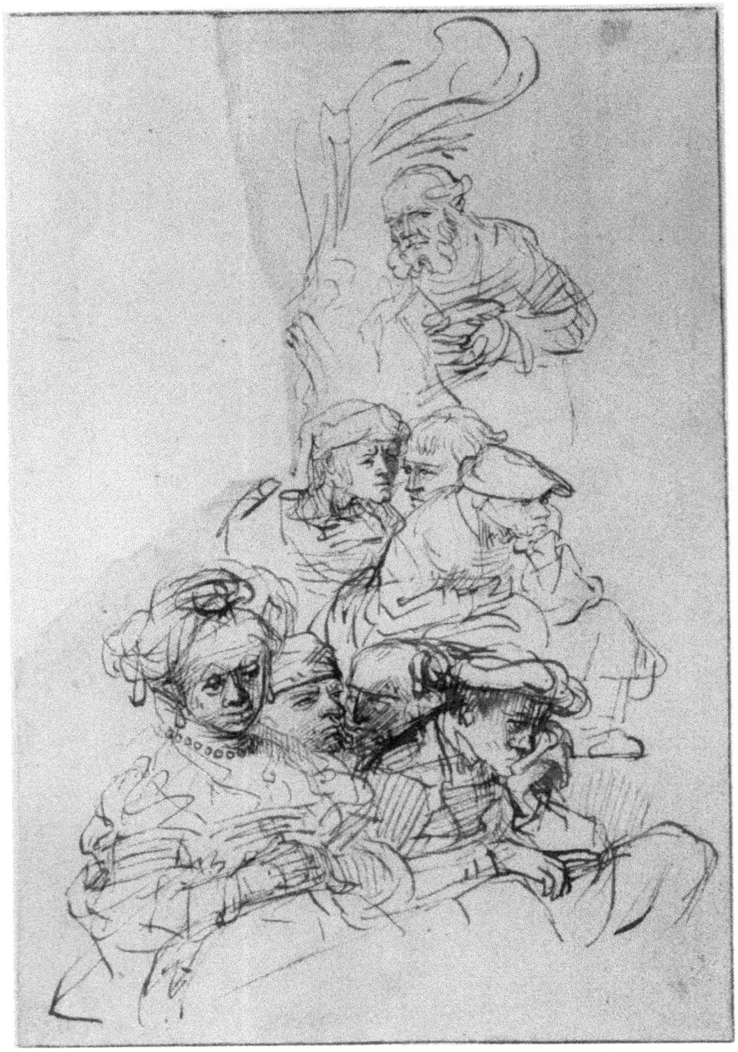

212. Rembrandt, *Different Listeners* (ca. 1637). Pen and brown ink, 19 × 12.5 cm. (irregular, torn and restored). Kupferstichkabinett, Staatliche Museen zu Berlin, Preussischer Kulturbesitz, Berlin (KdZ 5243 [Benesch 140]). Photo: Jörg P. Anders.

construct of listeners syntactic sequence follows graphic progression. Here, that sequence is spatial rather than narrative. We follow the course of Rembrandt's drawing: beginning with the woman in the lower left and moving in serpentine fashion up the fragmented field, first to the right and then to the left and, finally, to the right again. Each figure in this progress is overlapped by its predecessor, thereby signaling a retreat into notional space. As the number of figures decreases, each vertical stage becomes progressively more open, from the figural density of the base to the evaporating forms of the apex: first, two women framing two male heads; then, two men framing a single head, also male; and finally a lone figure whose contrapposto – body turned to the left, eyes to the right – summarizes the serpentine movement that it culminates and whose open situation is, in turn, confirmed by the swirling lines (of drapery, presumably) around him.

Rembrandt's pen traveled that same course, from linear constriction to calligraphic freedom. At the base, a complex structure of pictorial incident, of mimetic detail and hatching pattern, articulates planes and crystallizes form; its concentration of lines records the kind of attention and the duration of the draftsman's performance. Moving up the surface and back into notional space, the pen seems to overcome the gravity of its first representation; receding into that space, forms are freed of excess hatching – only enough to suggest the convexity of a body or the square cut of a costume – and open up. And the final gesture, escaping the ponderation and physicality of the figural groups, swings out into the ambient space that it itself inhabits and punctuates.

As Rembrandt's ascending pen disengages from its original haptic responsibilities to solid form, it asserts its own freedom of movement. And if we have been trained to read this transformation pictorially, as a move from foreground object to distant atmosphere, the very arbitrariness of the design calls us back to the reality of the drawing *qua* drawing. Isolated on the paper, a vignette, these sketched listeners lack the contextual rationale, narrative and pictorial, for their existence: the presence of a motivating speaker – that fuller scene that we as viewers are ready to imagine. Their colliding juxtapositions, disparate perspectives, and shifting scale hardly permit reconstruction of a consistent stage, despite the hint of a step. Without preestablished setting, then, and considered on their own, these figures seem without ulterior pictorial purpose – quite different from the communal dialogues or the focus of the functionally situated crowd in a drawing preparing the *Hundred Guilder-Print* (Figs. 213, 214).[23]

Whatever the narrative intention that inspired them, these figures have been

213. *Study for the Group of the Sick in the "Hundred-Guilder Print"* (ca. 1639–40). Pen and brown ink, wash, white body-color, 14.4 × 18.4 cm. Kupferstichkabinett, Staatliche Museen zu Berlin, Preussischer Kulturbesitz, Berlin (KdZ 2695 [Benesch 188]). Photo: Jörg P. Anders.

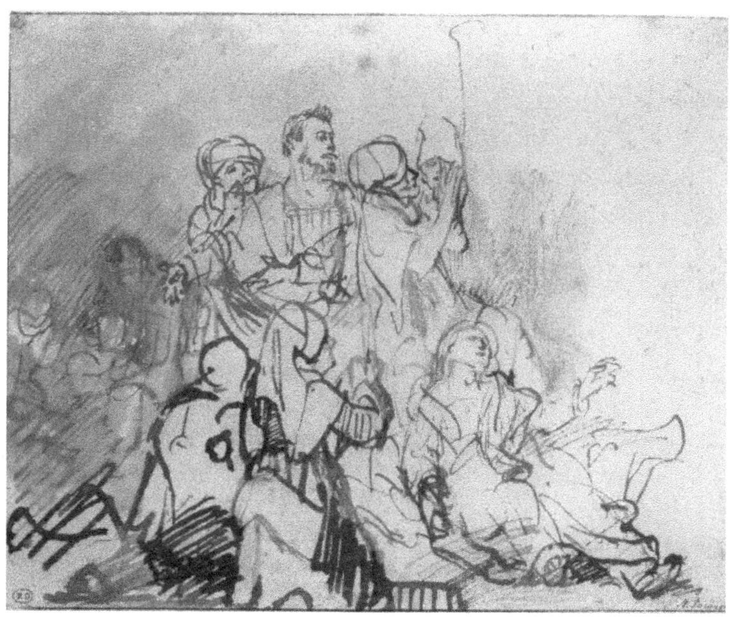

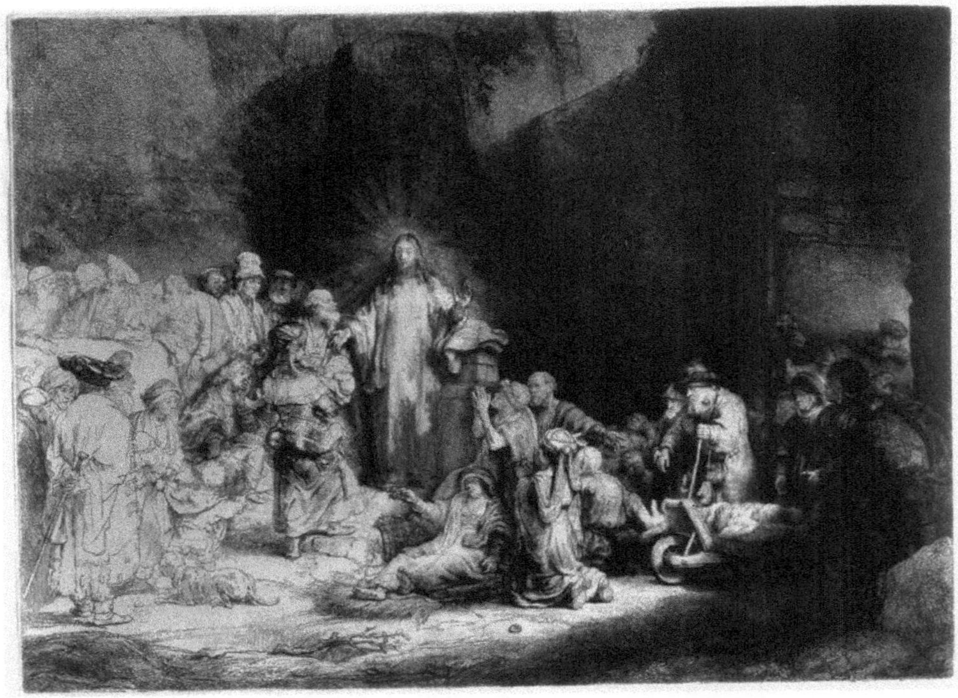

214. Rembrandt, *Christ with the Sick around Him, Receiving Little Children* (*"The Hundred-Guilder Print"*) (ca. 1639–49). Etching, with drypoint and burin, 27.8 × 38.9 cm. (B. 74). Metropolitan Museum of Art, New York. H. O. Havemeyer Collection, Bequest of Mrs. H. O. Havemeyer, 1929 (29.107.35).

graphically generated. The logic of their creation is the result of Rembrandt's penwork. We sense the dialectic of its operations: the first figure posited, leaning slightly to the left, gives rise to her neighbor, leaning to the right; one is openly pensive, the other closed in meditation. The dour squatter generates the elegant youth, who, in turn, seems to have inspired the culminating old man. This kind of dynamic is not unlike the imagining dialectic of Leonardo's drawing processes.

What we might term a dialogic imperative animates many of Rembrandt's drawings: in response to needs evidently both graphic and social, figures seem to generate their companions. Apparently born of and to dialogue, Rembrandt's creatures require company; once drawn, they seem naturally to surround themselves with others – even if only other views of their own bodies (Figs. 215, 216).[24] It is, of course, Rembrandt himself who imagines such need, and we recognize the process by which, to satisfy his own professional needs as a history painter, he transforms contemporary Amsterdammers into the anonymous crowds of ancient Galilee. But, beyond such representational aims, we also recognize the momentum of graphic creation. The wandering line of the draftsman's pen, having established one figure, keeps moving in search of others and thereby creates a compositional unit (Figs. 217, 218).[25] Rarely does Rembrandt construct a stage prior to populating it; the figure always takes precedence. Once established, it generates its own space, as the pen line extends beyond that initial body to colonize the surrounding paper.

In a compositional motif that epitomizes this generative process a cluster of

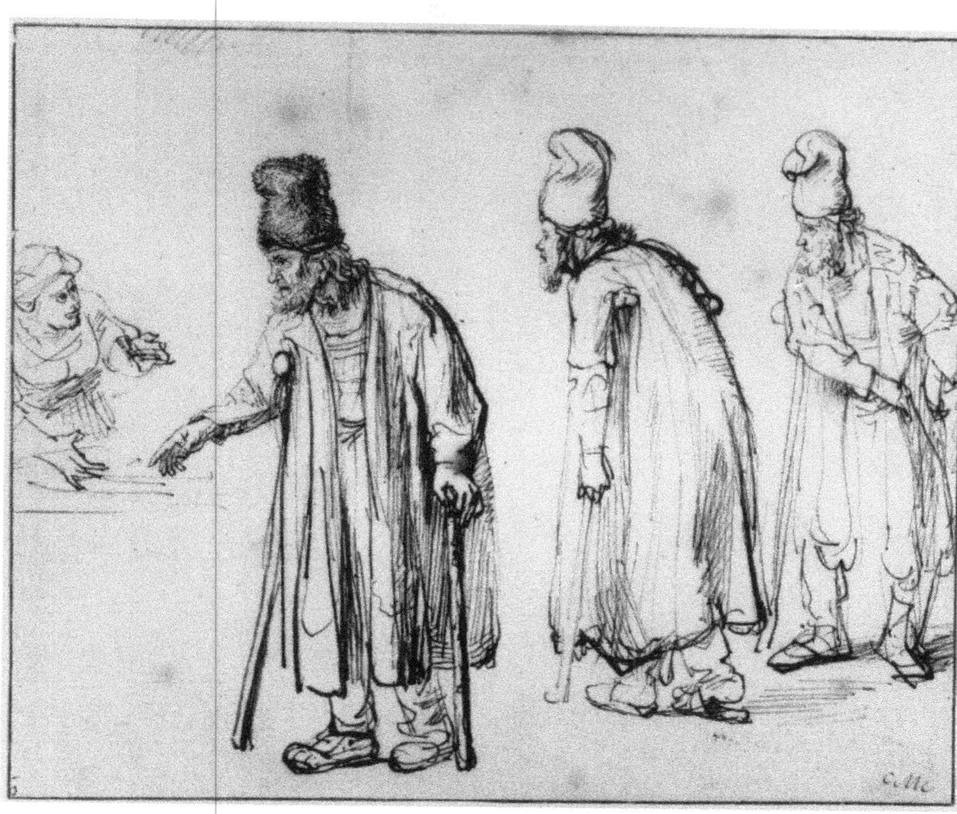

215. Rembrandt, *Three Studies of a Man on Crutches and a Woman* (ca. 1632–34). Pen and brown ink, 15.2 × 18.5 cm. British Museum, London (Gg.2-252 [Benesch 327]).

216. Rembrandt, *Three Studies of a Beggar* (ca. 1659–60). Reed pen and brown ink, shadows rubbed with the finger, 11.9 × 17.6 cm. Kupfterstichkabinett, Staatliche Museen zu Berlin, Preussischer Kulturbesitz, Berlin (KdZ 3108 [Benesch 1141]). Photo: Jörg P. Anders.

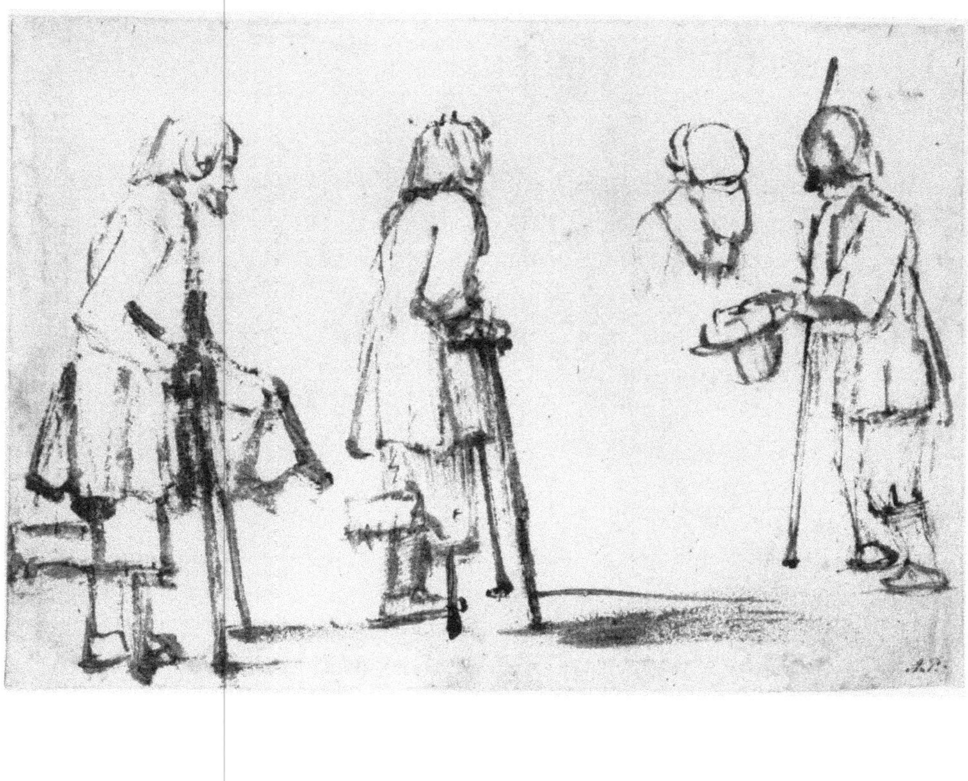

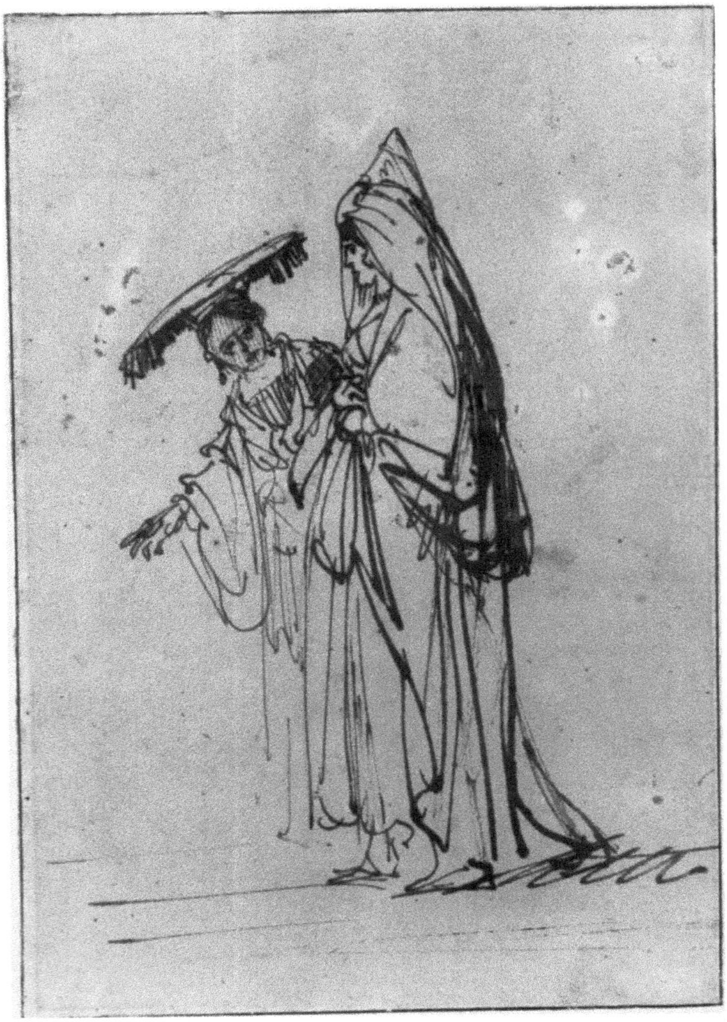

217. Rembrandt, *Ruth and Naomi* (ca. 1636). Pen and brown ink on tinted paper, 18 × 12.5 cm. Museum Boijmans Van Beuningen, Rotterdam (inv. MB 1958/T-32 [Benesch 161]).

mutually dependent figures constitute a dramatic core from which a hand or arm stretches into space beyond (Figs. 217, 219).[26] Such a gesture, extending dialogue, activates space, charging it with meaning as a potential part of a narrative, past or future. Acquiring a temporal as well as spatial aspect, it indicates a realm to be entered, both by the actors in the drawing and, imaginatively, by the viewer of it. Behind both is the imagining hand that conceived such a situation, that experienced it while rendering it. The hand of the draftsman, its course traced by ink or chalk, leads him – and subsequently us – across the paper's surface and through it into another realm.

In the intimacy of a small drawing of a child learning to walk (Fig. 219) we encounter the full dimensions of that projection. Around the central cylinder of the child, a solid form stable in its hesitancy, two women bend, enlarging the arena.

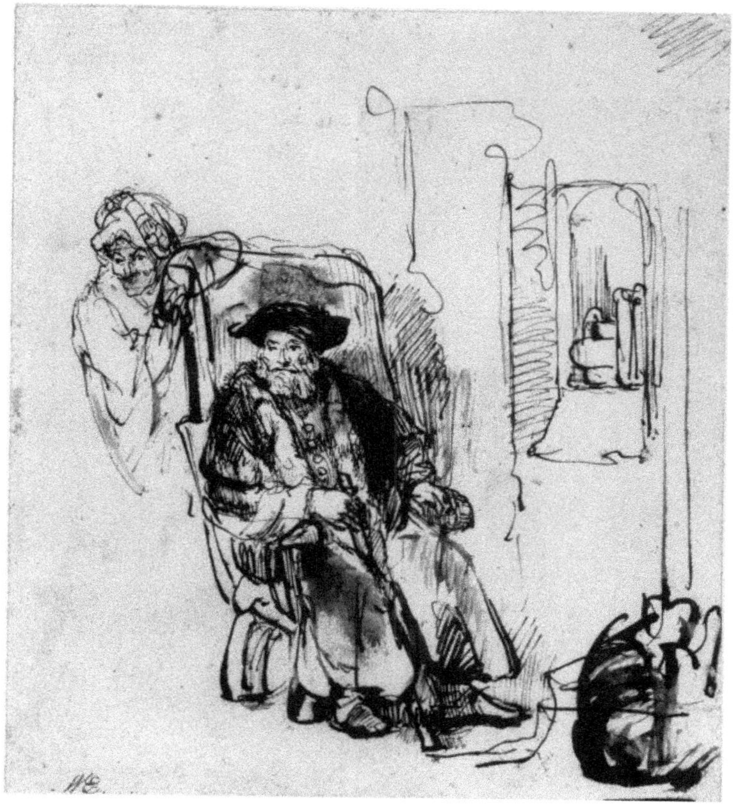

218. Rembrandt, *A Seated Old Man and a Woman (Jacob and Rachel)* (ca. 1640–45). Pen and brown ink, brown wash, touched with white, 18 × 16.3 cm. British Museum, London (1861-6-8-149 [Benesch 528]).

One, to the right, is clearly older: a grandmother, bent low and contained within her own bodily contours. The younger figure is taller, more energetic: the mother, taking the lead and by her outreach indicating space future. Responding to the simplicity of this drawing, its concept and its execution, we experience the gestures of its construction: the weighty concentration at the right; the internal focus of the supporting arms/strokes; the protective containment of the grandmother, slightly forward and turning inward; the cocked heads, each realized through graphic signs that establish spatial position; and the ultimate thrust beyond the security of the group. Rapidly sketched; rapidly felt. Even as it creates it, the draftsman's hand itself explores the world of the child.

In imagining even so apparently modest a world as this – but one ominously charged with the adventure of the unknown – the draftsman's exploration is thorough. Led by the red chalk that records as it charts the way, his exploring hand probes a fully three-dimensional world – its internal mechanics, its subtly inflected spatial facets, its boundaries and its extensions to a realm beyond immediate reach. We may admire the ability of his line to suggest so much, but our admiration recalls our own implication in those linear structures, our complicity in reinvesting them with animating energy. What we so readily respond to, what we feel in

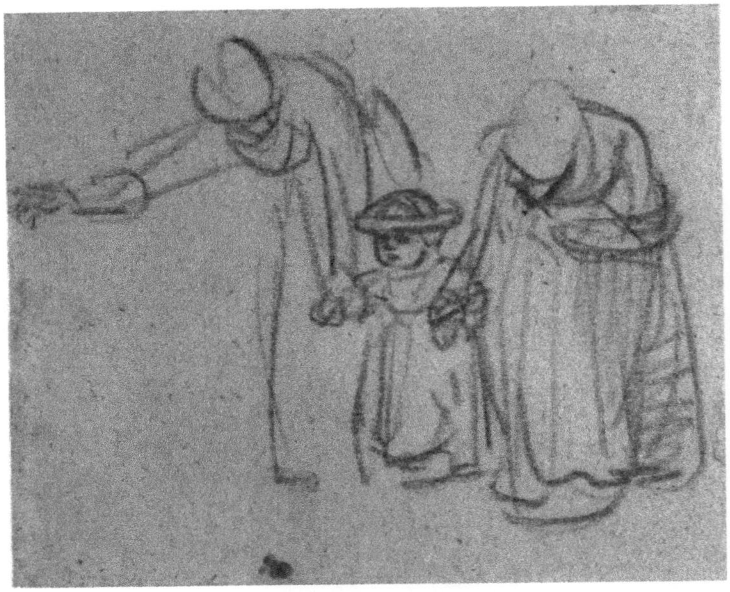

219. Rembrandt, *Two Women Teaching a Child to Walk* (ca. 1635–37). Red chalk on rough grey paper, 10.3 × 12.8 cm. British Museum, London (1910-2-12-187 [Benesch 421]).

and through the gestures recorded by the chalk, is Rembrandt's own sense of the body in the world. As orginally he did, so now do we gauge the meaning of those movements against our own image of the body, its coordinates of stability and balance. That is where we meet the artist most directly, in his sense of posture and of the possibilities of posturing.

Rembrandt's special sense of the body – unlike that of his Renaissance predecessors or of classicizing contemporaries like Rubens – is not particularly manifest in his studies of the nude model, although it can hardly be absent and is especially evident in his vigorous corrections to pupils' drawings (Fig. 220).[27] Rather, from early in his career, it is in the clothed body, the body weighted, that he finds the potential for movement, for motion and emotion (*beweechgelickheijt*): the body not in the protected artificial confines of the studio but in the more vulnerable social arena of the world. But even when he is drawing from a posing model, the pose, we are convinced, is his; not only is it so in that the master positioned the model, may have dictated the posture, but, more significantly, in that we as viewers know the pose, understand it, only through his drawing. In an early black chalk drawing (Fig. 221), for example, the old man bowing slightly but obsequiously before us, bending under the weight of his own cloak, finds his motion in the chalk itself. That is, we recognize it in the movements of the draftsman's defining hand: in its concentration on the core of the figure, the heaviness of the marking signaling a notional gravity; in its realization of weight firmly planted in and by a shadowed ground plane; in the counterpoint of hatching that bespeaks the internal contrapposto of the covered body. The very rapidity of the marking testifies to a priority of hand over eye. This is no sustained examination of a draped body, no

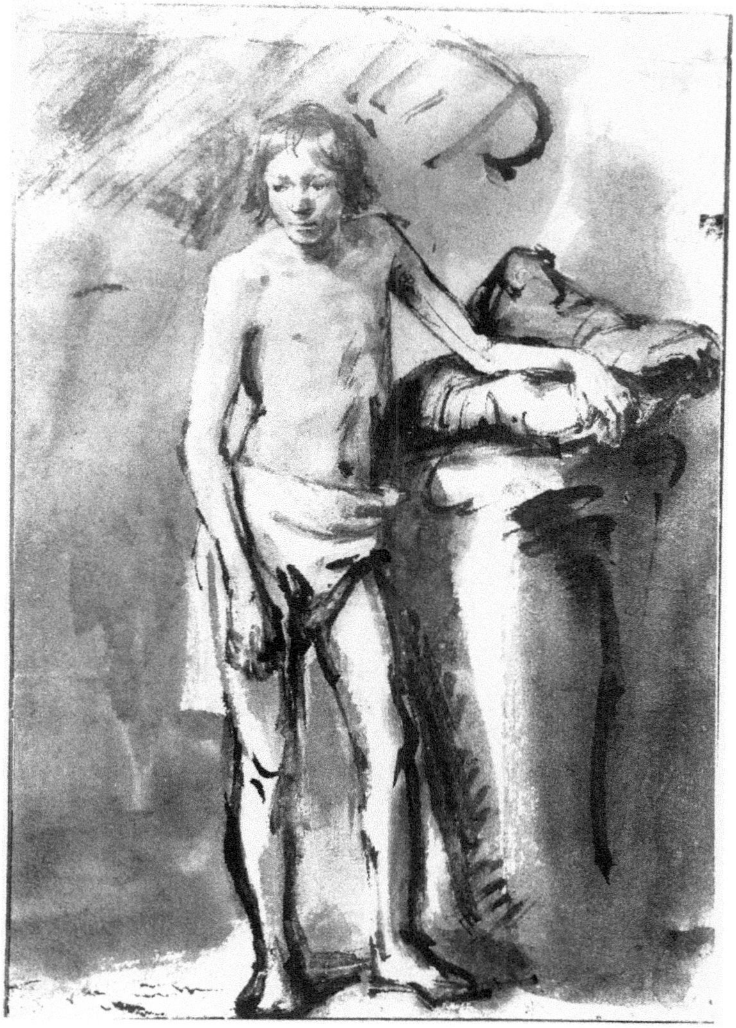

220. Rembrandt (or Rembrandt pupil corrected by Rembrandt), *Male Nude Standing* (ca. 1646). Pen and brown ink and brown wash, 19.8 × 13.3 cm. Graphische Sammlung Albertina, Vienna (inv. 8.827 [Benesch 709]).

studied analysis of the shape of folded cloth; we could hardly imagine such a drawing being squared for enlargement or transfer. Rather than objectively studied, the whole is instinctively felt, realized in and through the gestures of drawing. The drawing graphically records the imagining of such a figure, the external rendering of the draftsman's internal reenactment of bodily attitude, of Rembrandt posing for Rembrandt.

This is the mime of drawing, the artist investing himself in his model, projecting himself into the world. There is, admittedly, a degree of theatricality in all this: the draftsman imagining an other becomes that other during the drawing performance. Nonetheless, although Rembrandt's interest in theatrics is well established, we should be cautious about applying the term too loosely, assigning it too deter-

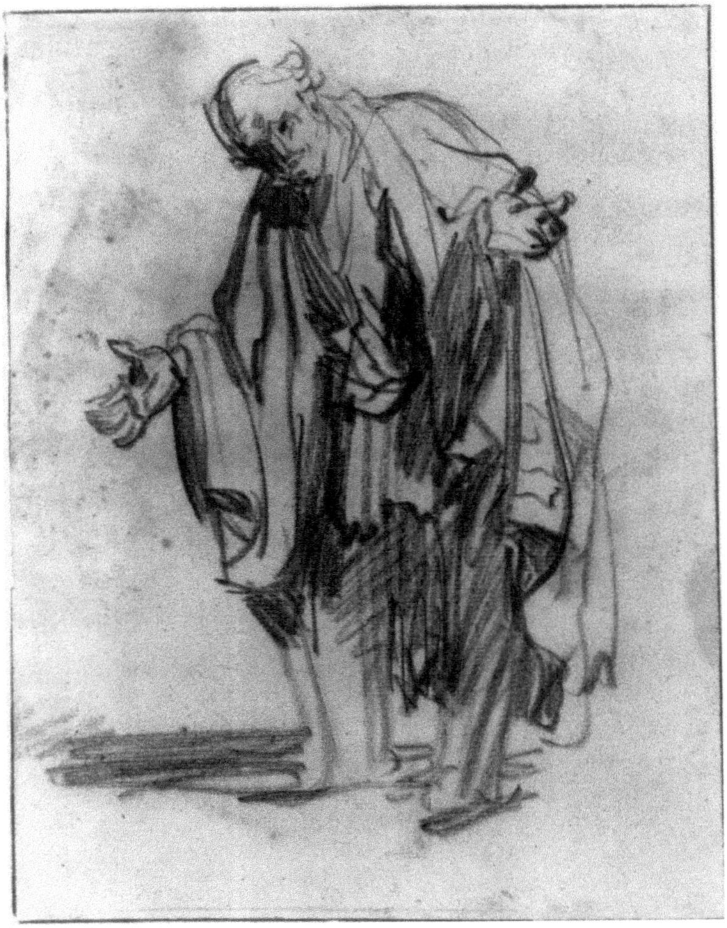

221. Rembrandt, *Old Man with His Arms Extended* (ca. 1629). Black chalk, 25.4 × 19.1 cm. Kupferstich-Kabinett, Staatlichen Kunstsammlungen, Dresden (inv. C 1971–26 [Benesch 12]).

mining a role in his creative operations. When he did study the comedians he may well have recognized kindred spirits, posers who made their bodies speak through conspicuous gestures (Fig. 222), but he had little to learn from them.[28] It is not the flamboyant actor who runs as a leitmotif through Rembrandt's graphic oeuvre; it is the beggar (Fig. 223).

Like the comedian, but for different reasons, the beggar presents a body out of the ordinary, bent and dependent, upon a cane or crutch. Just that prop, an extension and support of the body, unites Rembrandt's beggars with a larger community of marginalized beings in his work – Jews, the old, and the blind (Figs. 224, 225).[29] For these handicapped creatures, especially the blind, the cane serves as a sensory extension of the body, ocular surrogate, a tactile mode of seeing.[30] For the draftsman, that supporting staff becomes a ready standard of the supported body's posture, gauging stasis or movement. Indeed, absent that prop, Rembrandt often finds his own vertical coordinate to serve just such purpose in his graphic representations of the figure: an axis that establishes a basic stability, on which the irregular

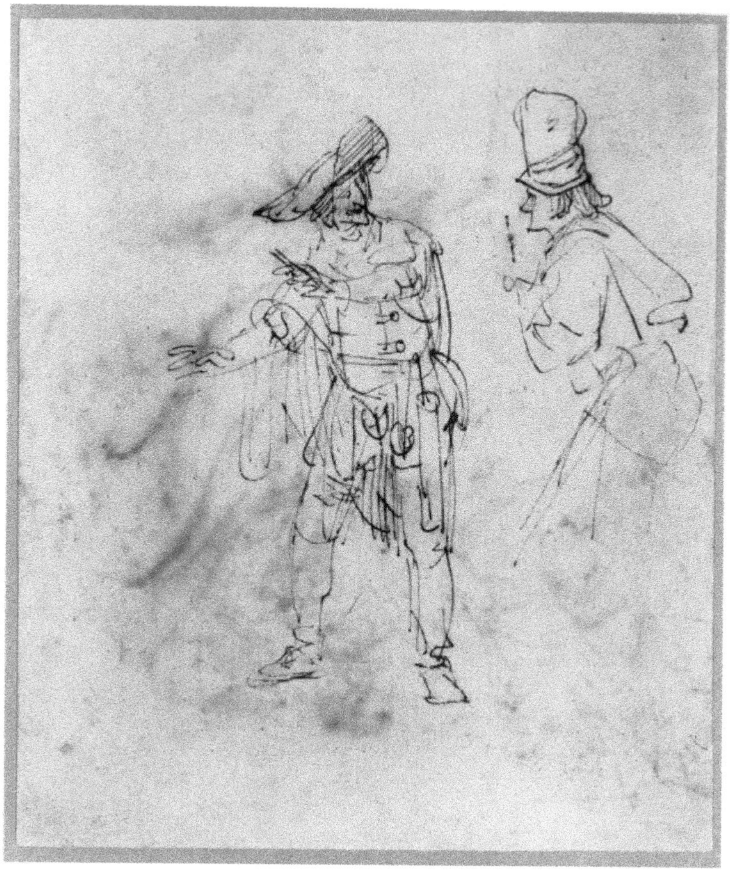

222. Rembrandt, *Two Actors in Dialogue* (ca. 1635). Pen and brown ink, 18.2 × 15.3 cm. Rijksmuseum, Amsterdam (inv. 1961:76 [Benesch 293 verso]).

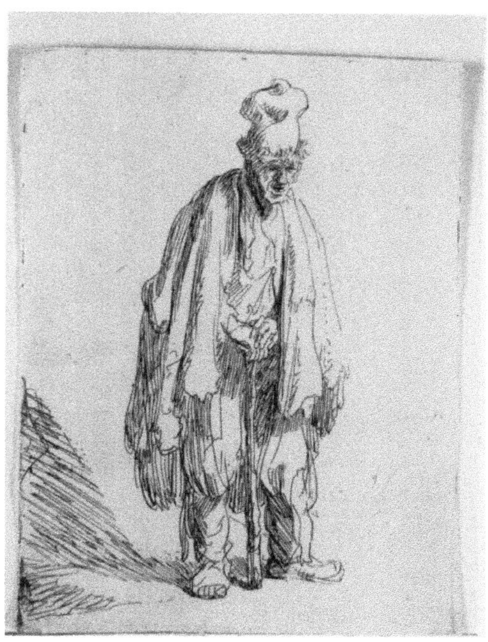

223. Rembrandt, *Beggar in a High Cap, Standing and Leaning on a Stick* (ca. 1629). Etching, 15.6 × 12 cm. (B. 162). Museum Het Rembrandthuis, Amsterdam.

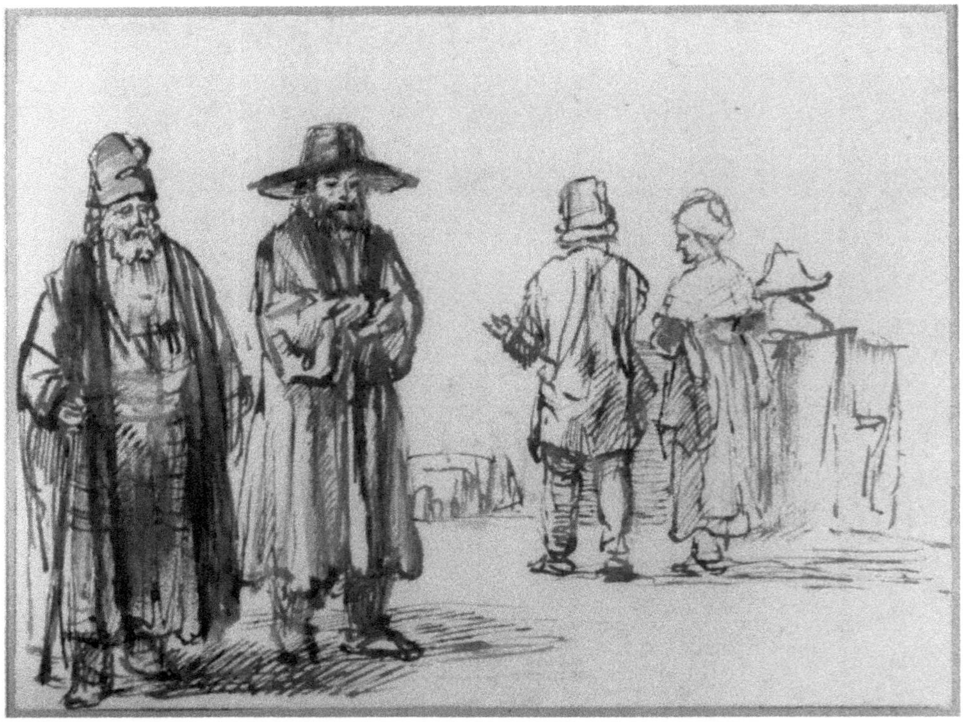

224. Rembrandt, *Two Standing Jews and Other Figures* (ca. 1647–48). Pen and brown ink, wash, corrections with white body-color, 17.5 × 23.7 cm. Haarlem, Teylers Museum (O*52 [Benesch 753]).

225. Rembrandt, *The Blindness of Tobit: The Larger Plate* (1651). Etching, with touches of drypoint, 16.1 × 12.9 cm. (B. 42). Metropolitan Museum of Art, New York. Harris Brisbane Dick Fund, 1937 (37.3.13).

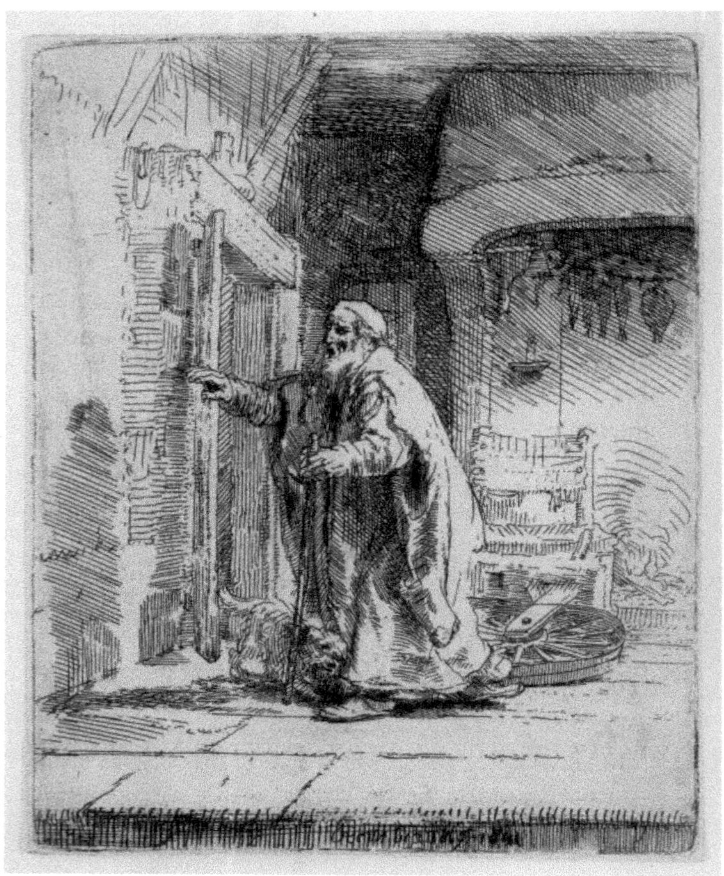

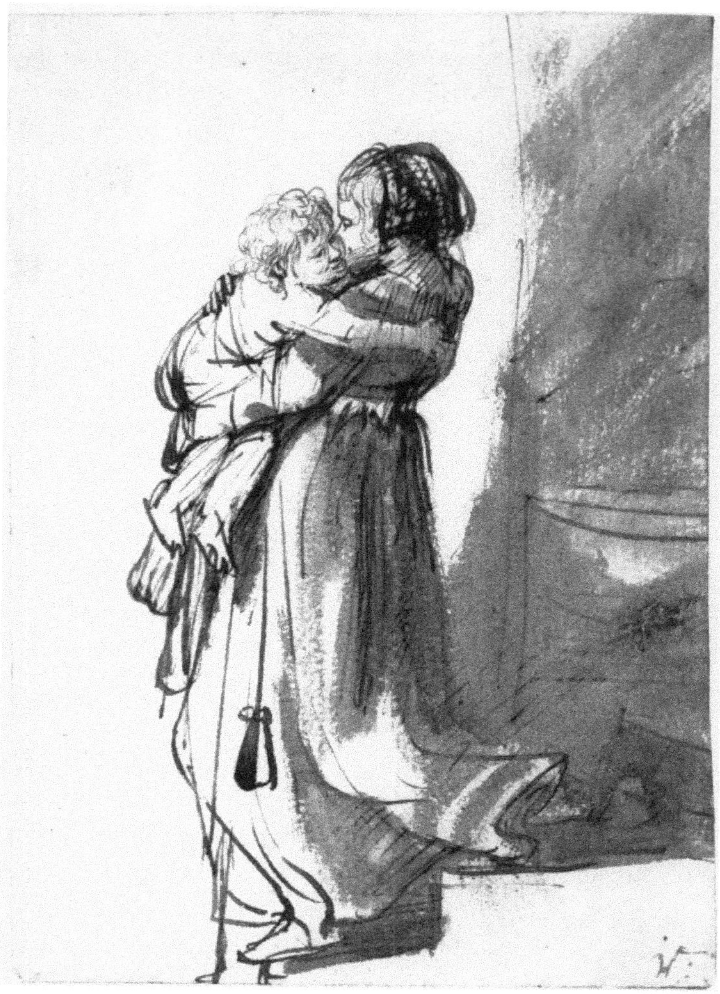

226. Rembrandt, *Woman Carrying a Child Down Stairs* (ca. 1636). Pen and brown ink, brown wash, 18.5 × 13.3 cm. Pierpont Morgan Library, New York (I,191 [Benesch 313]).

weight of the body depends – a carried child, hunched shoulders, a hanging paunch (Figs. 226, 227). There is something more instinctive than programmatic about this graphic strategy, a natural sense of rapport with the faulty but functional mechanics of the human frame.[31]

Aside from narrative subjects explicitly requiring physical energy, it is remarkable how little seems to be expended by most of the figures that fill Rembrandt's drawings, whether observed in Amsterdam or imagined in Galilee. The action represented is generally rather subdued, animated dialogue, a simple gesture extending the body into space, relating it physically and socially to a larger world. In these figure studies Rembrandt imagines a community of talkers and listeners, but, as he imagines it, the dialogic situation becomes a graphic occasion for narrative action. Significant figural movement – the tilt of a head, the hunch of shoulders, the shifting of weight – is realized by the course of the draftsman's implement recording

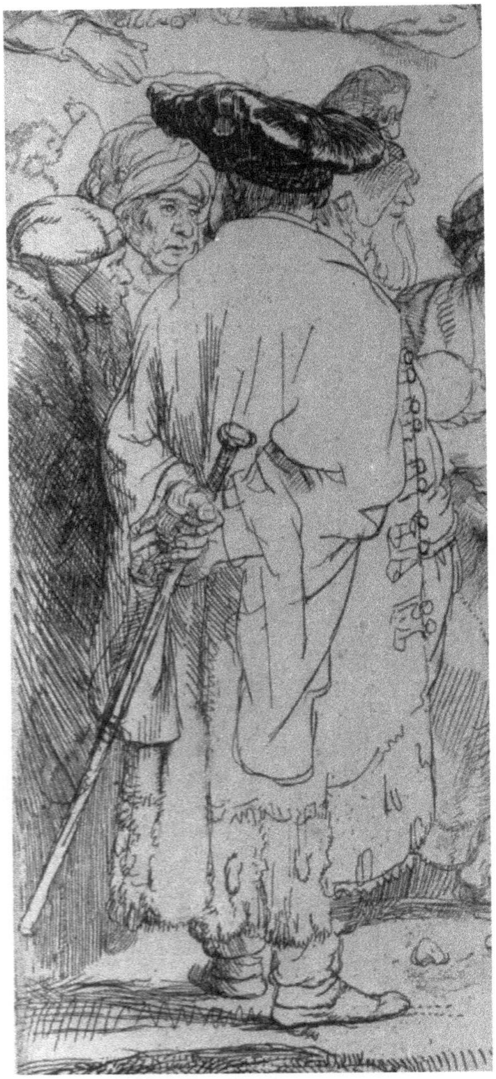

227. Rembrandt, *"The Hundred-Guilder Print,"* detail of Fig. 214.

his own playing out of pose and gesture. Transposed to a full narrative context, such corporeal inflection acquires greater dramatic import. As Rembrandt's imaginative stage expands, so do the potential roles of the imagined players.

2. The Physiology of Style

Worrying the issue of self-representation, Leonardo complained of painters "who in all their figures seem to have portrayed themselves from life," in whose figures one recognized "the motions and manners of their creator."[32] The "motions and manners of their creator" are decidedly what we encounter in figures drawn by Rembrandt, and especially in those narrative scenes sketched *uyt de geest.* We recognize a certain repertory of movements and gestures from which he built that rich corpus of biblical readings and from which we understand the language of his graphic mimes. Similarly, we recognize a repertory of drawing gestures, characteristic movements of the pen, as constituting a particular graphic style, which we call Rembrandt's. If those linear structures become animated, it is through our recognition of the originating anima of their creator, through our response to the draftsman's creating motions. In those motions imagining other bodies we sense the body behind the drawing hand, the body of the artist in the work. Neither that body nor the graphic style through which we know it is a constant, however; in acknowledging change in the latter ("stylistic development"), we necessarily implicate the former. Conventionally, we do talk about an artist maturing; we distinguish early, middle, and late styles, reserving special reverence for the *Altersstil* that presumably represents the full wisdom of age, wisdom gained through living – and, we tend to assume, suffering.[33] And yet, even in the case of Rembrandt, whose biography appears to be relatively well documented, we can know little of that life. The life we encounter in the art we know only through the art. Otto Benesch writes with lapidary eloquence of "the diagram of the mind that drawing means" and of Rembrandt's drawings expressing "the power of his inner vision."[34] But how do we get to that "mind" or that "vision" if not through the markings of the hand? Granting, then, that the draftsman "takes his body with him" (to reinvoke Valéry), to what extent can we explore a physiology of style?

Despite the modern revisions of the corpus of drawings, the basic course of Rembrandt's evolution as a draftsman over a period of four decades is generally well established – so that even the de-attributed drawings are considered datable with reference to the master's own stylistic development.[35] Thematically and formally, we can track that development from the dynamic and fluid activity of his earlier designs to the more solemn and stable monumentality of the later creations – from "Baroque" to "classical," we might once have said, applying a favorite polarity of historical style criticism, although "archaic" is a more appropriate term for that "breadth and squareness of execution" that characterizes Rembrandt's late style.[36] Still, such basic Wölfflinian terminology does seem relevant as we describe Rembrandt's gradual shift from the active diagonal thrust (Fig. 211) to a more tectonic conception of space (Fig. 228), one that respects the structuring dictates of the picture plane and the rectangular coordinates of the bounded field. Earlier, the circling pen, like the foreshortened figures it defines, seemed intent upon penetrating the barrier of the plane to a space beyond (Fig. 229); later, contours set into an angular geometry nearly devoid of curves, while rigid hatching patterns reinforce the tectonic faceting of form (Fig. 230).[37]

Rembrandt brings the rhetoric of his figures under increasingly stringent control. In a typical drawing of the 1630s, for example, they move with theatrical exuberance, their gestures large and open; later, especially in the course of the 1650s, his figures restrict their outward display to a more modest and restrained impulse. A child being taught to walk is no longer encouraged out into the world at large

228. Rembrandt, *Jacob Shown the Blood-Stained Coat of Joseph* (ca. 1656–57). Pen and brown ink, brown wash, corrections with white body-color, 16.2 × 22 cm. Fitzwilliam Museum, Cambridge (PD.40-1961 [Benesch 1020]).

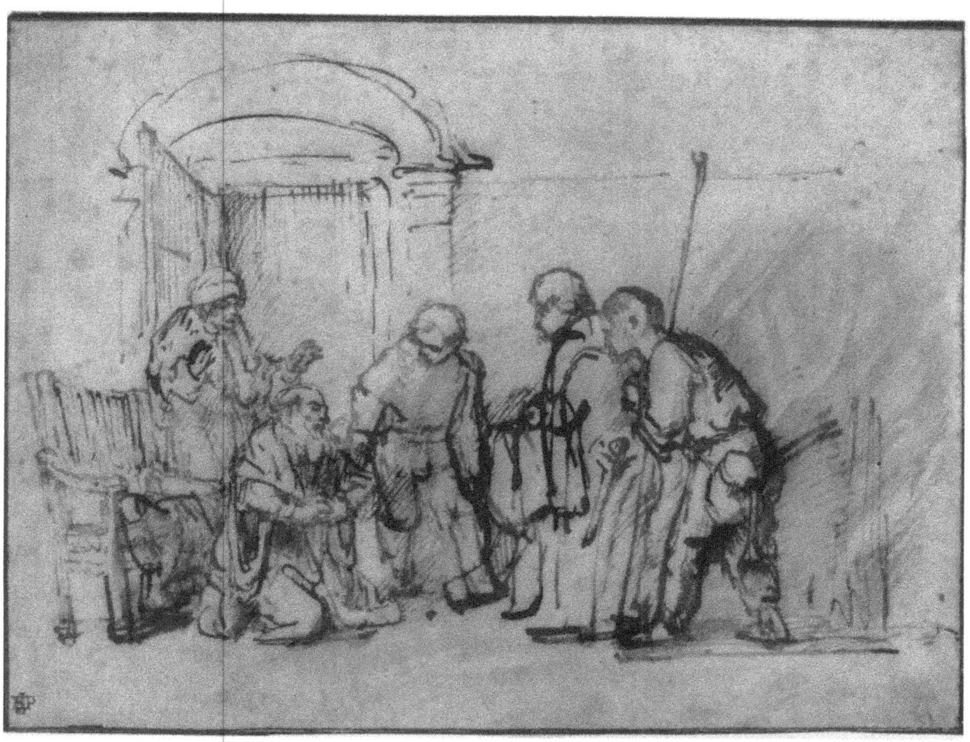

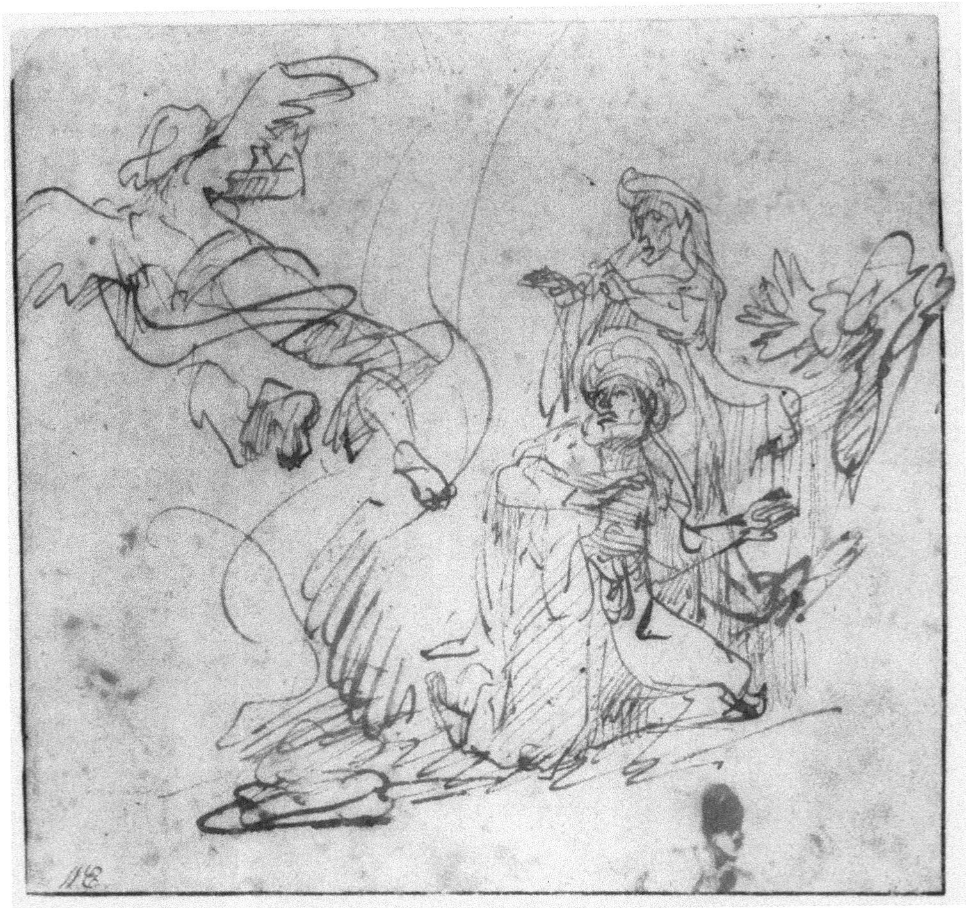

229. Rembrandt, *Manoah's Offering* (ca. 1639). Pen and brown ink, 17.4 × 19 cm. Kupferstichkabinett, Staatliche Museen zu Berlin, Preussischer Kulturbesitz, Berlin (KdZ 3774 [Benesch 180]).

(Fig. 219) but, rather, is guided into a protected circle (Fig. 231).[38] Where the earlier actors extend themselves deliberately and energetically into a space generated by their very actions, the later protagonists seem reticent, reluctant to break the limits of their own enclosing contours, to violate the boundaries that define their central cores (Fig. 232). Their subdued yet deeply affecting gestures are quite minimal; movement is no longer of the full arm but more usually of the hand alone, hardly daring to disturb the simple block of the figure's profile, to upset its stability.

Such observations, of course, apply to Rembrandt's stylistic evolution in general, in painting as well as in the graphic arts.[39] What interests us in the drawings in particular is the actual means by which these pathetic structures are established: Rembrandt's line, the pen stroke with its nuanced and differentiated qualities, the complexities and ambiguities of its mimetic operations. That line is invested with great expressive and imitative responsibility – "one can read the meaning from the very pen strokes themselves," to requote Houbraken. A record of a gesture, the line is a contingent mark; its particular qualities, as both trace and sign, are dependent not

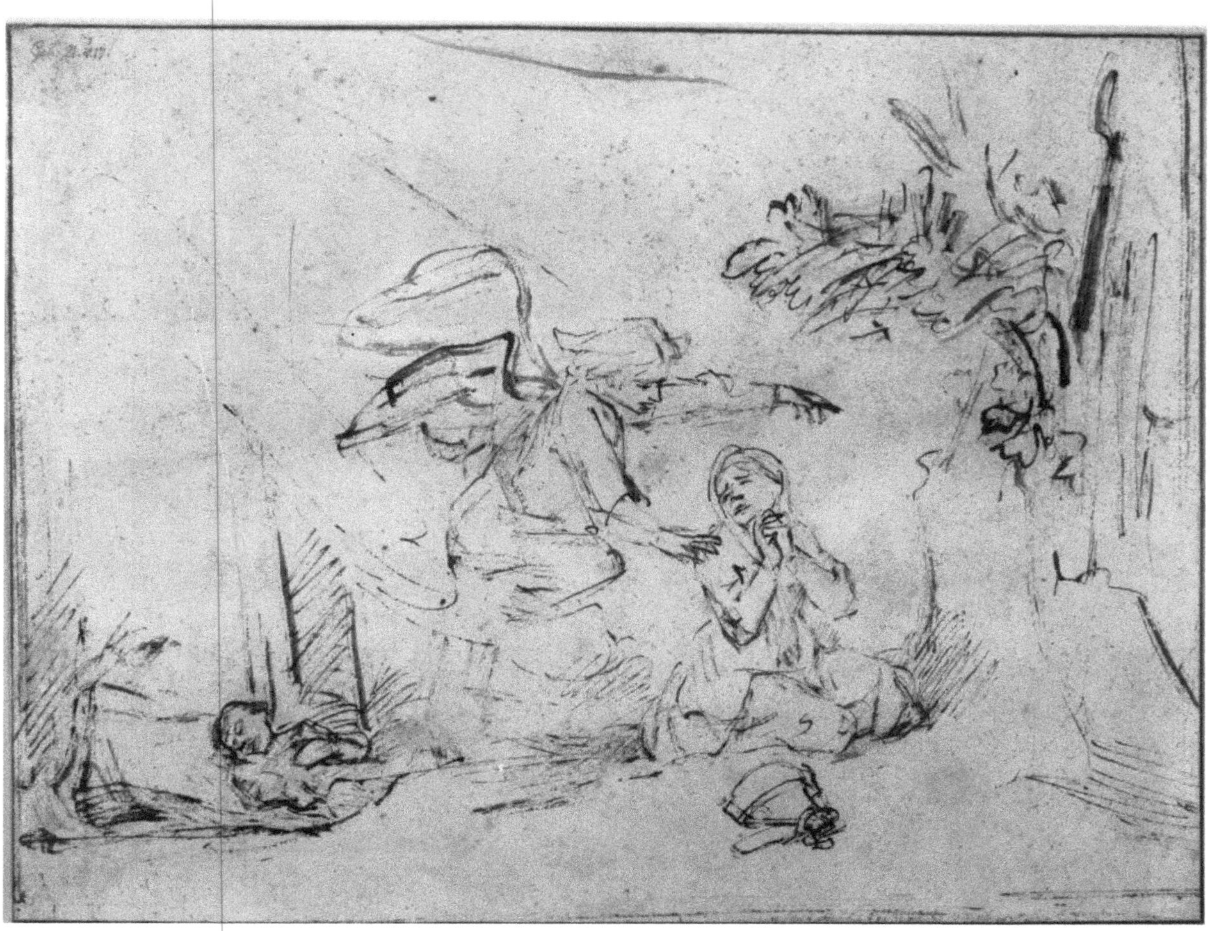

230. Rembrandt, *Hagar and Ishmael with the Angel in the Desert* (ca. 1652). Reed pen and brown ink, some corrections in white body-color, 18.2 × 25.2 cm. Kunsthalle, Hamburg (inv. 22411 [Benesch 904]). Photo: Elke Walford, Hamburg.

only on the drawing hand but also on the marking implement and the surface on which it leaves its mark.

Corresponding to the general development of Rembrandt's style is a relative shift of preference in drawing implement, from the quill to the reed pen – paralleling in a general way his shift from etching to drypoint in printmaking.[40] The "Baroque" manner of the drawings of the 1630s is fully realized by the fluid line of the quill, a long, calligraphic line that swells and tapers, often turning back upon itself, flowing in and out of space, and activating that space even as it defines it (Fig. 229). Flexible and hence responsive to nuances of pressure, the quill registers the slightest shifts in the draftsman's application, and that graphic sensitivity in turn encourages certain kinds of movement as the guided pen searches and feels its way into and around imagined form. A calligraphic instrument thriving on the linear continuity of script, the quill lends its grace to drawing.

The basic qualities of the reed pen, instead, confirm and enable the stiffer struc-

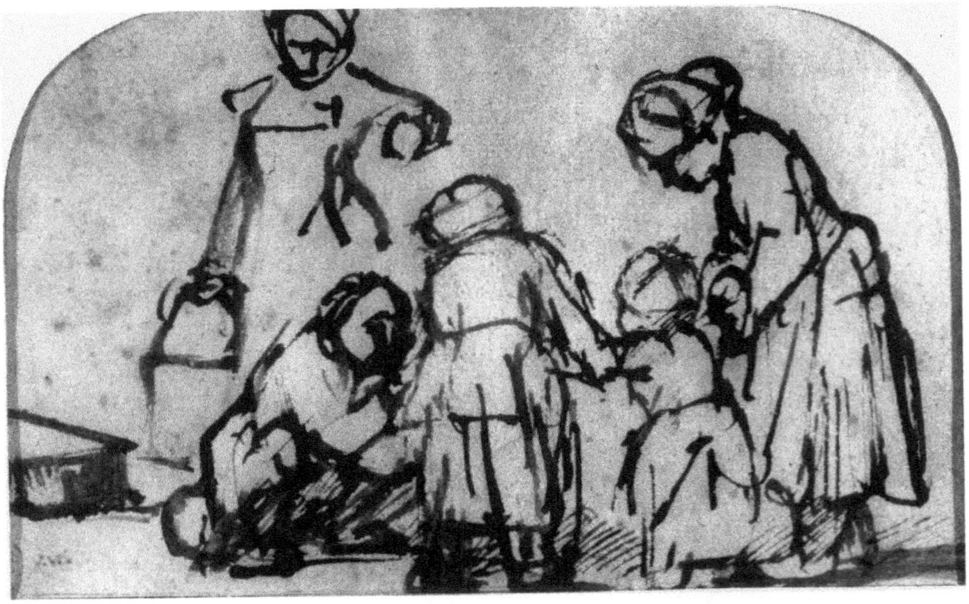

231. Rembrandt, *A Child Being Taught to Walk* (ca. 1656). Pen and brown ink on brownish-cream paper, 9.3 × 15.4 cm. British Museum, London (1912-4-16-2 [Benesch 1169]).

232. Rembrandt, *The Mocking of Christ* (ca. 1652–53). Pen and brown ink, rubbed with the finger, 15.5 × 21.8 cm. Pierpont Morgan Library, New York (I,189 [Benesch 920]).

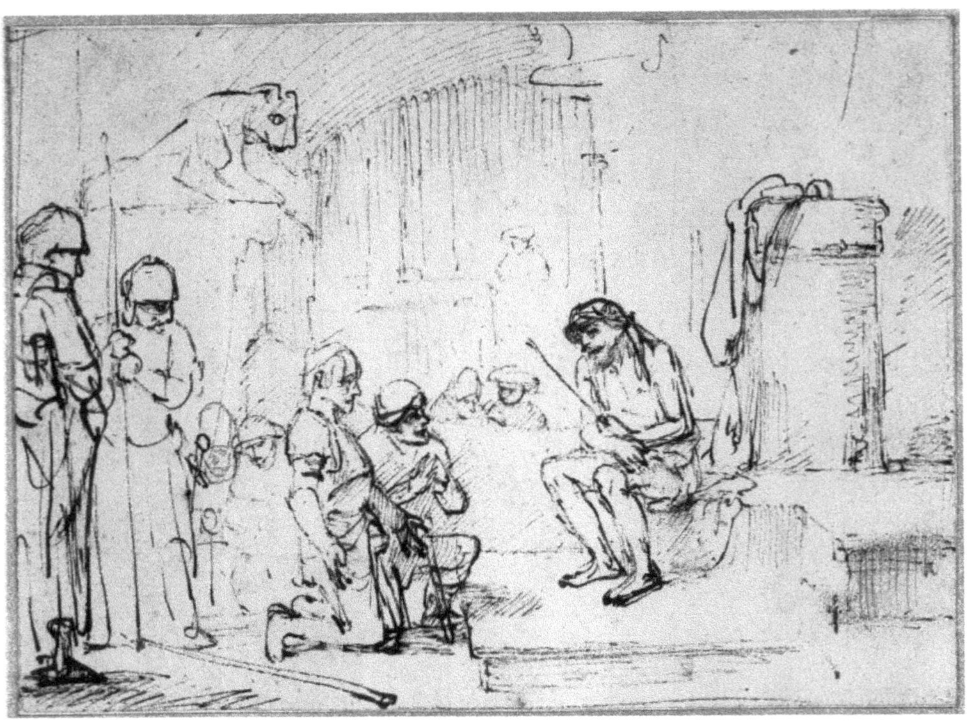

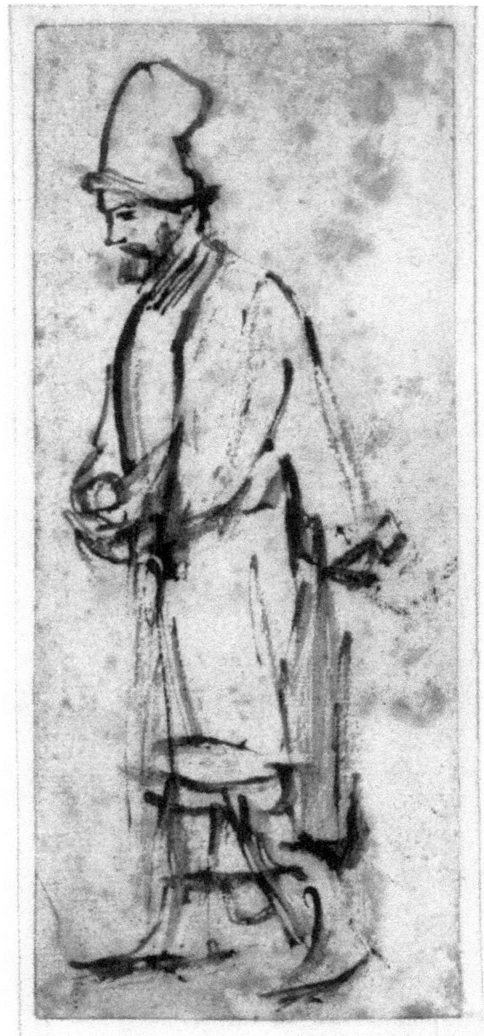

233. Rembrandt, *Man in a High Cap Walking* (ca. 1662–65). Reed pen and brown ink, 14.7 × 6.2 cm. Rijksmuseum, Amsterdam (inv. (RP-T-1930-40 [Benesch 1068B]).

tures of Rembrandt's later style. Less flexible than the quill and tending to lose its ink more quickly, the reed yields a line that is broader and blunter, bolder but sometimes grudging; tonally more luminous – especially as, in losing its ink, its dilute mark is double tracked by denser ink still clinging to the outer edges of the nib – its line is less elegantly varied in its course (Fig. 233).[41] Less a fluid writing instrument than a marker in his hands, the reed offered Rembrandt a strong tool – which he sometimes used to drive home a master's comment on a pupil's drawing.[42] Its very stiffness encourages direct attack, a more vigorous and abrupt gesture; and yet, in a softer or more pictorial mode, its mark, like the stroke of a brush, can dissipate into pure wash.[43]

The energies flowing through the dramatic spectacles of Rembrandt's earlier drawings are youthful; they derive their initial impetus from the active sweep of the pen, the expansive motion of the artist's own hand. Rembrandt underscores this identifi-

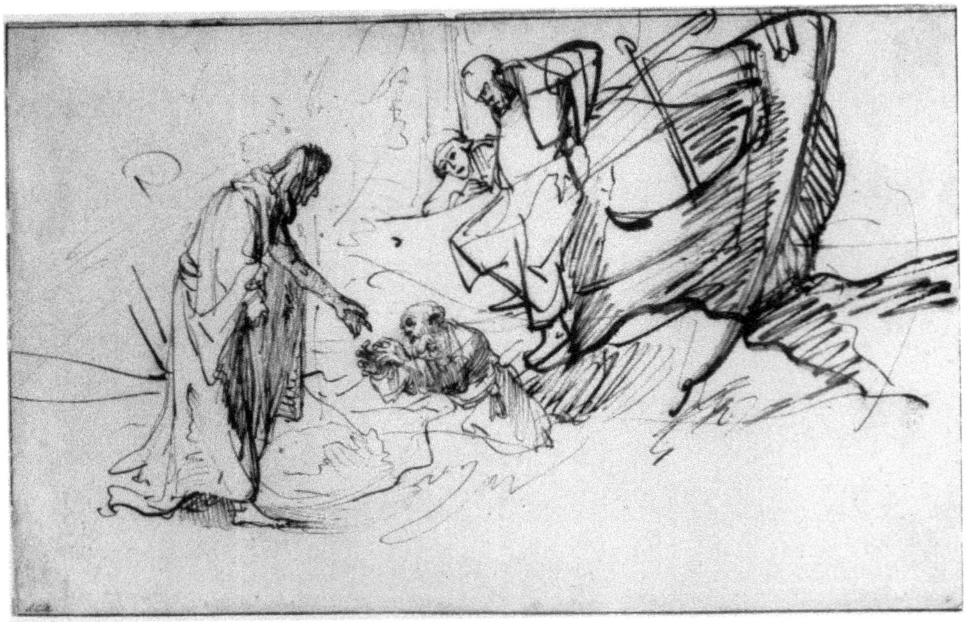

234. Rembrandt, *Christ Walking on the Waves* (ca. 1632). Pen and brown ink, 16.5 × 26.5 cm. British Museum, London (1895-9-15-1262 [Benesch 70]).

cation most explicitly when he punctuates the pathetic meaning of the larger figural posturing with detailed physiognomies, as fully mimed as the gestures (Fig. 211). In the graver drama of the later drawings, such masks play little part; instead, the most precise inflections of emotion are conveyed almost exclusively by the body, by the slight tilt of the head or shifting of weight – achieved by a single modifying stroke of the pen (Fig. 228).

More constant than the face as an expressive vehicle in Rembrandt's graphic art are hands. Like the full figures, hands too develop from a certain flexible rhetorical articulation (Fig. 234) to become simpler extensions of blocklike bodies (Fig. 235).[44] Within the apparent stiffness of their minimally indicated anatomy and apparently limited repertory of gestures, the hands of these later figures, often mittens without articulated fingers, compress a remarkable depth and range of expression. Within the self-containing restrictions of formal definition and movement of the style, they acquire a heightened significance; no longer public signs, the rhetoric of Baroque theater, their gestures are rather more personal and private, their reach more tentative and searching. Slow-moving and even ceremonious in their solemn deliberateness, these are, in effect, the gestures of age, of the body conserving its energies and thereby achieving the highest degree of expressive efficiency. And we assume that the reach of these figures, their bodily extension into the world around them, corresponds to – indeed, depends directly on – the movements of the draftsman's hand, the economy of his gesture.

Such observations are not intended to suggest a simple biological determinism. Style – that is, a characterizing consistency of operation – is a more complex phe-

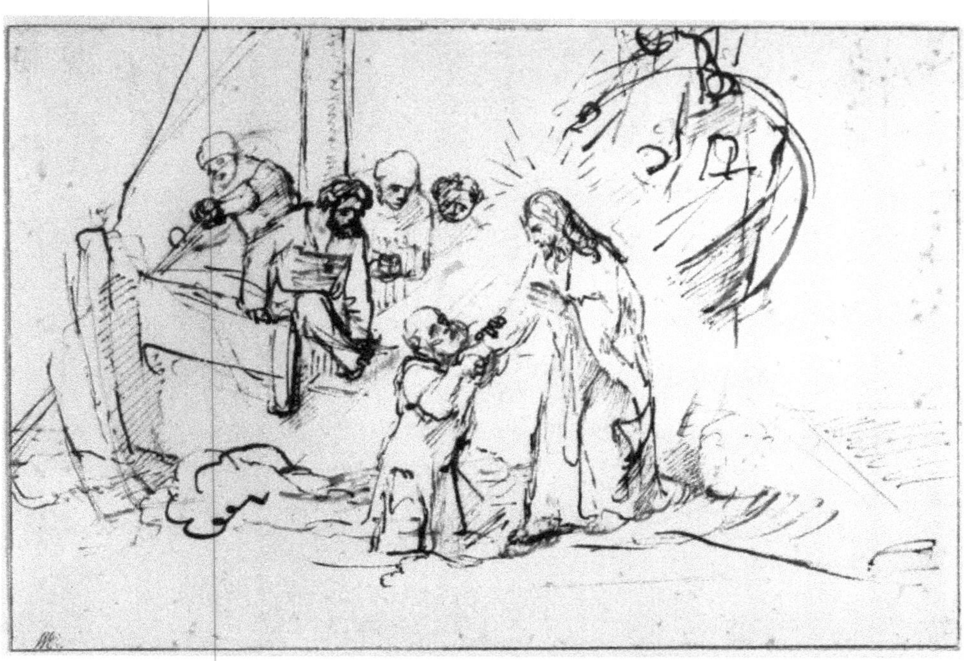

235. Rembrandt, *Christ Walking on the Waves* (ca. 1652–56). Reed pen and brown ink, touched with white, 19.1 × 29.1 cm. British Museum, London (1910-2-12-180 [Benesch 1043]).

nomenon. Whatever the natural inclinations of an artist's body, they are tempered by and only find expression through the techniques of art; the draftsman's motions are possible only because he has learned the technical procedures of the craft, usually from another master. What he acquires from his studies he may build upon, transcending the lessons learned to discover and affirm his own artistic self. Or, he may remain essentially dependent upon the model of the master – as the drawings of Rembrandt's disciples tend to reflect his graphic style during the period of their apprenticeship in the Rembrandt studio. Drawing may be a more spontaneous act than painting, but it too is a highly conscious one, with its own formulas and conventions; it too follows the rules of art. Rembrandt's gestures, then, those of the draftsman as well as those of his creatures, follow the rules.

Rembrandt was hardly unaware of the "breadth and squareness" of his own late manner; the tectonic deliberateness of both compositional structure and figural construction testifies to a high degree of aesthetic self-awareness – nowhere more so, perhaps, than in the imperial self-presentation in the Frick Collection (Br. 50). In the *Self-Portrait* at Kenwood House (Br. 52) the painter affirms his mastery of the rules of art with full pictorial eloquence: the two half-circles inscribed on the surface behind him introduce geometric precision within a most painterly setting, evoking the values of measure and control that since antiquity had been taken as signs of the pictorial intellect. Such perfectly inscribed forms on a painter's canvas could hardly avoid association with the celebrated "O" of Giotto, the great Renaissance topos of artistic skill.[45] And, in drawing, Rembrandt even more openly alludes to those clas-

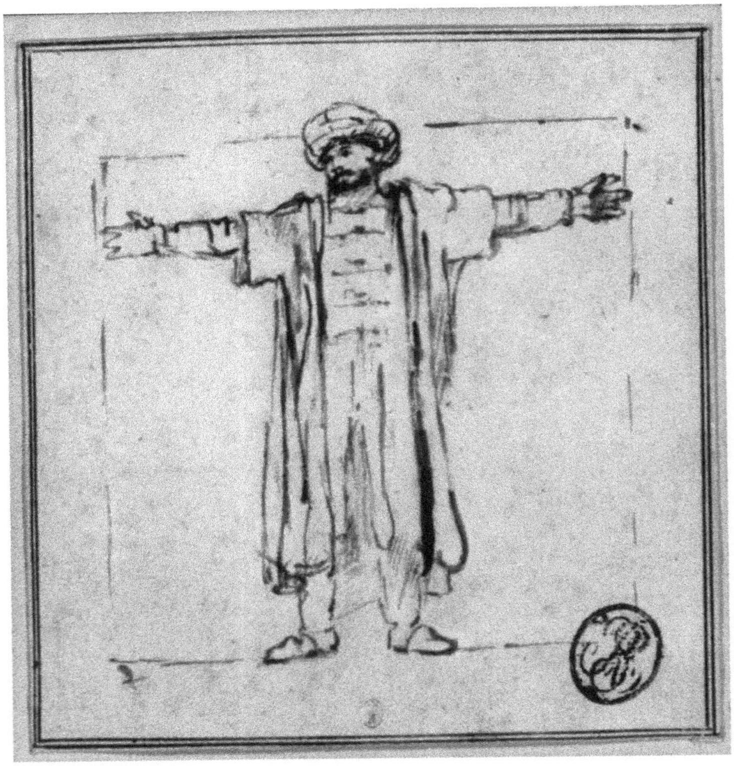

236. Rembrandt (copy?), *Man in Oriental Costume with Arms Outstretched* (ca. 1650–55). Pen and brown ink over black chalk, 13 × 12.5 cm. Musée du Louvre, Paris. Département des Arts Graphiques (inv. 22.914).

sical traditions in a declarative design of a turbaned man standing, arms outstretched, inscribed within a square (Fig. 236). Rembrandt seems to be testing his own sense of the body – significantly not nude and typically exoticized through costume – against a ground of classical theory, specifically, the traditional image of human proportions based on Vitruvius (cf. Fig. 119).[46] But, although translating the Latin canon into his northern vernacular, the Dutch master is no Dürer: the full measure of the human body for him is not quantifiable but remains affective, less intellectually analyzed than intuitively felt. The breadth and squareness embodied in Rembrandt's Vitruvian Oriental are internalized in the grand self-portrait of the artist in his painter's smock (Fig. 237), drawn during the years of financial and personal tribulation.[47] Rembrandt stands squarely in his field, arms akimbo, and claims his space, Vitruvian extension aggressively implicit in his out-thrust elbows.[48] The potential reach of the body is existentially charged, latent with affect.[49]

We recall how deeply moving Rembrandt found and made the theme of blindness, in particular that of the suffering Tobit (Figs. 225, 238) or of the reciting Homer (Fig. 239).[50] Deprived of sight, these venerable figures reach out in his art to know the world through their hands, literally groping to see. Articulating the fullest meaning of his own late gesture, Rembrandt's blind protagonists stand as symbols of his art, an art at once supremely visual and yet profoundly haptic, like

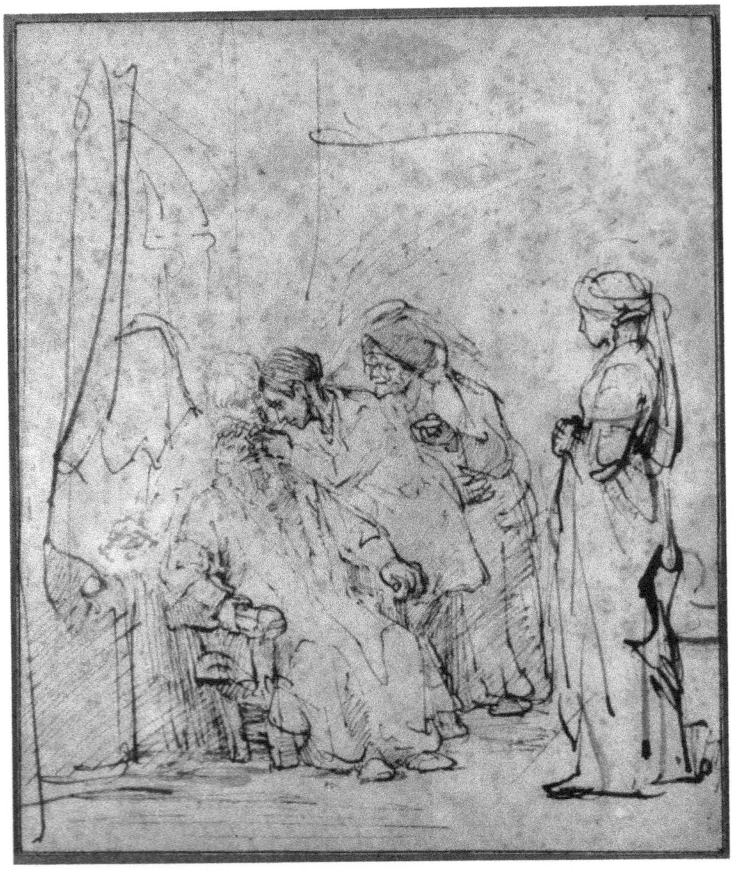

238. Rembrandt, *Tobias Healing His Father's Blindness* (ca. 1642–44). Pen and brown ink, corrected with white gouache, 21.1 × 17.7 cm. Cleveland Museum of Art, Purchase from the J. H. Wade Fund (1969.69 [Benesch 547]).

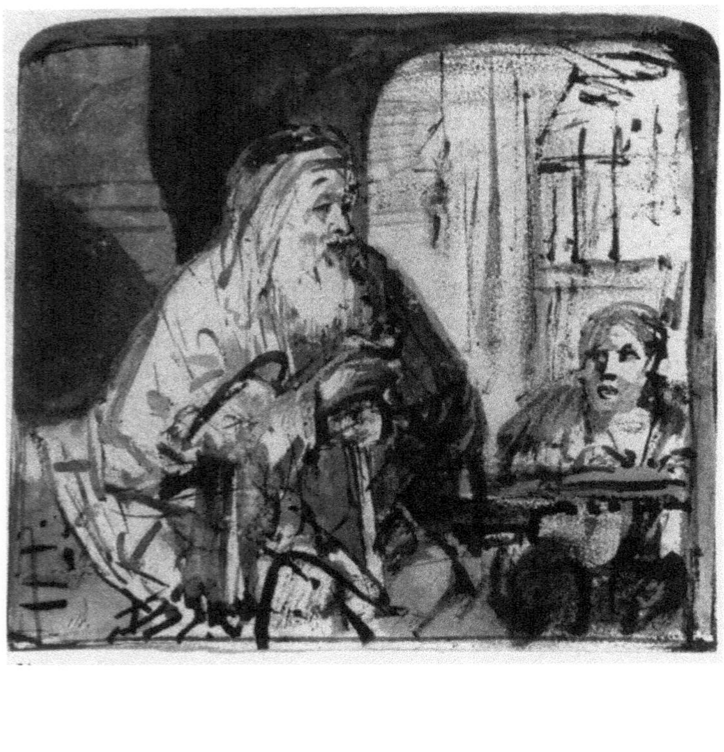

239. Rembrandt, *Homer Dictating to a Scribe* (ca. 1663). Reed pen and brown ink and India ink, brush and brown wash, heightened with white; yellow, gray washes added later, 14.9 × 16.8 cm. Nationalmuseum, Stockholm (H 1677/1863 [Benesch 1066]).

the broadly bounded yet luminous strokes of his reed pen. At the core of the dramatic pathos projected by this art is an essential physicality: figures reach out, however timidly, to communicate, to touch, to grasp, to know. Space is emotionally charged not by the grand gesture addressed to the multitude but rather by these quietly inflected, tentative efforts at personal, intimate contact. Proximity itself, expectant, latent with imminent possibility, acquires a weighted poignancy. Movement does not come easily; to realize itself, to give outward expression to inner feeling, it seems at times to have to overcome enormous inertia, psychic as well as physical.

The essentially graphic impulse that seemed to be the generating force in Rembrandt's earlier drawings, linking figures through sequential becoming, continues to animate his later groups (Figs. 240, 241). But now graphic interdependence assumes an even greater expressive urgency as the "breadth and squareness of execution" impose a tighter physical fit. We are less aware of the linear continuities of the drawn line than of a certain glyptic quality, a notional continuity maintained by planes of parallel hatching that further unite the separate bodies into a single unit, one adhering to the plane of the drawing surface.

This strong compacting of figures acquires most moving eloquence in strictly dialogic themes like the Agony in the Garden (Fig. 241) or the Return of the Prodigal Son (Fig. 242). Two figures come together as one, their union underscored by their distanced separation from other figures in the composition. The situation realized by

240. Rembrandt, *Christ Healing a Leper* (ca. 1652). Reed pen and brown ink, wash, rubbed with the finger, some white body-color, 18 × 24.7 cm. Kupferstichkabinett, Staatliche Museen zu Berlin, Preussischer Kulturbesitz, Berlin (KdZ 5247 [Benesch 900]). Photo: Jörg P. Anders.

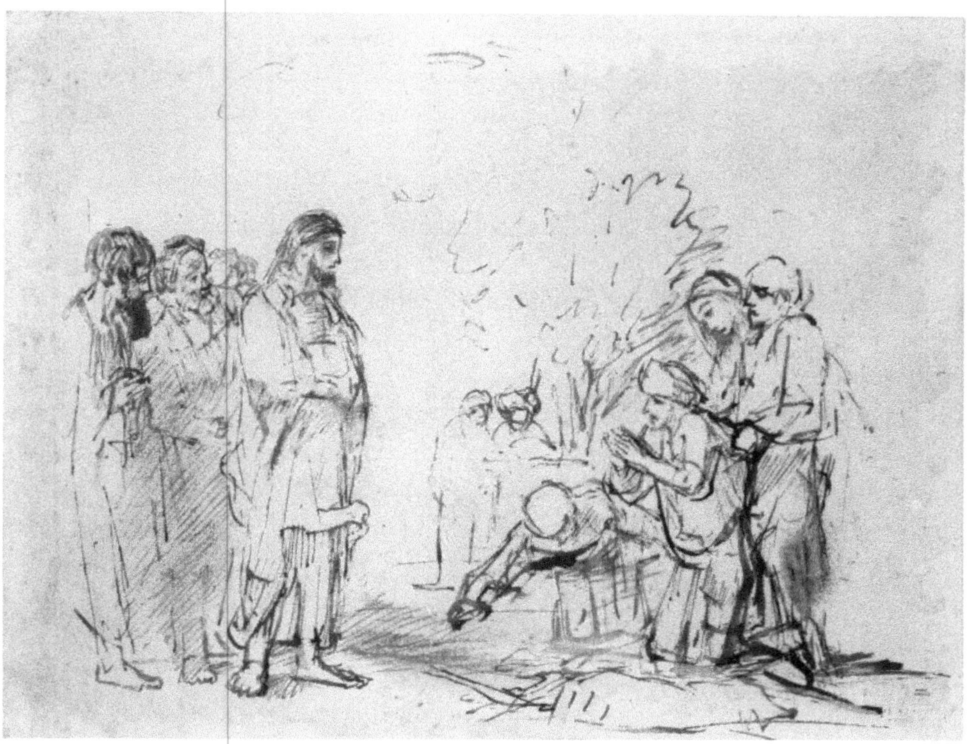

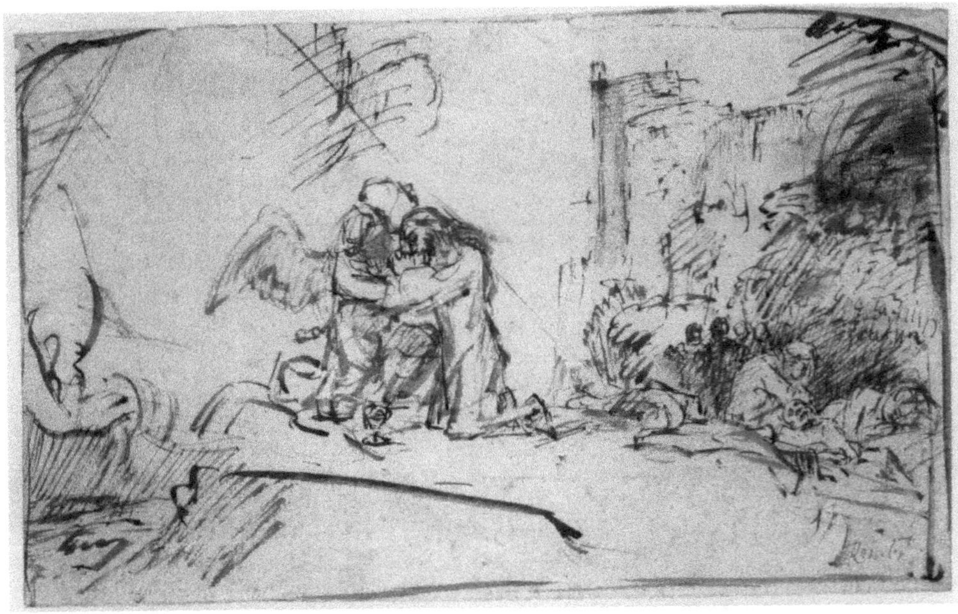

241. Rembrandt, *Christ Consoled by the Angel on the Mount of Olives* (ca. 1652). Reed pen and brown ink, rubbed with the finger, some white body-color, 18.4 × 30.1 cm. Kunsthalle, Hamburg (inv. 22413 [Benesch 899]). Photo: Elke Walford, Hamburg.

the draftsman's pen creates an intimate union of two human beings, a union effected in the course of drawing itself. Rembrandt enacts through drawing the kind of emotional bonding that he more programmatically represented in the tiny etching of *The Goldsmith* (Fig. 243). This moving image, in which touch – or better, holding – conveys feeling in the deepest sense, testifies with quiet poignancy to the artist's intimate relation to his work – significantly, a maternal Caritas group – and the man's to his family. We may even be somewhat embarrassed at our own access to these most personal imaginings, to this realization of human contact through art.[51]

Rembrandt's drawn lines once facilitated emotional flow. In the later drawings, as they lock into more rigidly structured patterns, they seem to speak of the difficulty as well as the gravity of personal expression – for the aging (though hardly aged) artist himself, as well as for his imagined dramatis personae. In the paradoxic reticence of the bold reed lines we intuit the psychological complexity of their maker, modest yet self-assertive, emotionally tentative and longing yet technically absolutely confident. In the roughness of his late manner, a roughness bordering at times on crudeness, and in the sincere awkwardness of some of his figures, in their lurching motion created through the blunt gestures of the reed, we may feel a clumsiness of the artist himself. Rembrandt's reach, the effort to make contact, is emotional as well as physical. The traces of that effort are his drawings.

The late graphic style of Rembrandt – or of Rubens or Poussin, about whose actual states of health we are better informed – necessarily reflects the draftsman's aging body; the drawings themselves seem to bear witness to the slower, more

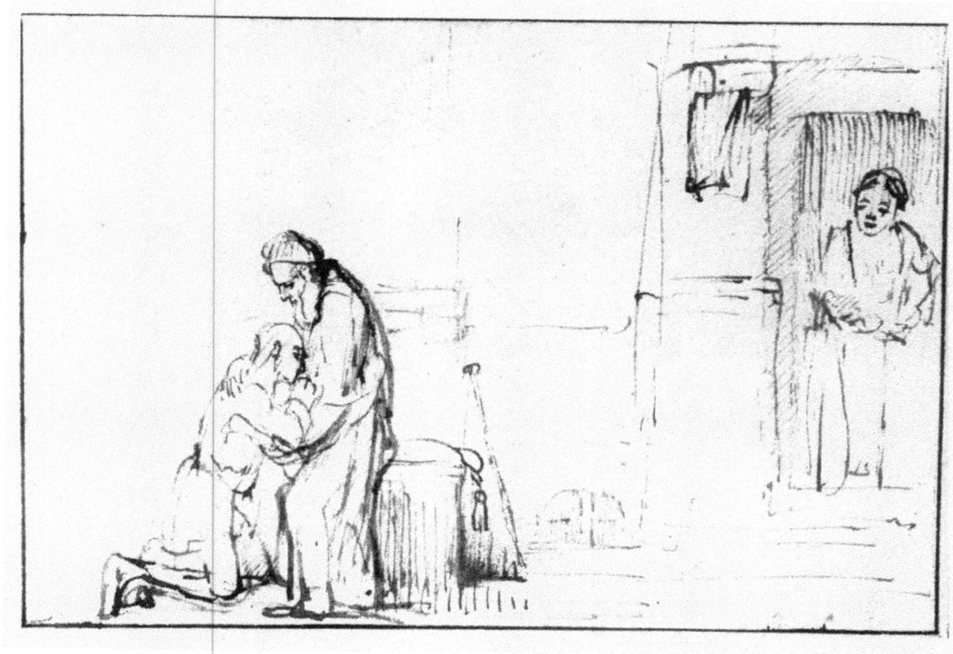

242. Rembrandt, *The Return of the Prodigal Son* (ca. 1658–59). Reed pen and brown ink, 13.3 × 19.9 cm. Graphische Sammlung Albertina, Vienna (inv. 8.805 [Benesch 1037]).

243. Rembrandt, *The Goldsmith* (1655). Etching with drypoint, 7.7 × 5.7 cm. (B. 123). Museum Het Rembrandthuis, Amsterdam.

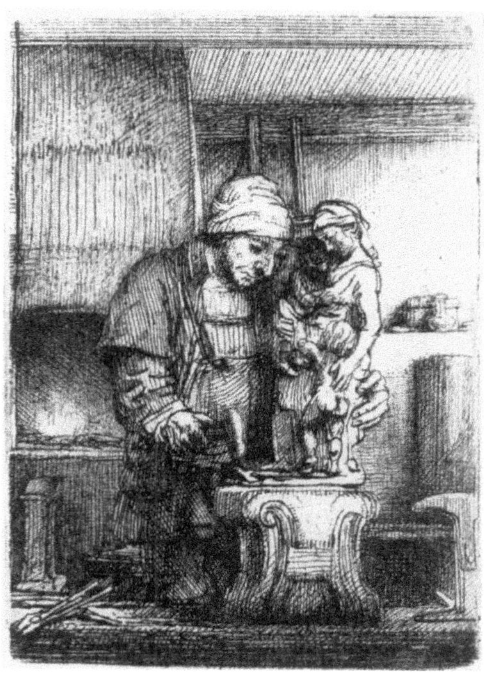

deliberate motions of that body.[52] Beyond the phenomenology of drawing, we may indeed want to explore a physiology of style.

3. The Body in the Landscape

In a number of drawings datable to the mid-1650s Rembrandt imagined a single figure in particularly poignant relationship to the surrounding landscape. His protagonists are prophets deliberately separated from the city: Elijah by the brook Cherith (I Kings 17:1–6) and Jonah before the walls of Nineveh (Jonah 4:5) (Figs. 244, 245).[53] Elijah sits upon a mound cut off from the landscape toward which he turns, hands clasped in prayer within the core of his body, a water vessel by his side. His stiff, upright posture and the profile turn of his head match the schematic structures of the drawing as a whole; indeed, the dry openness of the design, like the barren tree to the right, seems suggestive of the conclusion of the prophet's exile: "And it came to pass after a while, that the brook dried up, because there had been no rain in the land" (17:7).

244. Rembrandt, *The Prophet Elijah by the Brook Cherith* (ca. 1654–55). Pen and brown ink, wash, some white body-color, 20.5 × 23.3 cm. Kupferstichkabinett, Staatliche Museen zu Berlin, Preussischer Kulturbesitz, Berlin (KdZ 1111 [Benesch 944]).

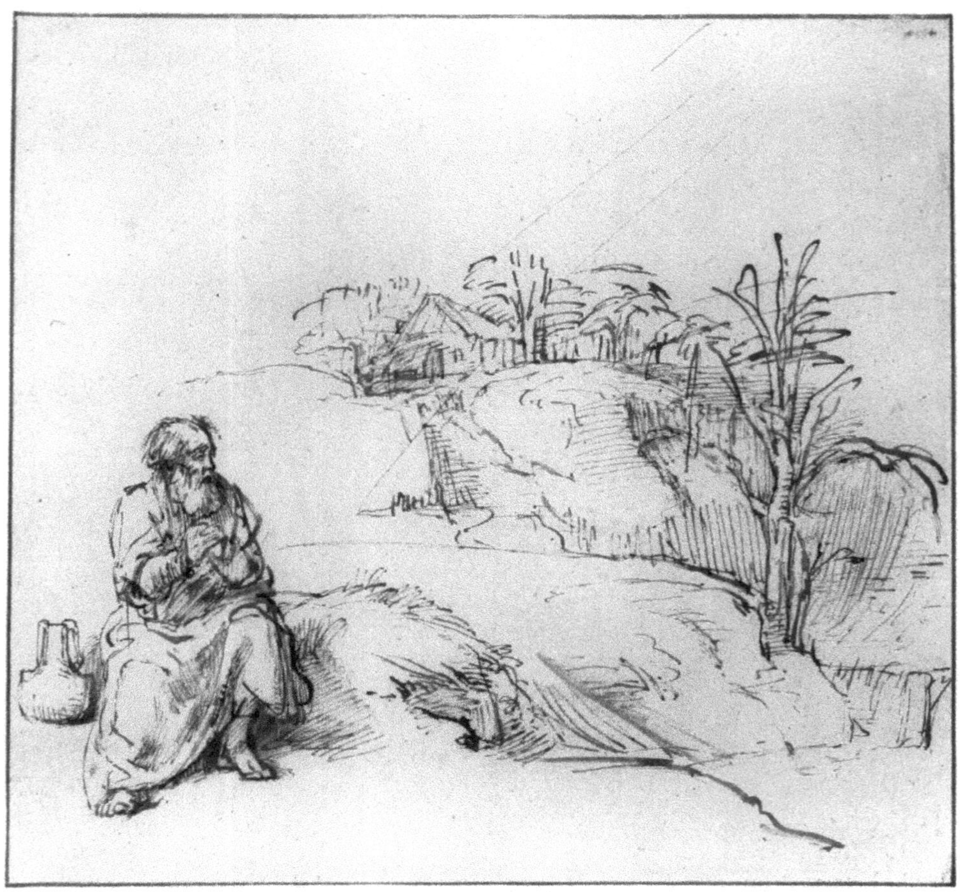

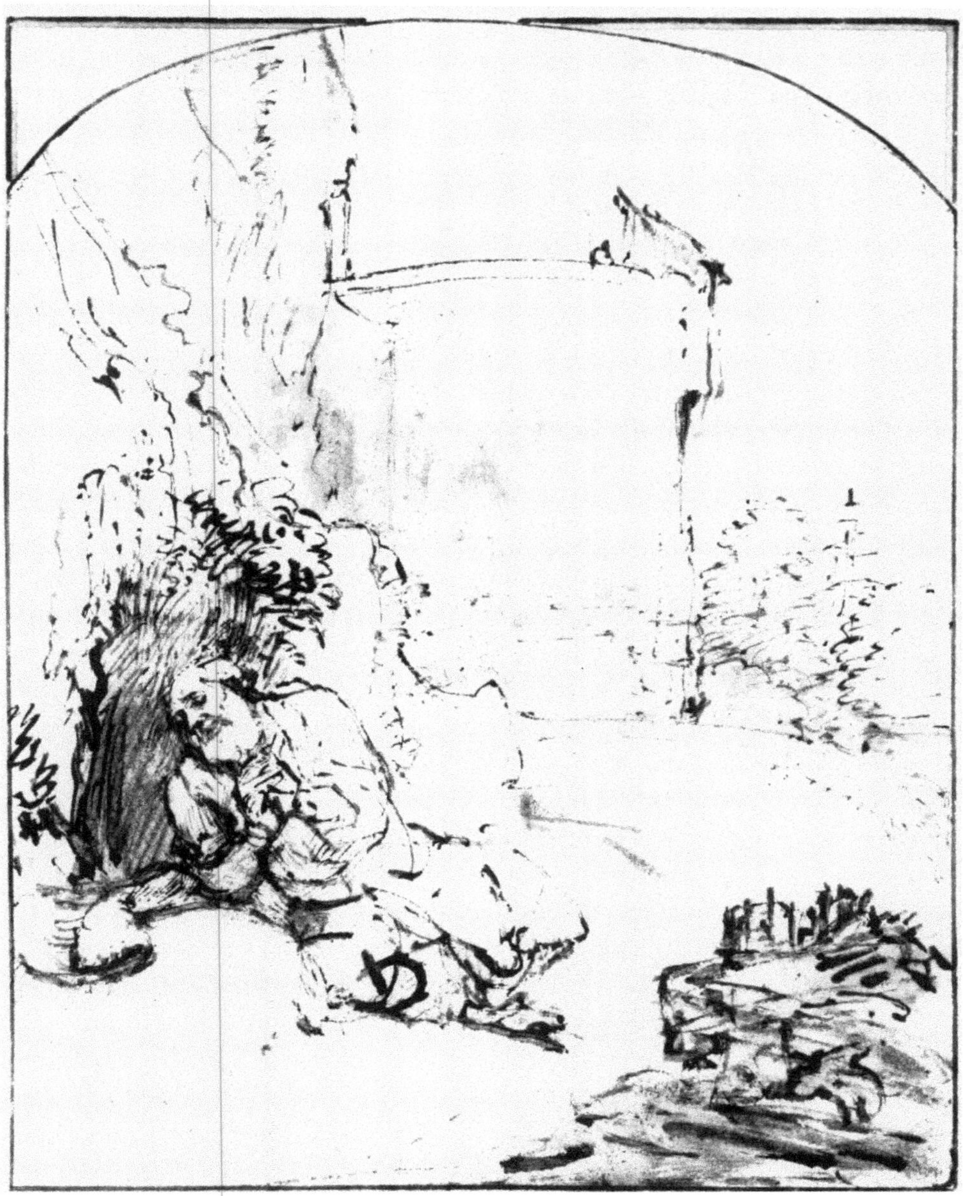

245. Rembrandt, *The Prophet Jonah before the Walls of Nineveh* (ca. 1654–55). Reed pen and brown ink, wash, 21.7 × 17.3 cm. Graphische Sammlung Albertina, Vienna (inv. 8.808 [Benesch 950]).

Even more responsive to its theme is Rembrandt's drawing of Jonah, a more dynamic figure in more intimate contact with his setting (Fig. 245): "So Jonah went out of the city, and sat on the east side of the city, and there made him a booth, and sat under it in the shadow, till he might see what would become of the city." It is precisely the pastoral motif of the shadowed booth that is the core of the design, as Jonah's body leans in desperate grief toward its protective enclosure, that has inspired Rembrandt's pen.[54] And yet, it is finally the pen that asserts its expressive priority over the word: at the base of the figure a few pen strokes, a short diagonal intersecting a curve, strongly accent that tilt, an abstract graphic epitome of the gravitational pull of Jonah's posture, a bold declaration of the draftsman's gesture.

Visual connection, the longing look of Elijah, bridges the horizontal distance separating the prophet from the brook. Physical proximity unites Jonah with his booth, the shadow itself embracing the prophet in haptic enclosure. These drawings manifest the range of rapport imaginable to Rembrandt's pen, the possibilities of its reach.

The projection of the draftsman in drawing, his identification with fictions beyond the surface of the paper, is not confined to the representation of the human figure. In the sense that the drawing gesture is both mark and mime, that representation involves enactment, we discover the presence of the artist in every drawing that he makes. As much as he is in his figure drawings, Rembrandt is in his landscapes. Indeed, he may be there even more immediately, for landscape carries with it no mask, no scripted scenario, no dramatis personae to be played out and through. More directly open and inviting, landscape offers itself as its own immediate stage, and in its creation Rembrandt the draftsman plays no role other than his own self, a wanderer in the world before him. That world, on and beyond the paper, is imagined as actively as the personal encounters of his narrative sketches; cottages and trees are felt as intensely as his dramatic figures, and space itself assumes a distinctive value as object in the landscape drawings.

In the more schematic of Rembrandt's graphic representations of the land, such as the *Winter Landscape* in the Fogg Art Museum (Fig. 246), we are made particularly aware of drawing as spatial reach. Each mark of the pen – according to its qualities of weight, velocity, and direction – assumes a spatializing function: the diagonal, heir to a long tradition of perspectival convention, recedes; the horizontal, confirming the rectangular values of the paper field, affirms that surface as it parallels its border at a notional distance; the verticals stand as figural constructs, punctuating moments in space, objects in the field of vision. Such dry description, however, is hardly adequate to the full affect of Rembrandt's lines. Recording the energies of their production, they carry a weight of feeling that, in turn, determines our perception of the space represented.

Typically, Rembrandt builds upon a base design, almost a diagram of a landscape, marked out by the pen in swift but stiff strokes. In both the format of the field and the essential composition, the horizon establishes the dominant coordinate, toward which fence and bare shrubs aspire and from which trees and buildings rise. This frozen skeleton of a landscape established, Rembrandt returned to his design with a broader nib and a heavier, more vigorous hand. With a few bold strokes he reinforced the receding fence, grounding it in a graphic figure as distinctive as a Chinese character and giving its recession a force now great enough to break triumphantly through the barrier of the paper surface, even as its marking strength reaffirms the integrity of that surface. To the right he constructed a barrier that further proclaims surface, a coulisse, set toward a middle ground, that serves to gauge spatial recession. And yet, for all its rectilinear pretense of stability, that

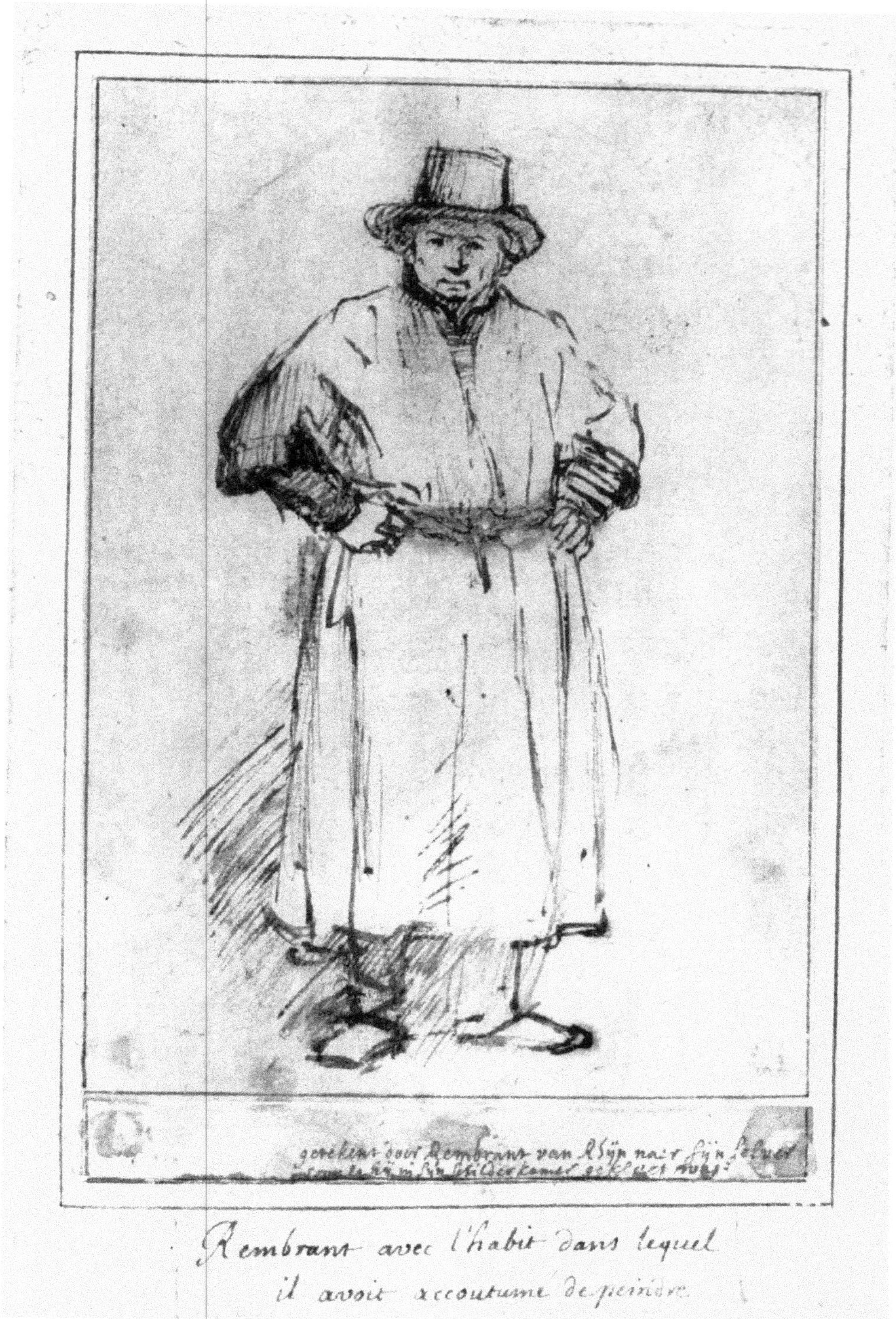

237. Rembrandt, *Self-Portrait* (ca. 1655–60). Reed pen and brown ink, on brownish paper, 20.3 × 13.4 cm. Museum Het Rembrandthuis, Amsterdam (Benesch 1171).

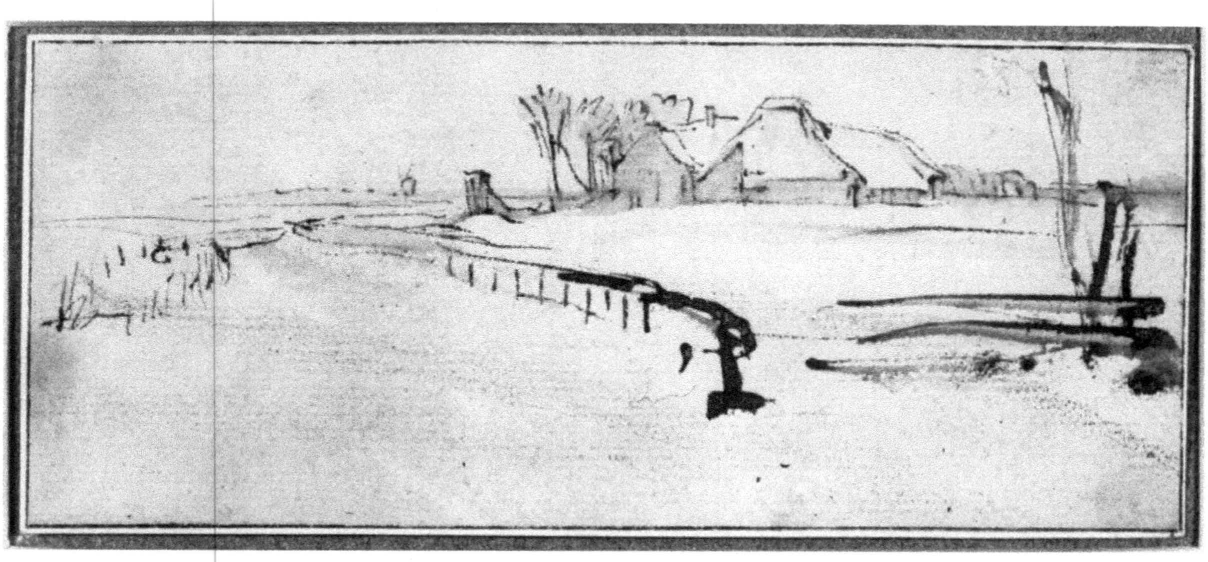

246. Rembrandt, *Landscape with a Farmstead ("Winter Landscape")* (ca. 1648–50). Reed pen and brown ink, wash, on cream paper, 6.6 × 15.8 cm. Fogg Art Museum, Harvard University Art Museums, Cambridge, Mass. (acc. no. 1932.368 [Benesch 845]).

structure is itself built of the most volatile and permeable marks of the drawing: rushing strokes of the reed, which is forced to spread its ink with pictorial irregularity, create an initial energy that is, in effect, gathered into the density of the central character, which then redirects it back into space – toward the crystalline structures along the horizon. And still, the dominant force in this drawing remains the paper itself, so much of which is untouched, a flat expanse transformed by marking, transcending its own flatness through the marks that it hosts, becoming an other world. Into that world we, like the draftsman before us, project our selves.

We relive an experience through drawing. In reconstructing the process of drawing, we retrace the gestures of the draftsman; in describing those gestures, we ascribe to them affective content, animation. The space we entered is that imagined by the draftsman. Our experience, however, is less of the Amstel area between Kostverloren and Ouderkerk, which has been suggested as the site represented in Rembrandt's *Winter Landscape*, than of the drawing itself.[55] The sense that a landscape drawing was indeed "artfully drawn from life" was understandably an important part of response; it was as important to assume the "truth" of the fiction on the other side of the picture plane in this genre as in history painting.[56] Nonetheless, the topography we respond to is not that which may (or may not) have been before the draftsman's eyes but rather that projected by his pen. If we insist on seeing beyond the drawing to the presumed site, considering the image merely as representational record, we deprive ourselves of the fuller experience of the drawing itself – of drawing itself – and lose a major dimension of its meaning.

In another landscape drawing (Fig. 247), also from about 1650, several farm buildings fuse to become the focus of the composition, the major object toward which other lines lead. The position of the buildings, expanding from the horizon, off to the right, establishes a dynamic asymmetry, activating the rest of the field. Established

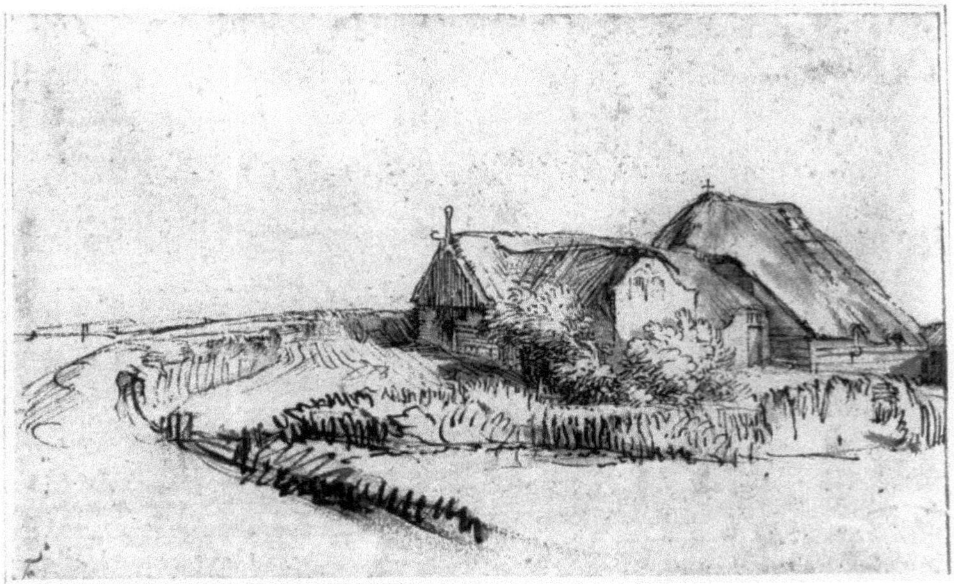

247. Rembrandt, *Farmstead* (ca. 1650). Pen and brown ink and wash, with touches of white, on paper toned with light brown wash, 10.5 × 17.8 cm. Collection A. Alfred Taubman, New York (Benesch 1228).

just below the center of the sheet, the horizon itself actually curves slightly, as though following the suggestion of the bend in the road; it thereby not only fixes the location of the buildings within the field but seems as well to contain them spatially, to embrace them. The road leading into space was first established by a series of diagonal strokes, spread to a dry texture at the base. These lines, in turn, were modified by a stronger scrawl zigzagging across their axis. We can read this reinforcement as just that, a strengthening of the border of the road by graphic means, establishing the foreground base from which spatial recession begins. That, surely, is its function within the representational economy of the design. Such a reading of visual experience, however, limits the referential charge of these marks to pictorial illusion, a rather simple mimetic algebra. It ignores the dynamic conflict inherent in this situation: over a series of flowing lines has been imposed a jagged scribble, as if to brake their progress, if not to cancel them. This kinesthetic complexity results, of course, directly from the draftsman's gestures. An initial rush into space has been checked, its linear continuity interrupted by a sequence of short, upright units – which themselves participate in another, more broken continuity of similar marks.[57] Acknowledging the dynamics of the drawing gesture, we participate more directly in the draftsman's imagining act; the landscape becomes less an abstractly constructed illusion of space than an arena defined by the very movements it contains, a space projected by the imagining subject, with whom we identify, an imagining body.

Rembrandt the draftsman projected himself into the landscape. The early landscape drawings are realized with the same energy that informs his figure sketches of the 1630s (Fig. 248). The quill sweeps across the long sheet, swiftly surveying terrain as it marks the way back to the tree-lined horizon where its energies are absorbed into the density of the wash; the wash, we sense, was applied as a confirmation of visual and physical arrival. The pen line, moving with vectorial purpose from the left, meandering with more concentrated purpose on the right – closer and weighting the focus on the low houses – articulates a broad stretch of ground, tracing the course of the draftsman's own path through that imagined space.

The horizontal format, conforming to an established convention in landscape representation, especially Dutch, offers the artist a field analogous to the realm of his own existence: horizon before him and stretching in either direction. Within that field, Rembrandt tends, unremarkably, to situate the horizon in the lower half. What is notable in his drawings, however, is a reluctance to touch the sky – as though the heavens were beyond physical grasp: the paper itself is appreciated and exploited for all its spatial potential. Indeed, as we have been seeing, he also leaves the base area of the design relatively untouched, certainly in the first imaginings. Setting the object of his representation along the horizon within the field, he may return to define means of visual access, a strong statement by the reed offering a foreground step (Fig. 249). Such a final gesture – equivalent to the repoussoir curtain in his narrative sketches – represents at once the draftsman's own final distancing from the object of his imagination and, by its very substantiality, a final claim upon the drawing as an extension of himself. The mark works both ways.

Spatial extension, a dominant experience in the panoramic views, involves the optical transformation of the flat opacity of paper into pictorial atmosphere. This is one phenomenological dimension of Rembrandt's graphic landscapes. There is another, more haptic, and hence more proximate; we know it best in his drawings and etchings of cottages and farm buildings (Figs. 250, 251). These thatched-roof structures, central to Rembrandt's landscape imagination from the beginning, offered themselves as ideally picturesque models for graphic exploitation; their roughly tex-

248. Rembrandt, *Landscape with Row of Trees and Farmhouses* (ca. 1633–36). Pen and brown ink and wash, 13.2 × 24.3 cm. Akademie der Bildenden Künste, Vienna (inv. 3.220 [Benesch 472]).

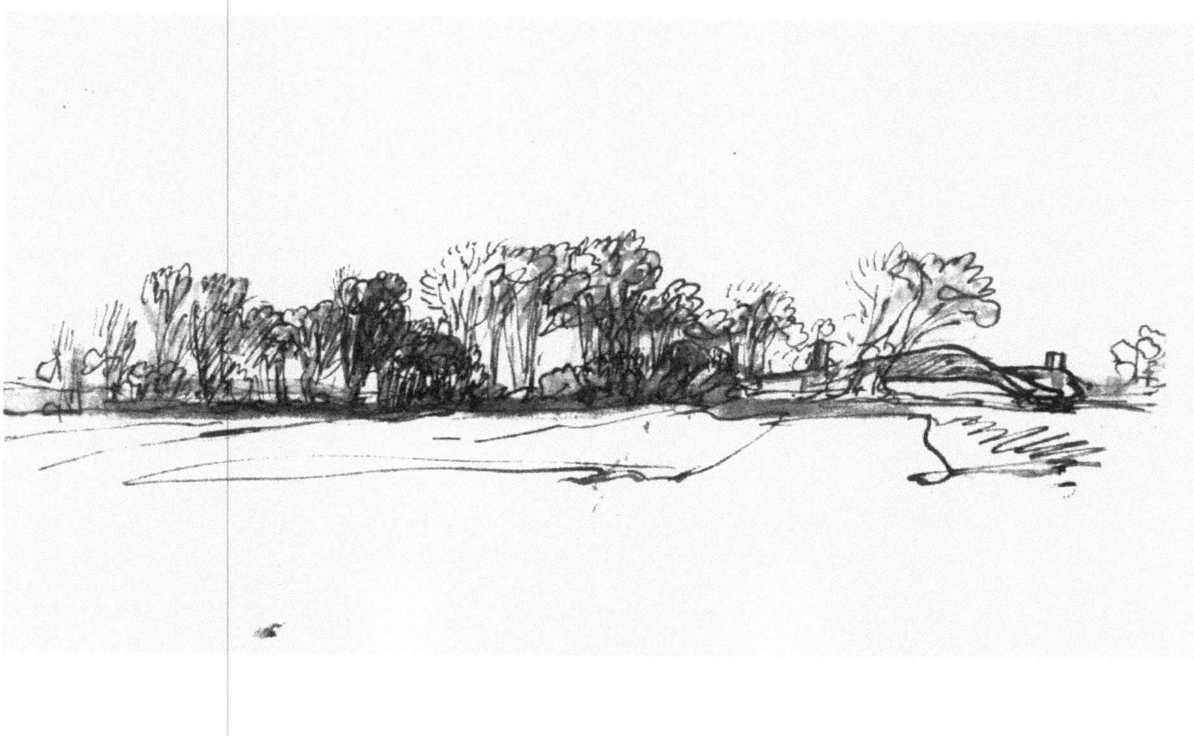

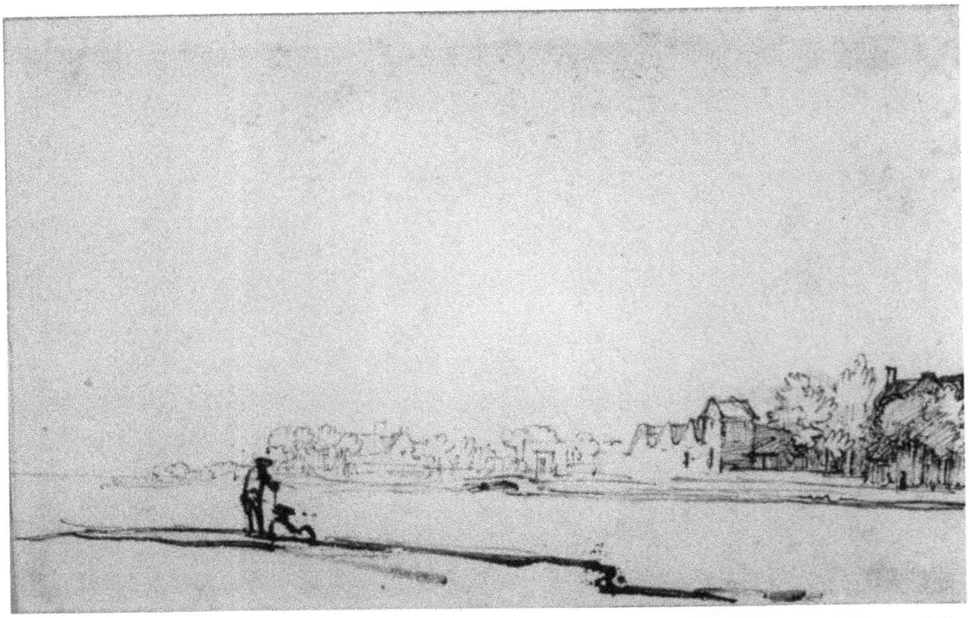

249. Rembrandt, *View across the Amstel* (ca. 1640–45). Pen and brown ink, 10.9 × 17.7 cm. Library of the Ossolinski National Institute of the Polish Academy of Science, Wroclaw (no. 8730 [Benesch 798]).

tured surfaces demanded and inspired free but controlled patterns of scribbling and hatching. Those very patterns – "curly crabby lines," as David Freedberg has characterized them, transposing a poetic line of Constantijn Huygens[58] – concentrating graphic energies, attest to the hand's close and sustained contact with the paper, to time invested in the execution/exploration of those imagined textures. The draftsman's reach is quite different here, more immediately tactile, more directly in touch with its imagined object. This much we know from the tracings of his pen or scratchings of his etching needle.

The thatched roof and ramshackle appearance of the cottage offered the occasion for a certain manner of penmanship; so too did the foliage of the surrounding trees (Fig. 252). Such motifs inspired that built-up scribble, the concentration of small hooks and loops representing shadowed texture; indeed, the deeper the shadow, especially in the landscape etchings, the more the imagination is invited to project its tactile sensors (Fig. 253). As these motifs developed over several decades, they adapted to Rembrandt's own changing style; stiffening with the predominance of the reed pen and drypoint technique, rendered with broader and simpler gestures, once organically distinct forms merge to become larger structural aggregates (Figs. 254, 255).

Carel van Mander had recommended that the artist introduce into his landscapes "strange and quaint shepherds' huts of farm hamlets in caves or hollow trees."[59] The thatched-roof cottage was indeed a commonplace in landscape representation, with a long pedigree in Netherlandish art as well as in Italian and German graphics of the Renaissance.[60] Heir to those traditions, Rembrandt, in appropriating the motif, nonetheless made it very much his own. He did so essentially by liberating it. Reducing the presence of the human figure, he allowed the cottage to emerge as

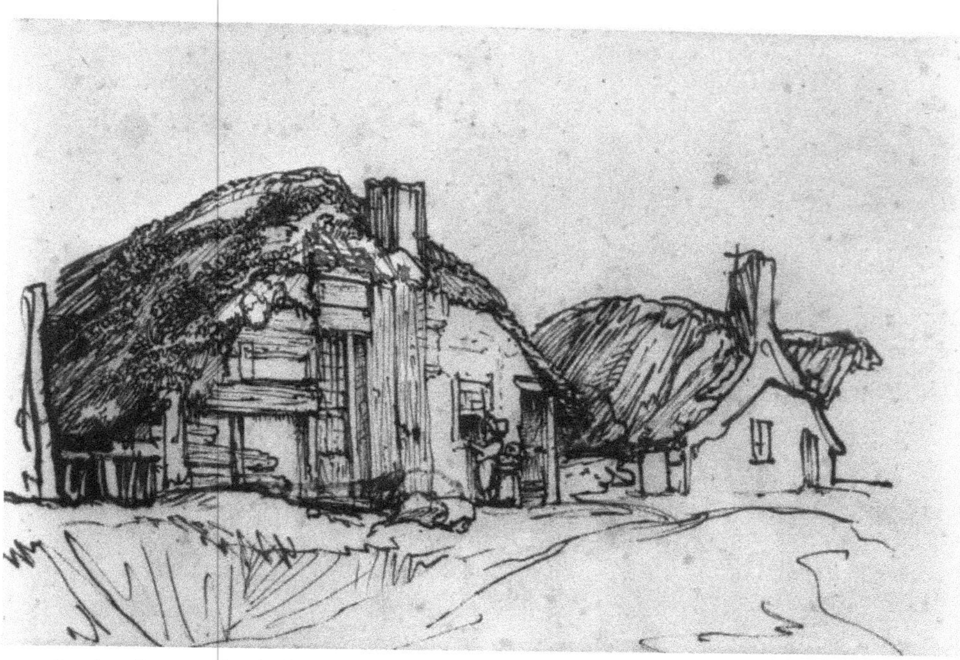

250. Rembrandt, *Two Thatched Cottages* (ca. 1635–40). Pen and brown ink, some white body-color, 13.7 × 20 cm. J. Paul Getty Museum of Art, Los Angeles (85.GA.93 [Benesch 796]).

the real protagonist of his designs, the expressive and dramatic focus. And, in granting it that pictorial independence, he invested it with new affective potential. From initial exploitation of their picturesque qualities, their irregularities of shape and texture, he developed a rather special feeling for these structures; they become increasingly sentient in his renderings. Isolating, exposing them, he in turn provides them with shelter, with ambient protection, by setting them under the shade of overarching foliage, that is, within a grove. Nestled within accommodating shadow, beneficiary of Rembrandt's drypoint burr, the cottage itself becomes a pas-

251. Rembrandt, *Landscape with a Cottage and Large Tree* (1642). Etching, 12.7 × 32 cm. (B. 226). Museum Het Rembrandthuis, Amsterdam.

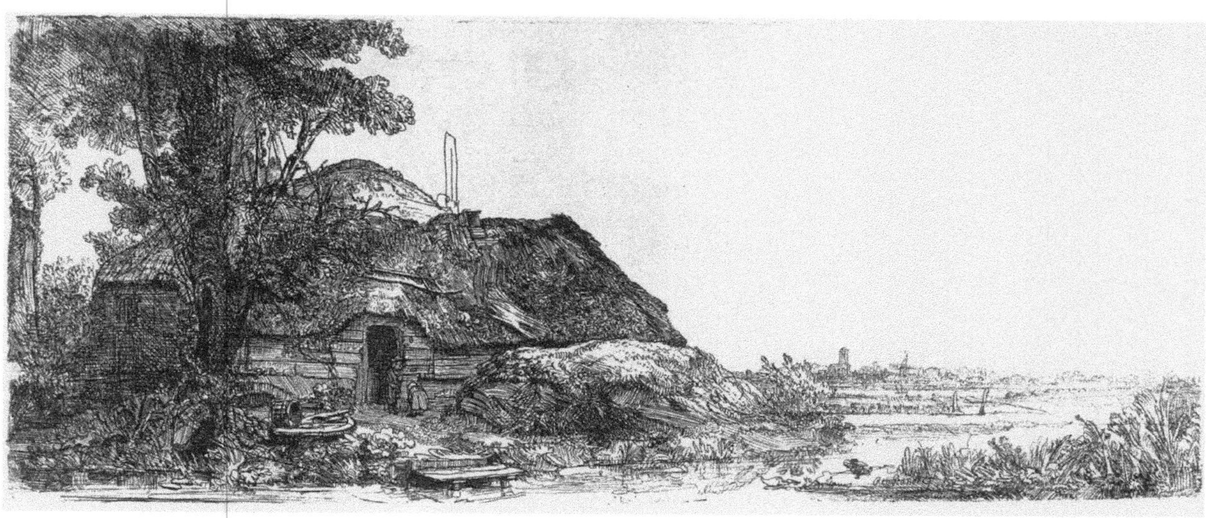

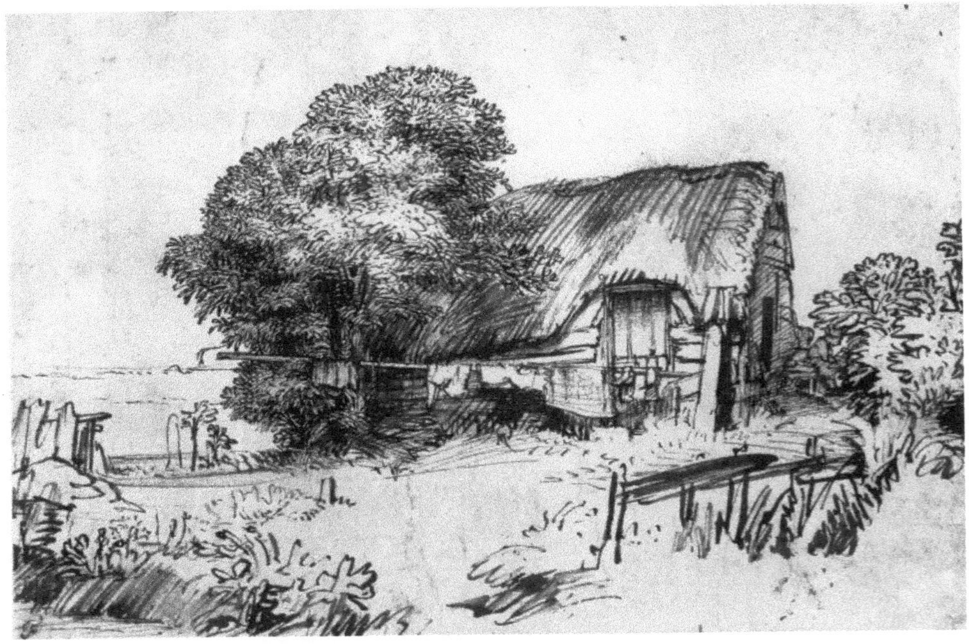

252. Rembrandt, *Thatched Cottage* (ca. 1648–50). Pen and brown ink and wash, 17.6 × 26.9 cm. Devonshire Collection, Chatsworth (no. 1046 [Benesch 1282]). Reproduced by permission of the Duke of Devonshire and the Chatsworth Settlement Trustees.

253. Rembrandt, *Three Gabled Cottages beside a Road* (1650). Etching and drypoint, 16.1 × 20.2 cm. (B. 217). Yale University Art Gallery, New Haven. Fritz Achelis Memorial Collection. Gift of Fritz George Achelis, B.A. 1907.

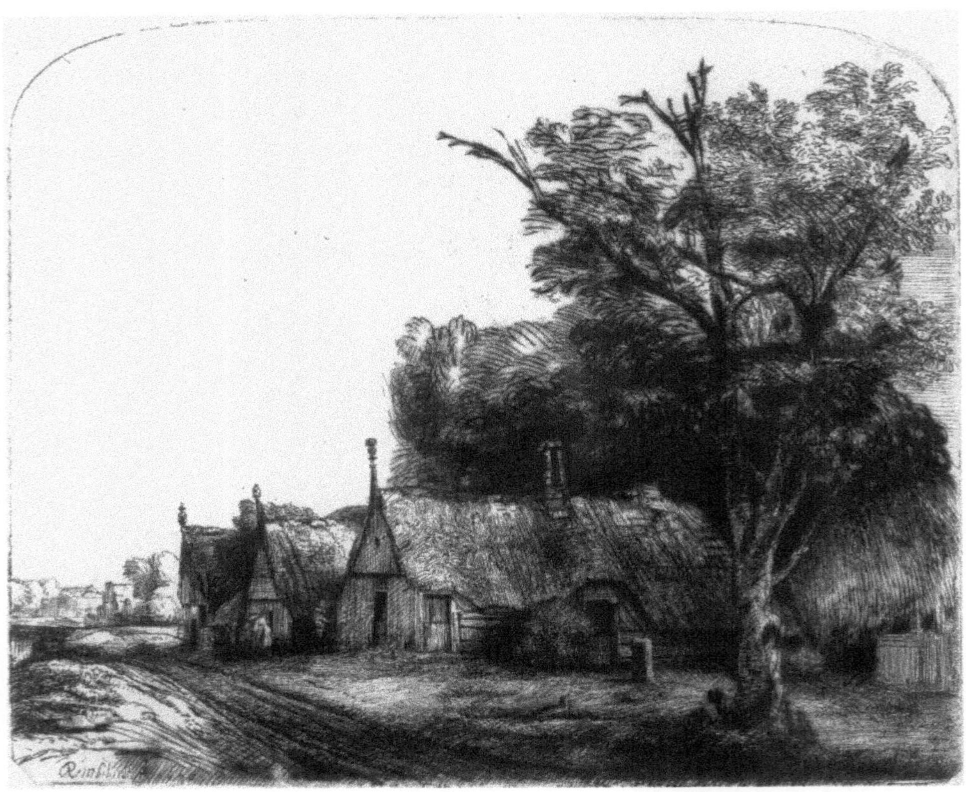

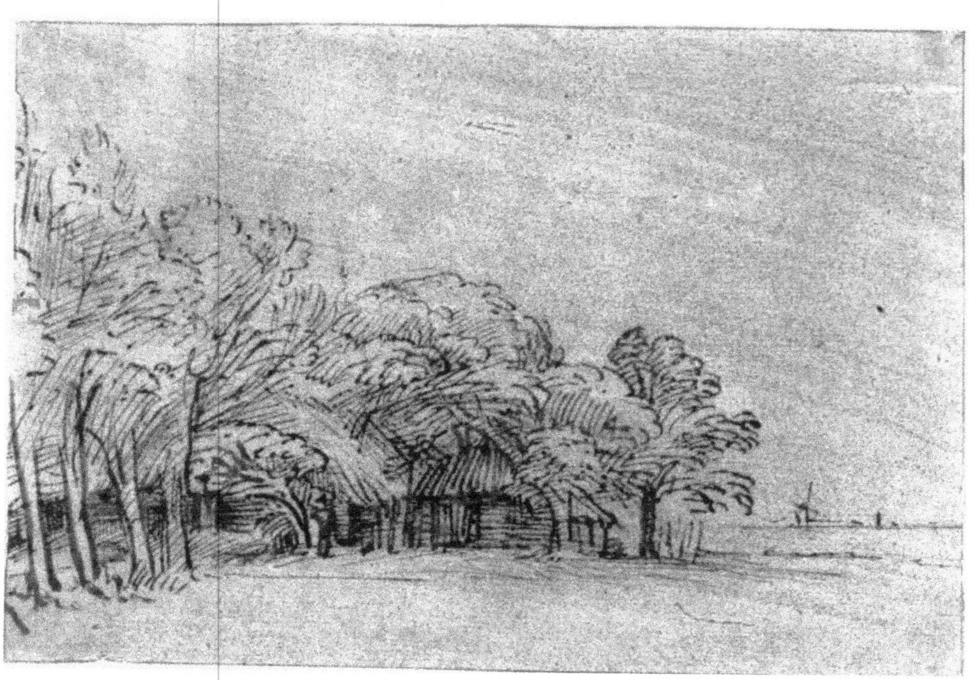

254. Rembrandt, *Farmhouse and Trees* (ca. 1653–54). Pen and brown ink on paper prepared with a light brown wash, 11.3 × 16.5 cm. Sterling and Francine Clark Art Institute, Williamstown, Mass. (acc. no. 993 [Benesch 1326]).

255. Rembrandt, *Clump of Trees with a Vista* (1652). Drypoint, 12.4 × 21.1 cm. (B. 222). Pierpont Morgan Library, New York.

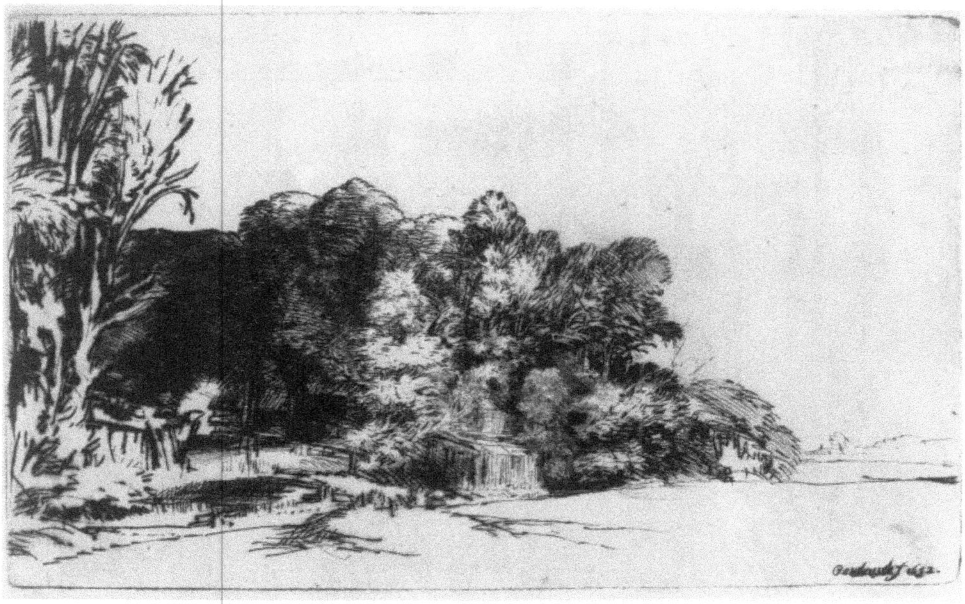

toral occasion; it enjoys a relationship to its immediate surroundings not unlike that of the saint in the landscape, set off from a larger world, protected – at once the inhabitant and location of a Batavian *locus amoenus*.[61]

Beyond those of his predecessors, Rembrandt's privileged cottages acquire a sensibility and an emotional presence, a humanity. That we so readily accord them life and feeling is owing, in large measure, to their situation: protected, they are by implication vulnerable. The very physicality of the cottage's relationship to the ambient shadow, to the trees that set it off and give it shelter, assumes an intimacy whose resonance is positively emotional. This union of forms in an affective bond must remind us of *The Goldsmith* (Fig. 243), for the same feelings of protection, expressed through tender contact, holding, inform these landscape family groups.

What was later to be identified as a pathetic fallacy was a tacit belief of the landscape traditions to which Rembrandt was heir. The "Book of Nature" was open to all who could read it, and landscape representations invited a range of exegetical responses: spiritualizing, moralizing, allegorizing, and, of course, the topographically epideictic.[62] Rembrandt's graphic landscapes, however, for the most part hardly encourage such efforts. This is partly due to their pictorial openness. Reluctant to take rendering to the very limits of the field, Rembrandt leaves broad areas of unmarked paper between viewer and object, areas leaving illusion to imaginative projection. Whatever their relation to the conventions of the pastoral or of the topographical vista, his imagined spaces are hardly so referential. Rather, they invite our direct participation through the very processes of their making. We become involved with the strokes of Rembrandt's pen or etching needle, with the concentration of ink, or the expanse of untouched yet totally transformed paper. These were his means of representing those imagined worlds, and through our reenactment of his drawing acts we enter them; through our participation we recreate them for ourselves. We feel ourselves into those depicted spaces because Rembrandt felt his way in, projected his own self into the landscape; toward cottage, tree, or horizon, we follow the reach of the draftsman.

CHAPTER EIGHT

Capriccio

The Antic Line

> Pray can you tell me, – that is, without anger, before I write my chapter upon straight lines – by what mistake – who told them so – or how it has come to pass, that your men of wit and genius have all along confounded this line, with the line of GRAVITATION?
>
> – Laurence Sterne

By chapter 40 of the sixth of its nine volumes the author of *The Life and Opinions of Tristram Shandy, Gent.* promises the reader that his narrative will proceed, finally, "in a tolerable straight line." Hitherto, Sterne admits, he had moved his story along with less-than-Euclidean efficiency (Fig. 256). His diagrams confirm with graphic clarity the reader's developed sense of indirection; with many starts, deflections, digressions, and returns, narrative progress has indeed been self-indulgently, yet quite pleasurably, slow. Henceforth, the author hopes to correct his capricious line, to follow a straight and narrow path, "even thus":

> which is a line drawn straight as I could draw it, by a writing-master's ruler, (borrowed for that purpose) turning neither to the right hand or to the left.
> The *right line*, – the path-way for Christians to walk in! say divines –
> – The emblem of moral rectitude! says Cicero –
> – The *best line!* say cabbage planters – is the shortest line, says Archimedes, which can be drawn from one given point to another. –
> I wish your ladyships would lay this matter to heart, in your next birth-day suits!
> – What a journey!

Invoking the culture of the line, its complex metaphoric status and signifying function, Sterne offers – indirectly, needless to say – an effectively semiotic analysis by demonstration. Horizontal, the line assumes a narrative function, moving, like text, from left to right through time ("What a journey!"). Inflecting "right" from a spatial to a moral mode, turning the horizontal line ninety degrees, the author reorients it to the verticality of rectitude – which operation provokes his incredulous recognition of the gravity that has generally been assigned to it. The line is a bearer of value. Resisting its moralizing invitation, however, Sterne insists upon returning the line to its spatial, and therefore temporal, status. Later, in the fourth chapter of volume 9, it reappears as pure movement in space, a punctuating gesture in a dialogue on the perils of matrimony:

> Whilst a man is free, – cried the corporal, giving a flourish with his stick thus –

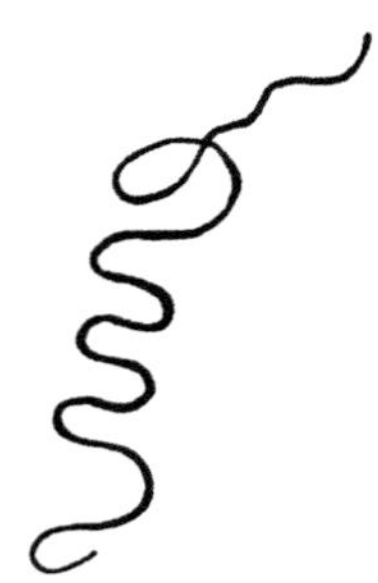

> A thousand of my father's most subtle syllogisms could not have said more for celibacy.

1. *Linear Analysis: Hogarth's Serpentine*

In the eighteenth century, an age of connoisseurship, line became fully theorized. What had been implicit in aesthetic thought and in studio practice was made explicit, the overt object of critical attention and interpretation. Long acknowledged as the basic unit in the creative process, the foundation of pictorial construction, its essential position in the re-creative process of connoisseurship received more artic-

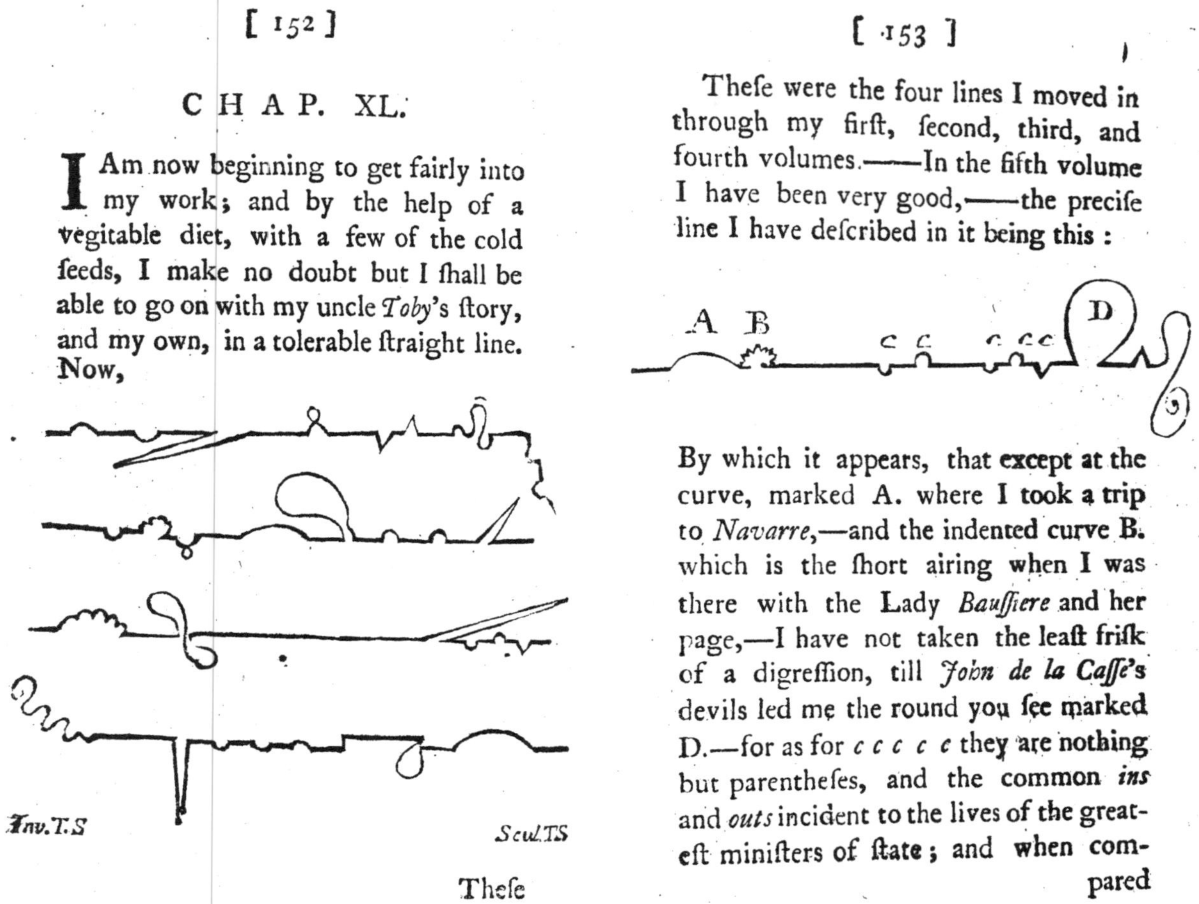

[152]

CHAP. XL.

I Am now beginning to get fairly into my work; and by the help of a vegitable diet, with a few of the cold ſeeds, I make no doubt but I ſhall be able to go on with my uncle *Toby*'s ſtory, and my own, in a tolerable ſtraight line. Now,

Inv. T. S *Scul. T. S*

Theſe

[153]

Theſe were the four lines I moved in through my firſt, ſecond, third, and fourth volumes.——In the fifth volume I have been very good,——the preciſe line I have deſcribed in it being this:

A B c c c c c D

By which it appears, that except at the curve, marked A. where I took a trip to *Navarre*,—and the indented curve B. which is the ſhort airing when I was there with the Lady *Bauſſiere* and her page,—I have not taken the leaſt friſk of a digreſſion, till *John de la Caſſe*'s devils led me the round you ſee marked D.—for as for *c c c c c* they are nothing but parentheſes, and the common *ins* and *outs* incident to the lives of the greateſt miniſters of ſtate; and when compared

256. From Laurence Sterne, *The Life and Times of Tristram Shandy, Gent.* (London, 1760–67), vol. 6 (1763), pp. 152–53. New York Public Library.

ulate recognition. Line led in both directions: forward to the final image and back to its maker.

Apelles' *linea summae tenuitatis*, the spatially inflected contour of Parrhasios, the freehand "O" of Giotto, Castiglione's *linea sola non stentata* – these tributes to artistic skill locate the test of such skill in the rendering of a single line. And, as Pliny implied, the understanding of the line was the true test of the connoisseur, one who was capable of recognizing the talent of the artist in the trace of the hand. In drawing a line, demonstrating his art, the artist declares himself. In responding to that line, to the mark of the artist, the sensitive viewer engages in a dialogic relationship, through that mark, with its maker. That engagement is predicated on an appreciation of the operations of the hand; it keeps the viewer at the surface of an image, attentive to the small constructive units of rendering rather than to the image as a whole, to the reality of marking rather than to the fiction of representation. In this respect, we might say, it professionalizes the viewer by locating him or her in effect in the studio, with the artist – brush or pen in mind, if not in hand. And that privileged position can extend to other dimensions of the creative process, to *invenzione* as well as to *disegno*.

Recognizing the line as fundamental to both expression and representation, the sensitive viewer learns to move between its referential poles, between the line as an actual mark and as a notional sign. Within the hermeneutic space defined by that polarity, we feel free to assign varying values to a line, a situation seized upon by Laurence Sterne to great effect. Sterne's invocation of linear weight, direction, velocity – phenomenological dimensions of the line – takes as axiomatic a basic assumption: that line is motion. Moreover, in a calculus well known to the draftsman, motion assumes time. A line is a movement through space, and latent in its trajectory is a narrative of its progress.

Sterne's appropriation of the drawn line for the writer's vocabulary – part of his larger arsenal of typo- and topographical strategies – owes much to the example of the artist whose work surely contributed to the ethos and the pictorialism of *Tristram Shandy,* who supplied illustrations for it and whose articulation of the very notion of line made it available to the writer. In 1753 William Hogarth's *Analysis of Beauty* made line part of public aesthetic discourse. For despite his apparent predecessors – mathematicians and philosophers as well as artists and writers on art – Hogarth's great originality may be found in his reification of line; he made the abstraction perceptible and available to sensual analysis. Perhaps only Leonardo may be said to have anticipated him in the focused precision of that analysis.

Corporal Trim's flourish traces a somewhat wayward version of Hogarth's "line of beauty" or, more accurately, a rather graceless version of his "line of grace."

> It is to be observed that straight lines vary only in length, and therefore are least ornamental.
>
> That curved lines as they can be varied in their degrees of curvature as well as in their lengths, begin on that account to be ornamental.
>
> That straight and curv'd lines join'd, being a compound line, vary more than curves alone, and so become somewhat more ornamental.
>
> That the waving line, or line of beauty, varying still more, being composed of two curves contrasted, becomes still more ornamental and pleasing, insomuch that the hand takes a lively movement in making it with pen or pencil.
>
> That the serpentine line, by its waving and winding at the same time different ways, leads the eye in a pleasing manner along the continuity of its variety, if I may be allowed the expression; and which by its twisting so many different ways, may be said to inclose (tho' but a single line) varied contents; and therefore all its variety cannot be express'd on paper by one continued line, without the assistance of the imagination, or help of a figure. . . .[1]

Knowing heir to the traditions of Leonardo and Michelangelo – and unwitting precursor to the pedagogics of Paul Klee – Hogarth, with a certain English bluntness, gives full expression to the kind of theorizing of the line that can be traced back, via Pliny, to the masters of ancient Greece. Rehearsing the story of Apelles' visit to Protogenes, Hogarth is in little doubt about the precise nature of the line in question: "if it was only a stroke (tho' as fine as a hair as Pliny seems to think) it could not possibly, by any means, denote the abilities of a great painter. But if we suppose it to be a line of some extraorinary quality, such as the serpentine line will appear to be, Apelles could not have left a more satisfactory signature of the compliment he had paid him." Protogenes' appropriate response to that compliment-cum-challenge, therefore, was to draw "a finer *or rather more expressive line* within it," thereby proving in turn his own genius. The culminating stroke in this graphic *agon* is Apelles' "correcting the line again, perhaps," Hogarth suggests, "by making it more precisely elegant. . . . The story thus may be reconcil'd to common sense, which, as it has generally been receiv'd, could never be understood but as a ridiculous tale" (p. 16).

Unlike artist predecessors such as Ghiberti (or art historian successors such as E. H. Gombrich), Hogarth resists accommodating the studio anecdote to a purely representational purpose. The Greek lines are not subject to mimetic responsibility. Writing in an age of connoisseurship, Hogarth recognizes the very professional nature of a competition in technical skill that yielded a panel prized especially by artists, as Pliny recalls, lines comprehensible only to the cognoscenti. Line, the foundation of the artist's work, offers the true test of the connoisseur.

"Written with a view of fixing the fluctuating IDEAS OF TASTE," *The Analysis of Beauty* was constructed on the basis of a natural truth Hogarth had discovered for himself, even as he rediscovered it in the history of art, a truth instinctively if inarticulately recognized by all painters. Hogarth had declared it earlier in the self-portrait published as the frontispiece to his engraved works in 1749, "in which I drew a serpentine line lying on a painter's pallette, with these words under it, THE LINE OF BEAUTY" (p. 10) (Figs. 257, 258). With this reification of line in space, rising above the tonal range of colors upon the palette – together an emblematic epitome of the conventional aesthetic values of *disegno* and *colore* – Hogarth celebrated the serpentine line that was the key to beauty. On the title page of *The Analysis of Beauty* he refined the concept in a device animating the line of beauty, now literally serpentine, within the other key to formal perfection, a pyramid – the two resting significantly on a base marked "VARIETY" (Fig. 259).

That essential combination, now of serpentine line around a cone, assumes theoretic pride of place in plate I, one of the two densely designed illustrations accompanying Hogarth's text (Fig. 260): the serpentinizing of the waving line "hath the power of super-adding grace to beauty" (p. 55). This is what Leonardo had indeed called the "serpeggiare" (or "serpeggiatura") of the line. For all the deliberately comic awkwardness of his application of these principles to representation, especially in plate II (Fig. 261), Hogarth's linear analysis recapitulates the efforts of his pioneering predecessors. Although his language may be couched in terms of aesthetic and social decorum – that is, of taste – he too is searching for fundamental principles of graphic construction, for the basic units of graphic expression. And like Leonardo, the Renaissance inventor of the *figura serpentinata,* the eighteenth-century English artist recognizes the crucial issue in the spatialization of line. Leonardo's deep concern with interlacing knots and helixes was inspired by self-

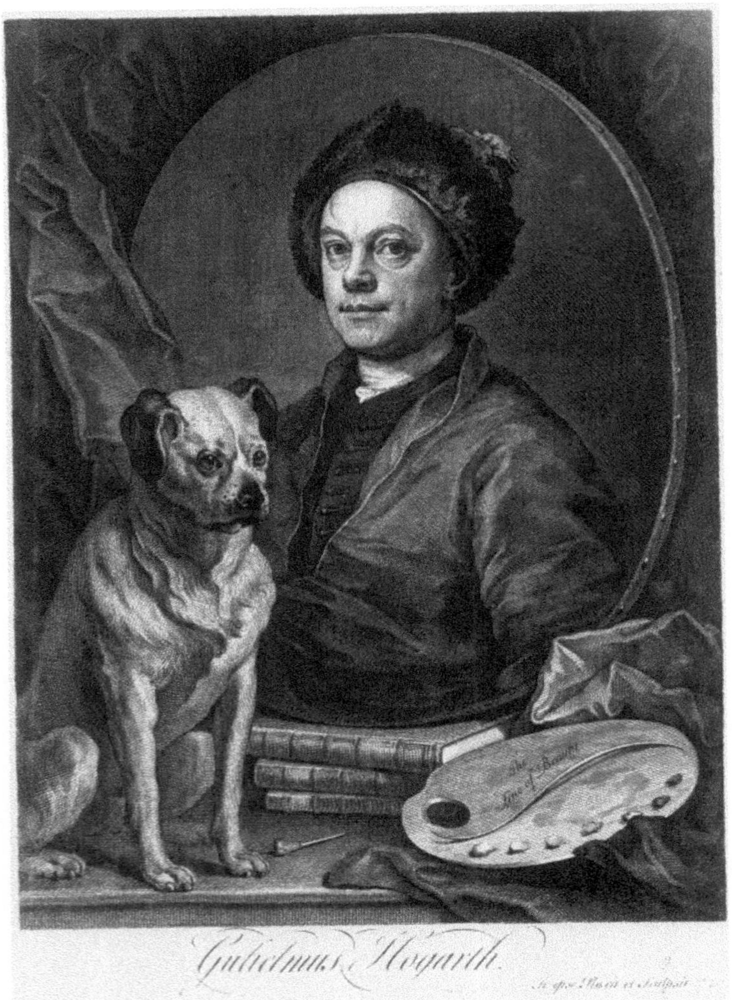

257. William Hogarth, *Self-Portrait* (1749). Etching and engraving, 34.3 × 26.2 cm. Washington, National Gallery of Art, Lessing J. Rosenwald Collection (1944.5.9).

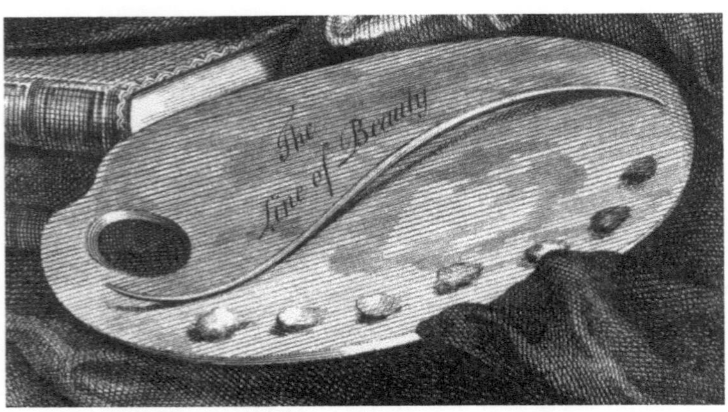

258. William Hogarth, *Self-Portrait*, detail of Fig. 257.

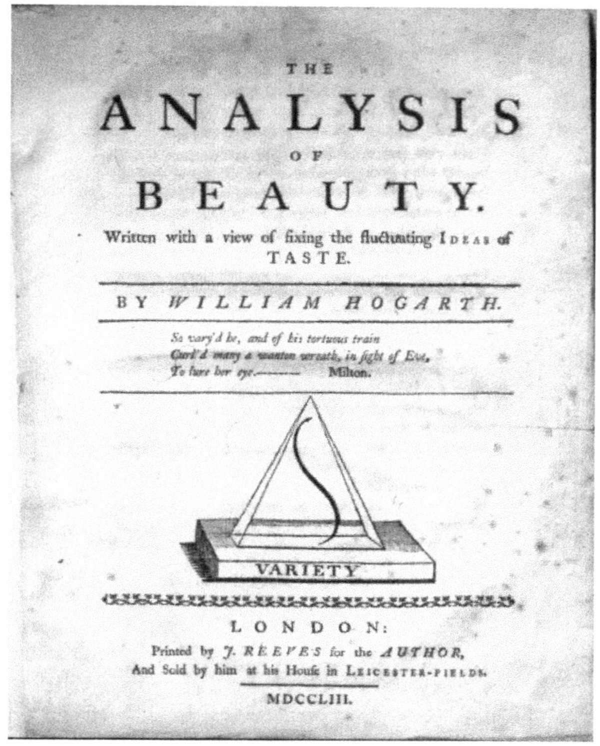

THE

ANALYSIS

OF

BEAUTY.

Written with a view of fixing the fluctuating IDEAS of TASTE.

BY *WILLIAM HOGARTH.*

So vary'd he, and of his tortuous train
Curl'd many a wanton wreath, in sight of Eve,
To lure her eye.—— Milton.

VARIETY

LONDON:

Printed by *J. REEVES* for the *AUTHOR,*
And Sold by him at his House in LEICESTER-FIELDS.

MDCCLIII.

259. William Hogarth, *The Analysis of Beauty* (London, 1753), title page. British Museum, London.

reflection, that is, by analysis of the motions of his own hand writing or drawing. In Leonardo's grapheme Hogarth might have recognized the antecedent to his own line of beauty turned gracefully in space. Both artists took pleasure in the well-turned line, "insomuch that the hand takes a lively movement in making it with pen or pencil." Both appreciated the pleasure of the hand in turning it, the very experience of drawing the line.

Pretentious and smug though it may seem at times, *The Analysis of Beauty* was written by an artist, a painter and, even more significant, engraver; it offers theory based very much on practice. Hogarth acknowledges his debt to predecessors, especially to Giampaolo Lomazzo, through whom he encountered "a certaine precept" of Michelangelo, namely, that figures should be pyramidal and serpentine. "For the greatest grace and life that a picture can have, is, that it expresse *Motion:* which the Painters call the *spirite* of a picture: Nowe there is no forme so fitte to expresse this *motion,* as that of the flame of fire," Hogarth continues to quote Lomazzo (in Haydock's Elizabethan translation). Fire is the most active of the elements and thus the ascending form of flame, twisting and conical, "is most apte for motion."[2] Continuing his search for the principles of beauty, the fundamentally empirical Englishman rejects the *Je ne sçai quoi* aesthetic, which had "become a fashionable phrase for grace" (p. 7). If grace exists – and we do indeed know it when we see it – then it must be subject to the objective control of reason.

Hogarth's theorizing is most compelling when he abandons the library for the

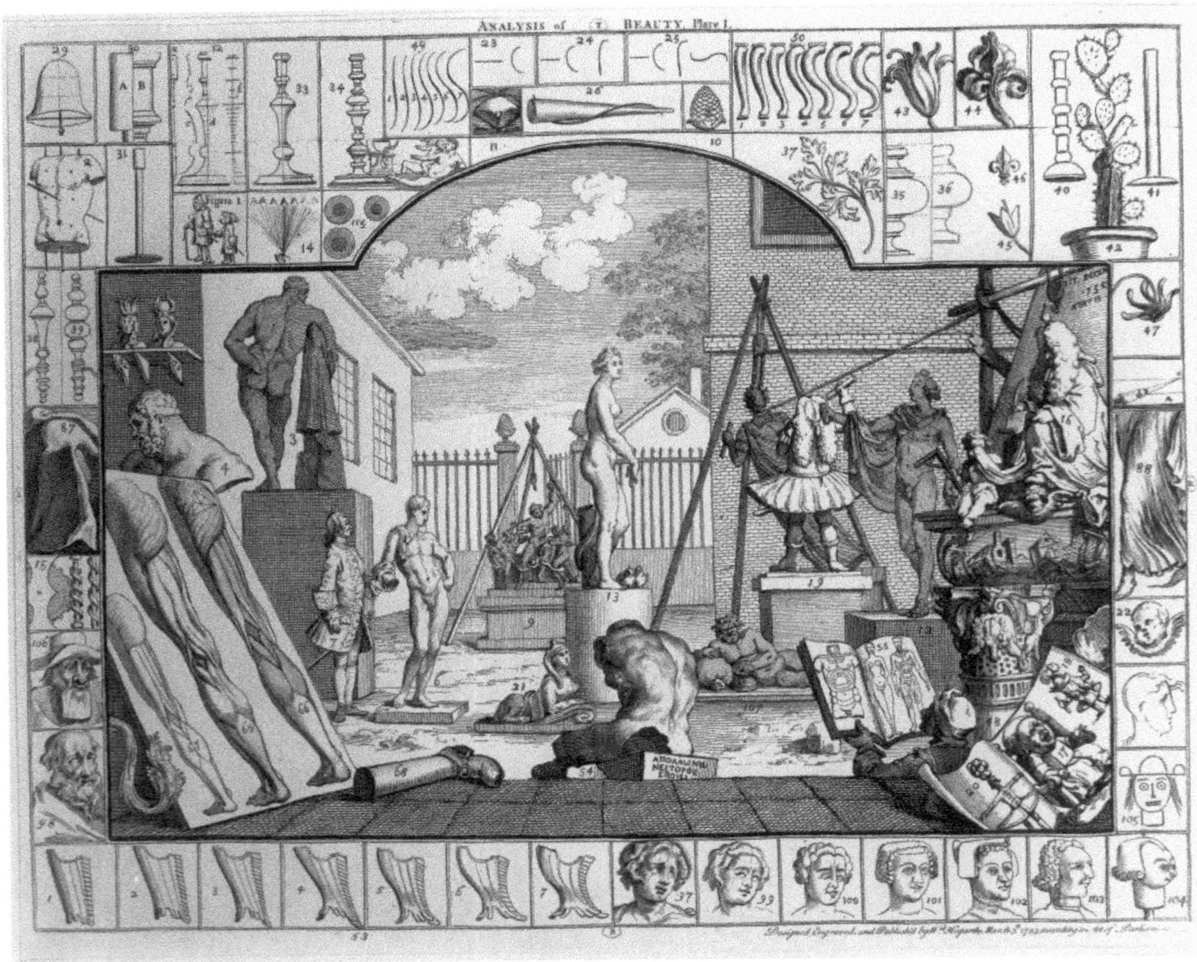

260. William Hogarth, *The Analysis of Beauty* (1753), Plate I. Etching and engraving, 38.5 × 49.8 cm. Metropolitan Museum of Art, New York. Harris Brisbane Dick Fund, 1932 (32.35[22]).

studio, when he leaves behind what he has read to engage the objects he knows in the world, how he knows them, and how he represents them. And his efforts, the efforts of an artist, are not unworthy of Leonardo, for they involve a similar imaginative projection, that kinesthesia of seeing and grasping in rendering: drawing as knowing. Hogarth confronts the paradox of drawing directly, the tension between two-dimensional representation and its three-dimensional model. His basic demonstrations involve the nature of line, to which, as a skilled engraver, he was naturally sensitive in practice. Without the mathematical deliberateness of Alberti or the visual penetration of Leonardo, Hogarth nonetheless subjects the world to a very practical linear analysis.

Objects are imagined as composed of an infinite variety of lines, "which serve to raise the ideas of bodies in the mind, and which are undoubtedly to be consider'd as drawn on the surfaces only of solid or opake bodies" (p. 26). To get beyond the flat representation of drawing, he urges "the endeavouring to conceive, as accurate

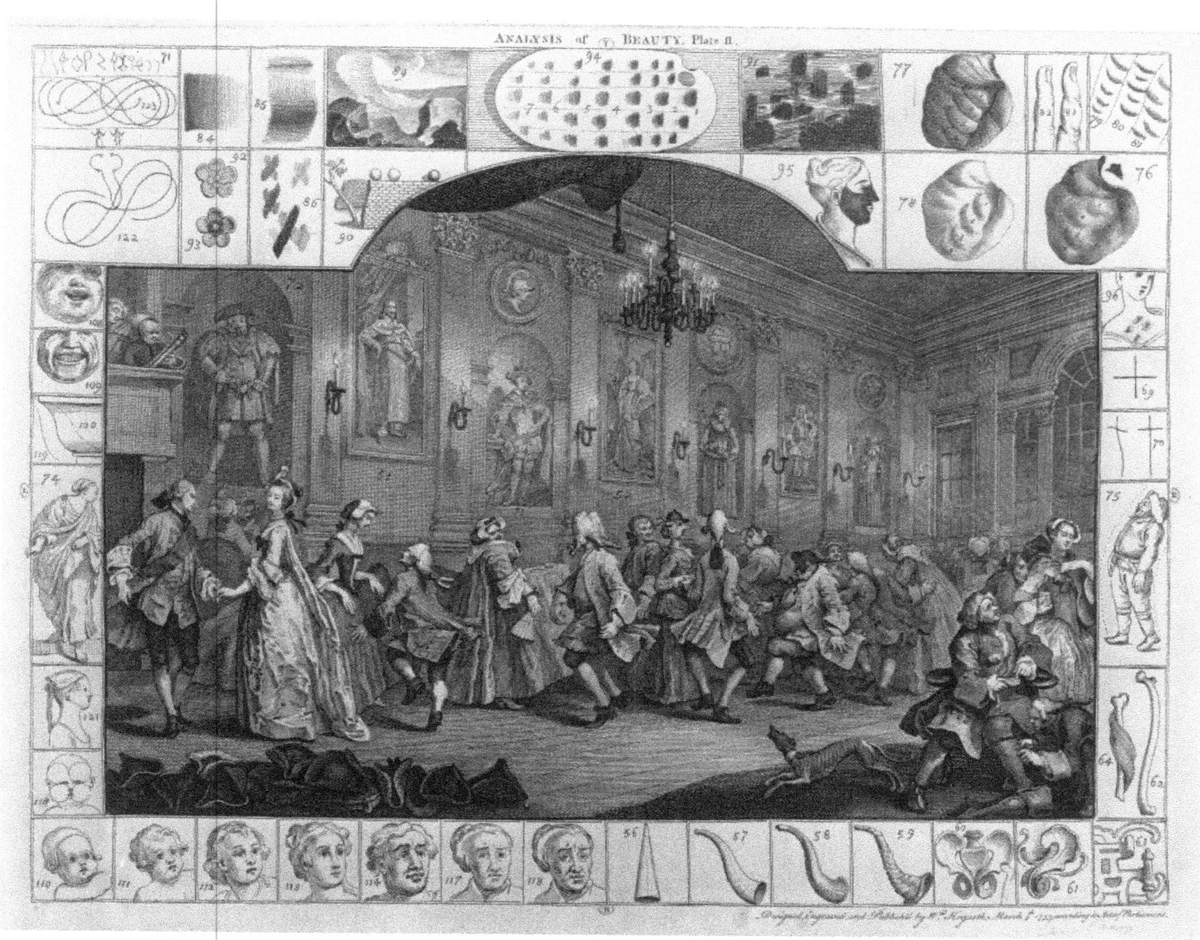

261. William Hogarth, *The Analysis of Beauty* (1753), Plate II. Etching and engraving, 42.5 × 53.2 cm. Metropolitan Museum of Art, New York. Harris Brisbane Dick Fund, 1932 (32.35[23]).

an idea as is possible, of the *inside* of those surfaces." In a remarkable passage, he invites the reader/draftsman to see in three dimensions:

> In order to my being well understood, let every object under our consideration, be imagined to have its inward contents scoop'd out so nicely, as to have nothing of it left but a thin shell, exactly corresponding both in its inner and outer surface, to the shape of the object itself: and let us likewise suppose this thin shell to be made up of very fine threads, closely connected together, and equally perceptible, whether the eye is supposed to observe them from without, or within; and we shall find the ideas of the two surfaces of this shell will naturally coincide. The very word, shell, makes us seem to see both surfaces alike.
>
> The use of this conceit, as it may be call'd by some, will be seen to be very great, in the process of this work: and the oftner we think of objects in this shell-like manner, we shall facilitate and strengthen our conception of any particular part of the surface of an object we are viewing, by

> acquiring thereby a more perfect knowledge of the whole, to which it belongs: because the imagination will naturally enter into the vacant space within this shell, and there at once, as from a center, view the whole form within, and mark the opposite corresponding parts so strongly, as to retain the idea of the whole, and make us masters of the meaning of every view of the object, as we walk around it, and view it from without. (p. 27)

The problem Hogarth puts before us is basic and recalls earlier efforts at imagining objects in the round – Renaissance artists recording several views of a body in order to render a fuller understanding of it (Pisanello) or projecting complex solids as transparent (Uccello). Hogarth imagines – and asks us to imagine – the body in space, to "reconnoitre" it with our minds. Thinking in lines affords the medium for such exploration:

> Another advantage of considering objects thus merely as shells composed of lines, is, that by these means we obtain the true and full idea of what is call'd the *outlines* of a figure, which has been confin'd within too narrow limits, by taking it only from drawings on paper; for in the example of the sphere . . . , every one of the imaginary circular threads has a right to be consider'd as an out-line of the sphere, as well as those which divide the half, that is seen, from that which is not seen; and if the eye be supposed to move regularly round it, these threads will each of them as regularly succeed one another in the office of out-lines, (in the narrow and limited sense of the word:) and the instant any one of these threads, during this motion of the eye, comes into sight on one side, its opposite thread is lost, and disappears on the other. (p. 28)

Seen as a continuous surface of lines, the object presents an infinite number of potential outlines, that is, the particular aspect of any one point of view. Seeing, or imagining, in this way allows the draftsman to comprehend the surface out of sight, beyond the horizon, as it were, of the bounding outline. Hogarth realizes, on a larger scale, the implications of the line of Parrhasios – the contour that seems to inflect itself spatially beyond and behind its own delineated limit.

The eye, in conjunction with the drawing hand, following a surface over the horizon: this was the experience celebrated by Leonardo – the line as vector, as lead, as both trace and lure. Free of the politics of the *paragone* that had animated the Renaissance painter in his defense of his art, Hogarth can more readily expand upon the pure pleasure of following the line, "this love of pursuit," as he so suggestively describes the sensuousness of the experience, an aesthetic experience. "With what delight does it [the mind] follow the well-connected thread of a play, or novel, which ever increases as the plot thickens, and ends most pleas'd, when that is most distinctly unravell'd?" In this more relaxed and professionally more generous recapitulation of Leonardo's praise of the eye, we are returned, in anticipation, to the intricately woven web and linear momentums of *Tristram Shandy*.

> The eye hath this sort of enjoyment in winding walks, and serpentine rivers, and all sorts of objects, whose forms, as we shall see hereafter, are composed principally of what I call the *waving* and *serpentine* lines.
>
> Intricacy in form, therefore I shall define to be that peculiarity in the lines, which compose it, that *leads the eye a wanton kind of chace,* and from the pleasure that gives the mind, intitles it to the name of beautiful: (p. 42)

In figure 26 at the top of plate I Hogarth reduced Lomazzo's Michelangelesque principle to a simple model: the serpentine line winding around a cone (Fig. 262). Surrounding that image are other didactic vignettes illustrating the linear principles behind that central truth as well as certain applications of it. At the bottom of plate II, figures 56–59 offer a more practical demonstration of the realization of serpentine form: the shaping of a basic cone, first by bending its axis into a reverse curve, then, "by giving the whole a twist" (p. 116), turning that curve into space, transforming a "waving" line into a "serpentine" (Fig. 263). A similar process of spatialization distinguishes the complex iris from simpler flora: the volution of its petals, turning with requisite variety, confirms its aesthetic superiority (Fig. 264). That Hogarth himself was fully aware of the "Rococo" implications of his principles is signaled in the lower left corner of plate I by the delightfully arbitrary intrusion of a full-grown arabesque: like the foliate tail of some unseen architectural creature, it swishes past the anatomical panel to assert its own organic vitality amidst the marmoreal remains of antiquity (Fig. 265).

The two framed compositions illustrating *The Analysis of Beauty* offer models in art and nature of Hogarth's principles and arguments. The frames themselves are composed of more deliberately pedagogic vignettes, analytic studio demonstrations in both constructive and deconstructive modes. Some of their sequences run through sets of lessons in drawing, parodic versions of the kind of exercises in rendering that had been part of the standard syllabus of printed drawing books since the Renaissance – moving reductively backwards from a head of pathos through wooden mannequin to primitive graffito (Fig. 266), or following the ages of woman from geometrically generated infant head (out of Dürer) to the wrinkles of old age (Fig. 267). In his draft notes Hogarth questioned the utility of the mere copying of objects; he would "rather read the language of them <and if possible find a grammar to it> and collect and retain a remembrance of what I saw by repeated observations."[3] Just as "the twenty four letters and their infinite combination" enable any one who can write to compose freely, so too the practiced draftsman may "draw by memory with facility," his alphabet "being but composed of lines" (p. 208). The graphic marginalia framing the illustrations to *The Analysis of Beauty* constitute the elements of Hogarth's pictorial alphabet, vocabulary, and grammar – academic lessons, but hardly without a sense of humor.

The "two explanatory Prints Serious and Comical" that accompany the book were also sold separately – "Engraved on large Copper Plates fit to Frame for Furniture," as the subscription ticket announced. Whatever their illustrative service to the text, these images are independently legible, as are the didactic diagrams of their frames.

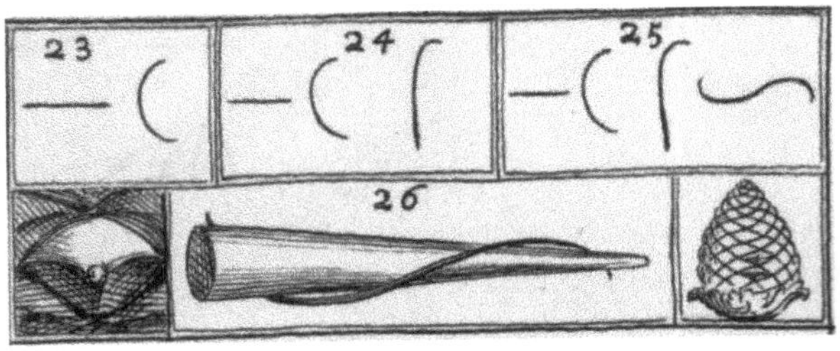

262. William Hogarth, *The Analysis of Beauty,* Plate I, detail of Fig. 260.

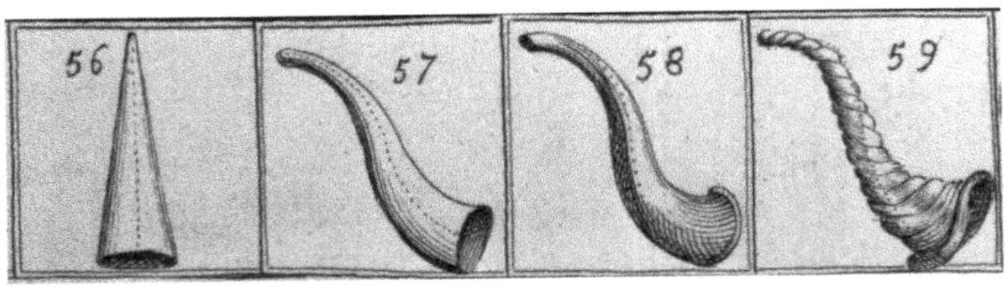

263. William Hogarth, *The Analysis of Beauty,* Plate II, detail of Fig. 261.

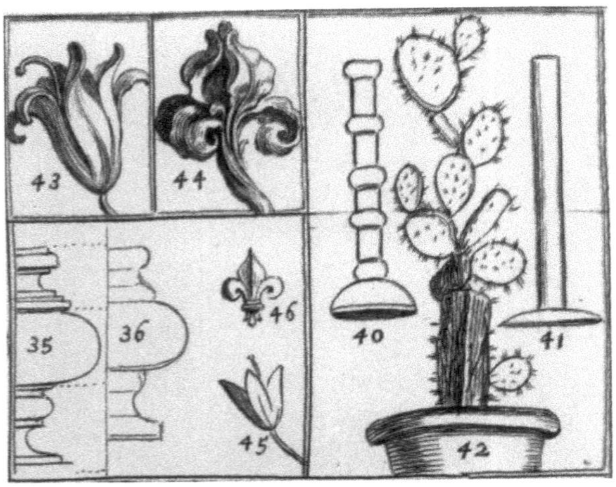

264. William Hogarth, *The Analysis of Beauty,* Plate I, detail of Fig. 260.

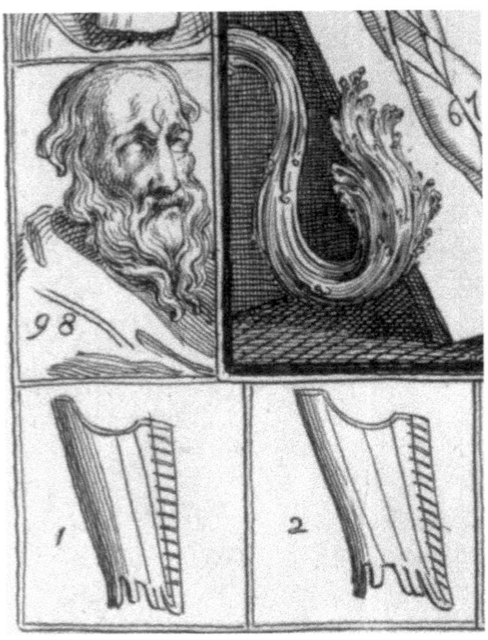

265. William Hogarth, *The Analysis of Beauty,* Plate I, detail of Fig. 260.

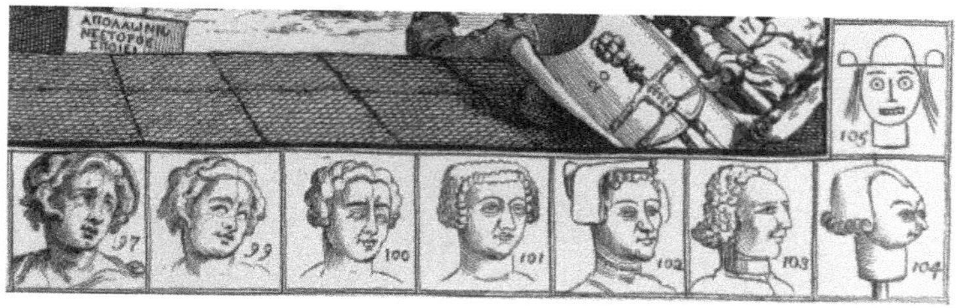

266. William Hogarth, *The Analysis of Beauty,* Plate I, detail of Fig. 260.

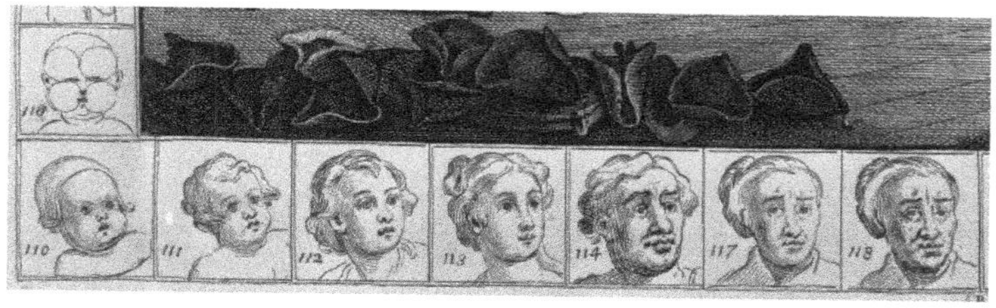

267. William Hogarth, *The Analysis of Beauty,* Plate II, detail of Fig. 261.

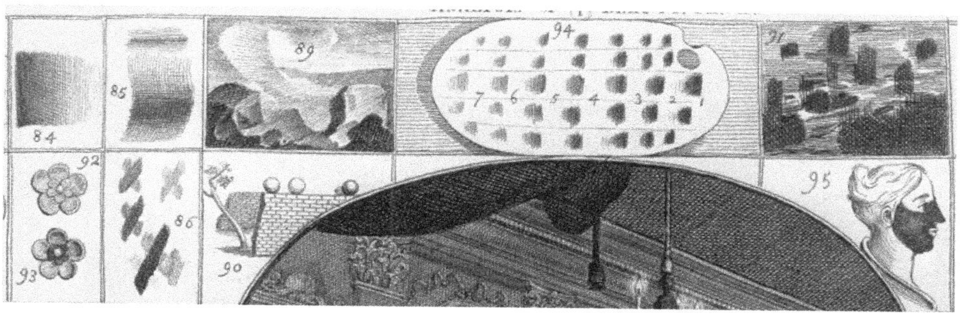

268. William Hogarth, *The Analysis of Beauty,* Plate II, detail of Fig. 261.

The latter, offering the elements of a grammar of drawing, are about rendering in line. The central vignettes at the top of the frame to plate II concern problems of tone and color (Fig. 268). Yet, in their visual presentation, they are – as they must be – above all, lessons in linear structure. The full palette Hogarth lays out in black and white (plate II, fig. 94) can only represent the tonal colors of the engraver's art.

> . . . the out-line of a globe is but a circle on the paper; yet, according to the manner of filling up the space within globular, or concave, in any of its positions with the eye; and as each manner of filling up the circle for those purposes must be very different, it evidently shews the necessity of distinguishing this shade into as many species or kinds, as there are classes or species of lines, with which they may have a correspondence. (pp. 111–12)

The "classes or species" are, of course, "straight, curved, waving, or serpentine lines." Hogarth speaks of a "conformity of shades" to the objects rendered, by which conformity "we have the same ideas of any of the objects composed of the above lines in their front aspects, as we have of them by their profiles; which otherwise could not be without feeling them." Linear pattern thus assumes a haptic dimension. The spatial implications of line lead to a fuller kinesthetic apprehension of the rendered object, which, although represented on a flat surface, must be imagined in the round. The groping of the draftsman must be satisfied by the line.

Hogarth's language – not unlike Leonardo's in this respect – represents a sometimes halting effort to describe experience. His appreciation of the variety of line, sharpened in the practice of his own graphic art, transcends his reading in aesthetics and art theory. His recognition of the spatial invitation of line, its notional extension of lived experience into an imagined space beyond the opaque barrier of the paper, is grounded in his own effort as draftsman to penetrate that space with "pen or pencil," even as those implements are defining it.[4]

2. *Col sporcar si trova*: Piranesi's Spiral

About the time that Hogarth published his "line of beauty" ruling the palette in his self-portrait, another testimony to the principled independence of line was issued, in Italy. Probably in the late 1740s Giovanni Battista Piranesi published a

269. Giovanni Battista Piranesi, from the *Grotteschi* ("The Skeletons") (1747–49). Etching, engraving, drypoint, burnishing, 39 × 54.6 cm. National Gallery of Art, Washington. Ailsa Mellon Bruce Fund.

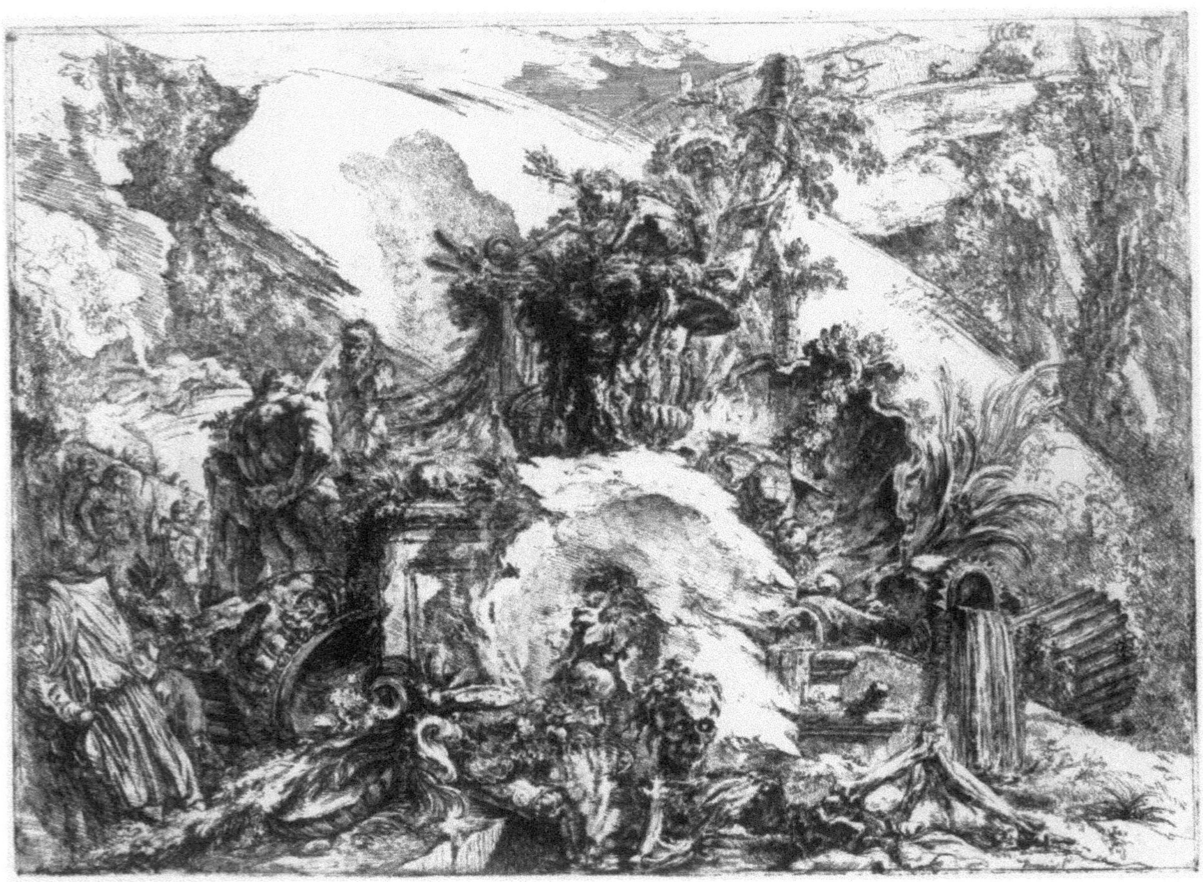

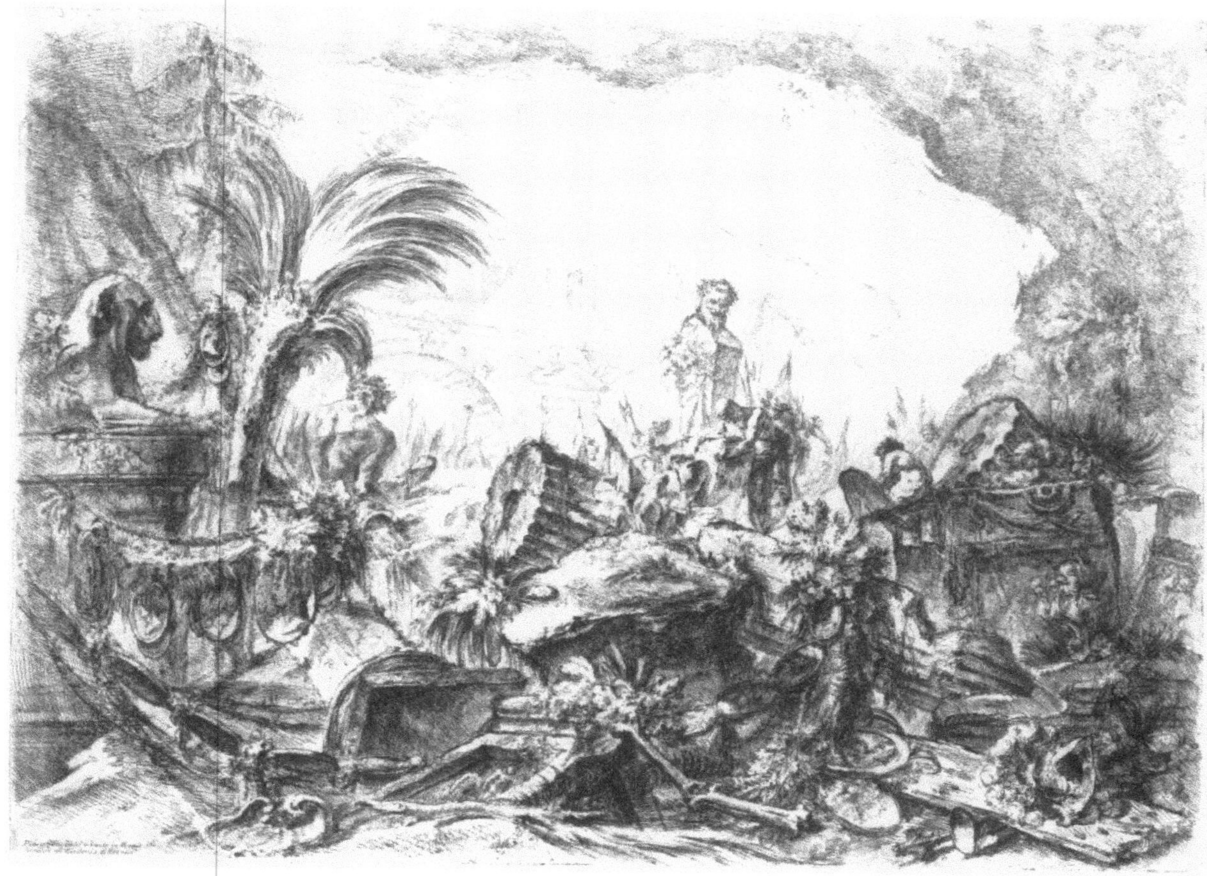

270. Giovanni Battista Piranesi, from the *Grotteschi* ("The Triumphal Arch") (1747–49). Etching, engraving, drypoint, burnishing, 39 × 54.2 cm. National Gallery of Art, Washington. Ailsa Mellon Bruce Fund.

suite of four fantastic etchings (Figs. 269–72). Modern critics, recognizing their generic status, tend to call them "capricci," but Piranesi referred to them as "grotteschi."[5] They are representations beyond reason – assemblages of ancient ruins, architectural and sculptural fragments, trophies and medals, skeletons and living figures, flora and fauna both organic and decorative – all juxtaposed with deliberate disregard for scale and set within atmospheric spaces of remarkable discoordination. These images seem to combine, disturbingly, Baroque moral seriousness with Rococo aesthetic wit: *memento mori* as *serio ludere,* with emphasis apparently on the ludic. The precise meaning of these prints – if such ever was intended – has eluded iconographers, even as the four-part constitution of the suite encourages their search: the four seasons, the four elements, the four humors, the four ages of . . . almost anything. Like form in these images, content too seems subject to the rules of some improvisational game.[6] *Invenzione,* the basic test of artistic creativity throughout the Renaissance tradition, has indeed become *capriccio.*

Defined as a disregard for rules, the *capriccio* dictated its own regulations, and, on a fundamental level, those involve the operations and materials of art. For participating audience, the capricious game requires players who know the rules. In

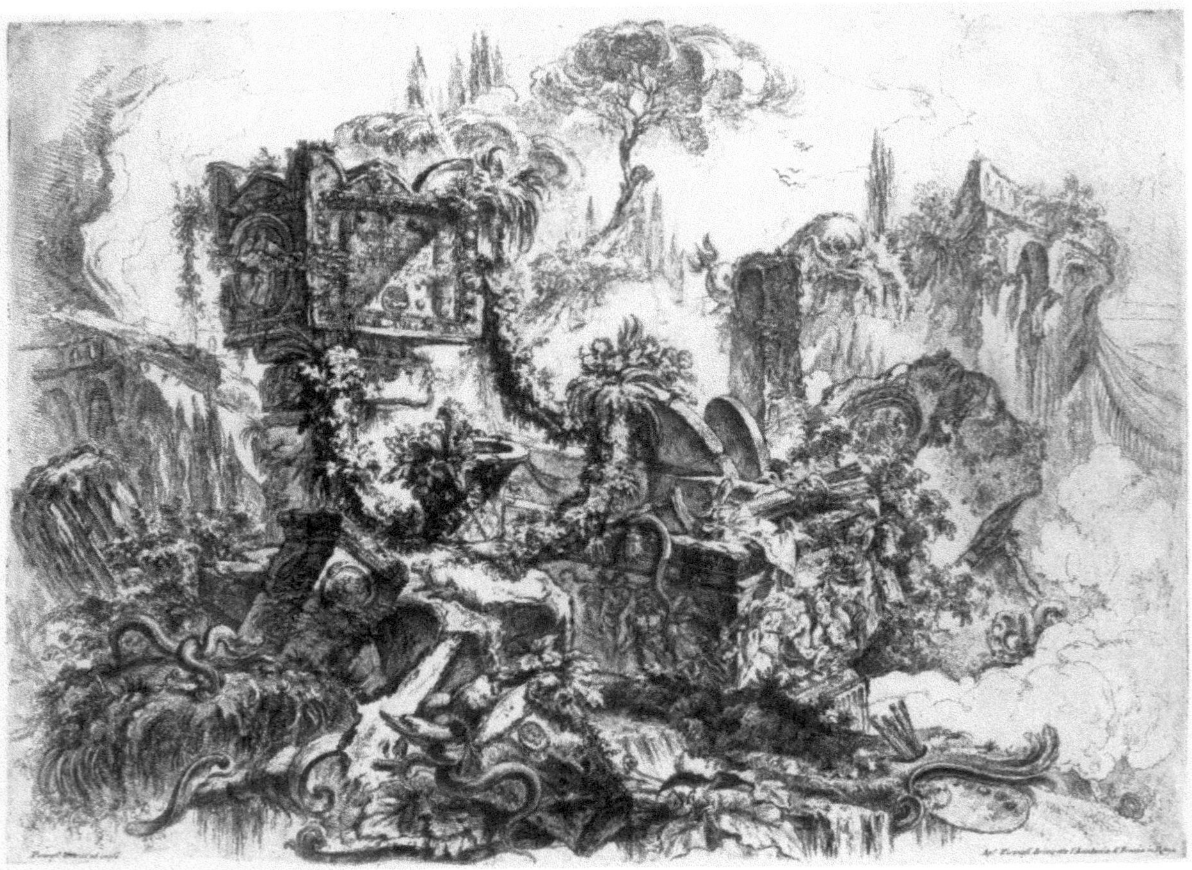

271. Giovanni Battista Piranesi, from the *Grotteschi* ("The Tomb of Nero") (1747–49). Etching, engraving, drypoint, scratching, 39.2 × 54.3 cm. National Gallery of Art, Washington. Ailsa Mellon Bruce Fund.

the graphic arts, those rules involve acknowledgment of the paper as the arena of play and line as the effective agent or marker of the game. The same rules include an inversion clause, however, allowing a reversal of roles. Paper may become the active agent, asserting the determining function of the ground in establishing or undermining mimetic truth: when lines assign a new reality to surface – curling the edges of the field, for example – the fiction of an image may be betrayed. It is particularly at the edges that Piranesi's fictive worlds flaunt their fiction, dissipating and dissolving into the reality of the paper on which they are printed – confessing to a truth known in the open form of the sketch and regularized in the floating image of the vignette. Piranesi's *grotteschi* are conceived as monumental vignettes, images unsecured by attachment to an enclosing border, whether edge of field or frame, and thereby mocking conventional window notions of pictorial representation. Rather, they tend to consolidate themselves internally; out of their own pictorial substance they create self-enclosed and self-enclosing worlds.[7]

All this, of course, is accomplished with requisite artifice and self-consciousness. Thus, for example, the tomb of Nero rises from a base built upon serpentine ener-

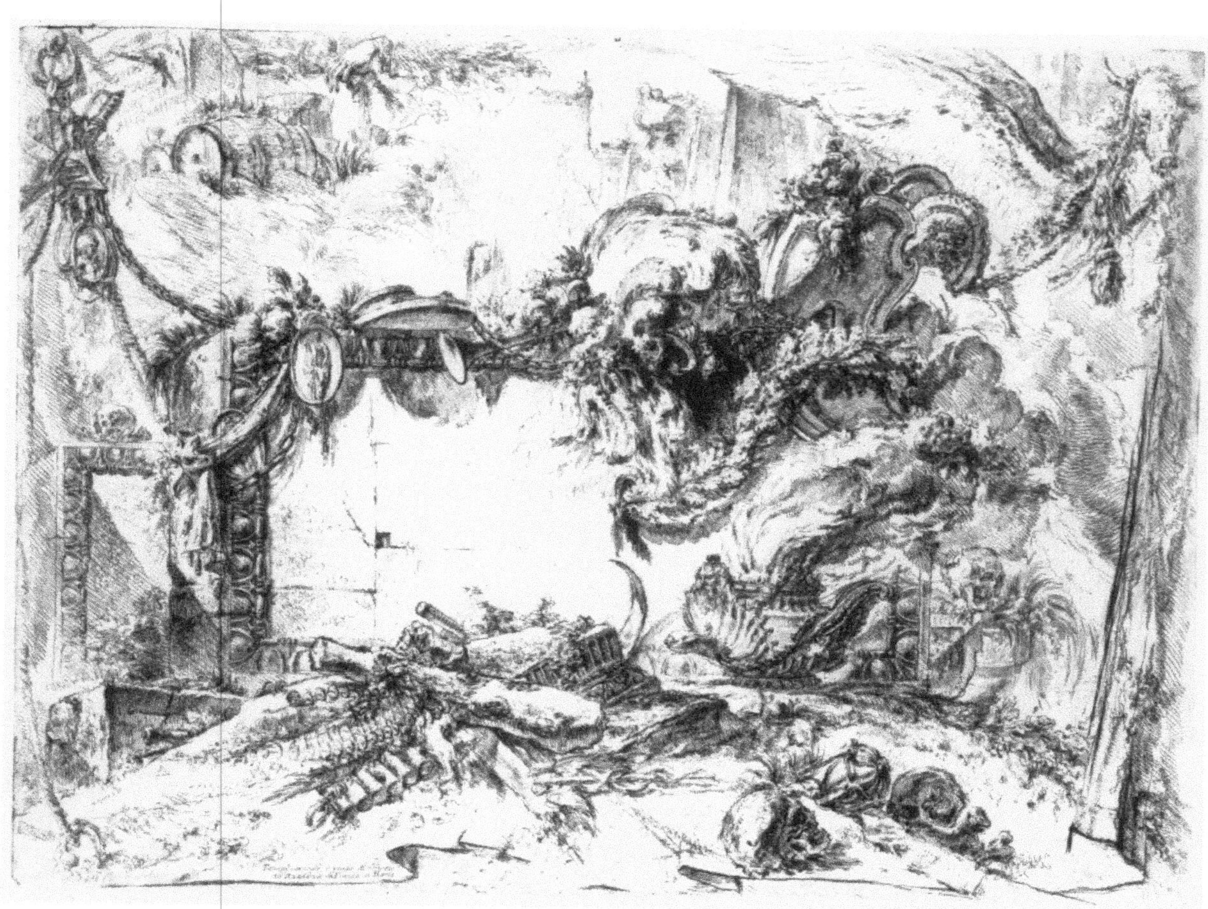

272. Giovanni Battista Piranesi, from the *Grotteschi* ("The Monumental Tablet") (1747–49). Etching, engraving, drypoint, scratching, 39 × 53.5 cm. National Gallery of Art, Washington. Ailsa Mellon Bruce Fund.

gies ultimately generated by the artist's palette in the lower right corner (Figs. 271, 273). From the sweep of its curving contours a linear continuity of rococo impulses is maintained by a sequence of feathered flourishes, floriated forms, decorative arabesques, animated, most determinedly, by the slithering bodies of serpents – a zoological reification of the line of beauty that more fully realizes the serpentine implications of Hogarth's frontispiece (Fig. 259).[8]

Although each of the *grotteschi* depends upon such sinuous vectoring for its basic compositional structure, one line in particular stands out for its refusal to participate in that notional world of fantasized space. At the left of the plate featuring a triumphal arch in the background (Figs. 270, 274), a sculpted lion frames the scene, sphinxlike, a guardian overlooking the ruins of time, yet separated from them by the swaying palm. The noble profile of this stone creature confirms its elevated status, allowing it to rise above the archaeological tumult it surveys. Over the shoulder of this lion is inscribed a spiral. This apparently perfect curl sits flat upon the surface of the paper; undistorted, it submits to no foreshortening, conforms in no way to the surface anatomy of the beast behind it. Thus dissociated from the illusion of representation, it declares itself an independent linear construct, abstract except for the organic resonance of its own form.

Actually, this spiral is not quite pure line, not quite totally independent. It is in fact a complex rendering of line. Only a few segments of pure arc are delineated; rather deeply bitten (possibly incised), these curves are modified and connected by sequences of scribble. The lateral energies of these scrawled patterns run counter to the geometric contours of the arcs; their directional impulse threatens to break radially or tangentially into the surrounding field, so much of which is itself defined by such scribbled patterns on both large and small scale. Like spreading shadow, these suggestive scribbles extend the spiral into pictorial space, embedding its pure flat form in the graphic texture of the etching, but not quite in the illusion of its image. As surely as any other self-conscious motif – the generating palette, for example, or the curling edge – the spiral declares the fiction of the image by recalling the eye to surface reality.

But the spiral is hardly a neutral mark upon a surface, a mute accident. This trace of fundamental organic growth carries profound cultural associations, well beyond any allusion to the headgear of Rome's Egyptian lions. A crucial link between art and nature, it evokes both Ionic volute and marine nautilus. Piranesi himself, some years later in his publication on the *Diverse maniere d'adornare i cammini* (1769), argued for the shell as the inspiration of the Ionic capital – as against the anthropomorphic etiology of Vitruvius, which saw it as an attempt to imitate the curls of the hair of matrons (pp. 19–20).[9] Earlier in the same text Piranesi associated the Ionic volute with the decorative potential of the ram's head: "by reason of the disposition which the horns of this animal have to form volutes" (p. 12). (In a different but not altogether unrelated mood, as historical justification of his line of grace, Hogarth too had invoked the twisted horn – along with the "twisted serpent, twisted cornucopia, or some symbol winding in this manner" – in the representations of Egyptian, Greek, and Roman deities [*Analysis of Beauty*, p. 17] [cf. Fig. 263].)

Defending the inventive and mimetic achievements of the Egyptians and arguing for the decorum of their adaptation of natural form to the tectonic aesthetic of architecture, Piranesi makes a further comparison that may throw some retrospective light upon the spiral in his early *grottesco.* "I have in view," he writes,

> among other works of theirs, the two Lions or Leopards which serve to adorn the fountain of the Felician aqueduct in Rome, together with two others studiously copied, both as to action and design from nature, that is worked after the Grecian manner. What majesty in the Egyptian ones, what gravity and wisdom! what union, and modification of parts! how artfully are those parts set of which are agreeable to architecture, while those are suppressed, which are not advantageous to it! Those other lions on the contrary, which are exactly copied from nature, and to which the artist capriciously gave what attitude he pleased, what have they to do there? they only serve to diminish the great effect which the Egyptian ones give to the architecture of that fountain; which however is not one of the most elegant. (p. 14)

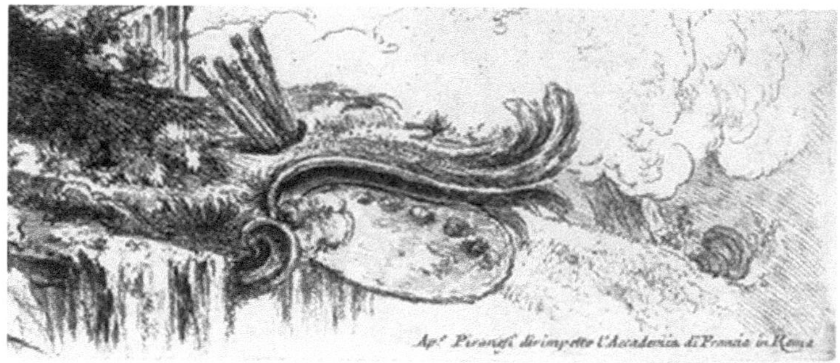

273. Giovanni Battista Piranesi, from the *Grotteschi* ("The Tomb of Nero"), detail of Fig. 271.

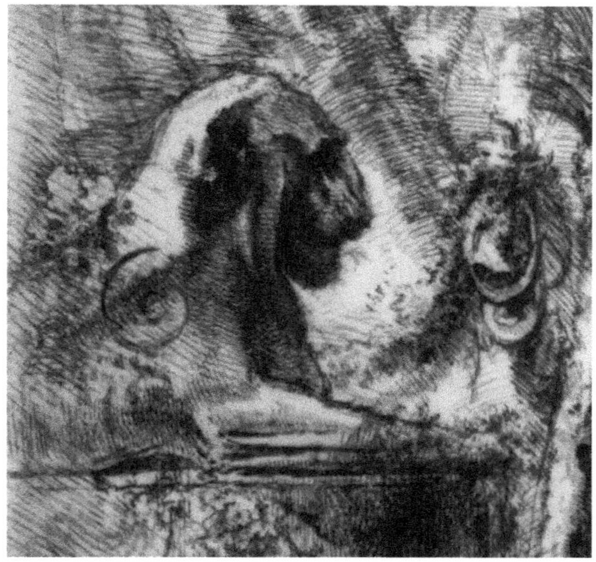

274. Giovanni Battista Piranesi, from the *Grotteschi* ("The Triumphal Arch"), detail of Fig. 270.

More than twenty years before so fully articulating his Egyptophilia, Piranesi rendered a reclining lion in sphinxlike manner, assigning to this adamantine beast the kind of high, supranatural formality he was to admire and defend in his *Diverse maniere*. And to the glyptic form of this lion the suspended spiral adds a special ornament, a mathematical hieroglyph – signaling, *avant la lettre*, that "perfect knowledge of all that is good and beautiful in nature." Adducing the later words of Piranesi the mature archaeologist to explicate an early *capriccio*, however, only underscores a fundamental aspect of his art and thought: namely, that his early explorations of antiquity were essentially imaginative, fantasies of mind and hand. Piranesi's spiral is less the programmatic declaration of a student of natural philosophy than it is the whim of a graphic artist.

Whether deliberately planned or creatively adapted – possibly inspired by the contour of the headgear gracing the Egyptian lions of Rome – the spiral itself nonetheless stands as commentary on the linear principles that govern Piranesi's compositions; it offers an epitome of "what there is in nature which could furnish . . . such a variety of ideas and forms," as he later wrote of shells (p. 18). And shells, with their expansive undulation of surface and contour, do, of course, play a central

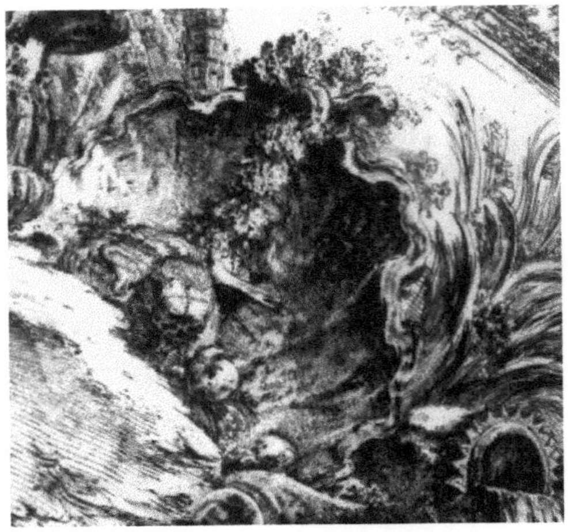

275. Giovanni Battista Piranesi, from the *Grotteschi* ("The Skeletons"), detail of Fig. 269.

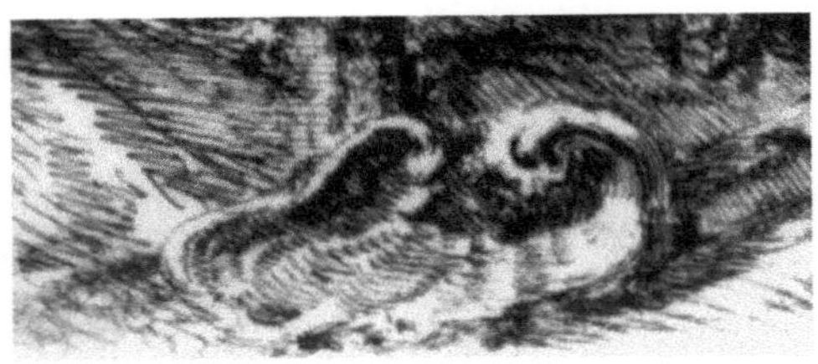

276. Giovanni Battista Piranesi, from the *Grotteschi* ("The Triumphal Arch"), detail of Fig. 270.

role in the compositional form of the *grotteschi* – whether as the monumental mollusk yielding its cranial pearl (Figs. 269, 275) or as the more modest rocaille with its inverted Ionic volutes (Figs. 270, 276).

The spiral is a two-dimensional form, adhering to the surface. To function pictorially, that is, as an integral part of a picture, it must be extended into space; it must be transformed helically into a "serpentine line." And yet that serpent's coil is an illusion; the line remains a mark on a flat surface, the trace of the draftsman's pen on the paper – or etching needle on the grounded plate. Here, we may recall Hogarth's comment on his waving line of beauty, which, "being composed of two curves contrasted, becomes still more ornamental and pleasing, insomuch that the hand takes a lively movement in making it with pen or pencil." The "lively movement" of the hand returns us to the making of the image, to the act of drawing.

Despite Hogarth's genuine appreciation of the drawn line as a negotiation of the world, of objects in space, his analysis remains somewhat divorced from the actual form of his art – his "two explanatory Prints Serious and Comical" notwithstanding. The young Piranesi, however, not yet the learned academician and archaeologist, analyzes line directly in his art, by graphic demonstration. If in the *grottesco* the spiral floats as epitome of a principle of swelling linear energy, it soon after asserts itself with greater controlling force in the *Carceri*, the suite of "invenzioni capricciose" first issued about 1749–50 (Fig. 277).[10]

Even more insistently than the *grotteschi*, the *Carceri* have challenged interpretation. Evidently related to the traditions of architectural fantasy, they recall in particular the scenographic conventions of the theater – the prison scene was a stan-

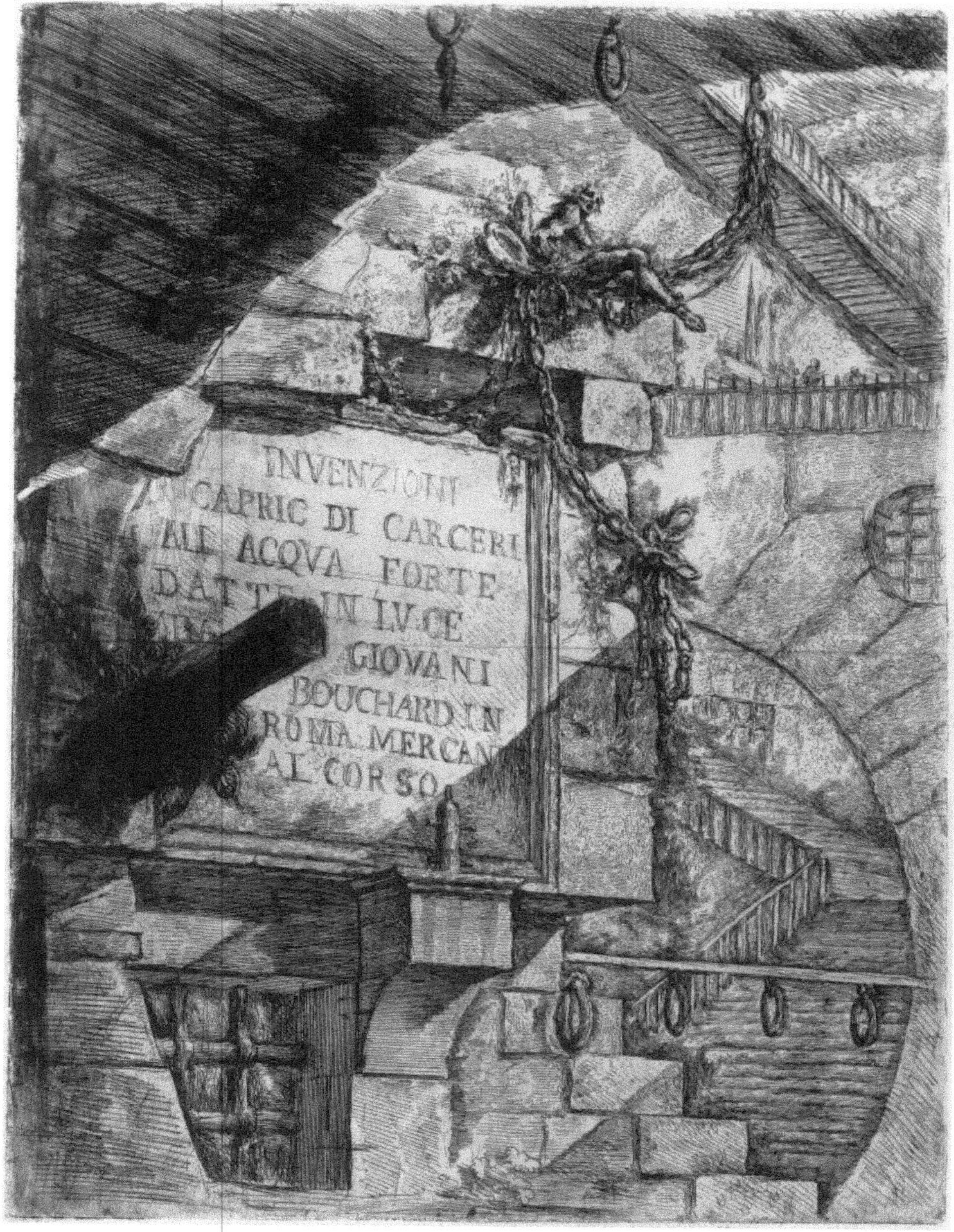

277. Giovanni Battista Piranesi, *Carceri*, title plate (second state) to first edition (1749–50), third issue (ca. 1758–60). Etching, engraving, sulphur tint or open bite, ink dabbing, 55.3 × 41.9 cm. Avery Architectural and Fine Arts Library, Columbia University, New York.

dard element in Italian Baroque opera – and are often compared with the publications of the Bibiena family. These images of monumental masonry vaults, heavy piers, and catwalks, bars and chains, ominous instruments, all dwarfing the human inhabitants, acquire a cumulative power through their presentation *en suite*, and they seem to require readings of commensurable gravity.

Without ignoring or denying that hermeneutic invitation, I propose to shift the focus of critical attention from "content" back to "form." The very title Piranesi

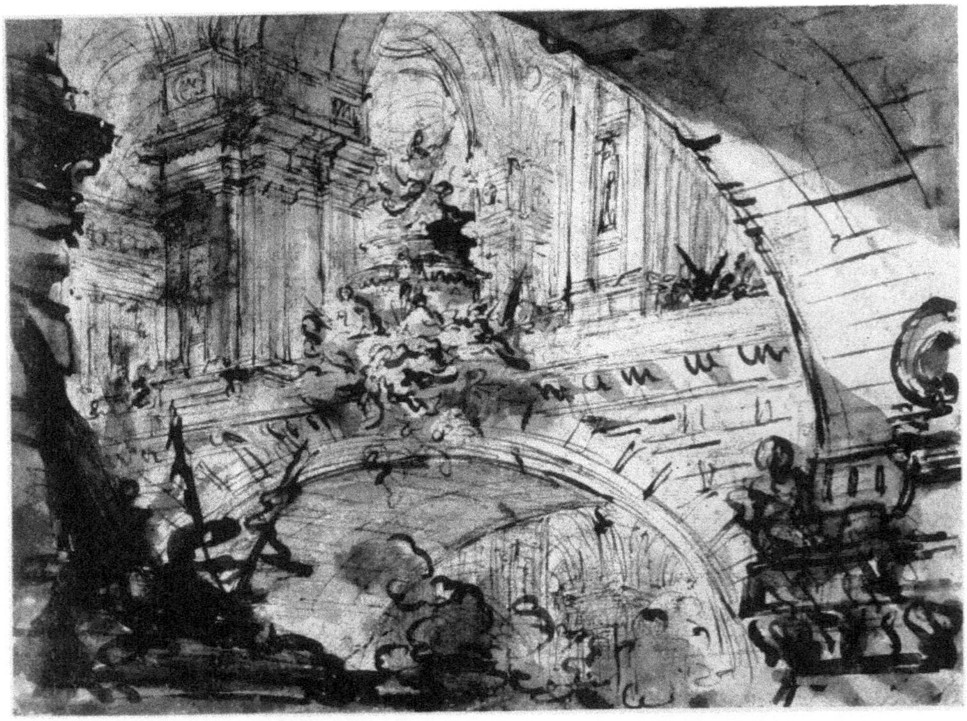

278. Giovanni Battista Piranesi, *Palatial Interior* (ca. 1748–49). Pen and brown ink, brown wash, over red chalk, 16.3 × 22.5 cm. British Museum, London (1908-6-16-20).

chose for the first edition alerts us to the primary demands of genre: "Invenzioni capric[ciose] di Carceri all'acqua forte" (capricious inventions of prisons in etching). The modal declaration is clear. As *capricci,* these images claim hermeneutic privilege, freedom from rules and laws – of perspective, of verisimilitude, of history. They present themselves as variations on a theme, exercises in invention but also in drawing (*disegno,* in the full Renaissance sense). The *Carceri* are, in the first instance, *dimostrazioni dell'arte,* demonstrations of the art of their maker – which includes, along with his scenographic imagination, his technical skill in drawing and in etching, his mastery of line.

Although there are a certain number of drawings that apparently served as preliminary to the project (Fig. 278), we have the sense that much of the invention took place more directly on the plate, in the course of the needlework on the grounded copper.[11] This was also true of the preceding graphic fantasies, the *grotteschi,* where the drawing needle, creating sequences of serpentine forms, finally dissipates its own momentum in the scribbles that extend its energies out into the space of the surrounding paper. The *Carceri,* however, are not monumental vignettes; their compositions do not float within an unbounded field but rather extend to secure themselves at the very limits of the plate, where they are quite deliberately enclosed by insistent framing lines or scribbles. Linear energy is maintained throughout, but there are variations. There are differences between the slower execution of the deliberately studied patterns that create the texture of particularized surfaces – of stone or moss – and the broader, more rapid sweep of the needle covering larger expanses, especially toward the edges of the field.

Piranesi's etching technique records the motions of his drawing hand, and it is precisely in those motions that we sense the inventive impulse behind many of his compositions, most especially in the title plate (Fig. 277). With its complex spatial ambiguities, surface ambivalencies, and scalar tensions, the title plate effectively introduces the ground theme and the game rules of variation that govern the series, for although the *capriccio* may mock the rules of the academy it necessarily substitutes rules of its own, however improvised. Very likely the last of the fourteen plates to be executed, the title plate in effect distills and epitomizes the design principles of the series, rehearsing them with a clarity possible only at the conclusion of the cumulative enterprise.

At the outset of his *Carceri*, then, Piranesi announces one dynamic structural motif that will remain crucial to the subsequent inventions: the spiral, now on a truly monumental scale (Fig. 279). Opening to fill the entire field, this form controls the spatial energies of the composition, initially by establishing the shadowed

279. Giovanni Battista Piranesi, *Carceri*, title plate to first edition (with diagrammatic overlay).

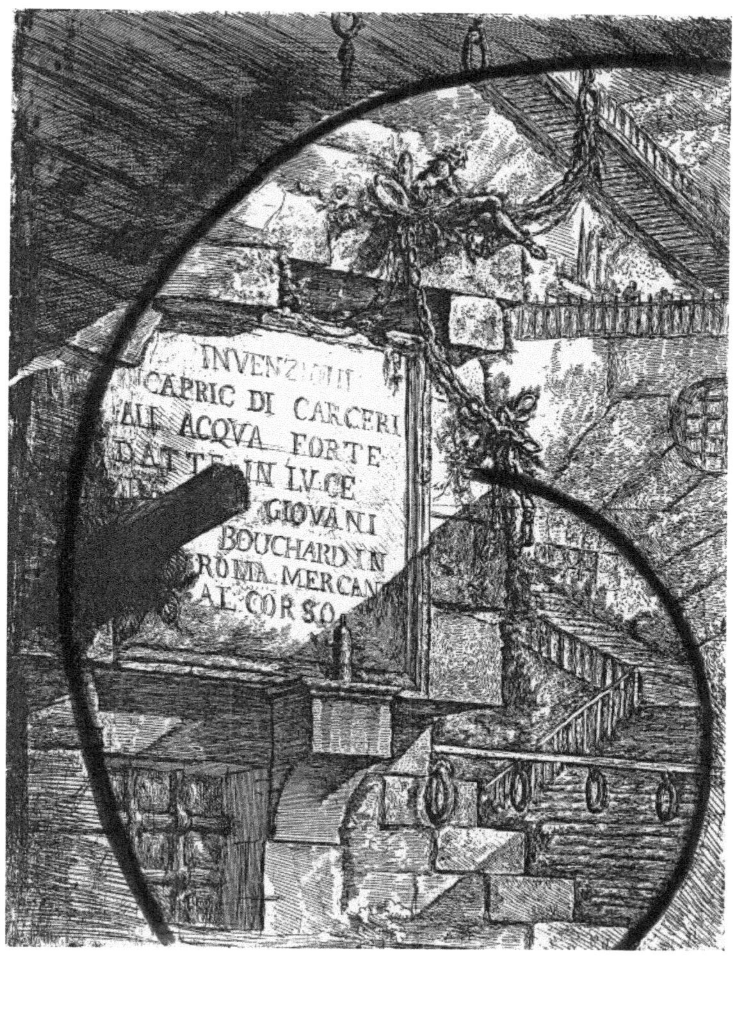

proscenium arch that frames the scene beyond. Winding centripetally to focus on the central core, this spiral implies its own spatial intrusion. Entering from the repoussoir of the proscenium shadows at top, its circling fragment pretends to follow the flight of the steps behind; and yet, playing its flat masonry against that flight, insisting on the unforeshortened purity of its own curve, this encircling line finally denies access to that background space. The cast of arbitrary shadow, flattening three-dimensional forms and collapsing distant planes, further frustrates perspective impulse. And the parallel thrust of foreshortened timber confirms the pictorial game being played, in which spatial contradiction finds resolution only at the pictorial surface. The composition itself seems to instruct us in the process of its own invention, generated by the spiraling, imagining hand of the artist sweeping broadly across the surface, laying out the basic controlling structure. The resulting large curving articulation of the field was then further refined and complicated by straight architectonic lines.[12]

In a more dynamic and searching way, but also less commandingly, these same designing motions – circling movement leading to spiraling form, patterns of shadow imposing linear continuities upon spatially differentiated surfaces – create the composition of the *Carcere* with a drawbridge (Fig. 280). Within the larger curvilinear structures of the composition smaller curves punctuate the field – rings, arcs, oculi, pulley – forms at once derivative and generative of those larger defining energies.

In the *Carcere* with a round tower that fundamental operation has been more consistently spatialized, as a monumental stairway, its curving flight postponed to the middle ground, extends the spiral backward and upward (Fig. 281). Yet its path too is subject to the ambivalence of surface. The heavy rusticated pier at the left and the great swing of rope interrupt the spatial progress of the stairway, reinforced by the cast shadow of the tower and the diagonal hatching of the pier; together, these elements conspire to suggest instead an alternative continuity: not back behind the round tower but rather directly up along the left margin of the field, an imagined path hidden from view by the pier. Such great curves tend to govern many of Piranesi's designs, whether as arches (Fig. 282), stairways, or sweeps of rope or chain – or, inverted and abstracted, as the inexplicable giant wheel (Fig. 283). It is the swing of the etching needle that seems to have determined form, a draftsman's motion in which Piranesi evidently recognized an affinity with the spiraling moves of natural generation – at least the ornamental volute on the arch in one plate seems acknowledgment of that affinity (Fig. 284), like the spiral on the lion of the *Grottesco* (Figs. 270, 274).

The *Carceri* of the first edition are informed by the energy of the drawing hand. Freely executed, they bear the character of monumental sketches, and they claim the privileges of that category: an openness and suggestiveness of form, a sweeping line that is at once exploratory and secure in its own trajectory, an indulgence of the scribble, of the shifting patterns of smaller motions, as surrogate for the

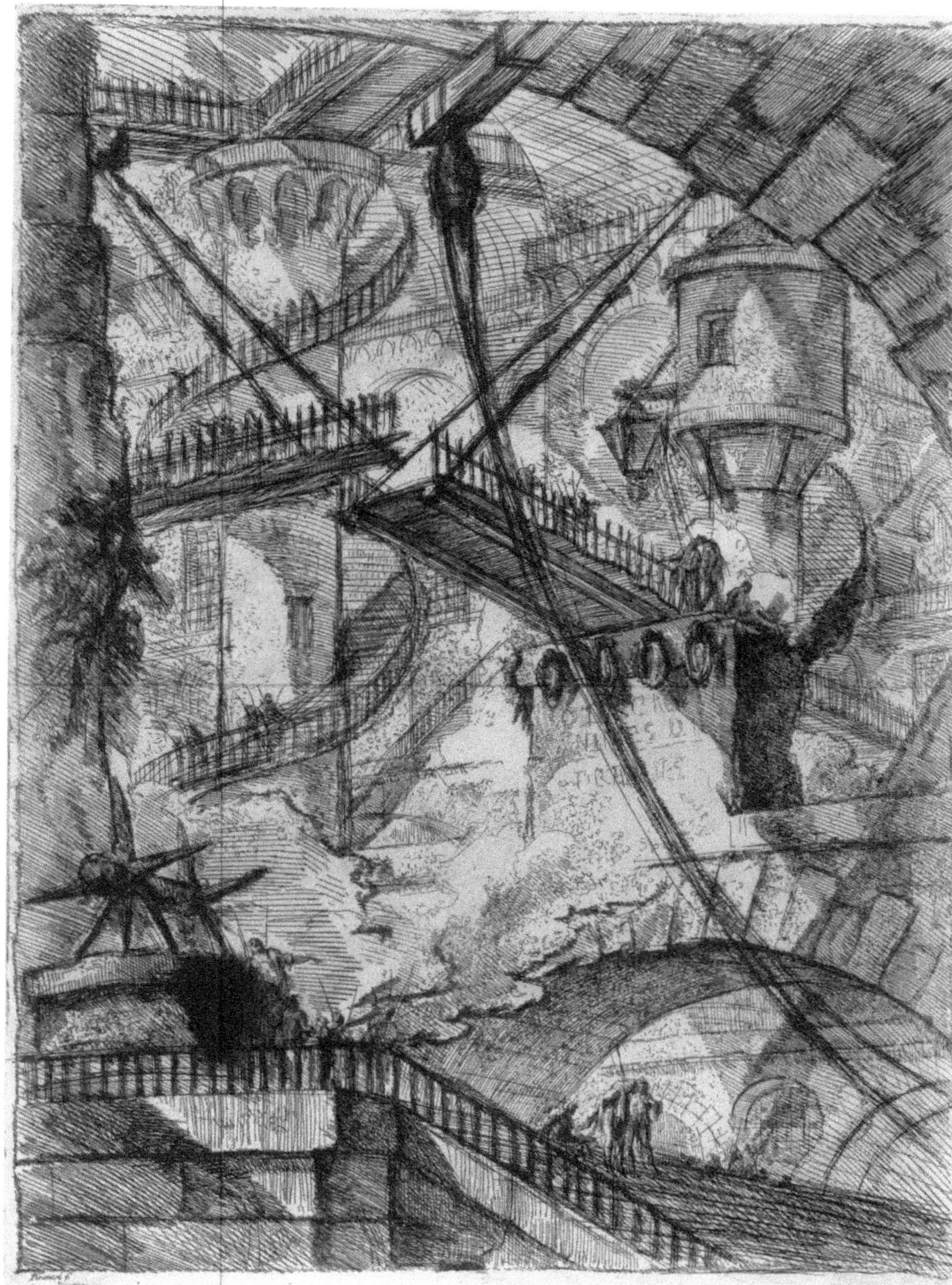

280. Giovanni Battista Piranesi, from the *Carceri* ("The Drawbridge," first state), first edition (1749–50), third issue (ca. 1758–60). Etching, engraving, scratching, ink dabbing, 56.1 × 41.5 cm. Avery Architectural and Fine Arts Library, Columbia University, New York.

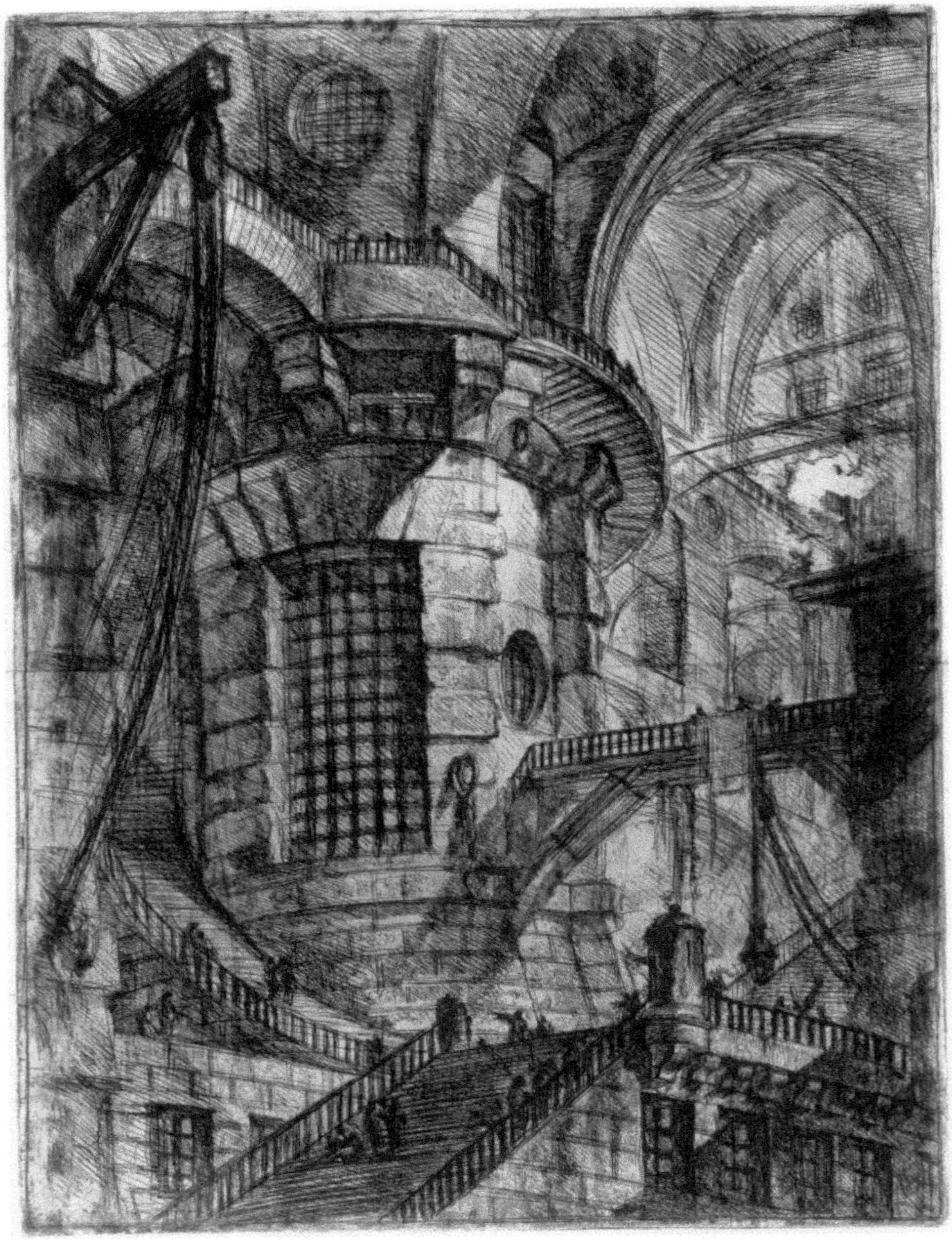

281. Giovanni Battista Piranesi, from the *Carceri* ("The Round Tower," first state), first edition (1749–50), third issue (ca. 1758–60). Etching, engraving, sulphur tint or open bite, burnishing, 55.6 × 41.8 cm. Avery Architectural and Fine Arts Library, Columbia University, New York.

mimetic information of representation. Comparing his etchings to those of Rembrandt, Piranesi's French biographer, J. G. Legrand, declared they were "like original drawings, in which the feeling of the artist is conveyed immediately on the copper plate."[13] And Piranesi himself, when asked later why he did not make more finished preparatory drawings, responded that he did not want his etchings to be

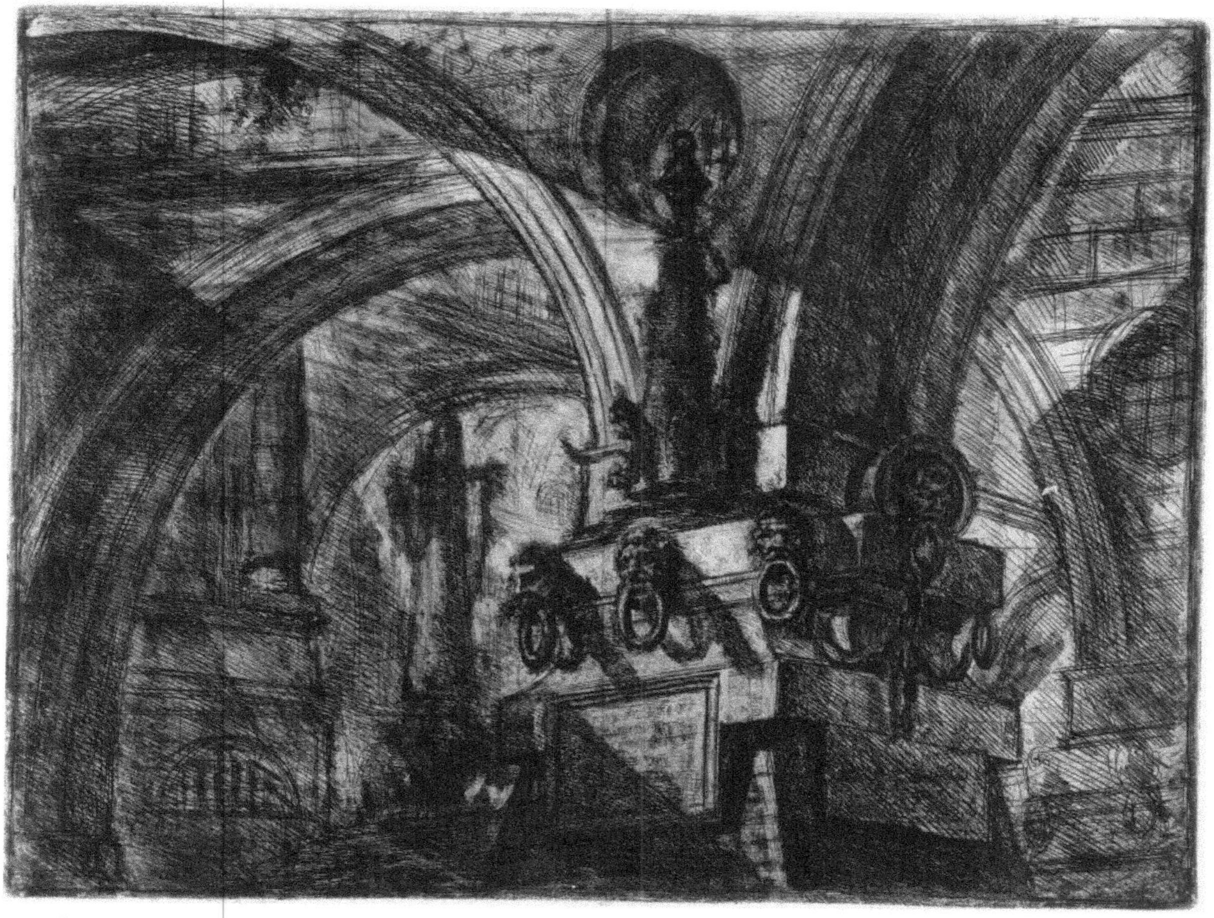

282. Giovanni Battista Piranesi, from the *Carceri* ("The Pier with a Lamp," first state), first edition (1749–50), third issue (ca. 1758–60). Etching, engraving, scratching, sulphur tint or open bite, burnishing, 41.5 × 55.8 cm. Avery Architectural and Fine Arts Library, Columbia University, New York.

mere copies: "when I create the effect on the copper, I make of it an original."[14] Generated by the drawing hand, Piranesi's *Carceri,* in their first edition, testify to the operations of the hand as an agent of invention.

Such a reading of these plates seems confirmed by the transformations they subsequently underwent when Piranesi prepared a second edition, first issued in 1761. Now he is his own publisher and declares himself Venetian architect (Fig. 285). Significantly, he changed the title of the series. No longer called *capricci,* "invenzioni capricciose," they are now primarily prisons: *Carceri d'invenzione.* The lettering of the title, originally only roughly sketched in, is chiseled with a new lapidary crispness and monumentality. The images have been subjected to new weight and deepening chiaroscuro, rendering them more ominous. They have also been subjected (or resubjected) to the ostensible regimen of perspective, as vaulted spaces are traversed by ruled lines, distances linked by beam and truss – although space has thereby become only more ambiguous (Figs. 286, 287). And, with the addition of

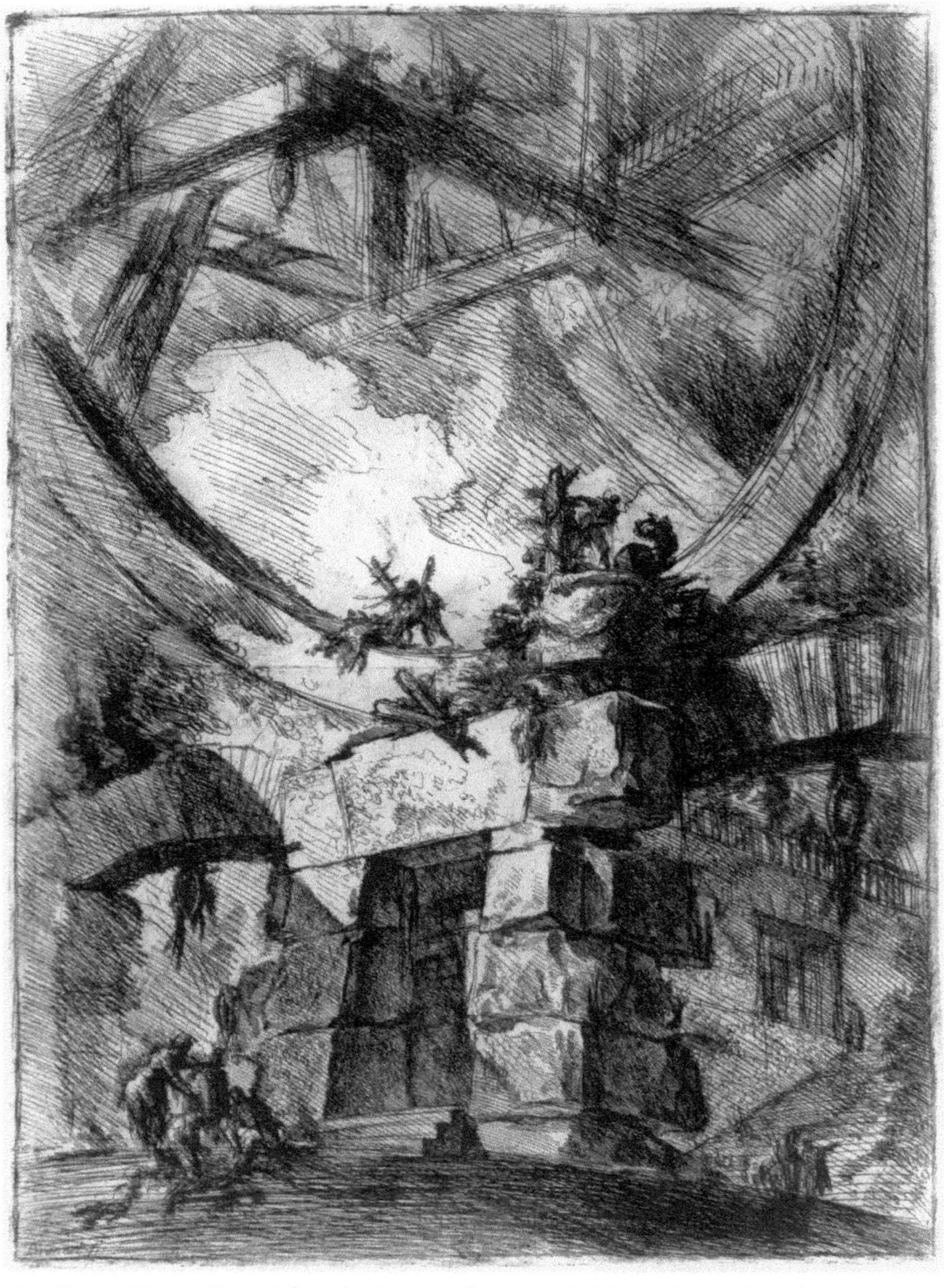

283. Giovanni Battista Piranesi, from the *Carceri* ("The Giant Wheel," second state), first edition (1749–50), third issue (ca. 1758–60). Etching, engraving, 56.1 × 41.1 cm. Avery Architectural and Fine Arts Library, Columbia University, New York.

two new plates evoking events of Roman antiquity, the *Carceri* seem destined to acknowledge the laws of history as well.[15] Now they do indeed seem to insist upon more serious, less capricious, interpretation. The compositions have become denser, weightier. Formally, the governing curves have been controlled (at least apparently)

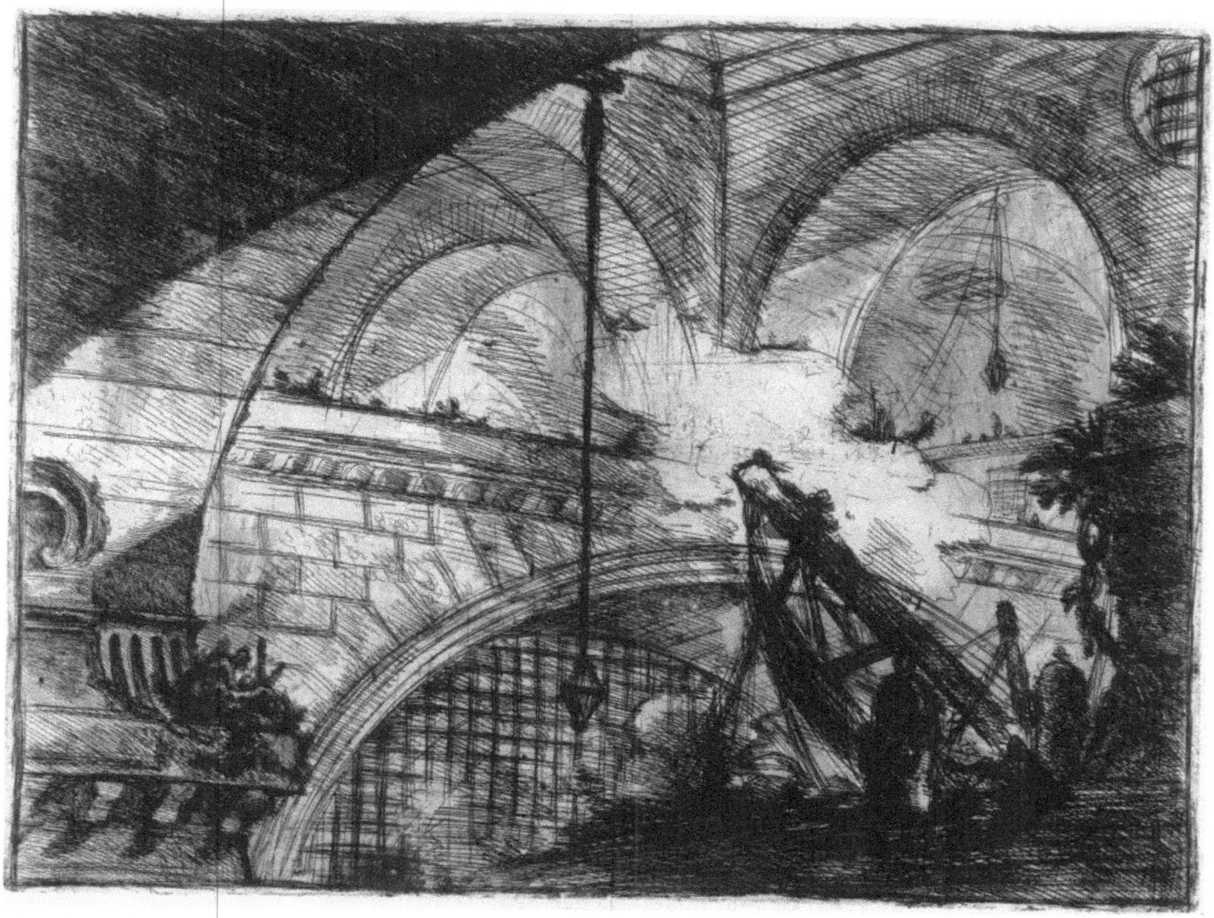

284. Giovanni Battista Piranesi, from the *Carceri* ("The Arch with a Shell Ornament," second state), first edition (1749–50), third issue (ca. 1758–60). Etching, engraving, scratching, sulphur tint or open bite, drypoint, 40.8 × 55.7 cm. Avery Architectural and Fine Arts Library, Columbia University, New York.

by tectonic orthogonals; the texture of the flowing lines of the sketch has been thickened, their movement slowed, their character more deliberately varied, as mimetic responsibility becomes more insistent. The inventing impulses of the hand have been disciplined.

In their second edition, the *Carceri* carry different meaning – or meanings. A decade after their initial conception, the artist evidently reconsidered his work and saw new possiblities. It was indeed the function of the sketch – a form open, unfinished, and suggestive – to challenge its maker to see new prospects in its linear chaos. Again, the biographer Legrand proves sensitive to this creative situation, in which from the graphic chaos of his rapid sketches the artist arrived at fully satisfying form working on the plate. Piranesi himself responded to the objection to his rough preparation that the drawing was not on the paper but rather entirely in his head, waiting to be realized on the plate.[16] We may recall how Leonardo, who first coined the word *schizzo,* viewed the *componimento inculto,* as a spur to further invention, and how

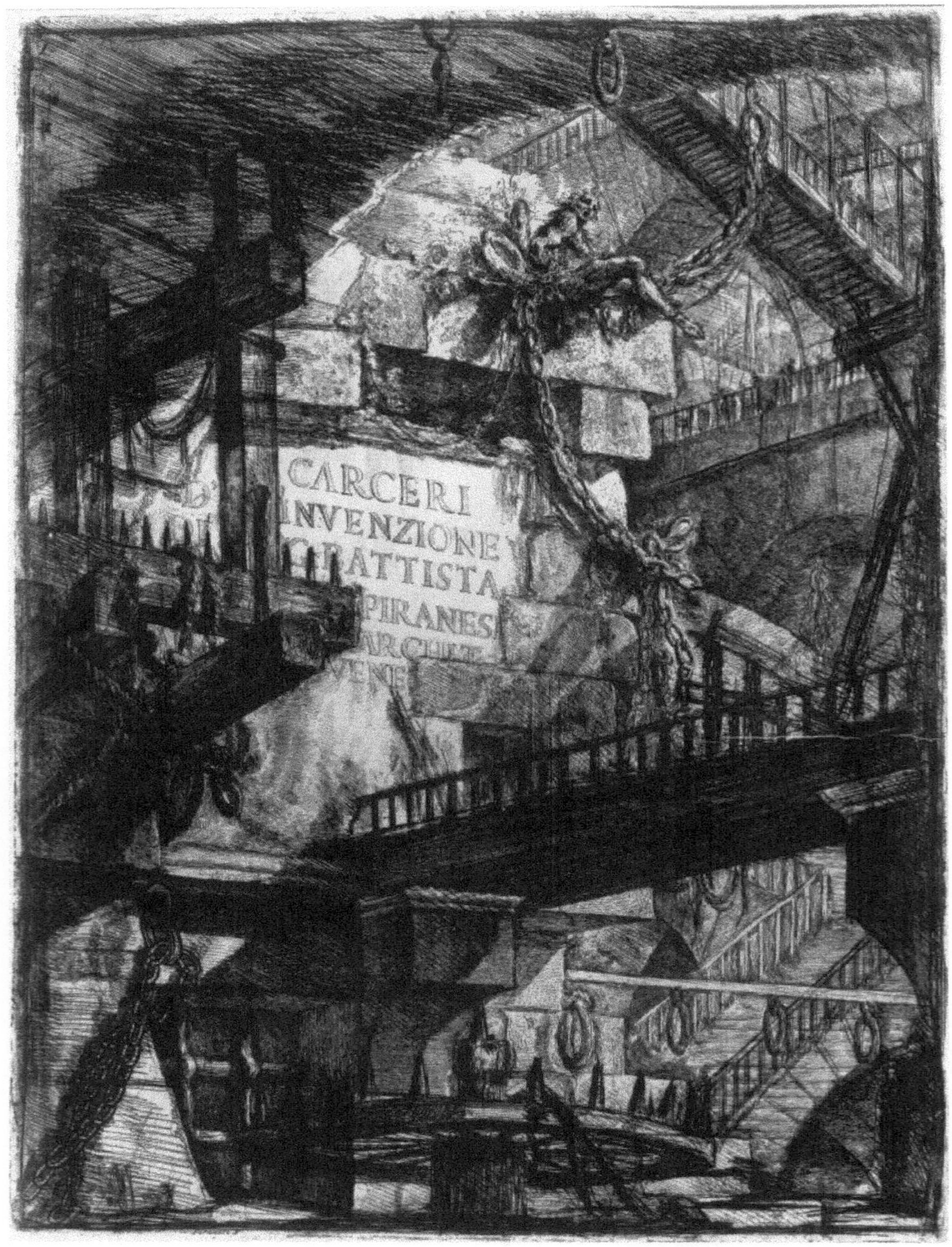

285. Giovanni Battista Piranesi, *Carceri*, title plate (sixth state) to second edition (1761), second issue (ca. 1765). Etching, engraving, sulphur tint or open bite, 55.3 × 41.9 cm. Avery Architectural and Fine Arts Library, Columbia University, New York.

he urged the artist to study the chaotic patterns of ashes, of clouds, of mud, of stained walls, to discover in those *macchie* new pictorial ideas. "Col sporcar si trova" – which we might translate, loosely, as "messing about, one finds."

The motto, however, is not Leonardo's; it is Piranesi's. In 1764 he published an album of etchings after drawings by Guercino and others – mostly the work of other printmakers (Fig. 288). The conceitful frontispiece – in which the severed

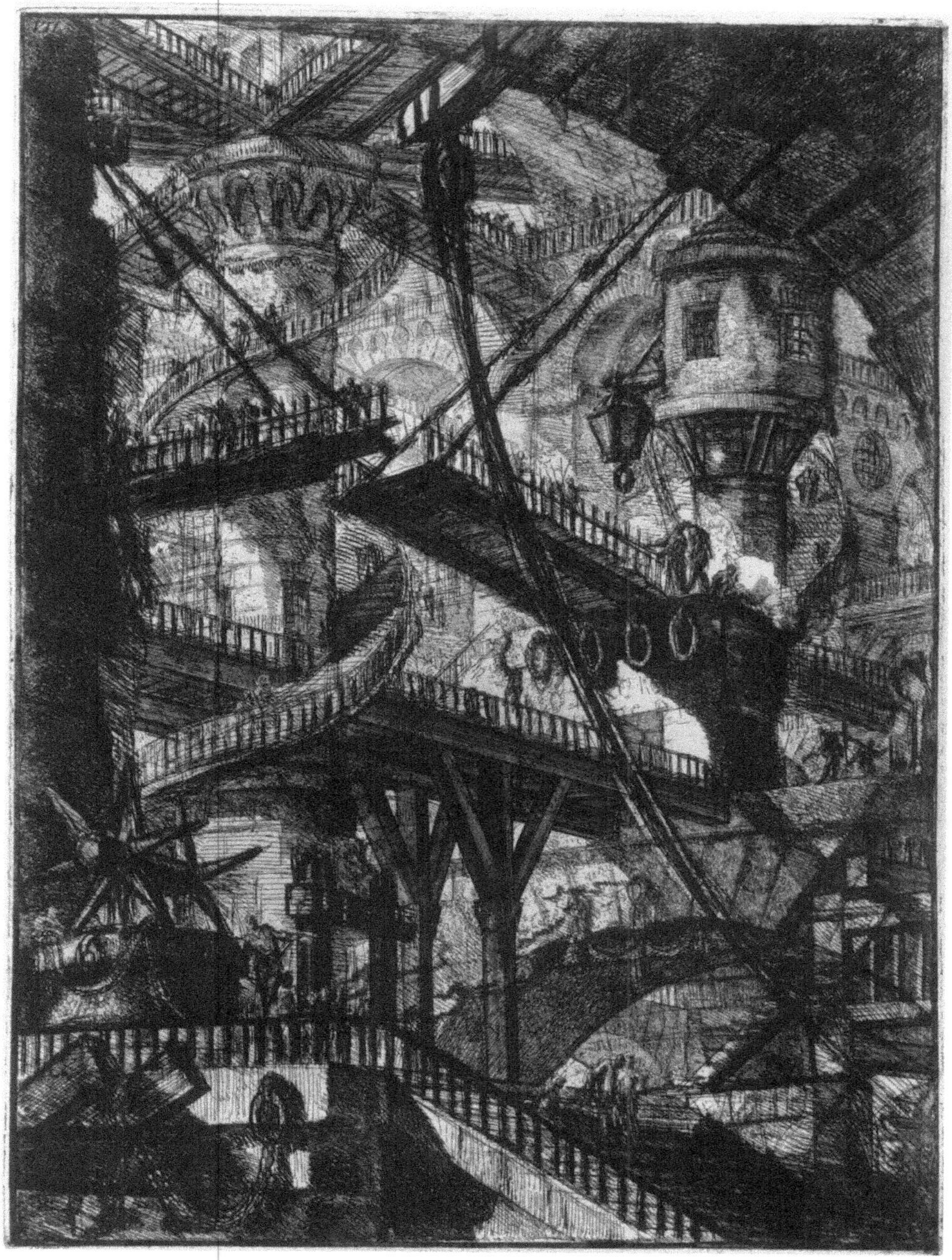

286. Giovanni Battista Piranesi, from the *Carceri* ("The Drawbridge," fourth state), second edition (1761), third issue (ca. 1770). Etching, engraving, scratching, 56.1 × 41.5 cm. Avery Architectural and Fine Arts Library, Columbia University, New York.

head of John the Baptist figures the artist's name – features an animated frame of studio trophies with an heraldic palette at its core, set upon an open drawing book. On that palette – almost a response to Hogarth's self-portrait – Piranesi has inscribed the motto that affirms belief in that Leonardesque aesthetic, in the open form, the *macchia,* as a source of new inventions (Fig. 289).[17]

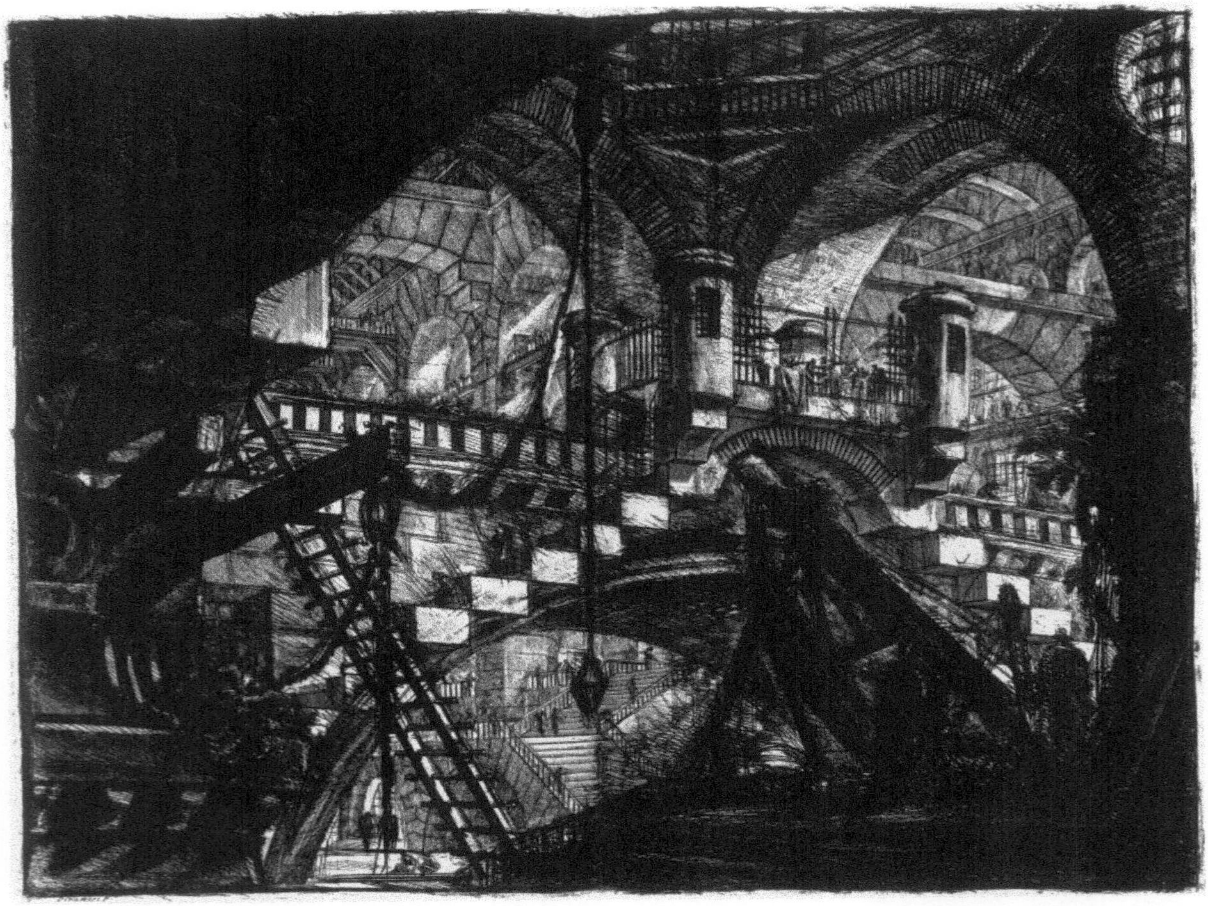

287. Giovanni Battista Piranesi, from the *Carceri* ("The Arch with a Shell Ornament," sixth state), second edition (1761), fourth issue (ca. 1775). Etching, engraving, scratching, sulphur tint or open bite, drypoint, 40.8 × 55.7 cm. Avery Architectural and Fine Arts Library, Columbia University, New York.

In the first edition of the *Carceri,* the "invenzioni capricciose," the capricious principle originated in the operations of the artist as *disegnatore*: here the creative energies of a searching hand in motion determine form, or, in the traditional vocabulary, the hand discovers form in its own tracing. In their second edition, where the new title assigns priority to the prisons of (and as) invention, these images become *capricci* in a rather different, combinatorial sense: here fantasy derives from architectural juxtaposition and contrast and the more sustained creative undermining of the rules of perspective and proportion. A more studied and deliberate technique, while deepening chiaroscuro, yields a more finished rendering, a more detailed and differentiated representation of objects and textures. To force the distinction somewhat, we might say that the principle now involves the operations of the artist as *inventore.* A second category of *capriccio* was, in effect, latent in the images of the first edition, in their "sporco," awaiting discovery and exploitation. That potential was then realized, and the brooding darkness of the second edition produces an effect that calls to mind yet a third category of *capriccio*: the terror provoked by the bizarre and the monstrous – the

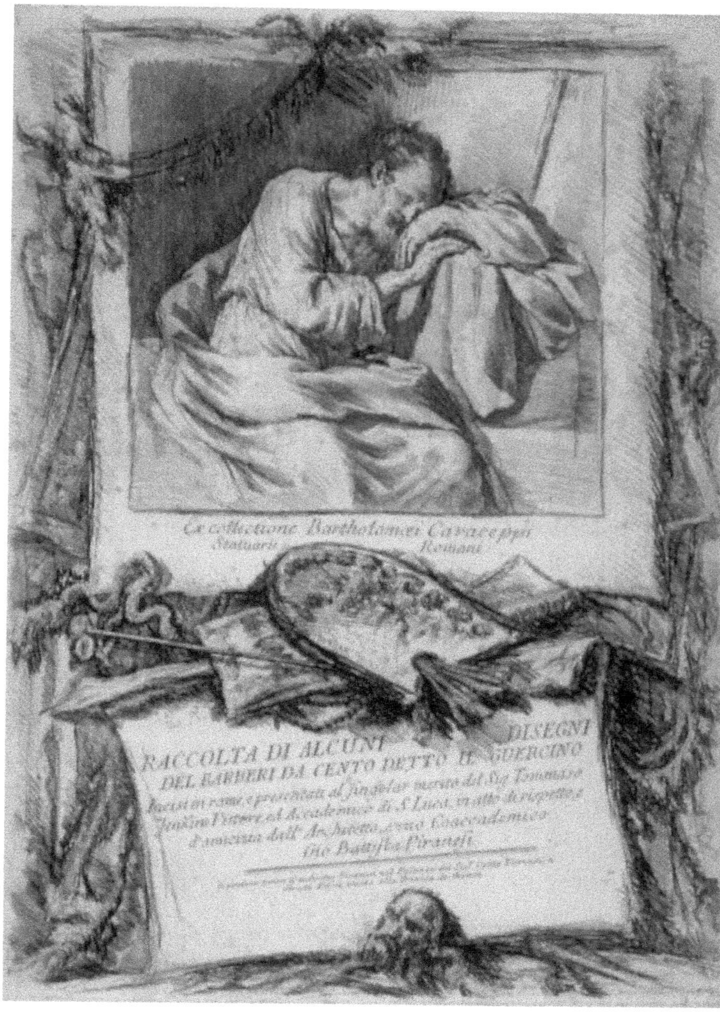

288. Giovanni Battista Piranesi, *Raccolta di alcuni disegni del Barberi da Cento detto il Guercino . . . ,* frontispiece (1764). Etching and engraving, printed in black and reddish-brown ink, 40.8 × 35.4 cm. Avery Architectural and Fine Arts Library, Columbia University, New York.

289. Giovanni Battista Piranesi, *Raccolta di alcuni disegni del Barberi da Cento detto il Guercino . . . ,* frontispiece, detail of Fig. 288.

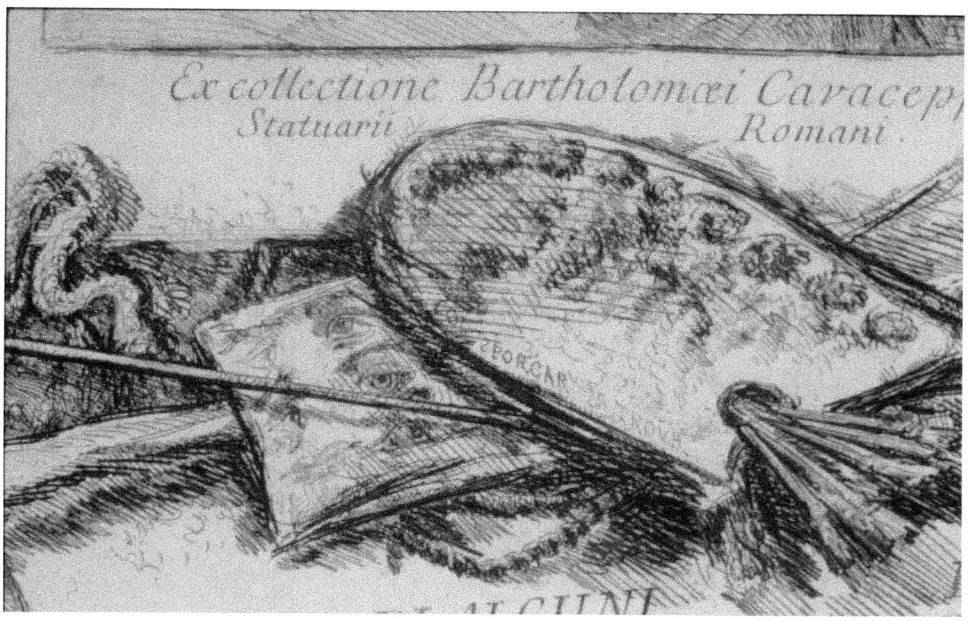

romantic gothic latent in the aesthetic grotesque.[18] It is an effect that anticipates the *Caprichos* of Goya.

3. *Invenzione* to *Capriccio*

"The drawing . . . is entirely in my head": Confirming a continuity in the Renaissance tradition, Piranesi's declaration recalls Cennino Cennini's "molto disegno entro la testa tua." A measure of the inventiveness of the artist was his ability to create, or discover, things never before seen. "Trovare cose non vedute," again recalling the words of Cennini, required both "fantasia" and "operazione di mano."[19] And that combination, of imagination and manual skill, continued to define the fundamentals of creativity. Since the early Renaissance, the concept of *inventio* had been borrowed for the visual arts from classical rhetoric and poetics. From *invenire,* to come upon or to find, the term itself allowed a particular cultural gloss on the language of Cennini.[20] Things never before seen were precisely the objects of invention, products of the imagination, of the artist's *fantasia,* which was defined as "the imaginative power of the soul" in Filippo Baldinucci's *Vocabolario toscano dell'arte del disegno* (1681): "La potenza immaginative dell'anima. Lat. *Phantasia, imaginatio.*" Artists, Baldinucci comments, say "far di fantasìa" or "di capriccio" when, without any model before them they work from their own imagination ("quando, senza esemplo, vanno operando di propria invenzione"), which is quite distinct from depending upon nature ("ricavare o fare dal Naturale"). The verb *fantasticare* means to wander with the imagination, to find or discover, to invent ("Andar vagando coll'immaginazione, per ritrovare, & inventare").[21] The practices of the artists described and prescribed by Cennini nearly three centuries before are here given proper academic expression and pedigree. Without immediate recourse to the external models of nature (although never quite independent of such models), the artist finds images in his own head – as Cennini, and Dürer, had long before acknowledged.

That the vocabulary of the imagination is quite varied is suggested by Baldinucci's entry in its implicit cross-reference to *capriccio:* "Proprio pensiero e invenzione. Quindi fatto a capriccio o di fantasìa, cioè di proprio pensiero e invenzione" (p. 28). Drawing was the natural way to realize such an idea, to empty the head, as it were, of its "molto disegno." "Per isfogare il capriccio" Renaissance artists picked up the pen or chalk and drew in off hours, after meals, keeping the hand in practice, in motion.[22] The graphic energies liberated in the act of drawing, as Leonardo had enthusiastically recognized, led to new inventions. In scribbling and sketching, discovering in the chaos of those very patterns new ideas, the draftsman spurred his own imagination, "for confused things rouse the mind to new inventions." *Col sporcare si trova.*

Drawing offered the most immediate outlet for a head "full of figures." Printmaking, as we have seen, afforded a means of disseminating the fruits of such inventive activity, a means of making public such *dimostrazioni dell'arte.* "Sfogare i suoi capricci" is how Vasari formulated it, writing of Dürer's great graphic enterprise, the suite of Apocalyptic woodcuts. Recognizing the imaginative dimensions of the German master's graphic art ("sua imaginative stravagante"), Vasari noted how many Italian artists looked to that imagery for ideas, profiting from its abundance of fantasy and invention ("dell'abondanze e copie delle belle fantasie e invenzioni").[23] Parmigianino's own graphic activity was a whim, the inspiration of a "cervello capriccioso."[24] His development of etching as a means of replicating the aesthetic of drawing as an art of rapid notation invested printmaking with the technical value of *disegno* as well as the imaginative value of *invenzione.* Through etching, in which the artist works directly on the grounded plate, the very motions of the draftsman's imagining hand were recorded and replicated – albeit in reverse.

Capriccio, in the vocabulary of Renaissance artistic discourse, carried connotations of license, of freedom from the rules of art, from the decorum of imitation – Michelangelo's "errors" in the depiction of the *Last Judgment,* for example, could be condemned as "capricci."[25] By the end of the sixteenth century Cesare Ripa's *Iconologia* figured *Capriccio* as a youth dressed as a jester, his many colors representing his inconstancy, the feathers in his hat the diverse ideas sprouting from the imagination; he holds a bellows in one hand, indicating his readiness to celebrate virtue, and a sharp spur in the other, ready to pierce vice: "Capricciosi are those whose actions follow ideas that differ from the ordinary ideas of others, but who shift from one idea to another of the same kind; and, by way of analogy, ideas in painting, in music, or in other media that appear far from the ordinary are called capricci."[26] And what was generally implicit in usage becomes explicitly codified in subsequent dictionary definitions of capricci, as in Antoine Furetière's *Dictionnaire universel* (1690): "pieces of poetry, music, and painting that succeed more by the force of imagination than by observation of the rules of art and which have no clear appelation" ("pièces de poésie, de musique, et de peinture qui réussissent plutôt par la force du génie que par l'observation des règles de l'art et qui n'ont aucun nom certain").

Precisely because it is not subject to rule, the *capriccio* resists any strict definition; it is in effect an illegitimate genre in search of a proper name. Furetière's first definition addresses the motivating behavior behind the product: "a disordering of the mind" ("un dérèglement d'esprit"). In reference both to product and to behavior, then, *capriccio* means beyond the norm, beyond measure.[27]

The performative and the improvisational define an essential dimension of the *capriccio,* the demonstration of art and its inventive capabilities, a virtuoso display. The term itself was first applied categorically in music, not to a particular form but rather to an attitude, a practice. Signifying no specific technique or structure, it denoted rather "a general disposition toward the exceptional, the whimsical, the fantastic and the apparently arbitrary."[28]

In the early seventeenth century the German music theorist Michael Praetorius defined the keyboard *capriccio* as "a sudden whim" ("phantasia subitanea"): "One takes a subject, but abandons it for another whenever it comes into the mind to do so. One can add, take away, digress, turn and direct the music as one wishes, but while one is not strictly bound by the rules, one ought not go too much out of the mode" (*Syntagma musicum*, 1619). The related word *fantasia* also finds early clarification in reference to music and musical practice: an instrumental composition whose form and invention spring "solely from the fantasy and skill of the author who created it," according to Luis de Milán (*Libro de musica*, 1535).[29] And it is in music that we find the term *capriccio* used regularly as part of the title of sets of pieces: *Diversi capricci* (1603, 1609), *Ricercate, & altre varij capricci* (1615).

In 1617 the term appears on the title page of a series of fifty small etchings published in Florence by Jacques Callot: *Capricci di varie figure . . . in aqua forte.*[30] The subjects of these prints vary from city views to battle scenes, a capricious combination of disparate themes; their primary function was to demonstrate the artist's inventiveness as a designer and his skill as a printmaker – the latter underscored by the final words of the title, declaring the graphic medium. The suite had long been a part of the printmaker's production, originating as a series of saints – such as those produced by Marcantonio, according to Vasari, to serve as models for those "poor painters who are weak in drawing" ("i poveri pittori che non hanno molto disegno") – or of virtues and vices, signs of the zodiac, seasons or months, or playing cards. Vasari characterizes one such set, of costumes of fifty nations engraved by Enea Vico, as something ingenious, beautiful, and fanciful ("cosa d'ingegno e bella e capricciosa").[31] It was in the context of a suite, a set of variations on a theme, that the artist could truly demonstrate his inventive talent. Callot's example was followed, toward the middle of the century, by graphic artists like Stefano della Bella, who issued similar sets of inventions upon popular genre themes – tavern scenes, street musicians, wanderers, soldier and battles – with titles such as *Diversi capricci, Varie capricij militarij, Raccolta di varii cappricii et nove inventionj,* as well as *Receuil de divers griffonnements & preuves deau forte* and *Diverses figures et griffonnemens inventez et gravez par Stef. de la Bella.*[32] *Griffonner* (to scrawl or scribble): Della Bella affirms the creative motions of his etching needle.

About 1656–57, Salvator Rosa produced a series of sixty-two small etchings of various figures – soldiers and assorted male and female figures, nude and clothed, domestic and exotic, posturing alone or in dialogue – *figurine,* as he called them. Although the series is not entitled *capricci,* the figure on the title page (Fig. 290) recalls Ripa's personification, and its dedicatory inscription confirms the underlying aesthetic: as a pledge of special friendship, the artist dedicated these prints of "playful leisure" ("SALVATOR ROSA/ Has Ludentis otij/ CAROLO RVBEO/ Singularis Amicitiae pignus/ D.D.D.").[33] Prints of "playful leisure": the description reads like a working definition of the *capriccio.*

In printmaking, then, the painter found the publishable means to *sfogare i suoi capricci,* to challenge and indulge his imaginative faculties and to broadcast his creative products. The degree to which an educated public responded may be gauged by a proclamation of Louis XIV, issued in 1660: etching and engraving are here defended as liberal arts; above the laws governing *métiers,* they are subject only to the imagination of their authors.[34] Although referring to the graphic arts in a more general sense, the formulation resonates with those values that had long been especially associated with prints and that were epitomized in the term *capriccio.*

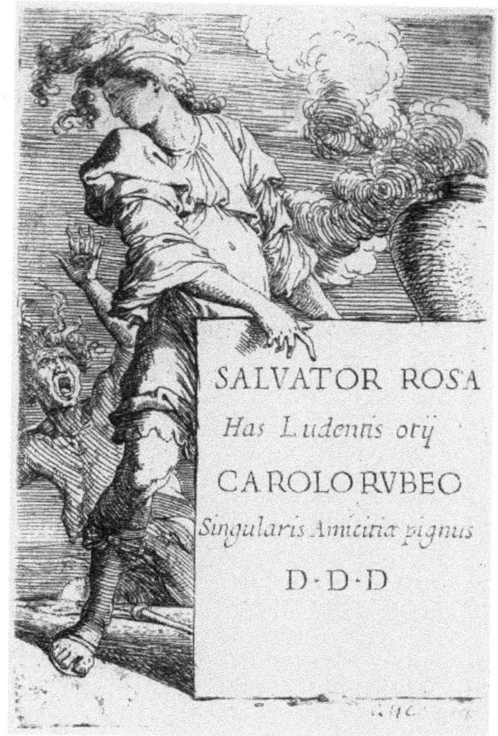

290. Salvator Rosa, *Figurine,* frontispiece (ca. 1656–57). Etching, 14.3 × 9.3 cm. British Museum, London.

The association of inventive genre and graphic medium achieves its grand climax, famously, in 1799 with the publication of *Los Caprichos,* "a collection of prints of capricious subjects, invented and etched by Don Francisco Goya." In his advertisement for the series, after defending the social utility of visual satire in the criticism of human folly, the artist has recourse to traditional notions of *capriccio,* inflecting them to his own, insistently original, ends.

> Since the majority of the objects represented in this work are ideal, it will not be too daring to expect that their defects may be forgiven by the connoisseurs, considering that the author has neither followed the examples of others, nor been able to copy from nature. And if imitating Nature is as difficult as it is admirable when one succeeds in it, then some esteem must be shown toward him, who, departing entirely from Nature, has had to put before the eyes forms and attitudes that have so far have existed only in the human mind, obscured and confused by lack of illustration or excited by uncontrolled passions.[35]

Goya's public offering was of images beyond reason, forms imagined, pulled from the darkness of an irrational mind.

Plate 43 (Fig. 291), conceived initially as authorial frontispiece until it was replaced by the proud self-portrait, declares by image and text that thesis: "El sueño de la razon produce monstruos." The dream or sleep – and the ambivalence is weighted – of reason is imagination itself. Long before, in probing their own experience, Renaissance artists had marveled at the power of forms imagined in the dark. "Why," Leonardo wondered, "does the eye see a thing more clearly in dreams than with the imagination being awake?" And Dürer marveled at his dreams: "Ah! how often in my sleep do I behold great works of art and beautiful things, the like whereof never appear to me awake, but so soon as I awake even the remembrance of them leaves me."[36] Goya's visions seem both to implode upon the sleeping creator and to explode from his fevered brain; creatures of a diabolic Platonic fury of inspiration, these malignant genii, ominous denizens of the night, are at once cause and effect.

Goya's advertisement goes on to appropriate other topoi of invention, invoking poetic license on behalf of the painter. As Cennini had done, he inverts the values of the Horatian caveat regarding grotesque combinations, justifying them as a legitimate extension of Zeuxian eclecticism, and claims them as the true demonstration of invention:

> Painting (like poetry) chooses from the universal what it considers suitable to its own ends: It brings together in a single fantastic personage circumstances and characteristics that nature has divided among many different persons. From such a combination, ingeniously arranged, results the kind of happy imitation for which a good artist deserves the title of inventor rather than that of servile copyist.[37]

Alseep at his drawing table, having dropped his drawing implement, Goya's draftsman suffers from that *cervello capriccioso* that is the source of imagination.[38]

4. Story Lines of the Tiepolo

In 1785 Domenico Tiepolo reissued a suite of ten of his father's etchings with a simple, unillustrated title plate that confirmed their generic identity: *Vari Capricci inventati ed incisi dal celebre Gio. Battista Tiepolo.* More ambitiously, to another suite of prints he added the text to an open tablet on the frontispiece: *Scherzi di Fantasia N. 24 del celebre Sig. Gio. Batta. Tiepolo Veneto Pitore morto in Madrid al serviggio di S:M:C:...* (Fig. 292).[39] Such titles invite a certain mode of response and intepretation, and Domenico, who was involved in the preparation and dissemination of these prints from the beginning, is not likely to have misunderstood his father's intent. Already in 1757 a group of Tiepolo's prints appeared in a price list as "essemplare con Capricci." The document is part of the negotiations between Anton Maria Zanetti the Elder and Pierre-Jean Mariette; among the prints being sent to the French connoisseur are "Capricci dal Tiepoletto il Padre." The following year, Domenico, acknowledging payment, explains that the four *capricci* were printed without the retouching his father had intended and so there are some gaps in the design; Monsieur Mariette is asked "to have the goodness to touch them up with a pen." Zanetti – connoisseur, collector, dealer, publisher, and printmaker himself – was constantly pressing both Tiepolo for more prints, to which Domenico complains that he barely has time to fulfill his commitments in painting ("mi continua, e mi tormenta per stampe, ed io non ho tempo di poter intagliar avendo molte cose da dipinger, non potendo ne meno suplir alli miei impegni").[40]

Not only does this correspondence validate the titles subsequently assigned to the etchings, it also suggests that they were indeed products of "playful leisure," ideas tossed off in moments of freedom from more demanding professional tasks, *per isfogare i capricci. Capriccio, fantasia, scherzo:* in music the terms inevitably call to mind compositional processes as well as products. But if such terms gener-

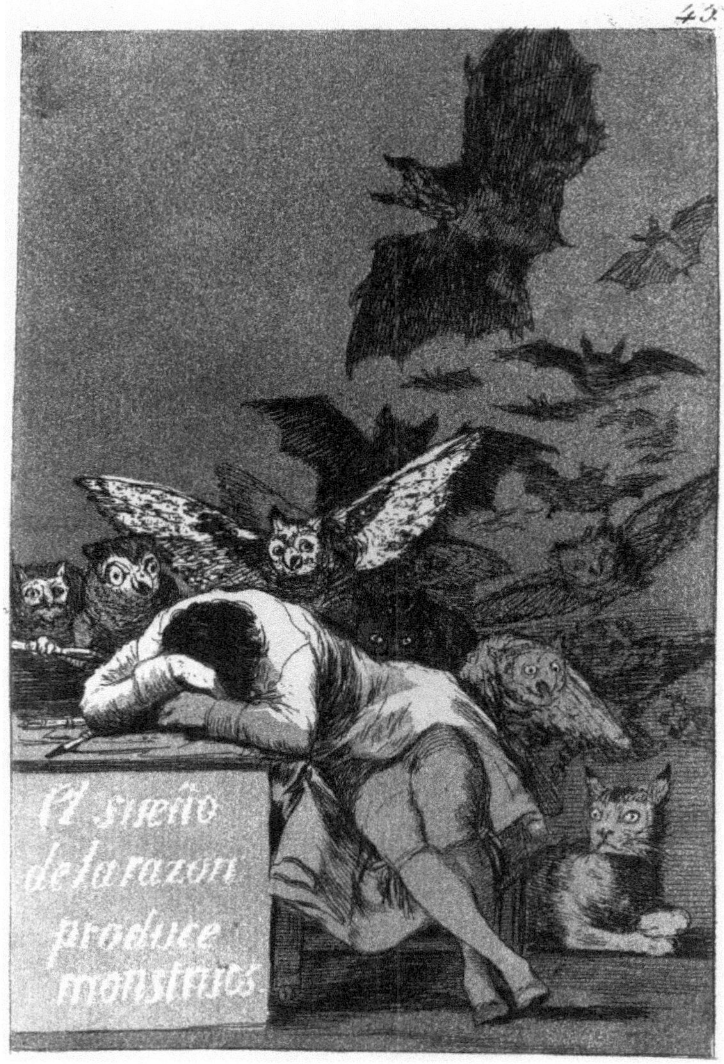

291. Francisco Goya, *Caprichos,* plate 43 ("El sueño de la razon produce monstruos") (1797–98). Etching and aquatint, 18.3 × 12.3 cm. (plate: 21.5 × 15 cm.). Brooklyn Museum of Art. A. A. Healy, Frank L. Babbett and Carl De Silver Funds.

ally imply a certain quickness of tempo and lightness of style, their playfulness is not frivolous. For all its self-liberation from the rules, as we have already seen in Piranesi's *Carceri,* the *capriccio* draws upon the conventions of art with new purpose. Indeed, it is precisely by playing with those conventions, whether formal or iconographic, that it acquires its particular eloquence, its legibility to an audience that is pictorially literate, that is, an audience of connoisseurs, of amateurs and professional colleagues. For Piranesi the conventions that were to be treated capriciously were those of architectural representation, the rules those of perspective. Tiepolo's *capricci* engage the conventions and expectations of figural invention.

In the suite entitled *Vari Capricci,* probably the earlier of the two – although the issue continues to be debated[41] – Tiepolo's needle moves rapidly, across broad areas,

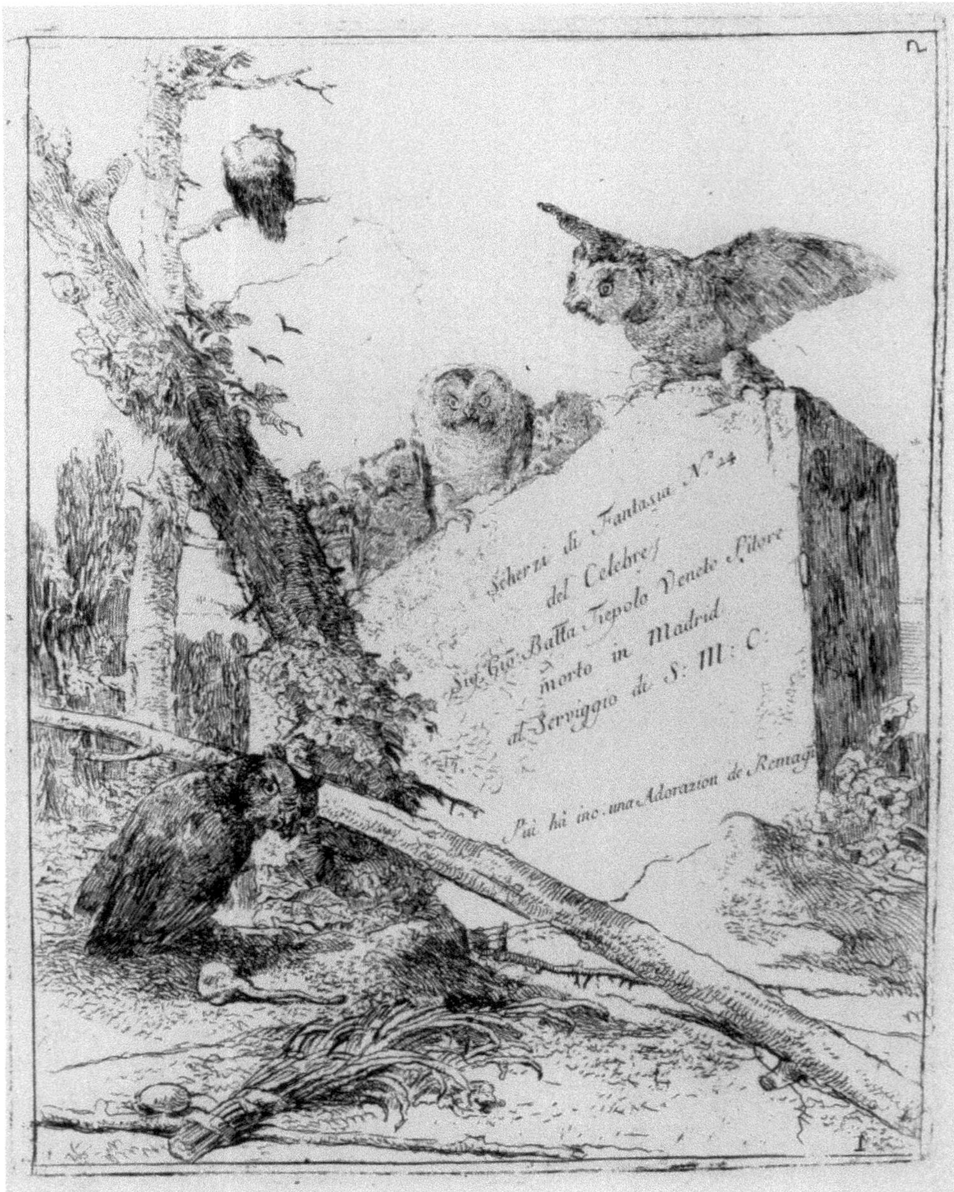

292. Giovanni Battista Tiepolo, *Scherzi di Fantasia,* frontispiece (lettering added by Domenico Tiepolo, ca. 1775/78). Etching (with engraved lettering), 22.5 × 18.2 cm. Cooper-Hewitt, National Design Museum, Smithsonian Institution/Art Resource, New York. Gift of Eleanor and Sarah Hewitt (1931-67-60-a).

in what are apparently among his initial efforts on the grounded copper (Figs. 293, 294). He then brings his instrument under more stringent control, slowing the movement and rendering in smaller, more concentrated units (Fig. 295). Still, form remains open, line light: the aesthetic of the sketch is modally appropriate to the generic concept of *capriccio.*

The images present groups of disparate figures in minimal landscape settings, usually gathered around a dominant tree or architectural monument – obelisk, column,

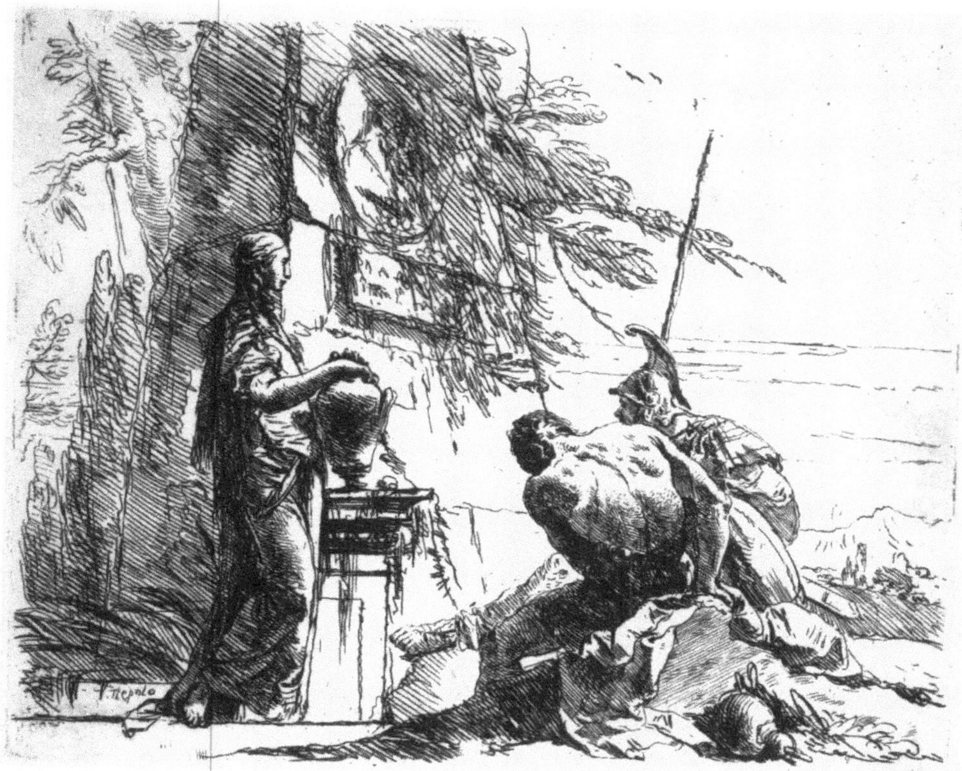

293. Giovanni Battista Tiepolo, from *Vari Capricci* ("Standing Woman and Seated Men before an Obelisk") (ca. 1741). Etching, 13.7 × 17.3 cm. National Gallery of Art, Washington. Rosenwald Collection (B-19,889).

294. Giovanni Battista Tiepolo, from *Vari Capricci* ("Women and Men Regarding a Burning Pyre of Bones") (ca. 1741). Etching, 13.6 × 17.4 cm. National Gallery of Art, Washington. Rosenwald Collection (B-19,887).

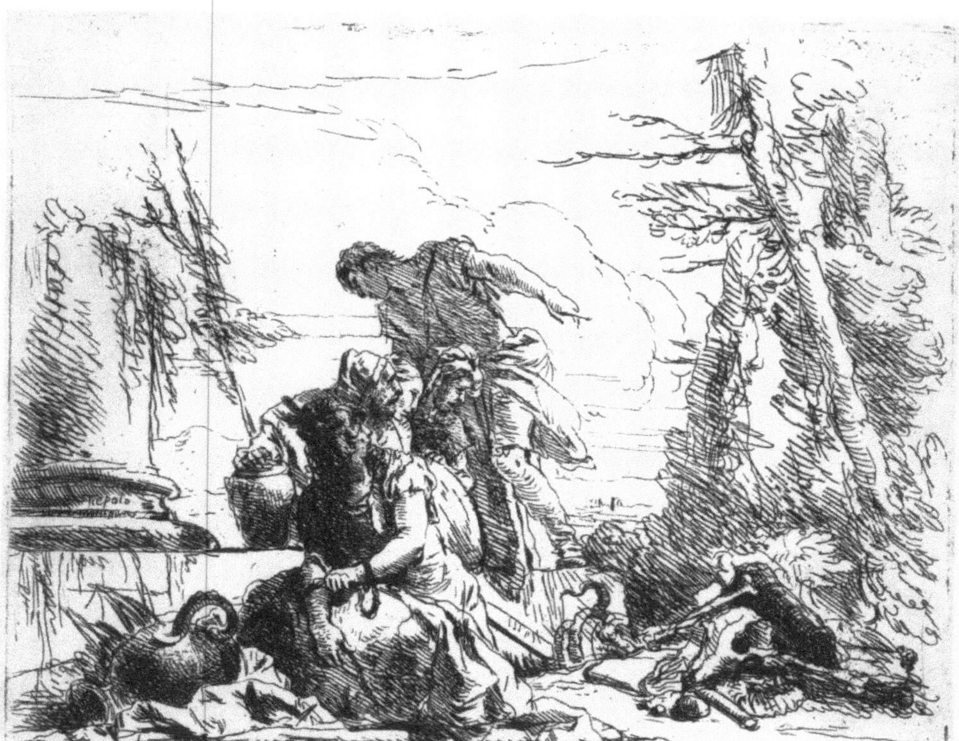

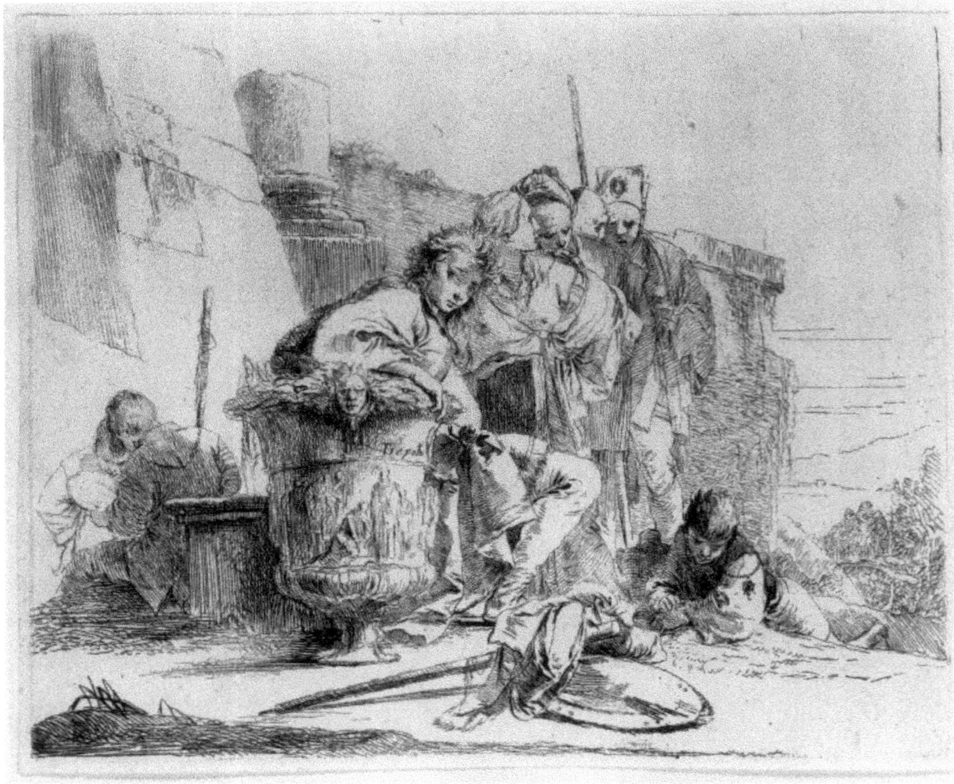

295. Giovanni Battista Tiepolo, from *Vari Capricci* ("Young Man Seated, Leaning against an Urn, with Other Figures") (ca. 1741). Etching, 13.6 × 18.1 cm. National Gallery of Art, Washington. Rosenwald Collection (B-19,981).

tomb, altar. If never quite the *locus amoenus* of pastoral tradition, the site is thus marked as one of special significance, however vaguely hinted. Such significance seems both to be confirmed by the presence of the figures and, in turn, to confer meaning upon their gathering. By their own gestures and exchanges the personages suggest their status as dramatis personae, players in some story; their variety of type – young and old, male and female, warrior, shepherd, sage, vestal and mother – further implies dramatic possibility. Occasionally, one of them will engage the viewer directly, either inviting entry (Figs. 295, 296) or resenting intrusion (Fig. 297). Their own internal dialogues may be muted or animated, focused or not: one contemplates the distance in silence (Fig. 298); another points excitedly, possibly toward a spent sacrificial pyre (Fig. 294). Pointing and looking dominate what little action there is. This is a world of romanticized antiquity, suggesting sorcery and myth, part of the popular diffusion of a classical tradition handed down especially in the graphic arts – in prints by Giovanni Benedetto Castiglione and Salvator Rosa.[42]

Tiepolo draws upon a rich heritage of images in the Western tradition, a particularly resonant dimension of which deal with themes of mortality, the contemplation of death. His *capricci,* then, appear as inventive variations on themes such as *et in Arcadia ego* or the quick and the dead. Even the apparently pastoral mood of the composition with a woman, child satyr, and goat (Fig. 299) can hardly escape the

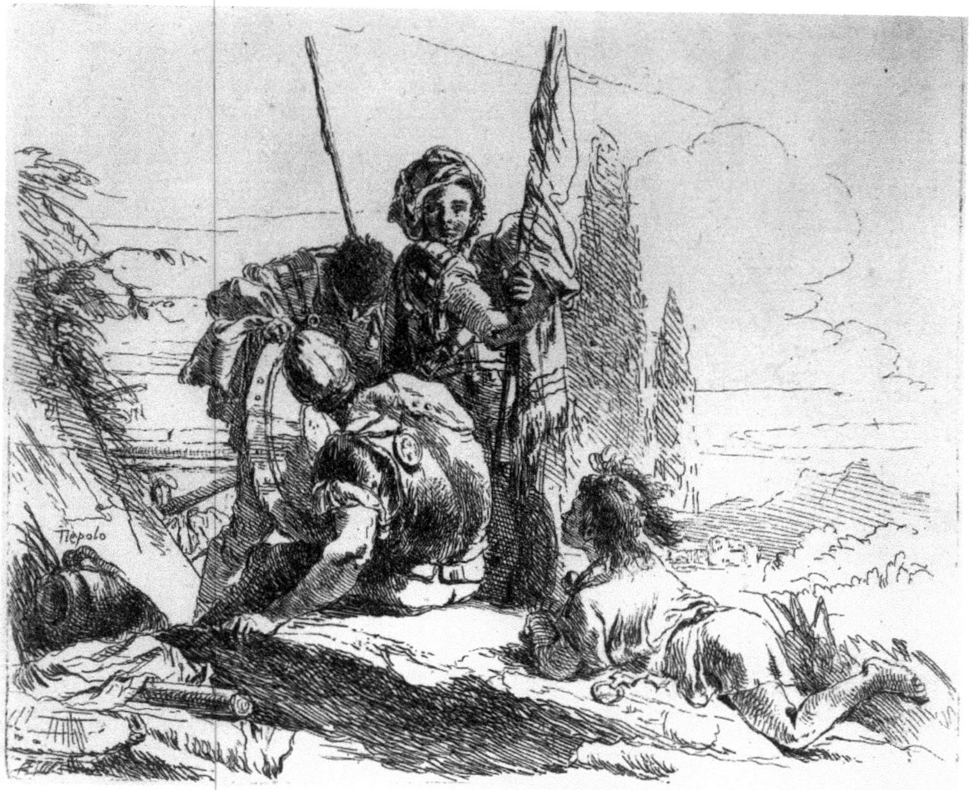

296. Giovanni Battista Tiepolo, from *Vari Capricci* ("Three Soldiers and a Youth") (ca. 1741). Etching, 14.1 × 17.5 cm. National Gallery of Art, Washington. Rosenwald Collection (B-19,893).

297. Giovanni Battista Tiepolo, from *Vari Capricci* ("Soldier Seated on a Tomb, with Other Figures") (ca. 1741). Etching, 13.3 × 17 cm. National Gallery of Art, Washington. Rosenwald Collection (B-19,888).

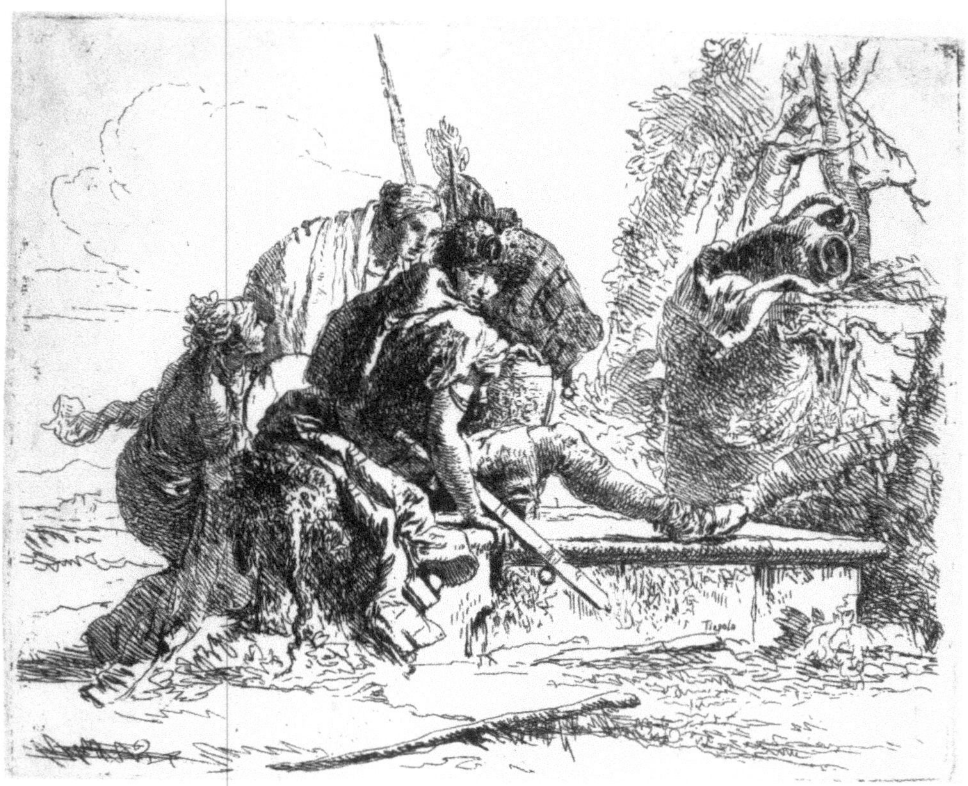

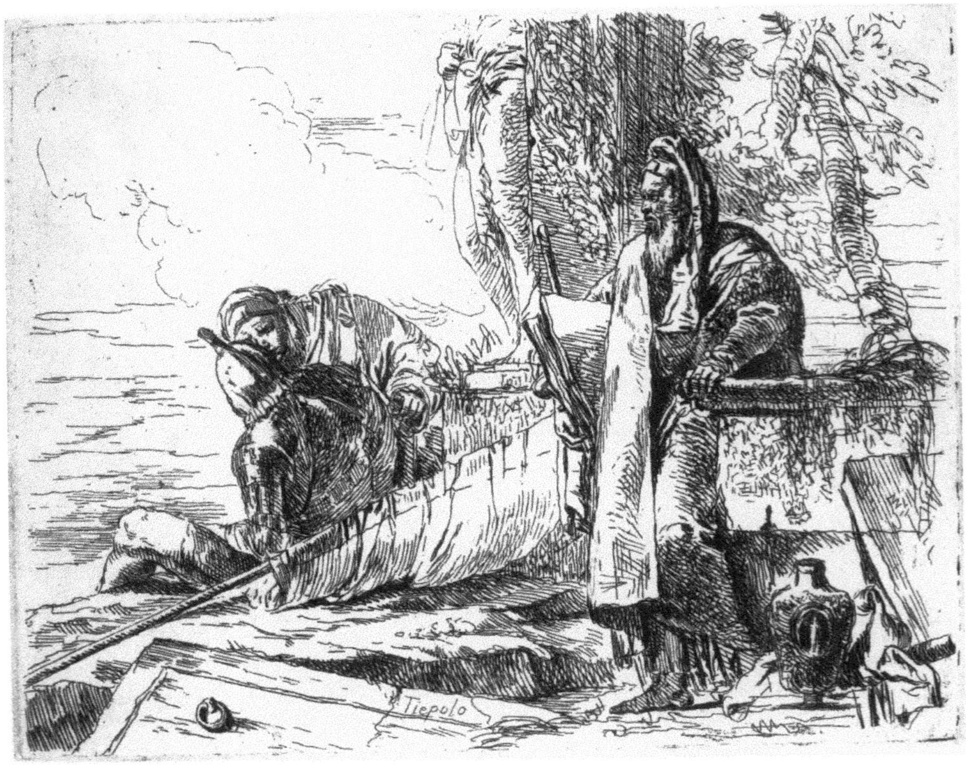

298. Giovanni Battista Tiepolo, from *Vari Capricci* ("Standing Philosopher and Two Other Figures") (ca. 1741). Etching, 13.3 × 17.2 cm. National Gallery of Art, Washington. Rosenwald Collection (B-19,890).

mood of pathos: on the one hand, its collection of creatures may evoke the classical iconography of the birth of Jupiter; on the other, the bloated infant so poignantly turning away from the maternal breast may be either sated or sick. The mood is only suggested, implicit in the imagery that lies behind this *capriccio,* imagery available on some level to the culturally literate viewer. And yet nothing is clear in this art of "aucun nom certain," nothing, that is, except the energies of invention.

In each of these images the artist invents a story, or implies one. Based upon the very compositional conventions that it undermines, the *capriccio* lures one into its own hermeneutic web, compelling the viewer to read significance into pictured dialogue and encounter, to meet the interpretive challenge of objects apparently latent with symbolic meaning – monuments, altars, urns, masks, serpents, bones. Collectively and cumulatively, these images maintain their common tone, reinforcing one another and the sense of common subject. As Praetorius said of the *capriccio* in music, "one ought not go too much out of the mode."

In "Death Giving an Audience" (Fig. 300), the most dramatic and overtly narrative of the *capricci,* the evolving narrative imagination can be followed in a sequence of drawings leading up to the etching, in particular, four sketches on two sheets. Three of these already include the cloaked skeleton of the final version (Figs. 301–4).[43] What is evidently the first in the series, however, is especially revealing,

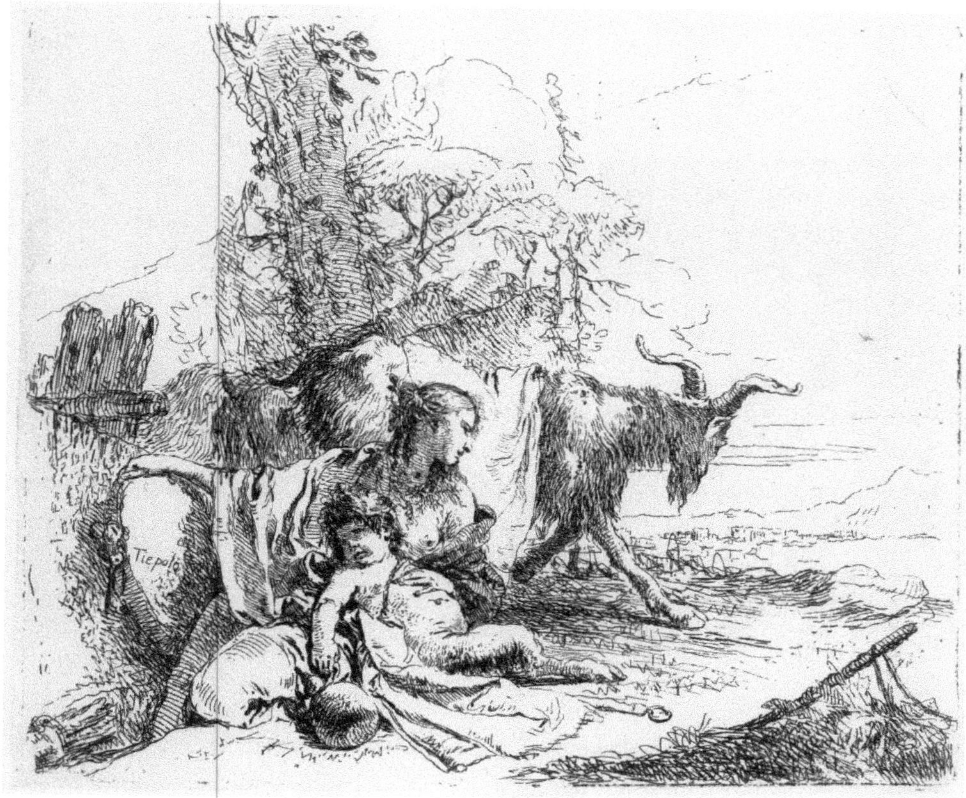

299. Giovanni Battista Tiepolo, from *Vari Capricci* ("Woman, Satyr Child, and Goat in a Landscape") (ca. 1741). Etching, 14 × 17.2 cm. National Gallery of Art, Washington. Rosenwald Collection (B-19,885).

300. Giovanni Battista Tiepolo, from *Vari Capricci* ("Death Giving an Audience") (ca. 1741). Etching, 14.1 × 17.9 cm. National Gallery of Art, Washington. Rosenwald Collection (B-19,886).

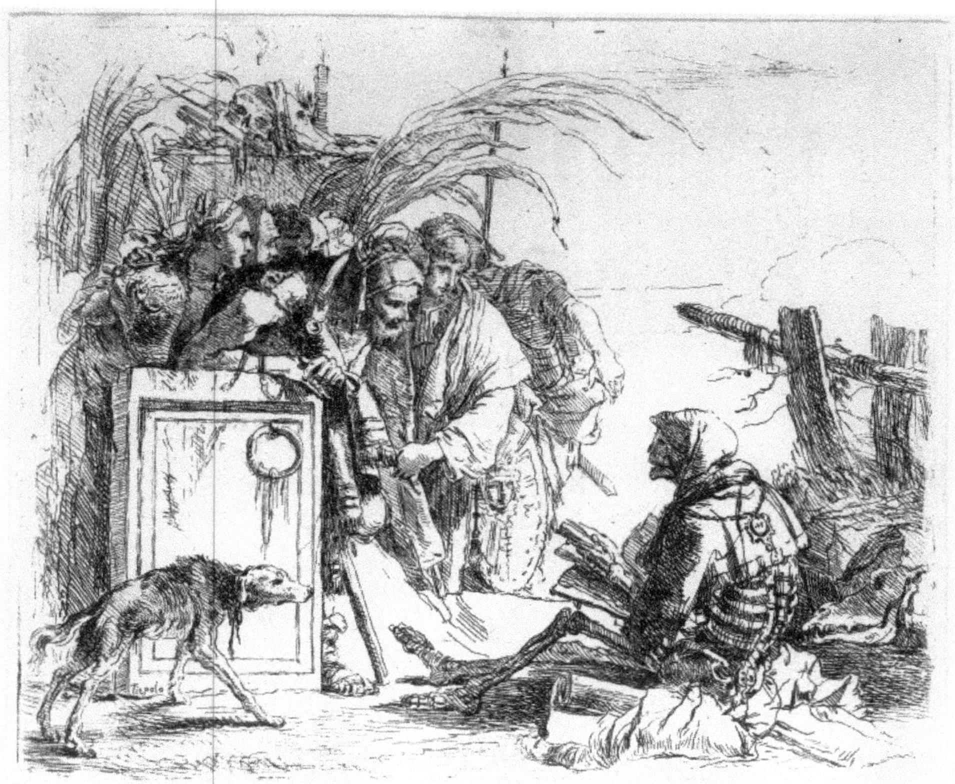

for the figure of Death is not yet present (Fig. 301). Rather, the scene is one of the opening of a tomb, a group of soldiers struggling to raise its heavy slab. And the presiding figure is not yet an exotic magus but rather a bearded Franciscan friar who offers a gesture of Christian benediction. Although establishing the basic mode of the idea, Tiepolo initially imagined a dramatic situation of different cultural dimension – the mangy hound, at least, is already present.

On the verso of this sheet, even more rapidly notated, Death makes its appearance, rising from the grave (Fig. 302), and with that skeletal epiphany the essential drama is inflected from expectation to confrontation; the new protagonist assumes control, commanding the dialogue and, evidently, banishing the Christian presence – as well as the hound. The place of the friar is taken by a soldier, armored *all'antica;* with one arm on an urn (or shield), he leans forward, pointing, to lead the interrogation of Death. In the two drawings on the next sheet the support for this figure becomes the upturned slab of the tomb itself, and, as he dissociates himself from his colleagues and refocuses his attention, his dialogue with Death becomes more intensely animated (Figs. 303, 304). In the ultimate version in this sequence, the leading interlocutor begins to assume the headdress and costume of the magus – and the dog reappears, now contributing the counterpoint of his own timidity to the encounter. Here, interestingly, Tiepolo experiments with a rather more casual attitude for Death, who now lies prone upon the ground – rather like the curious youth in another of the *Capricci* (Fig. 296). Dignity is restored in the etching, where Death, still fully emerged, is more sedately seated.

301. Giovanni Battista Tiepolo, Study for "Death Giving an Audience" (ca. 1741). Pen, brown ink, over red chalk, 15.3 × 23.7 cm. Victoria and Albert Museum, London (D.1825.219-1885, recto).

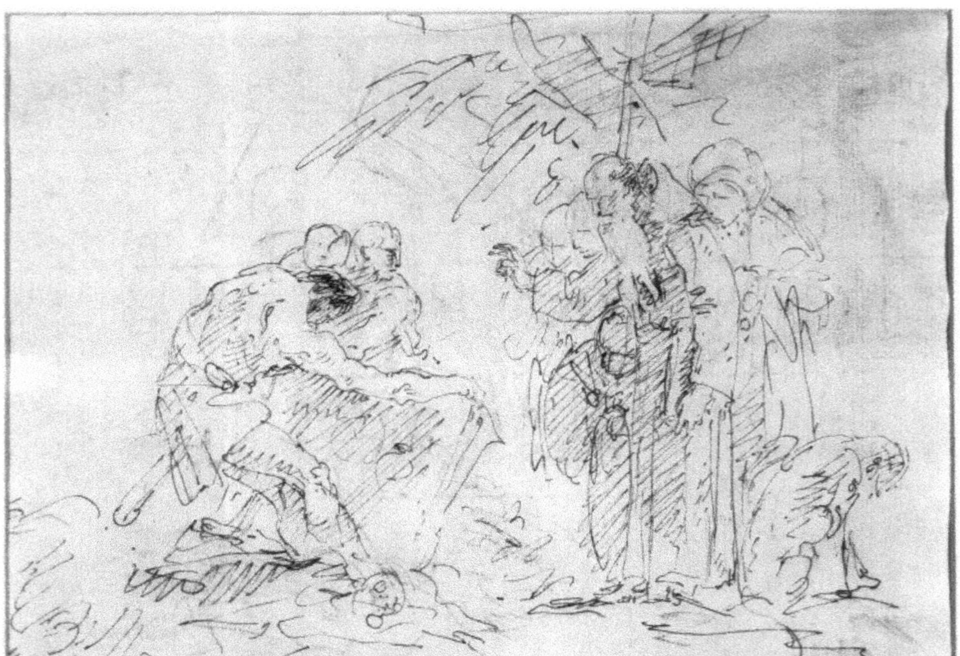

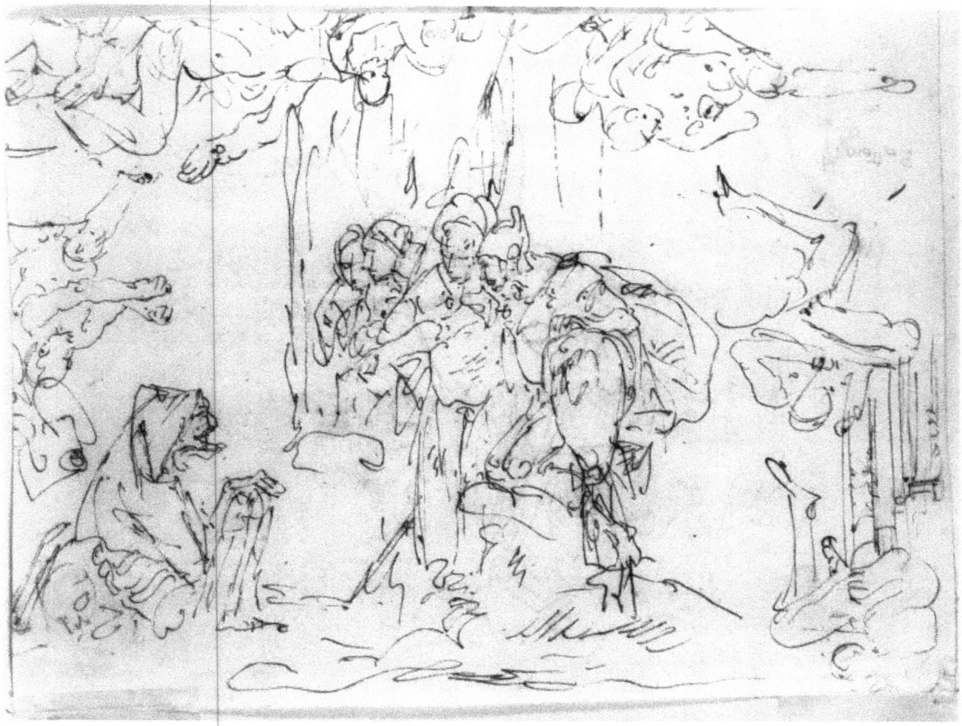

302. Giovanni Battista Tiepolo, Study for "Death Giving an Audience" (ca. 1741). Pen, brown ink, over red chalk, 15.3 × 23.7 cm. Victoria and Albert Museum, London (D.1825.219-1885, verso).

Throughout the development of the composition one essential principle has been followed, what might be termed figural generation, a process that lies at the core of the artist's inventive procedure. Tiepolo's choral groups grow from the seed of a single figure, a foreground protagonist who seems to project variations of his own form, radiating graphic shadows of himself. Within their formal bonding, the resulting community of figures offers a number of relational possibilities: the characters may share a common focus or disperse their attention; they may react in unison to an object or event, interact in dialogue or ignore one another entirely; some may, as we have seen, acknowledge the presence of the viewer and by that recognition co-opt him or her. In the drawings leading up to "Death Giving an Audience" we follow the expansion of the group, as the protagonist develops his own greater curiosity, bending with more dynamic contrapposto and increasing gravity, the profile of his figure finally fully contained within the contours of his heavy cloak. In the etching itself, adding a monumental note of support to the inquiring chorus, the tomb slab is presented with tectonic frontality – almost as a field awaiting text in a title plate.

Behind such figural invention, motivating and enabling it, is an essentially graphic momentum: the creating exploration of the draftsman's pen in dialectic motion, responding to the challenge of its own initial idea. Tiepolo's inventive process began with a basic idea: the confrontation of death. That theme established the essential mode in which variations on the sujects are then composed. Iconog-

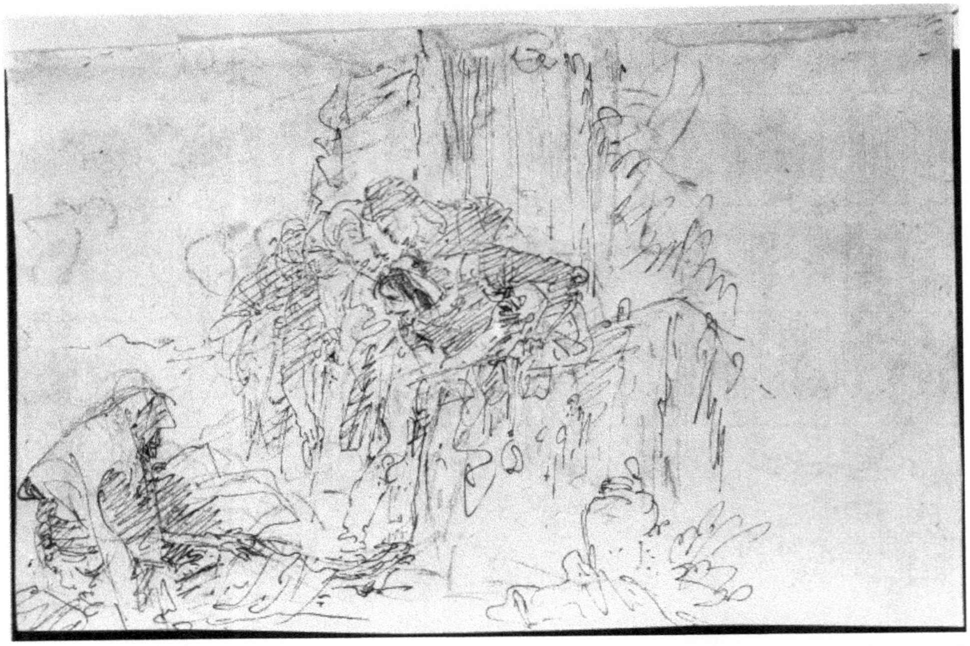

303. Giovanni Battista Tiepolo, Study for "Death Giving an Audience" (ca. 1741). Pen, brown ink, over red chalk, 17.3 × 23.4 cm. Victoria and Albert Museum, London (D.1825.22-1885, recto).

304. Giovanni Battista Tiepolo, Study for "Death Giving an Audience"(ca. 1741). Pen, brown ink, brown wash, traces of red chalk, 17.3 × 23.4 cm. Victoria and Albert Museum, London (D.1825.22-1885, verso).

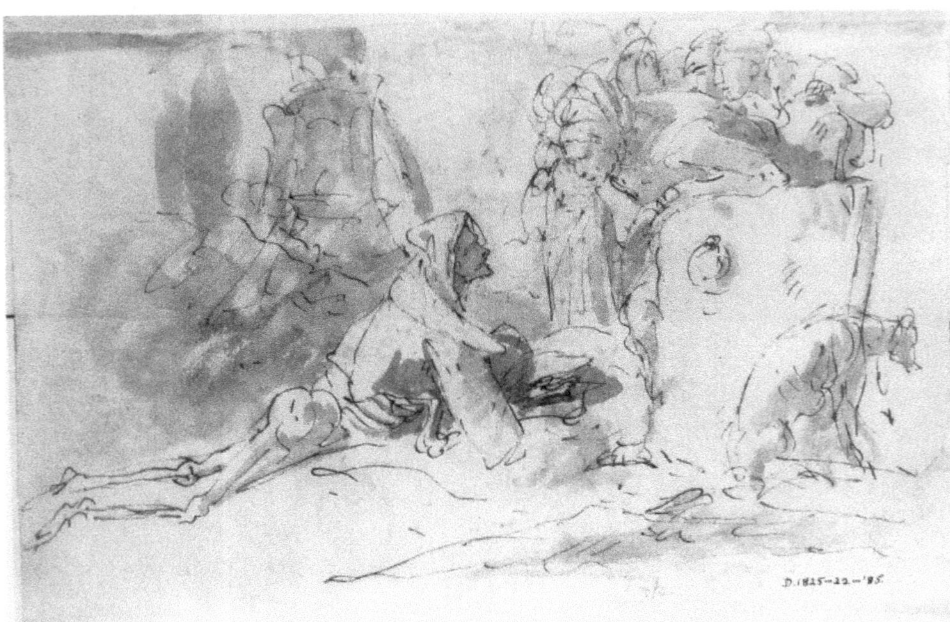

raphy per se – that is, subject matter in so far as it involves precise identity of players and attributes according to an a priori script – is less a determinant of design than a resource. Shifting from friar to soldier to magus, Tiepolo changes *personaggi* without going "too much out of the mode" of his *capriccio.* In his initial statement the key protagonist has not yet appeared: Death is imminent, its appearance promised with the opening of the tomb. The subsequent sketch then realizes that promise. Drawing sequence and narrative sequence are one, as the draftsman follows the logical progression of his own fiction, and the pen discovers new dramatic possibilities in its own creation.

The inventing game seems to pick up pace in the expanded field of the *Scherzi di Fantasia,* a suite comprising more and larger plates, for which Tiepolo did indeed execute a title plate, without, however, filling in the title himself (Fig. 305). Creative energies achieve greater focus here, as the linework is brought under more rigorous control, fulfilling its mimetic responsibilities with more studied variety of stroke and pattern, without, however, surrendering the independent value of its constituent marks. The surface of the image thereby assumes a higher degree of tautness, representation a greater density, without, however, entirely sacrificing the

305. Giovanni Battista Tiepolo, *Scherzi di Fantasia,* frontispiece (ca. 1757–62). Etching, 22.5 × 18.2 cm. National Gallery of Art, Washington. Rosenwald Collection (B-19,895).

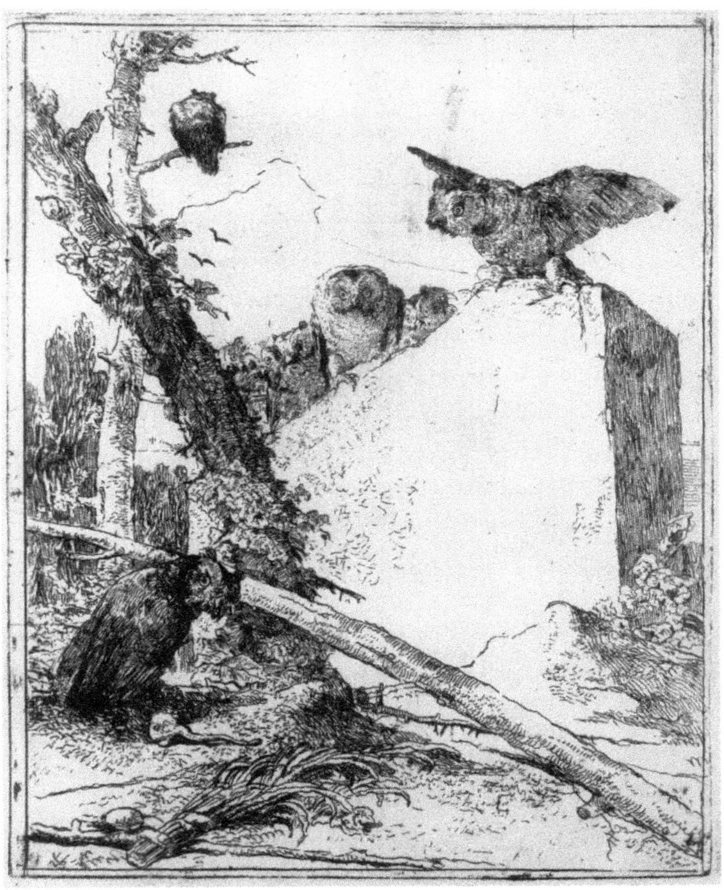

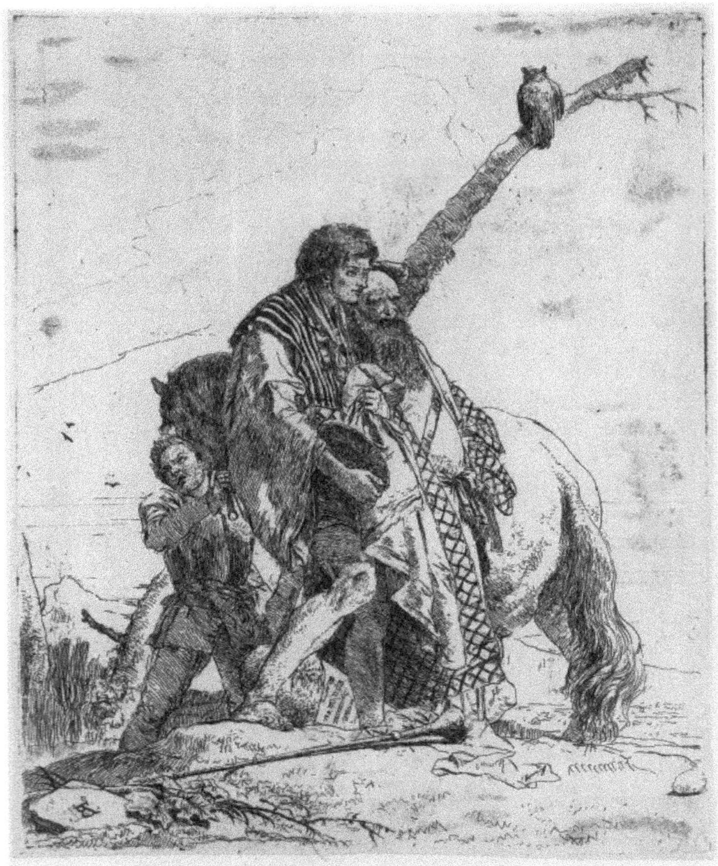

306. Giovanni Battista Tiepolo, from *Scherzi di Fantasia* ("Youth, Sage, and Attendant with Horse") (before 1757). Etching, 21.8 × 17.8 cm. National Gallery of Art, Washington. Rosenwald Collection (B-19,906).

lightness of touch so essential to maintaining aesthetic mood. Linear activity intensifies toward the core of the image, concentrating attention on the central figural nodes, but toward the margins it opens up, dissipating its energies in suggestive scribbles or yielding entirely to white ground. Within the borders of the plate, the image builds toward the center; extended lines – of a tree against the whiteness (Fig. 306) or a staff or shadow on the ground (Fig. 307) – tie it to the frame, keeping it from floating like a vignette. In their varied qualities of surface finish, their energies of line, and expanses of untouched paper, these etchings retain the qualities of the open drawing, a graphic structure in process.

As images, the *Scherzi* are even more insistently figure-generated: a single central personage spawning others. These appendages may turn to engage the originating figure dialogically, or they may extend attention elsewhere. The operating principle is clearest in the progressions of heads back into space; the generating figure creates his own chorus of followers. Fragments of relief sculpture comment on even as they exemplify the principle (Fig. 308). Their own cephalic sequences of

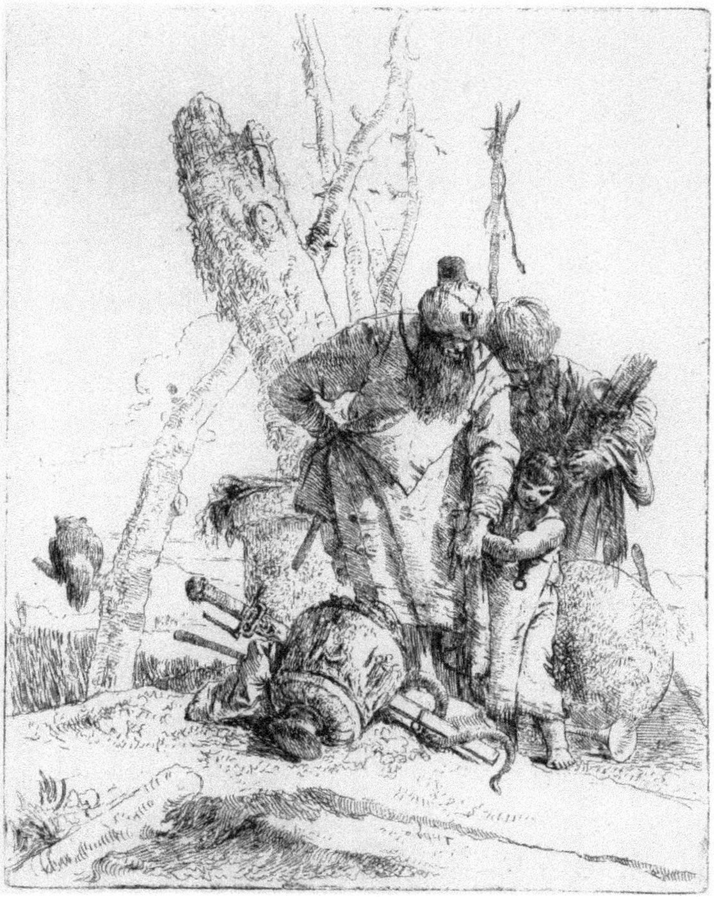

307. Giovanni Battista Tiepolo, from *Scherzi di Fantasia* ("Two Turbaned Magicians and a Boy") (before 1757). Etching, 22.6 × 17.6 cm. National Gallery of Art, Washington. Rosenwald Collection (B-19,915).

overlapping profiles recall a long tradition in drawing, one that we first encountered in Leonardo and in the exercises of subsequent draftsmen: a series of varied profile heads, one physiognomic contour generating another, each a variation on the basic linear theme (Fig. 309). What had become a standard academic exercise is predicated on the inventing impulse of the drawing hand, its instinctive desire to repeat yet vary its own motions.

Like his pen, Tiepolo's etching needle operates in this way. In dialectic response to its own initial idea, it creates a larger complex. The dynamic of the process is reflected in the compositional structure, which is founded on a large-scale counterpoint of diagonals. Not since Veronese has the leaning tree trunk assumed such pictorial responsibility, securing figural pose or balancing bodily momentum. Indeed, a series of pen and wash drawings of such trees attests to Tiepolo's studied interest in these structuring diagonals: hardly close studies of nature, these are rather arboreal inventions, natural staffage awaiting narrative assignment.[44] In the *Scherzi*

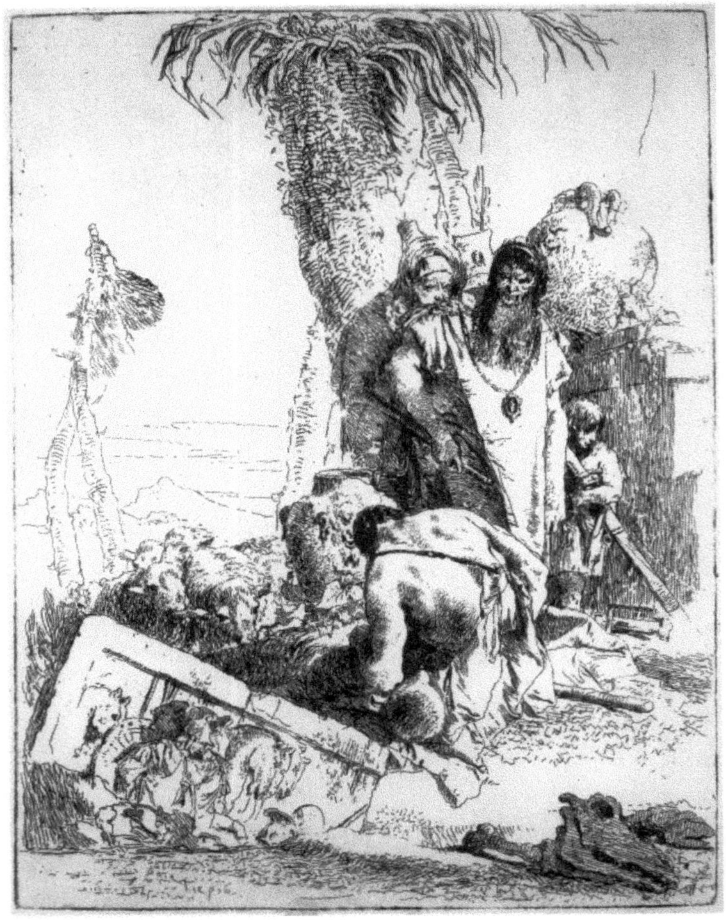

308. Giovanni Battista Tiepolo, from *Scherzi di Fantasia* ("Seated Man and Two Magicians with Attendant Boy") (before 1757). Etching, 22.5 × 17.5 cm. National Gallery of Art, Washington. Rosenwald Collection (B-19,912).

such forms become full participants in the composition, choral commentators on the figural action that they serve to fix within both the landscape and the pictorial field.

The range of dramatis personae in the *Scherzi* is expanded to include a fuller typological representation of young and old, male and female, mothers and children, magi and warriors, shepherds, satyrs and, the most intriguing addition, Punchinello (Figs. 310, 311). The leading role is claimed by the bearded elders, those theatrically costumed wise men, philosophers and sorcerers, whose task it is to confront and, presumably, interpret the signs of mortality scattered before them and their puzzled attendants (Fig. 309). Those signs include the tombs, altars, urns, skulls, and serpents that traditionally articulated the *vanitas* landscapes of the *et in Arcadia ego* tradition, along with the stilled eloquence of fragmented sculptural reliefs *all'antica*. The serpent, in particular, comes to embody some sacred mystery, a presence from the underworld – slithering through urns and fire, around scab-

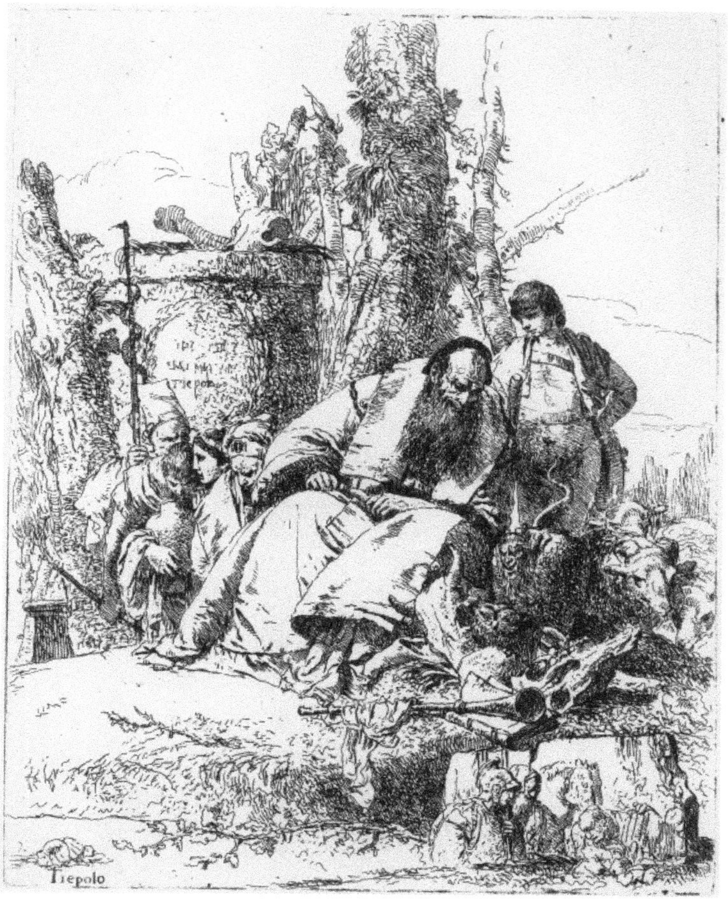

309. Giovanni Battista Tiepolo, from *Scherzi di Fantasia* ("Seated Magician Regarding Animal Skulls, and Other Figures") (before 1757). Etching, with some reworking in pen and brown ink, 22.5 × 17.8 cm. National Gallery of Art, Washington. Rosenwald Collection (B-19,910).

bards, poles, and torches – ominously enacting Hogarth's line of grace (Figs. 307, 311, 312, 313).

Confirming the dark brooding of the scene, lending a special note of foreboding, are the ubiquitous owls. Some of these creatures of the night, like so much of the iconographic paraphernalia of Tiepolo's etchings, are recalled from prints by Rosa and Castiglione, where they already carry their weight of dark wisdom. More starkly poised, however, Tiepolo's predatory birds strike a more ominous chord, especially when they assert their full hermeneutic power in the title plate, which they alone rule. Perched possessively upon the marble slab, they challenge entry to the suite, even as their fierce round eyes dare the viewer to essay interpretation.[45]

If Tiepolo's *capricci* in general play upon some basic themes of dark wisdom and sacred mystery, themes sounded in earlier prints, they introduce one totally new card into the game: the figure of Punchinello. However incongruous his presence in an Arcadia so insistently marked by signs of mortality, this beak-masked clown

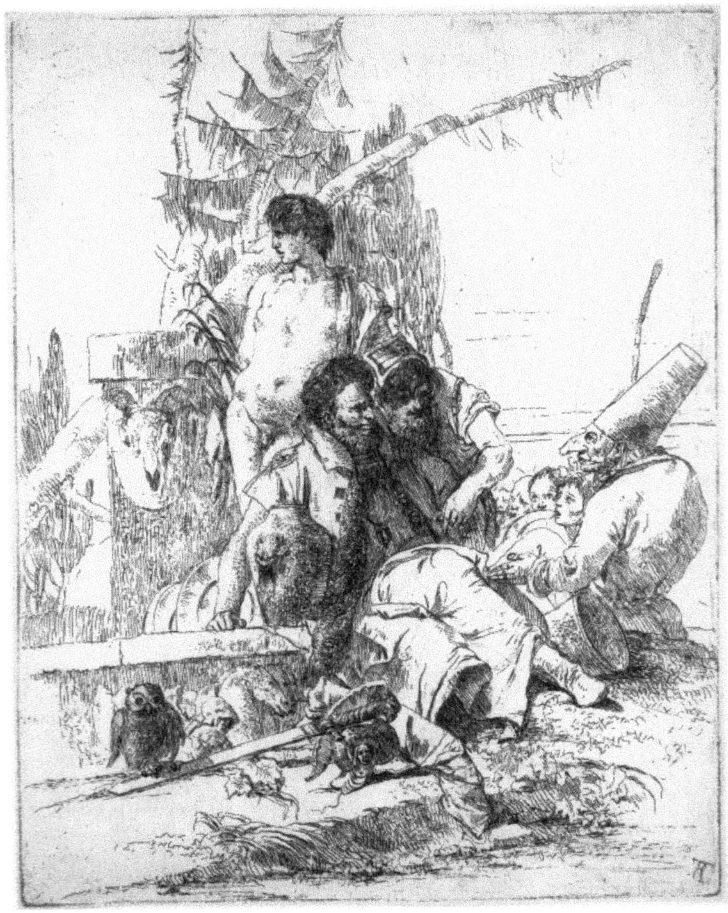

310. Giovanni Battista Tiepolo, from *Scherzi di Fantasia* ("Two Sages in Dialogue with Punchinello, with Other Figures") (before 1757). Etching, with some reworking in pen and brown ink, 23.2 × 18.4 cm. National Gallery of Art, Washington. Rosenwald Collection (B-19,899).

out of the *commedia dell'arte* actually assumes a role analogous to the skeleton in the *capriccio* of "Death Giving an Audience." In one of the *Scherzi* he appears in intense dialogue, even debate, with two elder magi; it is not quite clear who is interrogating whom (Fig. 310). In another he appears in effigy, a sculpture in high relief on the lid of his own tomb, pointedly the object of curious attention of the assembled personae (Fig. 311). Surrounded by the attributes of death and mortality – silhouetted bone and hourglass above, serpent, owl, and skeletal jaw below – Punchinello, as Death, here adds his own ironic poignancy to the basic theme of the *Scherzi*: *et in comoedia ego.*

Tiepolo's etchings, like so much of his art, already constitute a world of masks. Throughout, the viewer is challenged by faces – on urns, shields, helmets, buckles – faces that are more animated than those of the human actors, themselves no more than types. These decorating heads are part of a standard repertory of motifs in Tiepolo's painting, where they tend to be more fully absorbed into the overall pic-

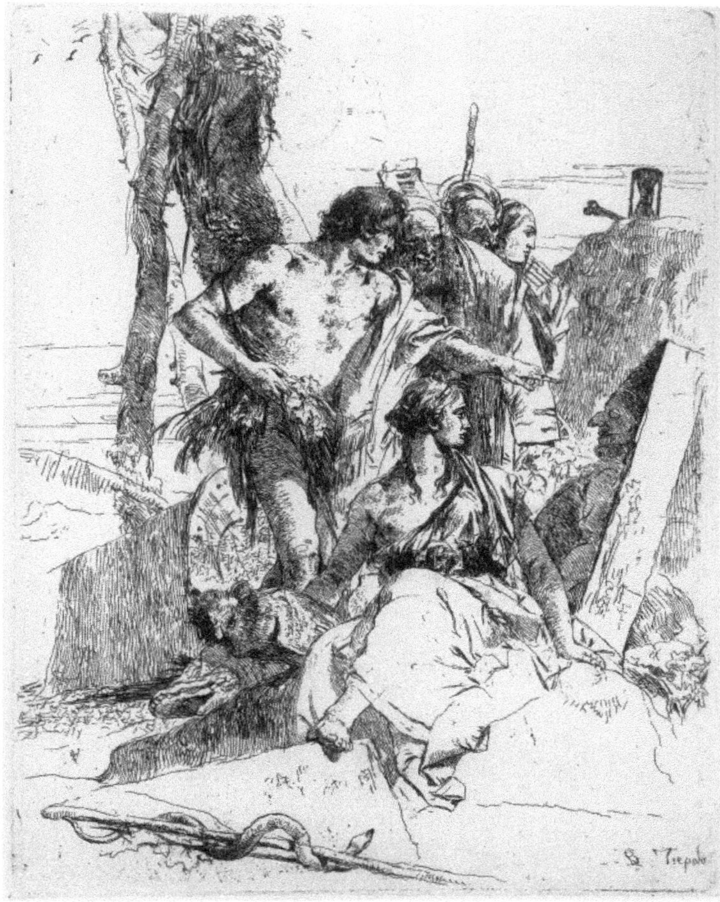

311. Giovanni Battista Tiepolo, from *Scherzi di Fantasia* ("Figures Regarding an Effigy of Punchinello") (before 1757). Etching, 23.1 × 17.9 cm. National Gallery of Art, Washington. Rosenwald Collection (B-19,902).

torial fabric. In the etchings, designed for more intimate reading, they become more insistent, as they distribute and reinforce the ocular motif established more immediately by the threatening glare of owls and the blind stare of skulls. Within this active physiognomic realm the mask of Punchinello appears curiously expressionless, and yet all the more human. His is most explicitly and clearly a mask, hiding a face behind. We are invited to penetrate its facade, to seek out that covered humanity; we project the affect – even to the dead eyes of the effigy. This clownish outlander in Arcadia, protean character of the urban stage, this fool intrudes a sudden note of reality into the fiction of Tiepolo's imagined world. And this irony is part of the artist's joking fantasy, his *scherzo di fantasia.*

Defined by his hunchback, his truncated conical cap, his beaked mask, and his simple white costume, Punchinello himself offered Tiepolo an object of figural fantasy. If traditional Arcadian iconography afforded a rich field for capricious invention – including its Felliniesque range of disparate characters – the figure of

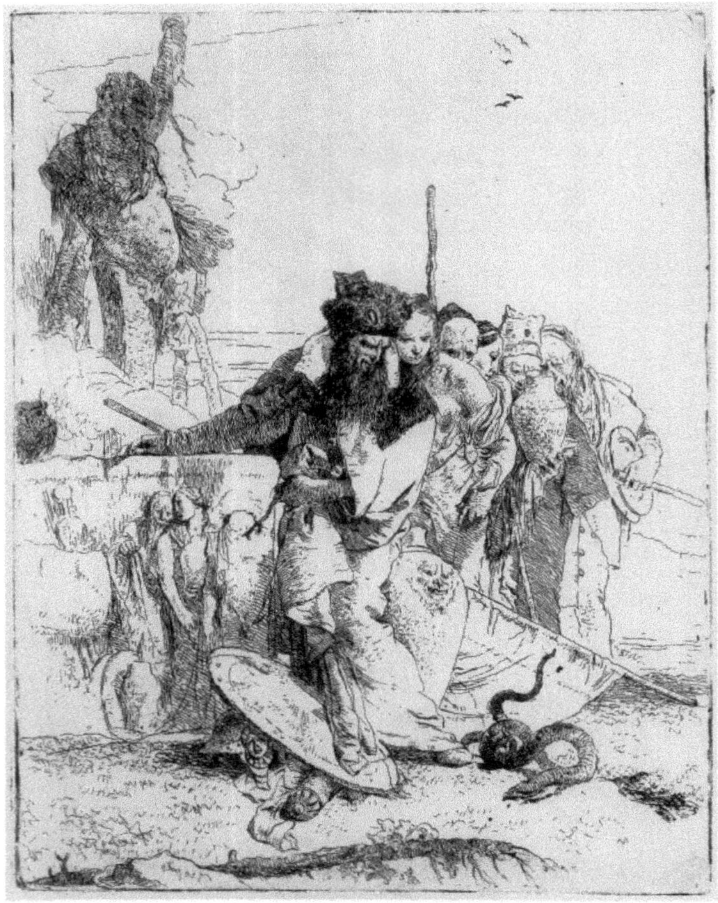

312. Giovanni Battista Tiepolo, from *Scherzi di Fantasia* ("Magician and Other Figures Regarding a Serpent") (before 1757). Etching, 22.6 × 17.6 cm. National Gallery of Art, Washington. Rosenwald Collection (B-19-915).

Punchinello presented a body latent with similar inventive possibilities. Deformed by both nature and art, the figure of the clown stood apart from those ideal and idealized worlds but, as Tiepolo instinctively recognized, ready to participate in both and by his participation to offer ironic commentary on them. Punchinello's affectless mask was adaptable, as was his ungainly body. Multiplied and assembled into groups, sometimes with narrative implications, he and his brethren play at reality (Fig. 314). Certainly theirs is a world more real than that figured by Tiepolo's Olympians; theirs is that lower, definitely sublunar realm of the senses in which the body functions fully – ingesting, digesting, evacuating (Fig. 315).

And it was so read and appreciated by connoisseurs like Count Francesco Algarotti, who boasted to Mariette:

> I truly believe that I possess the most beautiful Polichinelles in the world, by the hand of our illustrious Tiepolo. . . . One of them in partic-

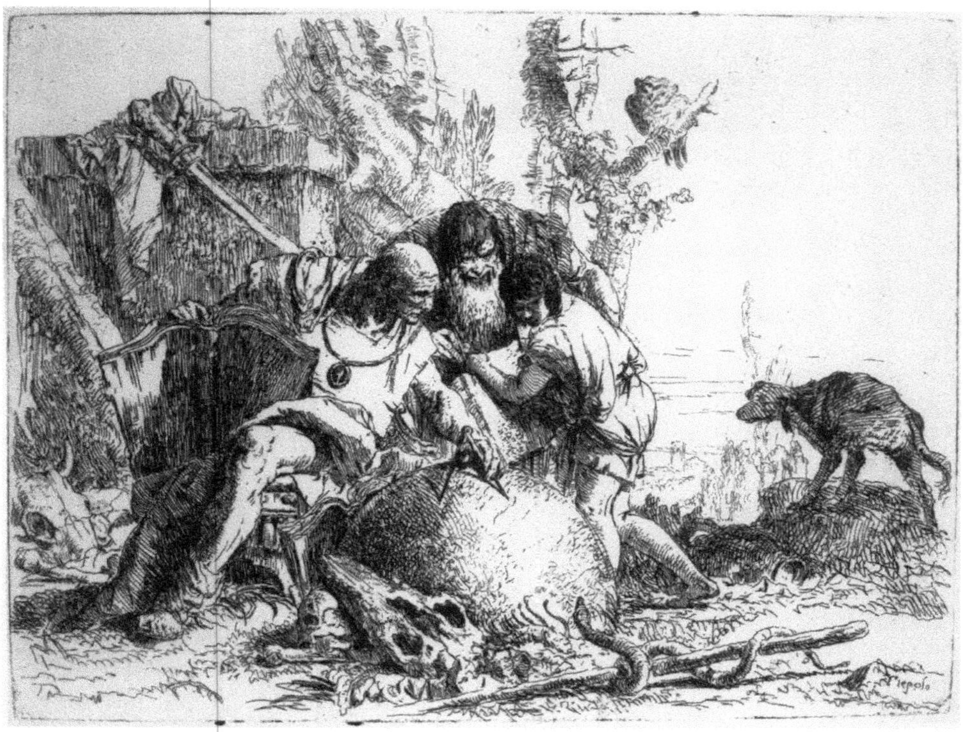

313. Giovanni Battista Tiepolo, from *Scherzi di Fantasia* ("Two Philosophers and a Youth Regarding a Serpent") (before 1757). Etching, with some reworking in pen and brown ink, 14.1 × 18.9 cm. National Gallery of Art, Washington. Rosenwald Collection (B-19,898).

> ular I recommend to you: he is seen from behind, and is making water against a wall, . . . all his body expresses by his contortions a sadness so significant that one could call him the Laocoon of Polichinelles.[46]

This, then, is the culture of the *capriccio,* in which the connoisseur participates fully in the game, ready to accept its appeal to the imagination, its invitation to interpret, to project.

Tiepolo's game included an artist's special appreciation of the less-than-non-idealized body. As in his caricatures – where the creation of character seems less a matter of satiric manipulation, of mocking distortion, than of graphic realization of a certain formal potential – in his drawing of Punchinello Tiepolo responds to the formal possibilities inherent in his corporal frame, the special dynamic of the deformed body that had inspired a controlled repertory of gestures on the stage – and in the etchings of Callot. The contrapuntal relationship between the dwarf's hunchback and the glutton's belly affords just the right challenge to the draftsman (Figs. 316, 317). Laying Punchinello on his back yields a delicious reversal: back becomes front, as belly rises triumphant in air – but, as nostrils extend to the length of the nose, we realize that mask itself has yielded to reality. Tiepolo's drawings of Punchinello, whether of the single figure or the fraternity, stand to his more

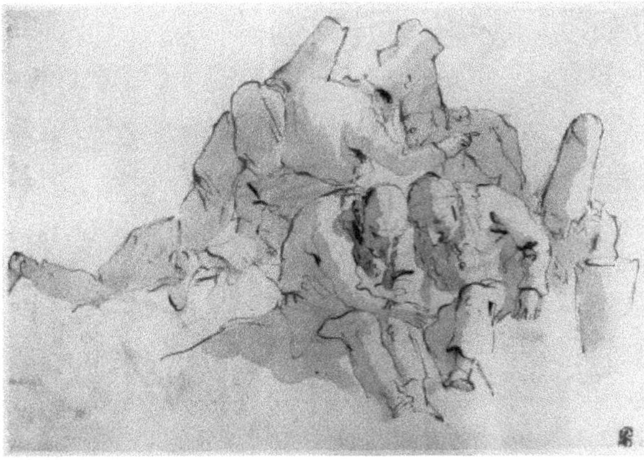

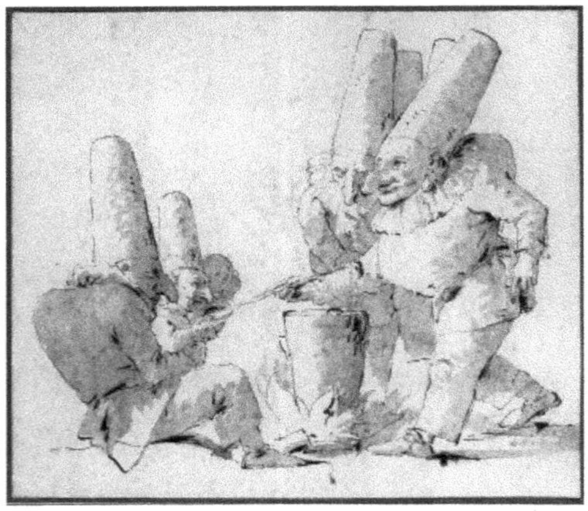

314. *(above)* Giovanni Battista Tiepolo, *A Group of Punchinellos* (ca. 1755–60). Pen and brown ink, brown wash, over graphite, 19.4 × 28.5 cm. Metropolitan Museum of Art, New York. Robert Lehman Collection, 1975 (1975.1.438).

315. *(left)* Giovanni Battista Tiepolo, *Punchinellos Cooking and Tasting Gnocchi* (ca. 1735–40). Pen and brown ink, brown wash, over graphite, 19.7 × 23.1 cm. Art Institute of Chicago. Helen Regenstein Collection (1972.108).

serious figure studies as studio *capricci,* parodic jokes on academic convention and heroic pretension.

Punchinello may be seen as the very embodiment of the *capriccio;* certainly his theatrical cousins inspired and sustained the capricious impulses of Tiepolo's predecessors like Callot. Like the *Vari Capricci* and *Scherzi di Fantasia,* Punchinello stands on the margins of the official, heroic art of Tiepolo. And yet both the mask and the etchings depend upon and derive from that more serious art. Deriving their hermeneutic potential from its conventions and traditions, they imply narrative significance, an *istoria,* and implication invites a more active interpretive response, a projection of meaning. Like drawing itself, the *capriccio,* whether as compositional idea or individual figure, remains open, incomplete, suggestive. It awaits closure in the mind of the viewer.

The potential for such closure in the *capricci* of Giambattista Tiepolo was more deliberately explored by his son. Domenico carried his father's suggestions of narrative situation and formal setting to paradoxical limits by abandoning the aesthetics of the sketch. His etchings are pictorially more fully realized in their detailed completeness, his forms more deliberately enclosed, settings more deeply shadowed. In hundreds of pictorially finished drawings, in pen and richly elaborated washes,

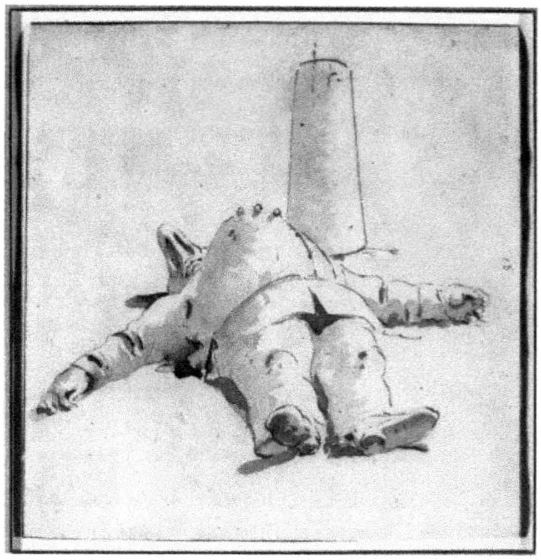

316. *(right)* Giovanni Battista Tiepolo, *Punchinello Lying on his Back* (ca. 1740–45). Pen and brown ink, brown wash, over graphite, 16 × 16 cm. Pierpont Morgan Library, New York. Eugene V. and Clare Thaw Collection. Photograph: Joseph Zehavi.

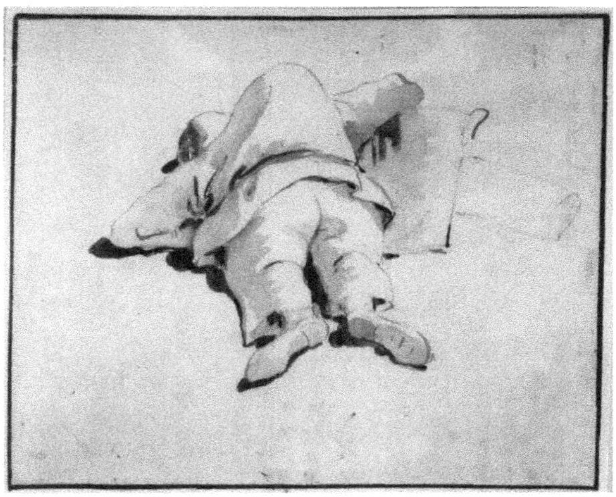

317. *(below)* Giovanni Battista Tiepolo, *Punchinello Lying Face Down* (ca. 1740–45). Pen and brown ink, brown wash, 16 × 19.7 cm. Present location unknown.

Domenico expanded the imaginative reach of his graphic world to include the fullest thematic range of Western iconography – biblical narrative and pagan mythology, pastoral landscape and domestic genre, caricature and animal life.

His earliest ambitious graphic project was the translation into etching of his own series of the Stations of the Cross painted for the church of San Polo in Venice; this *Via Crucis* was published in 1749 with a title plate proudly declaring the twenty-two-year-old artist as inventor, painter, and printmaker: *Domenico Tiepolo inventò, pinse, ed incise.*[47] Four years later, in Würzburg with his father, Domenico issued a suite of twenty-four variations on the theme of the Flight into Egypt: *Idee Pittoresche sopra la Fugga in Egitto di Giesu, Maria e Gioseppe. Opera inventata, ed incisa da me Gio: Domenico Tiepolo.*[48] Framed by scenes that announce departure and report arrival, the suite implies narrative sequence in the action of its individual images and, especially, in the cumulative serial momentum. At the same time, however, each of these "pictorial ideas" offers a particular response to the basic single subject, variation within repetition. In *pars* as well as in *toto*, the project is calculated to demonstrate the artist's powers of invention, which the title page declares with such insistence.

Much of Domenico's career was spent in the shadow of his father, with whom he studied and whose style he naturally assimilated, serving as chief assistant and collaborator on the great decorative projects. Nonetheless, the son did develop his own personality, especially in drawing – and particularly following Giambattista's death in Madrid in 1770 and his own return to Venice. It was in the latter part of his career, as taste shifted markedly away from the late Baroque (courtly) exuberance of the Tiepolo style toward the more sedate (bourgeois) structures of neoclassicism, that Domenico found increasing outlet in drawing. In the final decades of the eighteenth century, which saw the demise of the Republic of Venice with Napoleonic "liberation" in 1797, and into the opening years of the next, Domenico (who died in 1804) gradually retired from public painting projects to devote his time increasingly to more private matters, including the decoration of the family villa at Zianigo.[49]

The climactic achievement of his graphic activity was the series of 104 drawings devoted to the lives and times of Punchinello, collected in an album given its own title page: *Divertimenti per li Regazzi* (Fig. 318) – in choosing his musical title, Domenico turns a final variation on a theme, making the title itself the subject for capricious invention. In this entertainment for children the aged artist conjures a population of Punchinellos to rehearse not only a putative life, from cradle to grave – part picaresque novel, part *Bildungsroman* – but, even more ambitiously, an entire pictorial culture, a culture at the end of its own long life. Domenico had already, in the frescoes at Zianigo (in 1797), monumentalized his father's Punchinello into a taller, somewhat more gainly figure, permitting him a fuller social existence. Punchinello becomes at once protagonist, chorus, and audience in a vast theater of the world.[50]

Beginning with the title page, which parodies Domenico's own earlier plate for the *Via Crucis* suite, many of the drawings offer burlesque versions of celebrated themes from the traditional repertoire of Western art history – from heroic mythology to fêtes champêtres and galantes and domestic genre. Punchinello appears in an amazing array of roles, many of them implicit and dependent upon visual cultural association, an interpictoriality often inspired by his father's compositions. As painter, for example, Punchinello is both ancient Apelles (portraying Alexander's beloved Campaspe) (Fig. 319) and modern Giambattista Tiepolo (realizing ancient Timanthes' "Sacrifice of Iphegenia");[51] as mythic hero, he is young Achilles (with his centaur tutor),[52] Ganymede (abducted by the eagle) (Fig. 320), Deianira (abducted by a centaur) (Fig. 321), and Hercules (chasing the abductor),[53] companion to poor Actaeon (fully transformed and torn by his own hounds);[54] he is Joseph leading the flight into Egypt.[55] Finally, of course, he is himself, in his manifold guises – as clown, braggart, victim; as shepherd, farmer, laborer, lover; as child and as parent; as playful, curious, mischievous; as protagonist and witness.

The stories packed into the series seem beyond any reasonable plot. We are

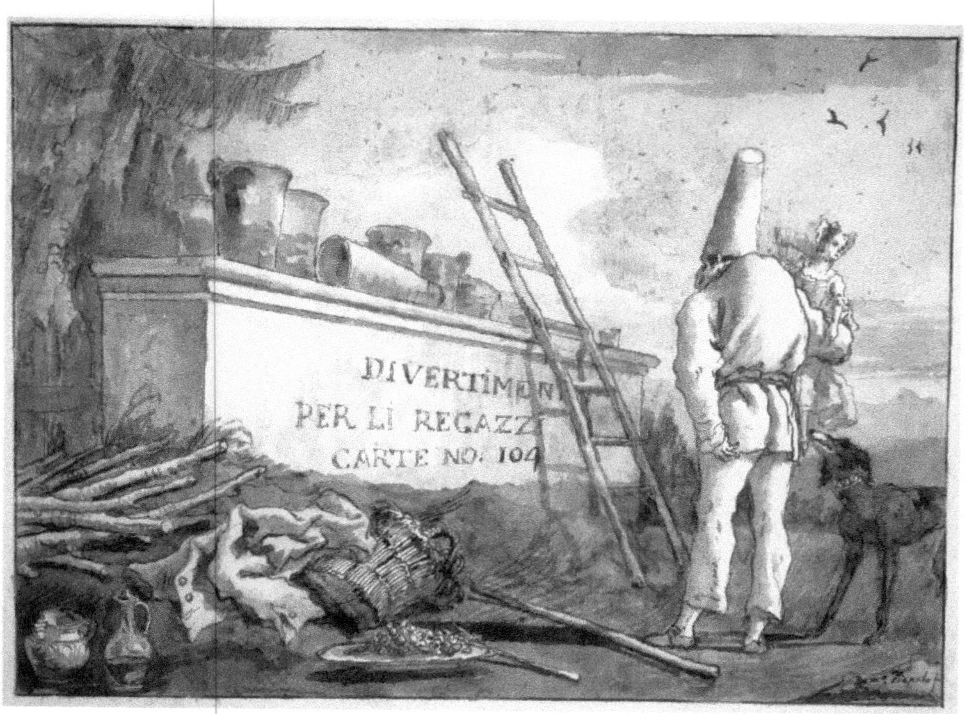

318. Domenico Tiepolo, *Divertimenti per li Regazzi,* frontispiece (ca. 1795–1800). Pen and brown ink, brown wash, over black chalk, 29.4 × 41 cm. (margin), 35.5 × 47 cm. (paper). Nelson-Atkins Museum of Art, Kansas City, Missouri. Purchase: Nelson Trust (32-193/9).

invited less to search out some lost libretto for this narrative richness than to supply one or, rather, many from our own imagination as we read each scene and follow apparent sequences. As with Goya's *Caprichos,* the cumulative effect of a sequence of related images strongly implies a correspondingly connected narrative line; viewing the drawings *en suite,* like turning the pages of a book, at once encourages and, in a sense, confirms narrative expectations. (Laurence Sterne knew well the rules of this game.)

The style of the drawings further encourages such expectation. Although based on his father's example, Domenico's drawing style, from the beginning, was the product of a heavier and more determined hand. To Giambattista's wash technique, which generally remained summary and suggestive, he assigned new mimetic responsibility. Domenico's washes are more slowly applied, more complex in their layering, sometimes mixing brown and black inks. They build shadow more deliberately and are more ambitious in their naturalism, seeking out and defining a range of materials and textures; moving between figure and ground, object and setting, they create a more sustained pictorial continuum. His contours, at first imitating those of his father – and, in a sense, never quite escaping their genealogy – eventually do settle into their own idiosyncratic rhythms, at once more insistent and more tremulous. Abandoning, in effect, the flexibility and suppleness that is the hallmark of Giambattista's poetic penmanship, Domenico's line accepts its own more prosaic manner. Its very consistency seems suited to an aesthetic that is less

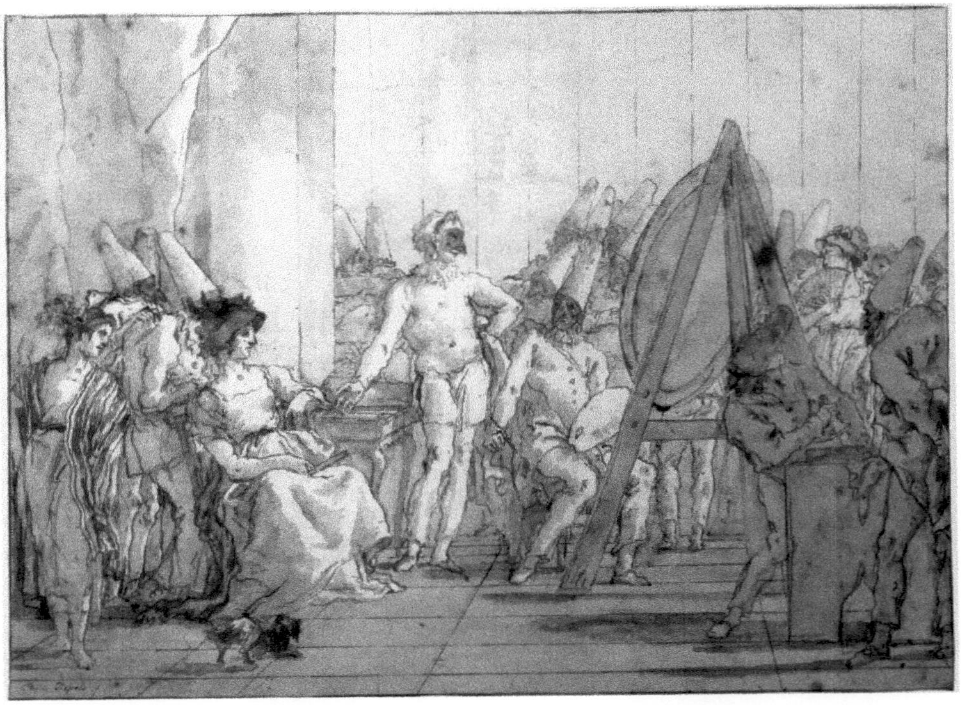

319. Domenico Tiepolo, *Punchinello as Portrait Painter* (ca. 1795–1800). Pen and brown ink, brown and ochre wash, over black chalk, 29.2 × 41.4 cm. (margin), 35.5 × 47 cm. (paper). Present location unknown.

320. Domenico Tiepolo, *Punchinello Abducted by an Eagle* (ca. 1795–1800). Pen and brown ink, brown wash, over black chalk, 29.5 × 41.3 cm. (margin), 35.5 × 47 cm. (paper). Formerly collection Sir Brinsley Ford, London.

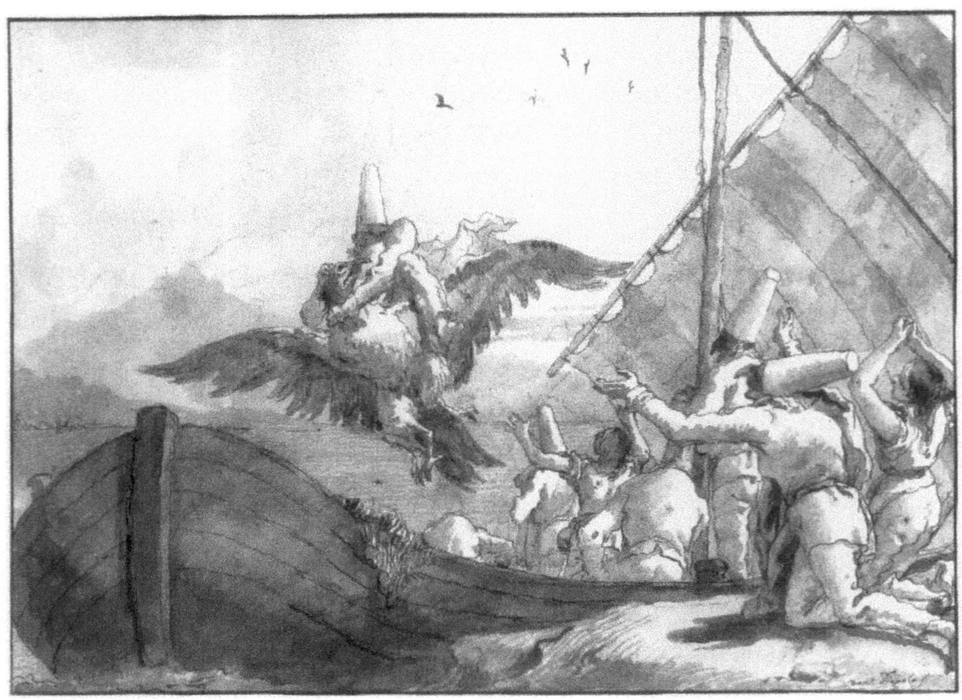

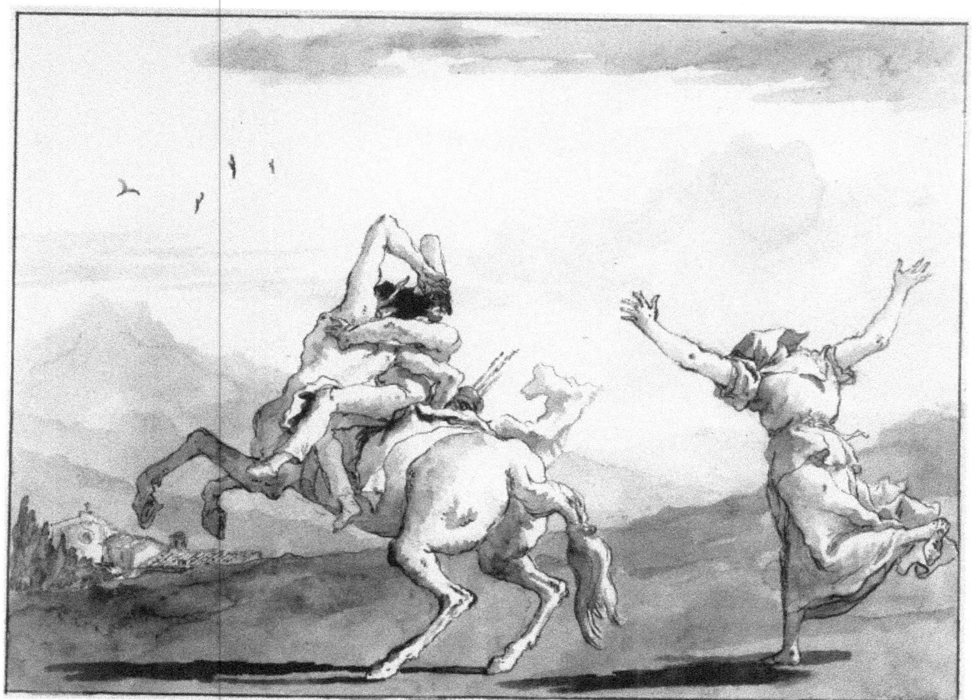

321. Domenico Tiepolo, *Punchinello Abducted by a Centaur* (ca. 1795–1800). Pen and brown ink, brown wash, over black chalk, 29.5 × 41.3 cm. (margin), 35.5 × 47.3 cm. (paper). British Museum, London (1925-4-6-1).

optical, more haptic; a broader, stiffer nib circumscribes form with firmness, bounding with determination. Only a certain nervousness of hand allows some variation; it is an irregularity of course that exaggerates formal features that are part of the paternal legacy, an overarticulation of anatomy that becomes a defining aspect of Domenico's own style. And that quality becomes increasingly marked as Domenico ages, a tremulousness that accords even a sense of lightness to his later drawings.

In the remarkable range of their iconographic reach, Domenico's drawings offer a valedictory to the centuries of Renaissance tradition, a capricious summa of a pictorial culture coming to its end during his lifetime. The *Divertimenti per li Regazzi* are among his very last works, probably his last, and they seem in every way the creations of an aged artist. A world of private fantasy exposed, made deliberately public, their mordant humor leads us to both laughter and tears. They joke, but the joke is heavy. Following the course of Punchinello's lives in these uniformly worked-up drawings, we become increasingly aware of the sheer effort of the project, the sustained, concentrated labor of the septuagenarian draftsman. Domenico must have devoted a major part of his final years to imagining a world of Punchinellos, throwing himself into his own fantasies even as he committed his drawing hand to realizing them. We can only wonder about "li regazzi" with whom he might have shared his joke. All that is clear is that he here lived through drawing, that drawing afforded the old man the means *per isfogare i suoi capricci.*

Epilogue:
Picasso's Rehearsal

With Picasso it is as if he had retraced the whole process of the invention of plastic forms, from anonymous arts to the sophistication of the present day.

– Tristan Tzara[1]

There is a truth in drawing, the most fundamental of representational media. It resides in the transparency of the line, the essential honesty of the deliberately dissimulating mark – even the line of Parrhasios by inflecting itself spatially along its course thereby demonstrates its very artifice. The transformative nature of the line fulfilling its mimetic responsibilities has inspired admiration since antiquity, and the nature of that transformation, as well as its tension with the materiality of the mark itself, has challenged critical interpretation. Pliny's comments reflect, with tantalizing laconicism, a rich studio tradition of professional self-awareness. Leonardo da Vinci's meditations on his art, like his own graphic practice, explore the possibilities of such linear transformation as a way of simultaneously knowing and representing the world. Raphael, in his figures as in his calligraphy, literally embodies the elegant linear aesthetic of graceful serpentine motion. The very motions of the drawing hand construct new realities.

Founded on the fundamental dynamics of linear transformation, drawing offers itself as the most efficient medium of imaginative projection. Drawing provides the means for realizing that *disegno* in the head (Cennini); the act of drawing releases those figures filling the head of any good artist (Dürer). Yet it is also the substance of those ideas, enabling their very conception. The night monsters surrounding Goya's dozing draftsman – like the figures informing Michelangelo's blocks of marble – are creatures of their medium, of drawing.

Drawing is expression. Through it the artist leaves his mark, signing himself. But drawing is also a means of reaching out, an extension of the self. "Drawing is like making an expressive gesture," Matisse observed, "but it has the advantage of permanency."[2] For Michelangelo that gesture carried the urgency of feeling directed toward an other; the expressive gesture was one both of graphic creation, the very act of drawing, and of an offering, a gift to an other. For Rembrandt the drawing gesture offered a way of projecting himself into worlds of his own imagining.

The truth or, rather, the truths of drawing, affirmed throughout the long history of graphic marking, find special articulation at certain moments in that history: tentatively in antiquity and most emphatically within the Renaissance tradition that culminated in the art of Goya – even as its conventions were transformed and transcended. And in the twentieth century drawing enjoyed another period of intense self-reflection. Such graphic awareness most obviously informs the pedagogic intentions of artists like Paul Klee and Wassily Kandinsky, both of whom rehearse, from their distinctive perspectives, the fundamental Albertian geometry of representation: from point and line to plane.[3] But the pedagogical link between early Renaissance and Bauhaus theory is less significant than the continuities in praxis that we encounter in the work of the most ambitious master draftsmen of the twentieth century, Matisse and, especially, Picasso. These creators of pictorial modernism carried with them the academic traditions that they may have rejected but that they never forgot. Essentially committed to the figure – and that commitment includes by extension still life, itself an articulation of lived space – they distilled their new art from basic studio practice.

> In drawing, nothing is better than the first attempt.[4]

The precosity of the child draftsman is a central element in the myth of the artist. Picasso, the son of an academic painter, claimed that he could draw before he could speak and that even as a child he drew like a Raphael. Like Leonardo long before, this Spanish prodigy too had a professional father with whom to contend, but his was a master in his own art. It is interesting (although hardly extraordinary) that Picasso's earliest graphic activity was supposedly devoted to drawing spirals, and, further recapitulation of a mythic topos, his first images were said to have been traced "in the sand where children played in the Plaza de la Merced."[5] Picasso's interest in children's drawings is of course visually confirmed by his own mature draftsmanship, with its willful yet sophisticated simplification and conceptual directness, and is further, if redundantly, attested by his later self-reflective comment at an exhibition of children's drawings: "When I was their age I could draw like Raphael, but it took me a lifetime to learn to draw like them."[6] However notorious the mythicizing element in the early biography of the artist, the terms of this narrative make a certain sense, as mythic topoi and graphic reality mutually validate each other.

A sheet that is generally dated to about 1898–99 affords an interesting document of the role of drawing in the young artist's imaginings (Fig. 322).[7] Around the sensitive Conté crayon portrait of a boy a series of marginal sketches transforms the reserved field into one of imaginative exploration. Rapid pen sketches of toreros and a bull follow a graphic momentum not unlike the kind we have traced before in the marginalia of Leonardo: form is generated out of the movements of the pen, and those movements are essentially circular, their cumulative effect one of spiraling into space – leading the two retreating figures trailing their capes in graphic flourish. Less spontaneous, more deliberately studied, is the kind of analytic deconstruction performed on the basic perspective box crayoned in the upper left corner: below, its simple geometry is reduced to component planes simultaneously floating in an orthogonally indicated space and interlocking on the surface, a proleptic cubist diagram. Along the lower edge of the field yet another analysis is carried out on the calligraphy of a telling word: *dibujo* ("drawing").[8] It is as though the word itself has instigated its own deconstruction by the motor means of its original inscription, as the writing hand becomes the drawing hand and linear will triumphs over verbal legibility.

In these linear analyses the adolescent Picasso explores the mechanics of graphic representation and writing, in a dialectic rapport with his own initial drawing. Like Leonardo, he seems to wonder at the motions of his own hand, the lines that it traces, and to delight in varying them; for both, the elision between writing and drawing is natural. The very operations of graphic production, the marking process itself, become the subject of the draftsman's interest. The paper becomes an inviting field for exploration and drawing the means of discovery, that is, of invention. "To find is the thing."[9]

> To know what you want to draw, you have to begin drawing it.[10]

Whatever primitive traces he may have left to be obliterated in the sand of the Plaza de la Merced, young Picasso was subjected to a standard academic education in drawing. Among his earliest extant drawings are a group that have sometimes been considered studies after plaster casts but are in fact copies made directly from French drawing manuals (Fig. 323). These books offered convenient illustrations of pre-

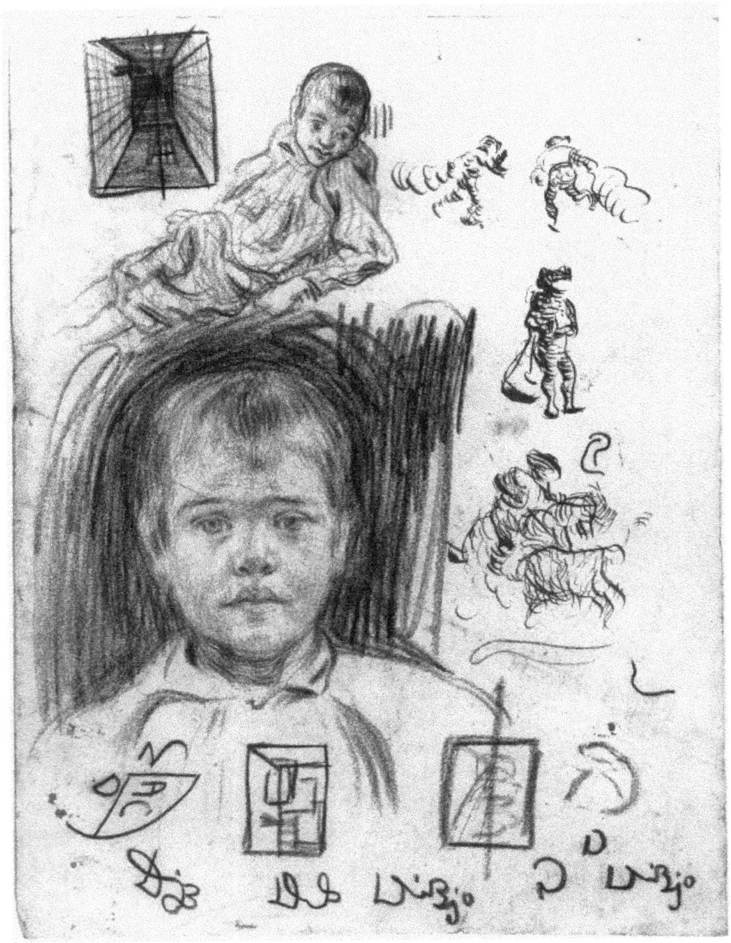

322. Pablo Picasso, *A Child's Face and Other Sketches* (1898–99). Conté crayon and pen on paper, 32.1 × 24.1 cm. Museu Picasso, Barcelona (inv. MPB 110.577).

dictable models, such as the Belvedere torso and other antique sculpture, classical guarantors of cultural as well as anatomical propriety. On a more fundamental level, they taught through schematic analyses of figure construction and simplified contours of chiaroscuro patterns. However innate the genius, the young Picasso perfected his drawing by drawing from drawings, copying ready graphic structures.[11] Supposedly instructing the novice how to draw like Raphael, the methodological reductiveness of such academic pedagogy naturally heightened awareness of its own mechanisms. The very artifice of such diagrammatic simplification of form and tone, as well as the parsing of the human body into a set of unit problems (standard in drawing books since the Renaissance) valorized the independent constituents of drawing, whether parts of anatomy or patterns of rendering. Those two aspects of his early training, anatomy and rendering, were to serve together, and especially at their intersection, as a basis for Picasso's subsequent adventures in graphic invention.

The formal deconstructions of early Cubism represent in effect an extension, a most creative one, to be sure, of the analytic approach instilled by the graphic

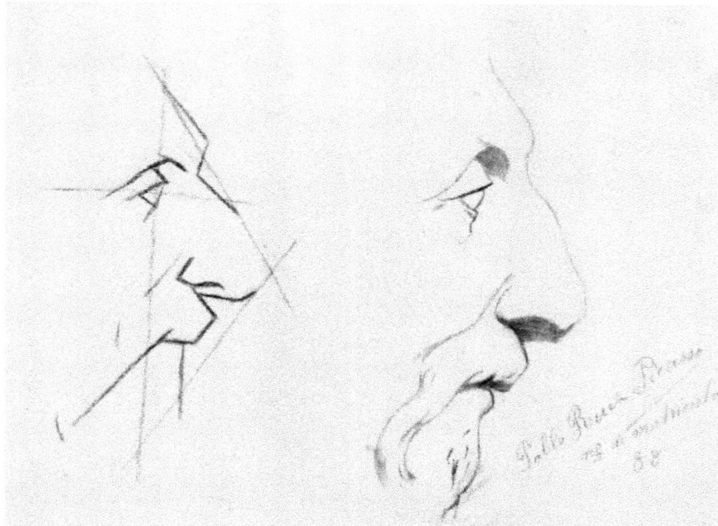

323. Pablo Picasso, *Profile Heads after Bargue* (1892–93). Conté crayon on paper, 23.7 × 31 cm. Heirs of the artist.

exempla of the academic drawing books, if not by their intent. In painting, the monochromatic palette of early Cubism, eliminating the superficial distraction of color, brings the analysis of three-dimensional form to ever clearer focus – even as such form yields to the insistent reality of painting. Modeling depends as much upon the rigorous control of touch, as independent marks work in concert to establish tonal pattern. The constructive stroke of the brush in this kind of painting may find a basic inspiration in Cézanne, but, drained of color, it recalls with equal insistence its origins in drawing. Repeated touches, sequences of strokes similar in length and orientation, define and affirm the continuity of planes in this art. Such repetition testifies to the gestures of application. In the patterning itself, the repetitive sequencing, we recognize the touch of the draftsman. The accumulation of marks, each respecting the autonomy of its neighbor, evokes the operations of drawing, the creation and modulation of tone through successive strokes of pen, pencil, or charcoal (Fig. 324). There is, in fact, a greater variety of such stroking in Picasso's drawing than in his painting. In the analytic Cubist paintings the brush is more deliberately controlled, and such control establishes a certain order. In the drawings, however, the stroke may be scribbled, hooked, or straight, executed rapidly or more systematically, as the draftsman's hand more instinctively searches out the ambiguities of formal representation and tests the ambivalence of surface.

> Cubism is no different from any other school of painting. The same principles and the same elements are common to all.[12]

Cubism proves the very means of representation. It tests the fundamental operations of painting even as it builds a new kind of imagery from them, one that presses the conventions of pictorial art. Threatening to undermine assumptions

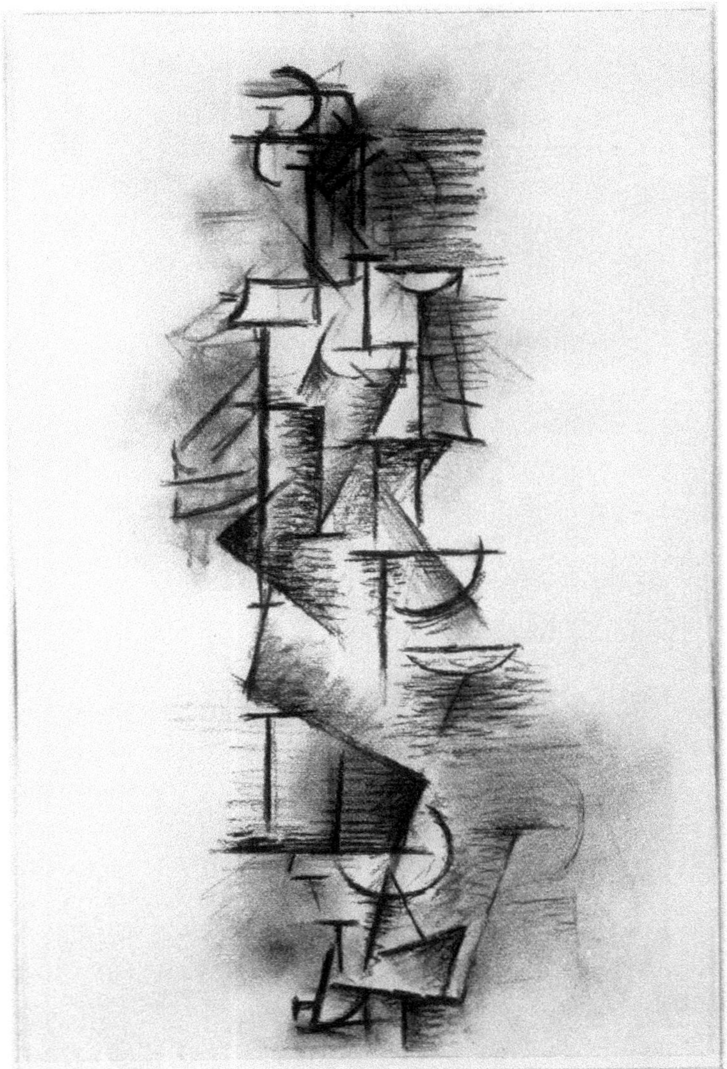

324. Pablo Picasso, *Standing Female Nude* (1910). Charcoal, 48.3 × 31.4 cm. Metropolitan Museum of Art, New York. Alfred Steiglitz Collection, 1949 (49.70.34).

and practices of representation that were in fact critical to its own achievement, this new discovery posed the most radical challenge yet to the art of painting. Perhaps in response to its deconstructive implications, Picasso was to insist that Cubism "kept itself within the limits and limitations of painting, never pretending to go beyond it."[13] On the level of pictorial construction, in so far as its essential operations play at and with the picture plane, Picasso was right.

Crucial to analytic Cubism are those basic lessons of tonal development, the mechanics of rendering. Shading establishes the implications of overlap that creates the ambivalence of the plane upon which this art depends. Suggesting tonal continuities through sequences of autonomous marks maintains constant reference to the single flat surface on which they are applied; where tone dissipates, the opening of the marked fabric to the ground itself returns the apparently recessive or shadowed plane to that surface. In the visual interchange that creates meaning in analytic Cubism the dialectic tension between mark and ground plays out a dynamic we recognize as inherent to the art of drawing.[14]

While hardly the exclusive prerogative of graphic media, the independence of the mark is essential to the graphic arts, to drawing and to printmaking (Fig. 325). Nor is the short dash the unique constitutive mark of Cubism. The longer line

325. Pablo Picasso, *Still Life with Bottle of Marc* (1911, published 1912). Drypoint, printed in black, plate: 50 × 30.5 cm. Museum of Modern Art, New York. Acquired through the Lillie P. Bliss Bequest. Photograph ©2000 The Museum of Modern Art, New York.

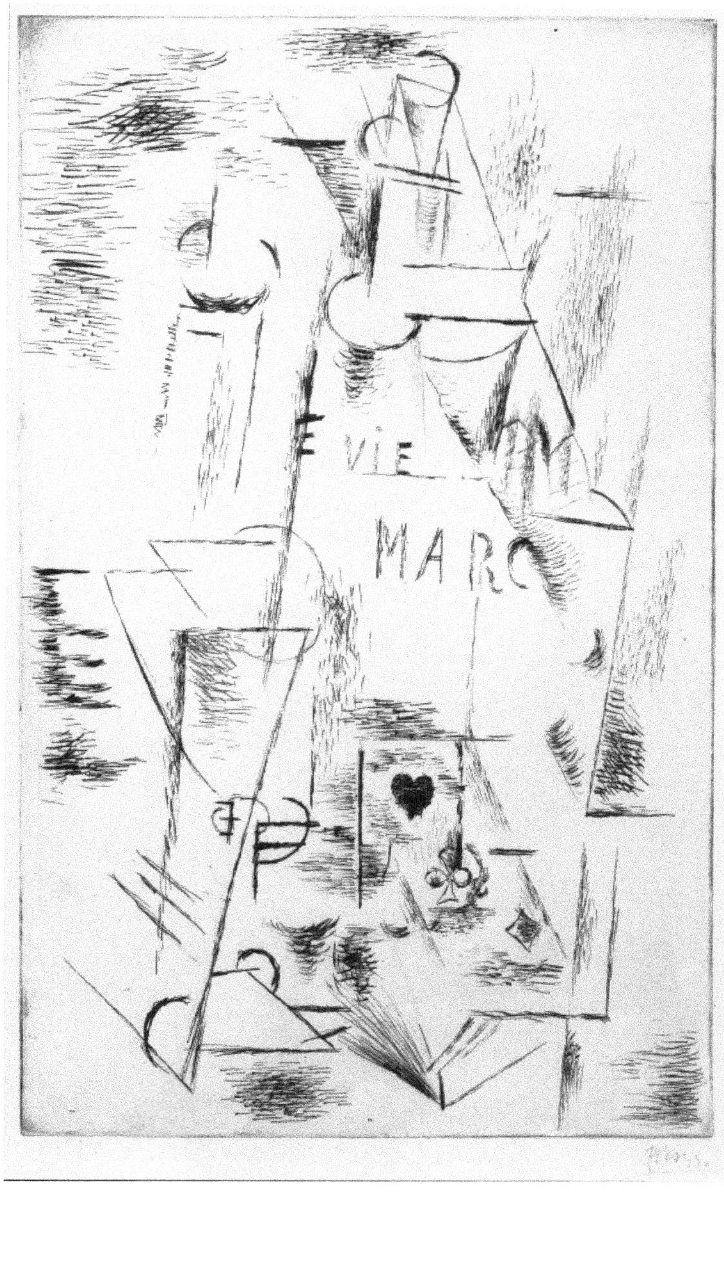

asserts itself even more insistently as drawing; it establishes the structural armature of the image, defines the edges of planes, traces the contours of objects: that is, it performs the basic functions of drawing. In his retreat from the implications of Cubism Picasso took refuge precisely in the security of the drawn line, its elemental quality and representational impulse. The (in)famous return to classicism was essentially a return to drawing, to linear styles of the past, including his own pre-Cubist draftsmanship, to the security of his own mimetic manual skills.

In the imagery of Cubism line conforms to a certain geometric regularity of straight strokes and curves; the mark functions as a constituent element of the larger structure. In Picasso's more conventionally representational figural art, whether from the blue and rose periods or the post-Cubist neoclassicism, line leads a freer, more self-indulgent life, even as it obeys mimetic directives. Contours may be firmly bound, the pencil in continuous touch with the paper or delicately tensile, or deliberately or tentatively probing, the contour itself the result of a hesitant, searching movement, the pencil pausing to confirm its direction (Fig. 326). It is less a matter of stylistic evolution than of the setting out of options, options offered by a classical linear tradition tracing back from Degas through Ingres and Raphael to

326. Pablo Picasso, *Portrait of Igor Stravinsky* (May 24, 1920). Pencil on gray paper, 62 × 48.5 cm. Musée Picasso, Paris.

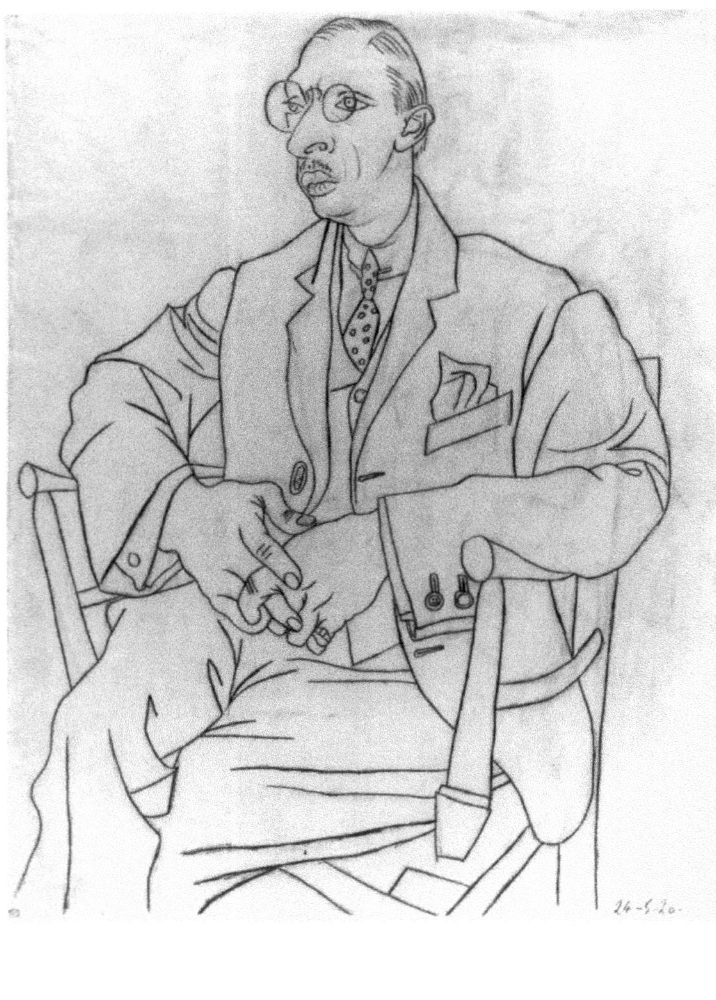

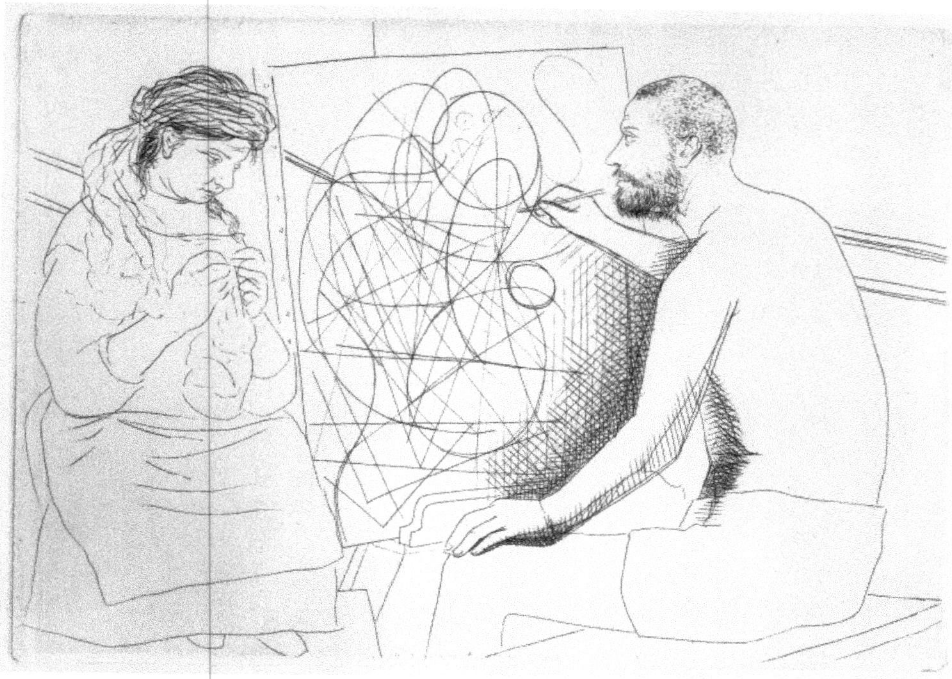

327. Pablo Picasso, *Painter with a Model Knitting,* from *Le Chef d'oeuvre inconnu,* by Honoré de Balzac. Paris, 1927. Published by Ambroise Vollard, 1931. Etching, 19.2 × 27.7 cm. Museum of Modern Art, New York. Louis E. Stern Collection. Photograph ©2000 The Museum of Modern Art, New York.

ancient vase painting. Once claimed, each manner remains a readily available resource.[15]

Picasso's concept of style was, we might say, essentially graphic, linear in that it depended upon formal structuring, the varieties of enclosing contour and modeling by discrete mark. In aesthetically self-conscious images like the etching for Vollard's edition of Balzac's *Le Chef d'oeuvre inconnu* (Fig. 327) the play of line defines the alternative modes of representation that are its subject: the reticent touch of the knitting model; the traced geometries of the composition on the easel; the closed classical contours of the artist, his form further articulated by regular, mechanical hatching patterns evocative of engraving. Transformation is both theme and means in Picasso's art, and the metamorphic operations tend to be fundamentally linear.[16]

In graphic series like the *Vollard Suite* Picasso explored and exploited the resources of line with sustained attention to its possibilities and its resonance, art-historical as well as expressive. The linear purity of the opening etchings at once revives and validates classical drawing, each a demonstration of the line of Parrhasios. And, appropriately, the linear conventions of inherited graphic traditions are revisited, rather like the technical vignettes of Hogarth's frames (cf. Figs. 267, 268): veils of cross-hatching and concentrations of scribbling, stereometric modeling, and deep chiaroscuro – as well as the printmaker's practices of drypoint and burin, of sugar-lift acquatint, of scraping and burnishing. Four of the plates portray images of Rembrandt, evidently the result of discovery in process (Fig. 328). As

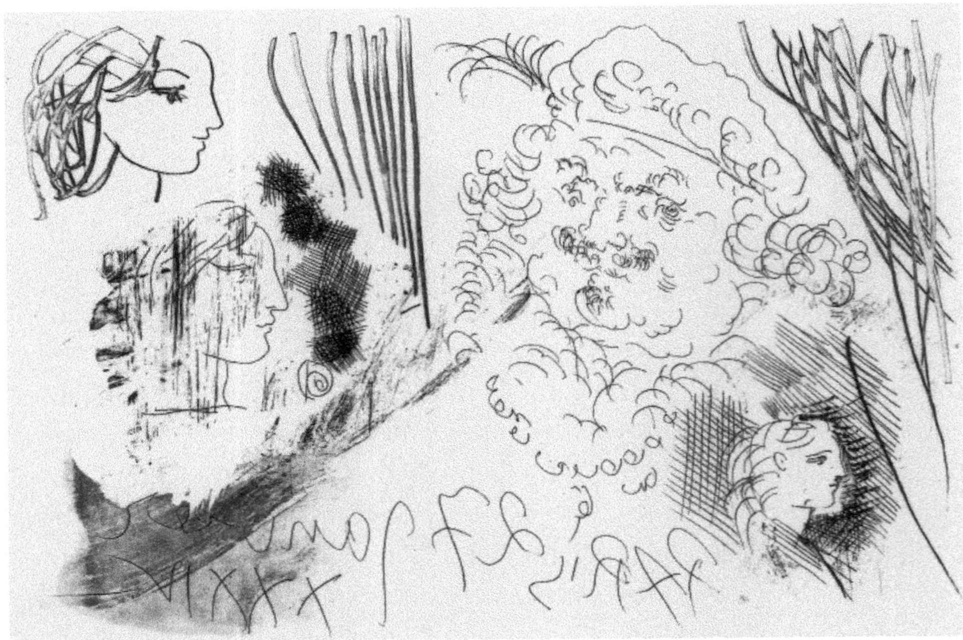

328. Pablo Picasso, *Head of Rembrandt and Profiles of Marie-Thérèse* (Paris, January 27, 1934, printed 1939), from the *Vollard Suite*. Etching on copper, printed in black, plate: 13.8 × 20.8 cm. Museum of Modern Art, New York. Abby Aldrich Rockefeller Fund. Photograph ©2000 The Museum of Modern Art, New York.

Picasso explained to Kahnweiler, "It's all on account of that varnish that cracks. It happened to one of my plates. I said to myself, 'It's spoiled, I'll just do any old thing on it.' I began to scrawl. What came out was Rembrandt. I began to like it, and I kept on. I even did another one, with his turban, his furs, and his eye – his elephant's eye, you know. Now I'm going on with the plate to see if I can get blacks like his – you don't get them at the first try."[17] Picasso's experience replays that of past discoverers, like Leonardo; the twentieth-century master might well have adopted Piranesi's motto: *Col sporcar si trova.*

We are not merely the executors of our work; we *live* our work.[18]

The prints that constitute the *Vollard Suite* document a series of findings by Picasso, discoveries of techniques of etching and engraving, of linear vocabularies, of the evolving iconography of his self, the artist. From designs of remarkably restrained linear purity (Fig. 329) to varied combinations of graphic construction (Fig. 330) and technique – drypoint, etching, engraving, and aquatint (Fig. 331) – these plates manifest the artist's graphic prowess, the metamorphic power of his art. Picasso's drawing hand creates a world of creative passions, impulses at once erotic and aesthetic, violent and tender. It is a felt world of his imaginings, invented by the *disegno* in *la testa sua,* populated by creatures of his mind, the figures in his head. Fauns and minotaurs, sleepers and watchers, models and artists: these are the dramatis personae of the *Vollard Suite,* for and through whom Picasso lives scenarios domestic and epic, professional and mythic.[19] Dominating the *Vollard Suite*

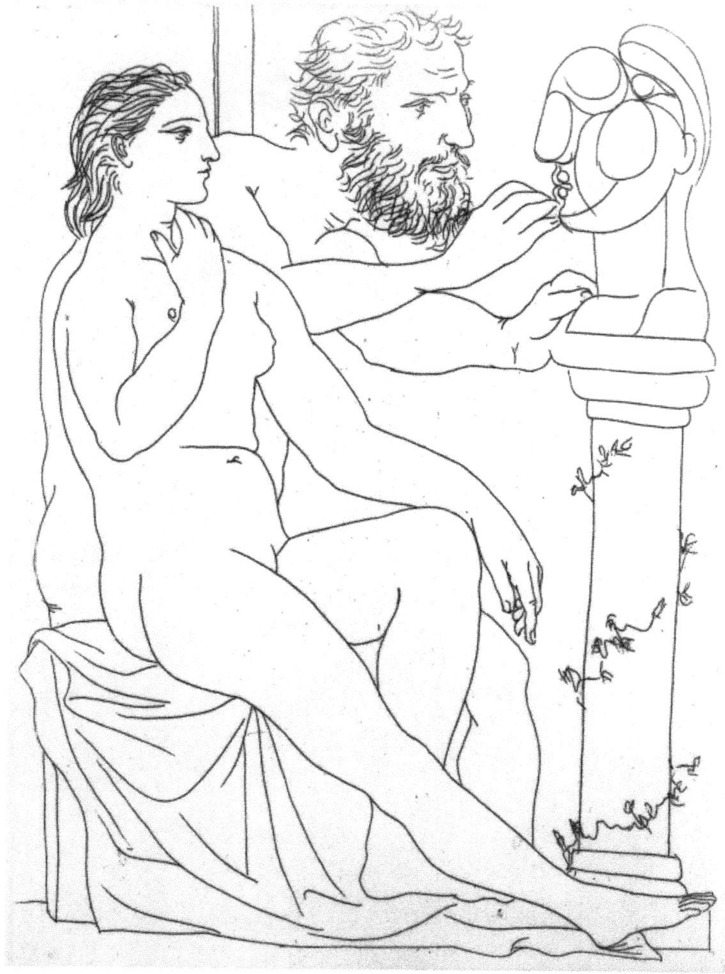

329. Pablo Picasso, *Model and Sculptor with His Sculpture* (March 17, 1933, printed in 1939), from the *Vollard Suite.* Etching, printed in black, plate: 26.7 × 19.3 cm. Museum of Modern Art, New York. Abby Aldrich Rockefeller Fund. Photograph ©2000 The Museum of Modern Art, New York.

is the theme of the sculptor's studio, scenes in which model and statue constantly exchange roles as the object of the creator's attention or desire, in which passion is projected, displaced from living to artificial beings, and then returned again in a grand conjugation of the Pygmalion myth.

Especially in his graphic art, in drawings and prints, Picasso enacted a fantasy life that assembled the living and the dead, the real and the imagined, into his own kind of family romance. Cavaliers and musketeers evoke the world of his seventeenth-century artistic ancestors, Rembrandt and Velázquez, and the parade of nude majas and old Celestinas, as well as his broad wash technique, testify to the continuing presence of Goya in the modern Spaniard's imagination (Fig. 332). With pen, pencil, or brush in hand, Picasso created his own human comedy; the drawn line becomes a story line, its plot running a course worthy of Tristram Shandy.

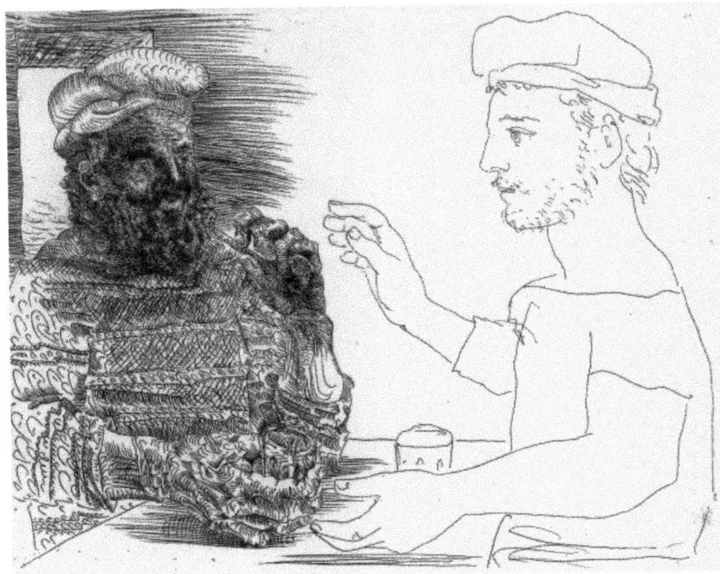

330. Pablo Picasso, *The Tavern: Two Catalan Fishermen* (November 29, 1934, printed 1939), from the *Vollard Suite.* Etching on copper, printed in black, plate: 23.7 × 29.7 cm. Museum of Modern Art, New York. Abby Aldrich Rockefeller Fund. Photograph ©2000 The Museum of Modern Art, New York.

331. Pablo Picasso, *Faun Unveiling a Sleeping Girl* (June 12, 1936, printed in 1939), from the *Vollard Suite.* Aquatint, lift-ground acquatint, and engraving, printed in black, 31.6 × 41.7 cm. The Museum of Modern Art, New York. Abby Aldrich Rockefeller Fund. Photograph ©2000 The Museum of Modern Art, New York.

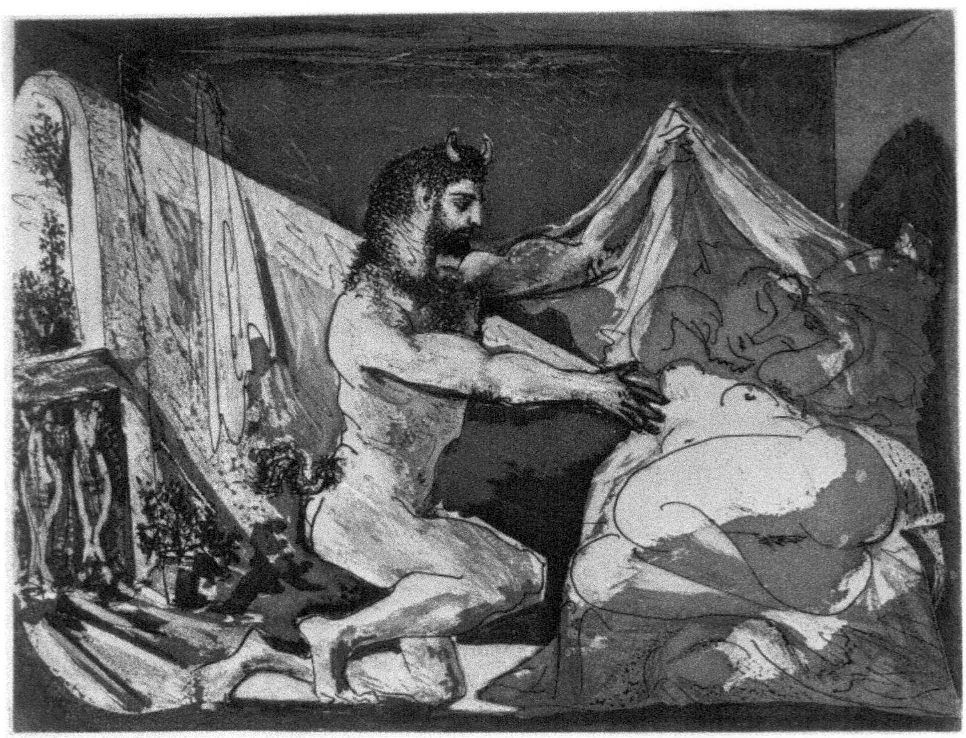

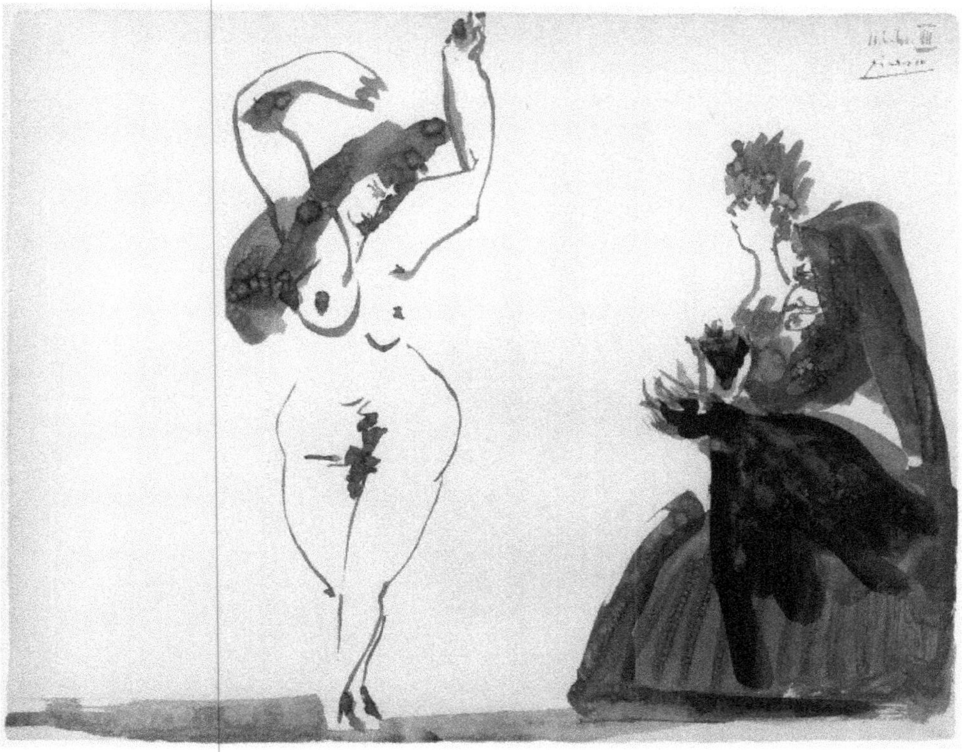

332. Pablo Picasso, *A Dancer and Two Women* (June 11, 1960). Ink and wash on paper, 50.5 × 65 cm. Present location unknown.

> Of course, one never knows what's going to come out, but as soon as the drawing gets underway, a story or an idea is born, and that's it. Then the story grows, like theatre or life – and the drawing is turned into other drawings, a real novel. It's great fun, believe me. At least, I enjoy myself no end inventing these stories, and I spend hour after hour while I draw, observing my creatures and thinking about the mad things they're up to; basically, it's my way of writing fiction.[20]

Goya himself or Domenico Tiepolo might have said as much.

Capricci, scherzi di fantasia, divertimenti: Like his predecessors, Picasso entered into a dialectic with his own creative energies, responding to the inventions of his hand and mind with yet new inventions, investing himself with deepening self-consciousness in the accumulated meditations on his art and its vital potential. In the graphic images he produced in series, Picasso signed and dated each one; fixing the image in time, the signature stands as testimony to the reality of its creation, affirming its truth – not unlike Leonardo's clear documentation of his earliest landscape drawing. Picasso lived his art.[21]

Wandering among his invented *personaggi* is the figure of the artist himself. He may be old, wrinkled, and potbellied, or he may be young, even a child, wreathed in laurel, but he is essentially an observing eye and possessing hand, standing before easel or model, or the desiring spectator at the margin of the world of his own creation; that world may be epitomized by the female nude in open display and the desire of the aged artist by the ambition of his libidinous brush.

Picasso's rehearsals restage scenes from the history of art, including his own art, through which he projected his self and his life. Through drawing the artist extends himself into the world and becomes part of the world, becomes, as Kokoschka said, "part of the world's imaginings" – or, more to the point, part of his own imagined world.

Notes

1. CRITICISM, CONNOISSEURSHIP, AND THE PHENOMENOLOGY OF DRAWING

1. Roland Barthes, preface to Roger Druet and Herman Grégoire, *La civilization de l'écriture* (Paris, 1976), p. 5, cited in Georges Jean, *Writing: The Story of Alphabets and Scripts*, trans. Jenny Oates (New York and London, 1992), p. 196.
2. For this notion, formulated in a text attributed to the eighth-century calligrapher Yang-pin, see John Hay, "Surface and the Chinese Painter: The Discovery of Surface," *Archives of Asian Art* 38 (1985): 98. The generative potential of paper has assumed a particularly radical function in recent Chinese calligraphy: see Yiguo Zhang, *Brushed Voices: Calligraphy in Contemporary China* (New York, 1998), pp. 14, 108.
3. Meyer Schapiro has emphasized the historical significance of the invention of prepared surface and its implications for the definition of a bounded pictorial space. See "On Some Problems in the Semiotics of Visual Art: Field and Vehicle in Image-Signs," *Semiotica* 1 (1969): 223–42; reprinted in volume 4 of his selected papers, *Theory and Philosophy of Art: Style, Artist, and Society* (New York, 1994), pp. 1–32. For a particularly suggestive extended consideration of the nature of drawing, see Philip Rawson, *Drawing*, 2d ed. (Philadelphia, 1987).
4. Bernard Berenson, *The Drawings of the Florentine Painters* (Chicago, 1938), II, p. 189, no. 1519[A]. More recently, Alexander Perrig has attempted to establish an objective basis for the critical evaluation of drawings: see *Michelangelo-Studien, I: Michelangelo und die Zeichnungswissenschaft – Ein methodologischer Versuch* (Frankfurt am Main and Bern, 1976), and *Michelangelo's Drawings: The Science of Attribution* (New Haven and London, 1991); for problems in practice of Perrig's theory, cf. my review, "More or Less Michelangelo," *Drawing* 13 (1992): 112f. For a good introduction to the historical development of connoisseurship, see Carol Gibson-Wood, "Studies in the Theory of Connoisseurship from Vasari to Morelli," Ph.D. dissertation (Warburg Institute, University of London, 1982). See as well Edgar Wind's "Critique of Connoisseurship," in *Art and Anarchy*, rev. ed. (New York, 1969), pp. 32–51.
5. Leonardo da Vinci, *Treatise on Painting [Codex Urbinas Latinus 1270]*, ed. A. Philip McMahon (Princeton, 1956), ¶ 506, c. 154: ". . . perchè termine d'una cosa in un'altra è di natura di linea matematicha, ma non linea; perché il termine d'un colore è principio d'un altro colore, e non è da essere però detta linea, perché nissuna cosa s'intramette infra il termine d'un colore che sia antiposto a un altro colore se non è il termine, il quale è cosa insensibile d'apresso. . . ."
6. Pliny the Elder, *Natural History*, XXXV, 15; trans. K. Jex-Blake, *The Elder Pliny's Chapters on the History of Art*, ed. E. Sellers, London, 1896, p. 85. Pliny proceeds to ascribe the "invention of linear drawing" to individual artists, to Philokles of Egypt or to Kleanthes of Corinth, and to record its subsequent progress in the work of other specific masters: "The first to practice it were Arideikes of Corinth, and Telephanes of Sikyon, who still used no colour, though they had begun to give inner markings. . . ."

   The invention of painting in the tracing of shadow and the corollary primitive virtue of pure line were frequent topics in ancient rhetoric: e.g., Quintilian, *Institutio Oratoria*, X, ii, 7–8; Dionysios of Halikarnassos, *De Isaeo* 4 (cited below, note 16).

Futher on *lineamenta* and *linea*, see J. J. Pollitt, *The Ancient View of Greek Art: Criticism, History, and Terminology* (New Haven and London, 1974), pp. 249–54. On primitive purity, see E. H. Gombrich, "The Debate on Primitivism in Ancient Rhetoric," *Journal of the Warburg and Courtauld Institutes* 29 (1966): 24–38.

Surviving Paleolithic cave art would seem to confirm the assumptions behind early accounts like that of Pliny: cf. S. Giedion, *The Eternal Present: The Beginnings of Art* (New York, 1962), pp. 19–22, 349–56, and "The Outline in the Early Beginnings of Art," *Leonardo* 2 (1968): 181–92. The myth itself became a standard topos in the Renaissance: e.g., in Leon Battista Alberti, *De Pictura*, ed. Cecil Grayson (Rome and Bari, 1975), ¶ 31, and Leonardo, *Treatise on Painting*, ed. McMahon, ¶ 98, c. 49v).

7. Pliny, *Natural History*, XXXV, 151; cf. also the variations in XXXVII, 9: "Linear drawing was discovered by Saurias, who traced the outline of the shadow cast by a horse in the sun, and painting by Kraton, who painted on a whitened tablet the shadows of a man and woman. The maiden invented the art of modeling figures in relief. She was in love with a youth, and while he lay asleep she sketched the outline of his shadow on the wall. Delighted with the perfection of the likeness, her father, who was a potter, cut out the shape and filled in the outline with clay; the figure is still preserved at Corinth" (trans. Jex-Blake, p. 227).

Giorgio Vasari included a scene of the invention of drawing, along with other professional legends, in a pictorial cycle in the Florentine house given him by Duke Cosimo I de' Medici: see F. H. Jacobs, "Vasari's Vision of the History of Painting: Frescoes in the Casa Vasari, Florence," *Art Bulletin* 66 (1984): 399–416. For later representations of the myth, see Robert Rosenblum, "The Origin of Painting: A Problem in the Iconography of Romantic Classicism," *Art Bulletin* 39 (1957): 179–290.

Joachim von Sandrart's illustrations (Figs. 1, 2) appeared as a single plate in the second part of his *Teutsche Academie der edlen Bau- Bild- und Mahlerey Künste* (Nuremberg, 1675), opposite page 2, executed by Georg Andreas Wolfgang. Other impressions of the same edition, it is interesting to note, carry variant compositions executed by his great-nephew, Johann Jacob Sandrart, and this version is used in Sandrart's *Academia Nobilissimae Artis Pictoriae* (Nuremberg, 1683), opposite page 40. The theoretical implications of these images have been discussed by Richard Schiff, "On Criticism Handling History," *Art Criticism* 3:1 (1986): 60–77, and "Performing an Appearance: On the Surface of Abstract Expressionism," in *Abstract Expressionism: The Critical Developments*, ed. Michael Auping (New York, 1987), pp. 94–123, esp. 100–103.

8. For example, the reflected image of Narcissus, as related, somewhat metaphorically, by Alberti in *Della pittura* (1435):

> . . . usai di dire tra i miei amici, secondo la sentenza de' poeti, quel Narcisso convertito in fiore essere della pittura stato inventore; ché già ove sia la pittura fiore d'ogni arte, ivi tutta la storia di Narcisso viene a proposito. Che dirai tu essere dipignere altra cosa che simile abracciare con arte quella ivi superficie del fonte? (*De pictura*, ed. Grayson,¶ 26)

9. Letter to Henry Clifford (1948), in Jack Flam, ed., *Matisse on Art*, rev. ed. (Berkeley and Los Angeles, 1995), p. 183. On the creative tension between color and drawing in Matisse's art, see Yve-Alain Bois, "Matisse and 'Arche-drawing,'" in *Painting as Model* (Cambridge, Mass., and London, 1990), pp. 3–63.

10. From an essay of 1927 on drawings by Cocteau, *Poésies graphiques*, quoted by Peter Dronke, "Curtius as Medievalist and Modernist," *Times Literary Supplement*, October 30, 1980, p. 1104. Cf. Aristotle, *Poetics* 6 [1450a–1450b]: ". . . the first essential, the life and soul, so to speak, of tragedy is the plot; . . . the characters come second – compare the parallel in painting, where the most beautiful colours laid on without order will not give one the same pleasure as a simple black-and-white sketch of a portrait" (*The Complete Works of Aristotle: The Revised Oxford Translation*, ed. Jonathan Barnes [Princeton, 1984], p. 2312). Cf. as well the modern connoisseur's moralizing pronouncement: "Drawing, then, as an art by itself, is one where the line predominates, where modelling should be procured as little as possible by *chiaroscuro*, as much as possible by contour. Light and shade are even more the murderers of pure drawing, than our latter-day orchestra of pure music" (Berenson, *The Drawings of the Florentine Painters*, I, p. 226).

11. *Natural History*, XXXV, 81–83; trans. Jex-Blake, pp. 121–23.

12. *Natural History*, XXXV, 84. The obvious studio relevance of Apelles' motto is attested by later anecdotes about artists drawing, often after the dinner table has been cleared, merely "per isfogare il capriccio." Cf., e.g., Carlo Ridolfi on Jacopo Palma il Giovane (*Le maraviglie dell'arte* [1648], ed. Detlev von Hadeln [Berlin, 1914–24], II, p. 203) and Carlo Cesare Malvasia on the Carracci (*Felsina pittrice: Vite de' pittori bolognesi* [1678], ed. Giampietro Zanotti [Bologna, 1841], I, p. 334. On the printed drawing manuals, see especially E. H. Gombrich, *Art and Illusion: A Study in the Psychology of Pictorial Representation* (New York, 1960), pp. 146–78; David Rosand, "The Crisis of the Venetian Renaissance Tradition," *L'Arte* 11–12 (1970): 5–53; Chittima Amornpichetkul, "Seventeenth-Century Italian Drawing Books: Their Origin and Development," in *Children of Mercury: The Education of Artists in the Sixteenth and Seventeenth Centuries* (Providence, 1984), pp. 109–18; Paul van den Akker,

Sporen van vaardigheid: De ontwerpmethode voor de figuurhouding in de Italiaanse tekenkunst van de renaissance (Abcoude, 1991).

13. The basic survey of this tradition is H. van de Waal, "The *Linea Summae Tenuitatis* of Apelles: Pliny's Phrase and Its Interpreters," *Zeitschrift für Aesthetik und allgemeine Kunstwissenschaft* 12 (1967): 5–32. Finding none of the interpretations reviewed by Van de Waal convincing, E. H. Gombrich offered a further reading of the story, always in an illusionistic key, as a parable of the invention of highlight: "The Heritage of Apelles," in *The Heritage of Apelles: Studies in the Art of the Renaissance* (Ithaca, 1976), pp. 3–18.

    For further discussion in a Renaissance context, see A.-M.L. [Anne-Marie Lecoq], "Apelle et Protogène: La signature-ductus," *Revue de l'art* 26 (1974): 46–47 (citing the printer's mark of Valentin Schaffner [or Valentin Curio], which shows the hand of Apelles drawing the third line), and Martin Warnke, "Praxisfelder der Kunsttheorie: Über die Geburtswehen des Individualstils," *Idea. Jahrbuch der Hamburger Kunsthalle* 1 (1982): 54–71. More recently, the problem has been addressed by James Elkins, "Marks, Traces, *Traits*, Contours, *Orli*, and *Splendores:* Nonsemiotic Elements in Pictures," *Critical Inquiry* 21 (1995): 822–60, who vigorously, and appropriately, challenges Gombrich's reading.

14. Ernst Kris and Otto Kurz, *Legend, Myth, and Magic in the Image of the Artist* (1934) (New Haven and London, 1979), p. 96. For the professional aspect of ancient criticism, its roots in studio tradition, see Pollitt, *The Ancient View of Greek Art*, pp. 12–31. Just that professionalism enabled the translation of the legend into studio contexts of the Renaissance, as in Camerarius's story of Giovanni Bellini's interest in Dürer's miraculous brush: see Alistair Smith, "Dürer and Bellini, Apelles and Protogenes," *Burlington Magazine* 114 (1972): 326–29.

    In his letter prefacing the second edition of Vasari's *Vite* Giovambatista Adriani, translating Pliny's passage rather exactly, keeps the stress on the precise technical accomplishment: "... tornato Apelle ..., vergognando d'esser vinto, con un terzo colore partì quelle linee stesse per lungo il mezzo, non lasciando più luogo veruno ad alcuna sottigliezza ..." (Giorgio Vasari, *Le vite de' più eccellenti pittori, scultori ed architettori*, ed. Gaetano Milanesi [Florence, 1878–85], I, pp. 33–34).

15. *Natural History*, XXXV, 67–68; trans. Jex-Blake, pp. 111–13. On the line of Parrhasios in its historical context, see R. Bianchi-Bandinelli, "Piccoli problemi da risolvere, I: Parrasio: Linea spazio volume," *Critica d'arte* 3 (1938): 4–11; also Vincent J. Bruno, *Form and Color in Greek Painting* (New York, 1977), pp. 31–40.

16. Dionysios of Halikarnassus, *De Isaeo* 4, quoted by E. Sellers in her introduction to *The Elder Pliny's Chapters on the History of Art*, p. xxxi. On such critical nostalgia, see Gombrich, "The Debate on Primitivism" (cited above, note 6). For an alternative voice, favoring such progress, cf. Quintilian, *Institutio Oratoria*, X, ii, 7–8: "For what, I ask again, would have been the result if no one had done more than his predecessors? ... We should still be sailing on rafts, and the art of painting would be restricted to tracing a line around a shadow thrown by sunlight" (trans. H. E. Butler, Loeb Classical Library, vol. 10 [Cambridge, Mass., and London, 1922], pp. 77–78).

17. On line in ancient criticism, see Pollitt, *The Ancient View of Greek Art*, pp. 249–54. The demonstrative calligraphy of archaic Greek draughtsmanship has been nicely analyzed by Richard T. Neer, "The Lion's Eye: Imitation and Uncertainty in Attic Red-Figure," *Representations* 51 (1995): 118–53. On "vase drawing" and the suggestiveness of Greek line, see the observations of Dyfri Williams, "The Drawing of the Human Figure on Early Red-Figure Vases," in *New Perspectives in Early Greek Art*, ed. Diana Buitron Oliver (National Gallery of Art: *Studies in the History of Art* 25) (Washington, 1991), pp. 285–301.

18. On Picasso's line, see especially Leo Steinberg, *Other Criteria: Confrontations with Twentieth-Century Art* (London, Oxford, and New York, 1972), pp. 125–234, esp. 174–92 ("Drawing as if to Possess"), but cf. as well Rosalind Krauss, *The Picasso Papers* (New York, 1998) – discussed below in the Epilogue. On Matisse, see John Elderfield, *The Drawings of Henri Matisse* (New York, 1984), esp. pp. 52–60, 113–18.

19. Leonardo, *Treatise on Painting*, ed. McMahon, ¶ 807, cc. 217v–218: "Li termini de'corpi opachi sono quelli delli quali in brevissima distanzia si perde la nottizia; questo di che si predice il perdimento della notizia è la superficie de' corpi, per altro modo detta termine de' corpi densi, la quale, non havendo corpo, non dà di sé ispiedita notizia e tanto meno ne dà quanto essa è più remota dal suo investigatore." Ibid., ¶ 506 (quoted above, note 5).

20. Reviewing an exhibition of contemporary drawings (in 1956), Leo Steinberg lamented a general inability to achieve "the linear description of plasticity" and offered an eloquent summary of the tradition:

    > Now the evocation of volume through line is a feat which, during four hundred years, most self-respecting artists in the West could take for granted. When a Renaissance draughtsman, or even a Baroque master like Rubens, drew the contour of, say, a man's shoulder, he conceived it as a localized, small-scale horizon, which made an apparent line only because his vision was not periscopic. But he knew that this edge he was drawing was not a thing, that it stood for a process, for the event of a curvature turning out of his sight. And he symbolized this event by the dark trace of his medium, even though nothing dark showed at the contour observed.

> In the drawing of contours as such there is of course nothing remarkable. Comics are drawn the same way; an outline is made and we are told that what's inside is a man. To which we assent from sheer habit.
>
> But the miracle of great draughtsmanship in the past was not its conventional use of outlines, but what it compelled us to read around and between the lines. Whether or not shading was used, the contour itself was tensed in a transverse direction – like the edge of a full-bellied sail with the wind sitting in it. Where no mark was made on the paper, precisely there the form swelled to its summit. The drawn line, passing through thick and thin, pressing down heavy or light, sometimes breaking and leaping and doubling, became prodigiously descriptive. ("Recent Drawings, USA," in *Other Criteria*, p. 255)

21. LaMonte Young's suggestive score is reproduced in its entirety. See H. Wiley Hitchcock, *Music in the United States: A Historical Introduction*, 3d ed. (Englewood Cliffs, N.J., 1988), p. 271. The narrative logic of such linear imperative is fully realized in the classic children's book by Crockett Johnson, *Harold and the Purple Crayon* (New York, 1955).
22. Paul Klee, *Pedagogical Sketchbook* (1925), trans. Sibyl Maholy-Nagy (London, 1953), pp. 16–18.
23. *Picasso on Art: A Selection of Views*, ed. Dore Ashton (New York, 1972) p. 103. Cf. Paul Valéry's observation in the marginal comments to his "Introduction to the Method of Leonardo da Vinci": "Corresponding to the *spatialization* of linear movements is something I once described as the *chronolysis* of space" (in *Leonardo, Poe, Mallarmé*, trans. Malcolm Cowley and James R. Lawler [Princeton, 1972], pp. 24–25).
24. "Matisse Speaks to His Students, 1908: Notes by Sarah Stein," in Alfred H. Barr, Jr., *Matisse: His Art and His Public* (New York, 1951), p. 551.
25. "How does the straight line feel? It feels, as I suppose it looks, straight – a dull line drawn out endlessly. It is unstraight lines, or many straight and curved lines together, that are eloquent to the touch. They appear and disappear, are now deep, now shallow, now broken off or lengthened and swelling. They rise and sink beneath my fingers, they are full of sudden starts and pauses, and their variety is inexhaustible and wonderful." Helen Keller's feeling exaltation of line is quoted by Meyer Schapiro, "On the Humanity of Abstract Painting," in *Modern Art, 19th and 20th Centuries: Selected Papers II* (New York, 1978), p. 230.
26. Paul Valéry, "Seeing and Copying," in *Degas, Manet, Morisot*, trans. David Paul (New York, 1960), p. 36. Valéry continues: ". . . the act of drawing a given object endows the eye with a posture of command which must be sustained by the will. In this case the *will* is necessary to *seeing*; and both the *end* and the *means* of this *willed seeing* is the drawing itself."
27. Cf. the pertinent observations on "the kinetic basis of drawing" in Rawson, *Drawing*, pp. 15–19 et passim, as well as Richard Wollheim's account of the problem, "On Drawing an Object," in *On Art and the Mind* (Cambridge, Mass., 1974), pp. 3–30.
28. Maurice Merleau-Ponty comments on Cézanne's urge "to make *visible* how the world *touches* us": see "Cézanne's Doubt" (1945), in *Sense and Non-Sense*, trans. Hubert L. Dreyfus and Patricia Allen Dreyfus (Evanston, 1964), pp. 9–25. For the personally charged significance of the subject, see Meyer Schapiro, "The Apples of Cézanne: An Essay on the Meaning of Still-life," in *Modern Art, 19th and 20th Centuries*, pp. 1–38.
29. Maurice Merleau-Ponty, "Eye and Mind," trans. Carleton Dallery, in *The Primacy of Perception and Other Essays*, ed. James H. Edie (Evanston, 1964), p. 162. Cf. Valéry: "Conceivably, drawing may be the most haunting obsession the mind can experience. . . . But is it quite, after all, a question of mind?" (*Degas, Manet, Morisot*, p. 66).
30. On the concept of body-image, see Paul Schilder, *The Image and Appearance of the Human Body* (1935; New York, 1950), and its elaboration by Merleau-Ponty, *Phenomenology of Perception*, trans. Colin Smith (London and Henley, 1962); also "An Unpublished Text by Maurice Merleau-Ponty: A Prospectus of His Work," trans. Arleen B. Dallery, in *The Primacy of Perception*, pp. 3–11, and, in the same volume, "The Primacy of Perception and Its Philosophical Consequences," trans. James M. Edie, pp. 12–42.
31. The terms are those developed by Schilder, *The Image and Appearance of the Human Body*. For a particularly sensitive critical response to these issues in studio practice, see John Elderfield, *The Language of the Body: Drawings by Pierre-Paul Prud'hon* (New York, 1996).
32. As Michael Polanyi has observed,

> Physiologists long ago established that the way we see an object is determined by our awareness of certain efforts inside our body, efforts which we cannot feel in themselves. We are aware of these things going on inside our body in terms of the position, size, shape, and motion of an object, to which we are attending. In other words we are attending *from* these internal processes *to* the qualities of things outside. These qualities are what those processes *mean* to us. The transposition of bodily experiences into the perception of things outside may now appear, therefore, as an instance of the transposition of meaning away from us, which we have found to be present to some extent in all tacit knowing. (*The Tacit Dimension* [Garden City, N.Y., 1966], pp. 13–14)

The concept of "tacit knowing," and the role of the body in such knowledge, is elaborated more circumstantially by Polanyi in *Personal Knowledge: Towards a Post-Critical Philosophy* (Chicago, 1962).

Cf. as well Merleau-Ponty, *Phenomenology of Perception,* esp. chap. 3: "The Spatiality of One's Own Body and Motility," pp. 98–147. Further on upright posture, see Erwin W. Straus, "The Upright Posture," in *Essays in Phenomenology,* ed. Maurice Natanson (The Hague, 1966), pp. 164–92, and Straus, "Born to See, Bound to Behold: Reflections on the Function of the Upright Posture in the Esthetic Attitude," in *The Philosophy of the Body: Reflections of the Cartesian Dualism,* Stuart F. Spicker (Chicago, 1970), pp. 334–61.

33. Valéry, *Degas, Manet, Morisot,* p. 37.
34. For an interesting attempt to apply such parameters in the critical analysis of one artist's practice, see Svetlana Alpers and Michael Baxandall, *Tiepolo and the Pictorial Intelligence* (New Haven and London, 1994), pp. 51–63.
35. "My line drawing is the purest and most direct translation of my emotion. The simplification of the medium allows that" (Henri Matisse, "Notes of a Painter on His Drawing" [1939], in *Matisse on Art,* ed. Flam, p. 130).
36. Extending this analogy in his response to the figure of a dancer, Mallarmé spoke of "une écriture corporelle" ("Crayonné au théâtre," in *Oeuvres complètes* [Paris, 1966], p. 304). Leo Steinberg returns it to drawing: ". . . the neutral paper becomes active brightness and light; the lines move with agility, and while they hold to the surface they contrive the third dimension dancingly, as if in play" ("Recent Drawings, USA," in *Other Criteria,* p. 255). The analogy between the performing brush and the choreographed body found natural expression in traditional discussions of Chinese calligraphy: see Jean François Billeter, *The Chinese Art of Writing,* trans. Jean-Marie Clarke and Michael Taylor (New York, 1990), pp. 176–78.
37. "Les Desseins touchés & peu finis ont plus d'Esprit, & plaisent beaucoup plus que s'ils etoient plus achevés, pourvu qu'ils aient un bon Caractère, & qu'ils mettent l'Idée du Spectateur dans un bon chemin. La raison en est que l'imagination y supplée toutes les parties qui manquent, on qui n'y sont pas terminées, & chacun les voit selon son Goût." Roger de Piles, *Abrégé de la vie des peintres, avec de réflexions sur leurs ouvrages, et un traité du peintre parfait; de la connoissance des desseins; de l'utilité des estampes* (1699), 2d ed. (Paris, 1715), pp. 69–70.
38. Ernst Kris, *Psychoanalytic Explorations in Art* (New York, 1952) p. 55.
39. Ibid., p. 56. On the somatic response to schematic drawing, cf. the remarks of Jean-Paul Sartre, *The Psychology of Imagination,* trans. Bernard Frechtman (New York, 1948), pp. 40–41: ". . . the perceptual intention becomes an imagined one. But this would not be enough: the figure must lend itself to interpretation. The collection of lines must be animated by a certain attitude of my body, namely, by my body enacting a certain pantomime. . . . At the same time we must supply an absent line. . . . This we accomplish by carrying our eyes from N to D: we *enact* the missing line, we mimic it with our body."
40. The notion of criticism as understanding of creation through reconstruction, reenactment, or reversal of its processes may be compared to Richard Wollheim's concept of "criticism as retrieval": see *Art and Its Objects,* 2d ed. (Cambridge, 1980), supplementary essay 4, pp. 185–204.
41. John Graham, *System and Dialectics of Art,* ed. Marcia Epstein Allentuck (Baltimore and London, 1971), p. 165.
42. The problem of the amateur as critic has a long history, going back at least to the anecdotes of Apelles telling the cobbler to "stick to his last" and advising Alexander the Great not to embarrass himself before the apprentices (Pliny, *Natural History,* XXXV.85). It is addressed more directly in the Renaissance, when knowledge of the visual arts was assumed to be part of a good education: cf., e.g., Lodovico Dolce, *Dialogo della pittura intitolato l'Aretino* (1557), ed. Paola Barocchi, in *Trattati d'arte del Cinquecento,* I (Bari, 1960), pp. 154–55.
43. On the "O" of Giotto, see Chapter Four.
44. Francisco de Hollanda, *Vier Gespräche über die Malerei geführt zu Rom 1538,* ed. Joaquim de Vasconcellos (Vienna, 1899), p. 119. For fuller commentary on this passage, see David Summers, *Michelangelo and the Language of Art* (Princeton, 1981), pp. 285–96, whose translation I have adapted; see also Van de Waal, "The *Linea Summae Tenuitatis,*" p. 14. On of the sixteenth-century context of this attitude, see Chapter Four.
45. See E. H. Gombrich, "Style," in *International Encyclopedia of the Social Sciences,* vol. 15 (1968), pp. 352–61, as well as the discussion by Willibald Sauerländer, "From Stilus to Style: Reflections on the Fate of a Notion," *Art History* 6 (1983): 253–70.
46. In *The Literary Remains of Albrecht Dürer,* trans. William Martin Conway (Cambridge, 1889), p. 137. The issue of automimesis will be more fully addressed in the context of Leonardo's drawings, Chapter Three.
47. An early Renaissance example (1457) of the metonymic use of hand for the style of the artist is offered by the professional judgment of the painter Pietro da Milano, distinguishing the work of Andrea Mantegna and Niccolò Pizzolo in the Ovetari Chapel: "Et quia inter pictores semper cognoscitur manu cuius sit aliaque pictura, maxime quando est manu alicuius solemnis magister" (Erice Rigoni, *L'Arte rinascimentale in Padova* [Padua, 1970], pp. 21–22, doc. 8). See the discussion by Warnke, "Praxisfelder der Kunsttheorie," esp. pp. 54–58; cf. also Martin Kemp, "'Equal excellencies': Lomazzo and the Explanation of Individual Style in the Visual Arts" *Renaissance Studies* 1 (1987): 1–26. Further on the status of "hand" *(manus)* as sign of authorial responsibility and the aesthetic acknowledgment of the sketch, see below, Chapter Two; for the question of the printed replication of the hand-drawn line, see Chapter Five.

48. Georges-Louis Leclerc, comte de Buffon, *Discours sur le style prononcé à l'Académie Française par M. de Buffon le jour de sa réception* (1753), ed. A. Noel (Paris, 1866), pp. 24–25. Buffon's now proverbial declaration was intended to distinguish style from content and should be read in that context: ". . . parceque les connaissances, les faits et les découvertes s'enlèvent aisément, se transportent, et gagnent même à être mises en oeuvre par des mains plus habiles. Ces choses sont hors de l'homme, le style est l'homme même."

49. "Les Desseins marquent davantage le caractère du Maître, & font voir si son génie est vif ou pesant; si ses pensées sont elevées ou communes; & enfin s'il a une bonne habitude & un bon Goût de toutes les parties qui peuvent s'exprimer sur le papier. Le Peintre qui veut finir un Tableau, tache de sortir, pour ainsi dire, de lui-même, afin de s'attirer les louanges qu'on donne aux parties dont il sent bien qu'il est dépourvu: mais en faisant un Dessein, il s'abandonne a son génie, & se fait voir tel qu'il est" (*Abrégé de la vie des peintres*, pp. 66–67).

50. Roger de Piles, *Conversations sur la connoissance de la peinture et sur le jugement qu'on doit faire des tableaux* (Paris, 1677), p. 10. De Piles invokes the analogy to handwriting that had become commonplace: "On connoist de qui est un Tableau comme vous connoissez de qui est une Lettre que vous recevez d'une personne qui vous a écrit déja plusieurs fois. Et il y a deux choses qui font connoistre ces sortes de lettres, le caractère de la main, & celuy de l'esprit" (p. 9).

Cf. Jonathan Richardson, *Two Discourses*, I: *An Essay on the Whole Art of Criticism as It relates to Painting* (London, 1725), pp. 101–2:

> . . . if 100 Boys learn of the same Master, at the same time, yet such will be the difference in Other respects that their Hands shall be distinguished even while they are at School, and more easily afterwards. . . .
>
> So 'tis therefore in the Works of Painters. . . . If in forming an A, or a B no two men are exactly alike, neither will they agree in the manner of Drawing a Finger, or a Toe, less in a whole Hand, or Foot, less still in a Face, and so on.

On Richardson, see Carol Gibson-Wood, "Jonathan Richardson and the Rationalization of Connoisseurship," *Art History* 7 (1984): 38–56. Further on drawing and writing, see Chapter Three and Chapter Four.

51. Giovanni Morelli, *Italian Masters in German Galleries: A Critical Essay on the Italian Pictures in the Galleries of Munich, Dresden, Berlin* (1877), trans. L. M. Richter (London, 1883), p. 7.

The assumption that drawing style represents the basic expression of national as well as individual character was developed along rather dogmatic lines by Bernhard Degenhart in a major study that combines acute visual observation with untenable racial assumptions: "Zur Graphologie der Handzeichnung," *Kunstgeschichtliches Jahrbuch der Bibliotheca Hertziana* 1 (1937): 223–43.

52. Vasari, *Le vite*, ed. Milanesi, I, p. 174. The development of a Renaissance aesthetic of drawing is the subject of Chapter Two.

53. "Inner vision" is Otto Benesch's term: *Rembrandt as Draughtsman* (London, 1960), p. 18. Further on Rembrandt: see Chapter Seven.

54. Philip Rawson has nicely articulated this notion, observing that the structure of a drawing "in fact is produced by actions carried out in time. Therefore in appreciating drawings, no less than in making them, one has to be continuously aware of the character and qualities of the sequences which went into their composition. To get at these one has to look into the drawing carefully to find the order in which the parts were executed" (*Drawing*, p. 15).

55. Charles de Tolnay, *History and Technique of Old Master Drawings: A Handbook* (New York, 1943), p. 14.

56. Ibid., p. 15.

57. Ibid., p. 16.

58. "L'imitation de la nature est constamment l'essence, la base, la propriété, enfin la mère commune de ces deux arts; mais l'imitation seule ne produit que des glaces; elle n'est qu'une esclave, si le génie cesse de l'accompagner; c'est lui qui fornit les grands moyens qui conduisent à l'expression; c'est à lui que l'on doit cette pénétration de l'objet, et ce transport juste et précise, dont l'ame est affectée, et qui se reporte à l'action" (Anne-Claude-Philippe, comte de Caylus, "Parallèle de la Peinture et de la Sculpture" [1759]; *Magasin encyclopédique* 3 [1814], pp. 91–92; *Vie d'artistes du XVIIIe siècle*, ed. André Fontaine [Paris, 1910], p. 185). Cf. Jean-Claude Lebensztejn, *L'Art de la tache: Introduction à la* Nouvelle méthode *d'Alexander Cozens* (Paris, 1990), p. 307.

59. "C'est pour cette raison que dans les Cabinets des Grans, on y voit non seulment des Tableaux, mais que l'on y conserve encore les Desseins des bons Maitres" (*Abrégé de la vie des peintres*, p. 67). Cf. Max J. Friedländer on the study of drawings:

> Whoever turns from the pictures of a master to his drawing has the feeling that a curtain rises before him, and that he is penetrating into the inner sanctuary. For more than one reason a drawing is superior to a picture as evidence, as an autograph. It came into being relatively quickly, as a result of spontaneous action, and did not have to take the long and toilsome road through craftsmanlike procedure; it is in consequence less closely tied to teaching, tradition and studio convention. When drawing, the artists of the 15th and 16th centuries were more of artists; when painting, more of craftsmen. . . . In many cases

> the draughtsman is not complying with any wish from outside, does not carry out an order: he feels himself free in mood and fancy, alone with himself, as it were, speaking a monologue. Moreover, a drawing has hardly ever suffered from distortion, subsequent alteration, restoration or falsification. Everything lies there open to the day, as at the moment of its birth. (*On Art and Connoisseurship,* trans. Tancred Borenius [London, 1942], pp. 218–19)

60. "Il y a une chose, qui est le Sel des Desseins, & sans laquelle je n'en ferois que peu on point du tout de cas, & je ne puis mieux l'exprimer que par le mot de Caractère. Ce Caractère donc consiste dans la manière dont le Peintre pense les choses, c'est le Cachet qui le distingue des autres, & qu'il imprime sur ses Ouvrages comme la vive image de son Esprit. C'est ce Caractère qui remuë nôtre imagination . . ." (*Abrégé,* pp. 71–72).
61. Antoine-Joseph Dézallier d'Argenville, *Abrégé de la vie des plus fameux peintres* (1745; Paris, 1762), I, pp. xxxii–xxxiii: "Les desseins . . . sont les premières idées d'un peintre, le premier feu de son imagination, son style, son esprit, sa manière de penser. . . . Un artiste, en peignant un tableau, se corrige, & réprime la fougue de son génie; en faisant un dessein, il jette le premier feu de sa pensée; il s'abandonne à lui-même; il se montre tel qu'il est."
62. "Le caractère de la main est la pratique que chaque maître se forme pour opérer; cette main doit obeir à la pensée, elle n'est que son esclave; la tête fait le dessin, & conduit la main que ne fait ensuite qu'exécuter" (*Abrégé,* p. xliv).
63. "On ne sçauroit croire combien l'opération de la main forme le goût, & donne d'intelligence à l'esprit; elle vous montre la route qu'ont suivie tant d'habiles gens" (*Abrégé,* p. lxiv).
64. Les grands maîtres finissent peu leur desseins; il se contentent de faire des esquisses, ou griffonnemens faits de rien, qui ne plaisent pas aux demi-connoisseurs. Ceux-ci veulent quelque chose de terminé, qui soit agréable aux yeux: un vrai connoisseur pense autrement; il voit dans un croquis, la manière de penser d'un grand maître, pour caractériser chaque object avec peu de traits; son imagination animée par le beau feu qui regne dans le dessein, perce à traverse ce qui y manque; elle apperçoit souvent ce qui n'y est pas & ce qui doit y être. C'est ainsi qu'un beau génie secondé par ce qu'il voit, supplée & s'accommode à tout. (*Abrégé,* pp. lxi–lxii)
65. "Cette manière est comme un genre d'écriture, qui distingue les hommes entr'eux; de sorte que le caractère de l'un n'est jamais celui de l'autre" (*Abrégé,* p. lii). ". . . la manière de dessiner d'un peintre se distingue comme le caractère de l'écriture, & mieux que le d'un auteur. On sçait que les gens de lettres, qui on le tact fin & le goût délicat, s'y trompent rarement" (p. xl). On drawing and handwriting, cf. the observations of de Piles and Richardson, cited above, note 50.

2. DISEGNO: THE INVENTION OF AN ART

1. *De pictura,* ed. Cecil Grayson (Rome and Bari, 1975), ¶ 26; subsequent references will be to paragraph numbers in Grayson's edition, which includes both the Latin text and Alberti's Italian version, *Della pittura.*
2. In general, I have preferred Alberti's Italian version to his Latin; this is the version explicitly addressed to the artists of Florence and is therefore closer in tone to studio practice. For the similar reasons, I have tended to favor (with modification) the translation of John R. Spencer (*On Painting* [New Haven, 1956]) to Cecil Grayson's, which is from the Latin (*On Painting and On Sculpture: The Latin Texts of* De Pictura *and* De Statua [London, 1972]). Spencer's seems to me closer in spirit to the author's intention of writing "as a painter" for painters. Although it is generally assumed that Alberti conceived his treatise in Latin and subsequently translated it into Italian for his artist friends, an argument for the priority of the Italian version has been made by Maria Picchio Simonelli, "On Alberti's Treatises of Art and their Chronological Relationship," *Yearbook of Italian Studies* (1971): 26–44.
3. On Alberti's models, see Creighton E. Gilbert, "Antique Frameworks for Renaissance Art Theory: Alberti and Pino," *Marsyas* 3 (1943–45): 87–106; and, for a somewhat different view, D. R. Edward Wright, "Alberti's *De Pictura:* Its Literary Structure and Purpose," *Journal of the Warburg and Courtauld Institutes* 47 (1984): 52–71. Cf. as well Richard Tobin, "Leon Battista Alberti: Ancient Sources and Structures in the Treatises on Art," Ph.D. dissertation (Bryn Mawr College, 1979); Michael Baxandall, *Giotto and the Orators: Humanist Observers of Painting in Italy and the Discovery of Pictorial Composition* (Oxford, 1971), pp. 121–39, and John R. Spencer, "Ut Rhetorica Pictura: A Study in Quattrocento Theory of Painting," *Journal of the Warburg and Courtauld Institutes* 20 (1957): 26–44.
4. The significance of commensurability was stressed by Rudolf Wittkower, "Brunelleschi and 'Proportion in Perspective,'" *Journal of the Warburg and Courtauld Institutes* 16 (1953): 275–91 (reprinted in *Idea and Image: Studies in the Italian Renaissance* [London, 1978], pp. 125–35, 243–45). In the ever-growing literature on perspective, the role of Brunelleschi remains a central problem; among recent studies, cf. Hubert Damisch, *The Origins of Perspective* (1987) (Cambridge, Mass., and London, 1994); Martin Kemp, *The Science of Art: Optical Themes in Western Art from Brunelleschi to Seurat* (New Haven and London, 1990); Norris Kelly Smith, *Here I Stand: Perspective from Another Point of View* (New York, 1994). To some degree, all modern studies of perspective respond to the ambi-

tious essay of Erwin Panofsky, "Die Perspective als 'symbolische Form'," *Vorträge der Bibliothek Warburg 1924–1925* (Leipzig and Berlin, 1927), pp. 258–330; trans. Christopher S. Wood, *Perspective as Symbolic Form* (New York, 1991).

5. Piero della Francesca, *De prospectiva pingendi,* ed. G. Nicco-Fasola (Florence, 1984), p. 63. In that it is concerned with the construction of geometric form rather than with pictorial disposition, Piero's "comensuratio" does not quite correspond to Alberti's "composizione."
6. Petrus Paulus Vergerius, *De ingenuis moribus* (ca. 1404), trans. William Harrison Woodward, in *Vittorino da Feltre and Other Humanist Educators* (1897) (New York, 1963), p. 107. Also in Eugenio Garin, ed., *L'Educazione umanistica in Italia* (Bari, 1959), p. 88, and Baxandall, *Giotto and the Orators,* p. 125. One basic source for this was Aristotle, *Politics* (VIII.3 [1338^{a}]). More immediately relevant, however, and a mine of topoi for the Renaissance conception of the learned artist, was the account of the Macedonian painter Pamphilos as recorded by Pliny the Elder (*Natural History,* XXXV, 77):

> . . . Pamphilos was the first painter who was thoroughly trained in every branch of learning, more particularly in arithmetic and geometry; without which, so he held, art could not be perfect. He taught no one for less than a talent – that is, five hundred denarii a year – the fee paid him both by Apelles and by Melanthios. It was owing to his influence that first at Sikyon, and afterwards throughout Greece drawing, or rather painting, on tablets of boxwood, was the earliest subject taught to freeborn boys, and that this art was accepted as the preliminary step towards a liberal education. It was at any rate had in such honour that at all times the freeborn, and later on persons of distinction practised it, while by a standing prohibition no slaves might ever acquire it, and this is why neither in painting nor in statuary are there any celebrated works by artists who had been slaves. (Trans. K. Jex-Blake, *The Elder Pliny's Chapters on the History of Art,* ed. E. Sellers [London, 1896], p. 119)

7. On Renaissance penmanship, see Chapter Four and, for further bibliography, Chapter Three, note 3.
8. For further discussion of this concept, see Kristin Patz, "Zum Begriff der 'Historia' in L. B. Albertis 'De Pictura,'" *Zeitschrift für Kunstgeschichte* 49 (1986): 269–87, and Jack M. Greenstein, *Mantegna and Painting as Historical Narrative* (Chicago, 1992), pp. 34–58.
9. On "la più grassa Minerva," see the comments of Spencer in his introduction to Alberti, *On Painting,* pp. 18–20.
10. See David Rosand, "*Ekphrasis* and the Renaissance of Painting: Observations on Alberti's Third Book," in *Florilegium Columbianum: Essays in Honor of Paul Oskar Kristeller,* ed. Karl-Ludwig Selig and Robert Somerville (New York, 1987), pp. 147–65, and Rosand, "Ekphrasis and the Generation of Images," *Arion,* 3d series, I, 1 (1990): 61–105. On ekphrasis in general, cf. as well the recent collection of studies *Beschreibungskunst-Kunstbeschreibung: Ekphrasis von der Antike bis zur Gegenwart,* ed. Gottfried Böhm and Helmut Pfotenhauer (Munich, 1995).
11. Cennino Cennini, *Il libro dell'arte o trattato della pittura,* ed. Fernando Tempesti (Milan, 1984), p. 32: "A che modo cominci a disegnare in tavoletta, e l'ordine suo." Trans. Daniel V. Thompson, Jr., *The Craftsman's Handbook* (New Haven, 1933), p. 4: "How you begin drawing on a little panel; and the system for it." On Cennini as a painter, see Miklós Boskovits, "Cennino Cennini – pittore nonconformista," *Mitteilungen des Kunsthistorischen Institute in Florenz* 17 (1973): 201–22.
12. Cf. Cennini, *Il libro dell'arte,* cap. 29, where he recommends making a portfolio in which to hold paper and drawings, the stock of motifs recorded in the course of study that will serve in future production. The relation of Alberti's passage to the modelbook tradition has been noted by Robert W. Scheller, *Exemplum: Model-Book Drawings and the Practice of Artistic Transmission in the Middle Ages (ca. 900–ca. 1470)* (Amsterdam, 1995), p. 80, n. 224.
13. On *sinopie,* cartoons, and fresco: Robert Oertel, "Wandmalerei und Zeichnung in Italien: Die Anfänge der Entwurfszeichnung und ihre monumentalen Vorstufen" *Mitteilungen des Kunsthistorischen Institutes in Florenz* 6 (1940): 217–314; Oertel, "Perspective and Imagination," in *Studies in Western Art,* II. *The Renaissance and Mannerism* (Acts of the Twentieth International Congress of the History of Art) (Princeton, 1963, pp. 146–59; Ugo Procacci, *Sinopie e affreschi* (Milan, 1960); Millard Meiss, *The Great Age of Fresco: Discoveries, Recoveries, and Survivals* (New York, 1970); Eve Borsook, *The Mural Painters of Tuscany from Cimabue to Andrea del Sarto,* 2d ed. (Oxford, 1980); Eve Borsook and Fiorella Superbi Gioffredi, eds., *Tecnica e stile: Esempi di pittura murale del Rinascimento italiano,* 2 vols. (Florence, 1986); and Carmen Bambach Cappel, "The Tradition of Pouncing Drawings in the Italian Renaissance Workshop: Innovation and Derivation," Ph.D. dissertation (Yale University, 1988), that study now complemented by Carmen C. Bambach, *Drawing and Painting in the Italian Renaissance Workshop: Theory and Practice, 1300–1600* (Cambridge, New York, Melbourne, 1999).
14. Borsook, *The Mural Painters of Tuscany,* pp. 58–63, 74–79.
15. Ibid., pp. 87–90. That Mantegna may have been using cartoons as early as the 1450s has been suggested by Keith Christiansen, "Some Observations on Mantegna's Painting Technique," in Jane Martineau, ed., *Andrea Mantegna,* exhibition catalogue (London and New York, 1992), p. 71.

16. Cf. Apelles' criticism of Protogenes for not "knowing when to take his hand from a picture," hence the memorable saying: "nocere saepe nimiam diligentiam" (Pliny, *Natural History* XXXV, 80). The anecdote is explicitly invoked, for example, by Paolo Pino, *Dialogo di pittura* (1548) (ed. Paola Barocchi, in *Trattati d'arte del Cinquecento,* I [Bari, 1960], p. 119), and again by Lodovico Dolce, *Dialogo della pittura intitolato l'Aretino* (1557) (ed. Barocchi, in *Trattati d'arte,* I, p. 185).
17. "E l'ingegno mosso e riscaldato per essercitazione molto si rende pronto ed espedito al lavoro; e quella mano seguita velocissimo, quale sia da certa ragione d'ingegno ben guidato." On the necessary combination of *ars et ingenium* in the early Renaissance, see Baxandall, *Giotto and the Orators,* pp. 15–17 et passim, and for the further, problematic appropriation of the term for artists, see Martin Kemp, "From 'Mimesis' to 'Fantasia': The Quattrocento Vocabulary of Creation, Inspiration and Genius in the Visual Arts," *Viator* 8 (1977): 347–98, esp. 384–95.
18. Horace opens his *Ars poetica* by invoking the absurdity of the combinatorial fantasy that comes to be associated with the grotesque:

> Supposing a painter chose to put a human head on a horse's neck, or to spread feathers of various colours over the limbs of several different creatures, or to make what in the upper part is a beautiful woman tail off into a hideous fish, could you help laughing when he showed you his efforts? You may take it from me, my friends, that a book will have very much the same effect as these pictures if, like a sick man's dreams, the author's idle fancies assume such a shape that it is impossible to make head or tail of what he is driving at. "But," you will say, "the right to take liberties of almost any kind has always been enjoyed by painters and poets alike." I know that; we poets do claim this licence, and in our turn we concede it to others, but not to the point of associating what is wild with what is tame, of pairing snakes with birds or lambs with tigers. (Trans. T. S. Dorsch, *Classical Literary Criticism* [Harmondsworth, Baltimore, and Victoria, 1965], p. 79; cf. Horace, *Satires, Epistles, and Ars Poetica,* trans. H. Rushton Fairclough [Loeb Classical Library: London and New York, 1926], pp. 450–51)

19. "Continuando ogni dì non manchi disegnar qualche cosa, ché non sarà sì poco che non sia assai; e faratti eccellente pro" (*Il libro dell'arte,* cap. 28).
20. On *inventare, trovare,* and *fantasticare,* see Martin Kemp, "From 'Mimesis' to 'Fantasia.'"
21. The gap between classical form and classical subject is what Erwin Panofsky termed the "principle of disjunction," a major theme in his *Renaissance and Renascences in Western Art,* 2d ed. (New York, 1969), p. 84f. and chapter 4: "Rinascimento dell'Antichità: The Fifteenth Century." On Alberti's programmatic *ekphraseis,* see the references cited above, note 10.
22. A humanist's rather blatant appeal for courtly patronage, the dedication of *De pictura* to Giovan Francesco Gonzaga, Marquis of Mantua, concludes: "You could know my character and learning, and all my qualities best, if you arranged for me to join you, as I indeed desire. And I shall believe my work has not displeased you, if you decide to enrol me as a devoted member among your servants and to regard me as not one of the least" (trans. Grayson, *On Painting and On Sculpture,* p. 35). Alberti's qualities as an architect were to be appreciated by the next Gonzaga generation in Mantua. On Alberti's achievement, see the various contributions to the recent exhbition catalogue, *Leon Battista Alberti,* ed. Joseph Rykwert and Anne Engel (Milan, 1994).
23. The distinction between Alberti's Latin and Italian reflects the fundamental difference between his intended audiences: "sed artem novissime recenseamus" refers to his own account of the art, to *De pictura* as a text; the Italian "fabrichiamo" refers to the making of the new art itself, the art that is the subject of his treatise.
24. For surveys of this tradition, see Scheller, *Exemplum;* Albert J. Elen, *Italian Late-Medieval and Renaissance Drawing-Books from Giovannino de' Grassi to Palma Giovane: A Codicological Approach* (Leiden, 1995); Francis Ames-Lewis, *Drawing in Early Renaissance Italy* (New Haven and London, 1981), chap. 4: "Model-Books and Sketch-Books," and the exhibition catalogue *Pisanello: Le peintre aux sept vertus,* ed. Dominique Cordellier (Paris, 1996).
25. For a survey of this graphic activity, see Bernhard Degenhart and Annegrit Schmitt, "Gentile da Fabriano in Rom und die Anfänge des Antikenstudiums," *Münchner Jahrbuch der bildenden Kunst* 11 (1960): 59–151.
26. The recent important literature on these drawing books includes: Bernhard Degenhart and Annegrit Schmitt, *Corpus der italienischen Zeichnungen 1300–1450,* Part II: *Venedig,* vols. 5–8 (Berlin, 1990), and Degenhart and Schmitt, *Jacopo Bellini: The Louvre Album of Drawings* (New York, 1984); Colin Eisler, *The Genius of Jacopo Bellini: The Complete Paintings and Drawings* (New York, 1989), with codicological analysis and reconstruction by Albert J. Elen; also Elen, *Italian Late-Medieval and Renaissance Drawing-Books,* pp. 425–63.
27. For Jacopo's reuse of sheets from a fourteenth-century Venetian model book, see Degenhart and Schmitt, *Corpus der italienischen Zeichnungen 1300–1450,* Part II, vol. 5, pp. 136–77, esp. 148–50, 168–77, and Degenhart and Schmitt, *The Louvre Album,* p. 23.
28. The index is published in Eisler, *The Genius of Jacopo Bellini,* Appendix C, p. 508f. It is reproduced in facsimile in Degenhart and Schmitt, *The Louvre Album,* pl. 114.
29. The popular legend of the quick and the dead (num-

ber 91) is noted as "La istoria de q[uei] tre re ch[e] andaua a oxelar. E trovo tre corpi morti" ("The story of those three kings going to Auxerre and finding three corpses").

30. We might imagine an attitude similar to that recorded in an inscription (not autograph) on the back of one of Paolo Veronese's elaborate chiaroscuro drawings, the Virgin and Child with six musical angels (Louvre, Inv. 4666). The text rehearses some of the infinite ways in which the subject has been treated, by, among others, Dürer and Michelangelo as well as in Byzantine art, and then goes on to declare the intention of presenting an entirely novel composition, a new invention, in which Mary is clothing the Child. See David Rosand, "Three Drawings by Veronese," *Pantheon* 29 (1971): 203–9, and Richard Cocke, *Veronese's Drawings* (Ithaca, 1984), no. 7.
31. In describing number 63 as "una Istoria de pasio con figure picole," the index to the Paris book acknowledges the panoramic aspect of the composition.
32. In many instances, especially in the British Museum volume, Jacopo first drew a composition on the right-hand page of the book and then expanded the composition, extending the space as either landscape or architectural setting.
33. This aspect of Jacopo's drawings has been sensitively studied by Emmanuel Lemakis, "The Crucifixion as Pictorial Narrative: Scene-Making and the Illusion of Place and Time," Ph.D. dissertation (Columbia University, 1990), pp. 138–228 (chap. 4: "The Crucifixion as Istoria: Jacopo Bellini"). For Jacopo's explorations of biblical narrative, see the Eisler, *The Genius of Jacopo Bellini*, pp. 265–441, esp. 286–381 for the lives of Christ and the Virgin.
34. A rich survey of the topic is offered by David Landau and Peter Parshall, *The Renaissance Print 1470–1550* (New Haven and London, 1994); see pp. 13–21, on paper production and price. See as well Dard Hunter, *Papermaking: The History and Technique of an Ancient Craft*, 2d ed. (New York, 1947), pp. 12–17, 60–61.
35. William M. Ivins, Jr., *Prints and Visual Communication* (Cambridge, Mass., 1953), remains the most ambitious analysis of the graphic structures of visual knowledge.
36. Michelangelo's painted copy after Schongauer demonstrated the youth's precocious talent, according to Condivi (*The Life of Michelangelo*, ed. Helmut Wohl, trans. Alice Sedgwick Wohl [Oxford, 1976], pp. 9–10). For Dürer's German translations of his Italian models, see Erwin Panofsky, *The Life and Art of Albrecht Dürer*, 4th ed. (Princeton, 1955), pp. 31–35.
37. Paul Kristeller, *Andrea Mantegna* (Berlin and Leipzig, 1902), p. 584, doc. 193. As a letter to Isabella d'Este in 1504 declared, "De invencione nesuno po arivare a messer Andrea Mantegna che invero l'è ecelentisimo e il primo" (Clifford Brown, *Isabella d'Este and Lorenzo da Pavia: Documents for the History of Art and Culture in Renaissance Mantua* [Geneva, 1982], pp. 83–84). Mantegna's actual graphic corpus remains a topic of intense debate: in the exhibition catalogue *Andrea Mantegna*, ed. Martineau, cf. the alternative views of David Landau ("Mantegna as Printmaker," pp. 44–54) and Suzanne Boorsch ("Mantegna and his Printmakers," pp. 56–66), as well as Keith Christiansen, "The Case for Mantegna as Printmaker," *Burlington Magazine* 135 (1993): 604–12.
38. On the aesthetic values and tastes of the humanists, see Baxandall, *Giotto and the Orators*, who suggests (pp. 133–35) a rather direct dependence of Mantegna on Alberti's concept of pictorial composition. Insisting instead on the priority of Mantegna's own pictorial intelligence, Leo Steinberg has questioned such assumptions: "Leon Battista Alberti e Andrea Mantegna," in *Leon Battista Alberti*, ed. Rykwert and Engel, pp. 330–35. In the same volume, cf. as well Keith Christiansen, "Rapporti presunti, probabili e (forse anche) effettivi fra Alberti e Mantegna," pp. 336–57. Further on the issue in general, see David Chambers, Jane Martineau, and Rodolfo Signorini, "Mantegna and the Men of Letters," in *Andrea Mantegna*, ed. Martineau, pp. 8–30.
39. See Jay A. Levenson, Konrad Oberhuber, and Jacquelyn L. Sheehan, *Early Italian Engravings from the National Gallery of Art* (Washington, 1973), nos. 73–76, and *Andrea Mantegna*, ed. Martineau, nos. 74–79. For particular interpretations of these images, associating them with specific ancient texts, cf. Michael Jacobsen, "The Meaning of Mantegna's *Battle of the Sea Monsters*," *Art Bulletin* 64 (1982): 623–39; Patricia Emison, "The Raucousness of Mantegna's Mythological Engravings," *Gazette des Beaux-Arts* 122 (1994): 159–76; Marcello Ciccuto, "Un'iscrizione di Andrea Mantegna," *Albertiana* 1 (1998): 61–79.
40. Cf. Giorgio Vasari, *Le vite de' più eccellenti pittori, scultori et architettori* (1568), ed. Gaetano Milanesi (Florence, 1878–85), III, p. 295:

    > E fu primo a mostrare il modo di cercare i muscoli, che avessero forma ed ordine nelle figure; e di quelli tutti, cinti d'una catena, intagliò in rame una battaglia: e dopo quella fece altre stampe, con molto migliore intaglio che non avevano fatto gli altri maestri ch'erano stati inanzi a lui.
    >
    > Per queste cagioni, adunque, venuto famoso infra gli artefici.

    On Pollaiuolo's engraving, see the entry by Jacquelyn L. Sheehan in *Early Italian Engravings from the National Gallery of Art*, no. 13, pp. 66–80, with previous bibliography; see also, with special attention to the engraving's visual *concetto*, Patricia Emison, "The Word Made Naked in Pollaiuolo's *Battle of the Nudes*," *Art History* 13 (1990): 261–75.
41. The drawings and the two versions of the print are more fully discussed in Chapter Four. Probably the earliest datable use of *invenit* in prints is in Marcantonio's engraving after a figure in Michelangelo's car-

toon of the *Battle of Cascina:* "IV.MI.AG.FL./.MAF." *(Invenit Michelangelo Florentinus / Marc'antonio Fecit)* (B.XIV,363,488). This was most probably executed ca. 1508–9, when the engraver himself was in Florence; in 1510 he produced a more elaborate version of the design, with three figures (B.XIV,361,487). See Innis H. Shoemaker, *The Engravings of Marcantonio Raimondi,* exhibition catalogue (Lawrence, Kansas, 1981), no. 19. On the signatures, dates, and inscriptions, see Landau and Parshall, *The Renaissance Print,* pp. 141–46. Wolfgang Braunfels, "Die 'Inventio' des Künstlers," in *Festschrift für Ludwig Heydenreich* (Munich, 1964), p. 20, cites the *Massacre of the Innocents* as the earliest use of the concept.

42. Vasari, *Le vite,* ed. Milanesi, V, p. 405f., writes that the Venetian Signoria responded to Dürer's complaint only by ordering Marcantonio to remove the German's monogram from his engraved copies of his woodcuts. Whatever the problems with Vasari's account, the copyright privilege for prints as well as books was evidently first developed in Venice, as part of a deliberate effort to establish the city as a printing center. See David Rosand and Michelangelo Muraro, *Titian and the Venetian Woodcut,* exhibition catalogue (Washington, 1976), pp. 10–11, 19, 22–23, with further references. For general comment on copyright privilege, see Landau and Parshall, *The Renaissance Print,* pp. 298–309, 360–62.

43. Alberti quite naturally moves on to cite Timanthes' celebrated painting of the Sacrifice of Iphigenia, a favorite topic of the ancient orators, in which the face of Agamemnon, whose grief was beyond representation, was veiled, leaving the emotion to the imagination of the viewer. Timanthes, Pliny adds, "is the only artist whose works always suggest more than is in the picture, and great as is his dexterity, his power of invention yet exceeds it *(atque in unius huius operibus intellegitur plus semper quam pingitur et, cum sit ars summa, ingenium tamen ultra artem)*" (*Natural History,* XXXV, 73–74, trans. Jex-Blake, p. 117).

44. "Il bozzar delle storie sia pronto, e'l membrificare no' sia troppo finito, sta contento solamente a' siti d'esse membra, i quali poi a' bel'aggio piacendoti potrai finire" (*Treatise on Painting [Codex Urbinas Latinus 1270],* ed. and trans. A. Philip McMahon (Princeton, 1956), ¶ 257, c. 34r [hereafter abbreviated as McM with paragraph number]). On this topic, see the classic essay by E. H. Gombrich, "Leonardo's Method for Working Out Compositions," in *Norm and Form: Studies in the Art of the Renaissance* (London, 1966), pp. 58–63.

45. McM ¶ 261, cc. 61v–62r:

> O tu componitore delle istorie non membrifficare con terminati lineamenti le membriffıcationi d'esse istorie che t'entervera come a molti e vari pittori intervenire suole li quali vogliano che ogni minimo segno di carbone sia valido e questi tali ponno bene acquistare richezze ma non laude della sua arte perche molte sono le volte, che lo animale figurato non a li moti delle membra apropriate al moto mentale e havendo lui fatta bella e grata membriffıcatione ben finita li parra cosa ingiuriosa a trasmutare esse membra piu alte o basse o piu indietro che inanzi e questi tali non sonno merittevoli d' alcuna laude nella sua sientia.

46. McM ¶ 261, c. 62r:

> Hor non ai tu mai considerato li poeti componitori de lor versi alli quali non da noia il fare bella lettera ne si cura di canzellare alcuni d' essi versi riffaccendoli migliori adonque pittore componi grossamente le membra delle tue figure e' attendi prima alli movimenti apropriati alli accidenti mentali de li animali componitori della storia, che alla bellezza e bonta delle loro membra perche tu hai a' intendere che se tal componimento inculto ti reussira apropriato alla sua inventione tanto maggiormente satisfara essendo poi ornato della perfettione apropriata a' tutte le sue parte. Io ho gia veduto nelli nuvoli e' muri machie che m'anno deste e belle inventioni di varie cose le quali machie anchora che integralmente fussino in se private di perfectione di qualonque membro non machavano di perfectione nelli loro movimenti o altre actioni.

47. McM ¶ 256, c. 38v:

> attenderai prima col dissegno a' dare con dimostrativa forma al ochio la intentione, e la inventione fatta in prima nella tua imaginativa di poi va levando e' ponendo tanto che tu ti satisfacia di poi fa aconciare homini vestiti, o nudi, nel modo ch'in sul'opera hai ordinato e' fa che per misura e' grandezza sotto posta alla prospettiva che non passi niente de l'opera che bene non sia considerata della ragione e' dalli effetti naturali e questa sia la via da farti honorare della tua arte.

48. The opening of technique, favoring the visible touch or mark over the highly polished surface, may be observed in a range of artistic production at this time: from the scratchy drypoint of the Housebook Master and the splintered brushwork of Hieronymus Bosch, which transformed the Eyckian tradition in painting, to Giorgione's exploration of a *pittura di tocco,* a painterly equivalent to Leonardo's open graphic touch. Indeed, the development of a *sfumato* aesthetic by these two Italian painters, obscuring contour in ambient shadow, produces a corresponding openness of viewing. I have addressed these issues in "Giorgione e il concetto della creazione artistica," in *Giorgione: Atti del Convegno Internazionale di Studi per il 5° centenario della nascita* (Castelfranco Veneto, 1979), pp. 135–39, and *Painting in Sixteenth-Century Venice: Titian, Veronese, Tintoretto,* rev. ed. (Cambridge and New York, 1997), pp. 10–25, 33–34.

49. See Ulrike Jenni, "The Phenomena of Change in the Modelbook Tradition around 1400," in *Drawings Defined,* ed. Walter Strauss and Tracie Felker (New York, 1987), pp. 35–47.
50. This lost book is mentioned in Madrid MS. II, fol. 3r, datable ca. 1504. See Carlo Pedretti, *Leonardo's Horses: Studies of Horses and Other Animals by Leonardo da Vinci from the Royal Library at Windsor Castle,* exhibition catalogue (Florence and New York, 1984), p. 52 (re Windsor 12326, and cf. Windsor 12327). In the *Codex Urbinas* a note added by Hand 3 reads: "*Precetto* intorno allo disegno del schizzare istorie e figure" (McM ¶ 257, c. 34).
51. *Dürer: Schriftlicher Nachlass,* ed. Hans Rupprich (Berlin, 1956–69), II, p. 113; trans. William Martin Conway, *The Literary Remains of Albrecht Dürer* (Cambridge, 1889), p. 177.
52.
> Gli schizzi . . . chiamiamo noi una prima sorte di disegni che si fanno per trovar il modo delle attitudini, ed i primo componimento dell'opra; e sono fatti in forma di una macchia, ed accennati solamente da noi in una sola bozza del tutto. E perchè dal furor dello artefice sono in poco tempo con penna o con altro disegnatoio o carbone espressi, solo per tentare l'animo di quel che gli sovviene, perciò si chiamano schizzi. (Vasari, *Le vite,* ed. Milanesi, I, p. 174)

The text is essentially the same in both editions.

53. I have elaborated on this reading in "Raphael's *School of Athens* and the Artist of the Modern Manner," in *The World of Savonarola: Italian Elites and Perceptions of Crisis,* ed. Christine Shaw and Stella Fletcher (Aldershot, 2000), pp. 212–32.
54. The ardent terminology is quoted from Vasari's celebration of Giulio Romano's drawings as more worthy than his paintings: ". . . si può affermare che Giulio esprimesse sempre meglio i suoi concetti ne' disegni che nell'operare o nelle pitture, vedendosi in quelli più vivacità, fierezza ed affetto: e ciò potette forse avvenire, perchè un disegno lo faceva in un'ora tutto fiero ed acceso nell'opera, dove nelle pitture consumava i mesi e gli anni" (*Le vite,* ed. Milanesi, V, p. 528). On Giulio as draftsman, see Janet Cox-Rearick et al., *Giulio Romano: Master Designer,* exhibition catalogue (New York, 1999).
55. McM ¶ 102, cc. 50–50v: "ma questo disegno e di tanta eccellentia che non solo ricercha l'opere di natura ma infinite piu che quelle che fa natura. . . . e per questo concluderemo non solamente esser scientia ma una deità essere con debito nome, ricordata la qual deità rippette tutte l'opere evidenti fatte dal sommo iddio."
56. Lorenzo Ghiberti, *I Commentari* (Biblioteca Nazionale Centrale di Firenze, II, I, 333), ed. Lorenzo Bartoli (Florence, 1998), pp. 46–47. Ghiberti's list of liberal arts is interesting for its peculiarly professional slant: in addition to *Gramatica, Geometria, Phylosophia, Medicina, Astrologia, Arismetrica,* and *Istorico,* it includes *Prospectiva* and *Notomia,* as well as *Teorica disegno.* On the *Commentari* and Ghiberti's humanist ambitions, see Richard Krautheimer, *Lorenzo Ghiberti,* 2d ed. (Princeton, 1970), pp. 294–334.
57. Piero della Francesco, *De prospectiva pingendi,* ed. Nicco-Fasola, p. 63f.:

> La pictura contiene in sè tre parti principali, quali diciamo essere disegno, commensuratio et colorare. Desegno intendiamo essere profili et contorni che nella cosa se contene. Commensuratio diciamo essere essi profili et contorni proportionalmente posti nei luoghi loro. Colorare intendiamo dare i colori commo nelle cose se dimostrano, chiari et uscuri secondo che i lumi li devariano. De le quali tre parti intendo tracta[re] solo de la commensuratione, quale diciamo prospectiva, mescolandoci qualche parte de desegno. perciò che senza non se po dimostrare in opera essa prospectiva; il colorare lasciaremo stare, e tracteremo de quella parte che con line angoli et proportioni se po dimostrare, dicendo de puncti, linee, superficie et de corpi.

58. Ghiberti, *I Commentari,* ed. Bartoli, p. 47. Pomponius Gauricus reports that Donatello is supposed to have declared drawing so essential to the sculptor that he used to say to his pupils that the art could could be taught in one word: draw (*De sculptura* [1504], ed. André Chastel and Robert Klein (Paris and Geneva, 1969), p. 73).
59.
> Il disegno non è altro che speculation divina, che produce un arte eccellentissima, talmente che tu non puoi operare cosa nessuna nella scoltura, & nella pittura senza la guida di questa speculatione & disegno. . . . Il primo disegno è un'inventione di tutto l'universo, imaginato perfettamente nella mente della prima causa, inanzi che venisse all'atto del rilievo, & del colore. (*Disegno del Doni* [Florence, 1549], pp. 7v–8; ed. Mario Pepe [Milan, 1970])

60. On the topos of *deus artifex,* see Ernst Kris and Otto Kurz, *Legend, Myth, and Magic in the Image of the Artist: A Historical Experiment* (1934) (New Haven and London, 1979), pp. 38–60.
61. This was not Alberti's own *Della pittura* but an Italian translation of his Latin text by Lodovico Domenichi: *La pittura di Leonbattista Alberti* (Venice, 1547). The Latin version had appeared in print as *De pictura praestantissima arte et nunquam satis laudata libri tres absolutissimi Leonis Baptistae de Albertis . . .* (Basel, 1540).
62. *Lezzione di Benedetto Varchi, nella quale si disputa della maggioranza delle arti e qual sia più nobile, la scultura o la pittura . . .* (Florence, 1547); this was then reissued in *Due lezzioni di M. Benedetto Varchi, nella prima delle quali si dichiara un sonetto di M. Michelagnolo Buonarroti. Nella seconda si disputa quale sia più nobile arte, la scultura*

o la pittura, con una lettera d'esso Michelagnolo e più altri eccellentissimi pittori e scultori sopra la quaestione sopradetta (Florence, 1549). The second *Lezzione* and the responding letters have been edited by Paola Barocchi in *Trattati d'arte del Cinquecento,* I [Bari, 1960], pp. 1–82.

63. Pontormo, for example, accorded primacy to neither painting nor sculpture, "perché una cosa sola c'è che è nobile, che è el suo fondamento, e questo si è el disegno, e tutte quante l'altre ragioni sono debole rispetto a questo (vedetelo, che chiunche ha questo, fa l'una e l'altra bene) . . ." (in *Trattati d'arte,* ed. Barocchi, I, p. 67). And Francesco Sangallo, arguing on behalf of sculpture, declares, "allo scultore gli saria necessario avere più disegno, lo quale, per essere il fondamento d'ogni arte, non solo di queste . . ." (ibid., I, p. 73). On the articulation of the concept in the second half of the sixteenth century, see Wolfgang Kemp, "Disegno: Beiträge zur Geschichte des Begriffs zwischen 1547 und 1607," *Marburger Jahrbuch für Kunstwissenschaft* 19 (1974): 219–40, and Maurice Poirier, "The Role of the Concept of *Disegno* in Mid-Sixteenth Century Florence," in *The Age of Vasari* (Notre Dame, Ind., 1970), pp. 53–66. On Varchi and his role as aesthetic provocateur, see Leatrice Mendelsohn, *Paragoni: Benedetto Varchi's* Due Lezzioni *and Cinquecento Art Theory* (Ann Arbor, 1982).

64.

> Perchè il disegno, padre delle tre arti nostre, Architettura, Scultura e Pittura, procedendo dall'intelletto, cava di molte cose un giudizio universale; simile a una forma ovvero idea di tutte le cose della natura, la quale è singolarissima nelle sue misure; di qui è che non solo nei corpi umani e degli animali, ma nelle piante ancora, e nelle fabbriche e sculture e pitture, conosce la proporzione che ha il tutto con le parti, e che hanno le parti fra loro e col tutto insieme. E perchè da questa cognizione nasce un certo concetto e giudizio, che si forma nella mente quella tal cosa che poi espressa con le mani si chiama disegno; si può conchiudere che esso disegno altro non sia che una apparente espressione e dichiarazione del concetto che si ha nell'animo, e di quello che altri si è nella mente immaginato e fabbricato nell'idea. (Vasari, *Le vite,* ed. Milanesi, I, p. 168f.)

In a letter of 1547, Doni had already acknowledged *disegno* as "padre della pittura e della scultura" (in *Scritti d'arte del Cinquecento,* ed. Paola Barocchi [Milan and Naples, 1971–77], I, p. 1906f.). Although there was general agreement on the generational responsibility of *disegno,* the gender of the parent was occasionally open to question. In his response to Varchi, published in 1549, Vasari himself had declared *disegno* to be "madre di ognuna di queste arti" (in *Trattati d'arte,* ed. Barocchi, I, p. 62). Benvenuto Cellini, in the inscription on one of his designs for a seal for the Accademia del Disegno, wrote that "l'arte del disegnio si è la vera madre di tutte le azioni del huomo," identifying *disegno* as "la vera dea della natura" and figuring her as the multibreasted Diana of Ephesus (British Museum: see Nicholas Turner, *Florentine Drawings of the Sixteenth Century* [London, 1986], no. 118). Another, probably earlier, design featured instead Apollo (Fig. 45), tribute to the patronage of Cosimo I de' Medici. For Cellini's other designs for the academy, see below, note 71.

65.

> L'arte della pittura . . . dividerò in tre parti a modo mio: la prima parte sarà disegno, la seconda invenzione, la terza et ultima il colorire. Quanto alla prima parte, detta disegno, io voglio anco dividerla in quattro parti: la prima diremo giudicio, la seconda circumscrizzione, la terza pratica, l'ultima retta composizione. . . . L'ultima poi è detta composizione: in questa s'include tutte l'altre, cioè il giudicio, la circoscrizzione e la pratica, imperò che questa retta composizione consiste nel formar integramente le superfizie, le quali sono parti de' membri, et i membri come parte del corpo, il corpo, poi come integrità dell'opera. (Paolo Pino, *Dialogo di pittura* [1548], ed. Barocchi, in *Trattati d'arte,* I, pp. 113–14)

On Pino and Alberti, see the pioneering study by Creighton Gilbert, "Antique Frameworks for Renaissance Art Theory," and Mary Pardo, "Testo e contesti del 'Dialogo di Pittura' di Paolo Pino," in *Paolo Pino teorico d'arte e artista: Il restauro della pala di Scorzé* (Scorzé, 1992), pp. 33–49, as well as her forthcoming edition and commentary, *True Alchemy: Paolo Pino's "Dialogo di pittura" and the Origins of Venetian Art Criticism.*

66. "Il disegno . . . è la forma che dà il pittore alle cose che va imitando, et è proprio un giramento di linee per diverse vie, le quali formano le figure; . . . né basta a un pittore di esser bello inventore, se non è parimente buon disegnatore, percioché la invenzione si appresenta per la forma, e la forma non è altro che disegno" (Lodovico Dolce, *Dialogo della pittura, intitolato l'Aretino* [1557], ed. Barocchi, in *Trattati d'arte,* I, p. 171f.).

67. See Zygmunt Wazbinski, *L'Accademia medicea del disegno a Firenze nel Cinquecento: Idea e istituzione* (Florence, 1987), p. 171. Michelangelo and *disegno* are the subject of Chapter Six.

68. Baldesar Castiglione, *Il libro del Cortegiano* (1528), ed. Bruno Maier (Turin, 1964), p. 173: "E benché diversa sia la pittura dalla statuaria, pur l'una e l'altra da un medesimo fonte, che è il bon disegno."

69. On the Florentine academy: Theodore Reynolds, "The Accademia del Disegno in Florence, Formation and Early Years," Ph.D. dissertation (Columbia University, 1974); Wazbinski, *L'Accademia medicea del disegno,* and Karen-Edis Barzman, *The Florentine Academy and the Early Modern State: The Discipline of* Disegno (Cambridge and New York, 2000). Further on Cosimo's patronage and the political

implications of *disegno* as a controlling concept, see Randolph Starn and Loren Partridge, *Arts of Power: Three Halls of State in Italy, 1300–1600* (Berkeley, Los Angeles, Oxford, 1992), pp. 205–11.

70. Vasari describes Bertoldo as the curator of a collection of drawings that served pedagogic purpose in the Medici garden, a collection including "molti disegni, cartoni e modelli" by Donatello, Brunelleschi, Masaccio, Uccello, Filippo Lippi, and "altri maestri paesani e forestieri" (*Le vite*, ed. Milanesi, IV, p. 259f.). Many of the drawings in his own collection were acquired from such professional sources, such as the Ghiberti studio (ibid., II, p. 249). On Vasari's collection, see Otto Kurz, "Vasari's Libro de' disegni," *Old Master Drawings* 12 (1937): 1–15, 32–44; Bernhard Degenhart and Annegrit Schmitt, "Methoden Vasaris bei den Gestaltung seines Libro," in *Studien zur toskanischen Kunst: Festschrift für Ludwig Heydenreich*, ed. Wolfgang Lotz and Lise Lotte Moller (Munich, 1964), pp. 45–64; Licia Ragghianti Collobi, *Il Libro de' disegni del Vasari*, 2 vols. (Florence, 1974). For the larger art-historical implications of Vasari's frames, cf. Erwin Panofsky, "The First Page of Giorgio Vasari's 'Libro': A Study on the Gothic Style in the Judgment of the Italian Renaissance," in *Meaning in the Visual Arts: Papers in and on Art History* (Garden City, N.Y., 1955), pp. 169–235.

A general survey of the development of drawing collections will be found in Charles de Tolnay, *History and Technique of Old Master Drawings* (New York, 1943), pp. 76–86. On the early collection of prints, see Michael Bury, "The Taste for Prints in Italy to c. 1600," *Print Quarterly* 2 (1985): 12–26, and Landau and Parshall, *The Renaissance Print*, pp. 91–94, 284–98, 342–58.

71. The inscription comments on a figure of Apollo, paying tribute to the patronage of Duke Cosimo: "La inscrizione d'intorno al sigillo è questa: Apollo è sol la Luce, Cosmo è principio à la gran scuola, e Duce. II F. e S." The longer inscription below moves from solar Apollo as light of the universe to *disegno* as the guiding light of human endeavor: ". . . et così io l'ho messo in disegno parendomi chè la nostra Academia del Disegno sia degna di questa bella Impresa: perchè sì come questo è la vera Lucerna dell'universo, cosi il Disegno è la sola et Lucerna di tutte le Azzioni che fanno gli Huomini in ogni professione, perchè il Disegno e di due sorte, il primo è quello che si fa nell'Imaginativa, et il secondo tratto da quello si dimostra con linee. . . ." For a full transcription, see Peter Halm, Bernhard Degenhart, and Wolfgang Wegner, *Hundert Meisterzeichnungen aus der Staatlichen Graphischen Sammlung München* (Munich, 1958), no. 56. Among his alternative designs, Cellini developed the sibling imagery of Diana of Ephesus, standing for Nature, whose fecundity is imitated by the creativity of *disegno* (see above, note 64). On Cellini's several drawings for the academy, see Wolfgang Kemp, "Disegno: Beiträge zur Geschichte des Begriffs," and John Pope-Hennessy, *Cellini* (New York, 1985), pp. 275–89.

72. Federico Zuccaro, *L'Idea de' pittori, scultori, et architetti* (Turin, 1607), II, p. 83 (in *Scritti d'arte*, ed. Barocchi, II, p. 2116).

73. Zuccaro, *Idea*, II, p. 17 (in *Scritti d'arte*, ed. Barocchi, II, p. 2087).

74. On Zuccaro's *Idea*, see the classic essay by Erwin Panofsky, *Idea: A Concept in Art Theory* (1924; 2d ed., 1960), trans. Joseph J. S. Peake (Columbia, 1968), pp. 85–95; David Summers, *The Judgment of Sense: Renaissance Naturalism and the Rise of Aesthetics* (Cambridge, 1987), pp. 283–308, and Ghislain Kieft, "Zuccari, Scaligiero e Panofsky," *Mitteilungen des Kunsthistorischen Institutes in Florenz* 33 (1989): 355–68.

75. On Zuccaro's Sala del Disegno, see Werner Korte, *Der Palazzo Zuccari in Rom: Sein Freskenschmuck und seine Geschichte* (Leipzig, 1935), pp. 35–47.

76. A standard late Cinquecento declaration (Raffaele Borghini, *Il Riposo* [Florence, 1584], p. 137) will be cited in an eighteenth-century edition of the *Vocabolario degli Accademici della Crusca* (Naples, 1746), II, p. 106, s.v. *Disegno:* "Il disegno non estimo io, che sia altro che una apparente dimostrazione con linee di quello che prima nell'animo l'uomo si avea concetto, e nell'idea immaginato." Interestingly, the passage does not occur in seventeenth-century editions of the dictionary, which tend to gloss over the more theoretical implications of the word.

For the historical challenge of translating the term, see Michael Baxandall, "English *Disegno*," in *England and the Continental Renaissance*, ed. Edward Chaney and Peter Mack (Woodbridge, 1990), pp. 203–14.

3. THE HANDWRITING OF THE SELF: LEONARDO DA VINCI

1. "Si dice che ogni dipintore dipinge se medesimo." Girolamo Savonarola, *Prediche sopra Ezechiele* (Venice, 1517), f. 71v.; ed. Roberto Ridolfi (Rome, 1955), I, p. 343.
2. Carlo Pedretti and Gigetta Dalli Regoli, *I disegni di Leonardo da Vinci e della sua cerchia nel Gabinetto Disegni e Stampe della Galleria degli Uffizi* (Florence, 1985), pp. 19–22, and no. 1.
3. Leonardo's earliest script is close to what would have been known as *mercantile*, rather than *cancelleresca*, which it approaches later in his development. For the evolution of his handwriting, see especially Gerolamo Calvi, *I Manoscritti di Leonardo da Vinci dal punto di vista cronologico, storico e biografico* (1925), ed. Augusto Marinoni (Busto Arsizio, 1982). For an illustrated history of notarial penmanship, see Vincenzo Federici, *La scrittura delle cancellerie italiane dal secolo XII al XVII* (Rome, 1934); also Alfred Fairbank and Berthold Wolpe, *Renaissance Handwriting: An Anthology* (London, 1960); James Wardrop, *The*

Script of Humanism: Some Aspects of the Humanistic Script 1460–1560 (Oxford, 1963). A basic introduction to the teaching of writing, with further bibliography, will be found in Paul F. Grendler, *Schooling in Renaissance Italy: Literacy and Learning, 1300–1600* (Baltimore and London, 1989), pp. 322–29. The cultural and manual dynamics of Leonardo's writing are subject to most intelligent analysis by Robert Zwijnenberg, *The Writings and Drawings of Leonardo da Vinci: Order and Chaos in Early Modern Thought* (Cambridge, New York, Melbourne, 1999), esp. pp. 83–111.

4. In a fragment of an autobiography, Raffaello da Montelupo celebrated his own left-handedness and his own wondrous manner of writing, which sounds very much like Leonardo's: "Ora questa mia maniera di schrivere con la mano mancha, perchè io tengo il foglio per lo lungo, molti che mi ànno veduto si maravigliano, parendo loro più presto a l'ebraicho che altrimenti, nè chredano mentre ch'io schrivo la non si possi legere. . . ." Raffaello also drew with his left hand, which, he claims, amazed Michelangelo and Sebastiano del Piombo when they saw him, for both of them were also born left-handed but had, as it were, gone over: "si fermorono a vedere, e perchè l'uno e l'altro era mancino naturale, inperò non facevano niente con la mano mancina salvo le cose di forza; e stetono un pezzo a vedermi, maravigliandosi forte; cosa che forse non à mai fatto nisuno di queste dua arte, che si sapia."

   Published by Gaetano Milanesi in his edition of Giorgio Vasari, *Le vite de' più eccellenti pittori, scultori et architettori* (Florence, 1878–85), IV, p. 552, Raffaello da Montelupo's testimony suggests further paths of inquiry into the question of *mancino* artists in the Renaissance. For now, cf. the brief observations by Agnes Mongan, "On Left-Handedness," in *Drawings Defined*, ed. Walter Strauss and Tracie Felcker (New York, 1987), pp. 160–64; Peter Parshall, "Albrecht Dürer and the Axis of Meaning," *Allen Memorial Art Museum Bulletin* 50, no. 2 (1997): 5–31; Philip Rawson, *Drawing*, 2d ed. (Philadelphia, 1987), pp. 85, 215, as well as the more extensive speculations on "Right and Left-Handed Men" of Thomas Andrea Cook, *The Curves of Life* (New York, 1914), pp. 239–65.

5. *The Literary Works of Leonardo da Vinci*, ed. Jean Paul Richter, 2d ed. (London, 1939), ¶¶ 1372 and 1373 (hereafter cited as Richter with paragraph number); see also Carlo Pedretti, *The Literary Works of Leonardo da Vinci: A Commentary to Jean Paul Richter's Edition* (Berkeley and Los Angeles, 1977), II, p. 319. In addition, the draft of a rather moving letter to his father (Richter ¶ 1373A) is also written properly, left to right: "Padre carissimo, A l'ultimo del passato ebbi lettera mi scrivesti, la quale in brieve spazio mi dette piacere e tristezia: piacere in quanto che per quella intesi voi essere sano di che ne rendo grazie a Dio; ebbi dispiacere intendendo il disagio vostro." See *Il Codice Atlantico di Leonardo da Vinci* (Edizione nazionale dei manoscritti e disegni di Leonardo da Vinci a cura della Commissione Vinciana), ed. Augusto Marinoni (Florence and New York, 1973–80), II, fol. 178v (hereafter references are to the new foliation: see Carlo Pedretti, *The Codex Atlanticus of Leonardo da Vinci: A Catalogue of its Newly Restored Sheets*, 2 vols. [New York, 1978–79]; also Augusto Marinoni, in *Leonardo all'Ambrosiana: Il Codice Atlantico, I disegni di Leonardo e della sua cerchia* [Milan, 1982]). Although rare in Leonardo's manuscripts and annotated drawings, conventional writing, from left to right, was clearly an option available to him, one that he exercised especially at this time in regard to the canalization of the Arno (ca. 1503–4), where his notations obviously had to be legible to others: e.g., Richter ¶¶ 766, 1463; Pedretti, *Commentary*, II, p. 42. Other examples may date as early as ca. 1479–80 (Richter ¶ 51; Pedretti, *Commentary*, I, p. 127) and from the later years of the first Milanese period, ca. 1497–99 (Richter ¶¶ 1466, 1468; Pedretti, *Commentary*, II, pp. 351–53). On the general problem, cf. Luca Beltrami, *La "destra mano" di Leonardo da Vinci e le lacune nella edizione del Codice Atlantico* (*Analecta Ambrosiana*, II) (Milan and Rome, 1919), who argues for Leonardo's ambidexterity.

6. Sigmund Freud, *Leonardo da Vinci and a Memory of His Childhood* (1910), trans. Alan Tyson (New York, 1964), pp. 69–73. For the subsequent debate over Freud's analysis of Leonardo, see the references cited below, note 31. For less speculative, more art-historical consideration of the issue, see James Beck, "Leonardo's Rapport with His Father," *Antichità viva* 28: 5–6 (1988): 5–12.

7. Quoted from the editor's note to Freud, *Leonardo da Vinci*, p. 7.

8. The verso of the Uffizi sheet presents a more problematic example of this relationship (Fig. 48). Over a rough landscape executed in black chalk, pen sketches of a highly calligraphic, almost caricature profile and of a running figure visually relate directly to the inscription above: "Jo Morando danto sono chontento" ("I, Morando d'Antonio, am content [sc. agree to] . . ."). The inscription reads from left to right and the figures are hardly persuasive as the work of Leonardo himself. Accepting the landscape drawing of the verso as autograph, Pedretti and Regoli (*I Disegni di Leonardo . . . degli Uffizi*, p. 20, n. 17) rejected the attribution of the pen notations to Leonardo. Commenting on the figure, Pedretti has identified it as a Mercury or a Perseus: see "A Proem to Sculpture," *Achademia Leonardi Vinci: Journal of Leonardo Studies* 2 (1989): 11–39, esp. p. 19, n. 26.

   Untroubled by the direction of the script, Raymond S. Stites has read the inscription as "I, remaining with Antonio, am content," and has identified this Antonio as Achattabrigha, the husband of Leonardo's natural mother: *The Sublimations of Leonardo da Vinci, with a Translation of the Codex Trivulzianus* (Washington, 1970), p. 7f.

9. Pedretti and Regoli, *I Disegni di Leonardo . . . degli Uffizi*, no. 7. The torn month has generally been reconstructed as December: cf. Pedretti, *Commentary*, I, p. 380, and Martin Kemp, *Leonardo da Vinci: The Marvellous Works of Nature and Man* (Cambridge, Mass., 1981), pp. 42, 53. Calvi, *I Manoscritti*, p. 45, allowed a possible reading as September.
10. On this particular inscription, see Calvi, *I Manoscritti*, p. 48f., and on the frequency of Leonardo's doodling "in dei nomine," see Kemp, *Leonardo da Vinci*, p. 81, and, especially, the observations of Renzo Cianchi, *Vinci, Leonardo e la sua famiglia* (Milan, 1952), p. 52. Stites, *The Sublimations*, p. 8, attaches more affective weight to the notarial formula than seems warranted.
11. I borrow the term from Paul Valéry's later gloss on his "Introduction to the Method of Leonardo da Vinci" (1894), in *Leonardo, Poe, Mallarmé*, trans. Malcolm Cowley and James R. Lawler (Princeton, 1972), p. 24f. For the full statement, see Chapter One, note 23.
12. Kenneth Clark, *The Drawings of Leonardo da Vinci . . . at Windsor Castle*, 2d ed., rev. with the assistance of Carlo Pedretti, 3 vols. (London, 1968), I, p. 3f.
13. The double-sided British Museum sheet (Figs. 55, 56) has been discussed recently by Martin Kemp in *Leonardo da Vinci: The Mystery of the* Madonna of the Yarnwinder, exhibition catalogue (Edinburgh, 1992), no. 8. For the drawing in Venice (Fig. 58), see Luisa Cogliati Arano, *Disegni di Leonardo e della sua cerchia alle Gallerie dell'Accademia*, exhibition catalogue (Milan, 1980), no. 9.
14. Further on these drawings: Virginia Budny, "The Sequence of Leonardo's Sketches for *The Madonna and Child with Saint Anne and Saint John the Baptist*," *Art Bulletin* 65 (1983): 34–50; Ilse E. Friesen, "Leonardo da Vinci's Unorthodox Iconography: The *Madonna with the Cat*," *RACAR* 16 (1989): 78–80.
15. In a fragmentary sketch in Venice, also datable to ca. 1478, in which he explored the theme of the adoration of the Christ child, Leonardo introduced the infant Baptist kneeling worshipfully before the reclining Jesus. For the drawing, see Luisa Cogliati Arano, *Disegni di Leonardo e della sua cerchia*, exhibition catalogue (Milan, 1980), no. 3, and, for a reconstruction of the sheet and fuller discussion, Carlo Pedretti, "Giorgione e Leonardo," in *Giorgione e l'umanesimo veneziano*, ed. Rodolfo Pallucchini (Florence, 1981), II, pp. 485–512, esp. 486–90. On the significance of the theme, see Marilyn Aronberg Lavin, "Giovannino Battista: A Study in Renaissance Religious Symbolism," *Art Bulletin* 37 (1955): 85–101, and "Giovannino Battista: A Supplement," *Art Bulletin* 43 (1961): 319–26.
16. For recent consideration of this moment, see the papers in *Leonardo, Michelangelo, and Raphael in Renaissance Florence from 1500 to 1508*, ed. Serafina Hager (Washington, 1992).
17. In a compositional epilogue, known only through copies, Leonardo may have extended this relationship, joining the two infants in kissing embrace. Elaborating on this motif – and citing Hella Krause-Zimmer, *Le problème des deux enfants Jésus et sa trace dans l'art* (Paris, 1977) – Carlo Pedretti has suggested an iconography of "the Christ Child and His Double" as possibly "the key to the true meaning" – unorthodox if not heretical – of the first version of the *Virgin of the Rocks:* see "Leonardo in Sweden," *Achademia Leonardi Vinci: Journal of Leonardo Studies* 6 (1993): 200–211, esp. 204–6. Whatever the theological implications of this motif, that Leonardo evidently conceived of a reconciliation of the two infants is hardly without psychological interest.
18. Leon Battista Alberti, *De pictura*, ed. Cecil Grayson (Rome and Bari, 1975), ¶ 36: ". . . ma come a vestire l'uomo prima si disegna ignudo, poi il circondiamo di panni, così dipignendo il nudo, prima pogniamo sue ossa e muscoli, quali poi così copriamo con sue carni che non sia difficile intendere ove sotto sia ciascuno moscolo."
19. See Kenneth D. Keele, *Leonardo da Vinci's Elements of the Science of Man* (New York and London, 1983), pp. 348–62.
20. The antique figure of a crouching Venus was adduced as a model for Leonardo's kneeling Leda by Kenneth Clark, "Leonardo and the Antique," in *Leonardo's Legacy: An International Symposium*, ed. C. D. O'Malley (Berkeley and Los Angeles, 1969), pp. 18–21; see also *The Drawings of Leonardo da Vinci . . . at Windsor Castle*, I, p. 32f., as well as Francis Ames-Lewis and Joanne Wright, *Drawing in the Italian Renaissance Workshop*, exhibition catalogue (London, 1983), no. 45. The development of the motif has been discussed, in essentially formal terms, by Ames-Lewis, "Leonardo da Vinci's 'Kneeling Leda': The Evolution of an Expressive Figure Composition," *Drawing* 9 (Nov.–Dec. 1989): 73–76; further observations on the presumed archaeology of Leonardo's inspiration are offered by Alastair Smart and Martin Kemp, "Leonardo's *Leda* and the Belvedere *River-Gods:* Roman Sources and a New Chronology," *Art History* 3 (1980): 160–71. Kemp has observed that the "compressed pose of the Madonna [in Windsor 12276r] recalls the kind of antique crouching Venus (the 'Doidalsas type') that Leonardo was later to use as a starting point for his *Leda*" (*The Mystery of the* Madonna of the Yarnwinder, no. 7).
21. The marble relief of Alexander the Great in the National Gallery of Art issued from the workshop of Verrocchio and implicates the young Leonardo with regard to physiognomy as well as, perhaps, to its conception. On Leonardo in Verrocchio's shop, see the extended discussion in David Alan Brown, *Leonardo da Vinci: Origins of a Genius* (New Haven and London, 1998), esp. pp. 68–73, for the Alexander relief. For the problem of its attribution, see Charles Seymour, Jr., *The Sculpture of Verrocchio* (Green-

wich, Conn., 1970), pp. 170–71, and Andrew Butterfield, *The Sculpture of Andrea Verrocchio* (New Haven and London, 1997), pp. 156–57, and cat. no. 25. A most strenuous, if not particularly persuasive, argument for ascribing the conception to Leonardo himself has been made by Susan V. Lenkey, *An Unknown Leonardo Self-Portrait: Revision of the Alexander the Great Relief in the National Gallery of Art . . .* (Stanford, 1963) – the "unknown" self-portrait being, however, not the profile itself but one of the little faces under the shoulder armor.

22. Kenneth Clark, *Leonardo da Vinci: An Account of His Development as an Artist* (1939), rev. ed. (Baltimore, 1967), p. 71.

23. The locus classicus for Leonardo's reputation is Vasari's life of the artist, drawing on earlier tradition, especially Paolo Giovio. See Vasari, *Le vite*, ed. Milanesi, IV, pp. 17–53; for Paolo Giovio's *Vita*, see Paola Barocchi, ed., *Scritti d'arte del Cinquecento*, I (Milan and Naples, 1970), pp. 7–9. Leonardo's reputation is summarized in Clark, *Leonardo da Vinci*, pp. 18–19, and Ludwig H. Heydenreich, *Leonardo da Vinci* (London, New York, Basel, 1954), pp. 19–21. Cf. the critique by Patricia Rubin, "'What Men Saw': Vasari's Life of Leonardo da Vinci and the Image of the Renaissance Artist," *Art History* 13 (1990): 34–46 (also in *Nine Lectures on Leonardo da Vinci*, ed. Francis Ames-Lewis and Anka Bednarek [London, n.d.], pp. 96–108), as well as A. Richard Turner, *Inventing Leonardo* (New York, 1993), pp. 55–68.

For an optimistically ambitious effort to trace Leonardo's features in and through his works, see Marco Carpiceci, *Leonardo allo specchio: Ritratti e autoritratti*, exhibition catalogue (Brescia, 1984). Stites, *The Sublimations*, p. 8, goes so far as to call the faces on the verso of Windsor 12276 a "family constellation," including Leonardo's father. On the other hand, for Michael Kwakkelstein, *Leonardo da Vinci as a Physiognomist: Theory and Drawing Practice* (Leiden, 1994), p. 102, they are purely studies in comparative physiognomy.

24. Among the frequently cited models in this regard are the elegant youth of Verrocchio's *David* and the "nutcracker warrior" of his *Colleoni* – beyond which lie the models of antiquity, Hellenistic ephebes and coins of Roman emperors. See Clark, "Leonardo and the Antique," and, especially, E. H. Gombrich, "Leonardo da Vinci's Method of Analysis and Permutations: The Grotesque Heads," in *The Heritage of Apelles: Studies in the Art of the Renaissance* (Ithaca, 1976), pp. 57–75. For more recent commentary, specifically on Windsor 12276, see Jane Roberts, in Kemp and Roberts, *Leonardo da Vinci*, exhibition catalogue (New Haven and London, 1989), no. 5; cf. also the entries by Martin Kemp: nos. 33–36. For the idealized female head, see Françoise Viatte, "Verrocchio et Leonardo da Vinci: A propos des 'têtes idéales,'" in *Florentine Drawing at the Time of Lorenzo the Magnificent* (Villa Spelman Colloquia, Vol. 4), ed. Elizabeth Cropper (Bologna, n.d.), pp. 45–53. The most ambitious recent study of Leonardo's physiognomic investigations is Kwakkelstein, *Leonardo da Vinci as a Physiognomist*, who, deliberately "disregarding a modern psychological approach," stresses their rhetorical context and purely professional intention.

25. Leonardo da Vinci, *Treatise on Painting [Codex Urbinas Latinus 1270]*, trans. and ed. A. Philip McMahon, 2 vols. (Princeton, 1956), ¶ 86 (hereafter abbreviated as McM with ¶ number):

> *Del massimo diffetto de pittori:* . . . e' havendo io piu volte considerato la causa di tal difetto mi pare che sia da giudicare che quella anima che reggie e' governa sciascun corpo si e' quella che fa il nostro giuditio in anti sia il proprio giuditio nostro[;] adonque ella ha condotto tutta la figura del homo com'ella ha giudicato quello stare bene o' col naso longo, o' corto, o' camuso e' cosí li afermò la sua altezza e' figura[.] et e' di tanta potentia questo tal giuditio ch'egli move le braccia al pittore et fagli replicare se medesimo parendo a' essa anima che quello sia il vero modo di figurare l'homo. . . . (c. 44v)

26. Other passages concerned with the danger of automimesis: McM ¶¶ 85, 87, 273, 276, 438.

27. Leonardo was hardly alone in his concern. Cf. Dürer's similar comment in a draft of 1512: "Many fall into error because they follow their own taste alone; therefore let each look to it that his inclination blind not his judgment. For every mother is well pleased with her own child, and thus also it ariseth that many painters paint figures resembling themselves" (*Dürer: Schriftlicher Nachlass*, ed. Hans Rupprich [Berlin, 1956–69], II, p. 119; trans. William Martin Conway, *The Literary Remains of Albrecht Dürer* [Cambridge, 1889], p. 180). Cf. as well Vasari's anecdote about Michelangelo's response to a painting in which the best thing was an ox: "Ogni pittore ritrae se medesimo bene" (*Le vite*, ed. Milanesi, VII, p. 280).

For further discussion of this issue in Leonardo's thought and its context, see Martin Kemp, "'Ogni dipintore dipinge se': A Neoplatonic Echo in Leonardo's Art Theory?" in *Cultural Aspects of the Italian Renaissance: Essays in Honour of Paul Oskar Kristeller*, ed. Cecil H. Clough (New York, 1976), pp. 311–23; and Frank Zöllner, "'Ogni Pittore Dipinge Sé': Leonardo da Vinci and Automimesis," in *Der Künstler über sich in seinem Werk* (Internationales Symposium der Bibliotheca Hertziana, Rome, 1989), ed. Matthias Winner (Weinheim, 1992), pp. 137–60; cf. also Carlo Pedretti, *Leonardo da Vinci on Painting: A Lost Book (Libro A)* (Berkeley and Los Angeles, 1964), p. 35 (carta 15). For the larger cultural resonance, see Martin Kemp, "'Equal excellences': Lomazzo and the Explanation of Individual Style in the Visual Arts," *Renaissance Studies* 1 (1987): 1–26, and, for the still broader intellectual context of faculty psychology, David Summers, *The Judgment of Sense: Renaissance Naturalism and the Rise of Aesthetics* (Cambridge and New York, 1987), esp. pp. 170–76, on Leonardo and the judgment of sense.

28. For the grotesques, see Gombrich, "The Grotesque Heads," and the more recent studies of Michael Kwakkelstein, *Leonardo da Vinci as a Physiognomist*, and "Leonardo da Vinci's Grotesque Heads and the Breaking of the Physiognomic Mould," *Journal of the Warburg and Courtauld Institutes* 54 (1991): 127–36.
29. Cf. McM ¶ 277: "*Of beauty and ugliness.* Beauty and ugliness seem more effective through one another."
30. See Charles D. O'Malley and J. B. de C.M. Saunders, *Leonardo da Vinci on the Human Body* (New York, 1952); Keele, *Leonardo da Vinci's Elements of the Science of Man*, and Kemp, *Leonardo da Vinci*, passim. For the best illustrations and commentary: Kenneth D. Keele and Carlo Pedretti, *Corpus of the Anatomical Studies in the Collection of Her Majesty the Queen at Windsor Castle*, 3 vols. (New York and London, 1979–80).
31. The subconscious relationship of these *leoni* to the name of Leonardo remains a topic for speculation. Cf. Cecilio Paniagua, "Notes on a Drawing by Leonardo da Vinci," *International Review of Psycho-Analysis* 13 (1986): 445–52, who does not hesitate to invest Leonardo's leonine interests with deeply overdetermined meaning (I thank Valerie Oltarsh for bringing this article to my attention). Modern psychoanalytic interest in Leonardo begins, of course, with Freud's *Eine Kindheitserinnerung des Leonardo da Vinci* (Vienna, 1910). Despite the difficulties inherent in any such approach to a subject accessible only through the screen of centuries, this subject in particular does indeed present a special challenge – and promise. But cf. the caveats of Meyer Schapiro, "Two Slips of Leonardo and a Slip of Freud," *Psychoanalysis* 4: 2 (Winter 1955–56): 3–8, and "Leonardo and Freud: An Art Historical Study," *Journal of the History of Ideas* 17 (1956): 147–78 (revised in volume 4 of his selected papers, *Theory and Philosophy of Art: Style, Artist, and Society* [New York, 1994], pp. 153–92, with "Further Notes on Freud and Leonardo," pp. 193–99). The most sustained effort at a psychoanalytic reading of Leonardo, responding to Schapiro's critique, is K. R. Eissler, *Leonardo da Vinci: Psychoanalytic Notes on the Enigma* (New York, 1961). Cf. also Stites, *The Sublimations*, and Sander L. Gilman, "Leonardo Sees Him-Self: Reading Leonardo's First Representation of Human Sexuality," *Social Research* 54 (1987): 149–71. For a recent psychoanalytic reading of Leonardo, see André Green, *Révélations de l'inachèvement: A propos du carton de Londres de Léonard de Vinci* (Paris, 1992). For a generally balanced consideration of the situation, see Bradley Collins, *Leonardo, Psychoanalysis, and Art History: A Critical Study of Psychobiographical Approaches to Leonardo da Vinci* (Evanston, 1997). Finally, and most important, Daniel Arasse has brought the discussion back to a more attentive analysis of the manuscript sources, which record the sequence of Leonardo's thoughts: *Léonard de Vinci: Le rythme du monde* (Paris, 1997), pp. 488–99.
32. Alberti, *De pictura*, ed. Grayson, ¶ 25.
33. Vasari, *Le vite*, ed. Milanesi, VII, pp. 427–28.
34. See the discussion in Chapter Two.
35. "*How one ought to make an imaginary animal seem natural.* . . . If, therefore, you would have an imaginary animal appear natural, and assuming, let us say, that it is a dragon, for the head take that of a mastiff or hound, and give him the eyes of a cat, the ears of a porcupine, the nose of a greyhound, the brow of a lion, the temples of an old cock, and the neck of a sea turtle" (McM ¶ 554).
36. *Schriftlicher Nachlass*, ed. Rupprich, III, p. 287; trans. Conway, *The Literary Remains*, p. 247.
37 Richter, ¶ 1144. Similar thoughts occur to Dürer, who, typically, formulates them less dispassionately: "Ah! how often in my sleep do I behold great works of art and beautiful things, the like whereof never appear to me awake, but so soon as I wake even the remembrance of them leaves me" (*Schriftlicher Nachlass*, ed. Rupprich, II, p. 119; trans. Conway, *The Literary Remains*, p. 180). On at least one famous occasion, however, in 1525, he did indeed remember one such dream vision, of a frightening deluge ("how many great waters fell from heaven") the recall of which left him "trembling all over" – but not too afraid to pick up his watercolor brush the next morning and record his nightmare (*Schriftlicher Nachlass*, ed. Rupprich, I, pp. 214–15.; trans. Conway, *The Literary Remains*, p. 145; for the watercolor: Fedja Anzelewsky, *Dürer: His Art and Life* [Fribourg, 1980], pl. 239). For a particularly sensitive consideration of this theme, see Mary Pardo, "Memory, Imagination, Figuration: Leonardo da Vinci and the Painter's Mind," in *Images of Memory: On Remembering and Representation*, ed. Susanne Küchler and Walter Melion (Washington and London, 1991), pp. 47–73; also David Rosand, "Remembered Lines," in *Memory and Oblivion* (Proceedings of the 29th International Congress of the History of Art), ed. Wessel Rinink and Jeroen Stumpel (Dordrecht, 1999), pp. 811–16.
38. But cf. Kwakkelstein, *Leonardo da Vinci as Physiognomist*, arguing for the priority of Leonardo's scientific interests.
39. For this sheet of pen sketches related to the *Battle of Anghiari*, see Carlo Pedretti, *Leonardo's Horses: Studies of Horses and Other Animals by Leonardo da Vinci from the Royal Library at Windsor Castle*, exhibition catalogue (Florence and New York, 1984), no. 24, and Kemp, in Kemp and Roberts, *Leonardo da Vinci*, exhibition catalogue, no. 87.

40. Leonardo recorded these same sensations in his notes for painting a battle scene, some of which were set down in Milan ca. 1490–92, more than a decade before his commission for the mural in the Palazzo della Signoria:

> You must make the conquered and beaten pale, their brows raised and knit, and the skin above their brows furrowed with pain, the sides of the nose with wrinkles going in an arch from the nostrils to the eyes, and make the nostrils drawn up – which is the cause of the lines of which I speak – and the lips arched upwards and revealing the upper teeth; and the teeth apart as with crying out and lamentation. (Richter, ¶ 502; see also Pedretti, *Commentary*, I, p. 353)

The passage becomes part of the *Treatise on Painting* (McM ¶ 283).

41. Cf., e.g., Leonardo's division of the animal kingdom into four species: man, lion, horse, and bull (Richter, ¶ 816; Pedretti, *Commentary*, II, p. 98), and his further comparative physiological notes on the lion (Richter, ¶ 827; Pedretti, *Commentary*, II, p. 102) – both on Windsor 19030 (see Pedretti's entry in *The Drawings of Leonardo . . . at Windsor Castle*, III, p. 14).
42. See Pedretti, *Leonardo's Horses*, exhibition catalogue, no. 22.
43. See Arthur Ewart Popham, "The Dragon-Fight," in *Leonardo: Saggi e ricerche* (Rome, 1954), pp. 221–27.
44. This complex, spiraling form was also imagined on a monumental scale in sculpture, in Leonardo's project for the statue of Gian Giacomo Trivulzio, a conception preserved in the smaller bronze version that presumably reflects his invention. The entire question is review by Michael Hall, *Reconsiderations of Sculpture by Leonardo da Vinci: A Bronze Statuette in the J. B. Speed Art Museum* (*J. B. Speed Art Museum Bulletin* 29) (Louisville, Ky., 1973).
45. For the drawings in the Accademia of Venice, see Cogliati Arano, *Disegni di Leonardo e della sua cerchia*, nos. 11–14.
46. See Pedretti, *Leonardo's Horses*, exhibition catalogue, no. 32, and, on the Neptune project, pp. 58–60; also Kemp, in Kemp and Roberts, *Leonardo da Vinci*, exhibition catalogue, no. 71.
47. See Carlo Pedretti, *Leonardo da Vinci Nature Studies from the Royal Library at Windsor Castle*, exhibition catalogue (New York, 1980), no. 29A.
48. The translation is that of E. H. Gombrich, "Leonardo da Vinci's Method of Analysis and Permutation: The Form of Movement in Water and Air," in *The Heritage of Apelles*, p. 47.
49. Ibid., p. 48.
50. On a drawing of the heart, trachea, and bronchial tree (Windsor no. 19071r): see O'Malley and Saunders, *Leonardo on the Human Body*, no. 173; also translated by Edward MacCurdy in *The Notebooks of Leonardo da Vinci* (1939; New York, 1956), p. 166f. That Leonardo may have known descriptions of meteorological phenomena in ancient literature should not lead us to assume the priority of reading over drawing: cf. John F. Moffitt, "The *Evidentia* of Curling Waters and Whirling Winds: Leonardo's *Ekphraseis* of the Latin Weathermen," *Achademia Leonardi Vinci: Journal of Leonardo Studies* 4 (1991): 11–33.
51. See Enzo Levi, "Leonardo precursore della scienza idraulica," in *Leonardo e l'età della ragione*, ed. Enrico Bellone and Paolo Rossi (Milan, 1982), pp. 399–419.
52. Reale Commissione Vinciana, *I manoscritti e i disegni di Leonardo da Vinci . . .*, I: *Il codice Arundel 263*, i (Rome, 1923), p. 88. On the poetic resonance of this theme – partly via Ovid – and its role in establishing meaning in the *Mona Lisa* as a portrait, see David Rosand, "The Portrait, the Courtier, and Death," in *Castiglione: The Ideal and the Real in Renaissance Culture*, ed. Robert W. Hanning and David Rosand (New Haven and London, 1983), pp. 91–129, esp. 109–15; see also Donald Strong, "The Triumph of Mona Lisa: Science and the Allegory of Time," in *Leonardo e l'età della ragione*, pp. 255–78.
53. See Pedretti, *Nature Studies*, exhibition catalogue, no. 42, and, for the series, pp. 47–50; also Kemp, in Kemp and Roberts, *Leonardo da Vinci*, exhibition catalogue, no. 63, and section 6 ("The Forces of Destruction"), pp. 132–40.
54. On the themes of time and destruction in Leonardo's thought: Joseph Gantner, *Leonardos Visionen von der Sintflut und vom Untergang der Welt* (Berne, 1958), pp. 62–71 ("Der Mikrocosmos und das Wasser"); V. P. Zubov, *Leonardo da Vinci*, trans. David H. Kraus (Cambridge, Mass., 1968), pp. 221–63 ("Time"); E. H. Gombrich, "The Form of Movement in Air and Water," in *The Heritage of Apelles*, pp. 39–56; Alexander Perrig, "Leonardo: Die Anatomie der Erde," *Jahrbuch der Hamburger Kunstsammlungen* 25 (1980): 51–80; also Jan Bialostocki, "Renaissance Artists as Philosophers in Meditation: Two Small Problems Concerning Two Great Masters," *Acta historiae artium* 24 (1978): 207–10. The most synthetic and satisfying account of Leonardo as thinker is offered by Kemp, *Leonardo da Vinci:* see especially chap. 5 ("The Prime Mover") and, for the deluge in particular, pp. 318–23. See also Kemp and Roberts, *Leonardo da Vinci*, exhibition catalogue, section 5 ("The Vortex"), pp. 118–33.
55. See especially Leonardo's explicit notation on Windsor 12579r (Fig. 54): "Observe the motion of the surface of water which resembles that of hair, and has two motions, of which one goes on with the flow of the surface, the other forms the lines of the eddies; thus the water forms eddying whirlpools one part of which are due to the impetus of the principal current and the other to the incidental motion and return flow" (Richter, ¶ 389).
56. On Leonardo's interest in Archimedes and the motion of the screw, see Kemp, *Leonardo da Vinci*,

passim, and Keele, *Elements of the Science of Man*, pp. 119f., 145f.

57. See Pedretti, *Nature Studies*, exhibition catalogue, no. 13.
58. See E. H. Gombrich, "Leonardo's Method for Working Out Compositions," in *Norm and Form: Studies in the Art of the Renaissance* (London, 1966), pp. 58–63, and the further discussion in Chapter Two.
59. "The true outlines of opaque bodies are never seen with sharp distinction" (McM ¶ 806). "The outlines which show the shapes of the surfaces of dense bodies are called contours and . . . do not have substance" (McM ¶ 807).
60. "L'aria é piena d'infinite linee, rette e radiose, insieme intersegate ed intessute senza occupazione l'una dell'altra; rappresentano a qualunque obietto la vera forma della loro cagione" (Leonardo da Vinci, *Manuscrit A de l'Institut de France*, ed. André Corbeau and Nando de Toni [Grenoble, 1972], p. 10 [fol. 2v]). This statement is discussed within the context of Leonardo's notions of vision and the power of sight by Zubov, *Leonardo da Vinci*, p. 143.
61. Codex Atlanticus, new fol. 520r: "corpo nato dalla prospettiva dj leonardo vincj djssciepolo della sperientia – sia fatto questo corpo sanza esenplo dalcun corpo (solido) Ma solamente con senplici linje." See Kenneth Clark, *Leonardo e le curve della vita* (XVII Lettura Vinciana) (Florence, 1979), pp. 7–8.; Pedretti, *Commentary*, II, p. 313, and Pedretti, *Leonardo da Vinci: A Study in Chronology and Style* (Berkeley and Los Angeles, 1973), p. 15. See also the observations on Leonardo's sense of form in space in Kemp, *Leonardo da Vinci*, pp. 252f., 270–72, 299, as well as Bern Dibner, "Leonardo and the Third Dimension," in *Leonardo da Vinci e l'età della ragione*, pp. 79–100.
62. "Del ritrar una cosa. Fa che quando ritrai e che tu movi alcun principio di linear che tu guardi per tutto il corpo che tu ritrai qualonque cosa si scontra per la drittura della principiata linear." Leonardo's own version, which is not quite faithfully transcribed in the Codex Urbinas, appears in B. N. 2038, fol. 29r (Richter, ¶ 522); cf. Pedretti, *Commentary*, I, p. 333, and the translation by MacCurdy, *The Notebooks*, p. 891.
63. Pedretti, *Leonardo's Horses*, exhibition catalogue, no. 13.
64. On metalpoint drawing: Joseph Meder, *Die Handzeichnung: Ihre Technik und Entwicklung*, 2d ed. (Vienna, 1923), pp. 72–100; trans. and rev. by Winslow Ames as *The Mastery of Drawing* (New York, 1978), pp. 58–79. See also James Watrous, *The Craft of Old-Master Drawings* (Madison, 1957), chap. 1.
65. Still a most rewarding account of Leonardo's drawing style, because of its active engagement of the problems of connoisseurship, is Kenneth Clark's introduction to the catalogue of Leonardo drawings at Windsor Castle. See also A. E. Popham, *The Drawings of Leonardo da Vinci* (London, 1946), and, more recently, Kemp and Roberts, *Leonardo da Vinci*, exhibition catalogue, and Martin Clayton, *Leonardo da Vinci: A Singular Vision*, exhibition catalogue (New York, London, Paris, 1996).
66. For this sheet, see Kenneth Keele and Jane Roberts, *Leonardo da Vinci: Anatomical Drawings from the Royal Library, Windsor Castle*, exhibition catalogue (Florence and New York, 1979), no. 8A.
67. Ibid., no. 27B.
68. In clarifying the nomenclature of his polarity between the "optical (visible) qualities, like color and light," and "the tactile (from *tangere* = to touch)," Riegl abandoned the latter term in favor of "haptic (from *haptein* = *fasten*)." In this he was inspired by the vocabulary of physiology, as he explained in a note to an essay of 1902, "Spätrömische oder Orientalische?" (*Münchner Allgemeine Zeitung*, no. 93–94) (trans. Peter Wortsman, "Late Roman or Oriental?" in *German Essays on Art History*, ed. Gert Schiff [New York, 1988], pp. 173–90).
69. Offering precise instructions on anatomical drawing, Leonardo correlates graphic technique and observed phenomenon: "When the muscles are separated one from the other you will show their outlines; and when they join together you will use only hatching" (Richter, ¶ 810; see Pedretti, *Commentary*, II, p. 96). The observation occurs on a sheet of comparative anatomical studies (Windsor 12625).
70. Leonardo's fascination with complex interlacing – which found monumental expression in his designs for the Sala delle Asse in the Castello at Milan – achieved wider circulation in the series of *nodi*, six engravings inscribed "Academia Leonardi Vinci" (A. M. Hind, *Early Italian Engraving* [London, 1938–48], V, pp. 93–95, nos. 19–24; Clelia Alberici et al., *Leonardo e l'incisione: Stampe derivate da Leonardo e Bramante dal XV al XIX secolo*, exhibition catalogue [Milan, 1984], no. 7); these were copied in woodcuts by Dürer (B. 140–145). For an intellectually ambitious reading of this "fantasia di vinci," in the context of Leonardo's concern with geometry and space, see Carlo Pedretti, "L'Organizzazione e simbolica dello spazio nelle cartelle dell' Accademia Vinciana," in *La prospettiva rinascimentale: Codificazione e trasgressioni*, ed. Marisa Dalai Emiliani (Florence, 1980), pp. 261–66. In "A Proem to Sculpture," p. 34, Pedretti notes Leonardo's earliest efforts in such "disegni di gruppi" on the verso of the Arno landscape drawing of 1473 (Fig. 47). For further consideration of the intelace motif with regard to calligraphy, see Carmen Bambach Cappel, "Leonardo, Tagliente, and Dürer: 'La scienza del far di groppi,'" *Achademia Leonardi Vinci: Journal of Leonardo Studies* 4 (1991): 72–98.
71. On Leonardo's ballistic curve, see the comments of Dibner, "Leonardo and the Third Dimension," pp. 87–88.
72. The passage concludes: ". . . it surpasses nature in dealing with things that are simply natural and finite, for the works which our hands do at the com-

mand of our eyes are infinite, as the painter shows in his representation of the infinite number of forms of animals, herbs, plants, and places."

On the *paragone:* Irma A. Richter, *Paragone: A Comparison of the Arts by Leonardo da Vinci* (London, New York, Toronto, 1949); Pedretti, *Libro A,* pp. 121–28; Claire J. Farago, *Leonardo da Vinci's* Paragone*: A Critical Interpretation with a New Edition of the Text in the* Codex Urbinas (Leiden, 1992). On the eye: Martin Kemp, "Leonardo and the Visual Pyramid," *Journal of the Warburg and Courtauld Institutes,* 40 (1977): 128–49, and James S. Ackerman, "Leonardo's Eye," *Journal of the Warburg and Courtauld Institutes,* 41 (1978): 108–46 (reprinted, with a postscript, in his *Distant Points: Essays in Theory and Renaissance Art and Architecture* [Cambridge, Mass. and London, 1991], pp. 97–150).

73. Richter, ¶ 916; cf. also MacCurdy, *Notebooks,* pp. 76f., 631f. For fuller discussion of this passage in the context of Leonardo's later involvement with geometry, see Kemp, *Leonardo da Vinci,* pp. 250–55.
74. Valéry, "The Method of Leonardo," p. 25. For an appeciation of Valéry's critical achievement, see Roger Shattuck, "The Tortoise and the Hare: Valéry, Freud, and Leonardo da Vinci," in *The Innocent Eye: On Modern Literature and the Arts* (New York, 1984), pp. 82–101.
75. *Picasso on Art: A Selection of Views,* ed. Dore Ashton (New York, 1972), p. 103.
76. Quoted in Edith Hoffman, *Kokoschka: Life and Work* (London, 1947), p. 287.

4. RAPHAEL AND THE CALLIGRAPHY OF CLASSICISM

1. Baldesar Castiglione, *Il libro del Cortegiano* (1528), ed. Bruno Maier (Turin, 1964), p. 129. For the full passage, see below, note 44.
2. Philip Pouncey and John Gere, *Raphael and His Circle (Italian Drawings in the Department of Prints and Drawings in the British Museum)* (London, 1962), no. 19; Paul Joannides, *The Drawings of Raphael* (Oxford, 1983), no. 180; Eckhart Knab, Erwin Mitsch, Konrad Oberhuber, and Sylvia Ferino-Pagden, *Raphael: Die Zeichnungen* (Stuttgart, 1983), no. 161 (catalogue entries by Ferino-Pagden, Konrad Oberhuber, and Ernst Wolfgang Huber: hereafter cited as Knab et al.).
3. Voglio ancora avertire, che quando il Pittore va tentando ne' primi schizzi le fantasie, che genera nella sua mente la historia, non si dee contentar d'una sola, ma trovar più inventioni, e poi fare iscelta di quella, che meglio riesce, considerando tutte le cose insieme, e ciascuna separatamente: come soleva il medesimo Rafaello: il quale fu tanto ricco d'inventione, che faceva sempre a quattro e sei modi, differenti l'uno dall'altro, una historia, e tutti havevano gratia, e stavano bene. (Lodovico Dolce, *Dialogo dell pittura intitolato l'Aretino* [1557], ed. Paola Barocchi, in *Trattati d'arte del Cinquecento,* I [Bari, 1960], p. 170; trans. Mark W. Roskill, *Dolce's "Aretino" and Venetian Art Theory of the Cinquecento* [New York, 1968], p. 129 [translation here modified])
4. Vincenzo Golzio, *Raffaello nei documenti, nelle testimonianze dei contemporanei e nella letteratura del suo secolo* (Vatican City, 1936), p. 10.
5. Giorgio Vasari, *Le vite de' più eccellenti pittori, scultori ed architettori,* ed. Gaetano Milanesi (Florence, 1878–85), IV, p. 317. On Vasari's life of Raphael, see Patricia Lee Rubin, *Giorgio Vasari: Art and History* (New Haven and London, 1995), pp. 357–401 (chap. 9: "Raphael, The New Apelles"). On the early Raphael in particular, see Rudolf Wittkower, "The Young Raphael," *Allen Memorial Art Museum Bulletin* 20 (1963): 156–68, and the papers in *Raphael before Rome,* ed. James Beck (National Gallery of Art, *Studies in the History of Art* 17) (Washington, 1986).
6. Meyer Schapiro, "Style," in *Theory and Philosophy of Art: Style, Artist, and Society: Selected Papers IV* (New York, 1994), p. 51.
7. Heinrich Wölfflin, *Die klassische Kunst* (1899; 8th ed., 1948), trans. Peter and Linda Murray: *Classic Art: An Introduction to the Italian Renaissance* (London, 1959), p. 251.
8. On Raphael's tondo composition, see the meditations of E. H. Gombrich, "Raphael's 'Madonna della Sedia,'" in *Norm and Form: Studies in the Art of the Renaissance* (London, 1966), pp. 64–80.
9. Joannides, *The Drawings of Raphael,* no. 181; Knab et al., *Raphael: Die Zeichnungen,* no. 163.
10. Although this side is generally cited as the verso of the sheet (e.g., by Joannides and, most recently by Achim Gnann in Konrad Oberhuber et al., *A Quintessence of Drawing: Masterworks from the Albertina,* exhibition catalogue [Milan, 1997], no. 12), Knab et al., *Raphael: Die Zeichnungen,* no. 162, assign it the priority of recto, presumably in recognition of the prepared ground necessary for its silverpoint execution as well as its direct development of the Bridgewater motif on the British Museum sheet.
11. Vienna, Albertina IV, 207 (Figs. 115–16): Joannides, *The Drawings of Raphael,* no. 110; Knab et al., *Raphael: Die Zeichnungen,* nos. 119, 122. Chatsworth 783 (Fig. 117): Joannides, *The Drawings of Raphael,* no. 111r; Knab et al., *Raphael: Die Zeichnungen,* no. 118.
12. On the significance of the circle: Dietrich Mahnke, *Unendliche Sphäre und Allmittelpunkt* (Halle-Saale, 1937); Marjorie Hope Nicolson, *The Breaking of the Circle,* rev. ed. (New York, 1960); S. K. Henninger, Jr., *The Cosmographical Glass: Renaissance Diagrams of the Universe* (San Marino, Calif., 1977); cf. as well Jorge Luis Borges, "The Fearful Sphere of Pascal," in *Labyrinths: Selected Stories and Other Writings,* ed. Donald A. Yates and James E. Irby (New York, 1962), pp. 189–92.

13. The classic discussion of the circle in Renaissance artistic thought and practice remains Rudolf Wittkower, *Architectural Principles in the Age of Humanism*, 4th ed. (New York, 1971), part I: "The Centrally Planned Church and the Renaissance," pp. 3–32.
14. See Millard Meiss, "Masaccio and the Early Renaissance: The Circular Plan," in *The Painter's Choice: Problems in the Interpretation of Renaissance Art* (New York, 1976), pp. 63–81.
15. On this most famous yet probably least typical of Leonardo's drawings, see the recent entries by Martin Kemp in *Circa 1492: Art in the Age of Exploration*, ed. Jay A. Levenson, exhibition catalogue (New Haven and London, 1991), no. 175, and Giovanna Nepi Sciré in *Leonardo and Venice*, exhibition catalogue (Milan, 1992), no. 12, as well as Michelle Murray, "Leonardo e Vitruvio," in *Roma, centro ideale della cultura dell'Antico nei secoli XV e XVI: Da Martino V al Sacco di Roma 1417–1527*, ed. Silvia Danesi Squarzina (Milan, 1989), pp. 210–14. For the position of Leonardo's solution within the larger context of Renaissance Vitruvian studies, see Frank Zöllner, *Vitruvs Proportionsfigur: Quellenkritische Studien zur Kunstliteratur im 15. und 16. Jahrhundert* (Worms, 1987).
16. In the geometry of the medieval imagination, it is the triangle intersecting with the circle that graphically links the mystery of the Incarnation with that of the Trinity – as in the *Roman de la Rose:* "C'est le cercles trianguliers,/ C'est li triangles circuliers/ Qui en la vierge s'ostela." See Georges Poulet, *The Metamorphoses of the Circle* (Baltimore, 1966), pp. xx–xxii.
17. I have offered a fuller structural analysis of the *Disputa* in "Raphael and the Pictorial Generation of Meaning," *Source: Notes in the History of Art* 5:1 (1985): 38–43, further elaborated in "'Divinità di cosa dipinta': Pictorial Structure and the Legibility of the Altarpiece," in *The Altarpiece in the Renaissance*, ed. Peter Humfrey and Martin Kemp (Cambridge, New York, Melbourne, 1990), pp. 143–64.
18. The phrase is from Leone Ebreo's *Dialogi d'amore* (1535), in *Scritti d'arte del Cinquecento*, ed. Paola Barocchi (Milan and Naples, 1971–77) II, p. 1632.
19. Wölfflin, *Classic Art*, p. 254.
20. Joannides, *The Drawings of Raphael*, no. 287; Knab et al., *Raphael: Die Zeichnungen*, no. 340. Another full compositional pen drawing (Budapest, Szépmüvészti Múzeum, inv. 2195) is difficult to evaluate owing to its poor condition (Joannides, no. 289; Knab et al., no. 345); in addition, there exist two sheets of red-chalk studies of individual figure groups (Vienna, Albertina, IV, 188 [Joannides, no. 253v; Knab et al., no. 344]; Windsor, Royal Library, 12737 [Joannides, no. 288r; Knab et al., no. 341]).

    On Marcantonio as engraver to Raphael, see David Landau and Peter Parshall, *The Renaissance Print: 1470–1550* (New Haven and London, 1994), pp. 120–46. For the *Massacre of the Innocents*, see Innis H. Shoemaker, *The Engravings of Marcantonio Raimondi*, exhibition catalogue (Lawrence, Kans., 1981), nos. 21 and 26. Of the two plates, I illustrate the version *sans le chicot*, which seems to me clearly more mature in its control of graphic structure; the version *avec le chicot* – which actually exists in two versions: one with an inscription, one without (different states or different plates?) – appears to be a copy by a follower – possibly Agostino Veneziano, as suggested by Patricia Emison, "Marcantonio's *Massacre of the Innocents*," *Print Quarterly* 1 (1984): 257–67. For a reading of the expressive function and significance of the engraving, see David Rosand, "Raphael, Marcantonio, and the Icon of Pathos," *Source: Notes in the History of Art* 3 (Winter 1984): 34–52.
21. In what is presumably the final modello (Budapest) these systems are further reconciled, synthesized to realize a smoother fluidity of surface (Joannides, *The Drawings of Raphael*, no. 289; Knab et al., *Raphael: Die Zeichnungen*, no. 345). Between the sheets in London and Budapest is the red-chalk drawing in Windsor (12737r), begun on the basis of a pricked transfer, possibly from the British Museum sheet, and which refines the details (Joannides, no. 288; Knab et al., no. 341). For further discussion of the techniques of transfer, see Carmen C. Bambach, *Drawing and Painting in the Italian Renaissance Workshop: Theory and Practice, 1300–1600* (Cambridge, New York, Melbourne, 1999), pp. 310–12.
22. Still the most satisfying critical account of Dürer's graphic technique and aesthetic is that of Erwin Panofsky, *The Life and Art of Albrecht Dürer*, 4th ed. (Princeton, 1955).
23. Wölfflin, *Classic Art*, p. 254.
24. George Cumberland, *An Essay on the Utility of Collecting the Best Works of the Ancient Engravers of the Italian School* (London, 1827), pp. 9–10.
25. Shoemaker, *The Engravings of Marcantonio*, no. 20. For further readings of the engraving, see Rosand, "Raphael, Marcantonio, and the Icon of Pathos," and Patricia Emison, "The Singularity of Raphael's *Lucretia*," *Art History* 14 (1991): 372–96. A drawing of the subject (now in the Metropolitan Museum of Art) has been suggested as the model used by Marcantonio for his engraving of *Lucretia:* see Julien Stock, "A Drawing by Raphael of 'Lucretia,'" *Burlington Magazine* 126 (1984): 423–24. Despite the quality of the draftsmanship, however – and even allowing for the irregular trimming of the paper – there remains something unconvincing about the figure herself; her proportions and affect lack the heroic dimensions of the printed image.
26. Joannides, *The Drawings of Raphael*, no,. 238v; Knab et al., *Raphael: Die Zeichnungen*, no. 374.
27. "Il disegno . . . è la forma, che da il Pittore alle cose, che va imitando: & è proprio un giramento di linee per diverse vie, lequali formano le figure" (Dolce,

Dialogo della pittura, ed. Barocchi, in *Trattati d'arte,* I, p. 171; trans. Roskill, *Dolce's "Aretino",* p. 131).

28. Joannides, *The Drawings of Raphael,* no. 233r; Knab et al., *Raphael: Die Zeichnungen,* no. 353.

29. Pliny, *Natural History,* XXXV, 79, trans. K. Jex-Blake, *The Elder Pliny's Chapters on the History of Art,* ed. E. Sellers (London, 1896), p. 121. Cf. Dolce on Raphael:

> ... le sue cose tutte movono sommamente, si trova in loro quella parte che avevano, come scrive Plinio, le figure di Apelle: e questa è la venustà, che è quel che non so che, che tanto suole aggradire, così ne' pittori come ne' poeti, in guisa che empie l'animo altrui d'infinito diletto, non sapendo da qual parte esca quello che a noi tanto piace. (*Dialogo della pittura,* ed. Barocchi, in *Trattati d'arte,* I, p. 195f)

For rewarding discussion of Raphael's virtue, see Daniel Arasse, "Raffaello senza venustà e l'eredità della grazia," in *Studi su Raffaello, Atti del Congresso Internazionale di Studi,* ed. Micaela Sambucco Hamoud and Maria Letizia Strocchi (Urbino, 1987), pp. 703–14, and Patricia Emison, "Grazia," *Renaissance Studies* 5 (1991): 427–60; see also Eduardo Saccone, "*Grazia, Sprezzatura, Affettazione* in the *Courtier,*" in *Castiglione: The Ideal and the Real in Renaissance Culture,* ed. Robert W. Hanning and David Rosand (New Haven and London, 1983), pp. 45–67.

30. Joannides, *The Drawings of Raphael,* no. 248; Knab et al., *Raphael: Die Zeichnungen,* no. 334.

31. As a construct, the *figura serpentinata* resolves into a single figure the multiple views said to have been achieved by Giorgione through the depiction of reflecting surfaces: see Paolo Pino, *Dialogo di pittura* (1548), ed. Barocchi, in *Trattati d'arte,* I, p. 131, and Vasari, *Le vite,* ed. Milanesi, IV, p. 98. Directly relevant to the single figure graphically seized in the round, as it were, are Leo Steinberg's observations on Picasso's "Drawing as if to Possess," in *Other Criteria: Confrontations with Twentieth-Century Art* (London, Oxford, New York, 1972), pp. 174–92.

32. Joannides, *The Drawings of Raphael,* no. 333; Knab et al., *Raphael: Die Zeichnungen,* nos. 429, 430.

33. "... lo spirito del qual Raffaello si diceva poi esser passato nel corpo di Francesco, per vedersi quel giovane nell'arte raro e ne' costumi gentile e grazioso, come fu Raffaello" (Vasari, *Le vite,* ed. Milanesi, V, p. 223f.).

34. A. E. Popham, *Catalogue of the Drawings of Parmigianino* (New Haven and London, 1971), no. 244. On the larger context of this aesthetic, see the now classic essay of Elizabeth Cropper, "On Beautiful Women: Parmigianino, Petrarchismo and the Vernacular Style," *Art Bulletin* 58 (1976): 374–94, as well as her more recent "The Place of Beauty in the High Renaissance and its Displacement in the History of Art," in *Place and Displacement in the Renaissance,* ed. Alvin Vos (Binghamton, 1994), pp. 159–205. See also Mary Vaccaro, "*Forma virginis:* Form as Meaning in Parmigianino's Art," Ph.D. dissertation (Columbia University, 1994), and "Resplendent Vessels: Parmigianino's Work in the Steccata," in *Concepts of Beauty in Renaissance Art,* ed. Francis Ames-Lewis and Mary Rogers (London, 1998), pp. 134–46.

35. For Guido Reni's appreciation of Parmigianino: Carlo Cesare Malvasia, *Felsina pittrice: Vite de' pittori bolognesi* (1678), ed. Giampietro Zanotti (Bologna, 1841), II, p. 55. For a more recent appreciation of Parmigianino's draftsmanship, see Mary Vaccaro, "Parmigianino and the Poetry of Drawing," in Sylvie Béguin, Mario Di Giampaolo, *Parmigianino: The Drawings* (Turin, 2000), pp. 61–93.

36. Popham, *Catalogue of the Drawings of Parmigianino,* no. 668.

37. Luca Ciamberlano's engraving of heads in profile, from the *Scuola perfetta per imparare a disegnare . . . ,* is based on the pedagogic models of Agostino Carracci. See Diane DeGrazia Bohlin, *Prints and Related Drawings by the Carracci Family: A Catalogue Raisonné* (Washington, 1979), pp. 58, 410. Further bibliography on the printed drawing book: below, note 61.

38. Paolo Giovio, "Raphaelis Urbinatis vita" (ca. 1523–27), in *Scritti d'arte del Cinquecento,* ed. Paola Barocchi (Milan and Naples, 1971–77), I, p. 15: ". . . verum in ducendis lineis, quae commissuras colorum quasi margines terminarent, et in mitiganda commiscendaque vividiorum pigmentorum austeritate iucundissimus artifex ante alia id praestanter contendit."

39. Vasari, *Le vite,* ed. Milanesi, IV, p. 11.

40. Dolce, *Dialogo della pittura,* ed. Barocchi, in *Trattati d'arte,* I, pp. 149, 185; trans. Roskill, *Dolce's "Aretino",* pp. 91, 157.

41. Ma avendo io già più volte pensato meco onde nasca questa grazia, lasciando quelli che dalle stelle l'hanno, trovo una regula universalissima, la qual mi par valer circa questo in tutte le cose umane che si facciano o dicano più che alcuna altra, e ciò è fuggir quanto più si po, e come un asperissimo e pericoloso scoglio, la affettazione; e, per dir forse una nova parola, usar in ogni cosa una certa sprezzatura, che nasconda l'arte, e dimostri, ciò che si fa e dice, venir senza fatica e quasi senza pensarvi. Da questo credo io che derivi assai la grazia: perché delle cose rare e ben fatte ognun sa la difficultà, onde in esse la facilità genera grandissima maraviglila; e per lo contrario, il sforzare, e, come si dice, tirar per i capegli, dà summa disgrazia, e fa estimar poco ogni cosa, per grande ch'ella si sia. Però si po dir quella esser vera arte, che non appare esser arte; né più in altro si ha da poner studio, che nel nasconderla: perché se è scoperta, leva in tutto il credito e fa l'omo poco estimato. (Castiglione, *Il Cortegiano,* I, 26, ed. Maier, p. 125; trans. Charles S. Singleton: *The Book of the Courtier* [Garden City, N.Y., 1959], p. 43)

42. Castiglione, *Il Cortegiano,* I, 26, ed. Maier, p. 125; trans. Singleton, *The Courtier,* p. 44, as "that cool *disinvoltura* [ease]."
43. Castiglione, *Il Cortegiano,* I, 28, ed. Maier, p. 128; trans. Singleton, *The Courtier,* p. 46. The anecdotal source is, of course, Pliny, *Natural History,* XXXV.79–80. In developing Castiglione's discourse on *sprezzatura* and returning it to the visual arts, Dolce appropriates the same sequence, citing "la troppo diligenza" of Protogenes as a cautionary lesson (*Dialogo della pittura,* ed. Barocchi, in *Trattati d'arte,* I, p. 185); trans. Roskill, *Dolce's "Aretino,"* p. 157.
44.

> Spesso ancora nella pittura una linea sola non stentata, un sol colpo di pennello tirato facilmente, di modo che paia che la mano, senza esser guidato da studio o arte alcuna, vada per sé stessa al suo termine secondo la intenzion del pittore, scopre chiaramente la eccellenzia dell'artefice, circa la opinion della quale ognuno poi si estende secondo il suo giudicio. (Castiglione, *Il Cortegiano,* I, 28, ed. Maier, p. 129; trans. Singleton, *The Courtier,* p. 47)

45. Vasari, *Le vite,* ed. Milanesi, I, p. 383. On the larger context of the topos, see Ernst Kris and Otto Kurz, *Legend, Myth, and Magic in the Image of the Artist: A Historical Experiment* (1934) (New Haven and London, 1979), pp. 96–97, with further references. In his brief allusion to the story Paul Valéry adds an interesting refinement: "Giotto could draw a perfect circle with the brush, in either direction." The observation concludes a paragraph in an essay on "Seeing and Copying" that is worth quoting in full:

> A sustained act of will is essential to drawing, for drawing demands the collaboration of separate means whose one instinct is to resume their own independent automatism. By nature, the eye tends to wander, the hands curl up, move at a tangent. To ensure the freedom of drawing, so that the draftsman can carry out his will, he must suppress these local autonomies. The question is one of control. . . . To free the hand *in the visual sense* is to take away its liberty *in the muscular sense;* particularly it has to be trained to draw in any direction, against its instinct. (*Degas, Manet, Morisot,* trans. David Paul [New York, 1960], p. 37)

46. On the artist as *alter deus,* see Kris and Kurz, *Legend, Myth, and Magic,* pp. 49, 61.
47. "Onde il papa e molti cortigiani intendenti conobbero per ciò quanto Giotto avanzasse d'eccellenza tutti gli altri pittori del suo tempo" (Vasari). When the young Rubens inscribed a circular *impresa* in the *album amicorum* of Philips van Valckenisse, he was evidently less concerned to demonstrate the genius of his hand than the inventiveness of his mind, for he used a compass: see Jeffrey Muller, "Rubens' Divine Circle," in *The Ringling Museum of Art Journal* (Papers Presented at the International Rubens Symposium) (Sarasota, 1983), pp. 220–25. On Rembrandt's circles, see Chapter Seven.
48. Francisco de Hollanda, *De pintura antigua* (1548); see Chapter One, note 44, for further references.
49. Paolo Pino, *Dialogo di pittura* (1548), ed. Paola Barocchi, in *Trattati d'arte,* I, p. 117.
50. On the creation of a humanist critical vocabulary, see Michael Baxandall, *Painting and Experience in Fifteenth-Century Italy: A Primer in the Social History of Pictorial Style* (Oxford, 1972), pp. 109–53 (chap. 3: "Pictures and Categories").
51. Castiglione, *Il Cortegiano,* I, 37, ed. Maier, p. 148; trans. Singleton, *The Courtier,* p. 60. On the development of stylistic discrimination in the visual arts within humanistic culture, see Michael Baxandall, *Giotto and the Orators: Humanistic Observers of Painting in Italy and the Discovery of Pictorial Composition 1350–1450* (Oxford, 1971), and Baxandall, *Painting and Experience;* for its refinement in the later Renaissance, see Martin Kemp, "'Equal excellences': Lomazzo and the Explanation of Individual Style in the Visual Arts," *Renaissance Studies* 1 (1987): pp. 1–26.
52. On the historical dimension of Vasari's collecting, see Erwin Panofsky, "The First Page of Giorgio Vasari's 'Libro': A Study on the Gothic Style in the Judgment of the Italian Renaissance," in *Meaning in the Visual Arts: Papers in and on Art History* (Garden City, N.Y., 1955), pp. 169–225. For further bibliography, see Chapter Two, note 69.
53. Vasari, *Le vite,* ed. Milanesi, VII, p. 727: ". . . che si faccia un dotto e pratico cancelliere i diversi e variati scritti de' suoi eguali, e ciascuno i caratteri de' suoi più stretti famigliari amici e congiunti."
54. Cf. Roger de Piles, *Conversations sur la connoissance de la peinture* (Paris, 1677), pp. 9–10, quoted in Chapter One, note 50.
55. See Chapter Two.
56.

> Voglio che i giovani, quali ora nuovi si danno a dipignere, così facciano quanto veggo di chi impara a scrivere. Questi in prima separato insegnano tutte le forme delle lettere, quali gli antiqui chiamano elementi; poi insegnano le silabe; poi apresso insegnano componere tutte le dizioni. Con questa ragione ancora seguitino i nostri a dipignere. In prima imparino ben disegnare gli orli delle superficie, e qui se essercitino quasi come ne' primi elementi della pittura. (Leon Battista Alberti, *De pictura,* ed. Cecil Grayson [Rome and Bari, 1975], ¶55)

Further on this pedagogical parallel, see J. Bolten, "Ut Grammatica Pictura: A Method of Learning," in *Ars Auro Prior: Studia Ioanni Bialostocki, Sexagenario Dicata* (Warsaw, 1981), pp. 71–74, and Paul van den Akker, *Sporen van vaardigheid: De ontwerpmethode vor de figuurhouding in de Italiaanse tekenkunst van de renaissance* (Abcoude, 1991), pp. 86–93, 149–59.

57. Poniamo caso, tu, lettore, guardi in una occhiata tutta questa carta scritta, e subito giudicherai questa essere piena di varie lettere: ma non cognoscerai in questo tempo che lettere sieno, né che voglieno dire; onde ti bisogna fare a parola a parola, verso per verso, a voler havere notitia d'esse lettere. (*Treatise on Painting [Codex Urbinas Latinus 1270]*, ed. A. Philip McMahon [Princeton, 1956], ¶ 60, c. 31)

58. Giovanni Battista Armenini, *De' veri precetti della pittura* (Ravenna, 1587) I.vii, in *Scritti d'arte*, ed. Barocchi, II, p. 2006; trans. Edward J. Olszewski, *On the True Precepts of the Art of Painting* (New York, 1977), p. 122 (here slightly modified).

59. Dopo, essendo alquanto cresciuto, tosto che ebbe la penna in mano per imparare a scrivere, cominciò, spinto dalla natura, che l'avea fatto nascere al disegno, a far cose in quello maravigliose: di che accortosi il maestro che gl'insegnava a scrivere, persuase, vedendo dove col tempo poteva arrivare lo spirito del fanciullo, ai zii di quello, che lo facessero attendere al disegno ed alla pittura. (Vasari, *Le vite*, ed. Milanesi, V, p. 219)

60. Erasmus, *De recta Graeci et Latini sermonis pronunciatione* (Basel, 1528); trans. in A. S. Osley, *Scribes and Sources: Handbook of the Chancery Hand in the Sixteenth Century* (Boston, 1980), p. 36. The rest of the paragraph is interesting for its fuller Renaissance elaboration of the argument:

> But, if you want more refined and exact teaching about this, there is the book of Albrecht Dürer, written in German but with immense learning. In it he follows the ancient worthies of the art – the Macedonian Pamphilus, well schooled in all sides of literature as well as geometry and arithmetic (for he stated that the art of lettering is not complete without these disciplines) and also Apelles, who himself corresponded with his disciple Perseus about his art – and presents clearly many facts about the mysteries of drawing derived from mathematical principles, including several that are concerned with the basic elements of the letters, their construction and their proportions.

The ancient examples are from Pliny, *Natural History*, XXXV, 76 and 111. Dürer's book is the first of his published volumes, *Unterweysung der Messung mit dem Zirckel und Richtscheyt* (1525).

61. Following the projects of the High Renaissance – including, above all, Leonardo's many efforts as well as Bramante's plans for a treatise on the *quadratura* of the human body and of the horse – the academic aspirations of subsequent generations of artists encouraged such didactic endeavors: cf., e.g., Benvenuto Cellini's text *Sopra i principii e 'l modo d'imparare l'arte del disegno* and Alessandro Allori's dialogue with Bronzino, *Ragionamenti delle regole del disegno*, both now published in *Scritti d'arte*, ed. Barocchi, II, pp. 1933–40, 1941–81. Among the earliest printed versions of such manuals, intended for an audience of amateurs and novices, were Odoardo Fialetti's *Il vero modo et ordine per dissegnar tutte le parti et membra del corpo humano* (Venice, 1608) and Giacomo Franco's *De excellentia et nobilitate delineationis libri duo* (Venice, 1611); interestingly, Franco also published his own calligraphy manual, *Modo di scrivere cancellaresco moderno . . .* (Venice, 1596). On these drawing books, see David Rosand, "The Crisis of the Venetian Renaissance Tradition," *L'Arte* 11–12 (1970): 5–53, and for broader discussion of their relationship to graphic pedagogy and practice, see E. H. Gombrich, *Art and Illusion: A Study in the Psychology of Pictorial Representation* (New York, 1960), pp. 156–72, and, especially, van den Akker, *Sporen van vaardigheid*, and van den Akker, "'Out of Disegno Invention is Born' – Drawing a Convincing Figure in Renaissance Italian Art," *Argumentation* 7 (1993): 45–66. The relevance of the writing manuals to instruction in drawing has also been explored by Carmen Bambach Cappel, "Leonardo, Tagliente, and Dürer: 'La scienza del far di groppi,'" *Achademia Leonardi Vinci, Journal of Leonardo Studies* 4 (1991): 72–98.

62. When he has the time, which will not be soon, Raphael writes, "ve designerò ne' bianchi le fighure che v'ànno a essere e ve farò el frontespitio de hordine doricho con un archo e le fighure drento de le virtù, con varie altre inventioni che me naschono per la fantasia. . . ." The letter is published in Golzio, *Raffaello nei documenti*, p. 35; also in *Raffaello: Gli scritti – lettere, firme, sonetti, saggi tecnici e teorici*, ed. Ettore Camesasca (Milan, 1993), pp. 199–204. For further discussion, see Cecil H. Clough, "Ludovico degli Arrighi's Contact with Raphael and with Machiavelli," *Bibliografia* 75 (1973): 293–98, and "Ludovico degli Arrighi and Raphael," *Journal of the Society for Italic Handwriting* 79 (1974): 13–16. On Fabio's Vitruvius in context, see Ingrid D. Rowland, *The Culture of the High Renaissance: Ancients and Moderns in Sixteenth-Century Rome* (Cambridge, New York, Melbourne, 1998), pp. 223–26.

63. As he writes in his letter to the reader, "Si come a chi vuol saper sonare e' bisogno per molte cose, che ponno intervenire sapere anchora accordare lo instrumento, così a chi dee saper scrivere, e necessario per molti rispetti saper temperare le penne." *Il modo de temperare le penne con le varie sorti de littere ordinato per Ludovico Vicentino* (Rome, 1523) is available in facscimile in *Three Classics of Italian Calligraphy: An Unabridged Reissue of the Writing Books of Arrighi, Tagliente, Palatino*, ed. Oscar Ogg (New York, 1953). The cutting of the nib was of obvious importance to both writer and draftsman: "El modo di saper temperar la penna per disegnare" is the topic of capitolo 14 of Cennino Cennini's *Il*

libro dell arte (ed. Fernando Tempesti [Milan, 1984], p. 36).

64. *La Operina di Ludovico Vicentino da imparare di scrivere littera cancellaresca* (Rome, 1522), fol. A V verso. Facsimiles of Vicentino's *Operina* are available in Ogg, ed., *Three Classics of Italian Calligraphy*, and, John Howard Benson, *The First Writing Book: An English Translation and Facsimile Text of Arrighi's Operina* (New Haven and London, 1954), which includes a translation in cursive.

65.
> Farai che la distantia da linea a linea de cose che tu scriverai in tal littera cancellaresca non sia troppo larga, ne troppo stretta, ma mediocre. Che la distantia da parola á parola sia quanto è uno n: Da littera ad littera poi nel ligarle sia quanto è il biancho tra le due gambe de lo n. Ma perchè seria quasi impossibile servare questa regola, te sforzarai di consigliarti con l'occhio, et á quello satisfare, il quale ti scusara bonissimo compasso. (Vicentino, *La Operina*, fol. A X)

66. In his life of Michelangelo Vasari writes:

> . . . egli usò le sue figure farle di nove e di dieci e di dodici teste, non cercando altro che, col metterle tutte insieme ci fussi una certa concordanza di grazia nel tutto, che non lo fa il naturale; dicendo che bisognava avere le seste negli occhi e non in mano, perchè le mani operano, e l'occhio giudica: che tal modo tenne ancora nell'architettura. (*Le vite*, ed. Milanesi, VII, p. 270).

He repeats the theme in his letter to Martino Bassi:

> . . . diceva il gran Michelangelo che bisognava aver le seste negli occhi e non in mano, cioè il giudicio; e per questa cagione egli usava tal volta le figure sue di XII e di XIII teste, secondo che le faceva raccolte o a seder o ritte e secondo l'attitudine; e così usava alle colonne et altri membri et a componimenti, di andar più sempre dietro alla grazia che alla misura. (In *Scritti d'arte*, ed. Barocchi, II, p. 1824)

On Michelangelo and the *giudizio dell'occhio*, see Summers, *Michelangelo and the Language of Art*, pp. 368–79.

The writing masters too had recourse to Vitruvian canons and their correspondence to the human proportions. See Emanuele Casamassima, *Trattati di scrittura del Cinquecento italiano* (Milan, 1966), p. 28.

67. Vasari, *Le vite*, ed. Milanesi, IV, p. 9. For an elegant discussion of the subjective factor in Cinquecento artistic attitudes, see Cropper, "The Place of Beauty in the High Renaissance."

68. *La Operina*, fol. A IIII; trans. Benson, *The First Writing Book*, p. 7.

5. DISEGNI A STAMPA: THE PRINTED LINE

1. Giorgio Vasari, *Le vite de' più eccellenti pittori, scultori ed architettori* (1568), ed. Gaetano Milanesi (Florence, 1878–85), V, p. 401. Vasari is commenting on Albrecht Dürer, who he assumes must have found engraving tedious and therefore turned to woodcut as a way of publishing his abundant inventions in drawing: "Dopo le quali opere vedendo con quanta larghezza di tempo intagliava in rame, e trovandosi avere gran copia d'invenzioni diversamente disegnate, si mise a intagliare in legno; nel qual modo di fare coloro che hanno maggior disegno, hanno più largo campo da poter mostrare la loro perfezione."

2. An introduction to these large themes is offered by Elizabeth L. Eisenstein, *The Printing Press as an Agent of Change: Communications and Cultural Transformations in Early-Modern Europe*, 2 vols. (Cambridge, 1979); see also the studies in *The Culture of Print: Power and the Uses of Print in Early Modern Europe*, ed. Roger Chartier (Princeton, 1989). For the cultural position of printed images, see the survey by David Landau and Peter Parshall, *The Renaissance Print, 1470–1550* (New Haven and London, 1994). Still a most provocative consideration of visual literacy, of the language of linear representation, is William M. Ivins, Jr., *Prints and Visual Communication* (Cambridge, Mass., 1953).

3.
> E perche impossibile era de mia mano porger tanti essempi, che sodisfacessino a tutti, mi sono ingegnato di ritrovare questa nuova inventione de lettere, e metterle in stampa, le quali tanto se avvicinano alle scritte a mano, quanto capeva il mio ingegno. E se puntualmente in tutto non possa in tutto ripresentarte la viva mano, spero nondimeno. . . . (*La Operina di Ludovico Vicentino, da imparare di scrivere littera cancellarescha* [Rome, 1522, fol. A II)

4. Strada's description comes in his letter to the reader of *Il Settimo libro d'architettura di Sebastiano Serglio* (Frankfurt am Main, 1575); it is reprinted in Vincenzo Golzio, *Raffaello nei documenti, nelle testimonianze dei contemporanei e nella letteratura del suo secolo* (Vatican City, 1936), p. 176.

5. The Vendramin inventories were published by Aldo Ravà, "Il 'Camerino delle anticaglie' di Gabriele Vendramin," *Nuovo Archivio Veneto* 22 (1920): 155–81; see as well Jaynie Anderson, "A Further Inventory of Gabriel Vendramin's Collection," *Burlington Magazine* 121 (1979): 639–48.

6. Vasari, *Le vite*, ed. Milanesi, VI, p. 587.

7. Erwin Panofsky, *The Life and Art of Albrecht Dürer*, 4th ed., Princeton, 1955, p. 284. On the equation of *manus* and *stilus*, see Chapter One, note 47, with further references.

8. On the drawing itself see Alice M. Kaplan, "Dürer's 'Raphael' Drawing Reconsidered," *Art Bulletin* 56 (1974): 50–58; Eckhart Knab, Erwin Mitsch, Konrad Oberhuber, *Raphael: Die Zeichnungen* (Stuttgart, 1983), no. 504; Paul Joannides, *The Drawings of Raphael* (Oxford, 1983), no. 371. For his part, Dürer had sent as a gift a self-portrait on fine linen, exe-

cuted in water color and of such transparency that, according to Vasari, Raphael considered it a marvel (Vasari, *Le vite*, ed. Milanesi, IV, p. 354). On Dürer's miraculous self-image, see Joseph Leo Koerner, *The Moment of Self-Portraiture in German Renaissance Art* (Chicago and London, 1993), pp. 95–96.

9. On the graphic aspects of Mantegna's art, see Evelyn Lincoln, "Mantegna's Culture of Line, *Art History* 16 (1993): 33–59, who tends, however, to deny personal intention in the development of style. The debate over Mantegna's handling of the burin, nonetheless, continues: cf. the opposing views of David Landau, "Mantegna as Printmaker," and Suzanne Boorsch, "Mantegna and His Printmakers," in Jane Martineau, ed., *Andrea Mantegna*, exhibition catalogue (London and New York, 1992), pp. 44–54, 56–66, and Keith Christiansen, "The Case for Mantegna as Printmaker," *Burlington Magazine* 135 (1993): 604–12. As one aspect of Mantegna's technical inventiveness, Landau argues his extensive use of drypoint, alone and in conjunction with the burin. Mantegna's instinct was evidently to draw on the plate rather than to engrave. The great variety and sheer complexity of his lines, which already distinguish them from any other engraver's, may record the work of an ambitious amateur, pushing the medium beyond its accepted limits, but in this instance inexperience proved to be a source of graphic invention. I have discussed some of these aspects of Mantegna's graphic creativity in my exhibition review in *The New Republic*, June 22, 1992, pp. 29–32. A cautionary note in evaluation of Mantegna's technique, however, has been sounded with regard to the Albertina impression of Mantegna's engraving of the *Virgin and Child*, "arguably the most beautiful print of the Italian Renaissance," as Landau writes in the exhibition catalogue (no. 48). Recent investigation has revealed that what has been considered the most subtle combination of engraving and drypoint is in fact an impression heavily retouched all over with the pen: see Shelley Fletcher, "A Re-evaluation of Two Mantegna Prints," *Print Quarterly* 14 (1997): 67–77.

10. Of Dürer's monogram Panofsky wrote: "Like the ships of a great merchant these giant woodcuts carried their cargo and their flag – Dürer's famous 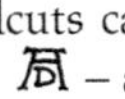 – all over the world. They had a threefold right to bear his initials. They were issued on his own responsibility; they were invented and designed by him; and most, if not all of them, were even cut by his own hand" (*Albrecht Dürer*, p. 46). For the monogram as a guarantee of "Dürer's presence of self within his images," see Koerner, *The Moment of Self-Portraiture*, pp. 204–5, 218–20, 236–38. On signatures and signature tablets in general, see Landau and Parshall, *The Renaissance Print*, passim.

11.
> Egli s'intese degl'ignudi più modernamente che fatto non avevano gli altri maestri innanzi a lui; e scorticò molti uomini per vedere la notomia lor sotto; e fu primo a mostrare il modo di cercare i muscoli, che avessero forma ed ordine nelle figure; e di quelli tutti, cinti d'una catena, intagliò in rame una battaglia: e dopo quella fece altre stampe, con molto migliore intaglio che non avevano fatto gli altri maestri ch'erano stati innanzi a lui. Per queste cagioni, adunque, venuto famoso infra gli artefici. (Vasari, *Le vite*, ed. Milanesi, III, p. 295)

Further on Pollaiuolo's engraving, see Louise Richards, "Antonio Pollaiuolo: Battle of the Naked Men," *Bulletin of the Cleveland Museum of Art* 55 (1968): 63–70; Laurie Smith Fusco in Jay A. Levenson, Konrad Oberhuber, Jacquelyn L. Sheehan, *Early Italian Engravings from the National Gallery of Art* (Washington, 1973), pp. 63–80; Patricia Emison, "The Word Made Naked in Pollaiuolo's *Battle of the Nudes*," *Art History* 13 (1990): 261–75.

12. "Fece in alcune carte i dodici Apostoli, piccoli in diverse maniere e molti Santi e Sante, acciò i poveri pittori che non hanno molto disegno, se ne potessero ne' loro bisogni servire" (Vasari, *Le vite*, ed. Milanesi, V, p. 417).

13. Vasari writes that his discussion of printmaking is intended to be of interest "non solo agli studiosi delle nostri arti ma a tutti color che di così fatte opere si dilettano" (Vasari, *Le vite*, ed. Milanesi, V, p. 442). On print collecting and collectors, see Landau and Parshall, *The Renaissance Print*, pp. 284–98, 342–58, et passim, with further bibliography.

14. Further on Titian's monumental woodcut of the *Sacrifice of Abraham* and related drawings, see below, note 30.

15. Still the best critical analysis of Dürer's graphic art and technique is to be found in Panofsky, *Albrecht Dürer*, passim.

16. Benvenuto Cellini, *Discorso sopra l'arte del disegno*, in *Scritti d'arte del Cinquecento*, ed. Paola Barocchi (Milan and Naples, 1971–77), II, p. 1929:

> Il disegnare si fa con il carbone e con la biacca, altrimenti con la penna stietta, intersegando l'una linea sopra l'altra; e dove si vuol fare scuro si soprappone più linee e dove manco scuro con manco linee, tanto che e' si viene a lasciar la carta bianca per e' lumi. Il qual modo di disegnare si è difficilissimo, e sono pochissimi che ànno disegnato ben di penna. E questo disegnar così fatto è stato causa al fare gli intagli col bulino in sul rame, sì come oggi si vede per tante stampe che vanno per el mondo; in fra le quali le meglio fatte che si sieno mai viste, cioè le meglio intagliate, sono state quelle di Alberto Duro di Germania.

17. Giovanni Battista Armenini, *De' veri precetti della pittura* (1587), in *Scritti d'arte del Cinquecento*, ed. Barocchi, II, p. 2006: "Il primo [modo di disegnare] adunque dicemo esser quello che si fa con la penna solamente, tratteggiando dove si vede che vanno l'ombre, e si fa su la carta bianca, et è simile a quei dissegni che son fatti su le stampe di rame." Trans.

Edward J. Olszewski: Giovanni Battista Armenini, *On the True Precepts of the Art of Painting* (New York, 1977), p. 123.

18. Armenini, *De'veri precetti*, in *Scritti d'arte*, ed. Barocchi, II, p. 2008:

> . . . io non intendo, né manco consiglio niuno, che si voglia invaghire su quei trattolini troppo minuti, i quali sono in alcune carte in stampa, sì come sono di quelle d'Alberto Durero, di maniera che da essi si consuma il tempo per non sapersi levare da quelle loro minutezze, perciò che, se ben quelli son bellissimi a verderli, quanto all'utile poi sono giovevoli alli intagliatori, ma non a i dessegnatori, a i quali li devono esser mostrate quelle vie, le quali per essi siano espedite e senza stento. (Trans. Olszewski: Armenini, *On the True Precepts*, pp. 124–25 [here modified])

19. See Walter S. Melion, "Karel van Mander's 'Life of Goltzius': Defining the Paradigm of Protean Virtuosity in Haarlem around 1600," in *Cultural Differentiation and Cultural Identity in the Visual Arts*, ed. Susan J. Barnes and Walter S. Melion (*Studies in the History of Art* 27) (Washington, 1989), pp. 113–33, and Melion, "Love and Artisanship in Hendrick Goltzius's *Venus, Bacchus and Ceres* of 1606," *Art History* 16 (1993): 60–94, and, for broader consideration of such linear skill, Martin Kemp, "Coming into Line: Graphic Demonstrations of Skill in Renaissance and Baroque Engravings," in *Sight & Insight: Essays on Art and Culture in Honour of E. H. Gombrich at 85*, ed. John Onians (London, 1994), pp. 221–44.
20. Vasari, *Le vite*, ed. Milanesi, I, p. 175. Vasari is contrasting this technique with full chiaroscuro drawing, with line and wash on tinted paper heightened with white, a method that is "molto alla pittoresca, e mostra più l'ordine del colorito." The difficulty of drawing with the pen alone, acknowledged long before by Cennino Cennini, will be picked up as well by Raffaele Borghini in *Il Riposo* (Florence, 1584): "Si può disegnare con la penna sola, lasciando i lumi della carta, il qual modo è molto difficile, ma molto a maestra mano conveniente" (in *Scritti d'arte*, ed. Barocchi, II, p. 1984f.). The larger implications of this valuation of pen drawing and its relation to engraving were the subject of an important paper by Julius S. Held, "The Early Appreciation of Drawings," in *Studies in Western Art*, III: *Latin American Art and the Baroque Period in Europe* (Acts of the Twentieth International Congress of the History of Art) (Princeton, 1963), pp. 72–95.
21. "Then Goltzius conceived of drawing with the pen on grounded or oil-paint-prepared canvas, since parchment, no matter how large the piece, in keeping with his great intentions and spirit, he felt was too small. Therefore he began, and drew with the pen on a rather large primed canvas the image of a nude woman with a laughing satyr, very handsomely and gracefully executed . . . ," wrote Carel van Mander (*Het Schilderboeck* [Haarlem, 1604], fol. 285) (see Lawrence W. Nichols, "The 'Pen Works' of Hendrick Goltzius," *Philadelphia Museum of Art Bulletin* 88 [Winter 1992], p. 4). Two of the three pen works on canvas mentioned by van Mander, both representing the maxim "Sine Cerere et Libero friget Venus," are known: one in the Hermitage, St. Petersburg (measuring 219 × 163 cm), the other recently acquired by the Philadelphia Museum of Art (105 × 80 cm). Both are excellently discussed by Nichols in relation to the full creative range of Goltzius's "artistic pen."
22. For an introduction to the problems of historical woodcut technique, see A. M. Hind, *An Introduction to a History of Woodcut* (London, 1935), I, pp. 1–63, with earlier bibliography; other general surveys: Max J. Friedländer, *Der Holzschnitt*, 4th ed. (Berlin, 1970); H. Th. Musper, *Der Holzschnitt in fünf Jahrhunderten* (Stuttgart, 1964); Landau and Parshall, *The Renaissance Print*, chap. 5 et passim.
23. The translation is from William Andrew Chatto and John Jackson, *A Treatise on Wood Engraving, Historical and Practical*, 2d ed. (London, 1861), p. 411. Hans Sachs's *Eygentliche Beschreibung aller Stände auff Erden* (Nuremberg, 1568), illustrated by Jost Amman, is available in a Dover paperback reprint, ed. Benjamin A. Rifkin (New York, 1973).
24. Panofsky, *Albrecht Dürer*, pp. 47–48.
25. Vasari, *Le vite*, ed. Milanesi, V, p. 401 (quoted above, note 1). In engraving, the young Dürer had surpassed Schongauer: "cominciò . . . , con più disegno e meglior giudizio, a dare opera alle medesime stampe, . . . : fece molte cose che furono tenute belle quanto quelle di Martino, e le intagliava di sua man propria, segnando col suo nome" (ibid., p. 398f.).
26. Exploration of that alternative was a major purpose of the quadricentennial exhibitions mounted in 1976: David Rosand and Michelangelo Muraro, *Titian and the Venetian Woodcut* (Washington, 1976); Italian version: *Tiziano e la silografia veneziana del Cinquecento* (Vicenza, 1976).
27. See Rosand and Muraro, *Titian and the Venetian Woodcut*, nos. 1, 2 *(Triumph of Christ)*, and 4 *(Red Sea)*. The *Red Sea* was one of three monumental woodcuts for which the publisher Bernardino Benalio requested a copyright privilege in 1515. According to Vasari (*Le vite*, ed. Milanesi, VII, p. 431), the *Triumph of Christ* was published in 1508. For the complex publishing history of the *Triumph of Christ*, see the more recent contributions of Michael Bury, "The 'Triumph of Christ' after Titian," *Burlington Magazine* 131 (1989): 188–197, and Landau and Parshall, *The Renaissance Print*, pp. 236–37; cf. as well Caroline Karpinski, "Il 'Trionfo della Fede': L''affresco' di Tiziano e la silografia di Lucantonio degli Uberti," *Arte Veneta* 48 (1994): 6–13, who follows Ridolfi's reference to a painted frieze (Carlo Ridolfi, *Le maraviglie dell'arte* [1648], ed. Detlev von Hadeln [Berlin, 1914–21], I, p. 156).

28. Panofsky, *Albrecht Dürer,* p. 48.
29. Giuseppe Mazzariol and Terisio Pignatti, *La pianta prospettica di Venezia del 1500 disegnata da Jacopo de' Barbari* (Venice, 1963); Terisio Pignatti, "La pianta di Venezia di Jacopo de' Barbari," *Bollettino dei Musei Civici Veneziani* 9 (1964): 9–49; Juergen Schulz, *The Printed Plans and Panoramic Views of Venice (1486–1797)* (= *Saggi e memorie di storia dell'arte* 7) (Florence, 1970), nos. 1–4, and Schulz, "Jacopo de' Barbari's View of Venice: Map Making, City Views, and Moralized Geography Before the Year 1500," *Art Bulletin* 60 (1978): 425–74; for the *View of Venice* in a monographic context, see Jay Alan Levenson, "Jacopo de' Barbari and Northern Art of the Early Sixteenth Century," Ph.D. dissertation (New York University, 1978), pp. 104–7, 278–81.
30. Rosand and Muraro, *Titian and the Venetian Woodcut,* no. 3. For the debate surrounding the related drawings, which Peter Dreyer has declared to be essentially forgeries, counterproofs of the print retouched to appear as original drawings, cf. Peter Dreyer, "Tizianfälschungen des sechszehnten Jahrhunderts: Korrekturen zur Definition der Delineatio bei Tizian und Anmerkungen zur Datierung seiner Holzschnitte," *Pantheon* 38 (1979): 365–75, and David Rosand, "Titian Drawings: A Crisis of Connoisseurship?" *Master Drawings* 19 (1981): 300–308. The situation is most recently reviewed by M. Agnese Chiari Moretto Wiel, *Titian Drawings* (New York, 1990), no. 9, who concludes in favor of the drawing's legitimacy.

    The edition of the *Sacrifice of Abraham* that, on the occasion of the exhibition, we knew only from the description of Mariette is in fact preserved in at least two impressions: at the Schlossmuseum, Gotha (as indicated to me by Werner Schade) and at Chatsworth (see Caroline Karpinski, "Some Woodcuts after Early Designs of Titian," *Zeitschrift für Kunstgeschichte* 39 (1976), p. 259, n. 4). For further consideration of the Chatsworth impression, see David Woodward, *Maps as Prints in the Italian Renaissance: Makers, Distributors and Consumers* (London,1996), pp. 59–62, and, for a broader review of the various editions, Jürgen Rapp, "Tizians frühestes Werk: der Grossholzschnitt 'Das Opfer Abrahams,'" *Pantheon* 52 (1994): 43–61.
31. Thus does Lodovico Dolce characterize the manner of drawing of the young Titian, impatient as an apprentice in the shop of Gentile Bellini: "Ma Tiziano, essendo spinto dalla natura a maggiori grandezze et alla perfezzione di quest'arte, non poteva sofferir di seguitar quella via secca e stentata di Gentile, ma disegnava gagliardamente e con molta prestezza" (*Dialogo della pittura intitolato l'Aretino* [1557], ed. Paola Barocchi, in *Trattati d'arte del Cinquecento,* I [Bari, 1960], p. 201).
32. On Titian's *pittura di macchia,* see David Rosand, "Titian and the Critical Tradition," in *Titian: His World and His Legacy,* ed. David Rosand (New York, 1982), pp. 1–39, and Rosand, "The Stroke of the Brush," in *The Meaning of the Mark: Leonardo and Titian* (Lawrence, Kans., 1988), pp. 49–89.
33. On inscriptions in prints, see Landau and Parshall, *The Renaissance Print,* pp. 162–68, 304–7, et passim, as well as the convenient glossary of abbreviations and lettering in Antony Griffiths, *Prints and Printmaking: An Introduction to the History and Techniques* (London, 1980), p. 133.
34. See Landau and Parshall, *The Renaissance Print,* pp. 262–70, 323–47, et passim.
35.

    > Non è anco stata se non lodevole invenzione l'essere stato trovato il modo da intagliare le stampe più facilmente che col bulino, se bene non vengono così nette; cioè con l'acquaforte, dando prima in sul rame una coverta di cera o di vernice o colore a olio, e disegnando poi con un ferro che abbia la punta sottile, che sgraffi la cera o la vernice o il colore che sia: perchè messavi poi sopra l'acqua da partire, rode il rame di maniera che lo fa cavo, e vi si può stampare sopra. (Vasari, *Le vite,* ed. Milanesi, V, p. 423)

36. For Marcantonio's use of etching, see Sue Welsh Reed and Richard Wallace, *Italian Etchers of the Renaissance and Baroque,* exhibition catalogue (Boston, 1989), no. 1; also Landau and Parshall, *The Renaissance Print,* pp. 264–65.
37. Reed and Wallace, *Italian Etchers,* no. 3.
38. Giorgio Vasari, *Le vite de' più eccellenti architetti, pittori, et scultori italiani* (1550), ed. Luciano Bellosi and Aldo Rossi (Turin, 1986), p. 798: "Prese assunto come cervello capriccioso ch'egli era, di fare carte stampate intagliate sul ferro e sul rame con acqua forte, et ancora di chiaro scuro se ne vede di suo in legno molte, come ancora di bulino intagliate per mano del Caralio, dilettandosi egli non meno de 'l disegno, che si facesse del colorito." The passage does not appear in the second edition (1568).
39. In his marginal notes to Daniele Barbaro's edition of Vitruvius. See Fernand Marías and Agustín Bustamante, *Las ideas artísticas de El Greco (comentarios a un texto inédito)* (Madrid, 1981), p. 236: ". . . e non desare de arecordar Parmigiano digo Francisco Parmijano que pare que solo nassio por mostrar con los yschizos ho rascunnos que ssi dicono la svelteza e grazia nelas figuras. . . ."
40. Our knowledge in this regard, however, is less than sure: As has recently been demonstrated, some of these effects are due to subsequent retouching with the pen (see above, note 9).
41. From those 91 separate plates, only 124 impressions are extant. On the artist, his complex oeuvre and personality, see Jane Campbell Hutchison, *The Master of the Housebook* (New York, 1972), and J. P. Filedt Kok et al., *Livelier than Life: The Master of the Amsterdam Cabinet or the Housebook Master, ca. 1470–1500* (Amsterdam, 1985).
42. Thus, Agostino Carracci, in his marginal comments

to Vasari, protested that Andrea Schiavone "fu così spiritoso e gratioso pittore, e così spedito e facile che avanzò di gran longa molti pittori fiorentini i quali il Vasari esalta fin al cielo" (Giovanna Perini, *Gli scritti dei Carracci* [Bologna, 1990], p. 160). Further on Schiavone as printmaker: Francis L. Richardson, *Andrea Schiavone* (Oxford, 1980), pp. 75–110; also Reed and Wallace, *Italian Etchers*, pp. 22–27.

43. For an introduction to Rembrandt's inventive procedures, see Christopher White, *Rembrandt as an Etcher: A Study of the Artist at Work*, 2 vols. (University Park and London, 1969). Further on Rembrandt: see Chapter Seven.

44. On this aspect of Rembrandt's inventive techniques, see especially the catalogue of the exhibition organized by the Museum of Fine Arts, Boston, and the Pierpont Morgan Library, New York: *Rembrandt: Experimental Etcher* (Boston, 1969).

45. This characterization of Rembrandt's late style is from John Smith, *A Catalogue Raisonné of the Works of the Most Eminent Dutch, Flemish, and French Painters*, VII (London, 1836), p. xxxv.

6. MICHELANGELO: THE URGENT GESTURE

1. John Addington Symonds, *The Life of Michelangelo Buonarroti*, 2nd ed. (London, 1893), I, p. 284.

2. Giorgio Vasari, *Le vite de' più eccellenti pittori, scultori ed architettori* (1568), ed. Gaetano Milanesi (Florence, 1878–85), VII, p. 270: "Ha avuto l'immaginativa tale e sì perfetta, che le cose propostosi nella idea sono state tali, che, con le mani per non potere esprimere sì grandi e terribili concetti, ha spesso abandonato l'opere sue, anzi ne ha guasto molte; come io so che, innanzi che morissi di poco, abruciò gran numero di disegni, schizzi, e cartoni fatti di man sua, acciò nessuno vedessi le fatiche durate da lui ed i modi di tentare l'ingegno suo, per non apparire se non perfetto. . . ."

   Cf. Michael Hirst, *Michelangelo and His Drawings* (New Haven and London, 1988), pp. 17–19. Rejecting Vasari's account of Michelangelo's motivation, Hirst argues that "this self-protectiveness seems to have sprung from, above all, a fear of plagiarism on the part of other artists" (p. 18).

3. Ascanio Condivi, *The Life of Michelangelo* (1553), ed. Helmut Wohl and trans. Alice Sedgwick Wohl (Oxford, 1976), p. 107. "E' stato di tenacissima memoria, di maniera che avend'egli dipinte tante migliaia di figure quante si vedono, non ha fatta mai una che somigli l'altra or faccia quella medesima attitudine. Anzi gli ho sentito dire che non tira mai linea, che non si ricordi se più mai l'ha tirata; scancellandola se si ha a vedere in pubblico" (*La vita di Michelangelo Buonarroti*, ed. Paolo D'Ancona [Milan, 1928], pp. 196–97).

4. "E' anco di potentissima virtù immaginativa; onde è nato, prima ch'egli poco si sia contentato delle sue cose e sempre l'abbia abbassate, non parendogli che la mano a quella idea sia arrivata, ch'egli dentro si formava" (Condivi, *La vita di Michelangelo*, ed. D'Ancona, p. 196).

5. The rare preserved fragment of the cartoon for part of Michelangelo's *Crucifixion of Saint Peter* in the Cappella Paolina reminds us that large, full-scale cartoons were physically transferred either to further subsidiary cartoons or directly to the painting surface, often several times over; they were inevitably cut up and tended to be consumed in the course of execution, unless they were deliberately preserved – as has been suggested for this fragment by Carmen Bambach Cappel,"Michelangelo's Cartoon for the *Crucifixion of St. Peter* Reconsidered," *Master Drawings*, 25 (1987): 131–41. For a thorough consideration of the topic, see now Carmen C. Bambach, *Drawing and Painting in the Italian Renaissance Workshop: Theory and Practice, 1300–1600* (Cambridge, New York, Melbourne, 1999).

6. See Zygmunt Wazbinski, *L'Accademia medicea del disegno a Firenze nel Cinquecento: Idea e istituzione* (Florence, 1987), p. 171. In a dialogue presumably recording Michelangelo's own words in 1538, Francisco de Hollanda writes that *desenho*, "or as it is called by another name, drawing [*debuxo*], constitutes the fountainhead and substance of painting and of sculpture and of architecture and every other kind of painting and is the root of all the sciences" (*Vier Gespräche über die Malerei geführt zu Rom 1538*, ed. Joaquim de Vasconcellos [Vienna, 1899], p. 112; trans. Aubrey F. G. Bell, *Four Dialogues on Painting* [London, 1928], p. 68). On this passage and its relation to Michelangelo, see David Summers, *Michelangelo and the Language of Art* (Princeton, 1981), pp. 258–60.

7. Vasari, *Le vite*, ed. Milanesi, VII, pp. 135–36:

   > Mentre gl'industriosi ed egregi spiriti col lume del famosissimo Giotto, e de' seguaci suoi, si sforzavano dar saggio al mondo del valore che la benignità delle stelle e la proporzionata mistione degli umori aveva dato agli ingegni loro; e desiderosi di imitare con la eccellenza dell'arte la grandezza della natura, per venire il più che potevano a quella somma cognizione che molti chiamano intelligenza, universalmente, ancora che indarno, si affaticavano; il benignissimo Rettore del Cielo volse clemente gli occhi alla terra, e veduta la vana infinità di tante fatiche, gli ardentissimi studi senza alcun frutto, e la opinione presuntuosa degli uomini, assai più lontana dal vero che le tenebre dalla luce; per cavarci di tanti errori, si dispose mandare in terra uno spirito, che universalmente in ciascheduna arte ed in ogni professione fusse abile, operando per sè solo a mostrare che cosa sia la perfezione dell'arte del disegno nel lineare, dintornare, ombrare e lumeggiare, per dare rilevo alle cose della pittura, e con retto giudizio operare nella scultura, e rendere le abitazioni commode e sicure, sane, allegre, proporzionate, e ricche di vari ornamenti nell'architettura.

8. It is in the second edition (1568) that Vasari brings his rhetoric to focus on "la perfezione dell'arte del disegno." In the first edition (1550) *disegno* has not yet assumed its synecdochic hegemony over the three arts: "operando per sé solo a mostrare che cosa siano le difficultà nella scienza delle linee, nella pittura, nel giudizio della scultura e nella invenzione della veramente garbata architettura" (*La vita di Michelangelo nelle redazioni del 1550 e del 1568*, ed. Paola Barocchi, I [Milan and Naples, 1962], p. 3). On the identification of Michelangelo and *disegno* Summers offers a particularly resonant discussion in *Michelangelo and the Language of Art*, pp. 250–261 (chap. 17: *"Panepistemon"*).
9. Although generally referred to as "presentation" drawings, following Johannes Wilde (cf. Hirst, *Michelangelo and His Drawings*, p. 127), that terminology risks confusing them with drawn models presented to patrons. Thus, a more accurate and satisfactory label as "gift" drawings has been proposed by William E. Wallace, "Studies in Michelangelo's Finished Drawings, 1520–1534," Ph.D. dissertation (Columbia University, 1983), pp. xvii, 1–3. Bernard Berenson had referred to them as "show-drawings" (*The Drawings of the Florentine Painters*, 2d ed. [Chicago-London, 1938], I, p. 225). For a related semantic problem concerning the term *modello*, although philologically subject to greater historical precision, see the review of Hirst by Carmen Bambach Cappel in *Art Bulletin* 72 (1990): 493–98, and the ensuing correspondence, *Art Bulletin* 73 (1991): 172–73. On the matter of gifts, see now Alexander Nagel, "Gifts for Michelangelo and Vittoria Colonna," *Art Bulletin* 79 (1997): 647–68, and Nagel, *Michelangelo and the Reform of Art* (Cambridge, New York, Melbourne, 2000), pp. 169–87.
10. After naming others who were favored by Michelangelo's affection, Vasari concludes:

   > ed infinitamente amò più di tutti messer Tommaso de' Cavalieri, gentiluomo romano, quale essendo giovane e molto inclinato a queste virtù, perchè egli imparassi a disegnare, gli fece molte carte stupendissime, disegnate in lapis nero e rosso, di teste divine; e poi gli disegnò un Ganimede rapito in cielo dall'uccel di Giove, un Tizio che l'avoltoio gli mangia il cuore, la cascata del carro del Sole con Fetonte nel Po, ed una baccanalia di putti, che tutti sono ciascuno per sè cosa rarissima, e disegni non mai più visti. Ritrasse Michelagnolo messer Tommaso in un cartone, grande di naturale, che nè prima nè poi di nessuno fece il ritratto, perchè aboriva il fare somiglilare il vivo, se non era d'infinita bellezza. Queste carte sono state cagione, che, dilettandosi messer Tommaso quanto e'fa, che n'ha poi avute una buona partita, che già Michelagnolo fece a Fra Bastiano Viniziano, che le messe in opera, che sono miracolose: ed in ver egli le tiene meritamente per reliquie, e n'ha accomodato gentilmente gli artefici. (Vasari, *Le vite*, ed. Milanesi, VII, pp. 271–72)

   In the 1550 edition Vasari mentions only three such drawings: a *Rape of Ganymede*, a *Tityus*, and a *Bacchanal* (*La vita di Michelangelo*, ed. Barocchi, I, pp. 121–22).
11. "Inconsideratamente, messer Tomao s[ignio]r mio karissimo, fui mosso a scrivere a Vostra S[ignori]a, non per risposta d'alcuna vostra che ricievuta avesse, ma primo a muovere.... E se pure delle cose mia, che io spero e promcto di fare, alcuna ne piacerà, la chiamerò molto più aventurata che buona ..." (*Il carteggio di Michelangelo*, ed. Paola Barocchi and Renzo Ristori [Florence, 1965–83], III, no. 897, pp. 443–44) English translation in E. H. Ramsden, *The Letters of Michelangelo* (Stanford, 1963), I, pp. 193–94 (draft 4); cf. also the version by Symonds, *The Life of Michelangelo*, II, pp. 134–35.
12. "In questo mezo mi pigliarò almanco doi hore del giorno piacere in contemplare doi vostri desegni che Pier Antonio me à portati, quali quanto più li miro, tanto più mi piacciono, et appag[h]erò in gran parte il mio male pensando alla speranza che 'l detto Piero Antonio mi à data di farmi vedere altre cose delle vostre" (*Carteggio*, III, no. 897, pp. 445–46).
13. A. E. Popham and Johannes Wilde, *The Italian Drawings of the XV and XVI Centuries ... at Windsor Castle* (London, 1949), no. 429; Charles de Tolnay, *Corpus dei disegni di Michelangelo* (Novara, 1976–80), II, no. 345; Michael Hirst, *Michelangelo Draftsman*, exhibition catalogue (Milan, 1988), no. 43; Paul Joannides, *Michelangelo and His Influence: Drawings from Windsor Castle*, exhibition catalogue (Washington and London, 1996), no. 12.
14. Popham and Wilde, *The Italian Drawings . . . at Windsor Castle*, no. 457; Joannides, *Michelangelo and His Influence*, no. 15.
15. The attribution to Michelangelo himself was made by Michael Hirst, "A Drawing of the 'Rape of Ganymede' by Michelangelo," *Burlington Magazine* 117 (1975): 166, and, more fully, "A Drawing of the Rape of Ganymede by Michelangelo," in *Essays Presented to Myron P. Gilmore*, II: *History of Art, History of Music*, ed. Sergio Bertelli and Gloria Ramakus (Florence,1978), pp. 253–60. It has been accepted by Tolnay, *Corpus*, II, no. 344, and by Alexander Perrig, *Michelangelo's Drawings: The Science of Attribution* (New Haven and London, 1991), pp. 43–44, but doubted by Joannides, *Michelangelo and His Influence*, pp. 72–74.
16. Within its larger Ovidian context, Correggio's *Rape of Ganymede*, painted for Mantua about 1530, makes such a Neoplatonic reading even clearer. See Egon Verheyen, "Correggio's 'Amori di Giove,'" *Journal of the Warburg and Courtauld Institutes*, 29 (1966): 160–92.
17. Cavalieri may have also possessed a version of the fuller *Ganymede* composition, since he arranged for a copy to be painted. See William Edward Wallace, "A New Letter, a Michelangelo Drawing, and a Lost Sebastiano?" *Source: Notes in the History of Art*, 4 (Summer 1985): 21–26.

18. Erwin Panofsky, "The Neoplatonic Movement and Michelangelo," in his *Studies in Iconology: Humanistic Themes in the Art of the Renaissance* (1939; New York and Evanston, 1962), pp. 171–230, esp. 212–18 on Ganymede and Tityus. Perrig, *Michelangelo's Drawings*, pp. 43–44, vehemently denying that Michelangelo's *Ganymede* is "a coded declaration of love," insists rather on reading it in a less emotional way, as part of the master's "course of instruction in drawing." One of the pupil's exercises, according to Perrig, is a variant *Rape of Ganymede* (Uffizi, no. 611E), a red-chalk drawing he attributes to Cavalieri – but which was given to Michelangelo himself by Johannes Wilde ("Notes on the Genesis of Michelangelo's Leda," in *Fritz Saxl: A Volume of Memorial Essays from his Friends in England* [London, 1957], p. 274), an opinion endorsed by Hirst ("A Drawing of the Rape of Ganymede" [1978], p. 256). "School of Michelangelo" seems closer to the mark, as in Paola Barocchi, *Michelangelo e la sua scuola: I disegni di Casa Buonarroti e degli Uffizi* (Florence, 1962), no. 277.
19. Enzo Noè Girardi, *Michelangelo Buonarroti: Rime* (Bari, 1960), no. 59 (subsequent references are to this edition [G]). See the bilingual edition of James M. Saslow, *The Poetry of Michelangelo: An Annotated Translation* (New Haven and London, 1991) – whose translation I have somewhat modified.
20. Panofsky, *Studies in Iconology*, p. 216, n. 145.
21. The pairing of Ganymede and Leda on a sarcophagus once on the Quirinal in Rome is recorded in several drawings of the fifteenth and sixteenth centuries: see Phyllis Pray Bober and Ruth Rubinstein, *Renaissance Artists and Antique Sculpture: A Handbook of Sources* (New York, 1986), no. 5, with further bibliography. On Michelangelo's *Leda*: Charles de Tolnay, *Michelangelo* (Princeton, 1947–60), III, pp. 106f., 190–93; Wilde, "Notes on the Genesis of Michelangelo's Leda," pp. 270–80. The homoerotic connotations of Ganymede, and of Michelangelo's representation in particular, have been the subject of much modern critical attention: see especially Robert S. Liebert, *Michelangelo: A Psychoanalytic Study of His Life and Images* (New Haven and London, 1983), pp. 173–80, 276–86 (part of chap. 16: "Tommaso de' Cavalieri and Other Young Men"); James M. Saslow, *Ganymede in the Renaissance: Homosexuality in Art and Society* (New Haven and London, 1986), chap. 1: "Michelangelo: Myth as Personal History"; Leonard Barkan, *Transuming Passion: Ganymede and the Erotics of Humanism* (Stanford, 1991), pp. 74–98.
22. This is the thesis of Wallace, "Studies in Michelangelo's Finished Drawings," pp. 131–76, who offers the most sustained discussion of the problem and the most intriguing alternative reading of the drawing. Locating the *Tityus* in the context of Michelangelo's troubled relationship with his native Florence, as well as confronting the motivic overlap with Prometheus, Wallace argues the personal political implications of the conflicted image of punished *superbia*. The most recent comment on the drawing is by Joannides, *Michelangelo and His Influence*, no. 12. A very summary black-chalk sketch in the Uffizi has been tentatively identified as a preliminary study for the composition, although its attribution remains debatable: see Barocchi, *Michelangelo e la sua scuola*, no. 132.
23. Unless, of course, the risen Christ actually preceded the reclining Tityus, as was proposed by Frederick Hartt, *Michelangelo Drawings* (New York, 1970), no. 184. Dating the entire group of resurrection drawings much earlier, Hartt assigned the drawing of the risen Christ to ca. 1517–18, that is, long before the *Tityus* and reversing the recto–verso relationship of the sheet. Barkan too (*Transuming Passion*, pp. 92, 135–36) has preferred the logic of Michelangelo's working up the verso of an already used sheet to the problematic tracing of a finished drawing presumably intended for presentation. Perrig, however, rejecting Michelangelo's responsibility entirely, has argued that Cavalieri himself traced on the verso of this precious gift (*Michelangelo's Drawings*, pp. 44, 76–77); the conviction of anatomical diagramming, however, the sheer confidence of its reductive notation, testifies in my view against an attribution to the pupil.
24. Condivi, *The Life of Michelangelo*, trans. Wohl, p. 105. A few years earlier (1545), Donato Giannotti reported Michelangelo's own supposed confession:

> You must know that I am, of all men who were ever born, the most inclined to love persons. Whenever I behold some one who possesses any talent or displays any dexterity of mind, who can do or say something more appropriately than the rest of the world, I am compelled to fall in love with him; and then I give myself up to him so entirely that I am no longer my own property, but wholly his. (*Dialoghi di Donato Giannotti de' giorni che Dante consumò nel cercare l'Inferno e 'l Purgatorio* [1545], ed. Deoclecio Redig de Campos [Florence, 1939], p. 68; trans. Symonds, *Michelangelo*, II, p. 132)

25. Vasari, *Le vite*, ed. Milanesi, VII, p. 275:

> Amò grandemente le bellezze humane per la imitazione dell'arte, per potere scierre il bello dal bello; che senza questa imitazione non si può far cosa perfetta; ma non in pensieri lascivi e disonesti: che l'ha mostro nel modo del viver suo, che è stato parchissimo, essendosi contentato quando era giovane, per istare intento al lavoro, d'un poco di pane e di vino. . . ." Cf. Condivi's explanation of the healthy state of Michelangelo's body: "sano sopratutto sì per natura, sì per l'esercizio del corpo e continenza sua tanto nel coito quanto nel cibo. . . ." (*La vita di Michelangelo*, ed. D'Ancona, p. 198)

26. On this relationship, see Christoph Luitpold Frommel, *Michelangelo und Tommaso dei Cavalieri* (Amsterdam, 1979); Liebert, *Michelangelo: A Psychoanalytic Study*, pp. 270–311; Saslow, *Ganymede in the Renaissance*, pp. 17–62. For the affective dimensions and vocabulary of the poems, see Saslow's introduction to *The Poetry of Michelangelo*. Perhaps too definitively, Barkan concludes, "Clearly, there is a discourse of secrecy surrounding all these communications" (*Transuming Passion*, p. 82).
27. *Carteggio*, III, pp. 443–44, no. 897; trans. Ramsden, *The Letters*, I, pp. 193–94, draft 4. The quoted line is from Petrarch's *Rime sparse*, XXIII, line 91. See Robert M. Durling, trans. and ed., *Petrarch's Lyric Poems: The* Rime sparse *and Other Lyrics* (Cambridge, Mass., and London, 1976), p. 65.
28. Vasari, *Le vite*, ed. Milanesi, VII, p. 271, cited above, note 10; cf. the briefer comment in the edition of 1550 (*La vita di Michelangelo*, ed. Barocchi, p. 121). For the most circumstantial consideration of Michelangelo's drawings for Cavalieri, see Wallace, "Studies in Michelangelo's Finished Drawings," pp. 122–203, and, for the "pedagogical" drawings, pp. 43–82. Perrig's bold effort to define Cavalieri as a draftsman (*Michelangelo's Drawings*, pp. 75–85), mainly at the expense of the traditional Michelangelo corpus, seems to me rather generous in its evaluation of the young man's talents (cf. my review, "More or Less Michelangelo," *Drawing* 13 [January–February 1992]: 112f.).
29. Johannes Wilde, *Michelangelo and His Studio* (Italian Drawings in the Department of Prints and Drawings in the British Museum) (London, 1953), no. 55; Tolnay, *Corpus*, II, no. 340; Hirst, *Michelangelo Draftsman*, no. 44.
30. Popham and Wilde, *The Italian Drawings . . . at Windsor Castle*, no. 430; Tolnay, *Corpus*, II, no. 343; Hirst, *Michelangelo Draftsman*, no. 45; Joannides, *Michelangelo and His Influence*, no. 9. For Cavalieri's letter: *Carteggio*, III, no. 932, p. 49.
31. Tolnay, *Corpus*, II, no. 342; Hirst, *Michelangelo Draftsman*, no. 46. For the conservation of the drawing, which revealed convincingly autograph figural sketches on the verso, see Giovanna Nepi Scirè, in *Restauri alle Gallerie dell'Accademia* (*Quaderni della Soprintendenza ai Beni Artistici e Storici di Venezia* 13) (Venice, 1987), pp. 50–60, pls. 15 and 16.
32. Alexander Perrig, "Bemerkungen zur Freundschaft zwischen Michelangelo und Tommaso de' Cavalieri," in *Stil und Überlieferung in der Kunst des Abendlandes* (Akten des 21. Internationalen Kongresses für Kunstgeschichte) (Berlin, 1967), II, pp. 164–71, has argued that the inscription on the Venice drawing actually confirms Cavalieri's own responsibility for the sheet – as well as for several other finished drawings traditionally ascribed to the master. See also Perrig, *Michelengelo's Drawings*, pp. 75–85. In a more radical rejection of the attribution to Michelangelo of the Accademia drawing, Hans Ost has declared it a late eighteenth-century forgery by Giuseppe Bossi: *Das Leonardo-Porträt in der Kgl. Bibliothek Turin und andere Fälschungen des Giuseppe Bossi* (Berlin, 1980), pp. 111–22.
33. Wallace, "Studies in Michelangelo's Finished Drawings," pp. 193–98. Wallace (pp. 185–203) offers a full discussion of the possible genesis of the Phaethon drawings, the inspiration and challenge of the ancient sarcophagus then at Santa Maria in Aracoeli, and the presumed continuing dialogue between Michelangelo and Cavalieri that seems reflected in the inscriptions on the drawings.
34. This was the conclusion of A. E. Brinckmann (*Michelangelo-Zeichnungen* [Munich, 1925], p. 55), followed by Wilde, and revived by Hirst (*Michelangelo and His Drawings*, p. 114), arguing that the message of the inscription confirms the execution of the drawing following Michelangelo's definitive return to Rome in 1534.
35. See above, note 12.
36.

> Ho auto la vostra et visto il crucifixo ilqual certamente ha crucifixe nella memoria mia quante altre picture viddi mai / non se po vedere piu ben fatta, piu viva et piu finita imagine et certo io non potrei mai explicar quanto sottilmente et mirabilmente e facta / . . . io l'ho ben visto al lume et col vetro et col speccio, et non viddi mai la piu finita cosa. (*Carteggio*, IV, p. 104, no. 968)

Both Vasari and Condivi celebrate the drawings for Vittoria Colonna: Vasari, *Le vite*, ed. Milanesi, VII, p. 275; *La vita di Michelangelo*, ed. Barocchi, I, pp. 120–22; Condivi, *La vita di Michelangelo*, ed. D'Ancona, pp. 186–90; *The Life of Michelangelo*, trans. Wohl, p. 103. For the British Museum drawing: Wilde, *Michelangelo and His Studio*, no. 67; Tolnay, *Corpus*, III, no. 411. On the *Pietà* drawing in the Isabella Stewart Gardner Museum, see Nagel, "Gifts for Michelangelo and Vittoria Colonna," and, on the marchesa herself, see Sylvia Ferino-Pagden, *Vittoria Colonna: Dichterin und Muse Michelangelos* (Vienna, 1997), both with further bibliography.
37. Berenson, *The Drawings of the Florentine Painters*, I, p. 226.
38. Symonds, *The Life of Michelangelo*, I, p. 295.
39. Popham and Wilde, *The Italian Drawings . . . at Windsor Castle*, no. 424; Tolnay, *Corpus*, II, no. 336; Joannides, *Michelangelo and His Influence*, no. 16.
40. Symonds, *The Life of Michelangelo*, I, p. 297. Cf. the response of Johannes Wilde: "The stippling is handled with the virtuosity of a professional engraver, and the gradations of light and shade are infinite" (Popham and Wilde, *The Italian Drawings . . . at Windsor Castle*, no. 424). Two inscriptions on the verso locate the drawing with a certain precision: one is dated 12 April 1530 and records ten ducats being taken to the artist's father by Andrea Quaratesi; the other, "D. Giulio Clouio copia di /

Michiel Angelo," documents the drawing in Clovio's collection and presumably identifies it as a copy. In light of the sheer quality of the drawing and the evidence of the *ricordo* of 1530, it is generally assumed that the second inscription is in error and that the drawing is indeed by the master (cf., e.g., Tolnay, *Corpus,* II, no. 336). Perrig, however, has resisted that logic and, insisting on the accuracy of the inventory scribe, has argued the drawing is indeed a copy by Clovio (*Michelangelo's Drawings,* pp. 31–34, 125, n. 64). Primarily, however, Perrig claims to base his argument on close technical analysis of the sheet itself. But his analysis is flawed in at least one important respect. He claims that the *Archers* at Windsor "has neither scratch marks nor other damages to the stroke system" (p. 34), which he takes as evidence of its never having served as the basis for copies. My own observation records precisely such surface markings: the contours of most of the major figures have indeed been traced with a stylus, which has in places damaged the original chalked surface. By Perrig's own criterion, the drawing at Windsor must have served as the model for copiests – like Clovio. For a reading of the desirous imagery itself in the context of the Cavalieri relationship, see Judith Anne Testa, "The Iconography of the *Archers:* A Study of Self-Concealment and Self-Revelation in Michelangelo's Presentation Drawings," *Studies in Iconography* 5 (1979): 45–72.

41. Popham and Wilde, *The Italian Drawings . . . at Windsor Castle,* no. 431; Tolnay, *Corpus,* II, no. 338; Hirst, *Michelangelo Draftsman,* no. 47.
42. Vasari, *La vita di Michelangelo,* ed. Barocchi, I, p. 122 (ed. 1550). For the drawing, see Popham and Wilde, *The Italian Drawings . . . at Windsor Castle,* no. 431; Tolnay, *Corpus,* II, no. 338; Hirst, *Michelangelo Draftsman,* no. 47, with full bibliography.
43. Francisco de Hollanda, *Four Dialogues on Painting,* trans. Bell, p. 80. For the original text, see *Vier Gespräche über dei Malerei,* ed. de Vasconcellos, pp. 134–36. In his treatise *De pintura antigua* (1548) de Hollanda offers a more expansive vision of his

> art of chiaroscuro illumination on virgin parchment, with touches of powdered gold: this is my art, and the truly celestial manner of painting. . . . a manner carried out entirely with a certain extremely fine stippling [*certos pontos sotilissimos*] which I call atoms [*átomos*] or mist [*nevoa*], which stippling covers the entire work in the manner of a veil of of smoke. . . . It must be practiced with much restraint (like all rare and excellent things), and to a very refined, and most consummate and breathed-on effect [*e que seja muito stremado e consumatissimo e soplado*]. And perfect illumination must be carried out . . . in such a way that it does not seem to have been made by the hand [*que pareça que nao foi feita co a mao*], but with the understanding and the breath [*do entendimento e asoplada*]. (*De pintura antigua,* ed. A. Gonzalez Garcia [Lisbon, 1983], pp. 164–65; translation by Mary Pardo, in *True Alchemy: Paolo Pino's Dialogo and the Origins of Venetian Art Criticism* [in press])

De Hollanda's pictorial art, "virgin parchment" being informed by the breath, becomes truly heavenly, an immaculist aesthetic. On the relative reliability of de Hollanda as a source for Michelangelo, see Summers, *Michelangelo and the Language of Art,* pp. 26–27, 508–9, et passim.

44. See Webster Smith, "Giulio Clovio and the 'Maniera di figure piccole,'" *Art Bulletin* 46 (1964): 395–401.
45. Johannes Wilde, *Michelangelo: Six Lectures* (Oxford, 1978), p. 156.
46. Ibid., p. 158. Although the term was not used in his Windsor catalogue entry for the *Phaethon* drawing, Wilde wrote, "Judging by the technical quality, it is natural to assume that the execution of the drawing must have taken a considerable time. The work is the result of an intense absorption by the artist with the problem of representation" (*Italian Drawings . . . at Windsor Castle,* no. 430, p. 254). "Stippling" became a consistent descriptive category only in Wilde's catalogue of the British Museum drawings (1953). Unfortunately, the term then entered standard catalogues as an enrichment, gratuitous as well as erroneous, of descriptions of medium – e.g., in J. A. Gere, *Drawings by Michelangelo from the British Museum,* exhibition catalogue, Pierpont Morgan Library (New York, 1979): "black chalk, partly stippled" (no. 19), "black chalk, to a great extent stippled" (no. 21); cf. my review, "The Elusive Michelangelo," *Art News* 78 (Summer 1979): 48–51.
47. For an earlier challenge to the stippling thesis, see David Rosand, "Michelangelo Draws: Communication and Revelation," in *World of Art: Themes of Unity in Diversity* (Acts of the 26th International Congress of the History of Art), ed. Irving Lavin (University Park and London, 1989), II, pp. 409–14. The wholesale acceptance of chalk stippling as a technique of Michelangelo's was also criticized by Alexander Perrig, *Michelangelo Studien I: Michelangelo und die Zeichnungswissenschaft, Ein methodologischer Versuch* (Frankfurt and Bern, 1976), pp. 46, 92, and by Wallace, "Studies in Michelangelo's Finished Drawings," p. 63; cf. also Perrig, *Michelangelo's Drawings,* pp. 65–66. Hirst, too, has acknowledged the absence of the technique in Michelangelo's gift drawings: *Michelangelo and His Drawings,* pp. 112–13.
48. The most circumspect general analysis of Michelangelo's drawing techniques is by Perrig, *Michelangelo Studien,* esp. pp. 41–67, on hatching, and *Michelangelo's Drawings,* esp. pp. 37–66.
49. P.-J. Mariette, *Abecedario . . . ,* ed. Ph. de Chennevières and A. de Montaiglon (Paris, 1851–60), I, p. 223.

50. Cf. Francisco de Hollanda's description of his miraculous art, quoted above, note 43.
51. Tolnay, *Michelangelo*, V, pp. 80, 223, has argued that the entire series must be considered preparatory to a multifigure group in marble.
52. Michelangelo seems often to have prepared his paper, strengthening (and whitening) its surface by the application of a chalk or bone substance. This is especially evident in the drawings for the *Last Judgment* in the British Museum. I would like to thank Eric Harding, then conservator in the Department of Prints and Drawings of the British Museum, for examining these drawings with me in 1986.
53. Charles de Tolnay, *The Art and Thought of Michelangelo* (New York, 1964), p. 81.
54. Berenson, *The Drawings of the Florentine Painters*, I, p. 225.
55. It must be noted that Michelangelo's authorship of these drawings has been denied by Perrig, *Michelangelo's Drawings*, pp. 94–101, who has attributed them instead to Marcello Venusti. Perrig observes that the figures of the crucified Christ derive ultimately from that drawn for Vittoria Colonna, and he aligns them as a series of problem-solving efforts, imitations of Michelangelo. His argument, in my view, fails to acknowledge the significance of the variations in design and the sheer intensity of the iconography, the emotional investment in their invention. Beyond the problem of Venusti as draftsman, then, Perrig must still demonstrate that this follower was indeed capable of such personal passion, such profound commitment to drawing as expression – that Venusti, like Michelangelo, poured such deep piety into his art.
56. Hirst, *Michelangelo and His Drawings*, p. 8. This situation was reported in letters to the duke of Urbino as early as 1537: see Georg Gronau, "Die Kunstbestrebungen der Herzöge von Urbino, II. Michelangelo," *Jahrbuch der Kgl. Preussischen Kunstsammlungen*, 27 (1906), Beiheft, pp. 7–9. On the general problem of "old-age style," see the references cited in Chapter Seven, note 32.
57. Perrig, *Michelangelo's Drawings*, p. 71f. Insisting that this style "has nothing to do with a change of aesthetic attitude," Perrig tends to overemphasize the "uncontrolled manual jerks" and "twitchings." Aesthetic attitude, after all, is not a priori; rather, it is the product of a complex dialectic with the medium. Nor can Perrig's reading of "the limits that were placed on the drawing efforts of a hand weak from age" be easily reconciled with our knowledge of Michelangelo wielding hammer and chisel only a few days before his death (see below, note 61).
58. In a sensitive discussion of these drawings, Paul Joannides has sought to locate their inspiration within the art-historical context of deliberate stylistic revival, a critical approach that may dilute to some extent the very personal dimension of their execution: "'Primitivism' in the Late Drawings of Michelangelo: The Master's Construction of an Old-age Style, in *Michelangelo Drawings*, ed. Craig Hugh Smyth, in collaboration with Ann Gilkerson (*Studies in the History of Art* 33, Center for Advanced Study in the Visual Arts, Symposium Papers XVII) (Washington, 1992), pp. 245–61.
59. The richest interpretation of this group, in the context of Michelangelo's life and religion, is that of Leo Steinberg, developed and refined over many years: "Michelangelo's Florentine *Pietà:* The Missing Leg," *Art Bulletin* 50 (1968): 343–59; "The Metaphors of Love and Birth in Michelangelo's *Pietàs*," in *Studies in Erotic Art*, ed. Theodore Bowie and Cornelia V. Christenson (New York and London, 1970), pp. 231–335; "The Case of the Wayward Shroud," in *Tribute to Lotte Brand Philip: Art Historian and Detective*, ed. William W. Clark, Colin Eisler, William S. Heckscher, Barbara G. Lane (New York, 1985), pp. 185–92; "Michelangelo's Florentine Pietà: The Missing Leg Twenty Years Later," *Art Bulletin* 71 (1989): 480–505. The inspirational force of Michelangelo's profound consciousness of death has been stressed in a recent study by Laura Camille Agoston, "Sonnet, Sculpture, Death: The Mediums of Michelangelo's Self-Imaging," *Art History* 20 (1997): 534–56.
60. Vasari, *Le vite*, ed. Milanesi, VII, p. 244f.: ". . . fu necessario trovar qualcosa poi di marmo, perchè e'potessi ogni giorno passar tempo scarpellando; e fu messo un altro pezzo di marmo dove era stato già abbbozzato un'altra Pietà, varia da quella, molto minore."
61. In a letter of June 11, 1564, Daniele da Volterra wrote that Michelangelo was still working on February 12, 1564: "io non mi ricordo se in tutto quello scritto io messi chome Michelagnolo lavoro tutto il sabbato della domenica di carnovale ellavoro in piedi studiando sopra quel corpo della pietà. . . ." See Tolnay, *Michelangelo*, V, pp. 154–57.

7. REMBRANDT'S REACH

1. Arnold Houbraken, *De Groote Schouburgh der Nederlandsche Kunstschilders en Schilderessen* (Amsterdam, 1718–21), I, p. 270: "Toren, haat, droefheit, blytschap, en zoo voort, alles staat zoo natuurlyk afgebeelt datmen uit de pentrekken lezen kan wat elk zeggen wil." Cited from Seymour Slive, *Rembrandt and His Critics 1630–1730* (The Hague, 1953), p. 189; see also William W. Robinson, "Rembrandt's Sketches of Historical Subjects," in *Drawings Defined*, ed. Walter Strauss and Tracie Felker (New York, 1987), p. 244.
2. Paul Valéry, "Reflections on Art, in *Aesthetics* (Princeton, 1964), p. 160.
3. For Calderón's legal defense of the art of painting, offered on July 18, 1677, see Ernst Robert Curtius, *European Literature and the Latin Middle Ages*,

trans. Willard R. Trask (New York, 1953), p. 561, with further references.

4. See Christian Tümpel and Astrid Tümpel, *Rembrandt legt die Bibel aus: Zeichnungen und Radierungen aus dem Kupferstichkabinett der Staatliche Museen Preussischer Kulturbesitz Berlin* (Berlin, 1970), no. 88.
5. Further on Rembrandt and children, see Peter Schatborn, "Over Rembrandt en kinderen," *De Kroniek van het Rembrandthuis* 27 (1975): 8–19, and "Kinderen door Rembrandt," *De Kroniek van het Rembrandthuis* 33 (1981): 1–32.

   The appreciation of naïve drawings in the Renaissance is attested by the story of Michelangelo's victory in a competition among professional artists to draw a figure that had "niente di disegno" but was "goffa," like those "fantocci" scrawled on walls by those who don't know how to draw – as reported by Giorgio Vasari, *Le vite de' più eccellenti pittori, scultori ed architettori* (1568), ed. Gaetano Milanesi (Florence, 1878–85), VII, p. 278. Julius S. Held has called attention to the portrait of *A Child with a Drawing* by the sixteenth-century Veronese painter Giovanni Francesco Caroto: "The Early Appreciation of Drawings," in *Studies in Western Art, II: Latin American Art and the the Baroque Period in Europe* (Acts of the Twentieth International Congress of the History of Art) (Princeton, 1963), pp. 72–95, esp. p. 78. See also the observations of Irving Lavin on graffiti and naïve drawing in *Past–Present: Essays on Historicism in Art from Donatello to Picasso* (Berkeley, Los Angeles, Oxford, 1993), pp. 214–21.
6. Among recent studies of this phenomenon: Joseph Leo Koerner, "Rembrandt and the Epiphany of the Face," *Res* 12 (Autumn 1986): 5–32; Frederic Schwartz, "'The motions of the countenance': Rembrandt's Early Portraits and the *Tronie*," *Res* 17/18 (Spring/Autumn 1989): 89–116, and H. Perry Chapman, *Rembrandt Self-Portraits: A Study in Seventeenth-Century Identity* (Princeton, 1990). Two recent books deal extensively with such issues of identity and self-representation: Simon Schama, *Rembrandt's Eyes* (New York, 1999), and Harry Berger, Jr., *Fictions of the Pose: Rembrandt against the Italian Renaissance* (Stanford, 2000).
7. Samuel van Hoogstraten, *Inleyding tot de Hooge Schoole der Schilder-konst* (Rotterdam, 1678), pp. 109–10. Translation from Chapman, *Rembrandt's Self-Portraits*, p. 20; also Peter Schatborn, *Dutch Figure Drawings from the Seventeenth Century* (The Hague, 1981), pp. 11–12.
8. *Ars poetica*, ll. 102–3; trans. T. S. Dorsch, *Classical Literary Criticism* (Harmondsworth, Baltimore, Victoria, 1965), p. 82. Precisely this affective truth is extended to painting by Alberti, *De pictura*, ed. Cecil Grayson (Rome-Bari, 1972), ¶¶ 41–42. I have discussed this affective dimension of Renaissance imagery in "'Troyes Painted Woes': Shakespeare and the Pictorial Imagination," *Hebrew University Studies in Literature* 8 (Spring 1980): 77–97, and "Raphael, Marcantonio, and the Icon of Pathos," *Source: Notes on the History of Art* 3 (Winter 1984): 34–52.
9. For the Carracci, see Carlo Cesare Malvasia, *Felsina pittrice: Vite de' pittori bolognesi* (1678), ed. Giampietro Zanotti (Bologna, 1841), I, p. 277. Even more dramatic accounts of affective projection are told of Bernini and Domenichino. See Filippo Baldinucci, *Vita di Gian Lorenzo Bernini* (1682), ed. Sergio Samek Ludovici (Milan, 1948), p. 78, and Domenico Bernini, *Vita del Cavalier Gio. Lorenzo Bernino* (Rome, 1713), p. 19, and, for Domenichino, Giovanni Pietro Bellori, *Le vite de' pittori, scultori e architetti moderni* (Rome, 1672), p. 415; cf. as well A. W. A. Boschloo, *Annibale Carracci in Bologna: Visible Reality in Art after the Council of Trent* (The Hague, 1974), II, pp. 235–36, n. 16, and Richard E. Spear, *Domenichino* (New Haven and London, 1982), I, p. 37.
10. Quoted from *The Rembrandt Documents*, ed. Walter L. Strauss and Marjon van der Meulen (New York, 1979), pp. 68–72. See also Slive, *Rembrandt and His Critics*, pp. 8–26. For the painting itself: A. Bredius, *Rembrandt: The Complete Edition of the Paintings*, rev. by H. Gerson (London, 1969), no. 539A (hereinafter Br.).
11. Letter of 12 January 1639: *The Rembrandt Documents*, pp. 161–62.
12. Franciscus Junius, *The Painting of the Ancients* (1638), ed. Keith Aldrich, Philipp Fehl, and Raina Fehl (Berkeley, Los Angeles, Oxford, 1991), I, p. 258.
13. The codification of Rembrandt's lamenting or grieving figure was established in part through variant copies like the etching by Joris van Vliet, in turn recast as the melancholy Heraclitus by Wenzel Hollar. See Svetlana Alpers, *Rembrandt's Enterprise: The Studio and the Market* (Chicago and London, 1988); also the discussion in Schwartz, "'The motions of the countenance,'" pp. 93–96, with further references. The compositional sketches preparatory to the painting of *Judas Returning the Thirty Pieces of Silver* have been discussed by Martin Royalton-Kisch, "Rembrandt's Sketches for His Paintings," *Master Drawings* 27 (1989): 128–45, esp. 130–33.
14. Otto Benesch, *The Drawings of Rembrandt*, enlarged ed. Eva Benesch, 6 vols. (London, 1973), no. 859 (hereinafter Benesch).
15. Recognizing the bloodied coat, Jacob said,

    > It is my son's coat; an evil beast hath devoured him; Joseph is without doubt rent in pieces. / And Jacob rent his clothes, and put sackcloth upon his loins, and mourned for his son many days. / And all his sons and all his daughters rose up to comfort him; but he refused to be comforted; and he said, For I will go down into the grave unto my son mourning. Thus his father wept for him. (Genesis 37:33–35)

16. Rembrandt's students recalled that he would often sketch a face "in ten different ways before he ever put it on canvas," as reported by Arnold Houbraken, *De Groote Schouburgh . . .*, I, pp. 257–58. See Slive, *Rembrandt and His Critics*, p. 178, for further discussion; also Koerner, "Rembrandt and the Epiphany of the Face," esp. pp. 23–30.
17. Junius, *The Painting of the Ancients*, ed. Aldrich, Fehl, and Fehl, I, pp. 55, 57. Junius then picks up the traditional topos of inspired speed vs. diligence of execution: "and it standeth an Artificer upon it, rather to trie all what may be tried, then to marre the vigorous force of a fresh and warme Imagination by a slow and coole manner of Imitation."
18. Hoogstraten, *Inleyding*, p. 192; trans. in Robinson, "Rembrandt's Sketches," p. 241. Further on the significance of *schets*, see J. Bruyn, "On Rembrandt's Use of Studio Props and Model Drawings during the 1630s," in *Essays in Northern European Art Presented to Egbert Haverkamp-Begemann* (Doornspijk, 1983), pp. 52–60.
19. Houbraken, *De Groote Schouburgh*, I, p. 270; trans. in Robinson, "Rembrandt's Sketches," p. 244.
20. The theatrical practices in Rembrandt's studio – posing, costuming, and playacting – have been emphasized by Alpers, *Rembrandt's Enterprise*, chap. 2: "The Theatrical Model." The master's dependence on posed models was argued even more insistently, indeed to the point nearly of denying Rembrandt's graphic imagination, by Nigel Konstam, "Rembrandt's Use of Models and Mirrors," *Burlington Magazine* 119 (1977): 94–98.
21. See Peter Schatborn in Bevers et al., *Rembrandt: The Master and His Workshop – Drawings and Etchings*, exhibition catalogue (New Haven and London, 1991), p. 46, with reference to Alison McNeil Kettering, *Drawings from the Ter Borch Studio Estate* (Catalogue of the Dutch and Flemish Drawings in the Rijksprentenkabinet, Rijksmuseum, Amsterdam) (The Hague, 1988), no. H51.
22. See Tümpel, *Rembrandt legt die Bibel aus*, no. 70, and Peter Schatborn's discussion of related drawings in Bevers et al., *Rembrandt: The Master and His Workshop – Drawings and Etchings*, no. 7, pp. 41–43. On forms of attention in Rembrandt's art, see especially Julius S. Held, "Rembrandt and the Spoken Word," in his *Rembrandt Studies* (Princeton, 1991), pp. 164–83.
23. See Tümpel, *Rembrandt legt die Bibel aus*, nos. 86, 87.
24. For recent commentary on the London drawing (Fig. 215), see Martin Royalton-Kisch, *Drawings by Rembrandt and His Circle in the British Museum* (London, 1992), no. 8.
25. Jeroen Giltaij, *The Drawings by Rembrandt and His School in the Museum Boymans-van Beuningen* (Rotterdam, 1988), no. 13; Royalton-Kisch, *Drawings by Rembrandt . . . in the British Museum*, no. 38.
26. Further on *Two Women Teaching a Child to Walk:* Royalton-Kisch, *Drawings by Rembrandt . . . in the British Museum*, no. 16.
27. The conviction of the Albertina drawing derives from the imposition of strong structural reinforcement with the reed pen, typical of Rembrandt's graphic commentary. The drawing itself evidently records a particular studio session, for the posed model, viewed from different angles, appears in other drawings by pupils as well as in an etching by the master himself (B. 194). See the observations of Peter Schatborn in his introduction to the exhibition catalogue Schatborn and Ornstein-van Slooter, *Bij Rembrandt in de leer / Rembrandt as Teacher* (Amsterdam, 1984), p. 10, and the entries by Eva Ornstein-van Slooten, nos. 20–23; cf. also Bevers et al., *Rembrandt: The Master and His Workshop – Drawings and Etchings*, no. 21.
28. On this double-side sheet of drawings of actors, see Peter Schatborn, *Drawings by Rembrandt, His Anonymous Pupils and Followers* (Catalogue of the Dutch and Flemish Drawings in the Rijksprentenkabinet, Rijksmuseum, Amsterdam) (The Hague, 1985), no. 8, and Bevers et al., *Rembrandt: The Master and His Workshop – Drawings and Etchings*, no. 12, pp. 54–56.
29. Although participating in a conventional social iconography, the theme itself of blindness had a more personal resonance for Rembrandt. See Julius S. Held, "Rembrandt's Interest in Beggars," in his *Rembrandt Studies*, pp. 153–63.
30. The famous illustration in Descartes's *La Dioptrique* (Leiden, 1637) of a blind man "seeing with sticks" was adduced by Svetlana Alpers as a way into the tactility of Rembrandt's painted surfaces: *Rembrandt's Enterprise*, p. 22. Descartes emphasized the doubling of the sticks, essential for the more complex coordination of fixing multiple points in space. These issues are more fully discussed by Michael J. Morgan, *Molyneaux's Question: Vision, Touch, and the Philosophy of Perception* (Cambridge, 1977). On the cane or staff as line of vision in drawings by Goya, see the observations of Hubert Damisch, *Traité du trait* (Paris, 1995), pp. 73–74.
31. The use of a perpendicular plumb line to gauge the vertical axis of a standing figure had been part of standard practice in the Renaissance studio, from Masaccio through Leonardo (e.g., *Treatise on Painting [Codex Urbinas Latinus 1270]*, ed. A. Philip McMahon [Princeton, 1956], ¶ 113).
32. *Treatise on Painting*, ed. McMahon, ¶ 86. On Leonardo and automimesis, see Chapter Three.
33. On the general problem, see the papers of the College Art Association symposium on "Old-Age Style" published in *Art Journal* 46 (1987): 91–133 – with contributions by David Rosand, Martin Kemp, Jerome Silbergeld, Catherine M. Soussloff, Gert Schiff, and Julius S. Held – and the symposium on "Artists and Old Age" published in *Allen Memorial Art Museum Bulletin* 35 (1977–78) – edited by

William Hood with contributions by Irving Lavin, Christopher White, Jean Sutherland Boggs, and Robert Rosenblum. Earlier literature on the issue includes A. E. Brinckmann, *Spätwerke grosser Meister* (Frankfurt am Main, 1925); Hans Tietze, "Earliest and Latest Works of Great Artists," *Gazette des Beaux-Arts* 26 (1944): 273–84; Joseph Gantner, "Der alte Künstler," in *Festschrift für Herbert von Einem*, ed. Gert von der Osten and Georg Kauffmann (Berlin, 1965), pp. 71–76; Herbert von Einem, "Zur Deutung des Altersstiles in der Kunstgeschichte," in *Album Amicorum J. G. van Gelder*, ed. J. Bruyn et al. (The Hague, 1973), pp. 88–92; Kenneth Clark, *The Artist Grows Old* (Cambridge, 1972); Hugo Munsterberg, *The Crown of Life: Artistic Creativity in Old Age* (New York, 1983).

34. Otto Benesch, *Rembrandt as a Draughtsman* (London, 1960), pp. 33, 18. Benesch's observations attest and affirm the fundamental assumptions of traditional connoisseurship:

> Drawing in its deepest sense is handwriting, an immediate emanation of personality, of its rhythm of life and its creative faculty. The greater, the more experienced an artist is, the simpler will be his means of artistic expression. He avoids the roundabout methods of complicated and refined technical processes. The simplest ones, which give direct expression of personality, are just the right ones. (pp. 30–31)

35. Typically, this revision has involved clarification of the graphic identities of some of Rembrandt's many pupils and followers – such as Govert Flinck, Ferdinand Bol, Philips Koninck, Gerbrandt van den Eeckhout, Carel Fabritius, Nicolaes Maes, Aert de Gelder, Willem Drost, Johannes Raven. See Werner Sumowski, *Drawings of the Rembrandt School*, nine volumes to date (New York, 1979–85), as well as the exhibition and museum catalogues by Peter Schatborn, *Drawings by Rembrandt . . .* (in the Rijksprentenkabinet); Schatborn and Ornstein-van Slooten, *Bij Rembrandt in de leer;* Bevers et al., *Rembrandt: The Master and His Workshop – Drawings and Etchings;* Giltaij, *The Drawings by Rembrandt . . . in the Museum Boymans-van Beuningen;* Emmanuel Starcky, *Rembrandt et son école: Dessins du Musée du Louvre* (Paris, 1988); and Royalton-Kisch, *Drawings by Rembrandt . . . in the British Museum.* Cf. the overview by Egbert Haverkamp-Begemann, "Rembrandt as a Draftsman: The Changing Image, 1956–1988," *Master Drawings* 27 (1989): 105–10.

36. The characterization is by John Smith, *A Catalogue Raisonné of the Works of the Most Eminent Dutch, Flemish, and French Painters*, VII (London, 1836), p. xxxv.

37. On the subject of the drawing of *Manoah's Offering* (Fig. 229), see Tümpel, *Rembrandt legt die Bibel aus*, no 21. A good comparison with the Berlin sheet is afforded by a drawing in the Morgan Library of *The Angel Departing from the Family of Tobit* (Benesch 893), in which the the flight of the angel runs parallel to the picture plane. Once considered a characteristic example of Rembrandt's late graphic style, the drawing has recently been reattributed to Willem Drost, reflecting the master's drawing style of the early 1650s: see Schatborn in Bevers et al., *Rembrandt: The Master and His Workshop – Drawings and Etchings*, pp. 144–46, no. 46. Further on the Hamburg drawing of *The Angel Appearing to Hagar and Ishmael in the Wilderness* (Fig. 230): Schatborn in ibid., p. 114, no. 32.

38. For recent discussion of these drawings, see Royalton-Kisch, *Drawings by Rembrandt . . . in the British Museum*, nos. 16, 60.

39. The most sustained study of Rembrandt's later drawing style remains Hans Hell, "Die späten Handzeichnungen Rembrandts," *Repertorium für Kunstwissenschaft* 51 (1930): 4–43, 92–136. More recently, Nicola Courtright has considered the late manner by locating it within broader cultural and historical contexts of rhetorical tradition and response, in "Origin and Meanings of Rembrandt's Late Drawing Style," *Art Bulletin* 78 (1996): 485–510.

40. The distinction between quill and reed provided a fundamental introduction to Hell's study, "Die späten Handzeichnungen Rembrandts," pp. 6–10. For further discussion of pens and inks, see Josef Meder, *Die Handzeichnung: Ihre Technik und Entwicklung*, 2d ed. (Vienna, 1923), pp. 34–71, rev. trans. by Winslow Ames, *The Mastery of Drawing* (New York, 1978), I, pp. 30–57; and the detailed account in James Watrous, *The Craft of Old-Master Drawings* (Madison, 1957), pp. 44–59.

41. Schatborn, *Drawings by Rembrandt . . .* (in the Rijksprentenkabinet), no. 48.

42. For recent discussion of such studio drawings retouched by the master, see Schatborn and Ornstein-van Slooten, *Bij Rembrandt in de leer*, nos. 26–30, and Royalton-Kisch, *Drawings by Rembrandt . . . in the British Museum*, nos. 87–89.

43. Van Gogh seems to have worked his reeds to the point of deconstructing their physical integrity, loosening the individual fibers and thereby effectively transforming pen into brush. Cf. the drawings in Ronald Pickvance, *Van Gogh in Arles*, exhibition catalogue (New York, 1984), nos. 35, 36, 38, 54.

44. Royalton-Kisch, *Drawings by Rembrandt . . . in the British Museum*, nos. 7, 56.

45. Giotto's "O" is discussed in Chapter Four. For Rembrandt's image in this context, see B. P. J. Broos, "The 'O' of Rembrandt," *Simiolus* 4 (1971): 150–84, and John F. Moffitt, "'Più tondo che l'O di Giotto': Giotto, Vasari, and Rembrandt's Kenwood House 'Self-Portrait,'" *Paragone* 35 (1984): 63–70. Chapman, *Rembrandt's Self-Portraits*, pp. 97–101, argues instead that Rembrandt's circles represent the beginnings of a double-hemisphere map, presumably declaring the artist master of the visible world – a

reading that, by conventionalizing the demonstration, deprives it of its full graphic force. For a review of interpretations of the Kenwood House *Self-Portrait,* see Jeanne Chenault Porter, "Rembrandt and His Circles: More About the Late *Self-Portrait* in Kenwood House," in *The Age of Rembrandt: Studies in Seventeenth-Century Dutch Painting,* ed. Roland E. Fleischer and Susan Scott Munshower, *Papers in Art History from The Pennsylvania State University* (1988): 188–212.

46. In light of its careful preparation (pen over a preliminary sketch in black chalk) and laborious execution, Frits Lugt considered the drawing a copy after a lost original of circa 1650–55: *Rembrandt, ses élèves, ses imitateurs, ses copistes* (Musée du Louvre. Inventaire général des dessins des écoles du nord. Ecole hollandaise, III) (Paris, 1933), no. 1301. Hell, "Die späten Handzeichnungen Rembrandts," pp. 106–7, strongly favored the attribution to the master – as does Julius Held. Whether original or copy, the style of the drawing reflects a period when Rembrandt was especially interested in the more formal structures of early Renaissance imagery, as well as the related rigidities of the Mughal miniatures he so assiduously studied toward the end of the decade. For this interest, see, of course, Kenneth Clark, *Rembrandt and the Italian Renaissance* (New York, 1964), esp. chap. 5, "Rembrandt and the Quattrocento." For Rembrandt's knowledge of classical academic tradition, J. A. Emmens, *Rembrandt en de regels van de kunst* (Utrecht, 1968).

47. J. P. Filedt Kok, *Rembrandt: Etchings and Drawings in the Rembrandt House: A Catalogue* (Maarssen, 1972), no. 1.

48. For the larger social context of this stance, see Joneath Spicer, "The Renaissance Elbow," in *A Cultural History of Gesture,* ed. Jan Bremmer and Herman Roodenburg (Ithaca, N.Y., 1991), pp. 84–128.

49. To quote a distant heir of Rembrandt, "If I stretch my arms next to the rest of myself and wonder where my fingers are – that is all the space I need as a painter" (interview with Willem de Kooning, "What Abstract Art Means to Me," *Museum of Modern Art Bulletin* 18 (Spring 1951), reprinted in Harold Rosenberg, *De Kooning* [New York, 1974], p. 146).

50. On blindness and Rembrandt, see Held, "Rembrandt and the Book of Tobit," in his *Rembrandt Studies,* pp. 118–43; see as well Christian Tümpel and Peter Schatborn, *Het boek Tobias, met etsen en tekeningen van Rembrandt en zijn leeringen* (Zeist, 1987). On the Cleveland drawing, see Schatborn in Bevers et al., *Rembrandt: The Master and His Workshop – Drawings and Etchings,* pp. 70–72, no. 18. The attribution of the drawing in Berlin of the *Healing of Tobit's Blindness* (Benesch 646) has been questioned by Robinson ("Rembrandt Sketches," p. 253), who assigns it to an anonymous Rembrandt pupil – although the structural logic of the cane supporting old Anna, its integral role in the conception of the figure, suggests a master with a sure sense of bodily posture.

51. For recent readings of *The Goldsmith* that recognize the high charge of the image, albeit from different perspectives, cf. Mieke Bal, *Reading "Rembrandt": Beyond the Word–Image Opposition* (Cambridge, 1991), pp. 374–80, and Alpers, *Rembrandt's Enterprise,* pp. 29–31.

52. The gout from which Rubens suffered led ultimately to the complete paralysis of his hands and the sad pronouncement of observers that he would never again be able to hold a brush. See Christopher White, *Peter Paul Rubens: Man and Artist* (New Haven and London, 1987), pp. 294–95. Cf. as well Julius Held's observations on the late self-portrait drawing in Windsor: "We look into a large face, impressive in its quiet dignity and mature wisdom. We see also, however, in its aging and slightly flabby forms the signs of fatigue, of a lassitude that at the end of the road may at times have overcome even this man of boundless energy and physical endurance" (*Rubens: Selected Drawings* [London: 1959], p. 83, and no. 126).

Poussin's trembling hand, presumably caused by the syphilis that he had contracted in 1630, marks his late pen drawings in particular. For the frequent references to the problem in the artist's correspondence and in the early biographies, see Claire Pace, *Félibien's Life of Poussin* (London, 1981), pp. 159, 161, 172. Mariette's observation on "une main tremblante et appesantie" are quoted in Anthony Blunt, *The Drawings of Poussin* (New Haven and London, 1979), pp. 2 and 191; see as well Blunt's own brief comments, p. 189, as well as those of Martin Clayton, *Poussin: Works on Paper: Drawings from the Collection of Her Majesty Queen Elizabeth II* (Houston and London, 1995), pp. 145–47.

53. On the Berlin drawing (Fig. 244), see Tümpel, *Rembrandt legt die Bibel aus,* no. 26; for recent comment on the Vienna drawing (Fig. 245), see the entry by Marian Bisanz-Prakken in Oberhuber et al., *A Quintessence of Drawing: Masterworks from the Albertina,* exhibition catalogue (Milan, 1997), no. 59.

54. The scribbled lines falling above the shadowed concavity may allude to the subsequent verse (4:6): "And the Lord God prepared a gourd, and made it to come up over Jonah, that it might be a shadow over his head, to deliver him from his grief."

55. Frits Lugt pioneered the topographical approach to Rembrandt's graphic landscapes; for the *Winter Landscape,* see *Wandelingen met Rembrandt in en om Amsterdam* (Amsterdam, 1915), p. 116 (German trans. *Mit Rembrandt in Amsterdam* [Berlin, 1920], p. 113). Further on the drawing, see Cynthia P. Schneider, *Rembrandt's Landscapes: Drawings and Prints,* exhibition catalogue (Washington, 1990), no. 77 – an important exhibition, organized by topographical and typological categories. On the question of landscapes drawn "from life" or developed in the studio, see as well Martin Royalton-Kisch,

"Rembrandt's Landscape Drawings," in *Drawing: Masters and Methods, Raphael to Redon* (Papers presented to the Ian Woodner Master Drawings Symposium at the Royal Academy of Arts, London), ed. Diana Dethloff (New York, 1992), pp. 114–35. The rural nostalgia read into Rembrandt's graphic landscapes by Linda Stone-Ferrier may well be implicit in a general way, without necessarily carrying programmatic intention: see "Rembrandt's Landscape Etchings: Defying Modernity's Encroachment," *Art History* 15 (1992): 403–33.

Chapter 8 of "Den Grondt der Edel Vry Schilderconst," the theoretical treatise in verse of Carel van Mander, *Het Schilder-boeck* (Haarlem, 1604), is devoted to landscape and opens with the following~ counsel: "Young painters need to practise landscape painting too. Therefore they should rise early if convenient, and go out of town to look at nature and spend time making sketches" (trans. in Christopher Brown, *Dutch Landscape: The Early Years, Haarlem and Amsterdam 1590–1650* [London, 1986], p. 36).

56. In the inventory of one Dutch collection we find "Een kleinder boek . . . daar in leggen 60 stuks Landscapjes, buiten Amsterdam, konstig na't leven, door Rembrandt zyn getekent." See Peter Schatborn, "Van Rembrandt tot Crozat: Vroege verzamelingen met tekeningen van Rembrandt," *Nederlands Kunsthistorisch Jaarboek* 32 (1981), p. 21. Further on the dialectic between natural observation and imaginative invention, see David Freedberg, *Dutch Landscape Prints* (London, 1980), and Claudia Swan, "*Ad vivum, naer het leven,* from the life: Defining a Mode of Representation," *Word and Image* 11 (1995): 353–72.
57. This is what Paul Klee, in the opening linear analyses of his *Pedagogical Sketchbook,* was to call a line "accompanied by complementary forms" or, more dynamically, "secondary lines moving around an imaginary main line." See Chapter One.
58. "En die cromme crauwel-pooten / Drijven 't naer den Leewen-neck." The verse is from Huygens's *Batava Tempe* (1621). "I don't know why," Freedberg comments, "but those 'crome crauwel pooten' seem almost to mimic the scratchiness of what one could call the 'cromme crauwel lijnen' of Rembrandt's etching needle and some of the late pen drawings" (David Freedberg, "The Landscapes of Rembrandt and Constantijn Huygens: 'Eenen Lust om te sien'" [unpublished lecture, Boston Museum of Fine Arts, 12 March 1988]).
59. Van Mander, "Den Grondt der Edel Vry Schilderconst," chap. 8, 31; trans. in Brown, *Dutch Landscape,* p. 40.
60. For this context, see Peter Schatborn, *Landscapes by Rembrandt and His Precursors,* exhibition catalogue (Amsterdam, 1983).
61. I have discussed this dimension of Rembrandt's graphic landscape art more fully in "Pastoral Topoi: On the Construction of Meaning in Landscape," in *The Pastoral Landscape,* ed. John Dixon Hunt (National Gallery of Art, *Studies in the History of Art* 36) (Hanover, N.H., and London, 1992), esp. pp. 169–77. See as well Robert C. Cafritz, "Reverberations of Venetian Graphics in Rembrandt's Pastoral Landscapes," in Robert C. Cafritz, Lawrence Gowing, and David Rosand, *Places of Delight: The Pastoral Landscape,* exhibition catalogue (Washington, 1988), pp. 131–47.
62. See M. A. Schenkeveld-van der Dussen, "Nature and Landscape in Dutch Literature of the Golden Age," in Brown, *Dutch Landscape,* pp. 72–78; Josua Bruyn, "Towards a Scriptural Reading of Seventeenth-Century Dutch Landscape Paintings," in Peter C. Sutton, *Masters of Seventeenth-Century Dutch Landscape,* exhibition catalogue (Boston, 1987), pp. 84–103, and Simon Schama, "Dutch Landscapes: Culture as Foreground," in ibid., pp. 64–83. On the possibilities of interpretation in the Netherlandish tradition, see Walter S. Gibson, *"Mirror of the Earth": The World Landscape in Sixteenth-Century Flemish Painting* (Princeton, 1989), and Lisa Vergara, *Rubens and the Poetics of Landscape* (New Haven and London, 1982).

8. CAPRICCIO: THE ANTIC LINE

1. William Hogarth, *The Analysis of Beauty* (1753), ed. Joseph Burke (Oxford, 1955), p. 35.
2. Hogarth, *Analysis of Beauty,* ed. Burke, pp. 5–6, quoting Richard Haydock's translation, *A Tracte containing the Artes of curious Painting Carvinge and Building written first in Italian by Jo: Paul Lomatius painter of Milan* (Oxford, 1598), p. 17. For fuller consideration of Hogarth's ideas on line in relation to contemporary thought as well as tradition, see J. Dobai, "William Hogarth and Antoine Parent," *Journal of the Warburg and Courtauld Institutes* 31 (1965): 336–82.
3. *The Analysis of Beauty,* ed. Burke, pp. 184–86; cf. Burke's introduction, pp. xxxviii–xl.
4. Cf. the observations of Michael Podro, "The Drawn Line from Hogarth to Schiller," in *"Sind Briten Hier?" Relations between British & Continental Art 1680–1880* (Augsburg, 1981), pp. 45–56:

> For Hogarth lines are, we must recall, not marks but are informed by the objects they form, they are gestures which issue into the world as they define a figure or a scene which would be insipid or inarticulate or commonplace without them. The additional point made by the analogy between drawing and gesture is that drawing is itself a social performance. In drawing as in speech we address other people, and in Hogarth's case, on social matters. (p. 49)

5. Thus they appear listed on the title page of *Opere Varie di Architettura, Prospettive, Grotteschi, Antichità,* first issued in 1750. For the publishing history

of the *Grotteschi,* the various states and editions, see Andrew Robison, *Piranesi: Early Architectural Fantasies: A Catalogue Raisonné of the Etchings* (Washington, 1986), pp. 25–32, 115–22, nos. 21–24.

6. The most ambitious effort at precise symbolic interpretation has been that of Maurizio Calvesi: see his introduction to the Italian edition of Henri Focillon, *Giovanni Battista Piranesi* (Bologna, 1967), pp. XXV–XXX; "G. B. Piranesi," in *Giovan Battista e Francesco Piranesi,* exhibition catalogue (Rome, 1967), pp. 5–53, reprinted in *Giovan Battista Piranesi: Dispensa per il corso monografico del prof. Maurizio Calvesi* (Rome, 1979–80), pp. 58–92, esp. 76–82, and "Nota ai 'Capricci' di Piranesi, in ibid., pp. 220–25.
7. Although addressing a later development, the observations on "the Romantic vignette" of Charles Rosen and Henri Zerner are critically relevant:

    > Apparently unassuming as an artistic form, the vignette launches a powerful attack on the classical definition of representation, a window on the world. The vignette is not a window because it has no limit, no frame. The image, defined from its center rather than its edges, emerges from the paper as an apparition or fantasy. The uncertainty of contour often makes it impossible to distinguish the edge of the vignette from the paper: the whiteness of the paper, which represents the play of light within the image, changes imperceptibly into the paper. (*Romanticism and Realism: The Mythology of Nineteenth-Century Art* [New York, 1984], pp. 81–84)

8. Two generations later, the serpent will be rejected by Humbert de Superville as a creature less animal than "animated line," linear embodiment of the low and the devious as opposed to the moral uprightness of the straight line. David Pierre Giottino Humbert de Superville, *Essai sur les signes inconditionnels dans l'art* (Leiden, 1827), as cited by Barbara Maria Stafford, *Symbol and Myth: Humbert de Superville's Essay on Absolute Signs in Art* (Cranbury, N.J., and London, 1979), p. 33, 45.
9. Published with English and French translations, its full title in English reads: *Divers Manners of Ornamenting Chimneys and all Other Parts of Houses, Taken from the Egyptian, Tuscan, and Grecian Architecture, with an Apologetical Essay in Defence of the Egyptian and Tuscan Architecture.* For a recent study, see Roberta Battaglia, "Le 'Diverse maniere d'adornare i cammini . . .' di Giovanni Battista Piranesi: Gusto e cultura antiquaria," *Saggi e memorie di storia dell'arte* 19 (1994): 191–273.
10. For the history of editions and states, see Robison, *Piranesi: Early Architectural Fantasies,* pp. 37–53, 139–210, nos. 29–44. For further consideration of their generic status, see Werner Busch "Piranesis 'Carceri' und der Capriccio-Begriff im 18. Jahrhundert," *Wallraf-Richartz-Jahrbuch* 39 (1977): 210–24, as well as Norbert Miller, "Giovanni Battista Piranesis Entdeckung der Imagination: Das Capriccio in den Zeichnungen und Radierungen seines Frühwerks," in *Das Capriccio als Kunstprinzip: Zur Vorgeschichte der Moderne von Arcimbolo und Callot bis Tiepolo und Goya,* ed. Joachim Rees (Milan, 1996), pp. 141–55.
11. For the relevant drawings, see Patricia May Sekler, "Giovanni Battista Piranesi's *Carceri* Etchings and Related Drawings," *Art Quarterly* 25 (1962): 330–63, and Robison, *Piranesi: Early Architectural Fantasies,* pp. 37–42.
12. The problems of perspective and architectural construction in the *Carceri* have been graphically analyzed by Ulya Vogt-Göknil, *Giovanni Battista Piranesi: "Carceri"* (Zurich, 1968).
13. J. G. Legrand, *Notice historique sur la vie et les ouvrages de J. B. Piranesi architecte, peintre et graveur né à Venise en 1720 mort à Rome en 1778,* in Gilbert Erouart and Monique Mosser, "A propos de la 'Notice historique sur la vie et les ouvrages de J.-B. Piranesi': Origine et fortune d'une biographie," in *Piranèse et les français,* ed. Georges Brunel (Rome, 1978), pp. 246–47.: ". . . les gravures peuvent être regardées comme des dessins originaux, où le sentiment de l'auteur est transmis immédiatement sur le cuivre et n'a point perdu son esprit et son charme en passant par une main timide."

    In his *Elogio storico del Cavalier Giambattista Piranesi* (1779), G. L. Bianconi explicitly acknowledges the artist's deliberate intention to transform the art of etching: "sulla quale fece assidui studj per uscir dal comune e per trovare un far nuovo." Seeking an adequate comparison, Bianconi concludes that Piranesi can only be acclaimed "il Rembrand delle antiche rovine." Bianconi's *Elogio* is reprinted in the exhibition catalogue *Grafica 2* (Rome, 1976), pp. 127–35.
14. Legrand, *Notice historique,* p. 246: ". . . et si on lui demandait pourquoi il ne faisait pas de dessins plus terminés, et où toutes les ombres fussent exprimées? *J'en serais bien fâché,* répondit-il, *ne voyez-vous pas que si mon dessin était fini ma planche ne deviendrait plus qu'une copie; lorsqu'au contraire je crée l'effet sur le cuivre, j'en fait un original."*
15. That a committed vision of ancient Roman justice and law inspired Piranesi has been most fully argued by Maurizio Calvesi, "Le Carceri," in *Piranesi nei luoghi di Piranesi* (Rome, 1979), pp. 7–28. In a magisterial review of the recent literature following the bicentennial of Piranesi's death, Robin Middleton offers a judicious but sympathetic critique of Calvesi's thesis (*Journal of the Society of Architectural Historians* 41 [1982]: 333–44, esp. 338–39).
16. Legrand, *Notice historique,* p. 231:

    > *Piranesi* ne faisait point de dessins finis, un gros trait à la sanguine, sur lequel il revenait ensuite avec la plume ou le pinceau et par parties seule-

ment lui suffisait pour arrêter ses idées, mais il est presque impossible de distinguer ce qu'il croyait fixer sur le papier, ce n'est qu'un cahos dont il démêlait seul les éléments sur le cuivre avec un art admirable.

Le peintre Robert avec lequel il dessinait quelques fois aussi d'après nature, et qui était si bien en état d'apprécier son talents, ne concevait pas ce qu'on pouvait fare de croquis aussi peu arrêtés; *Piranesi*, voyant son étonnement, lui disait: *le dessin n'est pas sur mon papier, j'en conviens, mais il est tout entier dans ma tête, et vous le verrez par la planche*, elle était fidèle, en effet, et rien n'y était omis.

17. For the publication, generally overlooked in the Piranesi literature, see Alessandro Bettagno, in *Piranesi: Incisioni-rami-legature-architetture*, exhibition catalogue (Vicenza, 1978), pp. 53–55, nos. 306–9. The fuller significance of this motto was suggestively explored by Michelangelo Muraro, "Giambattista Piranesi o dell'espressione," in *Piranesi tra Venezia e l'Europa*, ed. Alessandro Bettagno (Florence, 1983), pp. 75–87.
18. The first edition of the *Vocabolario degli Accademici della Crusca* (Venice, 1612), p. 156, offers this as its leading definition: "CAPRICCIO, quel tremore, che scorre per le carni, o per orrore di che sia, che ti fa arricciare i peli, o per febbre sopravvegnente. Lat. *horror*." And this remains essentially unchanged in later editions. On this dimension of the term, see Omar Calabrese, "Breve semantica del capriccio," in *Il capriccio nell'incisione francese del Seicento e del Settecento*, ed. Philippe Morel and Cesare Nissirio (Rome, 1982), pp. 14–15.
19. For Cennini's observation, see Chapter Two.
20. Cf., e.g., Filippo Baldinucci, *Vocabolario toscano dell'arte del disegno* (Florence, 1681), p. 78:

 Inventare. Essere il primo autore che sia, fare ritrovamenti.

 Inventiva f. Invenzione, ed è quello che noi diciamo propriamente, trovato. Lat. *Inventum, inventio.*

 Inventore m. Che inventa, che è autore di cosa inventata. Lat. *Inventor, author.*

21. Baldinucci takes this definition directly from the *Vocabolario degli Accademici della Crusca*, p. 320. In 1505, to describe Giovanni Bellini's creative imagining, Pietro Bembo used just such a vocabulary: "uso come dice di sempre vagare a sua voglia nelle pitture" (Rona Goffen, *Giovanni Bellini* [New Haven and London, 1989], p. 268, doc. 49).
22. See Chapter One, note 12.
23. Giorgio Vasari, *Le vite de' più eccellenti pittori, scultori ed architettori*, ed. Gaetano Milanesi (Florence, 1878–85), V, pp. 402–3. Vasari's use of the term has been surveyed by Alice Rathé, "Le *Capriccio* dans les écrits de Vasari," *Italica* 57 (1980): 239–54.
24. Prese assunto come cervello capriccioso ch'egli era, di fare carte stampate intagliate sul ferro e sul rame con acqua forte, et ancora di chiaro scuro se ne vede di suo in legno molte, come ancora di bulino intagliate per mano del Caralio, dilettandosi egli non meno de 'l disegno, che si facesse del colorito. (Giorgio Vasari, *Le vite de' più eccellenti architetti, pittori, et scultori italiani . . .* [1550], ed. Luciano Bellosi and Aldo Rossi [Turin, 1986], p. 798)
25. Giovanni Andrea Gilio, *Dialogo secondo . . . nel quale si ragiona de gli errori, e de gli abusi de' pittori . . .* (Camerino, 1564), p. 95v, condemns Michelangelo, who "più del capriccio dell'arte che del vero s'è compiaciuto." Chiding artists for disobeying Horace's injunctions against grotesque unnatural combinations – precisely the exercises claimed for the painter's imagination by Cennini – Gilio condemns such "disonanze" created "con pretesto de la poetica licenza" for such images "saranno regolate dal capriccio, che da la ragione, de le cose naturali de le quali l'arte è scimia" (p. 77). Cf. the opening of Horace's *Ars poetica*, quoted in Chapter Two, note 18.
26. Cesare Ripa, *Iconologia overo descrittione di diverse imagini cavate dall'antichità, & di propria inventione* (Rome, 1603), p. 48: "Capricciosi si dimandano quelli, che con Idee dall'ordinarie de gl'altri huomini diverse, fanno pendere le proprie attioni, ma con la mobiltà dall'una all'altra pur del medesimo genere, & per modo d'Analogia si dicono capricci le idee, che in pitture, ò in musica, ò in altro modo si manifestano lontane dal modo ordinario." The original edition of 1593 was unillustrated. For fuller discussion of the Ripa's personification, see Philipp P. Fehl, "The Capriccio in Prints," in *Capriccio: The Jest and Earnestness of Art*, exhibition catalogue (Urbana-Champaign, 1987), pp. 2–12.
27. See Louis Marin, "Il capriccio: A partir des Caprices de Saint Amant et de Jacques Callot," in *Il capriccio nell'incisione francese*, ed. Morel and Nissirio, pp. 17–23. For further discussion of the concept and its implications, see as well the essays in *Das* Capriccio *als Kunstprinzip*, ed. Rees, esp. Werner Hofmann, "Das Capriccio als Kunstprinzip," pp. 23–33, and Ekkehard Mai, "Phantasie, Invention, Capriccio-kunsttheoretische Splitter und Randbemerkungen zu einem grossen Thema," pp. 35–53.
28. Erich Schwandt, "Capriccio," in *The New Grove Dictionary of Music and Musicians* (London, 1980), III, pp. 758–59. The term was evidently first used for pieces of music in Jacquet de Berchem's set of madrigals on Ariosto's *Orlando furioso* (Venice, 1561); another early example is Giovanni Croce's *Triaca musicale* ("musical cure for animal bites") (Venice, 1595). For further discussion, see Peter Schleuning, "'Ungewöhnliche Gänge, versteckte Zierrathen, sinnreiche Drehungen und Verbrämungen.' Das Capriccio in der Musik," in *Das* Capriccio *als Kunstprinzip*, ed. Rees, pp. 179–85.
29. On "Fantasia" in music, see the articles by Christo-

i Capricci?" in *Giambattista Tiepolo nel terzo centenario della nascita* (Atti del convegno internazionale di studi), ed. Lionello Puppi (Venice, 1998), pp. 39–41.

42. Only the more or less contemporary cavalier (De Vesme 12; Rizzi 38; Russell, *Rare Etchings,* no. 10) seems out of place, although such military characters, soldiers and brigands, make up part of that same graphic legacy.
43. George Knox, *Catalogue of the Tiepolo Drawings in the Victoria and Albert Museum* (London, 1960), nos. 106, 107; Russell, *Rare Etchings,* pp. 20–21.
44. Detlev von Hadeln, *Handzeichnungen von G. B. Tiepolo* (Leipzig, 1927), figs. 175–85.
45. The most sustained effort at a consistent interpretation is that of Charles Dempsey, "Tiepolo Etchings at Washington," *Burlington Magazine* 114 (1972): 503–7, who sought to locate these images rather (too) precisely within a culture of magic and magicians.
46. Francesco Algarotti, *Opere,* VIII (Venice, 1792), p. 191. On these drawings, see George Knox, "The Punchinello Drawings of Giambattista Tiepolo," in *Interpretazioni veneziane: Studi di storia dell'arte in onore di Michelangelo Muraro,* ed. David Rosand (Venice, 1984), pp. 439–46.
47. See Russell, *Rare Etchings,* nos. 42–57.
48. Ibid., nos. 59–92.
49. Basic studies of Domenico include James Byam Shaw, *The Drawings of Domenico Tiepolo* (London, 1962), and Adriano Mariuz, *Giandomenico Tiepolo* (Milan, 1971). See also Adelheid M. Gealt and George Knox, *Domenico Tiepolo, Master Draftsman,* exhibition catalogue (Milan, 1996), and Linda Wolk-Simon, *Domenico Tiepolo: Drawings, Prints, and Paintings in The Metropolitan Museum of Art* (*Metropolitan Museum of Art Bulletin* 54 [Winter 1996/97]).
50. On these drawings in particular, see Byam Shaw, *The Drawings of Domenico Tiepolo,* pp. 52–59, and Marcia E. Vetrocq and Adelheid M. Gealt, *Domenico Tiepolo's Punchinello Drawings,* exhibition catalogue (Bloomington, 1979); the drawings themselves are well illustrated in the beautifully produced volume by Adelheid M. Gealt, *Domenico Tiepolo: The Punchinello Drawings* (New York and London, 1986). In addition, see George Knox, "Domenico Tiepolo's Punchinello Drawings: Satire, or Labor of Love?" in *Satire in the Eighteenth Century,* ed. J. D. Browning (New York, 1982), pp. 124–46; Philipp P. Fehl, "Farewell to Jokes: The Last *Capricci* of Giovanni Domenico Tiepolo and the Tradition of Irony in Venetian Painting," *Critical Inquiry* 5 (1979): 761–91 (reprinted in his *Decorum and Wit: The Poetry of Venetian Painting* [Vienna, 1992], pp. 330–48), and, most recently, Gealt and Knox, *Domenico Tiepolo: Master Draftsman,* nos. 155–176.
51. Gealt, *Domenico Tiepolo: The Punchinello Drawings,* no. 87 (present location unknown).
52. Ibid., no. 59; Gealt and Knox, *Domenico Tiepolo: Master Draftsman,* no. 171 (Boston, Collection Jeffrey E. Horvitz).
53. Gealt, *Domenico Tiepolo: The Punchinello Drawings,* no. 90 (present location unknown).
54. Ibid., no. 64 (private collection).
55. Ibid., no. 55 (private collection).

EPILOGUE

1. Tristan Tzara, "Picasso et la connaissance de l'espace," *Artès* 3–4 (1947–48): 3, trans. P. S. Falla, in Marilyn McCully, ed., *A Picasso Anthology: Documents, Criticism, Reminiscences* (Princeton, 1982), p. 233.
2. Sarah Stein's notes (1908), in Jack Flam, ed., *Matisse on Art,* rev. ed. (Berkeley and Los Angeles, 1995), p. 48.
3. Paul Klee, *Pedagogical Sketchbook* (1925), trans. Sibyl Maholy-Nagy (London, 1953); Wassily Kandinsky, *Point and Line to Plane* (1926), trans. Howard Dearstyne and Hilla Rebay (New York, 1947).
4. Dore Ashton, ed., *Picasso on Art: A Selection of Views* (New York, 1972), p. 164; originally published in Gyula H. Brassaï, *Picasso and Company* (New York, 1966), p. 56. This is the conclusion to an observation on Matisse:

   > Matisse makes a drawing, then he makes a copy of it. He recopies it five times, ten times, always clarifying the line. He's convinced that the last, the most stripped down, is the best the purest, the definitive one; and in fact, most of the time, it was the first. In drawing, nothing is better than the first attempt.

5. All this is recounted by Roland Penrose, *Picasso: His Life and Work* (1958), 2d ed. (New York, 1962), pp. 25–26:

   > One passion above all dominated Pablo from infancy. His mother was fond of telling how the first noise he learned to make, 'piz, piz,' was an imperative demand for 'la piz,' a pencil. For hours he would sit happily drawing spirals, which he managed to explain were a symbol for a kind of sugar called 'torruella,' a word formed from a verb which means to bewilder or entangle. He could draw long before he could speak, and many of his first pictures took their ephemeral shape in the sand where children played in the Plaza de la Merced.

   The larger implications of this juvenilia, especially in relation to nineteenth-century studies of children's drawings, are explored by Natasha Staller, "Early Picasso and the Origins of Cubism," *Arts Magazine* 61 (September 1986): 80–91.
6. Penrose, *Picasso,* p. 275.
7. Juan-Eduardo Cirlot, *Picasso: Birth of a Genius* (New York and Washington, 1972), no. 594.
8. For a sensitive reading of this drawing and its place within the young artist's graphic efforts, see Staller, "Early Picasso," p. 87.

9. In my opinion to search means nothing in painting. To find is the thing. Nobody is interested in following a man who, with his eyes fixed on the ground, spends his life looking for the pocketbook that fortune should put in his path. The one who finds something no matter what it might be, even if his intention were not to search for it, at least arouses our curiosity, if not our admiration. (Statement to Marius de Zayas [1923], in Ashton, ed., *Picasso on Art*, p. 3)

10. Ashton, ed., *Picasso on Art*, p. 107; originally in Brassaï, *Picasso and Company*, p. 55. The full comment reads: "Ideas are just simple points of departure. It's rare for me to be able to pinpoint them, just as they came into my mind. As soon as I set to work, others seem to flow from the pen. To know what you want to draw, you have to begin drawing it."
11. The most clearly documented sources are the publications of Charles Bargue and J. L. Gérome, *Cours de dessin* (Paris, 1868–1870), and Bargue's *Exercices au fusain pour préparer l'étude de l'académie d'après nature* (Paris, 1871). I owe my knowledge of these sources and their significance for Picasso's early development, as well as for aspects of cubism, to an unpublished study by Ronald Watson, "Drawing about the Art of Drawing: Academic Sources of Picasso's Late Cubism," presented in a NEH Summer Seminar in 1991. Irving Lavin has explored the implications of this material in the larger context of Picasso's relationship to earlier models of graphic pedagogy, including Dürer, in "Picasso's Lithograph(s) 'The Bull(s)' and the History of Art in Reverse," in *Past-Present: Essays on Historicism in Art from Donatello to Picasso* (Berkeley, Los Angeles, Oxford, 1993), pp. 203–61. For still broader discussion of the artist's early academic training, see Natasha Staller, "Gods of Art: Picasso's Academic Education and Its Legacy," in *Picasso: The Early Years, 1892–1906*, ed. Marilyn McCully, exhibition catalogue (New Haven and London, 1997), pp. 67–85.
12. Statement by Picasso (1923), in Alfred H. Barr, Jr., *Picasso: Fifty Years of His Art* (New York, 1946), p. 270.
13. Picasso's statement continues, "Drawing, design and color are understood and practiced in cubism in the spirit and manner that they are understood and practiced in all other schools" (Barr, *Picasso*, p. 271).
14. This dialectic is tested most aggressively and complexly in Picasso's early collages, in which the pasted paper so radically inflects the ground itself, simultaneously affirming and transforming surface. It is the introduction of collage that most seriously threatens to break the ties with pictorial representation and thrust the artist into still new, uncharted territory. The significance of this anxious situation is beautifully read by Rosalind E. Krauss, *The Picasso Papers* (New York, 1998).
15. As Rosalind Krauss observes, "with Picasso's neoclassicism, art becomes the *representational* content of art" (*The Picasso Papers*, p. 19). She views this phenomenon under the rubric of "pastiche," a particularly charged form of eclecticism. As a retreat from the consequences and implications of his own Cubist invention, Picasso's recourse to art-historical models is diagnosed a symptom of profound anxiety in response to the threat of modernist abstraction. Krauss invokes the psychoanalytic concept of reaction formation to describe that response, a transformational system the symptoms of which dialectically accommodate the threatening instinct by inversion. The psychodynamic model does indeed seem appropriate to the complexity of Picasso's volte-face. Krauss's analysis of Picasso's classical line sets it in competitive relation to the deliberately mechanical line of Picabia. However superficially similar the resulting linearity, the very ambition of Picasso's draftsmanship – its art-historical reach, the inflectional variety of his line and the visible manual work of its production – seems to me, rather, self-consciously to distinguish it from such mechanomorphic modernism.
16. "Just as his drawings in the drawer were all in black pencil, the original realistic painting was not in color and the majority of the successive studies were in black and white. To Picasso, form and line are all important. He even exclaimed, 'Color weakens.'" Alexander Liberman, "Picasso," *Vogue* (November 1, 1956): 132–34ff., in Ashton, ed., *Picasso on Art*, p. 89. On the problem of color and Cubism, see Krauss, *The Picasso Papers*, passim.
17. Quoted by Hans Bolliger, *Picasso's Vollard Suite* (New York, 1977), p. xii, from Daniel-Henry Kahnweiler, "Huit entretiens avec Picasso," *Le Point* 7 (October 1952): 22–30. For the fuller contexts of the *Vollard Suite*, see Lisa Florman, *Myth and Metamorphosis: Picasso's Classical Prints* (Cambridge, Mass., and London, 2000).
18. Ashton, ed., *Picasso on Art*, p. 43; originally quoted by Roland Penrose, *Homage to Picasso on His 70th Birthday* (London, 1951).
19. On "Picasso's Sleepwatchers," see the sensitive essay by Leo Steinberg, in *Other Criteria: Confrontations with Twentieth-Century Art* (London, Oxford, New York, 1972), pp. 93–114, the concluding sentence of which speaks directly to our theme: "For the flat picture surface is his whole working world, and Picasso reclaims it continually by projecting watchers and sleepers as the living coordinates of his realm."
20. Quoted by Roberto Otero, *Forever Picasso: An Intimate Look at his Last Years* (New York, 1974), p. 170. On the old Picasso's imaginative projections, see Gert Schiff, "The Musketeer and His *Theatrum Mundi*," introduction to *Picasso: The Last Years, 1963–1973*, exhibition catalogue (New York, 1983).
21. On the vexed question of biography and the artist-in-the-work, see the cautionary comments of Krauss, *The Picasso Papers*, pp. 213–41 ("Dime Novels").

Bibliography of Works Cited

Ackerman, James S. "Leonardo's Eye," *Journal of the Warburg and Courtauld Institutes* 41 (1978): 108–46; reprinted in *Distant Points: Essays in Theory and Renaissance Art and Architecture* (Cambridge, Mass., and London, 1991), pp. 97–150.

Agoston, Laura Camille. "Sonnet, Sculpture, Death: The Mediums of Michelangelo's Self-Imaging," *Art History* 20 (1997): 534–56.

Akker, Paul van den. *Sporen van vaardigheid: De ontewerpmethode voor de figuurhouding in de Italiaanse tekenkunst van de renaissance* (Abcoude, 1991).

"'Out of Disegno Invention is Born' – Drawing a Convincing Figure in Renaissance Italian Art," *Argumentation* 7 (1993): 45–66.

Alberici, Clelia, et al. *Leonardo e l'incisione: Stampe derivate da Leonardo e Bramante dal XV al XIX secolo* (Milan, 1984).

Alberti, Leon Battista. *La pittura di Leonbattista Alberti*, trans. Lodovico Domenichi (Venice, 1547).

On Painting, trans. John R. Spencer, rev. ed. (New Haven, 1966).

On Painting and On Sculpture: The Latin Texts of De Pictura *and* De Statua, trans. Cecil Grayson (London, 1972).

De Pictura, ed. Cecil Grayson (Rome and Bari, 1975).

Algarotti, Francesco. *Opere*, 17 vols. (Venice, 1791–94).

Alpers, Svetlana. *Rembrandt's Enterprise: The Studio and the Market* (Chicago and London, 1988).

Alpers, Svetlana, and Michael Baxandall. *Tiepolo and the Pictorial Intelligence* (New Haven and London, 1994).

Ames-Lewis, Francis. *Drawing in Early Renaissance Italy* (New Haven and London, 1981).

"Leonardo da Vinci's 'Kneeling Leda': The Evolution of an Expressive Figure Composition," *Drawing* 9 (Nov.–Dec. 1989): 73–76.

Ames-Lewis, Francis, and Anka Bednarek, eds. *Nine Lectures on Leonardo da Vinci* (London, n.d.).

Ames-Lewis, Francis, and Joanne Wright. *Drawing in the Italian Workshop* (London, 1983).

Amornpichetkul, Chittima. "Seventeenth-Century Italian Drawing Books: Their Origin and Development," in *Children of Mercury: The Education of Artists in the Sixteenth and Seventeenth Centuries* (Providence, 1984), pp. 109–18.

Anderson, Jaynie. "A Further Inventory of Gabriele Vendramin's Collection," *Burlington Magazine* 121 (1979): 639–48.

Anzelewsky, Fedja. *Dürer: His Art and Life* (Fribourg, 1980).

Arasse, Daniel. "Raffaello senza venustà e l'eredità della grazia," in *Studi su Raffaello, Atti del Congresso Internazionale di Studi*, ed. Micaela Sambucco Hamoud and Maria Letizia Strocchi (Urbino, 1987), pp. 703–14.

Léonard de Vinci: Le rythme du monde (Paris, 1997).

Aristotle. *The Complete Works of Aristotle: The Revised Oxford Translation*, ed. Jonathan Barnes, 2 vols. (Princeton, 1984).

Armenini, Giovanni Battista. *De' veri precetti della pittura* (1587), ed. Marina Gorreri (Turin, 1988); trans. Edward J. Olszewski, *On the True Precepts of the Art of Painting* (New York, 1977).

Aronberg, Marilyn. "A New Facet of Leonardo's Working Procedure," *Art Bulletin* 33 (1951): 235–39.

Arrighi, Ludovico degli. *La Operina di Ludovico Vicentino da imparare di scrivere littera cancellaresca* (Rome, 1522).

Il modo de temperare le penne con le varie sorti de littere ordinato per Ludovico Vicentino (Rome, 1523).

Ashton, Dore, ed. *Picasso on Art: A Selection of Views* (New York, 1972).

Bal, Mieke. *Reading "Rembrandt": Beyond the Word–Image Opposition* (Cambridge, 1991).

Baldinucci, Filippo. *Vocabolario toscano dell'arte del disegno* (Florence, 1681).

Vita di Gian Lorenzo Bernini (1682), ed. Sergio Samek Ludovici (Milan, 1948).

Bambach Cappel, Carmen. "Michelangelo's Cartoon for the *Crucifixion of St. Peter* Reconsidered," *Master Drawings* 25 (1987): 131–41.

"The Tradition of Pouncing Drawings in the Italian Renaissance Workshop: Innovation and Derivation," Ph.D. dissertation (Yale University, 1988).

Review of Michael Hirst, *Michelangelo and His Drawings*, in *Art Bulletin* 73 (1990): 171–73.

"Leonardo, Tagliente, and Dürer: 'La scienza del far di groppi,'" *Achademia Leonardi Vinci: Journal of Leonardo Studies* 4 (1991): 72–98.

Drawing and Painting in the Italian Renaissance Workshop: Theory and Practice, 1300–1600 (Cambridge, New York, Melbourne, 1999).

Barkan, Leonard. *Transuming Passion: Ganymede and the Erotics of Humanism* (Stanford, 1991).

Barocchi, Paola. *Michelangelo e la sua scuola: I disegni di Casa Buonarroti e degli Uffizi* (Florence, 1962).

Barocchi, Paola, ed. *Scritti d'arte del Cinquecento*, 3 vols. (Milan and Naples, 1971–77).

Trattati d'arte del Cinquecento, I (Bari, 1960).

Barocchi, Paola, and Renzo Ristori, eds. *Il carteggio di Michelangelo*, 5 vols. (Florence, 1965–83).

Barr, Alfred H., Jr. *Picasso: Fifty Years of His Art* (New York, 1946).

Matisse: His Art and His Public (New York, 1951).

Barthes, Roland. Preface to Roger Duret and Herman Grégoire, *La civilization de l'écriture* (Paris, 1976).

Barzman, Karen-Edis. *The Florentine Academy and the Early Modern State: The Discipline of* Disegno (Cambridge and New York, 2000).

Battaglia, Roberta. "Le 'Diverse maniere d'adornare i camini . . .' di Giovanni Battista Piranesi: Gusto e cultura antiquaria," *Saggi e memorie di storia dell'arte* 19 (1994): 191–273.

Baxandall, Michael. *Giotto and the Orators: Humanist Observers of Painting in Italy and the Discovery of Pictorial Composition 1350–1450* (Oxford, 1971).

Painting and Experience in Fifteenth-Century Italy: A Primer in the Social History of Pictorial Style (Oxford, 1972).

"English *Disegno*," in *England and the Continental Renaissance*, ed. Edward Chaney and Peter Mack (Woodbridge, 1990), pp. 203–14.

See Alpers, Svetlana, and Baxandall.

Beck, James. "Leonardo's Rapport with His Father," *Antichità viva* 17, nos. 5–6 (1988): 5–12.

Beck, James, ed. *Raphael before Rome* (National Gallery of Art, *Studies in the History of Art* 17) (Washington, 1986).

Bednarek, Anka. See Ames-Lewis, Francis, and Bednarek.

Bellori, Giovanni Pietro. *Le vite de' pittori, scultori e architetti moderni* (Rome, 1672).

Beltrami, Luca. *La "destra mano" di Leonardo da Vinci e le lacune nella edizione del Codice Atlantico* (*Analecta Ambrosiana*, II) (Milan and Rome, 1919).

Benesch, Otto. *Rembrandt as Draughtsman* (London, 1960).

The Drawings of Rembrandt, enlarged ed. by Eva Benesch, 6 vols. (London, 1973).

Benson, John Howard. *The First Writing Book: An English Translation and Facsimile of Arrighi's Operina* (New Haven and London, 1954).

Berenson, Bernhard. *The Drawings of the Florentine Painters*, 3 vols. (Chicago, 1938).

Berger, Harry, Jr. *Fictions of the Pose: Rembrandt against the Italian Renaissance* (Stanford, 2000).

Bernini, Domenico. *Vita del Cavalier Gio. Lorenzo Bernini* (Rome, 1713).

Bettagno, Alessandro, et al. *Piranesi: Incisioni-rami-legature-architetture* (Vicenza, 1978).

"Una data per i Capricci?" in *Giambattista Tiepolo nel terzo centenario della nascita, Atti del Convegno Internazionale di Studi*, ed. Lionello Puppi (Venice, 1998), pp. 39–41.

Bevers, Holm, Peter Schatborn, and Barbara Welzel. *Rembrandt: The Master and His Workshop – Drawings and Etchings* (New Haven and London, 1991).

Bialostocki, Jan. "Renaissance Artists as Philosophers in Meditation: Two Small Problems Concerning Two Great Masters," *Acta historiae artium* 24 (1978): 207–10.

Bianchi-Bandinelli, R. "Piccoli problemi da resolvere, I. Parrasio: Linea spazio volume," *Critica d'arte* 3 (1939): 4–11.

Billeter, Jean François. *The Chinese Art of Writing*, trans. Jean-Marie Clarke and Michael Taylor (New York, 1990).

Blunt, Anthony. *The Drawings of Poussin* (New Haven and London, 1979).

Bober, Phyllis Pray, and Ruth Rubinstein. *Renaissance Artists and Antique Sculpture: A Handbook of Sources* (New York, 1986).

Bohlin, Diane DeGrazia. *Prints and Related Drawings by the Carracci Family: A Catalogue Raisonné* (Washington, 1979).

Böhm, Gottfried, and Helmut Pfotenhauer, eds. *Beschreibungskunst-Kunstbeschreibung: Ekphrasis von der Antike bis zur Gegenwart* (Munich, 1995).

Bois, Yve-Alain. *Painting as Model* (Cambridge, Mass., and London, 1990).

Bolten, J. "Ut Grammatica Pictura: A Method of Learning," in *Ars Auro Prior: Studia Ioanni Bialostocki, Sexagenario Dicata* (Warsaw, 1981), pp. 71–74.

Bolliger, Hans. *Picasso's Vollard Suite* (New York, 1977).

Boorsch, Suzanne. "Mantegna and his Printmakers," in *Andrea Mantegna*, ed. Jane Martineau (London and New York, 1992), pp. 56–66.

Borges, Jorge Luis. "The Fearful Sphere of Pascal," in *Labyrinths: Selected Stories and Other Writings*, ed. Donald A. Yates and James E. Irby (New York, 1962), pp. 189–92.

Borghini, Raffaele. *Il Riposo* (Florence, 1584).

Borsook, Eve. *The Mural Painters of Tuscany from Cimabue to Andrea del Sarto*, 2d ed. (Oxford, 1980).

Borsook, Eve, and Fiorella Superbi Gioffredi, eds. *Tecnica e stile: Esempi di pittura murale del Rinascimento italiano*, 2 vols. (Florence, 1986).

Boschloo, A. W. A. *Annibale Carracci in Bologna: Visible Reality in Art after the Council of Trent* (The Hague, 1974).

Boskovits, Miklós. "Cennino Cennini – pittore nonconformista," *Mitteilungen des Kunsthistorischen Institutes in Florenz* 17 (1973): 201–22.

Boston, Museum of Fine Arts, and Pierpont Morgan Library, New York. *Rembrandt: Experimental Etcher* (Boston, 1969).

Brassaï, Gyula H. *Picasso and Company* (New York, 1966).

Braunfels, Wolfgang. "Die 'Inventio' des Künstlers," in *Festschrift für Ludwig Heydenreich* (Munich, 1962), pp. 20–28.

Bredius, A. *Rembrandt: The Complete Edition of the Paintings*, rev. by H. Gerson (London, 1969).

Brinckmann, A. E. *Michelangelo-Zeichnungen* (Munich, 1925).

Spätwerke grosser Meister (Frankfurt am Main, 1925).

Broos, B. P. J. "The 'O' of Rembrandt," *Simiolus* 4 (1971): 150–84.

Brown, Christopher. *Dutch Landscape: The Early Years, Haarlem and Amsterdam 1590–1650* (London, 1986).

Brown, Clifford. *Isabella d'Este and Lorenzo da Pavia: Documents for the History of Art and Culture in Renaissance Mantua* (Geneva, 1982).

Brown, David Alan. *Leonardo da Vinci: Origins of a Genius* (New Haven and London, 1998).

Bruno, Vincent. *Form and Color in Greek Painting* (New York, 1977).

Bruyn, J. "On Rembrandt's Use of Studio Props and Model Drawings during the 1630s," in *Essays in Northern European Art presented to Egbert Haverkamp-Begemann* (Doornspijk, 1983), pp. 52–60.

"Towards a Scriptural Reading of Seventeenth-Century Dutch Landscape Paintings," in Peter C. Sutton, *Masters of Seventeenth-Century Dutch Landscape* (Boston, 1987), pp. 84–103.

Budny, Virginia. "The Sequence of Leonardo's Sketches for *The Madonna and Child with Saint Anne and Saint John the Baptist*," *Art Bulletin* 65 (1983): 34–50.

Buffon, Georges Louis Leclerc de. *Discours sur le style prononcé à l'Académie Française par M. de Buffon le jour de sa réception* (1753), ed. A. Noel (Paris, 1866).

Bury, Michael. "The Taste for Prints in Italy to c. 1600," *Print Quarterly* 2 (1985): 12–26.

"The 'Triumph of Christ' after Titian," *Burlington Magazine* 131 (1989): 188–97.

Busch, Werner. "Piranesis 'Carceri' und der Capriccio'Begriff im 18. Jahrhundert," *Wallfraf-Richartz Jahrbuch* 39 (1977): 210–24.

"Die graphische Gattung Capriccio-der letztlich vergebliche Versuch, die Phantasie zu kontrollieren," in *Das* Capriccio *als Kunstprinzip: Zur Vorgeschichte der Moderne von Arcimboldo und Callot bis Tiepolo und Goya*, ed. Joachim Rees (Milan, 1996), pp. 55–81.

Bustamante, Augustín. See Marías, Fernand, and Bustamante.

Butterfield, Andrew. *The Sculpture of Andrea del Verrocchio* (New Haven and London, 1997).

Büttner, Frank. "Tiepolo und die subversive Kraft des Capriccio," in *Das* Capriccio *als Kunstprinzip: Zur Vorgeschichte der Moderne von Arcimboldo und Callot bis Tiepolo und Goya*, ed. Joachim Rees (Milan, 1996), pp. 157–67.

Byam Shaw, James. *The Drawings of Domenico Tiepolo* (London, 1962).

Cafritz, Robert C. "Reverberations of Venetian Graphics in Rembrandt's Pastoral Landscapes," in Robert C. Cafritz, Lawrence Gowing, and David Rosand, *Places of Delight: The Pastoral Landscape* (Washington, 1988), pp. 131–47.

Calabrese, Omar. "Breve semantica del capriccio," in *Il capriccio nell'incisione francese del Seicento e del Settecento*, ed. Philippe Morel and Cesare Nissirio (Rome, 1982), pp. 14–15.

Calvesi, Maurizio. "Le Carceri," in *Piranesi nei luoghi di Piranesi* (Rome, 1979), pp. 7–28.

Giovan Battista Piranesi: Dispensa per il corso monografico del prof. Maurizio Calvesi (Rome, 1979–1980).

Calvi, Gerolamo. *I manoscritti di Leonardo da Vinci dal punto di vista cronologico, storico e biografico* (1925), ed. Augusto Marinoni (Busto Arsizio, 1982).

Camesasca, Ettore, ed. *Raffaello: Gli scritti – lettere, firme, sonetti, saggi tecnici e teorici* (Milan, 1993).

Carpiceci, Marco. *Leonardo allo specchio: Ritratti e autoritratti* (Brescia, 1984).

Casamassima, Emanuele. *Trattati di scrittura del Cinquecento italiano* (Milan, 1966).

Castiglione, Baldesar. *Il libro del Cortegiano* (1528), ed. Bruno Maier (Turin, 1964); trans. Charles S. Singleton, *The Book of the Courtier* (Garden City, N.Y., 1959).

Caylus, Anne-Claude-Philippe, comte de. *Vie d'artistes du XVIIIe siècle*, ed. André Fontaine (Paris, 1910).

Cennini, Cennino. *Il libro dell'arte o trattato della pittura*, ed. Fernando Tempesti (Milan, 1984); trans. Daniel V. Thompson, Jr., *The Craftsman's Handbook* (New Haven, 1933).

Chambers, David, Jane Martineau, and Rodolfo Signorini. "Mantegna and the Men of Letters," in

Andrea Mantegna, ed. Jane Martineau (London and New York, 1992), pp. 8–30.

Chapman, H. Perry. *Rembrandt Self-Portraits: A Study in Seventeenth-Century Identity* (Princeton, 1990).

Chartier, Roger, ed. *The Culture of Print: Power and the Uses of Print in Early Modern Europe* (Princeton, 1989).

Chatto, William Andrew, and John Jackson. *A Treatise on Wood Engraving, Historical and Practical,* 2d ed. (London, 1861).

Chiari Moretto Wiel, M. Agnese. *Titian Drawings* (New York, 1990).

Christiansen, Keith. "Some Observations on Mantegna's Painting Technique," in *Andrea Mantegna,* ed. Jane Martineau (London and New York, 1992), pp. 68–77.

"The Case for Mantegna as Printmaker," *Burlington Magazine* 135 (1993): 604–12.

"Rapporti presunti, probabili e (forse anche) effettivi fra Alberti e Mantegna," in *Leon Battista Alberti,* ed. Joseph Rykwert and Anne Engel (Milan, 1994), pp. 336–57.

"The Capricci," in *Giambattista Tiepolo 1696–1770,* ed. Keith Christiansen (New York, 1996), pp. 348–57.

"The Fiery Poetic Fantasy of Giambattista Tiepolo," in *Giambattista Tiepolo 1696–1770,* ed. Keith Christiansen (New York, 1996), pp. 275–91.

"The Scherzi di Fantasia," in *Giambattista Tiepolo 1696–1770,* ed. Keith Christiansen (New York, 1996), pp. 558–69.

Cianchi, Renzo. *Vinci, Leonardo e la sua famiglia* (Milan, 1952).

Ciccuto, Marcello. "Un'iscrizione di Andrea Mantegna," *Albertiana* 1 (1998): 61–79.

Cirlot, Juan-Eduardo. *Picasso: Birth of a Genius* (New York and Washington, 1972).

Clark, Kenneth. *The Drawings of Leonardo da Vinci . . . at Windsor Castle* (1935), 2d rev. ed. with the assistance of Carlo Pedretti, 3 vols. (London, 1968).

Leonardo da Vinci: An Account of His Development as an Artist (1939), rev. ed. (Baltimore, 1967).

Rembrandt and the Italian Renaissance (New York, 1964).

"Leonardo and the Antique," in *Leonardo's Legacy: An International Symposium,* ed. C. D. O'Malley (Berkeley and Los Angeles, 1969), pp. 1–34.

The Artist Grows Old (Cambridge, 1972).

Leonardo e le curve della vita (XVII Lettura Vinciana) (Florence, 1979).

Clayton, Martin. *Poussin: Works on Paper: Drawings from the Collection of Her Majesty Queen Elizabeth II* (Houston and London, 1995).

Leonardo da Vinci: A Singular Vision (New York, London, Paris, 1996).

Clough, Cecil H. "Ludovico degli Arrighi's Contact with Raphael and with Machiavelli," *Bibliografia* 75 (1973): 293–98.

"Ludovico degli Arrighi and Raphael," *Journal of the Society for Italic Handwriting* 79 (1974): 13–16.

Cocke, Richard. *Veronese's Drawings* (Ithaca, 1984).

Cogliati Arano, Luisa. *Disegni di Leonardo e della sua cerchia alle Gallerie dell'Accademia* (Milan, 1980).

Collins, Bradley. *Leonardo, Psychoanalysis, and Art History: A Critical Study of Psychobiographical Approaches to Leonardo da Vinci* (Evanston, 1997).

Condivi, Ascanio. *La vita di Michelangelo Buonarroti* (1553), ed. Paolo D'Ancona (Milan, 1928); trans. Alice Sedgwick Wohl, *The Life of Michelangelo,* ed. Helmut Wohl (Oxford, 1976).

Cook, Thomas Andrea. *The Curves of Life* (New York, 1914).

Cordellier, Dominique, ed. *Pisanello: Le peintre aux sept vertus* (Paris, 1996).

Courtright, Nicola. "Origin and Meaning of Rembrandt's Late Drawing Style," *Art Bulletin* 78 (1996): 485–510.

Cox-Rearick, Janet, et al. *Giulio Romano: Master Designer,* exhibition catalogue (New York, 1999).

Cropper, Elizabeth. "On Beautiful Women: Parmigianino, Petrarchismo and the Vernacular Style," *Art Bulletin* 58 (1976): 374–94.

"The Place of Beauty in the High Renaissance and its Displacement in the History of Art," in *Place and Displacement in the Renaissance,* ed. Alvin Vos (Binghamton, 1994), pp. 159–205.

Crusca, Accademia della. *Vocabolario degli Accademici della Crusca* (Venice, 1612; Naples, 1746).

Cumberland, George. *An Essay on the Utility of Collecting the Best Works of the Ancient Engravers of the Italian School* (London, 1827).

Curtius, Ernst Robert. *European Literature and the Latin Middle Ages,* trans. Willard R. Trask (New York, 1953).

Dalli Regoli, Gigetta. See Pedretti, Carlo, and Dalli Regoli.

Damisch, Hubert. *The Origin of Perspective,* trans. John Goodman (Cambridge, Mass., and London, 1994).

Traité du trait (Paris, 1995).

Degenhart, Bernhard. "Zur Graphologie der Handzeichnung," *Kunstgeschichtliches Jahrbuch der Bibliotheca Hertziana* 1 (1937): 223–43.

See Halm, Peter, et al.

Degenhart, Bernhard, and Annegrit Schmitt. "Gentile da Fabriano in Rom und die Anfänge des Antikenstudiums," *Münchner Jahrbuch der bildenden Kunst* 11 (1960): 59–151.

"Methoden Vasaris bei den Gestaltung seines Libro," in *Studien zur toskanischen Kunst: Festschrift für Ludwig Heydenreich,* ed. Wolfgang Lotz and Lise Lotte Moller (Munich, 1964), pp. 45–64.

Corpus der italienischen Zeichnungen 1300–1450, Part II: *Venedig,* 8 vols. (Berlin, 1980–90).

Jacopo Bellini: The Louvre Album of Drawings (New York, 1984).

Dempsey, Charles. "Tiepolo Etchings at Washington," *Burlington Magazine* 114 (1972): 503–7.

De Vesme, Alexandre. *Le peintre-graveur italien* (Milan, 1906).

Stefano della Bella (1906), ed. Phyllis Dearborn Massar (New York, 1971).

Dézallier d'Argenville, Antoine-Joseph. *Abrégé de la vie des plus fameux peintres* (1745; Paris, 1762).

Dibner, Bern. "Leonardo and the Third Dimension," in *Leonardo da Vinci e l'età della ragione*, ed. Enrico Bellone and Paolo Rossi (Milan, 1982), pp. 79–100.

Dobai, J. "William Hogarth and Antoine Parent," *Journal of the Warburg and Courtauld Institutes* 31 (1965): 336–82.

Dolce, Lodovico. *Dialogo della pittura intitolato l'Aretino* (1557), ed. Paola Barocchi, in *Trattati d'arte del Cinquecento*, I (Bari, 1960).

See Roskill, Mark W.

Doni, Antonfrancesco. *Disegno del Doni* (Florence, 1549).

Drabkin, William. See Field, Christopher D. S., Helm, and Drabkin.

Dreyer, Peter. "Tizianfälschungen des sechszehnten Jahrhunderts: Korrekturen zur Definition der Delineatio bei Tizian und Anmerkungen zur Datierung seiner Holzschnitte," *Pantheon* 38 (1979): 365–75.

Dronke, Peter. "Curtius as Medievalist and Modernist," *Times Literary Supplement* (October 30, 1980): 1104.

Dürer, Albrecht. *Dürer: Schriftlicher Nachlass*, ed. Hans Rupprich, 3 vols. (Berlin, 1956–69).

The Literary Remains of Albrecht Dürer, trans. and ed. William Martin Conway (Cambridge, 1889).

Durling, Robert M., trans. and ed., *Petrarch's Lyric Poems: The Rime Sparse and Other Lyrics* (Cambridge, Mass., and London, 1976).

Einem, Herbert von. "Zur Deutung des Altersstiles in der Kunstgeschichte," in *Album Amicorum J. G. van Gelder*, ed. J. Bruyn et al. (The Hague, 1973), pp. 88–92.

Eisenstein, Elizabeth L. *The Printing Press as an Agent of Change: Communications and Cultural Transformations in Early–Modern Europe*, 2 vols. (Cambridge, 1979).

Eisler, Colin. *The Genius of Jacopo Bellini: The Complete Paintings and Drawings* (New York, 1989).

Eissler, K. R. *Leonardo da Vinci: Psychoanalytic Notes on the Enigma* (New York, 1961).

Elderfield, John. *The Drawings of Henri Matisse* (New York, 1984).

The Language of the Body: Drawings by Pierre-Paul Prud'hon (New York, 1996).

Elen, Albert J. *Italian Late-Medieval and Renaissance Drawing-Books from Giovannino de' Grassi to Palma Giovane: A Codicological Approach* (Leiden, 1995).

Elkins, James. "Marks, Traces, *Traits*, Contours, *Orli*, and *Splendores:* Non-semiotic Elements in Pictures," *Critical Inquiry* 21 (1995): 822–60.

Emison, Patricia. "Marcantonio's *Massacre of the Innocents*," *Print Quarterly* 1 (1984): 257–67.

"The Word Made Naked in Pollaiuolo's *Battle of the Nudes*," *Art History* 13 (1990): 261–75.

"Grazia," *Renaissance Studies* 5 (1991): 427–60.

"The Singularity of Raphael's *Lucretia*," *Art History* 14 (1991): 372–96.

"The Raucousness of Mantegna's Mythological Engravings," *Gazette des Beaux-Arts* 122 (1994): 159–76.

Emmens, J. A. *Rembrandt en de regels van de kunst* (Utrecht, 1968).

Erouart, Gilbert, and Monique Mosser. "A propos de la 'Notice historique sur la vie et les ouvrages de J.-B. Piranesi': Origine et fortune d'une biographie," in *Piranèse et les français*, ed. Georges Brunel (Rome, 1978), pp. 213–56.

Fabbri, Nancy Rush. "Salvator Rosa's Engraving for Carlo de' Rossi and His Satire *Invidia*," *Journal of the Warburg and Courtauld Institutes* 33 (1970): 328–30.

Fairbank, Alfred, and Berthol Wolpe. *Renaissance Handwriting: An Anthology* (London, 1960).

Farago, Claire J. *Leonardo da Vinci's* Paragone*: A Critical Interpretation with a New Edition of the Text in the* Codex Urbinas (Leiden, 1992).

Federici, Vincenzo. *La scrittura delle cancellerie italiane dal secolo XII al XVII* (Rome, 1934).

Fehl, Philipp P. "Farewell to Jokes: The Last *Capricci* of Giovanni Domenico Tiepolo and the Tradition of Irony in Venetian Painting," *Critical Inquiry* 5 (1979): 761–91.

"The Capriccio in Prints," in *Capriccio: The Jest and Earnestness of Art* (Urbana-Champaign, 1987).

Decorum and Wit: The Poetry of Venetian Painting (Vienna, 1992).

Ferino, Sylvia, ed. *Vittoria Colonna: Dichterin und Muse Michelangelos* (Vienna, 1997).

Ferino-Pagden, Sylvia. See Knab, Eckhart, et al.

Fialetti, Odoardo. *Il vero modo et ordine per dissegnar tutte le parti et membra del corpo humano* (Venice, 1608).

Field, Christopher D. S., Eugene Helm, and William Drabkin. "Fantasia," in *The New Grove Dictionary of Music and Musicians* (London, 1980), vol. 6, pp. 380–92.

Filedt Kok, J. P., et al. *Rembrandt: Etchings and Drawings in the Rembrandt House: A Catalogue* (Maarssen, 1972).

Livelier than Life: The Master of the Amsterdam Cabinet or the Housebook Master, ca. 1470–1500 (Amsterdam, 1985).

Flam, Jack, ed. *Matisse on Art*, rev. ed. (Berkeley and Los Angeles, 1995).

Fletcher, Shelley. "A Re-evaluation of Two Mantegna Prints," *Print Quarterly* 14 (1997): 67–77.

"A Closer Look at Mantegna's Prints," *Print Quaterly* 18 (2001): 3–41.

Florman, Lisa. *Myth and Metamorphosis: Picasso's Classical Prints of the 1930s* (Cambridge, Mass., and London, 2000).

Focillon, Henri. *Giovanni Battista Piranesi* (Bologna, 1967).

Franco, Giacomo. *Modo di scrivere cancellaresco moderno . . .* (Venice, 1596).

pher D. S. Field, Eugene Helm, and William Drabkin in *The New Grove Dictionary,* VI, pp. 380–92.

30. Jules Lieure, *Jacques Callot: Catalogue raisonné de l'oeuvre gravé* (1924–27), rev. ed. (San Francisco, 1989), nos. 214–63, 428–77. See as well Henri Zerner et al., *Jacques Callot 1592–1635* (Providence, 1970), no. 9, and H. Diane Russell, *Jacques Callot: Prints and Related Drawings* (Washington, 1975), nos. 2–8.
31. Vasari, *Le vite,* ed. Milanesi, V, p. 429.
32. For the frontispieces, see Phyllis Dearborn Massar's edition of Alexandre De Vesme, *Stefano della Bella* (1906) (New York, 1971), nos. 104, 128, 258, 389, 459, 1027.
33. See Richard Wallace, *The Etchings of Salvator Rosa* (Princeton, 1979), pp. 12–36, nos. 6–90, and Nancy Rush Fabbri, "Salvator Rosa's Engraving for Carlo de' Rossi and His Satire *Invidia,*" *Journal of the Warburg and Courtauld Institutes* 33 (1970): 328–30.
34. Marianne Grivel, *Le commerce de l'estampe à Paris au XVIIe siècle* (Geneva, 1986), p. 99.
35.
> Como la mayor parte de los objetos que en esta obra se representan son ideales, no será temeridad creer que sus defectos hallarán, tal vez, mucho disculpa entre los inteligentes: considerando que el autor, ni ha seguido los exemplos de otro, ni ha podido copiar tan poco de la naturaleza. Y si el imitarla es tan dificil, como admirable quando se logra; no dexará de merecer alguna estimacion el que apartandose enteramente de ella, ha tenido que exponer á los ojos formas y actitudes que solo han existido hasta ahora en la mente humana, obscurecida y confusa por la falta de ilustracion ó acalorada con el desenfreno de las pasiones.

Goya's notice appeared in *Diario de Madrid,* February 6, 1799. See Edith Helman, *Trasmundo de Goya,* 2d ed. (Madrid, 1983), pp. 48–49. The translation, slightly modified, is from José López-Rey, *Goya's Caprichos: Beauty, Reason and Caricature* (Princeton, 1953), I, pp. 78–79. More recent literature on the *Caprichos* as a graphic project includes a number of important exhibition catalogues: Eleanor A. Sayre et al., *The Changing Image: Prints by Francisco Goya* (Boston, 1974), pp. 54–121; Janis A. Tomlinson, *Graphic Evolutions: The Print Series of Francisco Goya* (New York, 1989), pp. 11–23; Alfonso E. Pérez-Sánchez and Eleanor A. Sayre, *Goya and the Spirit of Englightenment* (Boston, 1989), pp. xcviii–civ, 84–138, and Jutta Held, "Groteske Erotik: Zu Goyas frühen Karikaturen," in *Das* Capriccio *als Kunstprinzip,* ed. Rees, pp. 169–77. For the complex issues of Goya, the Enlightenment, and Romanticism, see Janis A. Tomlinson, *Goya in the Twilight of the Enlightenment* (New Haven and London, 1992).

36. On the nocturnal imaginings of Leonardo and Dürer, see Chapter Three, note 37.
37.
> La pintura (como la poesia) escoge en lo universal lo que juzga mas a proposito para sus fines: reune en un solo personage fantastico, circunstancias y caracteres que la naturaleza presenta repartidos en muchos, y de esta convinacion, ingeniosamente dispuesta, resulta aquella felíz imitacion, por la qual adquiere un buen artifice el titulo de inventor y no de copiante servil.

38. In 1788 Schiller had written to a friend complaining of writer's block:

> The ground for your complaint seems to me to lie in the constraint imposed by your reason upon your imagination. I will make my idea more concrete by a simile. It seems a bad thing and detrimental to the creative work of the mind if Reason makes too close an examination of the ideas as they come pouring in – at the very gateway, as it were. . . . where there is a creative mind, Reason – so it seems to me – relaxes its watch upon the gates, and the ideas rush in pell-mell. . . . (Quoted by Sigmund Freud, *The Interpretation of Dreams* (1900), trans. A. A. Brill (1913; New York, 1950), p. 15)

Needless to say, the interpretation of Goya's *Caprichos,* their private and public meaning, their relation to Enlightenment reason and morality and to the Romantic irrational, their very intention have been the subject of continuing debate. Cf. the recent literature cited above, note 35.

39. The text continues: *Più hà inc. una Adorazion de Remagi.* For the added etching of the *Adoration of the Magi* and the publishing situation of Tiepolo's etchings, see H. Diane Russell, *Rare Etchings by Giovanni Battista and Giovanni Domenico Tiepolo* (Washington, 1971). See also the recent discussion by Keith Christiansen, *Giambattista Tiepolo 1696–1770,* exhibition catalogue (New York, 1996), pp. 348–69, nos. 59 and 60, as well as his essay, "The Fiery Poetic Fantasy of Giambattista Tiepolo," pp. 275–91, and the essay by Frank Büttner, "Tiepolo und die subversive Kraft des Capriccio," in *Das* Capriccio *als Kunstprinzip,* ed. Rees, pp. 157–67. The standard catalogues of Tiepolo prints are: Alexandre De Vesme, *Le peintre-graveur italien* (Milan, 1906), and Aldo Rizzi, *Le acqueforti dei Tiepolo* (Milan, 1970).
40. Russell, *Rare Etchings,* Appendices A and B, pp. 33–34. The documents were first published by Lina Christina Frerichs, "Mariette et le eaux-fortes des Tieplo," *Gazette des Beaux-Arts* 78 (1971): 233–52, and "Nouvelles sources pour la connaissance de l'activité de graveur des trois Tiepolo," *Nouvelles de l'estampe,* No. 4 (1971): 213–14.
41. Tiepolo's *Capricci* were included in Zanetti's collection of *chiaroscuri,* which were ready by 1742 but which were in preparation some twenty years earlier. Alessandro Bettagno has recently argued that Tiepolo's etchings should be dated with the latest of Zanetti's *chiaroscuri,* that is, 1739–41: "Una data per

De excellentia et nobilitate delineationis libri duo (Venice, 1611).

Freedberg, David. *Dutch Landscape Prints* (London, 1980).

"The Landscapes of Rembrandt and Constantijn Huygens: 'Eenen Lust om to sien'" (unpublished lecture, Boston Museum of Fine Arts, 12 March 1988).

Frerichs, Lina Christina. "Mariette et les eaux-fortes des Tiepolo," *Gazette des Beaux-Arts* 78 (1971): 233–52.

"Nouvelles sources pour la connaissance de l'activité de graveur des trois Tiepolo," *Nouvelles de l'estampe,* No. 4 (1971): 213–14.

Freud, Sigmund. *The Interpretation of Dreams* (1900), trans. A. A. Brill (1913; New York, 1950).

Eine Kindheitserinnerung des Leonardo da Vinci (Vienna, 1910).

Leonardo da Vinci and a Memory of His Childhood (1910), trans. Alan Tyson (New York, 1964).

Friedländer, Max J. *On Art and Connoisseurship,* trans. Tancred Borenius (London, 1942).

Der Holzschnitt, 4th ed. (Berlin, 1970).

Friesen, E. "Leonardo da Vinci's Unorthodox Iconography: The *Madonna with the Cat,*" *RACAR* 16 (1989): 78–80.

Frommel, Christoph Luitpold. *Michelangelo und Tommaso dei Cavalieri* (Amsterdam, 1979).

Furetière, Antoine. *Dictionnaire universel, contenant généralement tous les mots français tant vieux que modernes et les termes de toutes les sciences et des arts,* 3 vols. (The Hague and Rotterdam, 1690).

Gantner, Joseph. *Leonardos Visionen von der Sintflut und vom Untergang der Welt* (Berne, 1958).

"Der alte Künstler," in *Festschrift für Herbert von Einem,* ed. Gert von der Osten and Georg Kauffman (Berlin, 1965), pp. 71–76.

Garin, Eugenio. *L'Educazione umanistica in Italia* (Bari, 1959).

Gauricus, Pomponius. *De Sculptura* (1504), ed. André Chastel and Robert Klein (Paris and Geneva, 1969).

Gealt, Adelheid M. *Domenico Tiepolo: The Punchinello Drawings* (New York and London, 1986).

Gealt, Adelheid M., and George Knox. *Domenico Tiepolo, Master Draftsman* (Milan, 1996).

See Vetrocq, Marcia E., and Gealt.

Gere, J. A. *Drawings by Michelangelo . . . at Windsor Castle, The Ashmolean Museum, The British Museum and other English Collections,* exhibition catalogue (London, 1975).

Drawings by Michelangelo from the British Museum, exhibition catalogue (New York, 1979).

See Pouncey, Philip, and Gere.

Ghiberti, Lorenzo. *I Commentari (Biblioteca Nazionale Centrale di Firenze, II,I, 333),* ed. Lorenzo Bartoli (Florence, 1998).

Giannotti, Donato. *Dialoghi di Donato Giannotti de' giorni che Dante consumò nel cercare l'Inferno e 'l Purgatorio* (1545), ed. Deoclecio Redig de Campos (Florence, 1939).

Gibson, Walter S. *"Mirror of the Earth": The World Landscape in Sixteenth-Century Flemish Painting* (Princeton, 1989).

Gibson-Wood, Carol. "Studies in the Theory of Connoisseurship from Vasari to Morelli," Ph.D. dissertation (Warburg Institute, University of London, 1982).

"Jonathan Richardson and the Rationalization of Connoisseurship," *Art History* 7 (1984): 38–56.

Giedion, S. *The Eternal Present: The Beginnings of Art* (New York, 1962).

"The Outline in the Early Beginnings of Art," *Leonardo* 2 (1968): 181–92.

Gilbert, Creighton E. "Antique Frameworks for Renaissance Art Theory: Alberti and Pino," *Marsyas* 3 (1943–45): 87–106.

Gilio, Giovanni Andrea. *Due dialogi* (Camerino, 1564).

Gilman, Sander L. "Leonardo Sees Him-Self: Reading Leonardo's First Representation of Human Sexuality," *Social Research* 54 (1987): 149–71.

Giltaij, Jeroen. *The Drawings by Rembrandt and His School in the Museum Boymans-van Beuningen* (Rotterdam, 1988).

Gioffredi, Fiorella Superbi. See Borsook, Eve, and Gioffredi.

Giovio, Paolo. "Raphaelis Urbinatis vita," ed. Paola Barocchi, in *Scritti d'arte del Cinquecento,* I (Milan and Naples, 1971), pp. 13–18.

Girardi, Enzo Noé. *Michelangelo Buonarroti: Rime* (Bari, 1960).

Goffen, Rona. *Giovanni Bellini* (New Haven and London, 1989).

Golzio, Vincenzo. *Raffaello nei documenti, nelle testimonianze dei contemporanei e nella letteratura del suo secolo* (Vatican City, 1936).

Gombrich, E. H. *Art and Illusion: A Study in the Psychology of Pictorial Representation* (New York, 1960).

"The Debate on Primitivism in the Art of the Renaissance," *Journal of the Warburg and Courtauld Institutes* 29 (1966): 24–38.

Norm and Form: Studies in the Art of the Renaissance (London, 1966).

"Style," in *International Encyclopedia of the Social Sciences,* vol. 15 (1968), pp. 352–61.

The Heritage of Apelles: Studies in the Art of the Renaissance (Ithaca, 1976).

Graham, John. *System and Dialectics of Art,* ed. Marcia Epstein Allentuck (Baltimore and London, 1971).

Green, André. *Révélations de l'inachèvement: A propos du carton de Londres de Léonard de Vinci* (Paris, 1992).

Greenstein, Jack. *Mantegna and Painting as Historical Narrative* (Chicago and London, 1992).

Grendler, Paul F. *Schooling in Renaissance Italy: Literacy and Learning, 1300–1600* (Baltimore and London, 1989).

Griffiths, Antony. *Prints and Printmaking: An Introduction to the History and Techniques* (London, 1980).

Grivel, Marianne. *Le commerce de l'estampe à Paris au XVIIe siècle* (Geneva, 1986).

Gronau, Georg. "Die Kunstbestrebungen der Herzöge von Urbino, II: Michelangelo," *Jahrbuch der Kgl. Preussischen Kunstsammlungen* 27 (1906), Beiheft.

Hadeln, Detlev von. *Handzeichnungen von G. B. Tiepolo* (Leipzig, 1927).

Hager, Serafina, ed. *Leonardo, Michelangelo, and Raphael in Renaissance Florence from 1500 to 1508* (Washington, 1992).

Hall, Michael. *Reconsiderations of Sculpture by Leonardo da Vinci: A Bronze Statuette in the J. B. Speed Art Museum* (*J. B. Speed Art Museum Bulletin* 29) (Louisville, 1973).

Halm, Peter, Bernhard Degenhart, and Wolfgang Wegner. *Hundert Meisterzeichnungen aus der Staatlichen Graphischen Sammlung München* (Munich, 1958).

Hartt, Frederick. *Michelangelo Drawings* (New York, 1970).

Haverkamp-Begemann. "Rembrandt as a Draftsman: The Changing Image, 1956–1988," *Master Drawings* 27 (1989): 105–10.

Hay, John. "Surface and the Chinese Painter: The Discovery of Surface," *Archives of Asian Art* 38 (1985): 95–123.

Haydock, Richard. *A Tracte containing the Artes of curious Painting Carvinge and Building written first in Italian by Jo: Paul Lomatius painter of Milan* (Oxford, 1598).

Held, Julius S. *Rubens: Selected Drawings*, 2 vols. (London, 1959).

"The Early Appreciation of Drawings," in *Studies in Western Art*, III: *Latin American Art and the Baroque Period in Europe* (Acts of the Twentieth International Congress of the History of Art) (Princeton, 1963), pp. 72–95.

"Commentary [on Old-Age Style]," *Art Journal* 46 (1987): 127–33.

Rembrandt Studies (Princeton, 1991).

Held, Jutta. "Groteske Erotik: Zu Goyas frühen Karikaturen," in *Das* Capriccio *als Kunstprinzip: Zur Vorgeschichte der Moderne von Arcimboldo und Callot bis Tiepolo und Goya*, ed. Joachim Rees (Milan, 1996), pp. 169–77.

Hell, Hans. "Die späten Handzeichnungen Rembrandts," *Repertorium für Kunstwissenschaft* 51 (1930): 4–43, 92–136.

Helm, Eugene. See Field, Christopher D. S., et al.

Helman, Edith. *Trasmundo de Goya*, 2d ed. (Madrid, 1983).

Henninger, S. K., Jr. *The Cosmological Glass: Renaissance Diagrams of the Universe* (San Marino, Calif., 1977).

Heydenreich, Ludwig H. *Leonardo da Vinci* (London, New York, Basel, 1954).

Hind, A. M. *An Introduction to a History of Woodcut*, 2 vols. (London, 1935).

Early Italian Engraving, 7 vols. (London, 1938–48).

Hirst, Michael. "A Drawing of the 'Rape of Ganymede' by Michelangelo," *Burlington Magazine* 117 (1975): 166.

"A Drawing of the Rape of Ganymede by Michelangelo," in *Essays Presented to Myron P. Gilmore*, II: *History of Art, History of Music*, ed. Sergio Bertelli and Gloria Ramakus (Florence, 1978), pp. 253–60.

Michelangelo and His Drawings (New Haven and London, 1988).

Michelangelo Draftsman (Milan, 1988).

Hitchcock, H. Wiley. *Music in the United States: A Historical Introduction*, 3d ed. (Englewood Cliffs, N.J., 1988).

Hoffman, Edith. *Kokoschka: Life and Work* (London, 1947).

Hofmann, Werner. "Das Capriccio als Kunsprinzip," in *Das* Capriccio *als Kunstprinzip: Zur Vorgeschichte der Moderne von Arcimboldo und Callot bis Tiepolo und Goya*, ed. Joachim Rees (Milan, 1996), pp. 23–33.

Hogarth, William. *The Analysis of Beauty* (1753), ed. Joseph Burke (Oxford, 1955).

Hollanda, Francisco de. *De pintura antiqua* (1548), ed. A. Gonzalez Garcia (Lisbon, 1983).

Vier Gespräche über die Malerei geführt zu Rom 1538, ed. Joaquim de Vasconcellos (Vienna, 1899); trans. Aubrey F. G. Bell, *Four Dialogues on Painting* (Oxford, 1928).

Hood, William, ed. "Artists and Old Age," *Allen Memorial Art Museum Bulletin* 35 (1977–78).

Hoogstraten, Samuel van. *Inleyding tot de Hooge Schoole der Schilder-konst* (Rotterdam, 1678).

Horace. *Satires, Epistles, and Ars Poetica*, trans. H. Rushton Fairclough (Loeb Classical Library: London and New York, 1926).

Ars Poetica, trans. T. S. Dorsch, in *Classical Literary Criticism* (Harmondsworth, Baltimore, Victoria, 1965).

Houbraken, Arnold. *De Groote Schouburgh der Nederlandsche Kunstschilders en Schilderessen*, 3 vols. (Amsterdam, 1718–21).

Hunter, Dard. *Papermaking: The History and Technique of an Ancient Craft*, 2d ed. (New York, 1947).

Hutchison, Jane Campbell. *The Master of the Housebook* (New York, 1972).

Ivins, William M., Jr. *Prints and Visual Communication* (Cambridge, Mass., 1953).

Jacobs, F. H. "Vasari's Vision of the History of Painting: Frescoes in the Casa Vasari, Florence," *Art Bulletin* 66 (1984): 399–416.

Jacobsen, Michael. "The Meaning of Mantegna's *Battle of the Sea Monsters*," *Art Bulletin* 64 (1982): 623–39.

Jackson, John. See Chatto, William Andrew.

Jean, Georges. *Writing: The Story of Alphabets and Scripts*, trans. Jenny Oates (New York and London, 1992).

Jenni, Ulrike. "The Phenomena of Change in the Modelbook Tradition around 1400," in *Drawings Defined*, ed. Walter Strauss and Tracie Felker (New York, 1987), pp. 35–47.

Joannides, Paul. *The Drawings of Raphael* (Oxford, 1983).

"'Primitivism' in the Late Drawings of Michelangelo: The Master's Construction of an Old-age Style," in *Michelangelo Drawings*, ed. Craig Hugh Smyth, in collaboration with Ann Gilkerson (*Studies in the History of Art* 33) (Washington, 1992), pp. 245–61.

Michelangelo and His Influence: Drawings from Windsor Castle, exhibition catalogue (Washington and London, 1996).

Johnson, Crockett. *Harold and the Purple Crayon* (New York, 1955).

Junius, Franciscus. *The Painting of the Ancients* (1638), ed. Keith Aldrich, Philipp Fehl, and Raina Fehl, 2 vols. (Berkeley, Los Angeles, Oxford, 1991).

Kandinsky, Wassily. *Point and Line to Plane* (1926), trans. Howard Dearstyne and Hilla Rebay (New York, 1947).

Kaplan, Alice M. "Dürer's 'Raphael' Drawing Reconsidered," *Art Bulletin* 56 (1974): 50–58.

Karpinski, Caroline. "Some Woodcuts after Early Designs by Titian," *Zeitschrift für Kunstgeschichte* 39 (1976): 258–74.

"Il 'Trionfo della Fede': L' 'affresco' di Tiziano e la silografia di Lucantonio degli Uberti," *Arte Veneta* 48 (1994): 6–13.

Keele, Kenneth D. *Leonardo da Vinci's Elements of the Science of Man* (New York and London, 1983).

Keele, Kenneth D., and Jane Roberts. *Leonardo da Vinci: Anatomical Drawings from the Royal Library, Windsor Castle,* exhibition catalogue (Florence and New York, 1979).

Keele, Kenneth D., and Carlo Pedretti. *Leonardo da Vinci: Corpus of the Anatomical Studies in the Collection of Her Majesty the Queen at Windsor Castle,* 3 vols. (New York and London, 1979–80).

Kemp, Martin. "'Ogni dipintore dipinge se': A Neoplatonic Echo in Leonardo's Art Theory," in *Cultural Aspects of the Italian Renaissance: Essays in Honour of Paul Oskar Kristeller,* ed. Cecil H. Clough (New York, 1976), pp. 311–23.

"From 'Mimesis' to 'Fantasia': The Quattrocento Vocabulary of Creation, Inspiration and Genius in the Visual Arts," *Viator* 8 (1977): 347–98.

"Leonardo and the Visual Pyramid," *Journal of the Warburg and Courtauld Institutes* 40 (1977): 128–49.

Leonardo da Vinci: The Marvellous Works of Nature and Man (Cambridge, Mass., 1981).

"Late Leonardo: Problems and Implications," *Art Journal* 46 (1987): 94–102.

"'Equal excellencies': Lomazzo and the Explanation of Individual Style in the Visual Arts," *Renaissance Studies* 1 (1987): 1–26.

The Science of Art: Optical Themes in Western Art from Brunelleschi to Seurat (New Haven and London, 1990).

Leonardo da Vinci: The Mystery of the Madonna of the Yardwinder (Edinburgh, 1992).

"Coming into Line: Graphic Demonstrations of Skill in Renaissance and Baroque Engravings," in *Sight and Insight: Essays on Art and Culture in Honour of E. H. Gombrich at 85,* ed. John Onians (London, 1994), pp. 221–44.

Kemp, Martin, and Jane Roberts. *Leonardo da Vinci,* exhibition catalogue (New Haven and London, 1989).

See Smart, Alastair, and Kemp.

Kemp, Wolfgang. "Disegno: Beiträge zur Geschichte des Begriffes zwischen 1547 und 1607," *Marburger Jahrbuch für Kunstwissenschaft* 19 (1974): 219–40.

Kettering, Alison McNeil. *Drawings from the Ter Borch Studio Estate* (Catalogue of the Dutch and Flemish Drawings in the Rijksprentenkabinet, Rijksmuseum, Amsterdam) (The Hague, 1988).

Kieft, Ghislain. "Zuccari, Scaligiero e Panofsky," *Mitteilungen des Kunsthistorischen Institutes in Florenz* 33 (1989): 355–68.

Klee, Paul. *Pedagogical Sketchbook* (1925), trans. Sibyl Maholy-Nagy (London, 1953).

Knab, Eckhart, Erwin Mitsch, Konrad Oberhuber, and Sylvia Ferino-Pagden. *Raphael: Die Zeichnungen* (Stuttgart, 1983).

Knox, George. *Catalogue of the Tiepolo Drawings in the Victoria and Albert Museum* (London, 1960).

"Domenico Tiepolo's Punchinello Drawings: Satire, or Labor of Love?" in *Satire in the Eighteenth Century,* ed. J. D. Browning (New York, 1982), pp. 124–46.

"The Punchinello Drawings of Giambattista Tiepolo," in *Interpretazioni veneziane: Studi di storia dell'arte in onore di Michelangelo Muraro,* ed. David Rosand (Venice, 1984), pp. 439–46.

See Gealt, Adelheid M., and Knox.

Koerner, Joseph. "Rembrandt and the Epiphany of the Face," *Res* 12 (Autumn 1986): 5–32.

The Moment of Self-Portraiture in German Renaissance Art (Chicago and London, 1993).

Konstam, Nigel. "Rembrandt's Use of Models and Mirrors," *Burlington Magazine* 119 (1977): 94–98.

Korte, Werner. *Der Palazzo Zuccari in Rom: Sein Freskenschmuck und seine Geschichte* (Leipzig, 1935).

Krause-Zimmer, Hella. *Le problème des deux enfants Jesus et sa trace dans l'art* (Paris, 1977).

Krauss, Rosalind E. *The Picasso Papers* (New York, 1998).

Krautheimer, Richard. *Lorenzo Ghiberti,* 2d ed. (Princeton, 1970).

Kris, Ernst. *Psychoanalytic Explorations in Art* (New York, 1952).

Kris, Ernst, and Otto Kurz. *Legend, Myth, and Magic in the Image of the Artist* (1934) (New Haven and London, 1979).

Kristeller, Paul. *Andrea Mantegna* (Berlin and Leipzig, 1902).

Kurz, Otto. "Vasari's Libro de' disegni," *Old Master Drawings* 12 (1937): 1–15, 32–44.

See Kris, Ernst, and Kurz.

Kwakkelstein, Michael. "Leonardo da Vinci's Grotesque Heads and the Breaking of the Physiognomic Mould," *Journal of the Warburg and Courtauld Institutes* 54 (1991): 127–36.

Leonardo da Vinci as a Physiognomist: Theory and Drawing Practice (Leiden, 1994).

Landau, David. "Mantegna as Printmaker," in *Andrea Mantegna,* ed. Jane Martineau (London and New York, 1992), pp. 44–54.

Landau, David, and Peter Parshall. *The Renaissance Print 1470–1550* (New Haven and London, 1994).

Lavin, Irving. *Past-Present: Essays on Historicism in Art from Donatello to Picasso* (Berkeley, Los Angeles, Oxford, 1993).

Lavin, Marilyn Aronberg. "Giovannino Battista: A Study in Renaissance Religious Symbolism," *Art Bulletin* 37 (1955): 85–101.

"Giovannino Battista: A Supplement," *Art Bulletin* 43 (1961): 319–26.

Lebensztejn, Jean-Claude. *L'Art de la tache: Introduction à la* Nouvelle méthode *d'Alexander Cozens* (Paris, 1990).

Lecoq, Anne-Marie. "Apelle et Protogène: La signature-ductus," *Revue de l'art* 26 (1974): 46–47.

Legrand, J. G. *Notice historique sur la vie et les ouvrages de J. B. Piranesi architecte, peintre et graveur né à Venise en 1720 mort à Rome en 1778*, in *Piranèse et le français*, ed. Georges Brunel (Rome, 1978), pp. 221–52.

Lemakis, Emmanuel. "The Crucifixion as Pictorial Narrative: Scene-Making and the Illusion of Place and Time," Ph.D. dissertation (Columbia University, 1990).

Lenkey, Susan V. *An Unknown Leonardo Self-Portrait: Revision of the Alexander the Great Relief in the National Gallery of Art . . .* (Stanford, 1963).

Leonardo da Vinci. *I manoscritti e i disegni di Leonardo da Vinci . . .*, I: *Il codice Arundel 263* (Reale Commissione Vinciana) (Rome, 1923).

The Literary Works of Leonardo da Vinci, ed. Jean Paul Richter, 2d ed. (London, 1939).

The Notebooks of Leonardo da Vinci, trans. Edward MacCurdy (1939; New York, 1956).

Treatise on Painting [Codex Urbinas Latinus 1270], trans. A. Philip McMahon, 2 vols. (Princeton, 1956).

Il Codice Atlantico di Leonardo da Vinci (Edizione nazionale dei manoscritti e disegni di Leonardo da Vinci a cura della Commissione Vinciana), ed. Augusto Marinoni, 12 vols. (Florence and New York, 1973–80).

Manuscrit A de l'Institut de France, ed. André Corbeau and Nando de Toni (Grenoble, 1972).

See Marinoni, Augusto.

See Marinoni, Augusto, ed.

See Pedretti, Carlo.

See Pedretti, Carlo, and Gigetta Dalli Regoli.

Levenson, Jay A. "Jacopo de' Barbari and Northern Art of the Early Sixteenth Century," Ph.D. dissertation (New York University, 1978).

Levenson, Jay A., ed. *Circa 1492: Art in the Age of Exploration* (New Haven and London, 1991).

Levenson, Jay A., Konrad Oberhuber, and Jaquelyn L. Sheehan. *Early Italian Engravings from the National Gallery of Art* (Washington, 1973).

Levi, Enzo. "Leonardo precursore della scienza idraulica," in *Leonardo e l'età della ragione*, ed. Enrico Bellone and Paolo Rossi (Milan, 1982), pp. 399–419.

Liebert, Robert S. *Michelangelo: A Psychoanalytic Study of His Life and Images* (New Haven and London, 1983).

Lieure, Jules. *Jacques Callot: Catalogue raisonné de l'oeuvre gravé*, rev. ed. (San Francisco, 1989), 5 vols. (Paris, 1924–27).

Limouize, Dorothy. "Engraving and Imitation: Goltzius and His Contemporaries," *Nederlands Kunsthistorisch Jaarboeck* 42–43 (1991–92): 439–41.

Lincoln, Evelyn. "Mantegna's Culture of Line," *Art History* 16 (1993): 33–59.

López-Rey, José. *Goya's Caprichos: Beauty, Reason and Caricature* (Princeton, 1953).

Lugt, Frits. *Wandelingen met Rembrandt in en om Amsterdam* (Amsterdam, 1915); German trans. *Mit Rembrandt in Amsterdam* (Berlin, 1920).

Rembrandt, ses élèves, ses imitateurs, ses copistes (Musée du Louvre. Inventaire général des dessins des écoles du nord. Ecole hollandaise, III) (Paris, 1933).

Mahnke, Dietrich. *Unendliche Sphäre und Allmittelpunkt* (Halle-Saale, 1937).

Mai, Ekkehard, "Phantasia, Invention, Capriccio-kunsttheoretische Splitter und Randbemerkungen zu einem grossen Thema," in *Das* Capriccio *als Kunstprinzip: Zur Vorgeschichte der Moderne von Arcimboldo und Callot bis Tiepolo und Goya*, ed. Joachim Rees (Milan, 1996), pp. 35–53.

Mallarmé, Stéphane. *Oeuvres complètes* (Paris, 1966).

Malvasia, Carlo Cesare. *Felsina pittrice: Vite de' pittori bolognesi* (1678), ed. Giampietro Zanotti, 2 vols. (Bologna, 1841).

Marías, Fernand, and Agustín Bustamante. *Las ideas artísticas de El Greco (comentarios a un texto inédito)* (Madrid, 1981).

Mariette, P.-J. *Abecedario de P.-J. Mariette et autres notes inédites de cet auteur sur les arts et les artistes*, ed. Ph. de Chennevières and A. de Montaiglon, 6 vols. (Paris, 1851–60).

Marin, Louis. "Il capriccio: A partir des Caprices de Saint Amant et de Jacques Callot," in *Il capriccio nell'incisione francese del Seicento e del Settecento*, ed. Philippe Morel and Cesare Nissirio (Rome, 1982), pp. 17–23.

Marinoni, Augusto, ed. *Leonardo and Venice* (Milan, 1992).

Mariuz, Adriano. *Giandomenico Tiepolo* (Milan, 1972).

Martineau, Jane, ed. *Andrea Mantegna*, exhibition catalogue (London and New York, 1992).

See Chambers, David, et al.

Mazzariol, Giuseppe, and Terisio Pignatti. *La pianta prospettica di Venezia del 1500 disegnata da Jacopo de' Barbari* (Venice, 1963).

McCully, Marilyn, ed. *A Picasso Anthology: Documents, Criticism, Reminiscences* (Princeton, 1982).

Meder, Joseph. *Die Handzeichnung: Ihre Technik und Entwicklung*, 2d ed. (Vienna, 1923); trans. and rev. by Winslow Ames, *The Mastery of Drawing*, 2 vols. (New York, 1978).

Meiss, Millard. *The Great Age of Fresco: Discoveries, Recoveries, and Survivals* (New York, 1970).

The Painter's Choice: Problems in the Interpretation of Renaissance Art (New York, 1976).

Melion, Walter S. "Kakrel van Mander's 'Life of Goltzius': Defining the Paradigm of Protean Virtuosity in Haarlem around 1600," *Studies in the History of Art* 27 (1987): 113–33.

"Love and Artisanship in Hendrick Goltzius's *Venus,*

Bacchus and Ceres of 1606," *Art History* 16 (1993): 60–94.

Mendelsohn, Leatrice. *Paragoni: Benedetto Varchi's* Due Lezzioni *and Cinquecento Art Theory* (Ann Arbor, 1982).

Merleau-Ponty, Maurice. *Phenomenology of Perception*, trans. Colin Smith (London and Henley, 1962).

The Primacy of Perception and Other Essays, ed. James H. Edie (Evanston, 1964).

Sense and Non-Sense, trans. Hubert L. Dreyfus and Patricia Allen Dreyfus (Evanston, 1964).

Meulen, Marjon van der. See Strauss, Walter L, and van der Meulen.

Middleton, Robin. Review of Piranesi exhibitions and publications, *Journal of the Society of Architectural Historians* 41 (1982): 333–44.

Miller, Norbert. "Giovanni Battista Piranesis Entdeckung der Imagination: Das Capriccio in den Zeichnungen und Radierungen seines Frühwerks," in *Das* Capriccio *als Kunstprinzip: Zur Vorgeschichte der Moderne von Arcimboldo und Callot bis Tiepolo und Goya*, ed. Joachim Rees (Milan, 1996), pp. 141–55.

Mitsch, Erwin. See Knab, Eckhart, et al.

Moffitt, John F. "'Più tondo che l'O di Giotto': Giotto, Vasari, and Rembrandt's Kenwood House 'Self-Portrait,'" *Paragone* 35 (1984): 63–70.

"The *Evidentia* of Curling Waters and Whirling Winds: Leonardo's *Ekphraseis* of the Latin Weathermen," *Achademia Leonardi Vinci: Journal of Leonardo Studies* 4 (1991): 11–33.

Mongan, Agnes. "On Left-Handedness," in *Drawings Defined*, ed. Walter Strauss and Tracie Felker (New York, 1987), pp. 160–64.

Morel, Philippe, and Cesare Nissirio, eds. *Il capriccio nell'incisione francese del Seicento e del Settecento* (Rome, 1982).

Morelli, Giovanni. *Italian Masters in German Galleries: A Critical Essay on the Italian Pictures in the Galleries of Munich, Dresden, Berlin* (1877), trans. L. M. Richter (London, 1883).

Morgan, Michael J. *Molyneaux's Question: Vision, Touch, and the Philosophy of Perception* (Cambridge, 1977).

Mosser, Monique. See Erouart, Gilbert, and Mosser.

Muller, Jeffrey. "Rubens' Divine Circle," in *The Ringling Museum of Art Journal* (Papers presented at the International Rubens Symposium) (Sarasota, 1983), pp. 220–25.

Munsterberg, Hugo. *The Crown of Life: Artistic Creativity in Old Age* (New York, 1983).

Muraro, Michelangelo. "Giambattista Piranesi o dell'-espressione," in *Piranesi tra Venezia e l'Europa*, ed. Alessandro Bettagno (Florence, 1983), pp. 75–87.

Muraro, Michelangelo, and David Rosand. *Tiziano e la silografia veneziana del Cinquecento*, exhibition catalogue (Vicenza, 1976).

See Rosand, David, and Muraro.

Murray, Michelle. "Leonardo e Vitruvio," in *Roma, centro ideale della cultura dell'antico nei secoli XV e XVI: Da Martino V al sacco di Roma, 1417–1527*, ed. Silvia Danesi Squarzina (Milan, 1989), pp. 210–14.

Musper, H. Th. *Der Holzschnitt in fünf Jahrhunderten* (Stuttgart, 1964).

Nagel, Alexander. "Gifts for Michelangelo and Vittoria Colonna," *Art Bulletin* 79 (1997): 647–68.

Michelangelo and the Reform of Art (Cambridge, New York, and Melbourne, 2000).

Neer, Richard T. "The Lion's Eye: Imitation and Uncertainty in Attic Red-Figure," *Representations* 51 (1995): 118–53.

Nepi Scirè, Giovanna. *Restauri alle Gallerie dell'Accademia (Quaderni della Soprintendenza ai Beni Artistici e Storici di Venezia* 13) (Venice, 1987).

Nepi Scirè, Giovanna, and Pietro C. Marani, et al. *Leonardo and Venice*, exhibition catalogue (Milan, 1992).

Nichols, Lawrence W. "The 'Pen Works' of Hendrick Goltzius," *Philadelphia Museum of Art Bulletin* 88 (Winter 1992): 4–57.

Nicolson, Marjorie Hope. *The Breaking of the Circle*, rev. ed. (New York, 1960).

Nissirio, Cesare. See Morel, Philippe, and Nissiro, eds.

Oberhuber, Konrad, et al. *A Quintessence of Drawing: Masterworks from the Albertina*, exhibition catalogue (Milan, 1997).

See Knab, Eckhart, et al.

See Levenson, Jay A., et al.

Oertel, Robert. "Wandmalerei und Zeichnung in Italien: Die Anfänge der Entwurfszeichnung und ihre monumentalen Vorstufen," *Mitteilungen des Kunsthistorischen Institutes in Florenz* 6 (1940): 217–314.

"Perspective and Imagination," in *Studies in Western Art*, II: *The Renaissance and Mannersim* (Acts of the Twentieth International Congress of the History of Art) (Princeton, 1963), pp. 146–59.

Ogg, Oscar, ed. *Three Classics of Italian Calligraphy: An Unabridged Reissue of the Writing Books of Arrighi, Tagliente, Palatino* (New York, 1953).

O'Malley, Charles D., and J. B. de C. M. Saunders. *Leonardo da Vinci on the Human Body* (New York, 1952).

Osley, A. S. *Scribes and Sources: Handbook of the Chancery Hand in the Sixteenth Century* (Boston, 1980).

Ost, Hans. *Das Leonardo-Porträt in der Kgl. Bibliothek Turin und andere Fälschungen des Giuseppe Bossi* (Berlin, 1980).

Otero, Roberto. *Forever Picasso: An Intimate Look at His Last Years* (New York, 1974).

Pace, Clare. *Félibien's Life of Poussin* (London, 1981).

Paniagua, Cecilio. "Notes on a Drawing by Leonardo da Vinci," *International Review of Psycho-Analysis* 13 (1986): 445–52.

Panofsky, Erwin. *Idea: A Concept in Art* (1924; 2d ed., 1960), trans. Joseph J. S. Peake (Columbia, 1968).

Perspective as Symbolic Form (1927), trans. Christopher S. Wood (New York, 1991).

Studies in Iconology: Humanistic Themes in the Art of the Renaissance (1939; New York and Evanston, 1962).

The Life and Art of Albrecht Dürer, 4th ed. (Princeton, 1955).

Meaning in the Visual Arts: Papers in and on Art History (Garden City, N.Y., 1955).

Renaissance and Renascences in Western Art, 2d ed. (New York, 1969).

Pardo, Mary. "Memory, Imagination, Figuration: Leonardo da Vinci and the Painter's Mind," in *Images of Memory: On Remembering and Representation*, ed. Susanne Küchler and Walter Melion (Washington and London, 1991), pp. 47–73, 212–24.

"Testo e contesto del 'Dialogo di Pittura' di Paolo Pino," in *Paolo Pino teorico d'arte e artista: Il restauro della pala di Scorzé* (Scorzé, 1992), pp. 33–49.

True Alchemy: Paolo Pino's "Dialogo di pittura" and the Origins of Venetian Art Criticism (in press).

Parshall, Peter. "Albrecht Dürer and the Axis of Meaning," *Allen Memorial Art Museum Bulletin* 50, no. 2 (1997): 5–31.

See Landau, David, and Parshall.

Partridge, Loren. See Starn, Randolph, and Partridge.

Patz, Kristin. "Zum Begriff der 'Historia' in L. B. Albertis 'De Pictura,'" *Zeitschrift für Kunstgeschichte* 49 (1986): 269–87.

Pedretti, Carlo. *Leonardo da Vinci on Painting: A Lost Book (Libro A)* (Berkeley and Los Angeles, 1964).

Leonardo da Vinci: A Study in Chronology and Style (Berkeley and Los Angeles, 1973).

The Literary Works of Leonardo da Vinci: A Commentary to Jean Paul Richter's Edition, 2 vols. (Berkeley and Los Angeles, 1977).

The Codex Atlanticus of Leonardo da Vinci: A Catalogue of its Newly Restored Sheets, 2 vols. (New York, 1978–79).

Leonardo da Vinci: Nature Studies from the Royal Library, Windsor Castle, exhibition catalogue (New York, 1980).

"L'Organizzazione e simbolica dello spazio nelle cartelle dell'Accademia Vinciana," in *La prospettiva rinascimentale: Codificazioni e trasgressioni*, ed. Marisa Dalai Emiliani (Florence, 1980), pp. 261–66.

"Giorgione e Leonardo," in *Giorgione e l'umanesimo veneziano*, ed. Rodolfo Pallucchini, 2 vols. (Florence, 1981), II, pp. 485–512.

Leonardo's Horses: Studies of Horses and Other Animals by Leonardo da Vinci from the Royal Library at Windsor Castle, exhibition catalogue (Florence and New York, 1984).

"A Proem to Sculpture," *Achademia Leonardi Vinci: Journal of Leonardo Studies* 2 (1989): 11–39.

"Leonardo in Sweden," *Achademia Leonardi Vinci: Journal of Leonardo Studies* 6 (1993): 200–211.

See Keele, Kenneth D., and Pedretti.

Pedretti, Carlo, and Gigetta Dalli Regoli. *I disegni di Leonardo da Vinci e della sua cerchia nel Gabinetto Disegni e Stampe della Galleria degli Uffizi* (Florence, 1985).

Penrose, Roland. *Picasso: His Life and Work*, 2d ed. (New York, 1962).

Pérez-Sánchez, Alfonso E., and Eleanor A. Sayre. *Goya and the Spirit of the Enlightenment* (Boston, 1989).

Perini, Giovanna. *Gli scritti dei Carracci* (Bologna, 1990).

Perrig, Alexander. "Bemerkungen zur Freundschaft zwischen Michelangelo und Tommaso de' Cavalieri," in *Stil und überlieferung in der Kunst des Abendlandes* (Akten des 21. Internationalen Kongresses für Kunstgeschichte) (Berlin, 1967), II, pp. 164–71.

Michelangelo-Studien, I: Michelangelo und die Zeichnungswissenschaft – Ein methodologischer Versuch (Frankfurt am Main and Bern, 1976).

"Leonardo: Die Anatomie der Erde," *Jahrbuch der Hamburger Kunstsammlungen* 25 (1980): 51–80.

Michelangelo's Drawings: The Science of Attribution (New Haven and London, 1991).

Pfotenhauer, Helmut. See Böhm, Gottfried, and Pfotenhauer.

Pickvance, Ronald. *Van Gogh in Arles* (New York, 1984).

Piero della Francesca. *De prospectiva pingendi*, ed. G. Nicco-Fasola (Florence, 1984).

Pierpont Morgan Library, New York. See Boston, Museum of Fine Arts, and Pierpont Morgan Library, New York.

Pignatti, Terisio. "La pianta di Venezia di Jacopo de' Barbari," *Bollettino dei Musei Civici* 9 (1964): 9–49.

See Mazzariol, Giuseppe, and Pignatti.

Piles, Roger de. *Conversations sur la connoissance de la peinture et sur le jugement qu'on doit faire des tableaux* (Paris, 1677).

Abrégé de la vie des peintres, avec de réflexions sur leurs ouvrages, et un traité du peintre parfait; de la connoissance des dessins; de l'utilité des estampes (1699), 2d ed. (Paris, 1715).

Pino, Paolo. *Dialogo di pittura* (1548), ed. Paola Barocchi, in *Trattati d'arte del Cinquecento*, I (Bari, 1960).

Pliny the Elder. *The Elder Pliny's Chapters on the History of Art*, trans. K. Jex-Blake, ed. E. Sellers (London, 1896).

Podro, Michael. "The Drawn Line from Hogarth to Schiller," in *"Sind Briten Hier?" Relations between British and Continental Art 1680–1880* (Augsburg, 1981), pp. 45–56.

Poirier, Maurice. "The Role of the Concept of *Disegno* in Mid-Sixteenth Century Florence," in *The Age of Vasari* (Notre Dame, Ind., 1970), pp. 53–66.

Polanyi, Michael. *Personal Knowledge: Towards a Post-Critical Philosophy* (Chicago, 1962).

The Tacit Dimension (Garden City, N.Y., 1966).

Pollitt, J. J. *The Ancient View of Greek Art: Criticism, History, Terminology* (New Haven and London, 1974).

Pope-Hennessy, John. *Cellini* (New York, 1985).

Popham, A. E. *The Drawings of Leonardo da Vinci* (London, 1946).

"The Dragon Fight," in *Leonardo: Saggi e ricerche* (Rome, 1954), pp. 221–27.

Catalogue of the Drawings of Parmigianino, 2 vols. (New Haven and London, 1971).

Popham, A. E., and Johannes Wilde. *The Italian Drawings of the XV and XVI Centuries . . . at Windsor Castle* (London, 1949).

Porter, Jeanne Cheneault. "Rembrandt and His Circles: More About the Late *Self-Portrait* in Kenwood House," in *The Age of Rembrandt: Studies in Seventeenth-Century Dutch Painting*, ed. Roland E. Fleischer and Susan Scott Munshower, *Papers in the History of Art from The Pennsylvania State University* 3 (1988): 188–212.

Poulet, Georges. *The Metamorphoses of the Circle* (Baltimore, 1966).

Pouncey, Philip, and John Gere. *Raphael and His Circle* (Italian Drawings in the Department of Prints and Drawings in the British Museum) (London, 1962).

Prat, Louis-Antoine. See Rosenberg, Pierre, and Prat.

Procacci, Ugo. *Sinopie e affreschi* (Milan, 1960).

Quintilian. *Institutio Oratoria*, trans. H. E. Butler (Loeb Classical Library, vol. 10) (Cambridge, Mass., and London, 1922).

Ragghianti, Licia Collobi. *Il Libro de' disegni del Vasari*, 2 vols. (Florence, 1974).

Ramsden, E. H. *The Letters of Michelangelo* (Stanford, 1963).

Rapp, Jürgen. "Tizians frühestes Werk: der Grossholzschnitt 'Das Opfer Abrahams,'" *Pantheon* 52 (1994): 43–61.

Rathé, Alice. "Le *Capriccio* dans les écrits de Vasari," *Italica* 57 (1980): 239–54.

Ravà, Aldo. "Il 'Camerino delle anticaglie' di Gabriele Vendramin," *Nuovo Archivio Veneto* 22 (1920): 155–81.

Rawson, Philip. *Drawing*, 2d ed. (Philadelphia, 1987).

Reed, Sue Welsh, and Richard Wallace. *Italian Etchers of the Renaissance and Baroque*, exhibition catalogue (Boston, 1989).

Reynolds, Theodore. "The Accademia del Disegno in Florence: Formation and Early Years," Ph.D. dissertation (Columbia University, 1974).

Richards, Louise. "Antonio Pollaiuolo: Battle of the Naked Men," *Bulletin of the Cleveland Museum of Art* 55 (1968): 63–70.

Richardson, Francis. *Andrea Schiavone* (Oxford, 1980).

Richardson, Jonathan. *Two Discourses*, I: *An Essay on the Whole Art of Criticism as It relates to Painting* (London, 1725).

Richter, Irma A. *Paragone: A Comparison of the Arts by Leonardo da Vinci* (London, New York, Toronto, 1949).

Ridolfi, Carlo. *Le maraviglie dell'arte* (1648), ed. Detlev von Hadeln, 2 vols. (Berlin, 1914–24).

Riegl, Alois. "Late Roman or Oriental?" trans. Peter Wortman, in *German Essays on Art History*, ed. Gert Schiff (New York, 1988), pp. 173–90.

Rigoni, Erice. *L'Arte rinascimentale in Padova* (Padua, 1970).

Ripa, Cesare. *Iconologia overo descrittione di diverse imagini cavate dall'antichità, e di propria inventione* (Rome, 1603).

Ristori, Renzo. See Barocchi, Paola.

Rizzi, Aldo. *Le acquaforti dei Tiepolo* (Milan, 1970).

Roberts, Jane. See Keele, Kenneth, and Roberts.
See Kemp, Martin, and Roberts.

Robinson, William W. "Rembrandt's Sketches of Historical Subjects," in *Drawing Defined*, ed. Walter Strauss and Tracie Felker (New York, 1987), pp. 241–57.

Robison, Andrew. *Piranesi: Early Architectural Fantasies: A Catalogue Raisonné of the Etchings* (Washington, 1986).

Rosand, David. "The Crisis of the Venetian Renaissance Tradition," *L'Arte* 11–12 (1970): 5–53.

"Three Drawings by Veronese," *Pantheon* 29 (1971): 203–9.

"The Elusive Michelangelo," *Art News* 78 (Summer 1979): 48–51.

"Giorgione e il concetto della creazione artistica," in *Giorgione: Atti del Convegno Internazionale di Studi per il 5° centenario della nascita* (Castelfranco Veneto, 1979), pp. 135–39.

"'Troyes Painted Woes': Shakespeare and the Pictorial Imagination," *Hebrew University Studies in Literature* 8 (Spring 1980): 77–97.

"Titian Drawings: A Crisis of Connoisseurship?" *Master Drawings* 19 (1981): 300–308.

"Titian and the Critical Tradition," in *Titian: His World and His Legacy*, ed. David Rosand (New York, 1982), pp. 1–39.

"The Portrait, the Courtier, and Death," in *Castiglione: The Ideal and the Real in Renaissance Culture*, ed. Robert W. Hanning and David Rosand (New Haven and London, 1983), pp. 91–129.

"Raphael, Marcantonio, and the Icon of Pathos," *Source: Notes in the History of Art* 3 (Winter 1984): 34–52.

"Raphael and the Pictorial Generation of Meaning," *Source: Notes in the History of Art* 5 (Fall 1985): 38–43.

"Editor's Statement: Style and the Aging Artist," *Art Journal* 46 (1987): 91–93.

"*Ekphrasis* and the Renaissance of Painting: Observations on Alberti's Third Book," in *Florilegium Columbianum: Essays in Honor of Paul Oskar Kristeller*, ed. Karl-Ludwig Selig and Robert Somerville (New York, 1987), pp. 147–65.

The Meaning of the Mark: Leonardo and Titian (Lawrence, Kans., 1988).

"Michelangelo Draws: Communication and Revelation," in *World of Art: Themes of Unity in Diversity* (Acts of the 26th International Congress of the History of Art), ed. Irving Lavin (University Park and London, 1989), II, pp. 409–14.

"'Divinità di cosa dipinta': Pictorial Structure and the Legibility of the Altarpiece," in *The Altarpiece in the Renaissance*, ed. Peter Humfrey and Martin Kemp (Cambridge, New York, Melbourne, 1990), pp. 143–64.

"Ekphrasis and the Generation of Images," *Arion*, 3d series, 1 (1990): 61–105.

"More or Less Michelangelo" (review of Alexander Perrig, *Michelangelo's Drawings: The Science of Attribution*), *Drawing* 13 (1992): 112–13.

"Pastoral Topoi: On the Construction of Meaning in Landscape," in *The Pastoral Landscape*, ed. John

Dixon Hunt (National Gallery of Art, *Studies in the History of Art* 36) (Hanover, N.H., and London, 1992), pp. 161–77.

Review of *Andrea Mantegna*, in *The New Republic* (June 22, 1992): 29–32.

Painting in Sixteenth-Century Venice: Titian, Veronese, Tintoretto (1982), rev. ed. (Cambridge and New York, 1997).

"Remembered Lines," in *Memory and Oblivion* (Acts of the 29th International Congress of the History of Art), ed. Wessel Rinink and Jeroen Stumpel (Dordrecht, 1999), pp. 811–16.

"Raphael's *School of Athens* and the Artist of the Modern Manner," in *The World of Savonarola: Italian Elites and Perceptions of Crisis*, ed. Christine Shaw and Stella Fletcher (Aldershot, 2000), pp. 212–32.

Rosand, David, and Michelangelo Muraro. *Titian and the Venetian Woodcut*, exhibition catalogue (Washington, 1976).

Rosen, Charles, and Henri Zerner. *Romanticism and Realism: The Mythology of Nineteenth-Century Art* (New York, 1984).

Rosenberg, Harold. *De Kooning* (New York, 1974).

Rosenberg, Pierre, and Louis-Antoine Prat. *Nicholas Poussin, 1594–1665: Catalogue raisonné des dessins*, 2 vols. (Milan, 1994).

Rosenblum, Robert. "The Origin of Painting: A Problem in the Iconography of Romantic Classicism," *Art Bulletin* 39 (1957): 179–290.

Roskill, Mark W. *Dolce's "Aretino" and Venetian Art Theory of the Cinquecento* (New York, 1968).

Rowland, Ingrid D. *The Culture of the High Renaissance: Ancients and Moderns in Sixteenth-Century Rome* (Cambridge, New York, Melbourne, 1998).

Royalton-Kisch, Martin. "Rembrandt's Sketches for His Paintings," *Master Drawings* 27 (1989): 128–45.

Drawings by Rembrandt and his Circle in the British Museum (London, 1992).

"Rembrandt's Landscape Drawings," in *Drawing: Masters and Methods, Raphael to Redon* (Papers presented to the Ian Woodner Master Drawings Symposium at the Royal Academy of Arts, London), ed. Diana Dethloff (New York, 1992), pp. 114–35.

Rubin, Patricia. "'What Men Saw': Vasari's Life of Leonardo da Vinci and the Image of the Renaissance Artist," *Art History* 13 (1990): 34–46; also in *Nine Lectures on Leonardo da Vinci*, ed. Francis Ames-Lewis and Anka Bednarek (London, n.d.), pp. 96–108.

Giorgio Vasari: Art and History (New Haven and London, 1995).

Rubinstein, Ruth. See Bober, Phyllis Pray, and Rubinstein.

Russell, H. Diane. *Rare Etchings by Giovanni Battista Tiepolo and Giovanni Domenico Tiepolo* (Washington, 1971).

Jacques Callot: Prints and Related Drawings (Washington, 1975).

Rykwert, Joseph, and Anne Engels, eds. *Leon Battista Alberti* (Milan, 1994).

Saccone, Eduardo. "*Grazia, Sprezzatura, Affettazione* in the *Courtier*," in *Castiglione: The Ideal and the Real in Renaissance Culture*, ed. Robert W. Hanning and David Rosand (New Haven and London, 1983), pp. 45–67.

Sachs, Hans. *Eygentliche Beschreibung aller Stände auff Erden* (Nuremberg, 1568).

Sandrart, Joachim von. *Teutsche Academie der edlen Bau- Bild- und Mahlerey-Künste* (Nuremberg, 1675).

Academia Nobilissimae Artis Pictoriae (Nuremberg, 1683).

Sartre, Jean-Paul. *The Psychology of Imagination*, trans. Bernard Frechtman (New York, 1948).

Saslow, James M. *Ganymede in the Renaissance: Homosexuality in Art and Society* (New Haven and London, 1986).

trans. and ed., *The Poetry of Michelangelo: An Annotated Translation* (New Haven and London, 1991).

Sauerländer, Willibald. "From Stilus to Style: Reflections on the Fate of a Notion," *Art History* 6 (1983): 253–70.

Saunders, J. B. de C. M. See O'Malley, Charles D., and Saunders.

Savonarola, Girolamo. *Prediche sopra Ezechiele* (1517), ed. Roberto Ridolfi, 2 vols. (Rome, 1955).

Sayre, Eleanor A., et al. *The Changing Image: Prints by Francisco Goya* (Boston, 1974).

See Pérez-Sánchez, Alfonso E., and Sayre.

Schama, Simon. "Dutch Landscapes: Culture as Foreground," in Peter C. Sutton, *Masters of Seventeenth-Century Dutch Landscape*, exhibition catalogue (Boston, 1987), pp. 64–83.

Rembrandt's Eyes (New York, 1999).

Schapiro, Meyer. "Two Slips of Leonardo and a Slip of Freud," *Psychoanalysis* 4:2 (1955–56): 3–8.

"Leonardo and Freud: An Art Historical Study," *Journal of the History of Ideas* 17 (1956): 147–78; revised in *Theory and Philosophy of Art: Style, Artist, and Society: Selected Papers IV* (New York, 1994), pp. 153–99.

"The Apples of Cézanne: An Essay on the Meaning of Still-Life," *Art News Annual* 34 (1960): 34–53; reprinted in *Modern Art, 19th and 20th Centuries: Selected Papers II* (New York, 1978), pp. 1–38.

"On the Humanity of Abstract Painting," in *Modern Art, 19th and 20th Centuries: Selected Papers II* (New York, 1978), pp. 227–32.

"On Some Problems in the Semiotics of Visual Art: Field and Vehicle in Image-Signs," *Semiotica* 1 (1969): 223–42; reprinted in *Theory and Philosophy of Art: Style, Artist, and Society: Selected Papers IV* (New York, 1994), pp. 1–32.

"Style," in *Theory and Philosophy of Art: Style, Artist, and Society: Selected Papers IV* (New York, 1994), pp. 51–101.

The Unity of Picasso's Art (New York, 2000).

Schatborn, Peter. "Over Rembrandt en kinderen," *De Kroniek van het Rembrandthuis* 27 (1975): 8–19.

Dutch Figure Drawings from the Seventeenth Century (The Hague, 1981).

"Kinderen door Rembrandt," *De Kroniek van het Rembrandthuis* 33 (1981): 1–32.

"Van Rembrandt tot Crozat: Vroege verzamelingen met tekeningen van Rembrandt," *Nederlands Kunsthistorisch Jaarboek* 32 (1981): 1–54.

Landscapes by Rembrandt and his Precursors, exhibition catalogue (Amsterdam, 1983).

Drawings by Rembrandt, his Anonymous Pupils and Followers (Catalogue of the Dutch and Flemish Drawings in the Rijksprentenkabinet, Rijksmuseum, Amsterdam) (The Hague, 1985).

See Bevers, Holm, et al.

See Tümpel, Christian, and Schatborn.

Schatborn, Peter, and Eva Ornstein-van Slooten. *Bij Rembrandt in de Leer / Rembrandt as Teacher*, exhibition catalogue (Amsterdam, 1984).

Scheller, Robert W. *Exemplum: Model-Book Drawings and the Practice of Artistic Transmission in the Middle Ages (ca. 900–ca. 1470)* (Amsterdam, 1995).

Schenkeveld-van der Dussen, M. A. "Nature and Landscape in Dutch Literature of the Golden Age," in *Dutch Landscape: The Early Years, Haarlem and Amsterdam 1590–1650* (London, 1986), pp. 72–78.

Schiff, Gert. *Picasso: The Last Years, 1963–1973*, exhibition catalogue (New York, 1983).

Schiff, Richard. "On Criticism Handling History," *Art Criticism* 3:1 (1986): 60–77.

"Performing an Appearance: On the Surface of Abstract Expressionism," in *Abstract Expressionism: The Critical Developments*, ed. Michael Auping (New York, 1987), pp. 94–123.

Schilder, Paul. *The Image and Appearance of the Human Body* (1935; New York, 1950).

Schleuning, Peter. "'Ungewöhnlich Gänge, versteckte Zierrathen, sinnreiche Drehungen und Verbrämungen.' Das Capriccio in der Musik," in *Das* Capriccio *als Kunstprinzip: Zur Vorgeschichte der Moderne von Arcimboldo und Callot bis Tiepolo und Goya*, ed. Joachim Rees (Milan, 1996), pp. 179–85.

Schmitt, Annegrit. See Degenhart, Bernhard, and Schmitt.

Schneider, Cynthia. *Rembrandt's Landscapes: Drawings and Prints*, exhibition catalogue (Washington, 1990).

Schulz, Juergen. *The Printed Plans and Panoramic Views of Venice (1486–1797)* (*Saggi e memorie di storia dell'arte* 7) (Florence, 1970).

"Jacopo de' Barbari's View of Venice: Map Making, City Views, and Moralized Geography Before the Year 1500," *Art Bulletin* 60 (1978): 425–74.

Schwandt, Erich. "Capriccio," in *The New Grove Dictionary of Music and Musicians* (London, 1980), III, pp. 758–59.

Schwartz, Frederic. "'The Motions of the Countenance': Rembrandt's Early Portraits and the *Tronie*," *Res* 17/18 (Spring/Autumn 1989): 89–116.

Sekler, Patricia May. "Giovanni Battista Piranesi's *Carceri* Etchings and Related Drawings," *Art Quarterly* 25 (1962): 330–63.

Seymour, Charles, Jr. *The Sculpture of Verrocchio* (Greenwich, Conn., 1970).

Shattuck, Roger. *The Innocent Eye: On Modern Literature and the Arts* (New York, 1984).

Sheehan, Jacquelyn L. See Levenson, Jay A., et al.

Shoemaker, Innis H. *The Engravings of Marcantonio Raimondi*, exhibition catalogue (Lawrence, Kans., 1981).

Signorini, Rodolfo. See Chambers, David, et al.

Silbergeld, Jerome. "Chinese Concepts of Old Age and their Role in Chinese Painting, Painting Theory, and Criticism," *Art Journal* 46 (1987): 103–14.

Simonelli, Maria Picchio. "On Alberti's Treatises of Art and their Chronological Relationship," *Yearbook of Italian Studies* (1971): 26–44.

Slive, Seymour. *Rembrandt and His Critics 1630–1730* (The Hague, 1953).

Smart, Alastair, and Martin Kemp. "Leonardo's *Leda* and the Belvedere *River-Gods:* Roman Sources and a New Chronology," *Art History* 3 (1980): 160–71.

Smith, Alistair. "Dürer and Bellini, Apelles and Protogenes," *Burlington Magazine* 114 (1972): 326–29.

Smith, John. *A Catalogue Raisonné of the Works of the Most Eminent Dutch, Flemish, and French Painters*, VII (London, 1836).

Smith, Norris Kelly. *Here I Stand: Perspective from Another Point of View* (New York, 1994).

Smith, Webster. "Giulio Clovio and the 'Maniera di figure piccole,'" *Art Bulletin* 46 (1964): 395–401.

Soussloff, Catherine M. "Old Age and Old-Age Style in the 'Lives' of Artists: Gianlorenzo Bernini," *Art Journal* 46 (1987): 115–21.

Spear, Richard. *Domenichino*, 2 vols. (New Haven and London, 1982).

Spencer, John R. "Ut Rhetorica Pictura: A Study in Quattrocento Theory of Painting," *Journal of the Warburg and Courtauld Institutes* 20 (1957): 26–44.

Spicer, Joneath. "The Renaissance Elbow," in *A Cultural History of Gesture*, ed. Jan Bremmer and Herman Roodenburg (Ithaca, N.Y., 1991), pp. 84–128.

Stafford, Barbara Maria. *Symbol and Myth: Humbert de Superville's Essay on Absolute Signs in Art* (Cranbury, N.J., and London, 1979).

Staller, Natasha. "Early Picasso and the Origins of Cubism," *Arts Magazine* 61 (September 1986): 80–91.

"Gods of Art: Picasso's Academic Education and Its Legacy," in *Picasso: The Early Years, 1892–1906*, ed. Marilyn McCully (New Haven and London, 1997), pp. 67–85.

Starcky, Emmanuel. *Rembrandt et son école: Dessins du Musée du Louvre* (Paris, 1988).

Starn, Randolph, and Loren Partridge. *Arts of Power: Three Halls of State in Italy, 1300–1600* (Berkeley, Los Angeles, Oxford, 1992).

Steinberg, Leo. "Michelangelo's Florentine *Pietà:* The Missing Leg," *Art Bulletin* 50 (1968): 343–59.

"The Metaphors of Love and Birth in Michelangelo's *Pietàs*," in *Studies in Erotic Art*, ed. Theodore Bowie and Cornelia V. Christenson (New York and London, 1970), pp. 231–335.

Other Criteria: Confrontations with Twentieth-Century Art (London, Oxford, New York, 1972).

"The Case of the Wayward Shroud," in *Tribute to Lotte Brand Philip: Art Historian and Detective*, ed. William V. Clark, Colin Eisler, William S. Heckscher, Barbara G. Lane (New York, 1985), pp. 185–92.

"Michelangelo's Florentine *Pietà:* The Missing Leg Twenty Years Later," *Art Bulletin* 71 (1989): 480–505.

"Leon Battista Alberti e Andrea Mantegna," in *Leon Battista Alberti*, ed. Joseph Rykwert and Anne Engel (Milan, 1994), pp. 330–35.

Stites, Raymond S. *The Sublimations of Leonardo da Vinci, with a Translation of the Codex Trivulzianus* (Washington, 1970).

Stock, Julien. "A Drawing by Raphael of 'Lucretia,'" *Burlington Magazine* 126 (1984): 423–24.

Stone-Ferrier, Linda. "Rembrandt's Landscape Etchings: Defying Modernity's Encroachment," *Art History* 15 (1992): 403–33.

Straus, Erwin W. "The Upright Posture," in *Essays in Phenomenology*, ed. Maurice Natanson (The Hague, 1966), pp. 164–92.

"Born to See, Bound to Behold: Reflections on the Function of the Upright Position in the Esthetic Attitude," in *The Philosophy of the Body: Reflections of the Cartesian Dualism*, ed. Stuart F. Spicker (Chicago, 1970), pp. 334–61.

Strauss, Walter L., and Marjon van der Meulen, eds. *The Rembrandt Documents* (New York, 1979).

Strong, Donald. "The Triumph of Mona Lisa: Science and the Allegory of Time," in *Leonardo e l'età della ragione*, ed. Enrico Bellone and Paolo Rossi (Milan, 1982), pp. 255–78.

Summers, David. *Michelangelo and the Language of Art* (Princeton, 1981).

The Judgment of Sense: Renaissance Naturalism and the Rise of Aesthetics (Cambridge, London, New York, 1987).

Sumowski, Werner. *Drawings of the Rembrandt School*, 9 vols. (New York, 1979–85).

Sutton, Peter C. *Masters of Seventeenth-Century Dutch Landscape*, exhibition catalogue (Boston, 1987).

Swan, Claudia. "*Ad vivum, naer het leven*, from the life: Defining a Mode of Representation," *Word and Image* 11 (1995): 353–72.

Symonds, John Addington. *The Life of Michelangelo Buonarroti*, 2d ed., 2 vols. (London, 1893).

Testa, Judith Anne. "The Iconography of the *Archers:* A Study in Self-Concealment and Self-Revelation in Michelangelo's Presentation Drawings," *Studies in Iconography* 5 (1979): 45–72.

Tietze, Hans. "Earliest and Latest Works of Great Artists," *Gazette des Beaux-Arts* 26 (1944): 273–84.

Tobin, Richard. "Leon Battista Alberti: Ancient Sources and Structures in the Treatises on Art," Ph.D. dissertation (Bryn Mawr College, 1979).

Tolnay, Charles de. *History and Technique of Old Master Drawings: A Handbook* (New York, 1943).

Michelangelo, 5 vols. (Princeton, 1947–60).

The Art and Thought of Michelangelo (New York, 1964).

Corpus dei disegni di Michelangelo, 4 vols. (Novara, 1976–80).

Tomlinson, Janis. *Graphic Evolutions: The Print Series of Francisco Goya* (New York, 1989).

Goya in the Twilight of the Enlightenment (New Haven and London, 1992).

Tümpel, Christian, and Peter Schatborn. *Het Boek Tobias, met etsen en tekeningen van Rembrandt en zijn leeringen*, exhibition catalogue (Zeist, 1987).

Tümpel, Christian, and Astrid Tümpel. *Rembrandt legt die Bibel aus* (Zeichnungen und Radierungen aus dem Kupferstichkabinett der Staatliche Museen Preussischer Kulturbesitz Berlin), exhibition catalogue (Berlin, 1970).

Turner, A. Richard. *Inventing Leonardo* (New York, 1993).

Turner, Nicholas. *Florentine Drawings of the Sixteenth Century*, exhibition catalogue (London, 1986).

Vaccaro, Mary. "*Forma virginis:* Form as Meaning in Parmigianino's Art," Ph.D. dissertation (Columbia University, 1994).

"Resplendent Vessels: Parmigianino's Work in the Steccata," in *Concepts of Beauty in Renaissance Art*, ed. Francis Ames-Lewis and Mary Rogers (London, 1998), pp. 134–46.

"Parmigianino and the Poetry of Drawing," in Sylvie Béguin, Mario Di Giampaolo, and Mary Vaccaro, *Parmigianino: The Drawings* (Turin, 2000), pp. 61–93.

Valéry, Paul. *Degas, Manet, Morisot*, trans. David Paul (Collected Works, Vol. 12) (New York, 1960).

Aesthetics (Collected Works, Vol. 13) (Princeton, 1962).

Leonardo, Poe, Mallarmé, trans. Malcolm Cowley and James R. Lawler (Collected Works, Vol. 8) (Princeton, 1972).

Varchi, Benedetto. *Due lezzioni di M. Benedetto Varchi, nella prima delle quali si dichiara un sonetto di M. Michelagnolo Buonarroti. Nella seconda si disputa quale sia più nobile arte, la scultura o la pittura, con una lettera d'esso Michelagnolo e più altri eccellentissimi pittori e scultori sopra la quaestione sopradetta* (Florence, 1549).

Vasari, Giorgio. *Le vite de' più eccellenti architetti, pittori, et scultori italiani* (1550), ed. Luciano Bellosi e Aldo Rossi (Turin, 1986).

Le vite de' più eccellenti pittori, scultori ed architettori (1568), ed. Gaetano Milanesi, 8 vols. (Florence, 1878–85).

La vita di Michelangelo nelle redazioni del 1550 e del 1568, ed. Paola Barocchi, 5 vols. (Milan and Naples, 1962).

Vergara, Lisa. *Rubens and the Poetics of Landscape* (New Haven and London, 1982).

Vergerius, Petrus Paulus. *De ingenuis moribus* (ca. 1404), ed. Eugenio Garin, in *L'Educazione umanistica in Italia* (Bari, 1959); trans. William Harrison

Woodward, in *Vittorino da Feltre and Other Humanist Educators* (1897; New York, 1963).

Verheyen, Egon. "Correggio's 'Amori di Giove,'" *Journal of the Warburg and Courtauld Institutes* 29 (1966): 160–92.

Vetroq, Marcia E., and Adelheid M. Gealt. *Domenico Tiepolo's Punchinello Drawings* (Bloomington, 1979).

Viatte, Françoise. "Verrocchio et Leonardo da Vinci: A propos des 'têtes idéales,'" in *Florentine Drawing at the Time of Lorenzo the Magnificent* (Villa Spelman Colloquia, vol. 4), ed. Elizabeth Cropper (Bologna, n.d.), pp. 45–53.

Vogt-Gölnik, Ulya. *Giovanni Battista Piranesi: "Carceri"* (Zurich, 1968).

Waal, H. van de. "The *Linea Summae Tenuitatis* of Apelles: Pliny's Phrase and Its Interpreters," *Zeitschrift für Aesthetik und allgemeine Kunstwissenschaft* 12 (1967): 5–32.

Wallace, Richard. *The Etchings of Salvator Rosa* (Princeton, 1979).

See Reed, Sue Welsh, and Wallace.

Wallace, William E. "Studies in Michelangelo's Finished Drawings, 1520–1534," Ph.D. dissertation (Columbia University, 1983).

"A New Letter, a Michelangelo Drawing and a Lost Sebastiano?" *Source: Notes in the History of Art* 4 (Summer 1985): 21–26.

Wardrop, James. *The Script of Humanism: Some Aspects of the Humanist Script 1460–1560* (Oxford, 1963).

Warnke, Martin. "Praxisfelder der Kunsttheorie: Über die Geburtswehen des Individualstils," *Idea: Jahrbuch der Hamburger Kunsthalle* 1 (1982): 54–71.

Watrous, James. *The Craft of Old-Master Drawings* (Madison, 1957).

Watson, Ronald. "Drawing about the Art of Drawing: Academic Sources of Picasso's Late Cubism" (unpublished paper).

Wazbinski, Zygmunt. *L'Accademia medicea del disegno a Firenze nel Cinquecento: Idea e istituzione* (Florence, 1987).

Wegner, Wolfgang. See Halm, Peter, et al.

Welzel, Barbara. See Bevers, Holm, et al.

Wetering, Ernst van de. *Rembrandt: The Painter at Work* (Amsterdam, 1997).

White, Christopher. *Rembrandt as an Etcher: A Study of the Artist at Work,* 2 vols. (University Park and London, 1969).

Peter Paul Rubens: Man and Artist (New Haven and London, 1987).

Wilde, Johannes. *Michelangelo and His Studio* (Italian Drawings in the Department of Prints and Drawings in the British Museum) (London, 1953).

"Notes on the Genesis of Michelangelo's Leda," in *Fritz Saxl: A Volume of Memorial Essays from his Friends in England* (London, 1957), pp. 270–80.

Michelangelo: Six Lectures (Oxford, 1978).

See Popham, A. E., and Wilde.

Williams, Dyfri. "The Drawing of the Human Figure on Early Red-Figure Vases," in *New Perspectives in Early Greek Art,* ed. Diana Buitron Oliver (National Gallery of Art, *Studies in the History of Art* 25) (Washington, 1991), pp. 285–301.

Wind, Edgar. *Art and Anarchy,* rev. ed. (New York, 1969).

Wittkower, Rudolf. "Brunelleschi and 'Proportion in Perspective,'" *Journal of the Warburg and Courtauld Institutes* 16 (1953): 275–91.

"The Young Raphael," *Allen Memorial Art Museum Bulletin* 20 (1963): 156–68.

Architectural Principles in the Age of Humanism, 4th ed. (New York, 1971).

Idea and Image: Studies in the Italian Renaissance (London, 1978).

Wölfflin, Heinrich. *Classic Art: An Introduction to the Italian Renaissance* (1899), trans. Peter and Linda Murray (London, 1959).

Wolk-Simon, Linda. *Domenico Tiepolo: Drawings, Prints, and Paintings in the Metropolitan Museum of Art* (*Metropolitan Museum of Art Bulletin* 54 [Winter 1996/97]).

Wollheim, Richard. *On Art and Mind* (Cambridge, Mass., 1974).

Art and Its Objects, 2d ed. (Cambridge, 1980).

Wolpe, Berthold. See Fairbank, Alfred, and Wolpe.

Woodward, David. *Maps as Prints in the Italian Renaissance: Makers, Distributors and Consumers* (London, 1996).

Woodward, William Harrison. *Vittorino da Feltre and Other Humanist Educators* (1897) (New York, 1963).

Wright, D. R. Edward. "Alberti's *De Pictura:* Its Literary Structure and Purpose," *Journal of the Warburg and Courtauld Institutes* 47 (1984): 52–71.

Wright, Joanne. See Ames-Lewis, Francis, and Wright.

Zerner, Henri, et al. *Jacques Callot 1592–1635,* exhibition catalogue (Providence, 1970).

See Rosen, Charles, and Zerner.

Zhang, Yiguo. *Brushed Voices: Calligraphy in Contemporary China,* exhibition catalogue (New York, 1998).

Zöllner, Frank. *Vitruvius Proportionsfigur: Quellenkritische Studien zur Kunstliteratur im 15. und 16. Jahrhundert* (Worms, 1987).

"'Ogni Pittore Dipinge Sé': Leonardo da Vinci and Automimesis," in *Der Künstler über sich in seinem Werk* (Internationales Symposium der Bibliotheca Hertziana, Rom 1989), ed. Matthias Winner (Weinheim, 1992), pp. 137–60.

Zubov, V. P. *Leonardo da Vinci,* trans. David H. Kraus (Cambridge, Mass., 1968).

Zuccaro, Federico. *L'Idea de' pittori, scultori, et architetti* (Turin, 1607).

Zwijnenberg, Robert. *The Writings and Drawings of Leonardo da Vinci: Order and Chaos in Early Modern Thought* (Cambridge, New York, Melbourne, 1999).

Index